Henry Francis Walling, Alexander Winchell

Atlas of the State of Michigan : including statistics and descriptions of its topography, hydrography, climate, natural and civil history, railways, educational institutions, material resources, etc.

Including Statistics and Descriptions

Henry Francis Walling, Alexander Winchell

Atlas of the State of Michigan : including statistics and descriptions of its topography, hydrography, climate, natural and civil history, railways, educational institutions, material resources, etc.
Including Statistics and Descriptions

ISBN/EAN: 9783743421981

Manufactured in Europe, USA, Canada, Australia, Japa

Cover: Foto ©Suzi / pixelio.de

Manufactured and distributed by brebook publishing software (www.brebook.com)

Henry Francis Walling, Alexander Winchell

Atlas of the State of Michigan : including statistics and descriptions of its topography, hydrography, climate, natural and civil history, railways, educational institutions, material resources, etc.

ATLAS

OF THE STATE OF

MICHIGAN,

INCLUDING STATISTICS AND DESCRIPTIONS

OF ITS

TOPOGRAPHY, HYDROGRAPHY, CLIMATE, NATURAL
AND CIVIL HISTORY, RAILWAYS, EDUCATIONAL INSTITUTIONS,
MATERIAL RESOURCES, ETC.

BY

ALEXANDER WINCHELL, LL.D., CHANCELLOR OF THE SYRACUSE UNIVERSITY, HON. C. I. WALKER,
ORAMEL HOSFORD, ESQ., HENRY M. UTLEY, ESQ., AND RAY HADDOCK, ESQ.

DRAWN, COMPILED, AND EDITED BY

H. F. WALLING, C. E.

LATE PROFESSOR OF CIVIL ENGINEERING IN LAFAYETTE COLLEGE.

AUTHOR OF MAPS AND ATLASES OF MAINE, NEW HAMPSHIRE, VERMONT, MASSACHUSETTS, RHODE ISLAND, NEW YORK,
PENNSYLVANIA, OHIO, INDIANA, ILLINOIS, IOWA, CANADA, ETC., ETC.

PUBLISHED BY

R. M. & S. T. TACKABURY,

DETROIT, MICH.

THE CLAREMONT MANUFACTURING COMPANY,
CLAREMONT, N. H.,
BOOK MANUFACTURERS.

NOTE.—ERRORS AND OMISSIONS.—It is quite impossible to avoid errors and omissions in a work of this extent. Some of them, indeed, arise from changes which occur while the work is in progress. Persons who notice them will confer a favor by indicating them so that they may be rectified in future editions.

Address R. M. & S. T. TACKABURY, DETROIT, MICH., or HENRY F. WALLING, 102 CHAUNCY ST., BOSTON.

CONTENTS.

CONTENTS.

MAPS.
BY R. F. WALLING.
County Maps of the Lower Peninsula; County Maps of the Upper Peninsula; City Maps; General Maps.   p. 51

CENSUS.
COMPILED FROM THE NINTH CENSUS BY GENERAL F. A. WALKER.
Population of the United States and Territories in 1860 and 1870; Population of the Principal Cities of the United States in 1860 and 1870.   p. 143

GAZETTEER.
BY H. F. WALLING.
Explanations; Abbreviations of names of Railroads; Landings; Lakes and Rivers; List of Cities, Towns and Villages, stating means of access, approximate amount of Population, etc.   p. 147

INDEX TO MAPS.

PREFACE.

SALUTATORY.

The Editor and Publishers to the Patrons of the Atlas of Michigan.

WE greet you with congratulations, which we feel should be mutual, on the completion of our arduous labors, editing, compiling, drawing, engraving and publishing the work now placed before you. The difficulties which attend the preparation of such a work by individual enterprise can be understood only by those who have been engaged in similar undertakings. We believe, however, that the great labor and expense bestowed upon this atlas have been productive of highly remunerative results, to you at least, as well as to all interested in the welfare of the State, if not to ourselves.

VALUE OF MAPS.

Maps of States, complete in comprehensive entirely as well as in plenitude of minute detail, such as we here present to you of Michigan, possess an intrinsic and a *practical* value far beyond that due to the mere pleasure they afford in regarding them as pictorial representations of the territory represented as it might appear, could it be looked down upon from a great elevation. . Only the more thoughtful, however, fully recognize how closely and extensively the prosperity of a country depends upon the existence of accurate maps of its domain with general facility of access to them. We take the liberty to suggest, to those who have not given much attention to the subject, a few of the many considerations which indicate this dependence.

EXPLORATIONS AND SURVEYS.

It will easily be seen that before a new country can become settled, it must be *explored*, to ascertain what portions of it, if any, are available for the residences of a future population. Exploration, to be serviceable, should be carefully and intelligibly recorded, and to accomplish this, accurate instrumental *surveys* are required. The original records of these surveys are taken in the surveyor's note-books in the field. The notes, however, are far from being in a convenient form for reference, and a stranger wishing to gain information from the note books or from a verbal abstract of them, would find himself involved in much difficulty and perplexity.

TOPOGRAPHICAL MAPS.

The most convenient and intelligible mode of presenting the results of the surveys is that of topographical maps drawn to a suitable scale. In this way the relative positions of all parts of the country are preserved, and every representation of an object upon the paper bears an invariable proportion to the corresponding object upon the ground. Thus the scale of the county maps in this atlas is ₁₉₀₀₈₀; or one inch upon the paper

represents a distance of 190,080 inches or three miles upon the ground. The same proportion holds good if any other standard of measure than that of inches is used. A length of one centimetre, for instance, on the paper would represent 190,080 centimetres or 1900.8 metres upon the ground.

IMAGINARY POINT OF VIEW.

The apparent size of an object depends upon the magnitude of the visual angle it subtends, or in less technical language, upon the size of the angle or opening between two straight lines extending from the opposite sides of the object to the eye. This angle diminishes as the distance increases and by the familiar law of proportion in similar triangles, we can calculate the elevation above the earth which would give the same apparent magnitude or visual angle to objects, which their representations have in the atlas. Supposing the atlas page to be viewed at a distance of fifteen inches from the eye, then, since the scale of the map is three miles to an inch, fifteen inches above the map correspond to forty-five miles above the ground. Of course the more comprehensive maps upon smaller scales represent the country as if seen from a correspondingly greater elevation of the point of view.

VALUE OF MAPS IN PROMOTING IMMIGRATION.

If the surveyor is accurate in his field work, and the topographer skillful in reproducing the results of the surveys in graphical form, we obtain reliable and valuable maps. In no other way could one who contemplated emigrating to a new country obtain so correct an idea of its topographical features, its rivers, lakes, marshes, forests, prairies etc., and their relations to each other as by a correct map of the country, particularly if the map also presents to view the means of access to the region, whether by sailing vessels or navigable rivers and lakes, or by artificially constructed roads and rail roads. The immigrant is thereby enabled to compare advantages held out to induce him to settle in different localities, in the way of convenience of access, proximity to earlier settlers and to markets for his produce, prospects of future increase in value, etc., and thus to come to a satisfactory decision in locating his new home. In the absence of such information most men would naturally shrink from a leap in the dark. Other things being equal, a country which has been explored and its attractive features intelligibly represented on a good map would far more rapidly become settled than a " terra incognita."

VALUE IN PROMOTING PUBLIC IMPROVEMENTS.

But the usefulness of maps does not cease with the first occupation of a country. On the

contrary the more a state becomes settled and improved the greater the need of an exact and minute knowledge of its topography. New facilities for conveyance and travel are continually required. Wagon roads, canals and railroads must be built to accommodate the ever increasing travel and traffic attendant upon the increasing population and the consequent development of agricultural and mechanic arts. Centres of trade, of manufactures, of the administration of government and of great educational institutions grow up to meet the wants of the people. Easy access to these cities and villages, and from them to more distant places, becomes indispensable, whence occurs a continued multiplication of the public highways. The location and construction of these public works must be preceded by a careful determination of the most favorable routes. The necessity for first constructing an accurate map of the different routes proposed is obvious. Upon it the peculiar advantages and disadvantages of each route will more distinctly appear than in any other way, and unnecessarily expensive if not irreparable errors of construction are thereby avoided. Officers and promoters of railroads and other public works, while constantly availing themselves of these important aids in their operations, frequently fail to appreciate their great indebtedness to them. If there is any one interest which, more than another, among the various branches of industry in the social economy, is indebted to topographical engineering, it is the enormously great and constantly increasing *Railroad* interest.

GENERAL USES.

It would be impossible to designate or enumerate all the various practical uses which are continually being made of maps by persons in nearly every class of life, from the traveller who, for business or pleasure, desires to ascertain the shortest and most convenient route from place to place, to the railroad engineer, county officer or state legislator who considers the relations of any particular engineering project or concomitant course of legislative action to the welfare of the parties for whom he is empowered to act. So clearly has the value, to a State, of accurate topographical maps been perceived by the Governments of Europe that, with scarcely an exception, they have each expended many millions of dollars to obtain them, instead of leaving the matter, as in this country, almost entirely to individual enterprise.

EDUCATIONAL USES.

Besides the direct practical uses of local maps they have an educational value, of which it is well not to lose sight. Instruction in the geography of the whole world is very properly taught, in an elementary way,

even in the primary schools, as a branch of the most common education. There can be no doubt that this would be most advantageously supplemented if not preceded, by a careful study of the minute geography of the student's own state, county and immediate vicinity. Even a child forms a better idea of the nature and uses of a map when he is able to observe and compare the relative position of familiar haunts and to trace out the routes of his rambles about his home. Clearly his conceptions of the relations, as to position and magnitude, between his town, county, state, country, and the entire world will be far more correct than would be possible without the aid of accurate local maps. No intelligent, public spirited citizen therefore, who feels interested in the prosperity of the community in which he resides, in his own personal prosperity and in the education and intellectual welfare of his children, can afford to be without the best maps attainable, of his township, county and state. This is especially true in a state like Michigan which is increasing with such wonderful rapidity, in population wealth and importance.

UNITED STATES SYSTEM OF LAND SURVEYS.

The sources of information made available in preparing the maps for this atlas were various. The basis of the whole work was obtained by carefully copying all the township plats in the State Land Office at Lansing, some eighteen hundred and fifty in number. These were originally made under the direction of the United States Land Commissioner, in accordance with the system of Surveying and Laying out the Public Lands established by Congress in 1785. This system was planned with a wise foresight of the needs of a new and growing country and its execution has, in general, been conducted in as faithful and skillful a manner as the circumstances would permit.

A brief description of the United States system as applied to the public lands of Michigan, will also describe, in its general features the uniform method for all the public lands of the United States except in a few special cases.

PRINCIPAL MERIDIAN AND BASE LINE.

A meridian line, running through the State from north to south, and a base line running across from east to west, were first surveyed out, very carefully, by competent engineers, great care being taken that the former should be truly on a meridian or due north and south line, and the latter on a parallel of latitude or due east and west line. These two lines serve as bases or datum lines for all the surveys in the State, including the upper and lower peninsulas and those islands belonging to the State. They correspond in some measure to the coordinate axes of analytical mathematics, affording a simple method of locating surveys. The Michigan meridian was the first one

located for the United States Public Lands, before the State was organized, and is known as the "First Principal Meridian." It forms the boundary between Lenawee and Hillsdale counties, passes through the middle of Jackson and Ingham, divides Clinton from Shiawassee and Gratiot from Saginaw, Crawford from Oscoda and Otsego from Montmorency, and, passing through the eastern part of Cheboygan county, strikes Lake Huron nearly south of the eastern extremity of Bois Blanc island. The Base Line for this meridian runs from Lake Michigan to Lake Huron, along the northern boundaries of Van Buren, Kalamazoo, Calhoun, Jackson, Washtenaw and Wayne counties.

RANGES AND TOWNSHIPS.

After the establishment of the Meridian and Base Line, the surveyor proceeds to lay off the country into Townships, six miles square. Each Township accordingly contains thirty-six square miles or 23,040 acres "as nearly as may be." Having measured a distance of six miles along the base line to the east or west of the Principal Meridian a monument is erected at the six mile point and another meridian is surveyed out north and south from this monument. The strip of land six miles wide lying between and extending in a north and south direction entirely across the State is called a Range. The Range adjacent to the Principal Meridian is called Range Number One East, if on the east side, or Range Number One West, if on the west side of the Principal Meridian. A second strip six miles wide adjoining the first, is called Range Number Two, east or west as the case may be, and so in the same manner on both sides of the Principal Meridian until the entire State is divided into Ranges.

These Ranges are subdivided into Townships, by east and west lines six miles apart. The Township adjoining the Base Line is called Township Number One North, if on the north side, and Township Number One South, if on the south side of the Base Line. The next Township is Township Number Two, north or south as the case may be, and so on to the northern and southern boundaries of the State. Portions of Townships which are not complete where the Ranges are bounded by irregular lines or bodies of water are called Fractional Townships.

By this comprehensive and simple method of designation the description of the smallest tract of land becomes admirably succinct and definite. An adequate description for purposes even of legal conveyance of a forty acre lot might read as follows,—"The southeast quarter of the north west quarter of section Seventeen in Township Eight North, Range Three East of the First Principal Meridian." No farther description could make its exact location plainer or more certain. Of course reference to other Principal Meridians would fix the position of the lands in other States or Territories.

Upon the county maps in this atlas the

numbers of the Ranges are indicated by Roman Numerals in the border at the top and bottom of the maps; the letters R. W. and R. E. near the corners signifying Ranges west and Ranges east of the Principal Meridian. Township numbers are in figures at the sides, $\frac{T}{N}$ and $\frac{T}{S}$ denoting Townships North and Townships South of the Base Line.

SECTIONS.

Each Township is cut up into thirty-six Sections by lines running parallel to the side of the Township. Each section is one mile square and contains 640 acres "as nearly as may be."

The accompanying diagram exhibits the manner of numbering the sections of a single township, commencing with Number One in the northeast corner.

6	5	4	3	2	1
7	8	9	10	11	12
18	17	16	15	14	13
19	20	21	22	23	24
30	29	28	27	26	25
31	32	33	34	35	36

In fractional Townships each section is numbered the same as the corresponding section in whole Townships.

It will be noticed that in this Atlas only those section numbers are engraved which mark the eastern and western sections of each lateral row, thus:— Crowding the map with figures is thereby avoided, while the number of any section is easily ascertained.

6		1
7		12
18		13
19		24
30		25
31		36

Each Section is usually subdivided into half mile squares called quarter Sections each containing one hundred and sixty acres, and sometimes the subdivision is carried still farther into half quarter or quarter quarter sections.

CONVERGENCE OF MERIDIANS.

It will be perceived, on a little reflection, that if north and south lines are true meridians, they will not be parallel, but will approach each other or converge towards the north. In fact if continued sufficiently far they would all meet in one point at the north pole. The convergence in a single township is small, though quite perceptible, the actual excess in length of its south over its north line being, in Michigan, about three rods. The townships north of the Base Line, therefore become narrower and narrower than the six miles width with which they commence, by that amount; and those south of it become as much wider than six miles.

CORRECTION LINES.

If continued for too great a distance this narrowing or widening would cause serious inconvenience, and to obviate this effect of the curvature of the earth's surface

it is found neccessary to establish, at stated intervals, *standard parallels* commonly called "*Correction Lines*." These are usually sixty miles apart, though in some localities it has been found convenient to establish them nearer together. It will be seen that Michigan has five Correction Lines, all north of the Base Line. The "First Correction Line" is sixty miles north of the Base Line and accordingly runs between Townships 10 and 11. The second is between Townships 20 and 21 and so on. On these parallels, which form new base lines, fresh measurements are made from the Principal Meridian, and the corners of new Townships are fixed six miles apart, as on the original Base Line. This method of proceedure not only takes up the error due to convergency of meridians, but checks and arrests errors which arise from want of precision or carelessness in the surveys already made. Its effects will be noticed on the maps at all the correction lines whose position is indicated above, by the offsets which occur there, in the north and south lines. These offsets, of course, increase in amount by a *cumulative* process, as their distance from the Principal Meridian increases. Another precaution against errors in surveying is taken by running, at convenient intervals, usually about forty-eight miles, " *Guide Meridians*". These are surveyed with more exact instruments and with greater care than the ordinary Range lines.

FRACTIONAL SECTIONS.

The reason is now apparent for using the words " as nearly as may be" in the law which defined the area of Townships and Sections. Upon the subdivision of a Township into sections, the surplusage or deficiency is by law " added to or deducted from the western or northern ranges of sections according as the error may be in running the lines from east to west or from north to south." The northern or western sections of a township, (and any others), which contain more or less than 640 acres are accordingly called *Fractional Sections.*

LAKE SURVEYS.

In accordance with Congressional Laws the War Department of the United States Government is carrying on elaborate surveys of the Northern and North western Lakes under the charge of the U. S. Engineer officers. These surveys are based upon very careful and accurate triangulations and astronomical observations and exhibit the topography and hydrography of the Lakes and navigable rivers with great minuteness, giving full sailing directions etc., for navigators. By the courtesy of the present directing officer, Brevet Brigadier General C. B. Comstock, Major of Engineers we have been supplied with all the published charts relating to Michigan as follows :—"West End of Lake Erie," Lieut. Col. James Kearney, 1849, "Maumee Bay," Capt. Geo. G. Meade, 1857, " River Ste. Marie (No. 1)," Capt. Geo. G. Meade, 1857. " River Sto. Marie (No. 2),"

Capt. Geo. G. Meade, 1858, " Lake Huron," Capt. Geo. G. Meade, 1860, "North End of Lake Michigan," Brev. Brig. Gen'l W. F. Raynolds, 1867, " Lake Superior (No. 1)," Brev. Brig. Gen'l W. F. Raynolds, 1868, " Lake Superior (No. 2)," Brev. Brig. Gen'l W. F. Raynolds, 1868, " Lake Superior (No. 3)," Brev. Brig. Gen'l C. B. Comstock, 1870, "St. Clair River," Brev. Brig. Gen'l C. B. Comstock, 1872. In this list the names of directing officers at the date of publication are given.

These charts have not only afforded a means of verifying the general outlines obtained by plotting the United States Land Surveys, and of correcting the coast and river details, so far as they extend, but they have furnished the only available data for projecting the map of Michigan upon correctly drawn meridians and parallels of latitude.

PROJECTION OF THE MAPS.

We have already shown that in drawing a map of a portion of the earth's surface we have to represent it on a reduced scale with all its parts maintaining a uniform proportion to the objects represented. In doing this of a territory of considerable extent we encounter the difficulty or rather the *impossibility* of representing in this way a spherically curved surface upon a flat or plain surface, like that of a map. In a single county the discrepancy arising from this source would be inappreciable, but it becomes quite apparent in a large map of the whole State of Michigan.

If we represent parallels of latitude by straight parallel lines, meridians cannot be accurately drawn for they must either converge, in which case only one of them can make right angles with the parallels of latitude, or if all are drawn at right angles they cannot converge, while on the ground both the convergence and the rectangularity occur.

As it was intended eventually to publish the map of Michigan entire, as a wall map as well as in atlas form, it became necessary to draw the map continuously and to adopt such a mode of " *projection*" as would best adapt it for both purposes by preserving the rectangularity of parellels and meridians without too great a disturbance of the scale or distortion of the true proportions of the map. Various projections have been devised by geographers with those objects in view and different plans are adopted by them for representing the whole earth, for a single hemisphere, for a portion of a hemisphere, near the equator, near the poles etc. The best now known for our present purpose is that devised by the officers of the United States Coast Survey and called by them the

" RECTANGULAR POLYCONIC PROJECTION."

Imagine huge hollow tin cones, like candle extinguishers, to be placed over the north part of the earth so as to just touch it all around on any particular parallel of latitude which we wish to draw. Of course as

we take parallels farther north the cones will become flatter or more blunt at the angle or apex. Suppose these cones removed by some mighty hand, slit from base to apex and then unrolled or "developed," as the mathematicians have it, so as to become flat. The line where the parallel of latitude touched the cone would roll out forming a part of a circle, the point which had formed the apex of the cone being its centre. Now this arc we draw upon the map for the corresponding parallel of latitude. The term " Polyconic" is used because it is necessary to develope a different cone for each different parallel of Latitude represented. For areas not too large all the meridians and parallels will cross at sensibly right angles. There will be more or less distortion on the sides of the map according to the extent of territory represented, but for a state no larger than Michigan the distortion will be practically inappreciable. The Coast Survey tables, published in the Report for 1853, are very convenient for drawing this projection and have been used in the construction of the large map from which all the county maps in this atlas are taken.

TOPOGRAPHICAL DETAILS.

The parallels and meridians being projected, we drew the Principal Meridian and its Base line, the latter on a parallel of latitude. Both were fixed as nearly as possible in their proper places by comparison with the Lake Charts already mentioned. The termini of these lines were approximately marked upon the charts by careful comparison of the adjacent topography with that of the Land Surveys and thus the true positions of the lines as to Latitude and Longitude were approximately determined.

We next proceeded to " build up" the surveys upon the projection about in the same order in which they were made, carefully measuring the distances recorded in the second or revised surveys made for subdividing townships into sections. This was a somewhat difficult and perplexing task but it was most faithfully performed. The Lakes and Water courses were next laid down from the Land Surveys and corrected from such more modern sources of information as could be obtained, and finally the villages, post-offices, highways, railroads etc., were carefully located.

CO-OPERATION.

The compilation of the details of the map has been attended with a vast amount of research and labor, including correspondence etc. We are happy to acknowledge the kind interest which has almost universally been manifested in the work throughout the State and the cordiality and effectiveness of the co-operation by numerous and well informed correspondents. It is hardly possible to enumerate all the persons to whom we are under deep obligations. The supervisors of nearly every organized township in the State have responded cheerfully and fully to our inquir-

8

PREFACE.

ies and have sketched upon maps sent to them, of their own townships, the locations of roads, villages, post-offices etc. Railway engineers have supplied plans of location of roads already built or in process of construction, and in many cases, surveyors, engineers and other well informed persons have undertaken the revision and correction of entire counties or large portions of them. Among the many persons to whom we are indebted for favors of this kind we take pleasure in mentioning the following:

Hon. Henry H. Holt, (Lieut. Gov.) Muskegon Co.
E. C. Martin, Dep. Co. Surv., Oakland Co.
Roys L. Cram, U. S. Civil Eng'r. Corps, Cheboygan Co.
M. J. Cross, Esq., Oceana Co.
J. H. Leavenworth, Co. Surveyor, Saginaw.
Louis D. Preston, Civ. Eng'r., Lansing.
Harry S. Beesley, Co. Surv., Houghton Co.
Alex. Sinclair, Esq., Port Sanilac.
Geo. B. Adair, Civ. Eng'r., Macomb Co.
H. M. Caukin.   "   "   Montcalm Co.
M. M. Stinson, Chief Eng'r., Grand Rapids and Ind. R. R.
W. H. Fuller, Chief Eng'r., Toledo and Ann Arbor R. R.
A. A. Blanchard, Co. Surv., Lake Co.
E. F. Guild, Co. Surv., Saginaw Co.
H. F. Olmstead, Co. Surv., Midland Co.
Wm. Mercer, Dep. Co. Surv., Bay Co.
D. A. Ballou, Esq., Kawkawlin, Bay Co.
Wm. Mirre, Co. Surv., Alpena Co.
E. Chapelle, Co. Treas., Alcona Co.
Jas. M. Colby, Reg. of Deeds, Mecosta Co.
J. S. Douglas, Co. Surv., Mackinac Co.
Richard Smith, Dep. Co. Surv., Huron Co.
A. C. Lewis, Esq., Missaukee Co.
Wm. Slawson, Co. Surv., Grand Traverse Co.
Geo. E. Steele.   "   "   Antrim Co.
Wm. Miller, Co. Surv., Charlevoix Co.
Hopkins Bros., Manistee Co.
Ed. Edwards, Dep. Co. Clerk, Newaygo Co.
C. L. Northrop, Esq., Wexford Co.
John Leatherby, Co. Surv., Kalkaska Co.

EARLIER STATE AND COUNTY MAPS.

We give a list of those county and State maps which we have seen. Most of them sustain a deservedly high character for accuracy and usefulness.

State of Michigan, by Silas Farmer (Revised and published from year to year.)

Washtenaw Co., by G. R. Bechler & E. Wenig,	1856.
Hillsdale Co., by S. Geil & S. L. Jones,	1857.
Oakland Co., by F. Hess,	1857.
Jackson Co., by S. Geil & S. L. Jones,	1858.
Branch Co., by Geil & Jones,	1858.
St. Joseph Co., by "	1858.
Calhoun Co., by Geil, Harley & Siverd	1858.
Monroe Co., " " "	1859.
Macomb & St. Clair Co's., by the same,	1859.
Ingham & Livingston Co's., by the same,	1859.
Genessee & Shiawassee, by Geil & Jones,	1859.
Saginaw & Tuscola by D. A. Pottibone,	1859.
Cass, Van Buren & Berrien Co., by Geil Harley & Siverd,	1860.
Eaton & Barry Co's., by the same,	1860.
Wayne Co., by the same,	1860.
Ionia Co., by Geo. W. Wilson,	1861.
Kalamazoo Co., by Geil & Harley,	1861.
Lapeer Co., by Samuel Geil,	1864.
State of Michigan Co's., by Sam'l Geil,	1864.
Clinton & Gratiot Co's., "	1864.

Allegan Co., by " "	1864.
Ottawa & Muskegon, by " "	1864.
Washtenaw & Lenawee Co's., by G. R. Bechler & E. Wenig,	1864.
Kent Co., by Sheldon Leavitt,	1871.
Ionia Co., By " "	1871.
Cass Co., (Atlas) by D. J. Lake,	1872.
Hillsdale Co., (Atlas) by D. J. Lake,	1872
Berrien " " " "	1872.
Oakland Co., (Atlas) by F. W. Beers & Co.,	1872.

We learn that Messrs. C. O. Titus & Co., and F. W. Beers & Co., are now engaged in the publication of atlases of several other counties in Michigan. We hardly need add that we consider works of this kind, if carefully prepared, to be eminently worthy of public patronage.

GENERAL DESCRIPTIONS OF THE STATE.

We take great pride and pleasure in referring to the descriptive articles which precede the maps in this atlas, and which have been placed in the order of their completion by the writers rather than in a natural sequence of subjects.

Those by Professor Winchell, who, since this work was commenced, has assumed his new position as chancellor of the Syracuse University, are especially remarkable for the great value and striking interest of the information they contain, as well to agriculturists and all classes of business men as to men of science. An immense amount of labor, habitual to this eminent savant, has been bestowed upon the collection of the necessary data and its elaboration into a form in which highly important and valuable features are disclosed and brought to view. We felicitate ourselves and our patrons that we are now enabled to receive the benefit of these valuable researches which have not hitherto been made public in their present comprehensive and popular form.

The Outlines of State History, by Judge Walker, and the History of Education, by Superintendent Hosford, are admirably comprehensive epitomes, sufficiently full to serve all ordinary purposes in a work of reference.

The attention of all who feel that they are concerned in the wonderful material prosperity of the state, and this must include every intelligent inhabitant, will be absorbed in the graphic descriptions of its Railroad Enterprises by Mr. Haddock and of its Forest and Mineral Wealth by Mr. Utley, as well on account of the artistic skill displayed in sketching, as by the great importance of the subjects portrayed.

FIELD AND OFFICE ASSISTANTS.

We take occasion to commend and thank our assistants for efficient services in preparing the maps and statistical matter. By the courtesy of Governor Baldwin, in 1872, and Governor Bagley, in 1873, we obtained access to all maps in the State archives, and were allowed to copy all the original land plats, maps of State Roads, etc., in the State Land Office. It was also necessary to travel extensively over the State in collecting information relative to various local matters. In these labors and in the final draughting and

compilation, we have been assisted by Herbert S. Packard, Ambrose S. Lovis, Frederick Endicott, Thomas B. Mann, Roger H. Pidgeon, Walter S. Mac Cormac, Annie Timmis, Mary C. Keeler, Lilian C. Sawyer, Jane Rosenberger and Mary J. Clapp.

ENGRAVING, PRINTING, AND MANUFACTURING.

Most of the engraving has been done upon stone by Mr. Louis E. Neuman, of New York; the lithographic printing by Messrs. Forbes & Co., of Boston, H. Seibert & Brothers, of New York, the Calvert Lithographing Co., of Detroit, and Julius Bien, of New York, who photo-lithographed the counties of the Upper Peninsula from drawings by H. S. Packard; the coloring by Miss Helen D. Findlay, of New York, and the letter press printing by the Claremont Manufacturing Co., of Claremont, N. H., who also made a portion of the paper. We are indebted to Messrs. G. W. & C. B. Colton & Co., of New York, for the included maps of the United States and of Europe; to Eugene Robinson, Esq., for the map of Detroit; and to the Calvert Lithographing Co., for the District maps. The binding was done by H. O. Houghton & Co., of the Riverside Press, Cambridge, Mass.

RAILROAD COURTESIES.

We gratefully acknowledge the uniform kindness and courtesy of Railroad officers towards our enterprise. Plans of routes have been promptly furnished, and facilities granted in the way of free passes over every road in the State to which application has been made.

PUBLICATION.

In conclusion, the topographer and editor upon whom the responsibility and care of preparing the draughts, etc., and manufacturing the atlases has fallen, takes the liberty to state that in engaging in this enterprise he had no encouragement to suppose that he would receive aid from the State, nor from any source except sales of atlases. Knowing by experience that works of this kind can only be successfully published by subscription, he would have been discouraged from the undertaking, had he not been able to contract with Messrs. R. M. & S. T. Tackabury, well known as energetic and successful subscription publishers, for a complete canvass of the State of Michigan. This has been to them an expensive and laborious undertaking, but up to the time of going to press their success warrants the belief that the people of Michigan are sufficiently alive to the value of our work to prevent us from incurring a loss in bringing it out.

The following persons have been employed by the Messrs. Tackabury as Assistant Publishers:

J. W. Porter,	S. L. Moffett,
W. W. Tackabury,	D. C. Bastine,
J. A. Horrigan,	Charles Hitchcock,
A. H. Proctor,	A. H. Nelson,
J. S. Sessions,	J. S. Lawson.

TOPOGRAPHY AND HYDROGRAPHY.

BY ALEXANDER WINCHELL, LL.D.,

PROFESSOR OF GEOLOGY, ZOÖLOGY, AND BOTANY IN THE UNIVERSITY OF MICHIGAN. LATE DIRECTOR OF THE STATE GEOLOGICAL SURVEY.

THE STATE OF MICHIGAN occupies a position approximating the centre of the continent of North America. The geographical centre of the continent is not far from the Lake of the Woods, which is 560 miles in a straight line from the centre of the State, and 260 miles from its western extremity. The centre of the State is marked by the position of Carp Lake, in Lelanau county, which is 670 miles in a straight line from New York, the nearest point on the Atlantic Seaboard. The State is limited by natural boundaries on all sides except the south. Politically,* it has 708.5 miles coterminous with the Dominion of Canada; 55.5 miles coterminous with Minnesota; 571 miles coterminous with Wisconsin; 58 miles bordering on Illinois; 129.2 miles on Indiana, and 92.8 miles on Ohio; making a total length of boundary line, amounting to 1615 miles.

The land area of the State consists of two natural divisions, known as the Upper and Lower Peninsulas, to which are attached the contiguous islands. The Upper Peninsula is bounded by portions of lakes Superior, Michigan and Huron, the river St. Mary and the State of Wisconsin. The Lower Peninsula is embraced by lakes Michigan, Huron, St. Clair and Erie, and the St. Clair† and Detroit rivers; and is bounded on the south by the States of Ohio and Indiana.

The main land of the State is embraced between the parallels of 41° 692 and 47° 478' north latitude, and the meridians of 82° 407 and 90° 536 of longitude west from Greenwich. The most northerly point is the north side of Keweenaw Point, five miles north of the Light House at Copper Harbor; and the most southerly is the north-west corner of Ohio. The most easterly point is at Port Huron, near the outlet of Lake Huron; and the most westerly is at the mouth of Montreal river. The most northern territory belonging to the State, is Gull Islet, off the extremity of Ile Royale, which attains the latitude of 48° 211.

The following table exhibits the latitudes and longitudes of the principal points of the State:

* The political boundaries of the State are defined by the following documents: Sixth Article of the Treaty of Ghent; Report of Commissioners provided by that Article, and dated June 18, 1822; Act admitting Michigan into the Union, June 15, 1836; Act of April 18, 1818, Sec. 2; Act admitting Wisconsin, Aug. 6, 1846; Act of April 18, 1818, Sec. 5. For the original boundary of Ohio on the north, see Act of April 30, 1802.

† The river St. Clair was originally named Sinclair from Patrick Sinclair, a British military officer, who purchased of the Indians, in 1765, 4000 acres of land on the river. Lake St. Clair was so named from a French officer. (American State Papers, Public Lands, Vol. I, p. 216.)

TABLE OF GEOGRAPHICAL POSITIONS.

STATIONS	LATITUDE	LONGITUDE
Detroit, St. Paul's Church,	42 19 43.85	83 02 22.73
" Congress'l Church.	42 19 45.64	83 02 29.07
" Intersection Fort and Griswold Sts.,	42 19 49.85	83 02 20.63
Fort Gratiot, Light House,	43 00 21.96	82 24 43.96
Pt. aux Barques, Light House,	44 01 23.35	82 47 09.87
Saginaw, Light House,	43 38 37.84	83 50 64.46
Tawas, Light House,	44 15 35.44	83 20 14.57
Mouth of Thunder Bay River,	45 03 38.90	83 25 32.63
Detour Light House,	45 57 20.11	93 54 21.71
Fort Holmes, Mackinac I.,	45 51 27.81	84 36 29.44
Waugoshance Light House,	45 47 13.38	85 04 56.83
N. E. cor. Big Beaver Island,	45 45 12.67	85 29 38.00
Sand Point, Escanaba,	45 44 35.04	87 02 25.65
Menominee,	45 05 19.31	87 35 22.20
Grand Haven, Court House,	43 03 47.25	
" Lake Survey Sta.,	43 03 50.14	86 14 21.30
Marquette, Light House,	46 33 55	87 22 12.45
Vulcan, near Copper Harbor,	47 26 44.25	
Ann Arbor, Observatory,	42 16 48.30	83 43 43.05
New Buffalo, Intersection of middle of Whitaker Ave. and Mechanics St.,	41 47 47.00	86 44 53.55
Niles, Steeple of Trinity Church,	41 49 46.10	93 55 36.60
Monroe, Light House,	41 53 26.77	83 19 22.29
Adrian,	41 54 26	83 50 42
Hillsdale,	41 55 19	84 35 40
Coldwater,	41 53 30	85 01 32
White Pigeon,	41 44 59	85 39 42
Ypsilanti,	42 14 12	83 37 06
Jackson,	42 14 46	84 23 01
Marshall,	42 23 38	84 56 09
Kalamazoo,	42 17 39	85 35 58
Allegan.,	42 31 49	85 52 37
Lansing,	42 43 53	84 30 42
Pontiac,	42 37 44	83 17 21
Owosso,	43 00 17	84 18 21
Grand Rapids,	42 57 59	85 39 59
Muskegon,	43 15 54	86 15 51
Flint,	43 01 01	83 40 58
Tuscola,	43 19 31	83 29 50
East Saginaw,	43 26 25	83 55 43
Manistee,	44 13 41	86 18 42
Traverse City, E. and Hannah, Lay & Co's Pier,	44 45 59.74	85 38 53.11
Ontonagon, Light House,	46 52 18.35	89 18 29.46
Houghton,	47 07 15.00	88 32 27.12

The foregoing positions, as far as Vulcan, inclusive, are selected from the numerous determinations of the United States Lake Survey; Ann Arbor has been determined by the Director of the Observatory; New Buffalo and Niles are from Col. Graham's determinations; Monroe, Traverse City, Ontonagon and Houghton are from the Lake Survey Charts, and the co-ordinates of the remaining localities have been calculated from Farmer's large sectional map of the State.

The following table exhibits the difference of time between Detroit and some important points in the State:

TABLE OF LOCAL TIME.

LOCALITIES	Time slower than Detroit Time.	LOCALITIES	Time slower than Detroit Time.
Port Huron,	2 30.57*	Battle Creek,	16 36.35
Pontiac,	0 59.85	Kalamazoo,	10 13.13
Monroe,	1 07.97	Traverse City,	10 18.00
Ypsilanti,	2 16.89	Grand Rapids,	10 20.33
Flint,	2 34.35	Allegan,	11 20.94
Ann Arbor (Obs.),	2 45.35	Grand Haven,	12 47.90
East Saginaw,	3 33.34	Niles (Trinity Ch.,)	12 52.93
Adrian,	3 48.62	Muskegon,	12 53.91
Owosso,	5 03.91	Manistee,	13 05.39
Hillsdale,	5 05.56	Escanaba,	18 00.19
Jackson,	5 22.54	Marquette (L. H.,)	17 18.65
Lansing,	5 53.30	Menominee,	19 12.16
Mackinac,	8 16.01	Houghton,	21 04.18
Marshall,	7 35.05	Ontonagon,	25 04.42
Coldwater,	7 52.64	Mouth Montreal River.	29 30.15

* Faster than Detroit Time.

FOREIGN LOCALITIES COMPARED WITH DETROIT.

Greenwich, England,	5 h. 32 m. 9.51 sec. faster.
N. Y. City, (Custom House,)	36 " 9.31 " "
Washington, D. C. (Observ.)	24 " 8.31 " "
Chicago, Ill. (Old Court House,)	19 " 22.34 " slower.
San Francisco, Cal.,	2 h. 37 " 32.00 " "

The geographical centre of the main land of the Upper Peninsula is on Sec. 35, T. 46, N. R. 25, W., about three miles east of the Peninsula Railroad, in Marquette County. The geographical centre of the main land of the Lower Peninsula is on Sec. 24, T. 13, N. R. 3, W., township of Coe, Isabella County. The geographical centre of the main land of the entire State is on Sec. 3, T. 21, N. R. 8, W., in Missaukee County. The geographical centre of the entire state, within its political boundaries (including the lake-areas belonging to the State) is on the S. W. ¼ Sec. 30, T. 30, N. R. 11, W, very near Provemont in Lelanau County.*

The extreme length of the main land of the Upper Peninsula is 318.104 miles, and its extreme breadth 164.286 miles. The extreme length of the main land of the Lower Peninsula, from north to south, is 277.000 miles; and its extreme breadth is 259.056 miles. The greatest actual width of the Peninsula, however, measured along a parallel of latitude, is between Forestville, on Lake Huron, and Little Point Sable, on Lake Michigan. The width here is 197.057 miles.†

The Base Line of the land surveys of the State runs "seven miles north of Detroit" (probably the Old Capitol), and the Michigan Meridian (which rules south to the old territorial boundary) is 84° 37' west of Greenwich. The land area of the State is 56,457 square miles, or 36,128,640 acres.

There are 179 islands included within the political boundaries of the State, which have an area from one acre upwards. The total area of these islands is 404,730 acres.

The total length of the lake-shore line within the State is 1620 miles. Besides the larger lakes lying upon the frontiers, the State includes within its bounds 5173 smaller lakes, having an area of 712,864 acres. The following Table sets forth the leading data respecting the "Great Lakes."

	Length miles	Width miles	Depth feet	Mean Lake Level feet	Elevation above sea feet	Area sq. miles
Superior,	460	160	988	601	599.2	32,000
Michigan,	360	108	900	637	580.6	20,000
Huron,	270	160	900	424	580.6	20,000
Erie,	250	80	200	39	565	6,000
Ontario,	180	65	500		262	6,000
	11,520		1,624			84,000

* These determinations have been made by ascertaining the centres of gravity of sheets of paper of uniform thickness, cut to the exact limits of the mapped boundaries of the areas whose centre were sought.

† These dimensions are based on the latitude and longitude of the points referred to, and the calculated length of the degree of latitude and longitude in the different positions.

Tho two natural divisions of the State are distinguished by marked physical characteristics. They are completely cut off from each other by the Straits of Mackinac. The northern is rugged, with numerous rocky exposures; tho southern consists of plains, plateaux, gentle undulations and moderate hills, with very few outcrops of rocky strata. The northern peninsula is a mineral region; the southern, agricultural. The climates of the two peninsulas are as distinct as their locations and their topography; and, in all statements respecting the climatic features of the State, the two peninsulas ought to be separately treated. The meteorological means for the whole State convey very inadequate impressions respecting either of its natural divisions.

The topographical configuration of the State has been the subject of very careful study. The attempt has been made to collect all the important information obtained in running the various levels for railroad and canal surveys, from 1836 to the present time. The recent progress of these enterprises is so rapid, that it has been impossible to make the tables of elevation absolutely complete, but over 6000 elevations have, nevertheless, been tabulated, which give the height of the surface at every point along the surveyed lines, at which the superficial slope exhibits any considerable change. The planes of reference of the various surveys have been elaborately compared with each other, and all the elevations reduced to the Chicago City Datum—which is low water in Lake Michigan in 1847. These elevations, transcribed upon the map of the State, have served, in the Lower Peninsula, for the construction of a system of contour lines, or lines drawn through points having the same elevation above a given plane. We have undertaken to draw a contour line for every fifty feet of elevation above Lake Michigan, and these are exhibited upon the accompanying map.

Throughout all that portion of the State south of Houghton Lake, this map presents a good general picture of the surface configuration. North of that latitude, the data are insufficient; and the contour lines must be regarded as only rudely approximative. Combining, however, the exact data at hand, with our personal familiarity with the northern portion of the Peninsula, and with the inferences to be drawn from a good map of the water courses, we have produced results which, with many persons, may be regarded as quite preferable to the absence of all information.

These tortuous lines, to the casual observer, may seem to be very easily laid down, and to possess little interest or value; but every intelligent person will be able to appreciate their importance, and to understand that they represent months of careful labor.

A general glance at the superficial configuration of the Lower Peninsula, reveals a surface swelling gently from the lake shores toward the interior regions. The lake waters are hemmed in by no mountainous barriers or rocky ranges of hills. Generally the lake shores are depressed. This is especially the case around the upper half of Saginaw Bay, and along the region from Lake Huron to Maumee Bay. Yet, in almost all cases, the land rises, within a few miles—sometimes quite rapidly, or even abruptly—to the height of one or two hundred feet above the contiguous lake. Steep, or even precipitous shores, are presented in the northern and eastern part of Huron county; through a large part of Presq' Ile county; around Little Traverse Bay in Emmet county; and throughout Charlevoix, Antrim, Leelanau and Benzie counties; and the statement may be extended to Manistee, Mason and Oceana counties. Sleeping Bear Point in Leelanau county is a bluff of incoherent materials facing the lake, and attaining an elevation of 500 feet. The limestone ridge forming the northern angle of the county, rises somewhat precipitously to altitudes of 200 to 300 feet.* Similar elevations approach the shore of Little Traverse Bay. The Sliding Banks on Hammond's Bay of Lake Huron are 77 feet high, and the rocky cliffs about Point aux Barques, rise to the height of 12 to 20 feet.

Along the border of Lake Michigan, stretches a series of sand-dunes or piles of fine, mostly silicious sand, blown up by the prevailing westerly winds. These attain elevations up to 100 and 200 feet. At Grand Haven, the highest reaches an altitude of 215 feet. This is on the north side of Grand river. The highest on the south side attains an elevation of 205 feet. In the neighborhood of New Buffalo, they reach heights of 30, 40, 50 and 93 feet. Back of these dunes the surface is generally depressed, and not unfrequently, occupied by a marsh, a lakelet, a lagoon or an estuary. As a rule, these sands are continually shifting before the wind. They are, accordingly, making constant encroachments upon areas occupied and improved by man. Sometimes, as at Grand Haven and Sleeping Bear, the forest becomes submerged beneath these accumulations, and presents the singular spectacle of withered tree tops projecting a few feet above a waste of sands.

The origin of these sands is in the disintegration or solution of rocks more or less arenaceous, and located along the shores to the windward, or in the bottom of the lake within reach of the agitations of the waters. The liberated silicious grains are either thrown directly upon the beach, or, through a process of bar formation, a new beach rises to the surface, with the characteristic lagoon between it and the original beach. Thus, in many situations, the land is extended lakeward, and, while the sands are encroaching on the landward side, compensation is made by the westward retreat of the sand-laden beach which supplies the encroaching sands.

Proceeding from the littoral belt of the Peninsula toward the interior, we find a region considerably more elevated and better drained than ancient official misrepresentations had led the general public to believe. Though presenting no mountainous districts, and no indications of the agency of forces of upheaval, we have a land-area attaining throughout a large portion of the peninsula, an elevation averaging from 400 to 1000 feet. Erosions, dating back into geological time, have pared down the original surface, and established the existing slopes to the lake shores, and even to the lake bottoms. Later fluviatile erosions have scored deep and broad valleys, which mark off the prominent portions into several distinct regions.

Viewing the Peninsula as a whole, we discover, first of all, a remarkable depression stretching obliquely across from the head of Saginaw Bay, up the valley of the Saginaw and Bad rivers, and down the Maple and Grand rivers, to Lake Michigan. This depression attains, nowhere, an elevation greater than 72 feet above Lake Michigan. This elevation is in the interval of three miles separating the waters flowing in the opposite directions. This spot was chosen, in 1837, as the location for a canal, connecting Saginaw Bay with Lake Michigan. It is obvious, that when the lakes stood at their ancient elevations, their waters communicated freely across this depression, and divided the Peninsula into two portions, of which the northern was an island. This depression, for convenience of reference, may be designated the "Grand-Saginaw Valley."

That lobe of the peninsular swell which lies to the south-east of the dividing belt, has its salient longitudinal axis stretching somewhat arcuately from north-east to south-west through Huron, Sanilac, Lapeer, Oakland, Washtenaw and Hillsdale counties. This, which may be called the South-eastern Water-shed, is not broken through by any of the streams, though it is deeply excavated by the Huron river, in Washtenaw county. Various passes exist across it, and the crest rises in four isolated summits. The Oakland Summit, located in the north part of Oakland county, attains an elevation, on the surveyed lines,* of 520 feet, and gives rise to tributaries of the Flint, Clinton and Belle rivers. The Washtenaw Summit, in the north-eastern portion of Washtenaw county, rises to the height of 394 feet, and over, and gives origin, on opposite sides, to tributaries of the Huron river. The Francisco Summit on the borders of Jackson and Washtenaw counties, is 411 feet high, on the measured lines, and divides the waters flowing into the Huron and Grand rivers. The Hillsdale Summit is located in the centre of Hillsdale county, and attains two culminations, one in the south-western part, between Cambria and Reading, where it reaches an elevation of 613 feet, and another in the north-eastern part, in the township of Somerset. This is, therefore, the highest summit south of the

---

* For a more particular account of the topography and hydrography of this portion of the State see the writer's *Report on the Grand Traverse Region.* 8 vo. pp. 92 with map, 1866.

* It must be remembered that the following discussion is based on elevations along lines of survey for railroads and canals. Generally, therefore, the numerical values given do not represent the highest elevations nor the lowest depressions.

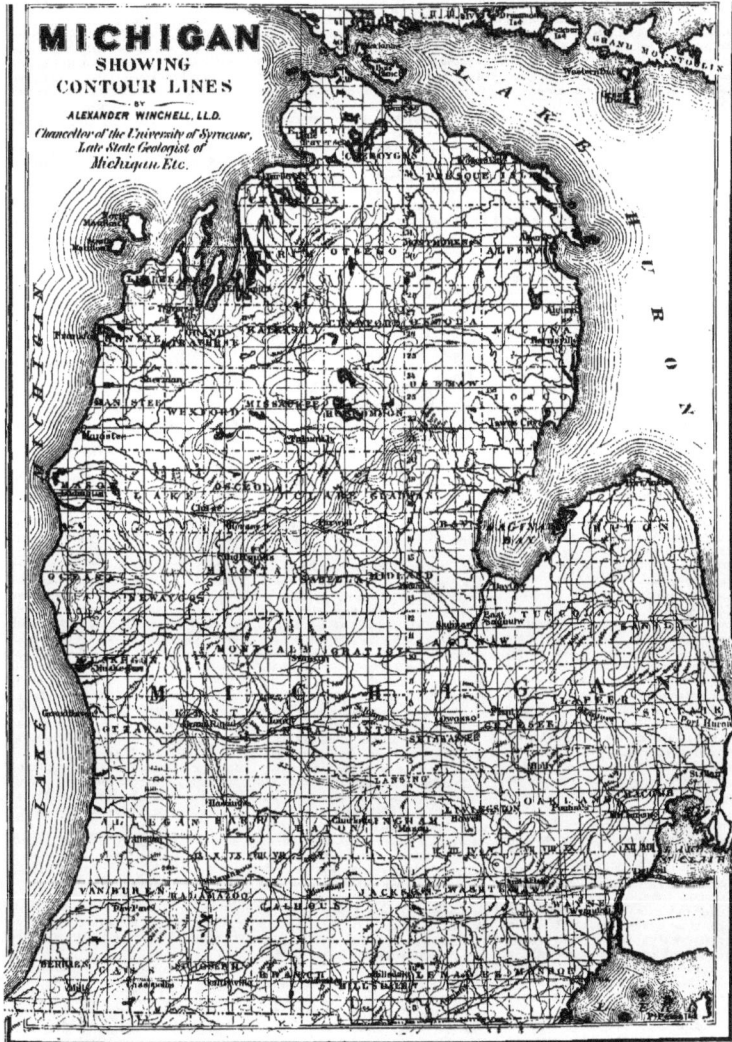

MICHIGAN
SHOWING
CONTOUR LINES
— BY —
ALEXANDER WINCHELL, LL.D.
Chancellor of the University of Syracuse,
Late State Geologist of
Michigan, Etc.

Grand-Saginaw valley. It stretches south-westward into Indiana, and, on the borders of that State, presents a culmination of 646 feet, while, through the southern portion of Branch county, it maintains an elevation of 400 to 500 feet. The Hillsdale Summit stretches also into the south-western part of Jackson county, with an elevation of 450 feet, while a spur 400 feet high, extends to Springport in the north-western corner of the county. From Hillsdale Summit rise the headwaters of the St. Joseph, Kalamazoo and Grand rivers, flowing into Lake Michigan, and the Maumee and Raisin, flowing into Lake Erie. Tributaries of the Maumee and St. Joseph rise within a mile of each other, in the townships of Reading and Allen. Tributaries of the Kalamazoo and St. Joseph rise within half a mile of each other, in the township of Adams; and these two streams approach again within two miles, at Homer, Calhoun county. The head waters of the Raisin are within a mile of those of the Kalamazoo, in the township of Somerset, and those of the Maumee approach equally near in the adjoining township of Wheatland. In the northern part of Somerset are two peaks which, perhaps, constitute the real culminations of the Hillsdale Summit. Here, within an area of two miles by three, we may view the head waters of the St. Joseph, Kalamazoo, Grand and Raisin rivers; and an area of four miles square would include, with these, the highest tributaries of the Maumee. The broad north-westerly slope of the south-eastern Water-shed is intersected by six great rivers—the Shiawassee, the Cedar and Grand, which unite at Lansing, the Thornapple, which unites with the Grand at Ada, the Kalamazoo and the St. Joseph rivers, all pursuing a general north-westerly course, except the latter, which flows south-westerly to South Bend in Indiana, and thence north-west. The surface between these river valleys rises into a corresponding number of swells. Of these, the one between the Shiawassee and Cedar rivers, lying chiefly in Livingston county, and reaching an elevation of 350 feet, may be regarded as a spur of the Oakland Summit. The Ingham Summit, which is the next, lies between the Cedar and Grand rivers, in the south-eastern portion of Ingham county and the contiguous parts of Jackson, attains an elevation of 391 feet, on the measured lines. The Grand Ledge Summit, between the Grand and Thornapple rivers, stretching across the northern part of Eaton county and into Ionia, attains an elevation of only 250 feet. The Barry Summit, between the Thornapple and Kalamazoo rivers, is a mass exscinded by Battle Creek from the northwestern prolongation of the Hillsdale Summit. It occupies the south-eastern part of Barry county, reaching, with an altitude of 250 feet, into Eaton, Calhoun and Kalamazoo. The north-western prolongation of this, out of Gun river, which unites with the Kalamazoo at Otsego, forms the Kent Summit, occupying the eastern part of Allegan county and the southern part of Kent, and having a culmi-

nation of 213 feet in the latter county. Between the Kalamazoo and St. Joseph rivers, is placed the north-easterly-elongated mass of the Cass Summit, which is cut off from the western extension of the Hillsdale Summit by the south-western reach of the St. Joseph river. It covers the north-eastern half of Cass county, extending into the south-western part of Kalamazoo, where it finds a culmination at an elevation of 349 feet, while another culmination in the vicinity of Cassopolis reaches an altitude of 384 feet.

Gathering together the foregoing results, we may here present the following compendious summary:

RELIEF FEATURES IN THE LOWER PENINSULA.

South-eastern Watershed.	Oakland Summit,	529 ft.
	Washtenaw Summit,	394 "
	Francisco Summit,	411 "
	Hillsdale { Somerset culmination,	600?"
	Summit. { Cambria "	613 "
	{ California "	546 "
North-western Slope.	Livingston Summit,	350 "
	Ingham Summit,	391 "
	Grand Ledge Summit,	250 "
	Barry Summit, }	250 "
	Kent Summit, }	213 "
	Cass Sum't { Oshtemo culmination,	349 "
	{ Cassopolis "	384 "

That Lobe of the Peninsular swell which lies to the north of the Grand-Saginaw Valley is placed, as a mass, midway between lakes Huron and Michigan, with its northwestern borders crowding somewhat upon the region of Grand and Little Traverse Bays of Lake Michigan. It exemplifies, like the Southern Lobe, a strong tendency to a north-east south-west disposition. The primary division of the Northern Lobe is effected by the valleys of the Manistee and Sable rivers, which take their rise upon the highest summit, and flow thence toward the south-west and south-east into their respective Lakes. The Sable has excavated a valley which, in Wexford county and the western part of Oscoda, sinks from 10 to 100 feet below the highest levels, and in the eastern part of Oscoda, and in Alcona County, 200 to 300 feet below the highest levels—the general plains being 90 to 125 feet above the river. The valley of the Manistee (as well as its tributary, the Pine) is similarly sunken in an undulating plateau. The southern division is bounded south-easterly by a continuous slope toward Saginaw Bay. In its central part it is indented by the hydrographical basin of Houghton and Higgins Lakes. In this rests Houghton Lake at an elevation of 589 feet above Lake Michigan. From this lake, the Muskegon river, the largest of the Peninsula, takes its rise, and, flowing south-westerly, marks the position of a broad deep valley, leaving, on the south-east, an elongated watershed stretching from Mecosta County through Clare and Roscommon, into Ogemaw County. This may be distinguished as the Central Watershed. It presents a general elevation of 700 feet and over, throughout its entire length. The Roscommon Summit of the Watershed, upon the eastern borders of the county by that name, attains an altitude of at least 820 feet, and the Clare Summit, in the central part of Clare County, is believed to attain an elevation of 750 feet.

The prolongation of the Central Watershed toward the north-east is nearly cut off by the South Branch of the Sable river, forming thus what may be designated as the Ogemaw Summit, occupying the region around the junction of the four counties, Ogemaw, Roscommon, Crawford and Oscoda. The culminating point is believed to be about 800 feet above Lake Michigan, while the pass separating it from the Roscommon Summit is not depressed below 625 feet.

To the north-west of the central lakes and the valley of the Muskegon, rise three summits detached from each other by shallow passes. The Crawford Summit, with an elevation of over 700 feet, besides occupying the south-western portion of the county by this name, stretches into Kalkaska, Missaukee and Roscommon Counties. Being bounded on the north-west by the valley of the Manistee, on the north-east by the bifurcated valley of the North and South Forks of the Sable, it is limited on the south-west by interlocking tributaries of the Manistee and Muskegon rivers.

The Wexford Summit, in the south-eastern portion of Wexford county and contiguous portions of Missaukee and Osceola counties, includes Clam Lake, and is believed to attain an elevation exceeding 700 feet. By the Pine river, a tributary of the Manistee, whose higher waters issue from the neighborhood of this Summit is isolated, on the south, from the Osceola Summit, located near the centre of Osceola County, and reaching an elevation of over 700 feet.

The northern division of the Northern Lobe of the Peninsula embraces the most elevated land south of the Straits of Mackinac. It appears to consist of two principal summits separated from each other by the pass which gives place to the head waters of the Thunder Bay river, and one of the affluents of the Sable. The eastern, which we may designate the Oscoda Summit, because located chiefly in the northern part of that county, has an elevation of 800 feet or more. The Otsego Summit, to the west, occupies a large part of Otsego county, and is said to attain an elevation of 1200 feet. Within its limits, take their rise the streams which water the Grand and Little Traverse regions, as well as those which find outlet in the vicinity of the Straits.*

RELIEF FEATURES IN THE LOWER PENINSULA.

Southern Division.	{	Roscommon Summit,	820? ft.
	{	Clare Summit,	750? "
	{	Ogemaw Summit,	850? "
	{	Crawford Summit,	700? "
	{	Wexford Summit,	700? "
Northern Division.	{	Osceola Summit,	700? "
	{	Oscoda Summit,	800? "
	{	Otsego Summit,	1200? "

The enumeration of the foregoing 18 Summits, in the whole Peninsula, must not be

* Otsego Lake is represented on the maps as having an outlet into the North Branch of the Sable river. This is an error. There are evidences, however, of an ancient outlet, at a time when the water of the lake stood at a higher level. Recently, moreover, a canal has been dug for "lumbering" purposes, which opens connection into the Sable. The lowering of this lake, like that of Houghton and Higgins Lakes, is one of the numberless evidences of a gradual process of desiccation taking place all over the continent—to the east as well as the west of the Rocky Mountains.

allowed to produce the impression of any very marked irregularities of surface. The summit-districts are not generally mere hill-tops, but level or gently undulating plateaux, through which atmospheric and fluviatile erosions have excavated drainage valleys of moderate depths or with gently bounding slopes. This conformation of the surface exists to a marked extent in the Northern Lobe of the Peninsula. There are, consequently, few precipitous hill-sides, and but very limited regions which cannot be subjected readily to the operations of agriculture. It may convey, in a more exact form, some idea of the nature of the surface, to present the following statistics of the construction of the Jackson, Lansing and Saginaw railroad. On the 120 miles of the road between Wenona and Otsego Lake, the average amount of earth-work per mile was 10,000 cubic yards; the maximum mile, 40,000, and the minimum, 1,000 cubic yards. The deepest cut is 33 feet; the deepest filling, 28 feet, and the longest cut, 5,000 feet. The total amount of culverting is 500,000 feet, board measure; total amount of bridging, 1,320 feet; number of bridges, 15; longest bridge, 200 feet; highest, 28 feet.

As to the Upper Peninsula, the data accumulated do not enable us to speak with so much detail; and no attempt has been made to lay off contour lines. It seems, nevertheless, appropriate to complete our account of Michigan topography by offering some descriptive statements in reference to that Peninsula.

The region between Lake Superior and the northern bend of Lake Michigan, limited on the east by St. Mary's river, and on the west by the Whitefish river, may be referred to as the Monistique Peninsula, from the large Lake Monistique, occupying nearly a central position in it. The principal portion of the drainage, to the west of this lake, is into Lake Michigan, the water-shed running east and west, by a zig-zag line, within six to ten miles of Lake Superior. East of Lake Monistique, the drainage is chiefly into Lake Superior and other waters east of the meridian of the Straits. The streams, however, throughout the whole interior of the Peninsula, are sluggish, and the regions to the east of Point Iroquois, and about the upper waters of the Tequamenon, are largely occupied by marshes abounding in peat and bog iron ore.

The southern border of the Monistique Peninsula is lined by ranges of limestone hills, which, in the vicinity of Point Detour, are but slightly elevated, with intervening marshes, but, further west, in the vicinity of Mackinac, attain elevations of 150 to 300 feet. Drummond's Island and the Manitoulin Islands are but the eastward prolongation of the same range of hills, and exhibit elevations quite as considerable as those in the vicinity of the Straits. The cliffs at the eastern extremity of Drummond's Island are over 100 feet high, while the surface toward the interior, rises to the height of 200 and 300 feet. The escarpments of Mackinac Island

are 140 feet high, and the central plateau is 300 feet high. Westwardly, the same range of hills extends to Little Bay de Noquet, where, as at Mackinac Island, it presents some strongly marked scenery. In approaching the coast, this elevated limestone region is cut by erosions into innumerable islands ranging in extent from a mere point of rock to several hundreds, or even thousands of acres. These, in the vicinity of Drummond's Island, and Point Detour, become a literal labyrinth with almost inextricable passages. Toward the north shore, a prominent range of hills begins in the region back of Point Iroquois, and extends in a nearly westerly direction, to the coast of Lake Superior, where it abuts in the famous escarpment known as the "Pictured Rocks," and re-appears in Grand Island with its towering promontories. These smoothly rounded and densely wooded hills attain elevations of 300 to 600 feet above Lake Superior. The streams which break through the range are interrupted by falls. The principal of these is the Tequamenon, which has falls of 40, 45 and 15 feet. The Au Train, eight miles above its mouth, has a fall of 95 feet, and nearer the lake, another of 40 feet.

The immediate shore, between Point Iroquois and the Pictured Rocks, is an alternation of low, sometimes marshy, plains, and rounded sand-hills and promontories. The latter, in the vicinity of Carp river, reach an elevation of 100 feet, while the Grand Sable stands 345 feet above the lake.

The Whitefish river marks the location of a well characterized Valley of Erosion, from one to three miles wide, and bounded by unconsolidated banks 100 to 120 feet above the limestone bottom. The river rises in a series of lakelets within nine miles of the shore of Lake Superior; and the Au Train river, flowing into the latter lake, takes its rise in the same vicinity. Along this valley, the most elevated point is not more than 150 feet above Lake Superior. The writer has elsewhere* suggested that this valley is probably the site of an ancient outlet of Lake Superior, whose waters then passed through Little Bay de Noquet, Green Bay, and the Wisconsin depression occupied by Lakes Winnebago, Horicon and Koshkonona, into the valley of Rock river, and thence to the Mississippi.

Of the region west of Whitefish river, the southeastern portion, between the Menominee river and Green Bay, is mostly a gently undulating surface, presenting a general slope in the direction of the water-courses. This slope, in the south-western part of Delta county, is 430 feet, and near the head waters of the Chocolate river, in Marquette county, 550 feet above Lake Michigan. North and north-west of this, is the mountainous dis-

trict, comprising the Iron and Copper regions, each of which is characterized by its own topography.

The water-shed of the mountainous region strikes in a serpentine course, north-west from the head-waters of the Chocolate river, to within ten miles of the head of Keweenaw Bay, whence it bends, by a course still more serpentine, south-westward to Lac Vieux Desert, on the boundary of Wisconsin. In the first reach of its course, it passes through the midst of the Marquette Iron District. The elevation at Negaunee is 775 feet above Lake Michigan; at Ishpeming, to the west of the water-shed, 865 feet, and at the Champion mine, near Lake Michigami, 1011 feet. The summit, on the Marquette, Houghton and Ontonagon railroad, is 1186 feet. Lake Michigami lies 966 feet above Lake Michigan. The hills north of the lake, reach an elevation of 1215 feet. The greatest elevation on the water-shed is in the vicinity of the sources of the Michigami river, which are 1250 feet above Lake Michigan. The Huron Mountains, east of Keweenaw Point, abut upon the shore of Lake Superior, and rise in rugged eminences which give a marked expression of the mountainous character of the Upper Peninsula. Mount Huron attains an elevation of 932 feet, and other Summits rise from 760 to 887 feet above Lake Superior. The region of the water-shed, south-west from Lake Michigami, becomes first less broken, and then a gently undulating plain, to the Wisconsin boundary.

Keweenaw Point is a rocky ridge, which, beginning with the promontory at the head of the Point, forms a water-shed nearly along the central line. From the base of the Point, the range trends south-west into Ontonagon county. Mount Houghton, near the head of the Point, is 884 feet above Lake Superior, and the range attains nowhere a greater elevation than 900 feet above the lake.

Beyond the Ontonagon river, the Porcupine Mountains may be regarded as a fresh development of the range. Rising somewhat abruptly from the immediate vicinity of the lake shore, they trend at first south-south-west for about 30 miles, whence their course is more westerly. The greatest altitude attained near Lake Superior, is 950 feet; but several knolls further inland, attain elevations from 1100 to 1380 feet above the lake.

In concluding this synoptical sketch of the topographical features of Michigan, it remains to direct attention to one interesting generalization which has not heretofore been pointed out. This is what may be styled the *diagonal system* in the physical features of the State. By this expression it is meant to say that the longitudinal axes of the topographical and hydrographical features of the State, especially of the Lower Peninsula, lie in directions which are diagonals between the cardinal points of the compass. It would extend this paper too far, to point out the leading facts which illustrate and establish this proposition; but it is believed that a brief study of the topographical Chart will render the truth of the proposition apparent.

---

* *American Naturalist*, Vol. IV., p. 558. Through inadvertence, it is stated in the *Naturalist* that the valley is hemmed in by "limestone" cliffs. The cliffs are of unconsolidated materials, though limestone frequently appears in the bottom of the valley. The existence of this valley is not the only evidence that it has been a water-course, since the limestone bed is, in some places, seen to be worn into pot-holes.

The subject will be elsewhere adequately amplified.

The diagonal system in American physiography is not by any means confined to Michigan. The Maumee river of Ohio, with its tributaries, is a striking reproduction of the Saginaw and its affluents. The Maumee, flowing east-north-east, is fed by the Au-Glaize and St. Mary's, from the south-east, the (little) St. Joseph from the north-east, and the Tiffin from the north-west—the last named, in its higher reaches, flowing from Hillsdale county, Michigan, first south-east and then south-west. In Wisconsin, the north-east south-west basin of Green Bay is prolonged through the Fox river into Lake Winnebago. The same trend is seen in the shore-lines about Chegowawegon Bay, the Apostle Islands and the western extremity of Lake Superior. Even the upper Mississippi, whose general course is meridional, divides itself into a succession of reaches, conforming strangely to the law of diagonism, while, on the other hand, the river and

Gulf of St. Lawrence are a further indication that something in the course of events which have fashioned the actual surface, has exerted a greater energy in the direction of the diagonals than in the direction of the cardinal points of the compass.

This is not the place to discuss the causes of this well-marked method in the surface-configuration of the north-west. It would be easy to show that these features sustain relations to the underlying rocky structure. It would be equally easy to demonstrate that they are closely connected with the movements of the continental glacier, which geologists believe to have moved, in the lake region, from north-east to south-west, during the epoch immediately preceding the advent of man upon the earth. But, at the same time, it would appear that these features do not conform exclusively to either set of agencies; and that their actual relation to each may be expressed in the following proposition : *The actual topographical and hydrographical axes of Michigan and the whole lake-*

region, are the resultant of two forces—a GLACIAL, *acting from the north-east, and a* STRATIGRAPHICAL, *acting along the lines of strike of the rocky formations.*

As a corollary, we should find that where the rocky formations are most consolidated, the resultant lies nearest the line of the stratigraphical force; and where the rocky formations are little consolidated, the resultant approximates the line of the glacial force.

As a second corollary, physical features determined by causes which have *obliterated* the glacial and stratigraphical trends, do not, necessarily, express relations to either force. Of this kind are the small streams whose courses over the diluvial beds have been determined by post-glacial erosions; and river courses, like the St. Clair and Detroit, marked out across lacustrine or other post-glacial deposits which have concealed the surface-features due to geological structure or glacial erosion.

BRIEF OUTLINE OF THE HISTORY OF MICHIGAN.

BY THE HON. C. I. WALKER.

MICHIGAN, although a comparatively new State, has a history not only of deep and romantic interest, but a history that reaches back beyond the clearly defined regions of fact into the dim and shadowy regions of romance. But a sketch of the limits to which this is confined can only deal with a dry and meager outline of fact. This, however, may not be without its use in awakening an interest in a wider and deeper research.

UNDER FRENCH DOMINION.

Precisely when the territory now included in the State of Michigan was first visited by civilized man cannot now be determined. The first authentic record of such visit is that of the Jesuit Fathers, Charles Raymbault and Isaac Jogues, to the Sault St. Mary in July, 1641. They planted the cross and preached its doctrines to the docile Chippeways. They left with the expectation of soon returning and establishing a mission, but Raymbault died of consumption the following year, and Jogues soon met a martyr's death among the Iroquois. Doubtless long previous to this time French traders had traversed both the woods and the waters of this distant wild.

In October, 1660, Father Mesnard, after a voyage of two months in which he suffered terribly from toil, and from the insults and cruelty of his savage attendants, reached one of the bays of Lake Superior, probably Keweenaw; where with no white man nearer to him than the region of Montreal he spent a long, cold winter, preaching the cross and bearing it. In the following summer he started to visit some Christianized Hurons,

and was never seen more. In 1665, the well known Jesuit Father, Claude Allouez, founded the Mission at Lapoint, Lake Superior, just over the Michigan boundary. In 1668, the revered Father Marquette founded the first Christian Mission within the limits of Michigan at Sault St. Mary, and in 1671, he founded the Mission of St. Ignace near Mackinaw, and these became permanent posts as well as great centres of Indian trade. In 1671, an envoy of the French King gathered a grand Indian Council, at Sault St. Mary, of all the Western tribes and formally took possession of all the country between Montreal and the South Sea. From this time, the North-West was under the dominion of France until it was ceded to Great Britain by the treaty of peace of 1763. For the most part, th : territory of Michigan, at this time, was occcpied by the Chippeways and Ottawas. Som : Pottawatomies and Miamis were on the southern borders, and the Sacs and Foxes skirted the southern shore of Lake Superior.

In 1679, La Salle passed through the Detroit River in the Griffin, on his way from Black Rock to Green Bay and the Illinois, and Father Hennepin, the historian of the voyage, who accompanied him, graphically describes the beautiful country bordering upon its banks.

In 1686, Fort St. Joseph was erected where Fort Gratiot afterwards stood near Port Huron by the De Luht or De Luth, and soon after another fort was erected upon the eastern border called Fort Detroit, but its precise locality is not known. One purpose of the erection of these Forts was to command

the passage, through which the Iroquois and the English of New York sought to gain access to the upper Lakes and share its rich fur trade. In 1688, a strong force of about sixty Englishmen and several Indians attempted to reach Mackinaw by this route with a large supply of goods, but were captured by the French.

About this time a Fort was built on the St. Joseph River, near its mouth, which continued to be occupied up to the time of the Revolutionary war.

Fort St. Joseph and Fort Detroit were temporary structures and were soon abandoned, so that when Detroit was founded in 1701 the only points in Michigan then occupied were Sault St. Mary, Mackinaw and the post on the St. Joseph River.

In 1694, De La Motte Cadillac, a man of noble birth, great ability and energy, was placed in command at Mackinaw, then the most important point in the Northwest. It had a garrison of one hundred soldiers, and was the center of a large and lucrative trade in furs, in which the English of New York were determined to share. It was while in command here, that he conceived the plan of founding a permanent post and settlement on the Detroit, with especial reference to holding the English and Iroquois in check. In 1699, he visited France, where his worth and services were well known, and in 1700, had interviews with Count Pontchartrain, the Prime Minister of Louis XIV, to whom he fully explained his plan.

It was cordially approved, and he was commanded to return without delay and pro-

ceed with its execution. The result was that, on the 24th day of July, 1701, he landed at Detroit with fifty soldiers and fifty traders and citizens, and at once proceeded to erect Fort Pontchartrain, a stockade of pickets with four wooden bastions. With characteristic energy, De La Motte took effective measures to draw around the new post Indians from Mackinaw and elsewhere, until in 1705, there were 2,000 Indians near the fort; 400 of whom were warriors. He also sought to encourage permanent agricultural settlements by the French, but with very limited success. In 1706, the Ottawas becoming dissatisfied, attacked the Miamis near the Fort, killed a priest and a soldier, and kept the fort in something like a state of siege for forty or fifty days. A still greater danger threatened the new post in the bitter hostility of the Jesuits, who disliked the commandant, and that of the Governor General of Canada, who was opposed to this whole project of a post at Detroit and made great efforts to bring about its abandonment.

The commandant however succeeded in retaining the confidence of the court and Detroit remained. In 1711, he was appointed Governor of Louisiana and left Detroit. The following year, 1712, while the Indians belonging to Detroit were absent on their hunting grounds, the post was surrounded by a large force of the Foxes, who threatened its destruction. The commandant, Du Buisson, "did not know on what Saint to call" as his force was very small. But the return of the friendly Indians not only raised the siege but the Foxes were in their turn besieged, and, for the most part, utterly destroyed under circumstances of peculiar and ferocious cruelty. About one thousand of them perished.

From this time, during the remainder of the French dominion, no great event occurred in Michigan history, although Indian hostility sometimes threatened its overthrow. About 1749, there was quite an emigration from France to the banks of the Detroit, and settlers were encouraged with grants of land and with advances of stock.

Major Rogers, in 1761, estimates the whole number of inhabitants of this settlement at 2500, of whom 500 were capable of bearing arms.

UNDER BRITISH RULE.

The victory of Wolfe upon the plains of Abraham in 1759, led to the surrender of Detroit and the other North-western posts to the English in the following year, and by the treaty of peace of 1763, France ceded her dominion over the Canadas, including Michigan and the North-West, to Great Britain; and the British power was firmly established. The French inhabitants submitted to this change with a much better grace than did their Indian allies. Pontiac, an Ottawa chief of remarkable ability, organized "The Conspiracy of Pontiac," being a combination among the Indian tribes for reducing, by a simultaneous attack, all the British posts from Niagara to Green Bay. Pittsburgh, Niagara and Detroit alone escaped the threatened destruction. In this State St. Joseph

and Mackinaw fell into their hands. Detroit was besieged by Pontiac in person for nearly four months. The history of this conspiracy and especially of the siege of Detroit forms one of the most remarkable chapters in the history of Indian warfare, and it has found in Parkman a fitting historian.

From this time, until the passage of the famous Quebec Act by Parliament in 1774, Michigan was without the pale of civil government. The commandant was not only the Military Commander but combined within himself the Legislative, judicial and executive powers. By the Quebec Act the North-West became a part of the Province of Quebec, and was brought nominally under civil government; and under it Col. Henry Hamilton was appointed "Lieut. Governor and Superintendent of Detroit." He had doubtless been selected because of his capacity, energy and zeal and with reference to the impending difficulties between the Colonies and the Mother Country. Henceforth, and during the entire revolution, Detroit became the center of British power in the North-West. The relentless and cruel Indian warfare, that was carried on against the border settlements of Pennsylvania, Virginia and Kentucky, received its inspiration and direction from this point. The Indian power of the North-West was at this period fearfully great. It was mainly under the control of British influence and British gold, and it was used without scruple to harass, cripple and destroy the struggling Colonies; and, in its cruel ferocity, it spared neither sex, infancy nor age. When George Rogers Clarke made the conquest of the British posts in Illinois in 1778, Governor Hamilton with a force of British and Indians left Detroit to reconquer them. He wintered at Vincennes; and on the 25th of February 1779 was captured by Clarke, and all his force taken prisoners. Major Lernoult, who was in command during the absence of Hamilton, was succeeded by Major De Peyster in October 1779, and it was under his command that the famous Indian expedition against Kentucky was sent forth under Capt. Byrd in 1780.

MICHIGAN AS A TERRITORY.

By the treaty of peace of 1783, Michigan, heretofore a part of Canada, became a part of the United States, but possession was not actually surrendered until July, 1796, and under the provisions of Jay's treaty.

It then became a part of the North-Western Territory, of which General St. Clair was the Governor; and on the 11th of August, 1796, Wayne County was organized, including all of Michigan, Northern Ohio and Indiana, and a part of Illinois and Wisconsin. It elected delegates to the first Territorial Legislature which met at Cincinnati, Sept. 16, 1799. By an Act of Congress April 30, 1802, the North-Western Territory ceased to exist, the State of Ohio was organized and the Territory of Indiana was formed, of which Michigan formed a part. Gen. Wm. H. Harrison was the Governor of this new Territory.

On the 11th of January, 1805, Congress

passed an Act for the organization of the Territory of Michigan, the Governor and Judges exercising the legislative power. On the 26th of February, the President nominated the Territorial Officers. Gen. Wm. Hull was made Governor. On the 11th of June following, and before the organization of the new government, Detroit was utterly destroyed by fire. Not a dwelling was saved. On the 1st of July, Governor Hull arrived, and on the following day the Territorial Legislature, consisting of the Governor and Judges was organized, and the Government of Michigan commenced its existence.

It included within its boundaries the present State of Michigan except the upper Peninsula. When Illinois was admitted as a State, in 1818, all of what is now Wisconsin was added to the Territory, and in 1834, Iowa and Minnesota were added for the purposes of temporary government. Gen. Hull continued Governor until the shameful surrender of Detroit to Gen. Brock on the 17th of August, 1812. On the breaking out of the war he was put in command of the army provided for the defence of this frontier. For this position he was utterly incompetent from his age and his habits; but of his patriotism there is no reasonable doubt. On the surrender of Detroit to the British, martial law was declared and they remained in possession until after the victory of Perry on Lake Erie, on the 10th of September in the following year, when on the approach of the army under Harrison, Detroit was evacuated and the subsequent victory of Harrison at the Thames secured it from further danger. On the 13th of October, 1813, Col. Lewis Cass was appointed Governor, an office which he held until he was called to the Cabinet of General Jackson in 1831. Under his wise administration Michigan commenced that career of prosperity which has made it what it now is.

In 1818, some of the public lands, which had recently been surveyed, were brought into market. This, with the introduction of steam navigation upon the lakes, the improvements of the roads leading from the east and the opening of the Erie Canal somewhat later, induced a large emigration to the Territory, so that her population increased from 8,876 in 1820 to 31,639 in 1830, and to 212,267, in 1840. In 1819, Michigan was authorized to elect a delegate to Congress, and in 1823 a Legislative Council was authorized; to consist of nine members to be appointed by the President, by and with the advice and consent of the senate, from eighteen persons elected by the people. From this time the Judges ceased to exercise Legislative power. In 1825, the council was increased to thirteen.

By the ordinance of 1787, it was provided that the Territory North-West of the Ohio, should be divided into not less than three States or more than five, as Congress should decide. Congress had the power to form one or two States of the territory lying "north of an East and West line drawn through the southerly bend or extreme of Lake Michi-

gen." By the creation of the three States of Ohio, Indiana, and Illinois, and leaving a large territory north of the line, Congress had clearly determined to create at least four if not five States out of this territory. The ordinance further provided that whenever any of the States had Sixty Thousand free inhabitants they might form a State Constitution and be admitted into the Union. In 1802 Congress authorized the inhabitants of Ohio to form a State Constitution, fixing for the northern boundary of the new State the line indicated by the ordinance viz.: "an East and West line drawn through the Southerly extreme of Lake Michigan." But the Constitution of Ohio described a different line, viz. "one running from the Southern bend of Lake Michigan to the Northerly cape of Maumee Bay." By the line of the Ordinance and the act of Congress the mouth of the Maumee and the site of Toledo would be in Michigan; by the line of the Constitution of Ohio they would be in Ohio. Congress admitted Ohio into the Union under her Constitution without any allusion to the boundary question. As early as 1812 Congress passed an act authorizing the Surveyor General to run and mark the line described in the act of Congress 1802, but the war with Great Britain came and nothing was done at the time. In 1831 Congress authorized a survey to enable them to determine the line.

ADMISSION INTO THE UNION.

In 1834, a census of the inhabitants of the Territory of Michigan was taken, under the authority of the Legislative Council, when it was ascertained that the population was 87,273, more than enough to enable it to be admitted as a State under the ordinance of 1787. In January, 1835, an act was passed by the Legislative Council, authorizing a convention to form a State Constitution. The convention met in May following, and formed a Constitution, which was submitted to and adopted by the people in October following. At the same time, State Officers and a Legislature were elected to act under the Constitution.

The Legislature met in November, 1835. The Governor, Stevens P. Mason, entered upon the duties of his Office and the whole machinery of State Legislation and action went into operation, except the judiciary, which was not organized until July 4th, 1836. At the same time John S. Horner claimed to be Governor of the Territory of Michigan under an appointment of President Jackson, and he continued to act as such until some time in 1836. The history of this contest, and of the admission of Michigan into the Union forms a very curious and interesting chapter in our annals, including as it does a history of that serio-comic performance "The Toledo War." But it can only be glanced at here.

Michigan claimed that the ordinance of 1787 was a compact of binding force, and that the line there described must govern. Ohio claimed that the ordinance had been superceded by the Constitution of the United States and that Congress had full power to regulate the boundary question.

When Michigan sought admission into the Union the question of boundary became a vital one, especially as the territory included the port and site of Toledo, and a decision became inevitable.

The Legislature of Ohio and the Council of Michigan in February and March 1835 passed acts asserting jurisdiction over the disputed territory and providing for its exercise.

In March, an army of Michigan braves, from 800 to 1200 strong, under the leadership of the young and gallant acting Governor Mason, marched to Toledo and took possession. Governor Lucas of Ohio was preparing for an attack on the invaders, but actual hostilities were prevented by the timely arrival of commissioners from Washington. A state of semi-war was kept up for many months, sometimes seriously threatening real hostilities, but the ludicrous incidents far outnumbered the tragic ones. In the meantime Michigan applied for admission under her new Constitution, and, on the 15th of June, 1836, Congress passed an act admitting Michigan into the Union, upon condition that she, by a convention of delegates elected by the people for that purpose, assented to the boundary line, as claimed by Ohio, and giving her, in the place of the territory claimed, the Upper Peninsula. A convention, elected under a call from the Governor, met at Ann-Arbor in September following, and rejected the proposed terms of admission, but the result was not acquiesced in. The machinery of a State government was already in operation, and there were many public and some private reasons for desiring full admission into the Sisterhood of States. The Democratic Central Committee called upon the people to elect another set of delegates, which they did. This second convention met at Ann Arbor on the 14th of December, 1836, and, on the following day, assented to the conditions of admission. A sharp debate ensued in Congress as to whether this assent of a second convention, called without authority, was such a one as the act of Congress contemplated; but on the 27th of January, 1837, Congress, by an act, declared such assent sufficient, and Michigan was admitted into the Union. The Constitution of 1835 remained the fundamental law of the State until superceded by the Constitution of 1850. A convention to revise the constitution was elected in 1867 and submitted to the people a new constitution which was rejected.

MICHIGAN AS A STATE.

The history of Michigan as a State of the Union has for the most part transpired within the memory of the present generation, and needs no especial record here. Then too, for the most part, it has been a history of peace, of growth, of material prosperity and of steady advancement in all the elements of real progress, including those higher interests upon which, in a great degree, the ultimate prosperity and greatness of a people depends. It is therefore a history marked by few incidents of stirring interest.

In no State have the interests of Education been more carefully and wisely promoted. One of the earliest acts of the State Government was the establishment of the University of Michigan upon a broad, firm basis and the making of ample provision for a system of Common Schools, and to-day her University and her common Schools are a just ground of State pride and of hope for the future.

Her Institutions for the care of the Insane, the Deaf and Dumb and the Blind, are worthy of the State; while a hopeful advance is being made in providing for the care of other helpless persons. Her Penal and Reformatory Institutions are being brought more and more into harmony with the true purposes for which they should exist, viz. the prevention of crime and the reformation of the offenders.

Michigan was among the earliest in abolishing imprisonment for debt, and in giving to married women the control of their own property.

No State in the Union poured forth more freely treasure and blood in defence of the Union. Few have shown greater enterprise in developing their natural resources and advantages.

Her mines, her forests, her soil and her waters are all contributing to her wealth and increase. Her past is secure and she may well be proud of it. Her future, under God, is in her own hands.

TERRITORIAL GOVERNORS.

William Hull,	1805 to 1812
Lewis Cass,	1813 to 1831
George B. Porter,	1831 to 1834
Stevens T. Mason, (Acting Gov.)	1834 to 1835
John S. Horner,	1835 to 1836

STATE GOVERNORS.

Stevens T. Mason,	Nov., 1835 to Dec. 31, 1839
William Woodbridge,	1840 and part of 1841
James Wright Gordon, (Acting Gov.)	part of 1841
John S. Barry,	1842, 1843, 1844, 1845
Alpheus Felch,	1846
William L. Greenly, (Acting Gov.)	1847
Epaphroditus Ransom,	1848, 1849
John S. Barry,	1850, 1851
Robert McClelland,	1852 and part of 1853
Andrew Parsons, (Acting Gov.)	Part of 1853, 1854
Kingsley S. Bingham,	1855, 1856, 1857, 1858
Moses Winser,	1859, 1860
Austin Blair,	1861, 1862, 1863, 1864
Henry H. Crapo,	1865, 1866, 1867, 1868
Henry P. Baldwin,	1869, 1870, 1871, 1872
John J. Bagley,	1873, 1874

LIEUTENANT GOVERNORS.

Edward Mundy,	1836, 1837, 1838, 1839
James Wright Gordon,	1840, 1841
Origin D. Richardson,	1842, 1843, 1844, 1845
William L. Greenly,	1846, 1847
William M. Fenton,	1848, 1849, 1850, 1851
Calvin Britain,	1852
Andrew Parsons,	1853, 1854
George A. Coe,	1855, 1856, 1857, 1858
Edmund B. Fairfield,	1859, 1860
James Birney,	1861, 1862
Charles S. May,	1863, 1864
Ebenezer O. Grosvenor,	1865, 1866
Dwight May,	1867, 1868
Morgan Bates,	1869, 1870, 1871, 1872
Henry H. Holt,	1873, 1874

SENATORS IN CONGRESS.

John Norvell,	1836 to 1841
Lucius Lyon,	1836 to 1840
Augustus S. Porter,	1840 to 1845
William Woodbridge,	1841 to 1847
Lewis Cass,	1845 to 1848

Thomas H. Fitzgerald, Session of . . 1848-9
Alpheus Felch, ... 1847 to 1853
Lewis Cass, ... 1850 to 1857
Charles E. Stuart, ... 1853 to 1859
Zachariah Chandler, . . . 1857 to 1875
Kingsley S. Bingham, . . . 1859 to 1861
Jacob M. Howard, ... 1861 to 1871
Thomas W. Ferry, ... 1871 to 1877

JUDGES OF TERRITORIAL SUPREME COURT.

Augustus B. Woodward, . . . 1805 to 1824
Frederick Bates, ... 1805 to 1808
John Griffin, ... 1806 to 1824
James Witherell, ... 1808 to 1828
Solomon Sibley, ... 1824 to 1836
John Hunt, ... 1824 to 1827
Henry Chipman, ... 1827 to 1832
William Woodbridge, . . . 1828 to 1832
George Morell, ... 1832 to 1836
Ross Wilkins, ... 1832 to 1836

CHANCELLORS OF THE STATE.

Elon Farnsworth, . . . 1837 to 1842 and 1846
Randolph Manning, . . . 1842 to 1846

JUDGES OF THE SUPREME COURT UNDER CONSTITUTION OF 1835.

William A. Fletcher, . . . 1836 to 1842
Epaphroditus Ransom, . . . 1836 to 1847
George Morell, ... 1836 to 1842
Charles W. Whipple, 1837 to 1848 and 1852 to 1855
Alpheus Felch, ... 1842 to 1845
David Goodwin, ... 1843 to 1846
Edward Mundy, ... 1848 to 1851
Warner Wing, . . 1845 to 1852 and 1854 to 1857
George Miles, ... 1846 to 1850
Sanford M. Green, . . 1848 to 1854 and 1856 to 1858
George Martin, ... 1851 to Jan., 1858
Joseph T. Copeland, . . . 1852 to 1857
Samuel T. Douglas, . . . 1852 to 1857
David Johnson, ... 1852 to 1857
Abner Pratt, ... 1851 to 1857
Nathaniel Bacon, . . . 1855 to 1858

E. H. C. Wilson, ... 1856 to 1858
Benjamin F. H. Witherell, vacancy in latter part 1857
Benjamin F. Graves, ... 1857
Josiah Turner, ... " " 1857
Edwin Lawrence, ... " " 1857

JUDGES OF SUPREME COURT UNDER PRESENT ORGANIZATION.

George Martin, ... 1858 to 1868
Randolph Manning, . . . 1858 to 1864
Isaac P. Christiancy, . . . 1858 to close of 1873
Jas. V. Campbell, 1858 to 1873—Term expires with 1879
Thos. M. Cooley, 1865 to 1873— " " 1877
Benj. F. Graves, 1868 to 1873— " " 1875

Population of Michigan at each Decade, according to Census of the United States—

CENSUS OF 1820,				8,896
" " 1830, (Territory)				31,639
" " 1840, (State)				212,267
" " 1850, "				397,659
" " 1860, "				749,113
" " 1870, "				1,184,059

A SUMMARY

OF THE

HISTORY OF EDUCATION IN MICHIGAN.

BY ORAMEL HOSFORD, Esq., SUPERINTENDENT OF PUBLIC INSTRUCTION.

THE first School Law of the Territory of Michigan, was enacted in 1827. That Law ordained that the citizens of any township, having fifty house-holders, should provide themselves with a schoolmaster, of good morals, to teach the children to read and write. Any township with two hundred house-holders, was required to have a schoolmaster who could teach Latin, French and English. For neglect to comply with the requirements of the law, the town became liable to a fine of $50 to $150.

In 1833, this law gave place to another creating the office of Superintendent of Common Schools, and providing for three Commissioners, and ten Inspectors, who were to have charge of the School lands, which had, by act of Congress, in 1828, been under the supervision of the Territorial Governor and Council.

As early as 1787, an ordinance was passed by Congress for the government of the North Western Territory, in which it was declared that "Schools and the means of education, shall forever be encouraged."

SCHOOL LANDS.

An act passed in 1804, providing for the sale of lands in the Indian Territory, afterwards formed into the States of Indiana, Illinois, Michigan and Wisconsin—expressly reserved from sale Section 16 in every township " for the support of schools."

All the rights and privileges which these acts conferred, were confirmed to the Territory of Michigan organized in 1805. The ordinance admitting the State of Michigan into the Union in 1836 declares, that "Section number 16 in every township of the public lands, and where such section has been sold, or otherwise disposed of, other lands equivalent thereto, and as contiguous as may be, shall be granted to the State for the use of schools." The original Constitution, as well as the present, required that the proceeds of these

lands, should " remain a perpetual fund for that object." The original design of Congress was to grant to each township the avails of the section found within its limits, or to give to the township, the section to be managed by them, as they might think best. In many of the townships, these lands were nearly worthless, being near swamps or covered with water. These grants led to most serious difficulties in other states, as they attempted to manage the lands, as proposed by Congress. Townships having worthless lands would apply to Congress for additional aid, and failing there, would apply to their Legislature. In addition to all this, different parts of the same township, and different townships, presented their conflicting claims, which could not possibly be adjusted, satisfactorily.

To escape these troubles the people of Michigan, when they came, in 1835, to form a State government, included in the ordinance submitted to Congress, that "Section 16, &c., shall be granted to the State, for the use of schools." The wisdom of this arrangement is seen in the ease with which the land grant has been managed, and the slight expense attending the sale of the lands and the appropriation of the School Fund.

Another great advantage has been, that all the schools of the State have shared in the School Fund as soon as such fund has accrued. Townships having poor or worthless sections, suffered no special loss on that account; it was a loss shared by the whole State, and those townships lying at a distance from the more settled portions of the State, were not compelled to go without schools, or conduct them at their own expense, until the school section of their township could be disposed of —but they at once shared, with all the schools of the State, in the Common School Fund.

The success of our school system is largely owing to this wise foresight of those who had the responsibility of its organization.

The first State Superintendent, Hon. J. D Pierce, estimated the amount of land thus donated by Congress for the use of public schools, to be 1,148,160 acres, and that there would be realized from them a sum not less than $6,000,000 This estimate, as it now appears, was too large, the actual amount being not far from 1,000,000 acres. A little more than one half has been sold, and the fund arising therefrom is $2,601,319, which added to $218,462 derived from swamp lands, gives a total of $2,819,781 as the present School Fund. The State pays 7 per cent. on the School land fund, and 5 per cent. on the swamp land fund. The school lands are sold at four dollars per acre. The purchaser can pay the full amount and secure his patent at once, or he can pay one fourth at the time of purchase, and the balance at his own convenience—the land reverting to the State, on a failure to pay the interest. About 440,000 acres are yet unsold. This should eventually increase the fund to nearly four and one half millions of dollars, and, adding the amount to be received from swamp lands, we may reasonably expect that ultimately the fund will reach $5,000,000.

UNIVERSITY LANDS.

The act of 1804, for the disposal of the public lands in the Indian Territory, reserved three townships "for the use of seminaries of learning,"—one of these was for that part of the Territory now constituting the State of Michigan.

In 1824, the township reserved for the University, not having been located, it was found difficult to secure a township of good land, of which none had been sold. Through the exertions of Gov. Woodbridge, and Hon. Austin E. Wing, then delegate to Congress, an act was passed, giving permission to select the land in detached sections, and adding another township, or its equivalent, to the original grant. The moneys arising from

the sale of those lands, together with that obtained from the three sections granted by Congress in 1817 to the "College of Detroit," constitute the "University Fund."

The Constitution provides that all lands granted for educational purposes "shall be inviolably appropriated and annually applied to the specific objects of the original gift, grant or appropriation."

Thus the University Fund, arising from these grants of lands, is inalienable, and can not be diverted from the University, without a gross breach of faith and a violation of the Constitution.

In addition to the permanent Fund, the University has received, from successive Legislatures, large appropriations. These will doubtless not only be continued, but largely increased.

THE UNIVERSITY AND ITS BRANCHES.

The University was established by the Legislature in 1837, but did not complete its buildings and make other necessary arrangements, so as to enter upon its appropriate work, until 1841.

The act establishing the University also provided for the creation of "Branches," as preparatory schools, to be located in various parts of the State. With no capital, and without any hope of any, except the anticipated income from the future sales of land, those having the responsibility erected the University buildings with borrowed capital. The State borrowed $100,000 and re-loaned it to the University with the understanding that it should be refunded, principal and interest, from the income from University Lands. The University was organized in 1842, having a preparatory school connected with it. There were but two Professors appointed to active duty, with a salary of $500 each, but they were also entitled to whatever tuition might be paid in the preparatory school. The University however soon rose to a commanding position among the Colleges of the country, notwithstanding the multitude of hindrances in the way of its advancement. It required the most vigilant and constant watchfulness, on the part of its friends, to prevent a diversion of its funds to other purposes during the great monetary pressure suffered by the State, during the early history of the University.

To these friends, is the Institution largely indebted for its present efficiency and standing. To these men the State will ever owe a debt of gratitude, for their untiring zeal and patience in caring for an Institution which is now the crowning work of our educational system.

Soon after the opening of the University, several Branches were established in different parts of the State. These were to be supported, in part, by appropriations from the University Fund. It was estimated that the income from this fund would be, at least, $50,000, and $25,000 was deemed an ample sum to meet the current expenses of the University, leaving $25,000 to be expended in these Branches, and the several Counties,

in which they were located, were to raise an amount equal to the sum appropriated, which would, together with a moderate tuition fee, meet the wants of these Branches. A few years' experience, however, satisfied the most ardent supporters, that the plan was impracticable, as all the money arising from the University Fund was not sufficient for the University alone, and the Branches could not be continued without endangering the University itself; indeed for a time, the danger of its suspension was imminent; consequently, the Branches were very soon closed or assigned to private corporations.

NORMAL SCHOOL.

The suspension of these schools was felt to be a great loss, as they gave much attention to the training of Teachers. Urgent petitions were sent to the Legislature, by parents and teachers, for the establishment of a Training School.

In 1849, an act was passed, creating a Normal School which was located at Ypsilanti. This school was opened in Oct. 1852.

The history of this Institution is familiar to all, and its influence has reached every primary school in the State.

OTHER COLLEGES.

During the years occupied in organizing and developing these State Institutions, there sprang up Academies and Seminaries in various places, either private or local in their character. None of them, however received aid from any public fund. All that was granted them, was permission to live. In 1856, there were about 40 of these chartered schools. Six of them have since received charters, giving them full College powers.

AGRICULTURAL COLLEGE.

The Agricultural College was established in 1855. From the first, it has met with violent opposition, but has overcome, thus far, every obstacle, and now stands first among the Agricultural Colleges of this country, and is honorably doing its peculiar work, as an efficient co-worker with the other educational institutions of the State.

PRIMARY SCHOOLS.

The Primary School Law was enacted in 1837, by the first State Legislature. This Law was a transcript of the Law of the State of New York. It provided for the division of the State into districts, containing a sufficient number of inhabitants to support a school having a single teacher. The schools were composed of pupils of all grades, pursuing the usual branches of study. As the population increased, and the school house became crowded, the district was divided. This process was continued in the villages, until there were five or six of these schools in the same village; many of the school houses, being hardly a stone's throw apart. Some of the schools were very good, others nearly worthless. Some were continued nine months, some six, and others not more than three. The purpose of the founders of our

school system, was to adopt that of Prussia, so far as it was found adapted to the genius of our government, and the character and condition of our people.

The Primary Schools constitute the foundation of the system, and the University its crowning glory. The design was, to have the primary schools connected with the University, by those of different grades, which should have courses of study, as would prepare the pupils to enter the University.

GRADED SCHOOLS.

The several Branches that were established having expired, a new system was devised. In the cities and villages, where a number of districts were contiguous, they were united, forming a single school district. These were, at first, called Union Schools. They were divided into several departments, called primary, intermediate, grammar and high school, and each department was divided into different grades or classes, for pupils of different degrees of advancement. These schools are now called by the more appropriate name of Graded Schools. The Curriculum for the High School department, is the same as that usually adopted by the best Academies, and pupils are here prepared for the Colleges and University.

SCHOOL HOUSES.

For ten or twelve years after the organization of our school system, but little attention was given to the building of School houses. They were of the cheapest character, small and insignificant and as inconvenient as they could well be made, and entirely inadequate to meet the wants of a rapidly growing population.

The successful management of a graded school, demanded a better class of school houses, and a new era in school architecture appeared. The various cities and villages vied with each other in erecting the best school edifice, and now it is no rare thing to find, in a village of two or three thousand inhabitants, a school house which cost $20,000 or $30,000, while in the cities and larger towns the cost of these edifices has been from $60,000 to more than $100,000.

There are now not far from five thousand five hundred school houses in the state, the value of which is estimated at about seven and one half millions of dollars.

EDUCATIONAL INSTITUTIONS.

The following is a list of the Educational Institutions of the State.

THE UNIVERSITY OF MICHIGAN.

This is under the control of a Board of Regents, consisting of eight members, elected by the people, and their term of office continues six years. The President of the University is, ex-officio President of the Board. The University is organized in three departments, as follows: the Department of Literature, Science and the Arts; the Department of Medicine and Surgery; and the Department of Law. Each department has its Faculty of Instruction, who are charged

with its special management. These several Faculties constitute the University Senate, which decides all questions of common interest in all the Departments.

THE STATE NORMAL SCHOOL.

This is under the control of the State Board of Education consisting of three members, chosen by the people, and their term of office is six years.

The Superintendent of Public Instruction is, ex-officio, Secretary of the Board.

THE AGRICULTURAL COLLEGE.

This is under the control of the State Board of Agriculture, consisting of six members, appointed by the Governor, with the approval of the Senate whose term of office is six years. The Governor and the President of the College are, ex-officio, members of the Board.

OTHER CHARTERED COLLEGES.

The following are the chartered Colleges of the State.

Hillsdale College, at Hillsdale.
Albion   "   " Albion.
Adrian   "   " Adrian.
Olivet   "   " Olivet.

Kalamazoo College, at Kalamazoo.
Hope   "   " Holland.

These are under the control of Boards chosen either by some religious body, or are made, by their charters, self-perpetuating.

All the above named Institutions are subject to visitation, by committees, appointed by the Superintendent of Public Instruction.

There are about 250 graded schools, taking the place and doing the work of Academies, and 5,500 district schools.

SCHOOL OFFICERS.

The State Superintendent of Public Instruction has the general supervision of the work of Education, and it is his duty to make an annual report of the condition of all the Institutions and public schools of the State. His term of office is two years.

Each County, having ten organized districts, has a County Superintendent, whose duty it is to examine all teachers, and visit the schools and make an annual report of their condition, to the State Superintendent. Their term of office is two years.

Each township has two School Inspectors who together with the township clerk, consti-

tute a Board of Inspection, whose duty it is to organize or alter school districts, and in case of a vacancy in the office of County Superintendent, to examine teachers, and visit the schools.

Their term of office is two years.

Each graded school has a Board of six Trustees ; two Trustees are elected annually, whose term of office is three years. The School Board thus elected, organize by choosing from their number, a Moderator, Director or Assessor.

The entire management of the school is committed to this Board.

Each district school is under the control of a Board of three members, whose term of office is three years, and they are elected as Moderator, Director or Assessor.

THE NUMBER OF TEACHERS AND CHILDREN REPORTED IN 1872.

Number of male teachers, . . 3,035
   "   " female   " . . 8,624
                            _____
   Total, ... 11,659
Number of children between the ages of five and twenty years,   404,235

THE FOREST AND MINERAL WEALTH OF MICHIGAN.

BY HENRY M. UTLEY, ESQ.

NO State in the Union has more varied and abundant resources than Michigan. The timber which must be cleared away to prepare the soil for the farmer brings a handsome profit for the labor employed in its removal. The vast primeval forests of pine which covered a large proportion of both peninsulas have proved a mine of wealth to the active and enterprising lumberman. In mineral wealth the State is unrivalled. Salt, gypsum and coal in the Lower Peninsula, and iron and copper in the Upper, lie but scantily hid beneath the surface and in quantities practically inexhaustible. As a grain-growing State, Michigan is unsurpassed. Its wheat is highly prized in European cities, ranking second in quality to none, while its corn and barley and other grains command the highest market values. As a fruit-growing State, it stands in the very front rank. Apples, peaches, grapes, pears, plums, etc., reward the industry of the horticulturist and are produced of such quality as to be sought for in all markets to which they are accessible, and in such quantities as to have become a source of enormous revenue. The peach and apple orchards of Michigan are widely celebrated, yielding an ample supply for less fortunate sister states, while small fruits are so abundant in their season as to be afforded for the scantiest tables. The pastures of the State are of excellent quality, sustaining herds of cattle and sheep, which are productive of wealth to their growers. With its vast coast-line and numerous interior lakes

and streams, the fisheries of the State are of no inconsiderable importance. They furnish employment to a large number of persons, and are a source of revenue, besides supplying cheap and healthy food to our own citizens.

The settlement of Michigan really began less than half a century ago, and the present development of its great resources of wealth has been made within fifteen or twenty years. The growth of the State, in population, has been rapid and the result of its material development satisfactory and highly promising for the future. It is the purpose of this article, however, to allude to only two features of the great material interests of Michigan—those classed under the heads of lumber and minerals.

LUMBER.

In the matter of pine, no other region of similar extent was ever so richly dowered by nature. The State embraces an area of about 40,000,000 acres, fully one half of which was covered by pine. Of the Lower Peninsula all that portion north of the third tier of counties may properly be called the pine region. It will not be understood, however, that the native forests were exclusively of pine. In some localities, and particularly along the margin of streams, the pine stood very densely, while in many townships it was liberally interspersed with hard wood. It is a well known fact that the pine thus mingled with hard wood is of the choicest

variety. The lumber region thus far developed is mainly that lying upon streams emptying into Saginaw River or Saginaw Bay, and extending to the upper Muskegon and thence to Lake Michigan.

The Thunder Bay region also embraces a large area of pine timber, and the Au Sable River of Lake Huron penetrates the large central pine country on the head waters of that stream, and on the Manistee and Muskegon. At the present time the two leading lumbering streams are the Muskegon on the west side of the State, and the Saginaw and its tributaries on the east side. The Saginaw River is formed by the confluence of the Tittabawassee, Cass and Shiawassee Rivers, and these streams together annually float out a very large proportion of the lumber produced in the State.

Until within the past year or two lumbering operations have been confined to the immediate vicinity of streams. In the winter logs are got out and hauled to the streams, down which they are floated by the spring freshets to the mills below. The trouble and expense of hauling the logs has been such that the lumbermen have not gone back from the streams more than eight or ten miles. Large tracts of intervening pine have been left untouched, and these are now being reached by railroads which have been rapidly pushed into the forest during the past two years. No sooner is the iron track laid than saw mills spring up along side it, as if by magic, and the railroads in the woods

find abundant employment and profitable remuneration in transporting lumber. In this way the older counties are being rapidly cleared of the timber which was left standing back from the streams. This is particularly the case in the counties of Lapeer, Genesee, Tuscola, Isabella, Clare, Osceola, Montcalm, Mecosta, Newaygo, etc. The newer lumber districts are those drained by the Rifle, Au Sable and Thunder Bay rivers on the east side, the great interior region penetrated by the Jackson, Lansing and Saginaw, Flint, and Pere Marquette and Grand Rapids and Indiana Railroads, and the region on the west side watered by the Great Manistee and Boardman Rivers and streams tributary thereto.

It is estimated that there are left in the Lower Peninsula from six to eight million acres upon which pine grows. But a large proportion of this is sparsely timbered and much of it would not, a few years since, have been deemed worthy of notice as pine land. During the past few years explorations have been made in all the wild portions of the State. Capitalists who are quick to foresee and prompt to take advantage of everything that may inure to their benefit have had their experts traversing the northern woods in every direction and have located every available tract of pine so far as discovered, taking at government prices lands which, in some cases, will not yield a thousand feet to the acre. These tracts are owned by men who can afford to hold them for a handsome profit on their investment, and this they are sure to get. It is estimated that there are in the Upper Peninsula about ten million acres which will produce probably about 7,000,000,000 feet of pine.

Michigan pine is of a superior quality for the purposes of lumber. It is what is known as white pine, and of this there are several varieties. The soft or "cork" pine, so called from the resemblance in softness and texture of the wood to the cork of commerce, is the least plentiful of all. It grows in huge trees sparsely scattered among the Oak, Beech and Maple, and consequently upon the very best quality of soil. Upon a somewhat similar soil is found the "Buckwheat," and "grove" pine, which are usually freely interspersed with hemlock. Some varieties of "grove" pine are found on a lighter soil, in which case they are apt to grow in dense forest groves, the trees straight and tall, towering in fair proportions sometimes a hundred feet or more before a twig is reached. In some instances these forests have been known to yield 30,000 feet of lumber to the acre. Norway Pitch, or Southern pine is found abundantly in some localities. It is the least valuable variety and grows upon an arid sandy soil. The best pine is found among trees of firmer grain and these are upon lands which also produce hardwood. It has been a widely prevailing but mistaken idea that lands upon which pine timber grows are worthless for farming purposes. Such is not the case in this State, as has been practically demonstrated. As intimated above in al-

luding to the varieties of pine, the soil upon which pine grows interspersed with Beech and Maple is the very best soil for agricultural purposes known. The soil which produces the grove pine, although of a lighter character, is as a rule found to be well adapted to cultivation, though requiring more artificial enriching than the loamy land on which the cork pine is found. On the best pine lands the quantity of hardwood is often considered greater than that of pine, and is not without its value also. In the older sections of the State considerable quantities of walnut and cherry have been left standing and these the furniture makers are now hunting up and paying liberally for. The trade in live Oak for shipbuilding is very great. Aside from that used in the construction of vessels in the Ship yards along our own coast, vast quantities of it are annually shipped to Quebec, Montreal, Cleveland and Buffalo. At interior points and back from streams where there are no facilities for forwarding heavy ship timbers, Oak is manufactured into Staves. Of these ten to twelve millions are annually shipped from this State, mainly to Europe and the West Indies.

The following figures show the annual shipments of Oak timber for the years named.

	Cubic feet.
1869	765,000
1870	1,105,000
1871	1,982,000
1872	2,560,000

The shipments of staves for the year 1872 were as follows:

Saginaw River,	8,963,200
Detroit,	2,102,000
Port Huron,	1,536,900
New Baltimore,	184,000
Lexington,	204,000
Total shipments in 1872,	12,090,100

To give an idea of the magnitude of the pine lumber manufacturing interests of the State the following facts and figures are condensed from the most reliable sources. They show, so far as can be ascertained, the number of feet of pine lumber cut in 1872 by the mills in the several districts named, includes very nearly, though not quite, all the mills in the State.

LOCALITIES.	FEET.
Saginaw Valley Mills,	837,798,484
Huron Shore "	175,500,000
F. & P. M. Railway Mills,	114,234,554
J. L. & S. " "	68,216,009
Detroit and St. Clair River Mills,	80,000,000
Muskegon Lake Mills,	316,031,400
White Lake "	85,302,347
Grand Haven "	150,000,000
Saugatuck "	50,000,000
Manistee "	161,900,000
Ludington "	47,912,646
Menominee "	136,115,360
Various other "	30,000,000
Total product of 1872,	2,253,011,000

In round numbers we may say that two and a quarter billion feet of pine lumber was

manufactured in Michigan in 1872. This takes no account of shingles and lath. Of these it is safe to say the product of the former reached 400,000,000, and of the latter 300,000,000.

By the best judges it is estimated that there are now invested in Michigan, in the production of pine lumber, over $20,000,000, giving constant employment in its direct manufacture to over 15,000 persons. This does not take into account the investment in pine lands, which is enormous, nor the number of persons employed in lumbering operations in the woods.

The population of prominent cities of the Michigan lumber regions is set down as follows by the best authorities: East Saginaw, 18,000; Grand Rapids, 20,000; Bay City, 14,000; Saginaw City, 9,500; Muskegon, 9,000; Manistee, 6,000; Wenona, 2,500; Midland, 2,500; Alpena, 3,000; Au Sable, 2,000; East Tawas, 1,000; Tawas City, 1,000; Standish, 1,000.

Of the probable future date of the exhaustion of the pine forests of Michigan there have been much discussion and several careful estimates. Upon this subject the Saginaw *Enterprise*, of Jan. 29, 1873, says:

Much has been said and written of late concerning the amount of standing pine in our forests. No accurate calculation can be made on this point, and of course opinions differ widely. The estimates lately made vary from seventeen billions to forty-three and a half billions of feet, for the amount standing in Michigan, and writers fix the time which will be required for the consumption of this pine at from twelve to thirty years. If the lower estimates were correct, the matter would even now be pressing itself uncomfortably upon the attention of lumbermen who have hundreds of thousands of dollars invested in mills and machinery. Our largest manufacturers of lumber, however, have apparently little confidence in small estimates of the pine supply, for the newest of the Michigan mills are the most costly. It is a subject with which lumbermen have been familiar for some years. We have now before us the *Enterprise* of June 2, 1866, in which is an editorial article calling attention to the proposition that "the lumber trade will not sustain the growth and prosperity of the Saginaw Valley for many years longer." At that time the product of our mills had reached 300,000,000, and the article mentioned refers to the "exhausted" lumber regions of Pennsylvania as an example of what this enormous consumption would soon do for our pineries. Nearly seven years have passed since that article was written, and the product of at least one of those "exhausted" Pennsylvania districts steadily and largely increased up to 1871, and would have done the same in 1872 had the season been a favorable one. In the same time the amount of lumber cut in the Valley has nearly doubled, while our mill capacity is sufficient to more than double it. It is true that logs are hauled greater distances to running streams, but the increasing price of lumber more than balances the enhanced cost of hauling. From the Cass river, which has long been spoken of as nearly exhausted of pine, there came last year more logs than ever before in a single year while hundreds of valuable tracts inaccessible before, are now, or soon will be, furnishing millions of feet of lumber by rail.

Now all this, on its face, would only go to show that we must be even nearer the end of our pine supply than was suspected in former years, because we are using it at more than double the old rate. But it really shows quite a different thing. It is plain that the old estimates of the amount of standing pine must be thrown aside in the face of later developments. In early days, for instance, when "short hauls" for logs were thought to be indispensable to profitable lumbering, many tracts of pine land were only "skimmed over," hardly taking even the cream of the pine thereon. Many tracts have been profitably re-cut, but even the present practice does not closely denude the land of its pine. Then again, former estimates took little account of the vast amount of pine standing off from rafting streams, but now being brought into market by our rapidly extended railroad system. There is one newly projecting railroad, not yet really commenced, that estimates as growing along its line, six billions of pine, in no wise accessible for market save by its rail, which would require all its available resources, if built and equipped to its full ability, at least forty years to roll to market.

We may therefore dismiss all present fear as to the duration of our pine supply. It will continue to be the chief source of our wealth and prosperity for many years, and to compensate for the increased cost of lumbering, by reason of long hauling of logs, we shall have the constantly advancing price of lumber, caused by the augmented demand. Upon this point the United States Commissioner of Agriculture says: "If for twenty years to come the demand for lumber shall increase in the same ratio to the population as in the past twenty, more than $200,000,000 worth of American sawed lumber will be needed each year, denuding more than 10,000,000 acres of land. About 7,000 acres are cleared of timber each week-day in this country. Of the annual crop $75,000,000 goes to fuel, and twice as much to fencing. The locomotives in this country consume no less than 7,000,000 cords a year, or 500 acres a day."

The price of pine land is rapidly advancing, in view of such facts as the above. Sales are no longer made at the old figures, and the prices one month are hardly to be taken as a guide to the ruling figure the next month. The forests of Michigan, yet clothed in primeval pine, sell at from $10 to $25 per acre, according to location. A good many lots will change hands at these prices the present winter.

There is another point to be taken into consideration, which doubly assures the permanent prosperity of this country. Our hard woods have hardly been touched yet, and the value of these products of our forests, unrivalled in excellence in many varieties, must continue to increase with every year. The time may not, indeed, be far distant when the hard wood product of this section will equal in yearly value the present pine lumber traffic. The oak stave trade and the business in ship timber have already assumed positions of importance, and their value is rapidly augmenting. The special industries which may grow up and be supplied by the hardwood forests are almost innumerable, and include all manufactures into which our native woods enter.

IRON.

The existence of iron ore in the Upper Peninsula was known to the Indians and white traders who visited that locality at an early day. In June, 1845, the Jackson Iron Co. was organized with a view to operations in the copper district. Mr. P. M. Everett, one of the original corporators, visited Lake Superior as the agent of the company to locate lands. He was provided with a number of permits from the Secretary of War for the location of such lands as he might select for the company. While on his way to that country Mr. Everett was informed by the Indians of the existence of iron, and through their instrumentality he was able to find it, and then located what are now the Jackson and Cleveland Mines. On his return to the lower country Mr. Everett brought with him some of the ore. A portion of this was sent to Pittsburgh to be tested and was there pronounced worthless. Another small quantity was sent to an old forge at Coldwater, and there was made the first iron from Lake Superior ore. This was a small bar, a portion of which Mr. Everett had made into a knife, the better to test its qualities. It was a year later before the Jackson company made the first opening and commenced the erection of a forge. This forge was put in operation in the Spring of 1847, and the first ore taken out at the Jackson mine was there manufactured into blooms. The first blooms were sold to E. B. Ward and the iron was used in the walking-beam of the Steamboat, "Ocean." Other forges were begun from time to time, but the business was slow at starting, owing to the difficulty of shipping. In 1853 three or four tons of Lake Superior iron were shipped to the World's Fair at New York, but regular shipments did not commence until the Spring of 1856.

The ores thus far developed, are mainly in the County of Marquette. They are generally found in hills, which are from 400 to 600 feet high, and which are nothing more nor less than solid masses of iron partially covered by layers of earth and rock. These hills are in a range of about six miles wide by one hundred miles in length, extending from Lake Fairbanks to Keweenaw Bay. There is another extensive range of equally rich hills in Menominee County, but which have not yet been much developed. This range also crops out near Bayfield, and at other points large deposits of magnetic ores have been found, which have been proved to be almost pure native iron. From a pamphlet on the Lake Superior Iron District, published some time since by the editor of the Mining Journal, I ascertain that five varieties of iron ore have been developed. The most valuable is the specular hematite, which is a very pure anhydrous sesqui-oxyde, giving a red powder and yielding in the blast-furnace from 60 to 65 per cent. of metallic iron, which is slightly red short. The ore occurs both slaty and granular or massive. The next in order of importance is probably the soft hematite, which much resembles the brown hematite of Pennsylvania and Connecticut. This ore is generally found associated with the harder ores, from which many suppose it is formed by partial decomposition or disintegration. It contains some water chemically combined, is porous in structure, yields about 50 per cent. in the furnace, and is more easily reduced than any other ore of the district. It forms an excellent mixture with the speculars. The magnetic ore of the district has thus far only been found to the west of the other ores—at the Michigan, Washington, Edwards and Champion mines—at which none of the other varieties have been found except the specular, into which the magnetic sometimes passes. The flag ore is a slaty or schistose silicious hematite, containing rather less metallic iron, and of a more difficult reduction than either of the varieties above named. It is often magnetic and sometimes banded with a dull red or white quartz. The iron is cold short, which is one of the best qualities of this ore, the other ores of the district being red short. It is believed to be the most abundant ore in the district. A silicious iron ore containing a variable amount of oxyde of manganese is found at several points accompanying the flag ore, and is of great value as a mixture.

As previously stated the first shipments of Lake Superior ore were from the Jackson mine in 1856, up to which year the aggregate product amounted to 25,000 tons. The Cleveland mine was opened about the same time and in 1856 shipped about 6,000 tons. The Marquette mine was the next one opened and made its first shipment in 1858. Other mines followed in due time, the attention of capitalists having been attracted in that direction. Railroads and immense docks have been built to facilitate the shipping of ores and furnaces have been erected to reduce the ores on the spot. At the close of the year 1872 upwards of 40 mines were shipping ore, and 14 furnaces were in operation in the Upper Peninsula. The statistics herewith given, for which I am indebted to the Marquette Mining Journal, indicate the magnitude of the iron interests of the State.

The following is a statement in gross-tons of the production of ore and pig iron in the Upper Peninsula, from 1856 to 1872, inclusive, together with the aggregate value:

YEAR.	SOFT ORE.	PIG IRON.	ORE AND PIG PER TON.	TOTAL.
1856	7,000	....	7,000	28,000
1857	21,000	....	21,000	60,000
1858	31,035	1,626	32,661	249,202
1859	65,679	7,258	72,937	575,929
1860	116,598	3,660	122,638	736,496
1861	45,436	7,970	53,406	419,501
1862	115,721	8,590	124,311	984,977
1863	185,257	9,813	195,070	1,416,935
1864	235,123	13,832	248,955	1,867,215
1865	196,256	12,283	208,530	1,590,430
1866	296,972	18,437	313,309	2,405,960
1867	466,076	30,911	496,987	3,475,820
1868	507,813	38,246	546,059	3,992,413
1869	633,238	39,003	672,241	4,958,435
1870	856,471	49,098	905,779	6,900,175
1871	813,379	51,225	864,604	6,115,895
1872	952,055	63,195	1,015,250	9,188,055
Total	5,567,873	357,880	5,925,253	44,373,833

The following table exhibits in gross tons the total product of each mine from 1856 to 1872, inclusive:

MINES.	GROSS TONS.	MINES.	GROSS TONS.
Jackson	1,197,225	S. C. Smith	13,445
Cleveland	1,025,261	Republic	11,025
Marquette	32,998	M. & P. Rolling Mill	6,772
Lake Superior	1,275,919	Allen	8,707
New York	450,780	Wilcox & Bagley	4,425
Lake Angeline	295,747	Mather	2,288

MINES.	GROSS TONS.	MINES	GROSS TONS.
Edwards.....	121,077	Green Bay......	7,633
Iron Mountain...	16,594	Franklin.......	2,007
Barnum........	126,977	Albion........	1,100
Foster........	73,781	Pittsburgh & Lake Superior	1,160
New England....	108,809	Michigan......	1,227
Washington.....	308,919	Quartz........	718
Champion......	243,867	Excelsior......	756
Cascade.......	39,340	Williams......	447
Grand Central..	14,755	Shenango......	197
McComber.....	44,153	Pendill.......	127
Parsons.......	1,896	Michigammi....	141
Winthrop......	25,027	Carr.........	18
Saginaw.......	19,160	Harlow........	83
Negaunee......	11,087	Belden........	7
Iron Cliffs red ore.	874		

Total.............................5,567,373

The following table shows the the total product of the Lake Superior furnaces from 1859 to 1872, inclusive:

FURNACE.	GROSS TONS.
Pioneer...............................	64,597
Northern.............................	15,068
Collins...............................	40,949
Michigan.............................	37,345
Greenwood...........................	29,352
Morgan..............................	35,991
Bancroft............................	36,251
Champion............................	23,566
Jackson..............................	34,242
Schoolcraft..........................	10,057
Deer Lake...........................	10,552
Bay.................................	11,995
Marquette & Pacific (pig metal)......	5,942
(muck bar and merch. iron	999
Lake Superior Company's Pent Furnace	200

Total...............................357,880

It has been demonstrated beyond all controversy that the Lake Superior iron is the best in the world. The following table, arrived at by analysis and actual tests by Prof. Johnson, shows the relative strength per square inch in pounds:

Salisbury, Conn., iron.................	58,009
Swedish (best)......................	58,184
English cable.......................	59,105
Centre County, Pa...................	50,400
Essex County, N. Y..................	59,962
Lancaster County, Pa................	56,661
Russia (best).......................	76,069
Common English and American.	30,000
Lake Superior......................	89,582

It has been practically tested in every use to which iron can be put. It is extensively used in rolling-mills, car-axle factories, boiler-plate factories and in iron works of every description, and the unanimous testimony of all is that it is far preferable to the best iron previously known, both for strength and ease of work.

Michigan now ranks as the second State in the Union in the production of iron, Pennsylvania only leading her. Of the entire product of the United States in 1872, Michigan furnished about one fifth; and of the entire product of the world, about one thirteenth.

The day is past when iron manufacturers east of the Alleghanies will furnish the West with iron. That important mission is reserved for Michigan, with her mountains of solid ore, covering square leagues of her territory, she can supply that race of men whose seat of empire this continent shall be a thousand years to come.

COPPER.

Copper mining operations are carried on in the Counties of Houghton, Keweenaw and Ontonagon in the Upper Peninsula. The existence of copper in those localities first attracted public attention in 1845, when numerous companies were organized and a mad speculation in stocks resulted. The Cliff mine was the first one developed, and was opened in that year. It is just back of Eagle Harbor in Keweenaw County. There is abundant evidence that copper was mined in this region ages previous and by an unknown race. In the Winter of 1847, Mr. S. Knapp, the agent of the Minnesota mine, discovered near the present location of this mine an ancient excavation and cavern in which were found several stone hammers and an immense mass of native copper resting on wooden supports, having evidently been raised some five feet and then abandoned. Since that time numerous discoveries of a similar character have been made. In some instances these pits have been found, containing tools and pieces of charred wood, with many feet of alluvial soil, and huge forest trees, apparently of centuries' growth, above them, indicating that ages have elapsed since the workings were made. The race of Indians who inhabited this country before its settlement by the whites knew nothing of the existence of copper there; nor had they any tools or implements like those found in the abandoned pits. From the skill and strength which these early miners possessed, it is evident that they belonged to a race antecedent to the aborigines whom the present settlers found there. It is conjectured that they were the same as, or cotemporaneous with, the Mound-builders of Ohio, Indiana and Michigan, and the Aztecs of Mexico. Their operations afford a field for curious inquiry and speculation, but history or tradition furnishes nothing concerning them.

The history of copper mining in Michigan presents a somewhat chockered phase. The Cliff mine was discovered in 1845, and worked three years without much sign of success. It changed hands at the very moment when the vein was opened which proved afterward to be exceedingly rich in copper and silver. The Minnesota mine was discovered in 1848, and for the first three years gave no very encouraging results. The discovery of the ancient pit with the large mass of native copper above alluded to, led to the operations at this mine, but it was long before any adequate return was received for the money expended. The Pewabic mine was commenced in 1855, with an expenditure of $26,357, which produced $1,080 worth of copper; the second year it expended $40,820 and produced $31,492 worth of copper; in 1857, $54,484 of expenses produced $44,068 worth of copper; in 1858, the amount expended was $109,152 and the receipts for copper $76,538. Other mines met with similar, or even more disastrous experiences. Mining operations were then carried on at a great disadvantage. Owing to the rapids in the St. Mary's River, the country could not be approached by water with large craft from below. Being more than a thousand miles distant from any centre of supplies or market for mine products, destitute of all the requirements for the development of mines; every tool, every part of machinery, every mouthful of provisions had to be hauled around the rapids, boated along the shores for hundreds of miles to the copper region, and there often carried on the back of man or beast to the place where copper was supposed to exist. Every stroke of the pick cost tenfold more than in populated districts; every disaster delayed the operations for weeks and months. But the opening of the Sault Ste Marie Ship Canal gave a new impetus to mining operations and tended largely to develop the mineral resources of the Upper Peninsula. The want of adequate scientific and practical knowledge, on the part of many who early embarked in the business, led to much loss of capital and often to the embarrassment of those interested, and the abandonment of enterprises which, if they had been conducted with the same care and judgment that is ordinarily bestowed upon other branches of business, would have proved profitable and permanent investments. The fact of an inexhaustible quantity of this valuable mineral, and of a quality which in richness is not surpassed in the world, led to numerous scientific explorations of the territory and to the employment of a large amount of capital, which has, for some years past, by judicious management, been yielding a rich percentage. It, in fact, ranks among the most important products of the North-west, and a careful study and exposition of the different geological peculiarities of the copper districts, and an attentive observation of the local and general mineralogical and vein phenomena are being bestowed upon these vast metallic deposits, which will lead to still more important developments, affecting very materially the wealth and the commerce of the country.

The ore now mined is of a very superior quality, yielding fully 80 per cent. of ingot copper. In many instances masses weighing hundreds of tons, of pure native copper, have been taken out. The copper is smelted at Portage Lake, Detroit, Cleveland and Pittsburgh. There are now about 25 mines in operation, employing about 7,000 men. The statistics of these mines, for 1872, are as follows:

	TONS.	LBS.
Portage Lake District	12,612	819
Keweenaw "	1,916	134
Ontonagon "	798	927
Total,	15,227	1380

STATEMENT OF THE LAKE SUPERIOR COPPER PRODUCT FROM 1845 TO 1872, INCLUSIVE.

	TONS.
1845 to 1854	7,542
1854 to 1858	11,312
1858	3,500
1859	4,200
1860	6,000
1861	7,460
1862	9,982
1863	8,548
1864	8,472
1865	10,790
1866	10,306
1867	11,735
1868	13,049
1869	15,288
1870	16,183
1871	16,071
1872	15,227
Total,	175,766

APPROXIMATE STATEMENT OF INGOT COPPER PRO-
DUCED, AND ITS VALUE.

		TONS.	VALUE.
1845 to 1858	. . .	13,955	$9,900,500
1858	. . . .	4,100	1,866,000
1859	. . . .	4,200	1,890,000
1860	. . . .	6,000	3,610,000
1861	. . . .	7,500	3,337,500
1862	. . . .	6,300	3,402,000
1863	. . . .	6,5 0	4,420,000
1864	. . . .	6,500	6,110,000
1865	. . . .	7,800	5,145,000
1866	. . . .	7,000	4,760,000
1867	. . . .	8,200	4,140,000
1868	. . . .	9,915	4,692,000
1869	. . . .	12,200	5,368,000
1870	. . . .	12,946	5,896,240
1871	. . . .	12,857	5,171,360
1872	. . . .	12,182	6,040,120
Total,	. . .	137,525	$75,560,720

It will be observed that while the number of tons mined last year falls somewhat short of the amount for the two or three preceding years, the value of the product considerably exceeds that of any previous year. It is predicted, by men qualified to judge, that the product of the mines in 1873 will be largely increased over preceding years.

TABLE OF ASSESSMENTS LEVIED,

As nearly as can be ascertained, since the commencement of operations in 1845.

Adams	$ 100,000	Kearsarge	$ 40,000
Adventure	100,000	Keweenaw	100,000
Etna	140,000	Knowlton	100,000
Albany & Boston	615,000	Lake, Superior	40,000
Algonah	65,000	Madison	121,000
Allouez	218,000	Mandan	65,300
American	40,000	Manhattan	110,000
Amygdaloid	470,000	Mass	98,800
Arnold	20,000	Medora	38,400
Atlas	40,000	Mendota	147,500
Aztec	150,000	Merrimac	117,900
Bay State	385,000	Menard	150,000
Bohemian	343,000	Michigan	40,000
Boston	45,000	Milton	30,000
Caledonia	140,000	Minnesota	436,000
Calumet	300,000	National	110,000
Central	100,000	Native	39,000
Concord	120,000	Naumkeag	20,000
Copper Creek	30,000	North Cliff	110,000
Copper Falls	510,000	Northwestern	227,300
Copper Harbor	20,000	Norwich	230,000
Dana	78,000	Ogima	140,000
Dacotah	56,500	Omipee	70,000
Delaware	350,000	Pennsylvania	500,000
Devon	20,000	Petherick	90,000
Dorchester	30,000	Pewabic	235,000
Douglass	130,000	Phl'del's & Boston	24,300
Dover	20,000	Phœnix	820,000
Dudley	20,000	Pittsburg & Boston	110,000
Eagle Harbor	80,000	Pontiac	100,930
Eagle River	85,000	Quincy	200,000
Edwards	32,500	Reliance	20,000
Empire	78,000	Resolute	51,000
Evergreen Bluff	150,000	Ridge	204,900
Everett	20,000	Rockland	360,000
Flint Steel River	244,000	Rhode Island	100,000
Franklin	370,000	St. Clair	140,000
Frue	50,000	St. Louis	29,900
Garden City,	156,000	St. Mary's	110,000
Girard	43,300	Salem	10,000
Grand Portage	50,000	Seneca	40,000
Great Western	40,000	Sharon	2,000
Hamilton	40,000	Shelden & Colum'n	450,000
Hancock	530,000	South Pewabic '69	500,000
Hanover	53,000	South Side	90,000
Hartford	30,000	Star	215,300
Hecla	600,000	Superior	225,500
Highland	20,000	Toltec	420,000
Hilton	50,000	Tremont	42,000
Hope	22,000	Victoria	87,500
Hulbert	18,000	Vulcan	30,000
Humboldt	100,000	Washington	20,900
Hungarian	20,000	West Minnesota	45,000
Huron	500,000	Winona	20,000
Indiana	200,000	Winthrop	90,000
Iroquois	20,000	Schoolcraft	580,000
Isle Royale	910,000		
Total			$ 17,298,500

TOTAL DIVIDENDS DECLARED.

Calumet and Hecla, ...	$ 5,250,000
Quincy, ...	1,480,000
Central, ...	630,000
Copper Falls, ...	100,000
Franklin, ...	260,000
Minnesota, ...	1,800,000

Pittsburgh & Boston,	. . . .	. 2,280,000
National,	. . . .	. 300,000
Pewabic,	. . . .	. 420,000
Ridge	. . . .	. 60,000
Total,	. . . .	. $ 12,570,000

TOTAL OF LAKE SUPERIOR COPPER BUSINESS.

Proceeds of Sales of Copper,	. . .	$ 76,560,720
Proceeds from assessments,	. . .	. 17,298,500
Total proceeds,	. . .	$ 93,859,220
Returned by Dividends,	. . .	. 12,570,000
Balance, .	. . .	$ 81,289,220
Percentage of dividends to assessments,		72.6

SALT.

The first steps taken to develop the saline resources of Michigan were in 1838, when the State geologist, Dr. Douglass Houghton, was authorized by the Legislature to commence boring for salt, as soon as practicable, at one or more salt springs in the State, the location to be selected by himself. In pursuance of this direction he selected a spot on the west bank of the Tittabawassee River, a short distance below the mouth of Salt River, a small tributary stream. The point thus selected was about ten miles above the now flourishing village of Midland, and in one of the wildest and most romantic spots in the State. The Legislature appropriated $3,000 to defray the expenses incident to the undertaking, and about the middle of June, 1838, actual operations were commenced. The work proved more laborious and expensive than had been anticipated; and when, at the end of the year, more than $2,000 of the appropriation had been expended, and a depth of less than 100 feet reached, the parties engaged in sinking the shaft felt that the work was almost hopeless. They persisted, however, until they had attained a depth of about 140 feet, with a poor show of brine, when the State, finding the undertaking too uncertain and onerous for the crippled condition of her finances at that period, abandoned it. Dr. Houghton still entertained the fullest confidence in the existence of rich saline deposits, and the result of later developments fully demonstrated the correctness of his opinions.

After the failure of his experiments, the matter was dropped for a time. Wells were sunk at Grand Rapids, St. Clair, Lansing and other points at various intervals, but with indifferent success. It was not until 1860 that the first paying well was established in the Saginaw Valley. In July, of that year, the first Michigan salt was shipped, and before the close of the year 4,000 barrels had been manufactured and forwarded to market. The character of Michigan salt is indicated by the following chemical analysis:

Chloride of sodium,	. . . .	97.288
" calcium,	. . . .	0.328
" magnesium,	. . . .	0.340
Sulphate of lime,	. . . .	0.697
Moisture,	. . . .	1.300
Insoluble matter,	. . . .	0.046
Total,	. . . .	100.000

The refuse from the salt manufactories is now being utilized, and proves of great chemical importance, producing aniline, one of the best known bases of color, bromo-chloralum, an excellent disinfectant, and

other chemical substances of commercial value.

Within the period of a little over twelve years since the manufacture of Michigan salt commenced, there have been made and shipped nearly six millions barrels. The following shows the amount made for each year, indicating a satisfactory increase:

YEAR.		BARRELS.
1860	. . . .	4,000
1861	. . . .	125,000
1862	. . . .	243,000
1863	. . . .	466,355
1864	. . . .	529,073
1865	. . . .	477,200
1866	. . . .	407,997
1867	. . . .	474,721
1868	. . . .	555,890
1869	. . . .	596,873
1870	. . . .	656,000
1871	. . . .	727,437
1872	. . . .	724,481
Total,	. . . .	5,981,827

At the close of the year 1872 there were 60 salt manufacturing firms in the State, with a capital invested of about $3,500,000, employing over 1,000 men, and with a manufacturing capacity of 1,158,000 barrels. These are distributed in the following districts, as arranged by the Salt Inspector of the State:

District No. 1, East Saginaw, has 4 salt companies, with 10 kettles, 1 steam and 2 pan blocks, having a capacity for manufacturing 140,000 barrels of salt.

District No. 2, South Saginaw, has 10 salt firms, with 10 kettle and 3 steam blocks, having a capacity for manufacturing 135,000 barrels of salt.

District No. 3, Saginaw City, has 8 salt firms, with 5 kettles, 7 steam and 1 pan block, having a capacity for manufacturing 150,000 barrels of salt.

District No. 4, Carrolton, has 6 salt firms, with 12 kettle, 2 steam and 1 pan block, and 500 solar salt covers, having a capacity for manufacturing 175,000 barrels of salt.

District No. 5, Zilwaukie, has 6 salt firms, with 3 kettle, 4 steam and 3 pan blocks, and 2,776 solar salt covers, having a capacity of 150,000 barrels of salt.

District No. 6, Portsmouth, Bay City and Salsburg, has 9 salt firms, with 6 kettle and 8 steam blocks, having a manufacturing capacity of 175,000 barrels of salt.

District No. 7, Bay, Banks and Kawkawlin, has 13 salt firms, with 4 kettle, 7 steam, 5 pan, and 521 solar salt covers, having a capacity of manufacturing 175,000 barrels of salt.

District No. 8, Huron County, has 3 salt firms,—one at Caseville, one at Port Austin, and one at White Rock. They have 2 kettle, 1 steam and 2 pan blocks, and 50 solar salt covers, having a manufacturing capacity of 50,000 barrels of salt.

District No. 9, Mount Clemens, has one salt firm, with one steam block, having a manufacturing capacity of 8,000 barrels.

In his report, for 1872, the Salt Inspector says:

"Since my last report the demand for Michigan salt has increased, and at the present time nearly the entire product of the year is either sold or contracted for.

"From all points reached by Michigan salt we are having the most favorable reports of its quality, and it is rapidly taking the precedence in all the markets of the West.

* * * * *

"The salt interests of the State are gradually extending, and I have to announce the commencement of the manufacture of salt at East Tawas, requiring a new inspection district for the next year."

GYPSUM.

Among the rich mineral productions of Michigan, gypsum holds an important position, as the fertility of the soil and the success of various crops depend more or less upon the application of it as a fertilizer. A chemical analysis of the gypsum found in the State shows the following result:

Sulphuric acid	48
Lime	32
Water	20
Total,	100

When applied in a powdered state it is so easily absorbed by the plant that its value as a manure is very great. This has been so frequently demonstrated by experiment that it is now almost universally used to a greater or less extent by the farmers of the State. Gypsum is known to exist in various parts of the State. There are extensive beds of it at Grand Rapids in Kent County, at Alabaster, Iosco County, and in the Upper Peninsula. It was first developed and the mining of it is now mainly carried on at Grand Rapids. About the year 1835, Degarmo Jones, of Detroit, purchased 80 acres of land in that vicinity, on account of its mineral value. In 1838, Douglass Houghton, State Geologist, visited the place, and wrote the first published statement in regard to the discovery of gypsum. From that time until the present the business of mining and grinding has steadily increased. The stratum of gypsum at Grand Rapids is about 18 to 20 feet in thickness, from 12 to 16 feet below the surface, and is probably about 1,000 acres in extent, offering an almost inexhaustible supply. When taken from the mine it is generally piled up in large blocks, and suffered to remain for several months exposed to the air, that some portion of the water which it contains may be carried away by evaporation. When taken to the mill the large lumps are broken and then ground to powder.

The manufacture of plaster at Grand Rapids has been steadily increasing from 500 tons a year until now it aggregates 40,000 tons of land plaster and 60,000 barrels of stucco per annum. The capital invested is about $500,000 and about 300 men find constant employment.

The mines at Alabaster are much more recent, their development having been begun but five or six years ago. They are located near the water's edge on an excellent harbor, and the facilities for mining and shipping are unsurpassed. Tram-ways have been constructed from the mines to the docks, and the gypsum is dumped from cars into the vessel's hold. This business is destined to assume even greater magnitude than it now possesses, as the agricultural portions of this and adjoining States are developed and the value of plaster, as a fertilizer, becomes more widely known and appreciated.

COAL.

The existence of a great coal basin underlying the central portion of the Lower Peninsula was long since demonstrated by geologists, and coal has in several localities been found cropping out on the banks of the streams. Mines have been opened at Jackson, at Corunna in Shiawassee County, and at Williamston, in Ingham County. At the first mentioned place operations were commenced about the year 1858, and have since been regularly continued. The coal is bituminous, and too soft and too strongly impregnated with sulphur to be popular for domestic uses. It is largely employed, however, in many branches of manufacture, for which it proves admirably adapted. As the shaft descends through the strata the quality of the coal improves.

Operations at Corunna have been carried on for the past eight or ten years. The quality of coal has been very similar to that mined at Jackson. Lately, however, a vein of a considerably superior quality has been opened and bids fair to prove of great importance. The railroad track has been extended to the mine—some two miles—and mining operations will be vigorously prosecuted during the coming season.

At Williamston very little has heretofore been done owing to lack of railroad facilities for transportation. This difficulty has now been overcome and mining has received a new impetus. The coal found here is said to be the best in the State, more nearly than any other resembling the famous block coal of Indiana. The development of this feature of the mineral resources of the State is still in its infancy. But the results thus far are quite satisfactory, promising well for the future.

OTHER MINERALS.

In addition to those enumerated there are other minerals of such value and found in such abundance in the State as to be worthy at least a brief allusion in this connection. Silver and gold have been found in the Copper mines of the Upper Peninsula, the former in no inconsiderable quantities. Lead and plumbago have been long known to exist in the Lake Superior region. Indeed the Indians abundantly supplied themselves with leaden bullets, but never revealed the sources from whence they came. Mines have been opened and worked to some extent, but the business has not yet attained much magnitude nor invited any outlay of capital, except by way of experiment. It is safe to predict that profitable mines will yet be opened and a new branch added to the already famous mining operations of Michigan.

The Huron grit stones are unrivalled in the market and the business of producing them has assumed considerable magnitude. Grindstones from those quarries now find their way into all the markets of the north and west, and from their superior quality are rapidly superseding all others.

In the Marquette iron region are deposits of marble that promise to develop into a product of commercial importance. Some samples are highly crystaline, others are beautifully clouded, others vary from pinkish to dove color, and are very fine grained. In the Menominee region are beds of beautiful white marble which possess the fineness of grain, and the purity and translucency of good statuary marble.

Unlimited qualities of coloring substances are afforded by the ochre and manganese beds of various parts of the State. Yellow and red ochres are especially abundant in the St. Mary's Peninsula.

A superior quality of building stone is found in various localities, equal in beauty, texture and durability to the free stone of New England. Various qualities of this Stone have been developed in Ionia, in the southern part of Jackson County, at Flushing in Genesee County, at Marquette, and in other localities.

The State is supplied with unlimited quantities of material for quick-limes and hydraulic limes. Its clays are of every variety, making a quality of brick which are a favorite and find a ready market far beyond the limits of the State. White and lemon-colored brick, which are so popular for building fronts, are made in many localities. The swamp lands of the State afford vast quantities of peat, which, fifty years hence, when the enhanced value of land and the crowded state of population shall have called the attention of agriculturists to it, will be found of incalculable value in replenishing decayed and worn-out soils. In nearly every town which has regard for its dignity and rank among its fellows, Artesian wells or springs exist, whose mineral properties have already gained wide notoriety for their therapeutic effects upon decayed or damaged human constitutions.

Indeed, so multifarious and valuable have the great natural resources of the State proven to be, that those classical gentlemen who constructed our armorial inscription would have been justified in writing it:

Si quæris Peninsulam locupletissimam, circumspice.

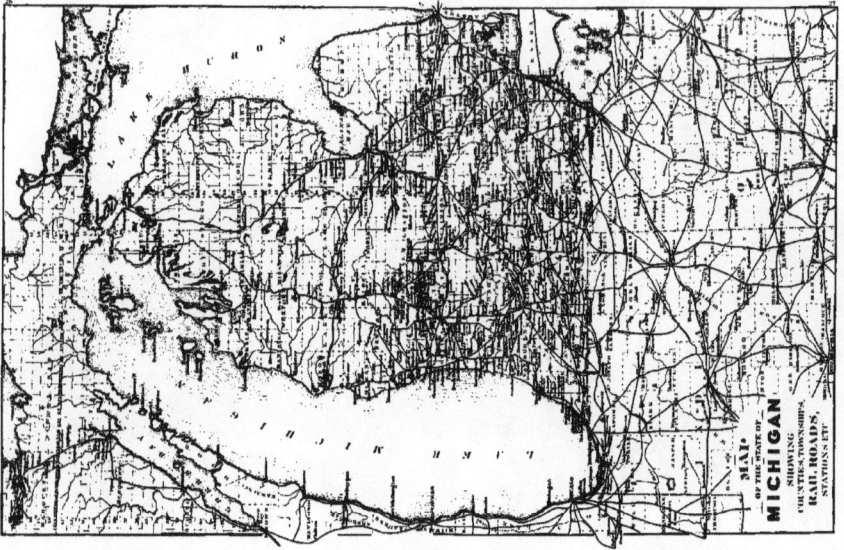

MAP
OF THE STATE OF
MICHIGAN
SHOWING
COUNTIES, TOWNSHIPS,
RAIL ROADS,
STATIONS, ETC.

RAILROADS OF MICHIGAN

NOW COMPLETED, WITH

STATIONS AND DISTANCES.

CHI. & MICH. LAKE SHORE.

New Buffalo to	
Town Line	4
Wilkinson's	5
Chickaming	7
Troy	10
Brown's	11
Bridgman's	15
Morris	16
Stevensville	20
Lincoln	22
St. Joseph	27
Benton Harbor	29
Hagar	33
Riverside	35
Coloma	39
Watervliet	41
Hartford	49
Deerfield	50
Bangor	54
Breedsville	57
Grand J'nc.	61
Black River	65
Hoppertown	66
Sherman	69
Clyde	71
Pennville	75
Manlius	78
Richmond	70
East Saugatuck	82
Holland	90
New Holland	95
Olive	98
Ottawa	100
Robinson	103
Spoonville	108
Nunica	110
Fruitport	116
Norton	121
Muskegon	126
Dalton	131
Califf	134
Sweet's	138
Whitehall	142
Montague	143
Greenwood	149
New Era	153
Barrett	157
Collins	162
Mears	163
Hart	164
Pentwater	170

GRAND RAPIDS DIV.

Holland to	
Zeeland	5
Vriesland	9
Hudson	14
Jennison's	18
Grandville	19
Grand Rapids	25

CHICAGO AND NORTH-WESTERN.

PENINSULA DIV.

Escanaba to	
Ore Siding	1
Flat Rock	3
Bay Siding	6
Mason	9
Day's River	13
Beaver	17
Campbell	20
Maple Ridge	25
Centreville	30
Helena	35
Little Lake	41
Plains	46
Sands	50
Harvey	54
Goose Lake	57
Partridge	59
Mineral Branch	60
Negaunee	62
N. Y. Mine	64
Ishpeming	65

DETROIT AND BAY CITY.

Detroit to	
M. C. & R. C. R. Junction	2
L. S. & M. S. & G. T. R. Cro.	6
D. & M. Junc.	7
Norris	11
Warren	14
Glenwood	17
Spinning's	18
Utica	24
Yates	29
Rochester	31
Goodison's	35
Orion	41
Oxford	44
Metamora	52
Hunter's Creek	-
Lapeer	60
Junction	61
Fish Lake	65
Millville	66
Columbiaville	70
Otter Lake	74
Millington	80
Vassar	87
Reese	90
Bay City	115

DETROIT, HILLSDALE & INDIANA.

Ypsilanti to	
Saline	11
Bridgewater	17
Manchester	25
Watkins	30
Brooklyn	36
Woodstock	41
Somerset	44
Somerset Centre	46
Jerome	49
North Adams	54
Hillsdale	61
Bankers	65

DETROIT, LANSING AND LAKE MICH.

Detroit to	
Grand Trunk Junction	3
Town Line	9
Redford	12
Fisher's	14
Elmwood	16
McKinney's	17
Livonia	18
Plymouth	23
Salem	29
South Lyon	34
Green Oak	37
Brighton	43
Genoa	46
Howell	52
Fleming	57
Fowlerville	61
Leroy	66
Dana	70
Williamston	71
Meridian	75
Okemos	78
College Farm	82
Lansing	85
North Lansing	86
Delta	94
Ingersoll's	96
Grand Ledge	99
Eagle	103
Danby	107
Portland	111
Stebbinsville	115
Lyons	119
Ionia	125
Orleans	131
Palmer's	134
Chadwick	136
Kiddville	138
Greenville	144
Kaywood	149
Trufant's	154
Maple Valley	157
Coral	159
Howard	164

STANTON BRANCH.

Ionia to	
Stanton Junc.	3
Wood's Corners	7
Shanty Plains	11
Fenwick's	12
Sheridan	17
Colby's	20
Stanton	22

DETROIT AND MILWAUKEE.

Detroit to	
L. S. & M. S. Junction	3
G'd Trunk J'nc.	4
Eight Mile Siding	8
Royal Oak	13
Birmingham	18
Pontiac	26
Drayton Plains	31
Waterford	33
Clarkston	36
Davisburgh	41
Holly	47
Fenton	50
Linden	55
Gaines	62
Vernon	70
Corunna	75
Owosso	78
J. L. & S. Junc.	79
Ovid	88
Shepardsville	92
St. Johns	98
Fowler	107
Pewamo	112
Muir	117
Ionia	124
Saranac	132
Lowell	139
Ada	148
Grand Rapids	158
G. R. and Ind. Junction	159
Berlin	167
Coopersville	173
Dennisonville	176
Nunica	180
Spring Lake	186
Ferrysburg	187
Grand Haven	189

FLINT AND PERE MARQUETTE.

Toledo to	
Monroe	25
Grafton	34
Wale	39
New Boston	43
Wayne	51
Plymouth	58
Waterford	60
Northville	62
Novi	66
Wixom	70
Milford	76
Highland	80
Clyde	83
Rose	86
Holly	91
Grand Blanc	100
Flint	108
F. H. B. Junc.	112
Mount Morris	116
Clio & Pine Run	120
County Line	124
Birch Run	128
Bridgeport	135
E. Saginaw	142
J. L. & S. R. R. Crossing	143
Freeland's	153
Midland	162
Averill	168
Sanford	170
Coleman	182
Loomis	186
Clare	192
Farwell	197
Remick	202
Lake	206
Orient	215
Evart	218
Hersey	228
Reed City	232

BAY CITY DIVISION.

East Saginaw to	
Portsmouth	11
Bay City	13

OTTER LAKE BRANCH.

Flint to	
Junction	4
Genesee	8
Otisville	14
Otter Lake	19

FORT WAYNE, JACKSON AND SAGINAW.

Jackson to	
Wilson's	6
Baldwin's	11
Hanover	14
Stony Point	16
Mosherville	19
Jonesville	25
Bankers	31
Reading	36
Camden	41
State Line	48
Angola	63
Auburn	77
Ft. Wayne	100

GRAND RAPIDS AND INDIANA.

Fort Wayne to	
Junction	1
Wallen	8
Huntertown	12
Bruces	17
Swans	18
Avilla	22
Lisbon	26
Kendallville	28
Rome City	35
Wolcottville	38
Valentine	42
Lagrange	46
Lima	51
Sturgis	57
Perrin	62
Nottawa	66
Air Line Crossing	67
Mendon	72
Portage Lake	77
Vicksburg	80
Austin	85
Kalamazoo	93
Cooper	99
Travis	101
Plainwell	104
Monteith	109
Martin	110
Shelby	114
Bradley	117
Wayland	120
Moline	125
Ross	528
Fisher	135
Grand Rapids	141
Mill Creek	147
Belmont	151
Child's Mill	153
Rockford	156
Edgerton	158
Burch's Mill	160
Cedar Springs	162
Lockwood	165
Sand Lake	167
Pierson	169
Wood Lake	171
Maple Hill	173
Howard City	175
Reynolds	176
Conger	179
Morley	181
Stanwood	188
Rust	189
Byers	193
L. Big Rapids	196
U. Big Rapids	197
Paris	202
Crapo	205
Mitchell's	207
Reed City	209
Ashton	215
Leroy	222
Clam Lake	238
Linden	241
Wexford	244
Manton	250
Walton	250
Fife Lake	264

TRAVERSE CITY BRANCH.

Walton to	
Kingsley's	10
Mayfield	13
Traverse City	27

GRAND RAP., GREENVILLE AND ALPENA.

Grand Rapids to	
Rockford	13
Cortland	17
Oakfield	22
Gould's Mills	26
Greenville	31
Crosby's Mills	38
Dickerson's Lake	40

GRAND RAPIDS, NEWAGO AND LAKE SHORE.

Grand Rapids to	
G. T. & L. Crossing	4
Alpine	8
Englishville	11
Sparta	14
Tyrone	19
Casinovia	21
Trent	23
County Line	25
Ashland	27
Grant	29
Brooks	33
Newaygo	36

GRAND TRUNK.

Detroit to	
Detroit Junc.	3
Mil. Junc.	8
Utica Plank	19
Mt. Clemens	25
New Baltimore	35
Ridgeway	41
Smith's Creek	51
Port Huron	62
Sarnia	63
Stratford	143
Toronto	231
Kingston	392
Montreal	564
Portland	861

HECLA AND TORCH LAKE.

Calumet to	
Hecla	1
Houghton Falls	3
Monroe Junc.	4
Torch Lake Mills	5

LAKE SHORE & MICHIGAN SOUTHERN.

Buffalo to	
Cleveland	183
Toledo	296
Sylvania	307
Ottawa Lake	311
Wood Sta.	313
Riga	317
Blissfield	319
Palmyra	323
Lenawee Junc.	325
Adrian	329
Dover	330
Clayton	340
Hudson	346
Pittsford Centre	349
Pittsford	352
Osseo	356
Hillsdale	362
Jonesville	368
Allen	371
Quincy	377
Coldwater	384
Batavia	390
Bronson	395
Wood Sta.	393
Burr Oak	402
Sturgis	408
Douglas	413
White Pigeon	420
Bristol	430
Elkhart	439
South Bend	454
La Porte	481
Chicago	539

DETROIT DIVISION. (Detroit to Toledo and Chicago.)

Detroit to	
Det. & Mil. J'nc.	3
Grand Trunk Junction	8
Wyandotte	17
Trenton	21
Rockwood	27
Newport	33
Strong Creek	36
Monroe Junction	40
Vienna	50
Toledo	65
Ida	50
Petersburg	57
Deerfield	61
Simon	64
Wellsville	66
Lenawee Junc.	70
Adrian	74
Chicago	284

KALAMAZOO DIV.

Grand Rapids to	
Eagle Mills	2
Grandville	6
North Byron	10
Byron	12
Dorr	18
Hilliards	22
Hopkins	26
Allegan	33
Abronia	39
Otsego	43
Plainwell	46
Argenta	49
Cooper	52
Kalamazoo	58
Portage	65
Schoolcraft	71
Flowerfield	75
Moorepark	78
Three Rivers	83
Florence	88
Constantine	91
White Pigeon	95
Chicago	218

JACKSON BRANCH.

Adrian to	
Lenawee Junc.	4
Chase's	7
Tecumseh	13
Clinton	18
River Raisin	21
Manchester	25
Norvell	32
Napoleon	36
Eldred	40
Jackson	46

LANSING DIVISION.

Jonesville to	
Litchfield	7
Homer	14
Condit	17
Albion	22
Devereux	27
Springport	33
Brockway	38
Eaton Rapids	42
Dimondale	51
Lansing	59

LAPEER AND NORTHERN.

Lapeer to	
Fish Lake	6

MANSFIELD, COLDWATER & LAKE MICH.

MICHIGAN DIVISION, (ONLY PARTLY COMPLETED.)

Coldwater to	
Ovid	6
Alaganee	9
Hall's Corners	12
Camden	16
Chester	19
Woodbridge	23
Amboy	27
Pioneer	32
Coldwater to	
Gerard	6
Burlington	13
Underwood's	18
Newton	22
Emmett	25
Battle Creek	30
Bedford	34
Augusta	38
Yorkville	42
Richland	45
Henneysett	48
Prairieville	51
Gun Marsh	56
Monteith	60
Allegan	72

MARQUETTE, HOUGHTON & ONTONAGON.

Marquette to	
Bancroft	3
Bruce	6
Morgan	7
Eagle Mill	8
Negaunee	12
Ishpeming	15
Ontonagon Junction	17
Saginaw	19
Greenwood	22
Clarksburg	26
Humboldt	27
Champion	32
Michigamme	39
Spurr Mine	41
Sturgeon	48
Summit	54
Hematite	59
L'Anse	64

BRANCHES:

At Ontonagon Junction: To New England and Saginaw Mines	5
At Humboldt: To Republic Mine	9
At Champion: To Champion and Chippewa Mines	8
At Hematite: To Sec. Nine	5

MICHIGAN AIR LINE.

Ridgeway to	
Armada	7
Romeo	14
Washington	20
Rochester	26

MICHIGAN CENTRAL.

Detroit to	
G. T. Junc.	3
Dearborn	10
Inkster	14
Wayne	18
Secords	23
Denton's	25
Ypsilanti	30
Geddes	34
Ann Arbor	38
Delhi	43
Scio	46
Dexter	47
Chelsea	55
Francisco	62
Grass Lake	60
Leoni	69
Mich. Centre	72
Jackson Junc.	75
Jackson	76
Trumbull	81
Parma	87
Bath Mills	92
Albion	96
Marengo	101
Marshall	108
Ceresco	113
White's	116
Battle Creek	121
Bedford	128
Augusta	130
Galesburg	136
Comstock	140
Kalamazoo	144
Oshtemo	149
Mattawan	156
Lawton	160
White Oaks	162
Decatur	168
Tietsort's	172
Dowagiac	179
Pokagon	185
Niles	191
Buchanan	197
Dayton	202
Galien	206
Avery's	209
Three Oaks	211
New Buffalo	218
Corymbo	223
Mich. City	228
Furnessville	234
Porter	240
Christman's	244
Lake	249
Tolleston	255
Gibson's	261
Calumet	270
Chicago	284

GRAND RIVER VALLEY DIVISION.

Detroit to	
Jackson	..
Van Horn's	7
Rives Junction	10
Arland	14
Onondaga	17
Eaton Rapids	24
Charlotte	35
Chester	40
Vermontville	46
Nashville	50
Sheridan	55
Quimby	66
Hastings	62
Irving	70
Middleville	73
Caledonia	79
Hammond	86
Bowen	88
Grand Rapids	94
D. & M. Junc.	97
Berlin	105
Coopersville	111
Nunica	117
Fruitport	123
Muskegon	133
Whitehall	149
Montague	150
Pentwater	177

JACKSON, LANSING & SAGINAW DIVISION.

Jackson to	
Van Horn's	7
Rives Junction	10
Leslie	15
Chapin's	20
Mason	26
Delhi	30
Lansing	37
No. Lansing	38
Chandlers	42
Bath	46
Laingsburg	55
Bennington	59
D. & M. Crossing	64
Owosso	65
Henderson's	72
Oakley's	76
Chesaning	80
Pine Grove	83
St. Charles	87
Swan Creek	93
Tittabawassee	97
Saginaw	101
East Saginaw	103
F. & P. M. Junc.	104
Carrolton	105
Zilwaukee	107
Salzburg	116
Wenona	116
Kawkawlin	121
Terry's	126
State Road	131
Pinconning	135
Saganin	140
Standish	144
Clyde	150
Wells	156
Culver	159
Bowens	161
Georgetown	163
Wright's	166
West Branch	169
Ogemaw	173
St. Helen's	184
Roscommon	193
Crawford	208

AIR LINE DIVISION.

Detroit	
Jackson to	
Fort Wayne Switch	1
Snyder's	7
Concord	14
Pulaski	16
Homer	23
Clarendon	27
Tekonsha	33
Burlington	37
Union City	41
Sherwood	48
Colon	53
Nottawa	60
Centreville	64
Three Rivers	69
Coreys	76
Jones	78
Vandalia	84
Cassopolis	89
Howard	96
Barren Lake	98
Niles	103

JOLIET DIV. (ILL.)

Lake to	
Ross	8
Dyer	15
Bloom	20
Matteson	24
Frankfort	32
Spencer	37
Joliet	45

SOUTH HAVEN DIV.

Kalamazoo to	
Alamo	8
Kendall's	14
Pine Grove	17
Goble's	18
Bloomingdale	22
Bear Lake	24
Columbia	27
Chi. & Mich. L. Shore Junc.	29
Genova	31
So. Haven	39

SOUTH BEND DIV.

Niles to	
Bertrand	4
South Bend	11

MICHIGAN LAKE SHORE.

Kalamazoo to	
Cooper	6
Travis	8
Plainwell	11
Monteith	16
Fisk	20
Kellogg	23
Allegan	28
Mill Grove	32
Dunning	36
Gilchrist	38
Hamilton	41
Fillmore	45
May	48
Holland	51
North Holland	56
Pigeon	61
Johnsville	64
Oconto	66
Grand Haven	71
Ferrysburgh	72
Black Lake	80
Muskegon	85

MUSKEGON & BIG RAPIDS.

Muskegon to	
Junction	4
Twin Lake	10
Holton	16
County Line	19
Fremont Centre	24
Alleyton	34
Morgansville	35
Monroeville	44
Big Rapids	55

PAW PAW.

Lawton to	
Paw Paw	4

PENINSULAR RAILWAY.

Lansing to	
Millet's	5
Sevastopol	10
Potterville	12
Charlotte	19
Moore's	25
Olivet	27
State Road	29
Bellevue	32
Madison's	37
Penfield	39
Verona	42
Battle Creek	45
Helmer's	49
Climax	55
Scott's	60
Indian Lake	64
Vicksburg	68
Schoolcraft	74
Flowerfield	79
Marcellus	85
Volinia	89
Jamestown	94
Cassopolis	98
Edwardsburg	108
Irvin's	110
Mishawaka	116
So. Bend	120
Crum's Point	129
Fish Lake	136
Stillwell	142
Kingsbury	146
Union Mills	151
Haskell's	157
Valparaiso	160

PORT HURON AND LAKE MICH.

Port Huron to	
G. T. Junc.	4
Thornton	10
Emmet	19
Capac	27
Imlay City	34
Attica	39
D. & B. C. Junc.	45
Lapeer	45
Elba	53
Davison	57
Flint	66

SAGINAW VALLEY AND ST. LOUIS.

Saginaw to	
J. L. & S. Junc.	4
Swan Creek	7
Graham's	9
Sand Ridge	11
Hemlock	14
Porter's	17
Meridan	21
Wheeler	24
Breckenridge	29
St. Louis	35

THE RAILROADS OF MICHIGAN.

BY RAY HADDOCK, ESQ.

THE history of the Railroads of Michigan is inwrought with the annals of the State, with her early struggles, her hopes, her progress, her destiny. Immigration hither was at its height during the period, particularly the latter part of it, extending from 1830 to 1835. A large proportion was from Western New York, an element belonging mainly to the New England stock, and quite naturally the maxims of thrift and enterprise came with them. The practical application of these maxims began to take shape in stupendous enterprises even before Michigan emerged from the chrysalis condition of a Territory. The name of these projects was legion, most of them being of a Utopian character, whose most important results consisted of fastening upon our then population an enormous load of indebtedness. This period constitutes the first of two epochs in our Railroad history. The first belongs to the era of wild speculation and "internal improvement" so vividly remembered by old citizens of the West, and, in view of the great results which our pioneers hoped for, taken in connection with the insignificant means at command, it may be regarded as eminently typical of that remarkable era. It is with entirely different emotions that we turn for a moment to the second epoch, in the midst of which we now are, the most gratifying reflection connected with which is that, magnificent as are the results, they are but a true index of the development of the great material resources of the State.

Of the numerous projects belonging to the earlier epoch, only three Roads of any considerable extent assumed substantial form and shape, viz. the Detroit and St. Joseph (the old corporate name of the Michigan Central); the Michigan Southern, and the Detroit and Pontiac (which alternately became merged in the Detroit and Milwaukee. In 1830, the population of Detroit numbered 2,200 souls. The citizens of that day were proverbially enterprising, to a degree more than commensurate with their ability. If the public interest required any work to be done, there were no capitalists to rely upon, for no fortunes had been made. A few of the old class of landed proprietors were comparatively well off, but those who were the most wealthy, as a general rule, had the least money, their possessions consisting of lands, and the necessity of borrowing money with which to pay their taxes was more nearly the rule than the exception. The community could boast of two or three banks, powerful institutions for those days, having more capital than could be conveniently used at home, and considerable of their surplus currency was absorbed by Ohio customers. There was comparatively little difficulty in borrowing money, and very naturally almost everybody

was in debt. Thus situated, with no trade with the outer world worth speaking of, except in the single item of furs, when we say that poor as Detroit was, it was rich compared with the settlements elsewhere in the Territory, something like a true idea may be formed as to the ability of Michigan to prosecute great works of internal improvement.

Such was the condition of affairs when the Detroit and St. Joseph Railroad was incorporated by the "Legislative Council of the Territory of Michigan." The act was consummated on the 29th June, 1832, and named as Commissioners the following gentlemen, all of whom, we believe, have passed from this earthly stage of action, viz. John Biddle, John R. Williams, Charles Larned, E. P. Hastings, Oliver Newberry, De Garmo Jones, James Abbott, John Gilbert, Abel Millington, Job Gorton, John Allen, Anson Brown, Samuel W. Dexter, W. E. Perrine, Wm. A. Thompson, Isaac Crary, O. W. Colden, Caleb Eldred, Cyrus Lovell, Calvin Brittain, and Talman Wheeler. By the terms of the charter, the State reserved the right to purchase the Road at a price not exceeding its original cost and fourteen per cent. interest.

This initial step, destined to be productive of great results in paving the way for an East and West through line, was due in a certain degree to the necessities of the case, as well as to enterprise and public spirit. There were at that time four thoroughfares leading into Detroit, the Chicago, Grand River, Fort Gratiot, and Saginaw, generally known as the Pontiac road, all of which had been built by government. They were all constructed upon a clay soil, and were well nigh impassable throughout a considerable portion of the year; hence the necessity for iron outlets. The Detroit and St. Joseph road was at the outset a local enterprise, and probably not a dollar of the original stock was taken at the East. Every one in Detroit who had a hundred dollars at command, present or prospective, subscribed, and upon this subscription, with what little could be obtained along the line, the work was commenced. Within two years from the date of the act of incorporation, the construction proceeded between Detroit and Ypsilanti, under the presidency of Major John Biddle. The civil engineer in charge was Col. John M. Berrien, then Lieut. Berrien, of the army, detached for civil service—a not uncommon proceeding, the valuable aid of officers being frequently called into requisition in laying out roads and furnishing drawings of harbors and "paper cities." Between Detroit and Ypsilanti the forest was almost entirely unbroken, and was so dense that it was with the greatest difficulty the surveyors

could run a line. Notwithstanding this and countless other drawbacks, the construction progressed at a fair rate for that period, when every necessary appliance was procured with great difficulty. The Albany and Schenectady (then Mohawk and Hudson) Railroad, the first Road built north of Pennsylvania, had been running only about a year when the Detroit and St. Joseph Railroad Company was chartered.

The construction of the Road progressed as rapidly as could be expected until Michigan was formally admitted as a State, in February, 1837. By this time, the subject of internal improvements by the State had begun to be agitated to a considerable extent, and an act was passed and approved March 20, 1837, entitled "An act to provide for the construction of certain works of public improvement, and for other purposes." This act provided for the purchase of the Detroit and St. Joseph Railroad, and under its provisions the Road passed into the possession of the State. It was after about $30,000 had been expended toward building the section between Detroit and Ypsilanti, in purchasing the right of way beyond the last named point. Laws were passed by which a loan of $5,000,000 was to be effected for the purpose of making internal improvements, and thus carrying out the popular idea. Somewhere between $2,000,000 and $3,000,000 was realized from this loan, but by the crash of 1837 the corporators who had taken the loan became insolvent, and the State was left financially powerless.

Upon the purchase of the Road by the State, the name was changed to the Michigan Central, and it became part and parcel of the famous plan of crossing the State by three parallel lines, namely, the Northern, having its eastern terminus at Port Huron, the Central, terminating at Detroit, and the Southern, at Monroe. By way of relieving the monotony attaching to so many land routes, a canal was projected from Clinton River to the Kalamazoo, upon which a large sum was expended before it was abandoned. The Northern road, after being graded for some distance west from Port Huron, was abandoned after the expenditure of a large sum for the right of way, grubbing and grading. The late Hon. James B. Hunt was the Acting Commissioner of the Northern route, Gen. Levi S. Humphrey, of Monroe, holding the same position in reference to the Southern, the works being in charge of a general Board of Internal Improvements. The first Acting Commissioner of Internal Improvements was Col. David C. McKinstry, father of Commodore J. P. McKinstry.

To convey a correct idea of the character of the railroads of that day, we ought to state

that up to this time, and for several years subsequently, the old-fashioned "strap rail" was the kind used. The rails, after a little wear, easily became displaced, the projecting ends being what were too familiarly known as "snake-heads." The T rail had been introduced upon Eastern roads, but the idea of its possession did not even enter into the thoughts of our pioneers of internal improvement. It was, in fact, the very cheapness of railroads that served as a powerful incentive to men with small means to undertake their construction. Even the strap rail was at times a luxury, the supply being eked out, in case of emergency, by the substitution of wooden material. The rolling stock was mostly of a character in keeping with that of the track. The cars were small, divided into three compartments, but entirely innocent of any of the "modern improvements," and having doors through the sides. The first cars in use were built in Troy, but their manufacture was soon commenced here. The first passenger car of Detroit make was christened the *Lady Mason*, and was built under the supervision of George and John Gibson, both now deceased.

The State built the Road as far west as Kalamazoo, but her reputation for railroad management was constantly on the descending scale. The Internal Improvement warrants sunk as low as forty cents to the dollar, there being no funds with which to meet them. The Roads were rapidly wearing out, and the State was so now and so poor that it had no credit to purchase iron, or even to buy the spikes required to fasten down the "snake-heads," to say nothing of a further extension of the track. The affairs of the Road were in such a strait that it would have stopped entirely, but for the interposition of Governor Barry, who advanced $7,000 in money from his individual means, and became personally responsible for $20,000 more. In this condition of affairs, the Legislature of 1846 assembled. Amongst the earliest proceedings, Judge Hand, the sole representative from Detroit in the House, moved a resolution for the appointment of a committee to consider the expediency of providing for the sale of the public works. This was carried, and a bill authorizing the sale was about being reported, when Mr. J. W. Brooks, of Boston, came forward as the representative of a number of Eastern capitalists, and made a tender for the purchase of the Road. Negotiations were at once entered into, the result of which was that the present charter was drawn up and reported, conditioned for the payment of $2,000,000 as purchase money, and after a protracted struggle, the required two thirds of each House was obtained, and the bill became a law. Previous to this time it is asserted that so large a sum as $100,000 had never been brought into the Western country from the East for investment in any one enterprise. Yet this act of incorporation contemplated the expenditure of $6,000,000 to $8,000,000, of which half a million had to be paid before the State would relinquish

possession. The Company were required to complete the Road to Lake Michigan with T rail of not less than sixty pounds to the yard—a very heavy rail for those days—and it was also stipulated that all the old Road should be relaid with similar rail. The Company were authorized to change the western terminus to any point in the State on Lake Michigan, and they were subsequently allowed to change it to Chicago. The carrying out of the provisions of the charter and the gradual change in equipment and outfit until the Road has become second to none in the country, if in the world, are matters upon which it is unnecessary to dwell at length. By an arrangement with the Great Western of Canada, the two interests have been practically consolidated so far as concerns their traffic.

The same committee reported a bill for the sale of the Southern Road. The charter of this Road, as granted by the State, was from Monroe to Lake Michigan. Subsequently it became a desideratum with the stockholders to have the terminus at Toledo, and they adopted measures finally resulting in the perpetual lease of the Erie and Kalamazoo road, whose indebtedness was assumed by the Southern to the extent of the amount of aid which had been afforded by the State. Previous to offering the Southern Road for sale, the State had completed it to Palmyra, four or five miles east of Adrian, at a cost of $1,100,000. The President, Mr. Noble, effected its purchase on behalf of himself and others, the corporators being as follows: James J. Godfroy, Samuel J. Holley, Harry V. Mann, Charles Noble, George W. Strong, Austin E. Wing, Henry Waldron, Stillman Blanchard, F. W. Macy, Jonathan Burch, Dan B. Miller, Benjamin F. Fifield, Wm. C. Sterling, W. Wadsworth, Edward Bronson, Daniel S. Bacon, and Thomas C. Cole. The Messrs. Litchfield, who subsequently figured so extensively in the history of the Road, then owned little or none of the stock. The price paid to the State was $500,000 for the whole Road, so far as completed, with the materials, right of way, etc., including also the Tecumseh branch, from Adrian to Manchester, which had been already built to Tecumseh, and also the franchises of the Palmyra and Jacksonburgh road, now known as the Jackson division of the Southern. The Company commenced operations the same year looking to the extension of the Road westward. The work progressed slowly, but public confidence steadily increased. Great difficulty was encountered for want of means, the corporators being mostly citizens of Monroe, who were mainly impelled by public spirit. Not long after the sale by the State, a controlling interest was obtained by the Messrs. Litchfield, and their coadjutors, who, with a little money, a great deal of boldness, and indomitable perseverance, succeeded in pushing the Road into Chicago, reaching that city in advance of the Central. There was no stoppage of the work from the period of the sale. While the construction was in

progress, Col. Bliss, of Springfield, Mass., also became prominently connected with it, and held the Presidency for several years. In 1855, an act was passed authorizing the consolidation of the Michigan, Southern and Northern Indiana Roads, and in 1856 the Detroit, Monroe and Toledo Road was chartered. The latter was promptly completed, and the company controlling the Southern obtained a perpetual lease. A reference to the other divisions controlled by the same interest, will come more properly hereafter in the portion of our article allotted to the enterprises of later date. By consolidation with Roads beyond the limits of the State, the Southern has become a gigantic corporation, the total length of the main line and the different divisions being about 1,200 miles. Like that of the Central, the building of the original line was attended with great difficulties, and the parallel is maintained so far as concerns equipment and general management,—both lines enjoying enviable and well-earned reputations.

Probably the history of no Railroad ever built is replete with so many amusing and grotesque incidents, or marked by so many financial perturbations, as that of the old Detroit and Pontiac Road. At an early period in the history of Detroit, it became a desideratum to establish railroad connection with the rich agricultural region of Oakland county, whose milling facilities were already in a fair stage of development. A charter was obtained of the Territorial Legislature on the 7th March, 1834, and the capital stock fixed at $100,000. Messrs. Alfred Williams and Sherman Stevens, of Pontiac, were the principal stockholders and managers, their control continuing until 1840, during which period their financial operations, if they could be presented in full, would make a most racy chapter. The building of the Road in the mean time made slow progress, banking enterprises engaging the principal attention of its managers. It was finally completed to Birmingham in 1839, and in September of that year the late Henry J. Buckley, agent and conductor, put forth his advertisement in the papers for two trips a day to Birmingham, the cars running in connection with "post coaches" to Pontiac and Flint, together with a semi-weekly line to Grand River.— The introduction of steam was regarded as a notable event, the cars, during the period for which Royal Oak had been the terminus, having been run by horse power. In 1840, parties in Syracuse, N. Y., having claims upon the Road, procured its sale under an execution. It was bid in by Gurdon Williams, of Detroit, and Giles Williams and Dean Richmond, of Buffalo, but was soon afterward transferred to other parties in Syracuse. It was finally completed to Pontiac in 1843. The Road was subsequently leased by the Syracuse owners for ten years to Gurdon Williams, who was to pay a graduated amount of rental, averaging about $10,000 a year. In 1848, before the expiration of the lease, steps were taken to rescue the Road

from the slough of despond into which it had been sunk by a heavy load of indebtedness, which finally resulted in its coming into the possession of a company headed by H. N. Walker, Esq., and that eminent but ultimately unfortunate financier, N. P. Stewart. Mr. Walker, who was elected President, negotiated bonds of the Company for a sufficient amount to relay the track. The accession of this company was the turning point in the fortunes of the Road. The laughable anecdotes of its early days, in which "snakeheads" and hair breadth escapes are among the leading staples, would fill a respectable sized volume.

On the 3d April, 1848, a charter was obtained by the "Oakland and Ottawa Railroad Company." The Company was poor, and its bonds were negotiated with difficulty, and it was only by the most strenuous exertions that any progress was made. In 1852 work was commenced, and in 1853 Mr. Walker went to Europe in the interest of the Road, where he purchased 2,600 tons of iron, being sufficient to lay the track to Fentonville.

The "Detroit and Pontiac" and "Oakland and Ottawa" Railroads were consolidated on the 13th February, 1855, under the name of the Detroit and Milwaukee Railway. In July of that year Mr. Walker made a second trip to Europe, where he negotiated the Company's bonds to the amount of $1,250,000. Subsequently Mr. W. visited Europe for the third time, during which visit an arrangement was made with the Great Western Railway Company, which was calculated to put an end to financial embarrassment. The mortgage was closed in 1860, and the name changed to the Detroit and Milwaukee Railroad. It may be added, as a curious fact, that, while those who were early engaged in pushing forward this enterprise made much greater sacrifices to promote the land grant policy than were made by any other interest in the country, the Road was ultimately deprived of all aid in the way of a grant. The Road was completed only by the most herculean efforts, but all these great sacrifices have been requited in the immense influence it has exerted in aiding the development of the country.

Our sketch of the Railroad enterprises belonging to the first epoch, is now brought to a close. For many years after the completion of our pioneer Roads, railway enterprise was at a low ebb, for want of the "sinews of war," but with the advent of a more favorable period in the money market, the attention of Eastern capitalists was directed to the flattering inducements held out by our State for investment in projects calculated to aid the development of our vast material wealth. It was not until the keels of countless merchantmen had vexed the waters of the bays and inlets of our Lower Peninsula, bearing away the rich spoils of our frontier forests, that our lumbermen began to work their way inward from the shore, a process that gradually became a matter of necessity as the supply began to show marked signs of diminution. By slow degrees the plow followed the paraphernalia of the mill, and in due time the important truth became revealed that the "pine barrens," which, according to tradition, constituted a very large share of our Peninsula, were almost entirely mythical so far as the term referred to the character of the soil. The choicest pine timber proved to be invariably interspersed with beech, maple, and other hardwoods, growing mostly on rolling lands, and having an arable and productive soil. The settlement of the north began in earnest; lands were constructed; lands became valuable for farming purposes, and the country began to feel the effect of the land grants that had been made by Congress in aid of railroads. These grants proved, indeed, the coup de grace in raising the value of lands along the line of the proposed Roads. They were granted in alternate sections, and a demand sprung up at advanced rates for the unappropriated sections, which in turn reacted upon and enhanced the value of the grants. The first specific grant by Congress for railroad purposes was made to the Illinois Central in 1850, but the first grant in aid of Michigan roads was not made until 1856. These grants were made to the State direct, and the details of the conditions were imposed by legislative enactment. The progress of the Roads was slow, and the effect in the enhancement of the value of the lands was on a corresponding scale. The unexampled progress which has been made within the past eight years is due in a very great degree to the interest controlling the Michigan Central, backed by Eastern capitalists. Within the brief period named this interest has either built with its own means, or materially aided in their construction, the following important lines, viz. The Jackson, Lansing and Saginaw; the Grand River Valley; the Jackson and Fort Wayne; the Michigan Air Line; the Detroit, Hillsdale and Indiana; the Kalamazoo and South Haven; the Chicago and Michigan Lake Shore; the Detroit, Lansing and Lake Michigan, and the Detroit and Bay City. The pushing forward of these great enterprises alone could not but exert a very marked influence upon the development of the State, to say nothing of the extension of the system by way of branches and the connecting lines that have been found expedient as that development progressed. In the mean time other causes have been at work, while local pride and local interests have been stimulated to the highest pitch, and within the past two or three years railroad enterprise has been at its height, and still shows no diminution except so far as that necessarily occasioned by the consummation of its objects. This rapid progress ought perhaps to excite no surprise when we duly consider the peculiar advantages presented by our State, bearing directly upon the case. While she stands confessedly without a peer in the extent and multiform character of her resources, her geographical position is at the same time strikingly favorable, situated as she is upon the very highway, both by land and water, of the mighty commerce of the northern part of the continent. Other, though less powerful causes, some of them subsidiary to the cardinal ones we have named, may be referred to, such as the comparatively easy gradients, and the incentives presented for spanning peninsular territory—a bribe held out by nature herself, as it were, to the spirit of progress. To these may be added the proverbially enterprising character of our people, a point which, so far from approaching to sitatingly, we desire to emphasize, and with respect to no class of our population more particularly than to the hardy tillers of the soil. The indomitable energy and public spirit of this class has, on numerous occasions, elicited admiring comments from capitalists, and has been brought most forcibly to the minds of the citizens of the commercial metropolis in connection with the noble efforts of the people upon all of the new lines by which it has been sought to reach the city—efforts which have finally, in almost every instance, been crowned with triumphant success.

Speculations have to some extent been indulged in, touching the effect of the final exhaustion of our pine timber upon the prosperity of the railroads whose interests are identified with the traffic of Northern Michigan, but no considerations touching this point have produced any influence—at least any unfavorable influence—upon the minds of investors. The conclusion is so obvious that he who runs may read, that the day that witnesses such exhaustion will see our railroads upon the very top wave of that prosperity that shall never know an ebb. A traffic quite as lucrative will be opened up in hardwood timber, the value of which will be greatly enhanced by numerous causes, among which may be named the very thinning out in question. Its prospective value and importance in fact baffles all computation. This commodity, which is produced among us in such profusion that the most prodigal disposition of it scarcely excites remark, is wanted at high prices in all the markets of Europe, and will be exported in limitless quantities as soon as a revolution is brought about in the carrying trade between the lakes and the ocean, an event which, in the very nature of things, cannot be much longer deferred. In the mean time the agricultural resources of the country will be developed, of whose effect some idea may be formed from the significant fact that several of the lines completed within the past two or three years have, in their very infancy, attained to prospects that warrant them in adopting means to provide for extensive lines of "feeders."

It is within the scope of our article to enumerate the roads already built,—but with no particular system as regards date of construction,—together with such projects as are certain or most likely to be matured, as well as to present a few leading facts concerning them respectively. The idea of doing full justice to them, in whole or in part, would

involve greater space than we have at our command.

The Jackson, Lansing and Saginaw road was the first ever aided by the Michigan Central, which was about eight years ago. When commenced, there was no thought of carrying the line as far as Saginaw, but upon its completion to Lansing, the idea was conceived of extending it to the former place. There lay in the way, between Lansing and Owosso, a segment of the old "Ramshorn Road," a familiar designation for a project whose corporate name was the Amboy, Lansing and Traverse Bay Railroad. The Jackson, Lansing and Saginaw Company purchased this segment, with all its franchises, including the land grant, under the authority of an act of the Legislature, made it part of their line, and carried it in triumph across the Saginaw Valley toward the Straits of Mackinac. It is the strength which the above land grant gave them which now enables them to be building toward the Straits. During the past season it has been completed to Otsego Lake, in the north part of Otsego County, within fifty miles of Cheboygan. At the present writing, it has not been decided whether the line is to be run to the Straits direct, or to that point via Cheboygan. Whichever may be the case, it will form a most important link in the chain of the Northern Pacific, and will afford, after the completion of the Detroit and Bay City road, virtually an air line from the Straits to Detroit. The Road from Mackinac to Marquette, it is now rendered certain, will be built at an early day, and the distance from Marquette to Detroit by rail will then be 340 miles shorter by this line than by any other existing route, which will enable it to control the entire traffic from Marquette during the protracted period of the year at which navigation is closed.

The Grand River Valley road was finished in 1870. It is 94 miles long, running from Jackson to Grand Rapids, intersecting the Detroit and Milwaukee road, and connecting, by means of the latter, with the Chicago and Michigan Lake Shore road, which runs north to Montague, on White Lake. This Road runs through the county seats of Eaton and Barry counties, through a fertile and to some extent a heavily timbered country, and has done and is still doing well, although it had not the benefit of a land grant. Like the Jackson, Lansing and Saginaw road, it was undertaken by the people of Jackson, but they finally applied to the Central for help, without which it could not have been finished for many years. The governing consideration in taking hold of it was to control the traffic of the important region through which it passes and bring the same to Detroit.

The Jackson and Fort Wayne road, which was completed about two years since, is 100 miles in length, and affords direct communication with Indiana, a connection which has been rendered a very important one by the completion of the Detroit, Eel River and Illinois road. It also forms, in connection with the Jackson, Lansing and Saginaw

road, a great route for lumber from Northern Michigan to Cincinnati, Louisville and other cities on the Ohio River.

The "Michigan Air Line" was projected as a short line from Chicago to Buffalo, and was intended to run across the State from Chicago, striking the St. Clair river just above the town of St. Clair, and there connect with what is now known as the Canada Southern. The Michigan Central, which aided in building so much of this line as lies between Jackson and Niles, and furnished almost the entire capital with which it was built, finally made it a feeder for Detroit and the Central. Cassopolis, Three Rivers, Union City, Centreville, Homer, and other thriving towns are located on this line, and it passes through as fine and productive region as any in Michigan. This Road, which was completed in 1871, is, in point of construction, equal to any in the West, and shortens the distance between Detroit and Chicago about 15 miles. Distance from Jackson to South Bend, 111 miles.

The Detroit, Hillsdale and Indiana Road was built by an arrangement with the managers of the Michigan Central, whereby it was enabled to sell its bonds, and raise money with which to go forward and build; but it may be proper to add that the Great Western was also a party to the arrangement. The new Road runs on the track of the Central from Ypsilanti to Detroit. Distance from Ypsilanti to Hillsdale, about 65 miles. Nearly all the business of the region traversed by this Road has hitherto gone to Toledo. The Hillsdale Company took the franchise of the Eel River road, extending from Butler, Indiana, to Logansport, and the Road has recently been finished to the last named point. The fact that it affords the shortest route to St. Louis from New England and the region having its outlet at Buffalo, coupled with the almost unrivaled fertility of the region which it penetrates, renders this Road of vast importance. It also affords a direct route between Detroit and Indianapolis via the Indianapolis, Peru and Chicago road.

The Kalamazoo and South Haven is another Road whose capital stock is owned chiefly by the Michigan Central, and the latter company has also guaranteed its bonds and obtained a lease of the Road, which is an important feeder of itself—40 miles in length—and important also as affording an eligible connection with another Road in the same interest—the Chicago and Michigan Lake Shore—the traffic of which it brings to Kalamazoo. It runs through a country partly timbered and partly farming.

The line of the Chicago and Michigan Lake Shore road extends from New Buffalo, 66 miles east of Chicago, to Pentwater, but it will ultimately be extended to Manistee, a distance of 200 miles in all, and a branch has been built from Holland to Grand Rapids, 24 miles. These lines have both been finished within 18 months. The main line north of Grand Haven is operated in the interest of the Michigan Central, and consti-

tutes, with the Grand River Valley road, a direct line from Detroit to the western coast of the State, trains leaving daily from the Michigan Central depot. The Chicago and Michigan Lake Shore road was consolidated, October 23, 1872, with the Muskegon and Big Rapids road, which has recently been completed. The pine lumber trade of these roads is assuming immense proportions.

The Detroit, Lansing and Lake Michigan road, an important artery of the commerce of Detroit and of the State, was completed in the Fall of 1871 to Howard City, at the junction with the Grand Rapids and Indiana road. From thence it has been surveyed and will be built during the Spring of 1873 to Fremont, a point near the centre of Newaygo County, where it will connect with the newly constructed Muskegon and Big Rapids road. A branch of this Road extending from Ionia to Stanton has already been built, and will be extended beyond Stanton at an early day. The Detroit, Lansing and Lake Michigan road was formed by the consolidation of three companies. The first consolidation was that of the Detroit and Howell with the Detroit and Lansing, the latter, however, being organized in the interest of the Detroit and Howell. The next was that of the Detroit, Howell and Lansing with the Ionia and Lansing, which took place in March last. The Hon. James F. Joy, President of the Michigan Central, first aided in raising the money to build the section from Lansing through Ionia to Greenville, some 56 miles in length, about four years ago. The parties who had it in charge became embarrassed, and Mr. Joy was obliged to take charge of it in order to save those who had invested in it from loss, and, in order to make it valuable, took up the Detroit and Howell project—an enterprise which had failed—with the view of extending the Road to Detroit, and from Greenville northwest to Lake Michigan.— The parties above referred to had put in a large amount of capital, which would have been hopelessly sunk but for this last consolidation.

The Detroit and Bay City road, which has already been incidentally referred to as part of a direct line to Mackinac and thence to a connection with the Northern Pacific, completes the present category of the Roads which have been built or aided by the Michigan Central. It is but a short time since its commencement, yet, before our work reaches its readers, it will have been completed. Its length is something over 100 miles, passing through a rich agricultural region, while the lumber and salt trade will contribute very materially to swell its traffic.

To appreciate the full significance of the great enterprises to which we have thus far referred, as belonging to our modern railway epoch, with a solitary exception these projects have all been matured within a period of a little more than two years! While the expenditure of capital in building branches and feeders is of common occurrence with railroad corporations, the large scale upon which the managers of the Michi-

gan Central have aided kindred enterprises that are neither branches nor "feeders," is unparalleled in railway annals. Without dwelling upon the incalculable benefits of this liberal policy to local interests or to the State at large, it is a fair inference that that policy has been inaugurated and pursued mainly as the means of judicious investment of capital—a theory that suggests a most flattering commentary on the estimate placed upon the vast latent wealth of our State by those most competent to form a just idea on the subject.

As next in order, we may properly refer to the branches or divisions of the Lake Shore and Michigan Southern Railway, of which quite an important one was completed last year, namely, the "Northern Central Michigan," now known as the Lansing Division, extending from Jonesville, on the main line, to Lansing, a distance of 59 miles. This division, which traverses a wealthy region, succeeded to the franchises of the southern section of the old Amboy, Lansing and Traverse Bay, or "Ramshorn" Road. The old company built a road from Lansing to Owosso, but it was constructed in primitive style. Financial difficulties arose, and, in September, 1864, the Hon. C. C. Trowbridge was appointed Receiver, who remained in possession about two years. The Road was managed under the direction of Mr. Trowbridge, by the Superintendent of the D. & M. Road, and the rolling stock necessary to its proper working was supplied by that Road. The Receivership was, of course, only temporary, and near the close of 1866 the road was sold to the Jackson, Lansing and Saginaw Company. It is the southern division of this once famous corporation, as already intimated, that is now practically represented in the Lansing division of the Lake Shore and Michigan Southern Railway. An extension has been projected from Lansing to St. Johns, and thence northward, which has already been mostly graded to St. Johns. This improvement will ensure connection with quite a number of enterprising and thriving towns.

The Kalamazoo Division, familiarly known as "Gardner's Road," was built by piecemeal, having been commenced (about seven years ago) without any clearly defined reference to the points now constituting its termini. The Southern Road has had for several years a "strap" road from White Pigeon to Three Rivers, and the company agreed that if Mr. Gardner would relay it, they would give him a lease of it, as a link in a project of his own, namely, the construction of a road from Three Rivers north to Schoolcraft, the latter point being the outlet of a rich prairie region. This arrangement was concluded, and the Road was extended to Schoolcraft, after which another corporation was formed by Mr. Gardner and his friends, to build from that point to Kalamazoo, which project was finally carried forward to completion, and at the last named point Mr. Gardner rested. He ultimately succeeded in carrying the Road to Grand Rapids, having been enabled to dis-

pose of the bonds by means of a stipulated traffic arrangement with the Michigan Central, which corporation was desirous of obtaining an outlet to Grand Rapids. The Road, however, finally passed into the hands of the Michigan Southern, and the Central built the Grand River Valley road, as already stated. Mr. Gardner also built a branch of his Road from Allegan to Holland, which was ultimately extended to Muskegon (known as the Michigan Lake Shore road.) The "Continental Improvement Company" (an association nearly identical in interest with the Pennsylvania Central) have obtained control of all this line beyond Allegan, and have completed a Road from that place to Martin's Corners, on the Grand Rapids and Indiana road.

The Detroit, Monroe and Toledo Division was built in part by subscriptions at Detroit and at other points on the line. It has proved of great value to Detroit merchants in affording communication with the South, and has grown into importance as a channel for shipment to various points in Pennsylvania and elsewhere.

The company that constructed the Jackson Division was organized under a special charter, and the Road was built about thirteen years ago. The effect of this Division is to draw off a certain portion of the traffic of the Central for the benefit of Toledo.

The Adrian and Monroe Division is practically part of the main line, Adrian being the point of divergence for the lines respectively to Toledo and Detroit, the latter via Monroe.

That portion of the main line from Toledo to Adrian, 33 miles, was acquired by a perpetual lease from the old "Erie and Kalamazoo Railroad Company."

The Roads hereafter named, including a number of highly important lines, have, it is hardly necessary to say, no connection with either of the great interests upon which we have heretofore dwelt. Like the lines already described, however, they are almost invariably first class in their construction and general equipment.

The Grand Rapids and Indiana road is a most important channel from a number of considerations, especially in view of its great length, the immense natural wealth of the vast region tributary to it, and from its connections, having the Straits of Mackinac as its northern terminus, and tapping the Grand River Valley with its network of railways and its rich stores of lumber, plaster, and other leading commodities, for which it has opened a market in the rich State of Indiana. Its financial history has been a checkered one. There were heavy losses from various causes, including inefficient management at the outset, quarrels with contractors, the failure of financial agents, etc.

In 1852 and 1853, the "Fort Wayne and Southern Railroad Company" made such advances toward the construction of a railroad from Louisville to Fort Wayne as seemed to insure its completion. The President of that company made propositions that led to the

organization of the Grand Rapids and Indiana Railroad Company in 1854. The proposed southern terminus was Hartford City, running north to the Michigan State line in the direction of Grand Rapids. The Grand Rapids and Southern Railroad Company was organized in 1854, and the two were consolidated under the present name. In 1855 the southern terminus was changed to Fort Wayne, and, the same year, application was made for a land grant, which was obtained in 1856, followed by another in 1864, the whole amount granted aggregating 1,160,382 acres. In 1857, the Company was consolidated with two other organizations, the "Grand Rapids and Mackinaw" and the "Grand Rapids and Fort Wayne" Companies, the name of Grand Rapids and Indiana Railroad Company being retained by the new organization. Early in 1857, the Company organized three full corps of engineers, one to operate direct from Grand Rapids to Grand Traverse Bay, the second west of that, nearer the Lake, and the other as direct from Grand Rapids to Little Traverse Bay, and thence to the Straits, as was practicable. On the data thus acquired, the present line was located. Owing to the embarrassments to which we have referred, the Company asked for and obtained numerous extensions in order to enable it to take advantage of the terms of the land grants, the time being finally extended to June 3, 1874, the Continental Improvement Company (organized for this specific purpose) took the contract to build the Road for the full length, from Fort Wayne to Little Traverse, 50 miles beyond Traverse City, in all 330 miles. This contract, owing to the greatly enhanced value of the bonds turned over to the Improvement Company (the Pennsylvania Central guaranteeing them, thus making them par), has given that company the lion's share of the avails of the enterprise, and thrown the original corporation completely into the shade. The Road has been built as far north as Rapid River, in Antrim County, and will be completed during the present year to Mackinac. A branch has been completed and is in operation to Traverse City, diverging from the main line at Walton, in the northeast part of Wexford County. Distance from Fort Wayne to the Straits, 352 miles.

The Flint and Pere Marquette road, another of the great arteries that are diffusing life and material health throughout our State, owes its inception and existence to the combined influence of a land grant and the enormous lumber trade of the region tributary to it. It has already been of inestimable value in stimulating the settlement and drawing out the resources of Northern Michigan. The Road was commenced at Flint and built to East Saginaw about seven years ago, and in the Fall of 1866 the construction of the second division was commenced, running from the east bank of the Saginaw River, at East Saginaw, 26½ miles, to Averill's, on the Tittabawassee River, six and one half miles west of Midland. Twenty miles were laid, ballasted and opened for traffic on the

1st of December, 1867. On the 24th of April, 1868, a lease was effected of the Flint and Holly Railroad—17 miles in length—for the term of 100 years. The latter Road had been opened for traffic in November, 1864. In December, 1868, a lease of the Bay City and East Saginaw Railroad was executed. The work on the main line has been steadily pushed forward. At the close of 1869, 77 miles were opened; in January, 1870, 20 additional miles were brought into use. During the ensuing Summer the Road will be finished to Ludington, on Lake Michigan, its western terminus, the contract having been concluded for the unfinished portion. A branch has recently been built from Flint to Otter Lake fifteen miles in length, and another has been surveyed and will probably be completed the present year, extending from East Saginaw by a very direct line through Vassar and Capac to St. Clair or Port Huron. A branch will also be built from East Saginaw to Caro, in Tuscola County, and at several distant points short branches will be constructed for the especial accommodation of the lumber trade.

The Holly, Wayne and Monroe road, which has been built within the past two years, has been consolidated with the Flint and Pere Marquette, giving the latter a Toledo connection. It also brings to Detroit the business of a circumscribed but wealthy region before inaccessible, via Plymouth, on the Detroit, Lansing and Lake Michigan road, and Wayne, on the Michigan Central. Distance from Holly to Monroe, 63½ miles.

The line of the Port Huron and Lake Michigan road is from Port Huron to Flint, where it connects with the Detroit and Milwaukee Road, affording direct communication between Port Huron and Grand Haven, and giving Port Huron the benefit of the connections of the D. and M. Road. It was projected as long ago as 1836, constituting one of the three pet schemes of crossing the State heretofore referred to. At that time a line was marked out all the way to Grand Rapids, and a few miles were graded, but owing to the great financial embarrassments of 1837, the scheme fell through. In 1841 the Port Huron and Lake Michigan Railroad Company was formed, but its progress was confined to locating the line and obtaining the right of way. In 1856 the Port Huron and Milwaukee Railroad Company was organized, the line located, and a considerable sum expended, but the property was sold under its mortgage in 1864, and the company dissolved. In 1865, the property and franchises came into the possession of the present Company. It is the present intention of the management to extend the line to Lansing, although Owosso has also been named as a possible objective point.

The route of the Peninsular Road extends southwest from Lansing and has been carried into Indiana, securing a Chicago connection. At Charlotte it crosses the Grand River Valley road; at Brady, the Grand Rapids and Indiana; at Schoolcraft, the Kalamazoo division of the M. S. and L. S. R. R.; at Battle Creek, the main track of the Michigan Central; at Cassopolis the Michigan Air Line; at South Bend, the Lake Shore and Michigan; at Stillwell, the Peru and Indianapolis; at Haskell, the Louisville, New Albany and Chicago; and at Valparaiso, the Pittsburgh, Fort Wayne and Chicago. The Road was undertaken by Mr. Dibble, of Battle Creek, some four or five years ago. He has built thus far on municipal aid, and the proceeds of bonds sold in Europe. Distance from Lansing to South Bend, 118 miles; Lansing to Chicago, 205. The project known as the Michigan Midland, from Lansing to Flint, is encouraged by the Peninsular, as a means of securing an eastern connection.

The Ohio and Michigan is the corporate name of a Road generally denominated the Mansfield, Coldwater and Lake Michigan Road, which is being constructed under the auspices of the "Continental Improvement Company." The line extends from Mansfield, Ohio, through Coldwater, Burlington, Battle Creek and Augusta to Allegan, from which point the route to Grand Haven and Muskegon, 56 miles in length, is controlled by the same interest.

The Michigan division of the Grand Trunk Railway, extending from Port Huron to Detroit, 59 miles, was completed in the autumn of 1859, the whole expense having been borne by the gigantic corporation by which it is owned and controlled. The Road has proved of substantial advantage to a part of the State not otherwise accommodated with a railway outlet, while the connection has proved invaluable to our merchants and shippers—and thereby to our producers—in affording a competing route to the East as well as connection with points not reached by any other line. Distance from Detroit to Portland, Maine, 861 miles.

The Saginaw Valley and St. Louis road, extending from East Saginaw to St. Louis, 34 miles, has been built during the past year, and the cars are running. The extension of this line to Grand Rapids was in contemplation at the period of the inception of the enterprise, and it may yet be built.

The Grand Rapids and Newaygo Railroad, 36 miles in length, also belongs to the list of railroads completed last year. An extension has been projected northward to Fremont, the junction of the Detroit, Lansing and Lake Michigan with the Muskegon and Big Rapids Railroad.

Considerable earth-work has been done at intervening points on the line of the proposed Marshall and Coldwater road, and an extension has been projected from Marshall to Elm Hall, in the northwest part of Gratiot county.

A Road has been projected from Wenona opposite Bay City via Midland, to Big Rapids, where it is proposed to form a junction with the Muskegon and Big Rapids road. The road-bed has been finished from Wenona to Midland, and that section will be ironed, it is expected, early the present season.

The new Canada Southern, which for a considerable period has occupied a prominent place in the public mind, now approaches completion. The last rail on the portion between St. Thomas and Amherstburg, Ontario, was laid some time since. From Trenton on Detroit River, the Road will have three branches, viz., one direct through to Chicago, passing through Flat Rock, Blissfield and Morenci; one to Toledo, where it will connect with the Toledo, Wabash and Western, with which it has been consolidated; and another to Detroit.

The Owosso and Northern road is a new project, with Frankfort, on Lake Michigan, as its ultimate objective point. It has been graded for the distance of forty miles northward from Owosso. The proposed route crosses the Flint and Pere Marquette road at Evart, and the Grand Rapids and Indiana at Clam Lake.

The Toledo, Ann Arbor and Northern road is another comparatively new project, but the line between Toledo and Ann Arbor will soon be ironed. The bridges are already built, and the road-bed completed.

The capital stock has all been subscribed for a railroad from Elkhart, Indiana, to Benton Harbor, opposite St. Joseph.

A railway will be eventually built, in all probability, from the main line of the Jackson, Lansing and Saginaw road to Alpena. As yet, very little has been done.

The Michigan Air Line, projected from St. Clair to Jackson—of which the Road in operation between Ridgway and Romeo is a segment—has disposed of its franchises to Pontiac parties who have been endeavoring the past summer to raise funds to complete the Road. They have induced some English capitalists to look over the ground with the view of investing, but the result is somewhat uncertain.

An Air line from Detroit to the southwest through Adrian has been a favorite project with the citizens of the rich region directly interested, but its culmination has been postponed through various causes, and is at present retarded by a conflict of interests. The line has already been graded from Tecumseh to Adrian, and a contract was let some time since from Adrian to Morenci.

A Road has been projected from Rockford to Greenville in the interest of the Continental Improvement Company, and some work has been performed.

A Road has been projected from Lapeer to Port Austin, which, if built, will run for the distance of six miles over a branch of the Detroit and Bay City road, which has already been completed northeasterly from Lapeer.

A Company has been organized for the construction of a Road from Utica to Almont, with some prospect of success.

We have now enumerated, in addition to the Roads actually built, the more meritorious of the new projects which are agitating the Lower Peninsula. New ones are being constantly urged upon the public attention, many of which have nothing very substantial to rest upon, but are projected as a means of

furthering purely local interests, without due deference to the question whether they can command the volume of business necessary to sustain them.

We will now invite the attention of the reader to the Upper Peninsula, where the stupendous interests at stake are beginning to enlist the serious attention of capitalists, and the development of a railway system on a scale corresponding with the magnitude of those interests has commenced in earnest within a recent period. We have already referred, incidentally, to the probable early completion of the link in the chain of the Northern Pacific, extending from the Straits of Mackinac to Marquette.

The formation of the Marquette, Houghton and Ontonagon Railroad Company is the result of the consolidation of the "Marquette and Ontonagon" and the "Houghton and Ontonagon" roads. The former road, extending from Marquette to Champion, opened to a market the iron district, embracing twenty of the largest mines, as well as a large timber, mineral and agricultural country. The latter road, from L'Anse, at the head of Keweenaw Bay, to a junction with the Marquette road, opened an immense additional mineral district, with an outlet at L'Anse, and the consolidated roads and branches, extending nearly a hundred miles, are rapidly accomplishing the development of the largest and richest mineral district in the world. The line is now completed and in full operation from Marquette to L'Anse, with a magnificent harbor and freight facilities at each terminus, and is doing a business, proportioned to the investment, greater than any other railroad in the United States. The iron traffic alone will amount in 1873 to at least 1,500,000 tons. The chief towns and cities located upon this important line are Negaunee, Ishpeming, Clarksburg, Champion, Michigammi, and L'Anse. The Road will be extended to Ontonagon within the next four years, and will eventually connect at Montreal River with the Northern Pacific. It will thus form a most important connecting link between Duluth and the Lower Peninsula of Michigan, and through the State to all points throughout the country.

The gap of 65 miles in the Chicago and Northwestern Railroad from Escanaba to the Wisconsin line has recently been built, forming a continuous route by rail from Marquette to Chicago. This road was built by W. B. Ogden and his friends, and finally consolidated with the Northwestern.

The aggregate length of the Railroads of Michigan is stated by Governor Bagley, in his message, at about 3,200 miles. The following is believed to be a correct statement of the number of miles actually ironed in 1872:—

The theodolite of the railroad surveyor has been to our beautiful Peninsula the wand of Prospero. It has caused the wilderness to blossom as the rose, and throughout the length and breadth of the land have risen schools, and colleges, and temples to the Most High. The rapid development of our resources has reacted upon the means by which it was wrought. Insignificant railroad machinery has given place to engines which are seemingly the perfection of human invention; the old-fashioned, ill-contrived cars have been succeeded by palatial coaches; and "strap rails" have been displaced by a kind more worthy to bear the teeming commerce of the mighty West. The history of our early enterprises has not been without its moral. We are commanded not to despise the day of small beginnings, and the lesson in this case is emphasized by the striking fact that the mightiest channels of the State and of the West are the legacy of a period chiefly remembered as the era of wild speculation. Thus did the strong man of old gather sweets from the carcass of the dead lion.

GEOLOGY.

BY ALEXANDER WINCHELL, LL.D.,

CHANCELLOR OF THE SYRACUSE UNIVERSITY, MEMBER OF THE PHILADELPHIA ACADEMY OF NATURAL SCIENCES, THE BOSTON SOCIETY OF NATURAL HISTORY, ETC., ETC. ALSO MEMBER OF THE GEOLOGICAL SOCIETY OF FRANCE; CORRESPONDING MEMBER OF THE GEOLOGICAL SOCIETIES OF LIVERPOOL, GLASGOW, DRESDEN, ETC.

A synoptical sketch of Michigan geology will naturally be embraced under three general heads: 1. STRUCTURAL GEOLOGY. 2. HISTORICAL GEOLOGY. 3. ECONOMICAL GEOLOGY.

I. STRUCTURAL GEOLOGY.

The Lower Peninsula occupies the central part of a great synclinal basin, toward which the strata dip from all directions. The basin structure is bounded on all sides by anticlinal swells and ridges. Thus, north of Lake Ontario, Georgian Bay and Lake Huron, is a portion of the great Laurentian ridge whose branches extend from this region toward the north-east and north-west. On the north-west is the elevated granitic and dioritic region stretching from Marquette south-west through northern Wisconsin. On the south-west, south and south-east is a bifurcating gentle swell of the outcropping Devonian and Silurian strata, which stretches southward to Cincinnati and central Kentucky.

The limits of this great geological basin exceed, somewhat, the bounds of the Lower Peninsula, as the centripetal dip can be traced, on the east, as far as London, Ont.; on the west, to Madison, Wis.; on the north-west, to the vicinity of Marquette, and on the north, to the Sault Ste. Marie. Within these limits, the outcropping edges of strata older and older in the series, are passed over in traveling from the centre of the Peninsula outward. The whole series of strata may be likened to a nest of wooden dishes. The great hydrographic features of the region present a striking conformity to the trends of these outcropping strata, as will readily be seen by comparing the longitudinal axes of Lakes Erie, Huron and Michigan, as of Georgian, Little Traverse and Green Bays, with the strikes of the neighboring formations, as delineated on the Geological Map.

The Upper Peninsula is divided by the Marquette-Wisconsin anticlinal into two geological areas. The eastern, as just stated, belongs to the great Michigan basin, while the western belongs to what may be styled the Lacustrine Basin, since Lake Superior covers a large part of its surface. The southern rim of the latter is seen uplifted along Keweenaw Pt., and the south shore of the Lake, while, from this rim, the strata dip north-westerly under the Lake, re-appearing in Ile Royale, and, to a limited extent, along the north shore of the Lake. Between the Michigan and Lacustrine basins the metalliferous Marquette-Wisconsin axis interposes a separating belt of about 50 miles. We here present, in tabular form, a list of the geological formations of the State.

TABLE OF FORMATIONS.

EOZOIC GREAT SYSTEM.
 I. LAURENTIAN SYSTEM.
 II. HURONIAN SYSTEM.
PALÆOZOIC GREAT SYSTEM, 2680 ft.
 III. SILURIAN SYSTEM,   920 ft.
   Lake Superior Sandstone,   300 ft.
   Calciferous Sandrock,   100
   Trenton Group,   60
   Cincinnati Group,   60
   Niagara Group,   250
     Niagara Limestone,   218
     Clinton Sub-group,   32
   Salina Group,   50
   Lower Helderberg Group,   100
 IV. DEVONIAN SYSTEM,   1040 ft.
   Corniferous Group,   120
   Little Traverse Group,   200
   Huron Group,   720

Black Shale,	20
Portage Sub-Group,	500
Chemung Sub-Group,	200
V. CARBONIFEROUS SYSTEM,	720 ft.
Marshall Group,	160
Michigan Salt Group,	185
Carboniferous Limestone,	70
Coal-bearing Group,	305
Perma Conglomerate,	100
Coal Measures,	125
Woodville Sandstone,	80

CÆNOZOIC GREAT SYSTEM.
VI. QUATERNARY SYSTEM.
    Boulder Deposits,
    Modified Drift,
    Lacustrine Clays,
    Bogs, Marls, Dunes, Soils, etc.

I. The LAURENTIAN SYSTEM.—This System embraces the oldest known stratified deposits. It therefore underlies all the other strata, and its outcropping border constitutes the barrier which limits the great geological basins. Only a small portion of the Laurentian falls within the State of Michigan, and its geographical limits have not been completely determined. It rises in four distinct bosses within the bounds of the Upper Peninsula, three of which lie between the meridians of Keweenaw Bay and Marquette, while the fourth lies south of Ontonagon, on the State boundary, and stretches far into Wisconsin. This System is composed largely of granitic, syenitic and gneissoid rocks. The latter, in Michigan, are known to embrace gneiss, hornblendic and syenitic gneiss, and micaceous and hornblendic schists. Granite proper rarely occurs; syenite is common. It is probable that some of the deposits of white crystalline marble north-west of Menominee will be found to belong to this System.

II. The HURONIAN SYSTEM.—This System comprises the mass of imperfectly stratified rocks with which the great deposits of iron ore, in Michigan, are associated. The area occupied by them stretches in a widening belt from Marquette south and south-westward into Wisconsin,—the Laurentian bosses protruding through the belt. Lithologically, the rocks consist chiefly of diorites, quartzites, chloritic and talcose schists, marbles and iron ores. The results of the most recent studies in these rocks have not as yet been published; but Major T. B. Brooks, under the direction of the State Survey of 1869, '70, determined the usual order of superposition of the rocks; in the Marquette iron region, to be as follows: 1. Laurentian rocks; 2. Quartzite; 3. Talcose schist; 4. Diorite; 5. Ferruginous Quartzite; 6. Diorite; 7. Ferruginous Quartzite; 8. Diorite; 9. Ferruginous Quartzite; 10. Diorite; 11. Ferruginous Quartzite; 12. Hæmatitic and magnetic ores; 13. Quartzites. The quartzites are whitish or rusty, and vitreous. The diorites are composed of feldspar and hornblende—the feldspar being generally albite, but sometimes orthoclase or oligoclase. These minerals vary greatly in degree of coarseness, but the rock is generally distinctly granular. The talcose schist ranges from an almost pure talc rock to chloritic, argillaceous, and sometimes, micaceous, talcite. The ferruginous quartzites are, in other words, silicious or lean hæmatites, which have been many

times mistaken for productive deposits, and so reported, to the great disappointment of investors. The productive iron ores are chiefly hæmatite, undergoing alteration, in contact with water, to red chalk and limonite ("soft hæmatite"), though magnetite occurs abundantly. The mode of occurrence of these ores is not in eruptive outbursts (as formerly supposed), but in vast lenticular masses crowded into the stratification of the schists. Their origin is yet a matter of discussion, but they seem to be masses segregated from the contiguous rocks by some geologic action—perhaps through heat. One of these masses, consequently, is not inexhaustible. Indeed, several of them have already been worked out.

The Laurentian and Huronian Systems are, in this State, wholly destitute of organic remains, as far as known. For this reason, they were styled, collectively, "Azoic" by Foster and Whitney. It is yet uncertain whether the supposed animal structures found in rocks of Laurentian age in Canada and Massachusetts, are truly of organic origin.

III. The SILURIAN SYSTEM.—1. *Lake Superior Sandstone.*—This is the whitish, reddish, mottled or drab sandstone—sometimes shaly—occurring along the south shore of Lake Superior, from the St. Mary's river to Superior City, and beyond. There has been much discussion in reference to its geological age. The prevailing opinion, at present, makes that portion of it east of Keweenaw Point the equivalent of the Calciferous and Chazy formations of New York. The portion west of the Point is thought by some to be of the same age, while others regard it as the equivalent of the sandstones in Wisconsin and Minnesota, which are generally ranged in the horizon of the Potsdam of New York. As the uplift of Keweenaw Point has tilted the sandstones on the west, while those on the east have retained their horizontality, there is reason for supposing that the eastern strata are of more recent origin. It may nevertheless be true that the sandstones on both sides of the Point are of the same age, though those on the eastern side were not permanently tilted by the convulsion which upheaved the others. As we find apparently superincumbent strata which answer to the Calciferous, we shall continue to parallelize the Lake Superior Sandstone, presumptively, with the Potsdam.

The geographical extent and surface features of this formation are set forth in the article on Topography. In its geological structure, it consists, as first pointed out by Dr. Houghton, of an upper division composed chiefly of gray sandrock, and a lower division composed of thinner beds of reddish sandrock. These two divisions are further subdivided, as follows:

(f) Sandstone, light colored, thick bedded, rather incoherent, with bands of conglomerate, one of which caps the mass,	20 to 45 ft.
(e) Sandstone, whitish, friable, thin-bedded, with shaly seams,	75 to 100 ft.
(d) Sandstone, white, friable, massive,	50 ft.
(c) Sandstone, laminated, micaceous, banded with white and red layers, alternating with red arenaceous shales,	35 ft.

(b) Sandstone, uniformly red, somewhat argillaceous, thick-bedded,	12 ft.
(a) Sandstone, red or speckled, thick-bedded, hard and coarse-grained,	20 ft.

In the Ontonagon district, the upper division of the sandrock seems to be wanting, and its character is generally laminated or shaly, sometimes becoming decidedly argillaceous.

Keweenaw Point is a ridge of more recent origin than the Huron mountains and the associated upheavals. It consists of an immense dyke or wall of volcanic rock, constituting the axis of the Point, against which rest, on the westerly side, alternating strata of sandstone, conglomerate and bedded dolerite, aggregating many thousand feet in thickness. These features, due to igneous action, continue westward to the Porcupine mountains. Ile Royale marks the site of another igneous outburst, which has also brought into view, along the south-easterly side of the island, a reddish sandstone undoubtedly the equivalent of that upon the southern shore.

No animal remains have been discovered in the Lake Superior Sandstone; but the writer has described some forms of fucoids found near the Montreal river and in the Porcupine mountains, under the names of *Palæophycus arthrophycus* and *Palæophycus informis*.

2. The *Calciferous and Chazy Formation.*—This formation enters the Upper Peninsula at the Grand Rapids of the Menominee river, and, trending nearly north in a broad belt, as far as township 45, bends eastward to follow the strike of the Lake Superior Sandstone, and crosses the St. Mary's river at Sugar island. Its contact with the underlying sandstone is seen near Munising Furnace, on Sailor Encampment island and elsewhere; and the limestones of the following group are seen in contact with it at the rapids of the Menominee, on the Escanaba river, on Sailor Encampment island, and at other localities.

The formation is a more or less calcareous, often coarse-grained, sandstone, with alternations of dolomitic limestone, recalling the prevailing character of the Calciferous formation west of the Mississippi river. The following is a section on the Menominee river:—

(f) Limestone, fine, crystalline, evenly and thinly bedded, with argillaceous partings,	4 ft.
(e) Limestone, nodular, concretionary,	3 ft.
(d) Dolomitic limestone, compact, arenaceous,	2 ft.
(c) Limestone, finely argillo-arenaceous, red-banded or variegated with red blotches, in thin and even-bedded layers,	3 ft.
(b) Limestone, hard, dolomitic, with oölitic belts,	4 ft.
(a) Sandstone, white, coarse, with seams of arenaceous shales,	5 ft.

The formation is almost destitute of fossils.

3. The *Trenton Group.*—These rocks are predominantly calcareous. They form an outcropping belt, about four miles wide, across St. Joseph and Great Sailor Encampment islands, stretching thence westerly in a gradually widening band which bends around to the south-west, lying with its southern border on the west shore of Little Bay de Noquet and Green Bay, and continuing thence across Wisconsin into northern Illinois.

The limestones of this Group form the Little and part of the Grand Rapids, in the Menominee river, and the so-called falls of the Escanaba and other affluents of Little Bay de Noquet, from the west.

The following section from the Escanaba river will serve as a representation of the stratigraphical constitution of the western portion of the Group :

(g) Limestone, impure and dolomitic, in beds 4 to 10 inches thick, 8 ft.
(f) Limestone, thin-bedded, nodular, with irregular seams of argillaceous and cherty matter, 12 ft.
(e) Shales, alternating with arenaceous limestones, highly fossiliferous, 30 ft.
(d) Limestone, light, sub-crystalline, underlaid by dark-blue, crystalline limestone, 7 ft.
(c) Limestone, thin-bedded, uneven, nodular, with silicious veins and concretions, 15 ft.
(b) Dolomitic limestone, thick-bedded and crystalline, 8 ft.
(a) Limestone, greenish-ashen, with concretions, 6 ft.

In the region of the eastern outcrops, we may dispose the strata of the Group into three divisions, as follows :

III. Limestone, light, brittle, breaking with conchoidal fracture, weathering into uneven, wedge-shaped slabs. Highly fossiliferous.
II. Limestone, dark, thin-bedded, nodular, with shaly intercalations. Highly fossiliferous.
I. Arenaceous shales, dusky-green or bluish. Abounding in fossils.

Besides the main outcropping belt, an isolated area of horizontally stratified Trenton limestones, 75 feet thick, covering about four square miles, is found about 14 miles northwest of the head of L'Anse Bay. Sulphur island, also, four miles north of Drummond's island, seems to be an uplifted dome of Huronian quartzite, flanked by steeply inclined strata of silico-argillaceous limestone belonging to this group.

4. The *Cincinnati Group* (Formerly "Hudson River Group.")—The outcropping belt of these prevalently argillaceous limestones is nearly concentric with the preceding formations, but lies nearer the centre of the geological basin. The strata are well seen on the north side of Drummond's island, in a belt about four miles wide, which extends with equal width across St. Joseph island, and intercepts the southern extremity of Sailor Encampment island. On the northwest, the Group occupies the space between Great and Little Bays de Noquet, forming cliffs 15 to 50 feet high along the shore of the latter. Excavated along its outcropping border to form the basin of Green Bay, it reappears at the southern extremity, and continues in the direction of Winnebago and Horicon lakes in Wisconsin. Dipping from the regions exterior to the Lower Peninsula of Michigan concentrically toward the centre of the Peninsula, the formation underlies the whole of it, making its appearance, on the south, in southern Ohio, and thence to Cincinnati and central Kentucky.

The following section of strata belonging to this Group, is furnished on the east side of Little Bay de Noquet, SE ¼ Sec. 26 T 39 N 22 W :

(f) Limestone, massive, argillaceous, bluish or ashen, and highly fossiliferous, 20 ft.
(e) Blue indurated shale, 2½ ft.
(d) Limestone, very argillaceous and fossiliferous, with irregular patches of shale intermixed, 2½ ft.
(c) Blue shale, greenish on fresh exposures, 5½ ft.

(b) Limestone, very argillaceous, bluish and fossiliferous, 11 ft.
(a) Blue shale, greenish on fresh exposures, 6½ ft.

The fine exposure upon the north shore of Drummond's island presents strata of a similar character, and abounding in beautiful fossil corals.

5. The *Niagara Group*.—This eminently calcareous group of strata forms a belt arching around the northern borders of lakes Michigan and Huron. Constituting the principal mass of Drummond's island, it trends westward, underlying the region west of the southern half of St. Mary's river, and dipping beneath the water of the lakes, where it remains visible, sometimes, to the depth of thirty or forty feet. It is deeply and irregularly eroded along the lake shores, presenting innumerable passes through a labyrinth of small rocky islands. Continuing westward, it underlies the peninsula between Lake Michigan and Big Bay de Noquet, and forming the islands south of Pt. Detour, reappears in the Wisconsin peninsula east of Green Bay, and follows the coast of Lake Michigan thence to Chicago. Along the shore of Big Bay de Noquet, it rises in picturesque cliffs to the height of 100 and 175 feet.

Eastward from Drummond's island, the solid masses of this group constitute the Little and Great Manitoulin islands, and reappear at Cape Hurd, to form the peninsula between Lake Huron and Georgian bay. Thence it strikes south-east to the Niagara river, which gives its name to the group.

In Michigan, the group divides itself into two divisions, consisting of the Niagara limestone above, and the Clinton limestone below. In New York, further divisions are noted. The Niagara limestone, as a whole, may be described as a gray, crystalline, rather fine-grained, compact, moderately fossiliferous, dolomitic mass, attaining a maximum measured thickness (on Green Bay, Wisconsin) of 217 ft. 10 in. A portion of the mass is generally very thick-bedded, more coarsely crystalline, vesicular, and abounding in *Pentamerus oblongus*, which it was styled by Dr. Houghton the "Pentamerus limestone." These beds seem generally to occupy a middle position, but observations in the vicinity of Bay de Noquet tend to indicate that the Pentamerus beds are not always in the same horizon. The Clinton limestone is more homogeneous, aluminous and fine-grained, and contains a paucity of fossils.

This group is finely exhibited on the eastern portion of Drummond's island, where the following section of limestones was carefully measured by the writer :

(p) Hard, crystalline, light gray, weathering rough, abounding in *Pentamerus* and corals, constituting the highest ledge, 6.00 ft.
(o) Very thin layers, much broken, 8.00
(n) Rough, crystalline, geodiferous, abounding in *Pentamerus* and corals, 26.93
(m) Concealed slope, which, allowing for dip, makes, 18.87
(l) Gray, crystalline, hard, highly calcareous, burned for lime. Forms upper ledge south of the quarry, 7.00
(k) Arco-calcareous, weathering harsh, abounding in fossils. Uppermost rock seen in the quarry, 5.00

(j) Argillo-calcareous below, resembling (h); arcno-calcareous above, resembling (k); weathers unequally ; some *Cyathophylloids* at top, 2.75
(i) Dark, coarsely crystalline, exceedingly tough, .25
(h) White layer, very fine-grained, weathering white, cherty-mottled in the lower part, 3.50
(g) Arcto-calcareous with some cherty mottlings ; the lower half very hard, the upper, softer and striped with brown, 4.25
(f) Arenaceous, with hard, interlaminated layers ; becomes vesicular, 2.00
(e) Dark gray, very hard, with small geodes. Beautifully ripple-marked at top, 2.00
(d) Arenaceous, thinly laminated, dark colored ; traces of fucoids or branching corals on the upper surface. Gashed with lamellar crystal cavities, 1.25
(c) Brown limestone, exceedingly tough, .75
(b) Dark, areno-calcareous, with alumina disseminated and in wavy streaks, 1.75
(a) Argillo-calcareous, ashen colored, very fine-grained, thick-bedded—a single stratum being 4½ feet. Contains *Cytherina*, an *Articuloid* and *Murchisonia*, 6.00
Distance to the water surface, 1.50
Total Elevation, 98.30 ft.

North of this locality, lower strata are seen which, added to the above, give us a thickness here of 75 feet for the Niagara limestones, and 32 feet for the Clinton.

On the opposite side of the State, in the vicinity of the Jackson Iron Furnace, on Big Bay de Noquet, the following detail of limestones appears :

(j) Thin-bedded and argillaceous, 8 ft.
(i) Talus, sloping back 20 rods, 20
(h) Coarse, vesicular, massive, fossiliferous, 14
(g) Very hard, sub-crystalline, fine-grained, compact, flint-like, argillaceous, unfossiliferous, weathering buffish, 8 ft. 2 in.
(f) Rough, massive, vesicular, fossiliferous, 5 ft. 10 in.
(e) Fine-grained, crystalline, very compact and hard, 2 ft.
(d) Rather thin-bedded, banded with argillaceous matter, fine-grained, unfossiliferous, 1 ft. 8 in.
(c) Hard and sub-crystalline, with conchoidal fracture, unfossiliferous, 11 ft.
(b) Rough, vesicular, coarse, weathering into irregular flags or chips, fossiliferous, 8 ft.
(a) Fine, hard, sub-crystalline, in beds of 11 to 14 inches, resembling (c), 7 ft. 8 in.
Total thickness of exposure, 83 ft. 4 in.

The total thickness of the Clinton strata in this part of the State is 38 ft. 10 in., with a persistent, mixed conglomeritic bed of 8 to 12 inches or more, separating them from the Niagara.

The Niagara limestones pass southward beneath the Lower Peninsula, but do not reach the surface within the southern limits of the State, though they have been penetrated in Artesian borings at London in Monroe county.

6. The *Salina Group*. (Formerly "Onondaga Salt Group.")—This is a thin series of argillaceous magnesian limestones and marls, embracing beds and masses of gypsum, and, in some regions, strata of rock salt. It is the lowest stratified rock in the Lower Peninsula. In the Upper Peninsula, its belt of outcrop stretches across the point of land north of the Straits of Mackinac, from Little Point au Chene to near the mouth of Carp river, and following the vicinity of the shore, from that Point to West Moran Bay. The formation, with the characteristic gypsum, is seen, beneath the water-surface, at the Little St. Martin island, and at Goose island near Mackinac. Dipping beneath the Southern Peninsula, it re-appears in Monroe county, where it has been exposed in some of the

MAP
OF THE STATE OF
MICHIGAN
coloured to shew the
GEOLOGICAL FORMATIONS
by
ALEXANDER WINCHELL, M.A.
Chancellor of the University of Syracuse,
Late State Geologist of
Michigan &c.

EXPLANATION OF COLORS

deepest quarries. Near Sandusky, Ohio, it affords valuable deposits of gypsum. The formation has also been reached in numerous Artesian borings, as at Mt. Clemens, Caseville and Alpena. At the two latter places, a thick bed of rock-salt was penetrated, which is undoubtedly the equivalent of the bed worked at Goderich, on the opposite side of Lake Huron. The total thickness of the formation is not accurately established, but probably, aside from the salt-bed, it does not exceed 50 or 60 feet. The stratification, by combining observations at remote outcrops, may be set down as follows:

III. Calcareous clay, seen at Bois Blanc.
II. Fine ash-colored limestone, with acicular crystals, as at Ida, Otter Creek and Plum Creek quarries, Monroe County, and at Mackinac, Round and Bois Blanc islands.
I. Variegated gypseous marls, with imbedded masses of gypsum, as at Little Point au Chêne and the St. Martin islands.

7. The *Lower Helderberg Group*.—This group of argillaceous and magnesian limestones was not known to the public to exist within the State until announced by the writer in 1870. They form some of the lower portions of Mackinac island and the contiguous shores, and, passing under the Peninsula, outcrop along the western end of Lake Erie, and constitute a large part of some of the islands in that region of the lake. At their northern outcrop, they consist of a series of chocolate-colored, magnesian limestones, more or less argillaceous, occurring in regular layers 4 to 8 inches in thickness, and passing upward by irregular gradations into the brecciated mass of the next group, showing a thickness of perhaps 50 feet. At the southern outcrops, the strata are evenly bedded, rather dark-ashen in color, argillaceous, and lined, sometimes, with darker argillaceous seams. They are often exposed in the quarries of the eastern part of Monroe county, and may be stated to attain the thickness of about 60 feet. They seem to correspond to the Waterlime group of the New York series. The fossils seen in Michigan are *Leperditia alta* and *Spirifer modesta*. *Eurypterus remipes* is also found on Put-in Bay and other contiguous islands of Lake Erie.

III. The DEVONIAN SYSTEM. 8. The *Corniferous Group*.—This comprises the conspicuous and durable limestone which forms the mass of Mackinac, Round and Bois Blanc islands, and the elevated promontories of that vicinity on both sides of the Straits. It underlies a large part of Emmet and Presqu' Ile counties, and forms the Fox and Beaver islands of Lake Michigan. On the south, it underlies a large part of Monroe county, and stretches southward into Ohio and Indiana. It is the prominent limestone seen at Columbus and Sandusky, Ohio; at Monroe and London, Michigan; and at London and Woodstock, Ontario. This and the Niagara are the great limestone masses which enter into the relief of the physiognomy of the northern states, from New York to the Mississippi river, and furnish sites for the most valuable limestone quarries. The for-

mation everywhere abounds in fossils, and furnishes us, in the form of fish-remains, the relics of the oldest vertebrates which inhabited our planet. Within the limits of Michigan, it is everywhere divisible into two well marked divisions: a lower, brecciated mass, about 150 feet thick, and an upper, somewhat evenly stratified mass, about 100 feet thick. At Mackinac and vicinity the stratification may be generalized, as follows:

IV. Limestone, more or less oölitic, regularly bedded, 25 ft.
III. Limestone, unevenly and thinly bedded, with silicious veins, and cherty nodules, 75 ft.
II. Brecciated limestone, the individual fragments being angular, various in composition, and sometimes little displaced from original juxtaposition, all re-cemented by an indurated calcareous mud, 150 ft.
I. Conglomeritic bed, consisting of a mass of cherty and agatoid pebbles. This occupies the place of the "Oriskany Sandstone" of New York, though not yet identified with it. 3 ft.

In the southern part of the State, the brecciated division presents conspicuous and remarkable features along the shore of Lake Erie, in the vicinity of Pt. aux Peaux and Stony Pt., where it abounds, also, in the mineral strontianite. A generalized section of the group in this part of the State is here presented:

IV. Brown bituminous limestone, seen in most of the quarries of Monroe county; also in Presqu' Ile and Emmet counties, 75 ft.
III. Arenaceous limestone, sometimes resolving itself into beds of friable sandstone and incoherent sand. Monroe county; also Crawford's quarry.
II. Oölitic limestone, as in Bedford and Raisinville, Monroe county, 25 ft.
I. Brecciated limestone, sometimes concretionary, 50 ft.

The Corniferous limestone, as its name implies, abounds everywhere in masses of hornstone. These however, do not occur in all parts of the formation. The very general presence of bituminous matter imparts a prevailing dark color to the rock. This is also frequently seen disposed in very thin partings between the strata. Petroleum often saturates the formation, and, in many places, imparts its characteristic odor. In some localities, it may be seen to ooze from the crevices and float upon the surface of water. Naturally, these manifestations have led to an unlimited amount of confident, but ignorant and wasteful well-boring. In consequence of the more or less shattered condition of the whole formation, streams of water have coursed through it, and worn out extensive subterranean passages and caverns. In these, considerable creeks sometimes wholly disappear; while they serve also, as means of communication between Lake Erie and some of the inland lakes.

9. The *Little Traverse Group*.—This is composed chiefly of the "Hamilton Group" proper, of the New York geologists; but, as the lower limits of the Hamilton have not yet been clearly fixed upon in this State, we apply the above term to a series of limestones outcropping in the vicinity of Little Traverse and Thunder Bays, and constituting physically a single mass. They have been made the subject of considerable study. In 1860 we made an official survey of the Little Traverse strata; in 1866, a special

survey and report; and in 1869 the ground was again officially examined. As the result of all our studies, we submit the following generalized arrangement:

IV. Chert Beds.
III. Buff, vesicular magnesian limestones, overlaid by characteristic crinoidal beds.
II. Bituminous shales and limestones, composed of
(b) Acervularia Beds above and
(a) Bryozoa Beds below.
I. Pale-buff, massive limestones, comprising
(b) Conostroma Beds above, and
(a) Fish Beds below.

The total thickness was set down provisionally at 141 feet, which is probably too low.

This grouping will apparently hold good over extensive regions. The Conostroma and Acervularia Beds are extremely conspicuous on the opposite side of the State, while the Acervularia Beds outcrop at Iowa City, and the Bryozoa Beds at New Buffalo, Iowa. The following is a section of the Conostroma Beds near the head of the Bay.

(d) Dolomitic limestone, pale-buff, very massive, breaking into regular blocks, somewhat arenaceous, 12 ft.
(c) Dolomitic limestone, similar to above, vesicular, brecciated in places, having a rude concretionary structure, 20 ft.
(b) Limestone, thin-bedded below, thicker above, broken, with a 10 inch band of dark bituminous soil at top, and thinner ones below, 10 ft.
(a) Talus, or sloping beach of fragments, 4 ft.

Section of Bryozoa Beds (SE ¼ Sec 1 T 34 N 6 W)

(e) Limestone, argillaceous, sub-crystalline, the thinner layers shaly, terminated by a few inches of black shale, 14 ft.
(d) Limestone, very dark chocolate-colored, argillaceous, compact, much broken, 3 ft.
(c) Limestone, very dark, bituminous, in beds from 8 inches to one foot thick, shaly or sub-crystalline, 12 ft.
(b) Limestone, dark brown, argillaceous, unevenbedded, breaking with a ragged uneven fracture, 5 ft.
(a) Limestone, dark, compact, argillo-calcareous, breaking with smooth, conchoidal fracture, much shattered, 1 ft.

Section of Acervularia Beds (SW ¼ Sec 2 T 34 N 6 W)

(d) Shale, bluish, argillaceous, imperfectly seen at, top of bank.
(c) Limestone, varying from dark to light gray, in beds from one to four feet thick, with a rough, somewhat granular fracture. Few fossils, 2 ft.
(b) Limestone, light or yellowish-buff, varying to dark chocolate, argillo-calcareous, breaking with smooth fracture into irregular, sharply angular fragments, rather even-bedded in layers 6 inches to 2 feet thick. In the upper part, alternating with bands of black bituminous calcareous shale and blue clay. The clay beds abounding in beautifully preserved corals, 23 ft.
(a) Limestone, grayish-brown, compact, argillaceous, uneven-bedded, with smooth conchoidal fracture, embracing in its upper part a 4 inch stratum of black, bituminous argillaceous limestone replete with characteristic fossils, 17 ft.

14 ft.

The strata embraced in the above section seem to be the equivalents of the eminently fossiliferous and often argillaceous beds well known at Partridge Point in Thunder Bay, at Widder and Saul's Mills, Ontario, and Eighteen-mile Creek, N. Y., and the less known localities near the head of Cheboygan lake and in Alpena county.*

The belt of strata of the group under consideration, arches across the northern portion of the Lower Peninsula, occasionally outcropping, and everywhere manifesting their proximity by characteristic fossils in the soil

* For further particulars, see "Report on the Grand Traverse Region," pp. 40 to 49 and 83 to 97.

(especially *Acervularia*, *Cænostroma* and *Atrypa reticularis*) and appearing again in extensive exposures in Alpena county, especially along Thunder Bay river, and in the bluffs and islands about Thunder Bay. Without entering here into details of stratification, we may offer the following summarized statements:

The Cænostroma Beds are extensively developed at the water-surface on Thunder Bay island and contiguous localities.

The Bryozoan Beds are seen immediately overlying, on the island, and at Nine-mile Point, and are extensively exposed along the lower valley of the Thunder Bay river.

The Acervularia Beds are seen in the cliffs along the lake shores north of the mouth of the Bay, and in the interior, in Sunken Lake and at the head of Cheboygan Lake.

The Crinoidal Beds are observed at the top of the bluff on Cheboygan Lake; and the gray, coarse, magnesian limestones are found in Sunken Lake.

The strata of this age, passing from Thunder Bay under Lake Huron, reappear in Ontario, and passing under the eastern part of Lake Erie, traverse centrally the western half of the State of New York. On Kelley's island, in Lake Erie, generally reputed to be formed of the Corniferous limestone, we find many of the fossils of this group, and it hence appears that the limits of the Hamilton and Corniferous are as obscure here as in northern Michigan.

The Little Traverse group abounds in most interesting fossil remains. Besides a large number of new species, we have signalized the occurrence of three new genera of corals occurring in the northern part of the Peninsula.

10. The *Huron Group.*—(The "Genesee Shale," the "Portage" and the "Chemung" groups of New York.) This series of preeminently argillaceous strata constituting a single mass, physically, not only in Michigan, but also in Ohio, Indiana, Kentucky and other regions, we perpetuate the general designation first employed by us in 1859. These strata underlie extensive areas in the northern and the southern portions of the Peninsula. Northward their outcropping belt strikes arcuately across the Peninsula between the regions south of Grand Traverse and Thunder Bays; while, southward, a considerable part of Allegan, Van Buren, Kalamazoo, Branch and Lenawee counties is underlaid by it. The physiognomy of these regions is generally plain without rocky outcrops.

The general features of the group may be stated as follows:

The *Black Shale*, at the bottom, attains a thickness of perhaps 20 feet. It is sometimes laminated and fissile, but frequently somewhat massive and indurated. It is a very persistent formation, known, with increasing thickness, in Ontario and all the western States east of the Mississippi river. In Michigan, we see it outcropping in Grand Traverse Bay, on Pine Lake, on Sulphur island of Thunder Bay, on the coast east of

Pt. aux Barques, at several localities in Sanilac and St. Clair counties, and in Kalamazoo and Branch counties; and it is pierced in numerous Artesian borings. It is often mistaken for a coal shale, or even for coal itself; but, though it blazes in a fire, its geological position is far below any valuable coal deposits.

The *Portage Shales* come next in order above, and consist of a series of whitish and greenish, more or less calcareous shales and clays almost wholly destitute of fossils, and attaining a thickness of probably 600 feet. They outcrop at several points around the shores of Grand Traverse Bay, and again, extensively, at Port Hope and other localities on Lake Huron, southward. They are frequently encountered in river bluffs and artificial excavations in the southern part of the State. Nodules of Kidney Iron ore are everywhere characteristic of the formation, as may be seen at Coldwater and Union City. At the latter place they have been worked for iron. These nodules are found abundantly in the surface deposits of the whole southern portion of the Peninsula. At Pt. aux Barques, the shales are seen to be interstratified with thin beds of crystalline and fossiliferous limestone; and such strata are also encountered to a limited extent in the Artesian borings further south.

The *Chemung Shales*, following next in ascending order, cannot be sharply distinguished from the preceding. They may be assigned a thickness of 200 feet. If these are more, the Portage shales are correspondingly less, since the thickness of the two has generally been found in Artesian borings, to attain about 700 feet. Toward their upper portion, they become more arenaceous, and terminate in a series of laminated, argillaceous, micaceous, friable sandstones, and pass into the lower beds of the next group.

IV. The CARBONIFEROUS SYSTEM. 11. The *Marshall Group*. This arenaceous and generally ferruginous series of strata corresponds to the upper or fossiliferous portion of the "Waverly Sandstone Group" of Ohio, and is probably represented by the Catskill Group of New York, as now restricted. It answers, probably, to the upper portion of the Old Red Sandstone series of Scotland, which, with the Catskill, seems to occupy the base of the Carboniferous System. The Marshall Group was, for a long time, confounded with the Portage and Chemung, but was assigned a distinct place and designation by the writer, in 1859 and 1860. It is seen outcropping in the sandstone bluffs of Pt. aux Barques; and, trending thence southward through Huron, Sanilac, Oakland and Washtenaw counties, it forms the southeastern watershed of the Peninsula. In the southern part of Jackson and most parts of Hillsdale county, it rises in frequent outcrops, and is not unfrequently worked as a quarry stone. It is mostly a somewhat friable rock, with a reddish, buffish or olive color, though in some regions becoming gray or bluish gray. The coloring ferruginous matter is very often arranged in imperfect concentric layers, presenting, on a

large scale, a rude concretionary structure. At Battle Creek, it becomes decidedly calcareous, and thence toward the northwest, this consolidating constituent causes the formation to present a marked contrast with the friable condition of the rock on the eastern side of the Peninsula.

This formation is generally rich in fossils, though they exist, chiefly, in the form of casts and impressions. Marshall, Battle Creek, Holland, Pt. aux Barques and numerous localities in Hillsdale county, are quite productive. Fish and crustacean remains are not abundant. The molluscous fauna embraces many species of *Nautilus*, *Goniatites*, *Orthoceras*, *Bellerophon*, besides *Nuculana*, *Solen*, *Cardiomorpha*, and many other genera. Brachiopoda, except *Rhynchonella*, are of infrequent occurrence.

12. The *Michigan Salt Group.*—This is eminently argillaceous, but the included stores of Gypsum and brine confer upon it a great degree of commercial importance. Stratigraphically, it consists of beds of clay and shale, with thin intercalated strata of limestone, and an apparently persistent bed of gypsum, having a thickness of ten to twenty feet. As the group embraces no porous stratum capable of serving as a reservoir of the brine, no considerable supplies of brine are obtained in the formation, but they occur in the underlying sandstones of the Marshall group.

This Group outcrops characteristically, near Grand Rapids, and, on the eastern side of the State, on the shore of Saginaw Bay, at Alabaster. At both these localities the gypsum is extensively worked. Evidences of the persistence of the gypseous deposits are known to exist many miles toward the interior. The formation becomes excessively thinned in the southern bend of its circuit.

The only fossils discovered in the Group are obtained from Alabaster. They present marked affinities with the fauna of the Carboniferous limestone; and the writer entertains little doubt that this Group is a mere local condition of the lower portion of the Carboniferous limestone. This phenomenon is understood to be reproduced in Nova Scotia. Thickness about 185 feet.

13 The *Carboniferous Limestone.*—This formation answers to some portion of the great calcareous deposits of the Mississippi Valley, which, for that reason, might be styled the Mississippi River Group. In Michigan, it outcrops quite frequently in Spring Arbor and neighboring portions of Jackson county, and very extensively at Bellevue and Grand Rapids, and, on the opposite side of the Peninsula, at Pt. au Gres, the Charity islands and Wild Fowl Bay. In the eastern outcrops, it presents a mass of calciferous sandstone at bottom, while elsewhere the formation is almost exclusively calcareous. At Grand Rapids it encloses a stratum of red ferruginous, argillaceous limestone, five feet thick, which, like some of the other argillaceous strata, possesses hydraulic properties. Total thickness does not exceed 70 feet.

The limestones are generally quite fossil-

iferous. *Lithostrotion Canadense* may be regarded as indicating some representation of the St. Louis member of the Mississippi Valley limestones, while *Spirifera Keokuk*, and perhaps other forms, establish the existence of the Keokuk member. It is probable that the highest member—the Chester limestone, is unrepresented, as in other northern regions, while the lowest member may yet be shown to be present in the Michigan Salt Group.

14. The *Coal-bearing Group.*—This occupies the central portion of the Peninsula, extending from Jackson on the south, to Town 20 on the north, and from Range X. west, to Range VIII. east, of the meridian. We may distinguish three members, as follows:

(a) The *Parma Conglomerate* is the well-known " Conglomerate" of the coal regions of Ohio and other western States. This is the oldest geographical designation bestowed upon the formation, and is derived from Parma, Jackson county, where it outcrops in a quarry of whitish, glistening, somewhat friable, massive sandstone, with scattered pebbles. It attains a somewhat uniform thickness of 100 feet.

(b) The *Coal Measures*, consisting essentially of a series of carbonaceous shales, sandstones, clays, and one persistent bed of bituminous coal, from three to four feet thick. To these are added local beds of black-band iron ore and considerable Kidney ore, though neither ore possesses economical importance in Michigan. The total thickness of these measures does not exceed 125 feet. The following is an average section:

V. Bituminous shales and clays, 40 ft.
IV. Black-band, passing into black limestone, 2 ft.
III. Bituminous and cannel coal, in one or more seams, with aggregate thickness of 3 to 11 feet.
II. Fire-clay and sandstone, 23 ft.
I. Shale, clay, sandstones and thin seams of coal, 50 ft.

(c) The *Woodville Sandstone*, a persistent deposit, presenting variable characters, but generally more or less friable, ferruginous and gritty. At Woodville it is buffish in color, in Shiawassee county, buffish-gray, in Ionia county, red and gray-mottled. Thickness 80 feet.

The Coal-bearing Group of strata presents no general dip. Their normal position is nearly horizontal; but local dips are of frequent occurrence. Slight geological disturbances have caused numerous anticlinal ridges on which the denudation which leveled the country has worn to a greater or less depth—sometimes leaving the Woodville sandstone at the surface, sometimes exposing the coal measures, and at other times even bringing to view the Parma Sandstone. Hence the local details of the geology within the geographical bounds of the Group, are exceedingly complex and difficult to settle.

V. The QUATERNARY SYSTEM.—The surfaces of the Laurentian, Huronian and Palæozoic rocks above described are overlaid generally by a sheet of unconsolidated materials consisting of clay, boulders and sand, with frequent superincumbent beds of marl and peat. Along the shores of the great lakes, these are seen to consist chiefly of

strictly and horizontally stratified clays, mostly of bluish and coppery colors. In the interior, we find partially and obliquely stratified, alternating beds of sands and clays, with occasional courses of boulders. In the Northern Peninsula, and, to a great extent, in the Southern, a bed of wholly unstratified clay and rounded boulders rests immediately upon the rocky surface. The superficial beds of marl and peat, with not infrequent bogs of iron and manganese, connect the history of the past with the present. The sand dunes along the lake shores are merely piles of sand blown up by the winds, as explained in the article on topography.

2. HISTORICAL GEOLOGY.

The first land within the limits of the State, was that which we have mapped as Laurentian and Huronian. No part of the existing continent is older; while nearly all other portions were still sea-bottom, except an angulated belt north of the Great Lakes and the river St. Lawrence. This original area has been subjected to a vast amount of subsequent erosion, and correspondingly diminished in its elevation and contracted in its dimensions. Its upheaval marked the close of Eozoic, and the dawn of Palæozoic, Time.

At the end of the first period of Palæozoic Time, an igneous outburst called into existence Keweenaw Point, the Porcupine Mountains, and the intervening copper ranges, together with Ile Royale and limited areas, upon the immediate shore of Lake Superior.

After this time, there were no local disturbances of special importance. The whole continental mass, east of the Rocky Mountain region was, by degrees, bodily uplifted. The Michigan region slowly emerged. The valley which was to become the basin of Lake Superior, was, at first, a bay of salt water. With the progress of continental upheaval, it became isolated from the sea, and was, for ages, a salt lake. The sea still set up the valley of the St. Lawrence to the head of the present hydrographical basin of Lake Ontario.

At the end of the Silurian Age, the whole Upper Peninsula had emerged, but the Lower Peninsula was still sea-bottom. On the west, the continent reached down to Chicago, and, on the opposite side, its shore trended southeast to London and the Niagara river. At the close of Devonian Time, the Lower Peninsula marked the position of a vast bay opening southward. It is not certain whether the anticlinals on the south of the Peninsula had an existence at this early period, or not. It is more probable that the coal-making marshes of Michigan were continuous with those of Ohio, Indiana and Illinois, but this is far from certain.

At the end of the Carboniferous Age, all Michigan was dry land. But none of the great lakes existed, except Superior. The region which is now the centre of the Lower Peninsula was probably less elevated than the regions which now lie upon the borders and in the beds of Lakes Huron and Michigan. The surface denudations going for-

ward through Mesozoic and Cænozoic Time, isolated the coal regions of Michigan and Ohio, if they were ever connected, depressed the regions which were to become the basins of Lakes Michigan, Huron and Erie, and excavated the first Niagara gorge. The drainage of the great northern sea changed it to a lake of fresh water, in which rose the St. Lawrence, flowing into the Atlantic, and probably another great stream flowing through the hydrographical basin now occupied by Lake Michigan and the Illinois river, to the Mississippi and the Gulf of Mexico. No traces of the Flora and Fauna of Michigan, during this long period, have been preserved; but without doubt, forms of animal and vegetable life adapted to the physical situation, were abundant.

At length the region which was to become Michigan, was buried, in common with the entire northern part of the continent, beneath a burden of accumulated snow and ice. This, like modern glaciers, underwent a slow motion which imparted a grinding action to the sheet of ice, and materially modified the surface features of the underlying country. The direction of this movement, on the eastern side of the State seems to have been from the north-east; on the western side, it may have been more from the north. The erosion of the continental glacier gave origin to the boulders and finer materials which occupy the present surface, and its movement transported them southward. By such action were deepened, if not originated, the valleys of Lake Erie, Lake Huron, Saginaw Bay and Lake Michigan with its appended bays. This action, combined with the strike of the underlying strata, has determined those trends in the physiographic features of the State, which we have designated as the "Diagonal System."

In due time, a change of climate, dissolving the glacier, originated torrents of water which imparted an imperfect stratification to the superficial portion of the drift materials. There was, perhaps, a subsidence which buried the whole State again beneath the waters of the ocean. Whether this were so or not, the great valleys excavated by Mesozoic and glacier agencies, were left filled with the water which either was, originally, or in time became, fresh water. The breadth of the great lakes exceeded vastly their present dimensions. Lakes Erie, St. Clair and Huron were one. Through Saginaw Bay and the valley of the Grand River, Lake Huron connected with Lake Michigan. The latter spread over the prairie region of Illinois. By the removal of the eastern barriers, the lakes were slowly drained to their present dimensions.

The surface of the Lower Peninsula was, at first, dotted with almost numberless small lakes. Many of these, by filling with sediments, marl and peat, have become converted into marshes or even meadows and arable lands; and the remainder of them are undergoing the same process.

It is likely that in America, as in Europe, man made his appearance while the dissolu-

tion of the continental glacier was in progress. We have, at least, some evidence of his presence in Illinois, while the prairies were a lake-bottom.

3. ECONOMICAL GEOLOGY.

As the commercial statistics of Michigan are presented in a separate article, we shall content ourselves, in this connection, with little more than a catalogue of the economical products of the geology of the State.

I. METALS AND THEIR ORES. 1. IRON.—(a) *Hæmatite* and *Magnetite*, in immense lenticular masses of unsurpassed purity, in the Huronian rocks of the Upper Peninsula. The Hæmatite presents itself as granular, slaty, micaceous, specular, crystalline, and earthy. Under the action of water, it becomes soft hæmatite and red chalk, and by a chemical union with water, assumes the character of Limonite, which is also styled by the miners, soft hæmatite. It also occurs to a limited extent in crystalline forms. The magnetite is generally massive and granular, with distinct crystallizations, which are sometimes also disseminated through the contiguous chloritic schists. (b) *Limonite*, altered from the Huronian hæmatites, as an earthy ore or ochre, or, not unfrequently, re-deposited in stalactitic, mammillary, botryoidal and velvety forms of great beauty. Limonite occurs, also, in immense quantities, and widely distributed over the State, in the forms of bog ore, shot ore, yellow ochre, or even in some cases, massive rock-like beds. (c) *Kidney Ore* abounds in the Huron clays, presenting, like the bog ores, various degrees of purity, and, like them, employed to a limited extent, for iron-making. (d) *Black-band* in the Coal Measures, but not known to possess economical importance.

2. COPPER.—(a) *Native* in the "trap" of Lake Superior, in sheets, and strings, and masses; also in certain conglomerates and grits associated with the beds of trap, where it occurs in grains and in powder, like the other detrital materials. This is its condition in the famous so-called "Calumet Vein," also in parts of the Porcupine mountains. (b) *Chalcopyrite* or Copper Pyrites and other ores, in the Eozoic and other metamorphic rocks. While these ores sustain an important industry in the dominion of Canada (Bruce and Wellington mines) native copper is the chief resource in Michigan.

3. SILVER.—(a) *Native*, existing, to some extent, in most of the native copper, and not unfrequently associated with it in a state of purity. (b) Existing as a *vein ore*, in limited abundance, in the trappean rocks; and, at Silver islet (Canada) and vicinity, developing an important special industry. Also, as a sulphide in union with galena, in the dolerites of Lake Superior, but not existing to any important extent.

4. LEAD.—*Galena* in unimportant and unpromising veins in the dolerites.

5. GOLD.—*Native*, existing, to a limited extent, in the Lake Superior region.

6. MANGANESE.—(a) In connection with certain hæmatites of Lake Superior. (b) In numerous bogs in the Lower Peninsula, where it is sometimes used as a black pigment.

II. SALT.—Occurring in the form of brine which has its origin in three different formations: 1. The *Salina Group*, which underlies the Lower Peninsula, and has been pierced and found to afford brine at Port Austin, Caseville, Mt. Clemens, Jackson, Lansing, Grand Haven, Alpena and other localities. Only in the first three does the supply sustain the manufacture of salt. At Alpena and Caseville rock salt occurs as at Goderich. 2. The *Michigan Salt Group*, which supplies most of the wells along the Saginaw river and vicinity, and affords a brine of remarkable strength, but containing considerable chloride of calcium which, nevertheless, as manipulated, does not interfere seriously with the manufacture of salt. These wells average about 800 feet in depth, and pass through the whole thickness of the coal-bearing group to the Marshall sandstone, into which the brine descends and accumulates. The brine is obtained from these Artesian borings by pumping. 3. The *Coal Measures*. Some of the shallow wells in the lower portion of the Saginaw Valley are supplied from this source with weaker but purer brine than that obtained from the group below. The Parma conglomerate serves as the reservoir for this group of salt-bearing strata. It may be added that the dish-like conformation of the strata of the Lower Peninsula, preventing the passage of water from side to side, retains the soluble constituents of the rocks, and hence they are all somewhat saliferous.

III. MINERALS USED IN CERTAIN CHEMICAL MANUFACTURES.—1. The BITTERNS rejected in the salt manufacture, are now extensively employed in the production of soda. 2. IRON PYRITES occurs in the Huron Group in such abundance as to promise availability, at some future time, in the process of alum-making. 3. LIMESTONE suitable for fluxing, occurs in unlimited quantities in the Trenton and Huronian rocks of the Upper Peninsula, as also in the form of calc-spar veins in the cupriferous region. In the Lower Peninsula the limestones of the Little Traverse and Corniferous Groups are equally available.

IV. MINERALS USED IN AGRICULTURE.—1. GYPSUM in remarkable abundance, purity and beauty, in the *Michigan Salt Group*, at Grand Rapids and Alabaster. Occurs also in the *Salina Group* at Little Pt. au Chene, and may be found, perhaps, in Monroe county. 2. MARL, generally distributed, and occuring at the bottom of lakelets and marshes. 3. PEAT, as the uppermost layer on the sites of filled lakelets, and around the low borders of existing lakelets.

V. MINERALS USED AS PIGMENTS.—1. IRON and MANGANESE OCHRES, in bogs and marshes through the Lower Peninsula and the Monistique Peninsula. 2. FERRUGINOUS SHALES.

VI. COMBUSTIBLE AND CARBONACEOUS MATERIALS. 1. COAL underlying about 6000 square miles of the central portion of the Lower Peninsula. Generally bituminous and of the character of the average Illinois coals. Cannel coal exists to some extent, but has not yet been developed. The principal coal mines are at Corunna and Jackson. At Grand Ledge and other points, the facilities for mining are equally good. The undisturbed condition of the strata has left the coal deposit generally so low that drainage of the mines is impracticable except by pumps. 2. BITUMINOUS SHALE, in the Huron Group, capable of furnishing oil, gas, stearine &c. 3. PETROLEUM in the Huron Shales; but which, from the absence of anticlinal axes and overlying porous strata, has not accumulated in reservoirs. 4. PEAT, in bogs, throughout the State.

VII. REFRACTORY MATERIALS. 1. SANDSTONE. 2. FIRE-CLAY of superior quality, in the Coal Measures. 3. MOULDING SAND: (a) *White*, in the Corniferous Limestone of Monroe County; (b) *Colored*, in the drift.

VIII. MATERIALS FOR BRICKS 1. CLAY, in the Huron Group (as at Coldwater) and in the lacustrine deposits and the ordinary drift, suitable for (a) *Common Bricks* and pottery, (b) *Buffish* (or "Milwaukie") *bricks*, and even *white* bricks and pottery, as at Spring Lake. 2. WHITE SAND of superior quality for glass, in Monroe county, and in the Woodville Sandstone of Jackson county.

IX. MATERIALS FOR CEMENTS AND MORTARS.—1. HYDRAULIC LIMESTONES, in the Salina and Lower Helderberg Groups of Monroe County, and probably, also, in the Hamilton of Alpena County and elsewhere; also, in the Michigan Salt Group of Grand Rapids and Alabaster. 2. STONE FOR QUICK-LIME, in great abundance. Used extensively from the Corniferous, in Monroe County, and from the Carboniferous, in Eaton and Kent counties. 3. PLASTER, in the Michigan Salt Group and the Salina Group.

X. GRINDING AND POLISHING MATERIALS.—1. GRITSTONES, of superior quality, from the Marshall Group at Pt. aux Barques, and coarser ones at Napoleon. The Huron grindstones have a national celebrity. 2. HONESTONES, in the Huronian strata near Marquette, from the silicious schists. 3. POLISHING POWDERS, in the drift in many places.

XI. BUILDING MATERIALS.—1. GRANITE, SYENITE, DIORITE, GNEISS, etc., equal to any in the world, in the Upper Peninsula. 2. ROOFING SLATES, in the vicinity of L'Anse and at other points. 3. SANDSTONES: (a) *Brown freestone*, somewhat reddish or mottled; otherwise very similar to the Portland (Ct.) brown sandstone. Occurs near Marquette, and somewhat inferior qualities at many other points in the Upper Peninsula. (b) *Reddish* and *mottled freestone*, from the Woodville formation at Ionia and vicinity. (c) *Bluish* and *gray freestone*, at Pt. aux Barques—same as Cleveland stone. (d) *Buffish freestone*, at Napoleon and Hanover, Jackson County. (e) *Whitish freestone*, in

Parma formation at Parma. 4. LIMESTONES, in the Corniferous, at London, Monroe County, and in Presqu' Ile County; also in the Hamilton in Little Traverse Bay; also in the Niagara of Drummond's island and Little Bay de Noquet—the same as at Lockport, N. Y., and Joliet, Ill. 5. SAND and GRAVEL, from the drift. 6. BOULDERS, from the drift, extensively used for foundations, and even sometimes for superstructures.

XII. MATERIALS FOR ORNAMENTAL PURPOSES.—1. MARBLES: (a) *Statuary* in the Menominee region. (b) *Mottled* and silicious in the Huronian of Marquette County. (c) *Coralline* from the Little Traverse Group of Presqu' Ile and Alpena counties. 2. ALABASTER, variously colored, from the Michigan Salt Group of Grand Rapids; also, *white* and *clouded*, from the same group at Alabaster. 3. PRECIOUS STONES. *Agates:* banded, fortification and moss agates; *jasper,*

chalcedony, chrysocolla, chlorastrolites, etc.,— all in the doleritic rocks of the Upper Peninsula.

XIII. MINERAL WATERS. 1. SALINE WATERS.—(a) *Brines,* used for salt-making, as before stated. (b) *Medicinal,* of insufficient strength for salt-making, but containing carbonate and sulphate of potash, soda and iron, with sometimes traces of lithia and other ingredients, occurring in the form of springs, as at Ann Arbor, St. Joseph and other localities, or obtained by boring, as at St. Louis, Lansing, Spring Lake and many other points. 2. CARBONATED waters, with more or less of soluble salts, as at Eaton Rapids. 3. SULPHUR WATERS, issuing in springs, as occurs most copiously at Raisinville and on the shore of Lake Erie in the town of Erie, Monroe County; also at Ann Arbor and many other points. Also, issuing from Artesian borings, especially in

the Corniferous limestone and the Huron Group. As before remarked, the conformation of the strata has retained all their original soluble constituents; hence, all Artesian waters in the State, save some outlying, leached-out patches of the Parma sandstone, will be found mineralized. The so-called "Magnetic" waters of the State are not themselves magnetic; but marked magnetic phenomena manifest themselves about the wells. These certainly arise, in part, through induction from the earth, without regard to the waters; but some experiments seem to indicate a power of *excitation* of magnetism possessed by the waters themselves.

XIV. MISCELLANEOUS. 1. LITHOGRAPHIC STONES, of coarse quality, in the Clinton and Salina Groups. 2. STATIONERS' SAND. Magnetic iron-sand assorted by the waves upon the lake-beaches. 3. PAVING STONES from the drift.

CLIMATE.

BY ALEXANDER WINCHELL, LL.D.,

CHANCELLOR OF THE SYRACUSE UNIVERSITY, VICE-PRESIDENT OF THE AMERICAN ASSOCIATION FOR THE ADVANCEMENT OF SCIENCE; MEMBER OF THE AMERICAN PHILOSOPHICAL SOCIETY, ETC., ETC.

THE meteorology of the region of the "Great Lakes" is singularly interesting, and is, also, closely connected with the industrial resources and the civilization of that portion of our country. We have accordingly, bestowed upon this subject, a large amount of study, some of the general results of which will be embodied in the present paper. Our investigations have extended to all the elements of climate—temperature, pressure, moisture, precipitation, cloudiness, winds and occasional phenomena; and we have compiled voluminous tables giving mean monthly results for series of years at a large number of localities, both within and without the State of Michigan. Our tables and results represent all the meteorological observations ever published from within the limits of the State, as well as many observations yet unpublished. For purposes of comparison, we have collected similar data, respecting more than fifty selected localities lying outside of the State of Michigan. The Michigan observations aggregate 284 years, and those of other localities, 493 years.

In the present paper we direct especial attention to the subject of temperature; and, instead of offering a body of statistical tables, we present the reader a series of *isothermal charts,* which, with the explanatory remarks with which we accompany them, will exhibit intelligibly to the eye, the general thermometric features of the different parts of the State. For the purpose of exhibiting a comparison between the climate of Michigan and that of the states contiguous, on the west, we have extended the territory covered by these charts, as far west as the Missouri river, and as far south as Springfield, Illinois. The

sinuosities of the several lines will demonstrate, at a glance, the peculiar character of the climate of Michigan, and the fact that, both in summer and winter, it is better adapted to the interests of agriculture and horticulture, and probably, also, to the comfort and health of its citizens, than the climate of any other northwestern state.

The marked peculiarity of the climate of Michigan, in these respects, is attributable to the influence of the Great Lakes, by which the State is nearly surrounded. It has long been known that considerable bodies of water exert a local influence in modifying climate, and especially, in averting frosts; but it has never before been suspected that Lake Michigan, for instance, impresses upon the climatic character of a broad region, an influence which is truly comparable with that exerted by the great lakes. That such is the fact will become apparent when we turn our attention, for a few moments, to the charts.[*]

We take first into consideration the chart or set of curves for July. Each of these curves—that for 73°, for instance—passes through all the places having the same mean temperature for the month of July. The mean July temperature for several places along each curve, has been determined from good observations continued through a series

---

[*] We think it will be conceded that the present writer was foremost in bringing into notice these great climatic facts. The conclusions of this paper were first foreshadowed in a *Report on the Grand Traverse Region* in 1860, and a paper read, the same year, at the Buffalo Meeting of the American Association for the Advancement of Science, entitled " *The Fruit Belt of Michigan.*" The subject was followed up in a carefully elaborated memoir on *The Isothermals of the Lake Region* read at the Troy Meeting of the Association, in 1870. This paper was appended to the writer's *Report on the Progress of the State Geological Survey,* 1870; and an abstract was published in the *Journal of the Austrian Society for Meteorology,* at Vienna, Vol. VII. p. 351, et seq.

of years; and the July means for the places between the principal ones, along the curve, are reasonably assumed to be the same as those of the principal places.

Turning our attention, then, to the curves, or isothermal lines for July, we are at once impressed by the magnitude of the deflections of the isothermals in passing the great lakes. These deflections are toward the south, in consequence of the cooling influence of the lakes. In the presence of this influence one must pass to a more southern latitude to find the same degree of warmth as exists in the regions removed more or less from the influence. In the lower peninsula of Michigan, the lines all form loops opening southward, showing that the mean temperature of July, in the interior, is much higher than along the lake borders. And yet, within the peninsula of Michigan, the isothermals do not attain so high a northern limit as in the continental region west of Lake Superior. The isotherm of 70°, for instance, first appears within the limits of the chart in the latitude of 48°, in the valley of the Red River of the North. Passing southeastward and eastward to the valley of the Menominee river, it comes within the influence of Lake Michigan, and bends directly southward through Green Bay and Milwaukie to latitude 42° 40', and thence trends northward to Traverse City, in latitude 44° 40'. Here it is deflected southward again, under the influence of Lake Huron, and, passing Saginaw and Sanilac, finally bends north-eastward to attain its normal position, striking Penetanguishene on Georgian Bay of Lake Huron. West of Lake Michigan, this isotherm sweeps across a latitudinal belt

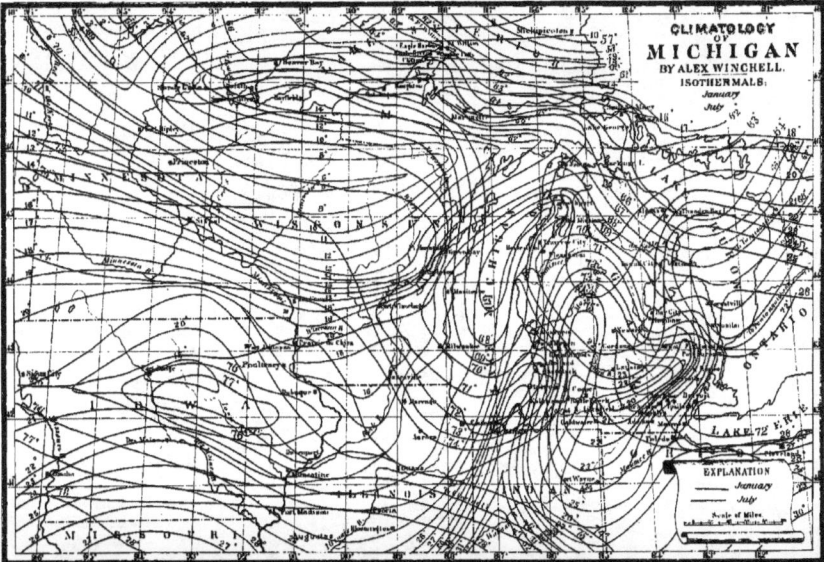

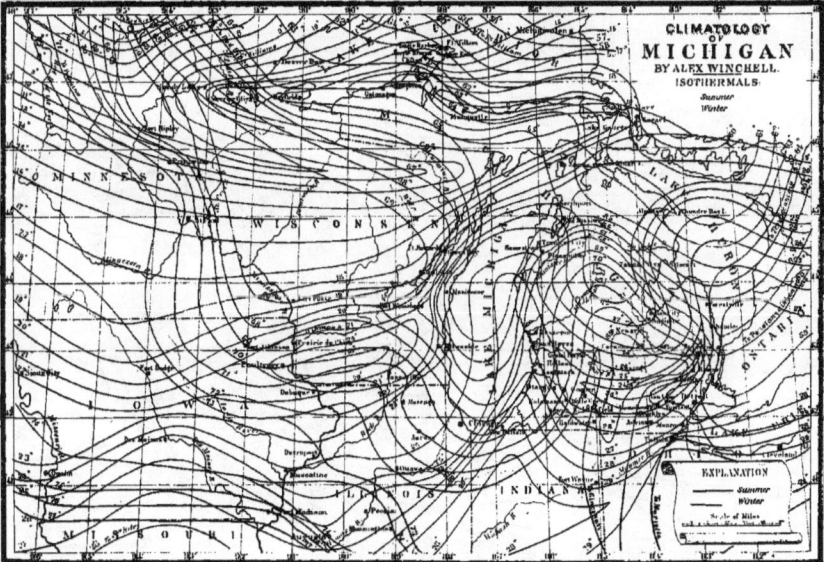

CLIMATOLOGY
OF
MICHIGAN
BY ALEX WINCHELL.
ISOTHERMALS.
January
July

EXPLANATION
January
July
Scale of Miles

CLIMATOLOGY
OF
MICHIGAN
BY ALEX WINCHELL.
ISOTHERMALS.
Summer
Winter

EXPLANATION
Summer
Winter
Scale of Miles

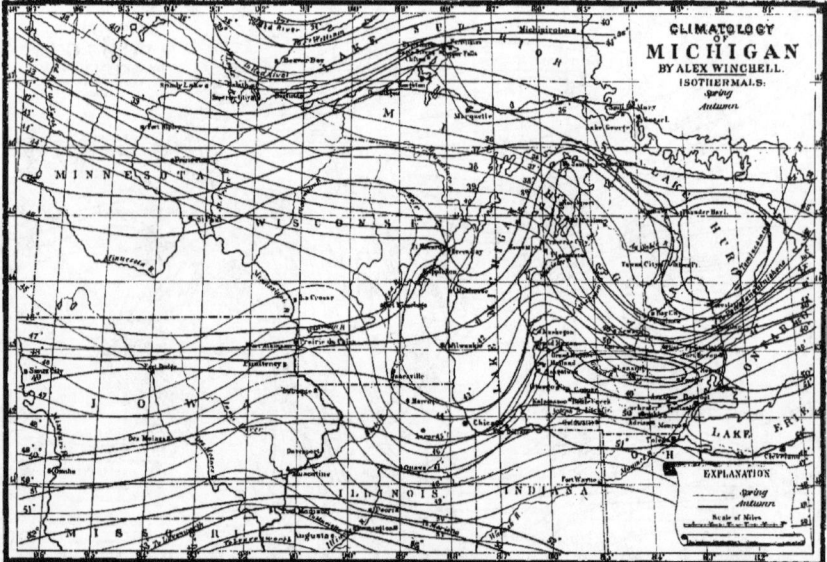

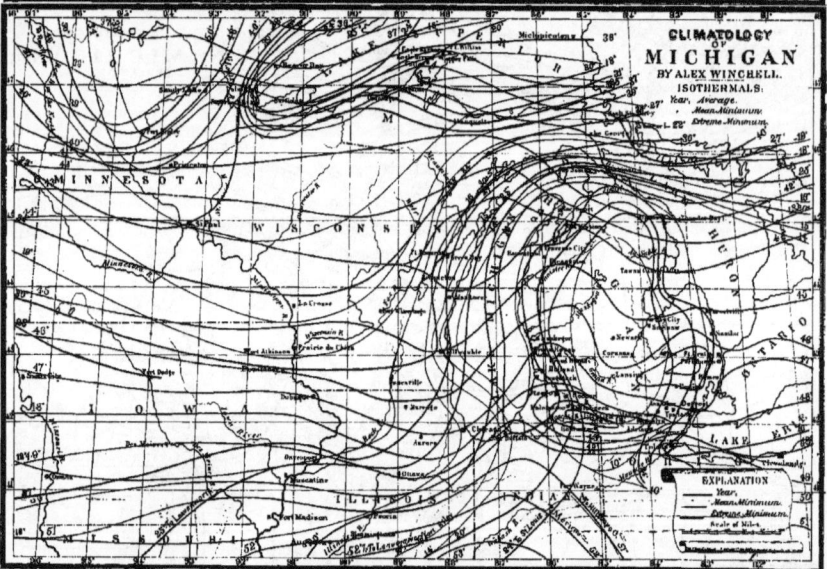

of five and a half degrees. Within the peninsula of Michigan, it is deflected first northward two degrees, and then southward one and a half degrees.

Similar deflections are experienced by the isotherms between 67° and 72°. The isotherms of 73°, 74°, and 75° appear to escape much of the influence of Lake Huron. The isotherm of 74° divides in southern Michigan —one branch passing eastward through northern Ohio and the other through central Indiana and southern Ohio. The state of Ohio, consequently, constitutes an area of uniform temperature in July, which is identical with the mean temperature of central Michigan to the limit of four and a half degrees of latitude, or 300 miles, further north.

An area in the southeastern part of the peninsula of Michigan seems to be an area of cold; since the temperature is two or three degrees colder than it is on either side. There exists a region in this part of the State which is topographically elevated about 300 feet above the general level of the peninsula. It is the region of outcrop of the sandstones of the Marshall Group, but it is not entirely coincident with this area of cold. An area of warmth seems to be indicated in northern Iowa.

It will be observed that the cooling effect of Lake Michigan is somewhat greater on the west side than on the east. Not only are the isotherms deflected from a higher latitude on the west side, but they likewise attain a somewhat lower latitude. The lowest deflection of the curve of 75°, for instance, is at Ottawa, Ill., to the west of the meridian of the lake. The curves of 71° and 72° are also somewhat more southern on the west side than on the east. This circumstance is undoubtedly accounted for by the slight preponderance, during July, of winds from the east of the meridian. Thus, at Chicago, this preponderance is as 60 : 33=1.82; at Milwaukie, as 47 : 36=1.30. But at Milwaukie and further north, northerly and even northwesterly winds feel the influence of Green Bay.

Contrasting with these results those represented on the isothermal chart for January, we are at once struck with these phenomena: 1st, the great deflection of the isothermal lines; 2d, their northward deflection; and 3d, the exertion of an excessive amount of lake influence upon the east side. All this is illustrated by tracing the isotherm of 22°. Coming within the limits of the chart a few miles southwest of Omaha, it pursues an undulating course eastward to Ottawa, in Illinois, when it bends abruptly northward, passing west of Chicago, and east of Milwaukie, to Northport, at the mouth of Grand Traverse Bay, whence it bends southward to Corunna, in the middle of the lower peninsula of Michigan, and northward again to Thunder Bay Island of Lake Huron, and thence east to Penetanguishene on Georgian Bay. The isotherm of 23° reaches almost as far north; but, in crossing the peninsula of Michigan, it strikes southward into northern Indiana and Ohio, thence northward again almost to Thunder Bay Island. The sinuosi-

ties of this isotherm spread over a belt of four and one half degrees, or 300 miles in width. In other words, the influence of the lakes is such that the mean temperature of January at Northport and Thunder Bay Island is identical with that of Omaha, Peoria, Chicago and Fort Wayne. The January temperature of Mackinac and Marquette is the same as that of Green Bay and Fort Winnebago.

An island of cold is again indicated in the southeastern part of the peninsula of Michigan. In this case, its form and position correspond quite exactly with a region of elevation. The area in northern Iowa which, in July, is an island of warmth, appears to be in January, an island of cold. A similar one exists in the elevated region of southern Wisconsin, while a remarkable axis of cold stretches through northern Wisconsin and Minnesota. The axis is not entirely coincident with the crest of the ridge dividing the tributaries of Lake Superior from those of the Mississippi; since the warming influence of Lake Superior crowds it about 60 miles southward.

One of the most striking phenomena exhibited by the chart for January, is the excess of the warming influence along the eastern side of Lake Michigan. The isotherm of 23½° strikes from Chicago directly to Northport, almost at the opposite end of the lake. The contrast in January temperature between the opposite shores of the lake is, for the northern half, four degrees, and for the southern, six degrees. This circumstance is due to the fact that the prevailing winds of the region, during January, and indeed during the entire winter, come from the west and south-west, and are at the same time, the coldest winds. The precise ratios of all the winds from the east and the west of the meridian, in January, are, at Chicago, according to eleven years' observations, as 72 : 5=14.4 ; at Milwaukie, for thirteen years, as 60 : 19= 3.33 ; at Manitowoc, for eleven years, as 67 : 11=6.09. These results embody all January winds, except those directly from the north or south. Thus the winds from the west of the meridian are greater in amount as well as severity. The reason why the excess of warming influence on the east side is greater toward the south than toward the north is evidently because north, and even northwest, winds coming from Green Bay, add their warming effect to that of Lake Michigan, in all the region north of Milwaukie.

The isothermal charts for the summer and winter contrast in the same way as those for July and January, though the contrast is naturally less marked. From the summer chart we perceive that the isothermal of 72° makes its advent upon the northern limit of the chart, and disappears upon its southern limit, only 12° of longitude further east. Coming from the Winnipeg country, it passes near Dubuque and Ottawa, thence into the centre of the peninsula of Michigan. Sweeping around this region, it strikes directly south to Germantown and Portsmouth

in Ohio. The summer temperature of the Winnipeg region and of central Michigan, is identical with that of northern Illinois and southern Ohio. Areas of cold exist in southern Michigan and northern Minnesota ; and large areas of uniform temperature in Wisconsin, Indiana and Ohio.

The excess of cooling influence upon the west side of the lake, during the entire summer, is quite noticeable. The isothermals, in approaching the Lake Superior region, make an angle of 45° with the meridian ; and, under the influence of Lake Michigan, they become quite parallel with the meridian. It does not appear that, in the Lake Superior region, any excess of winds from that lake exists ; but, in the vicinity of Lake Michigan, such excess is well established. At Chicago, the winds from the lake are to those from the land, during summer, as 151 : 119=1.27 ; at Milwaukie, the lake winds are to the land winds as 142 : 104= 1.27 ; at Manitowoc, the lake winds are to the land winds as 153 : 123=1.24.

From the winter chart we notice that the isotherm of 24° undulates over a breadth of more than 200 miles. Other isotherms are similarly situated. The mean winter climate of Mackinac is 20°; and is identical with that of Green Bay, Fort Winnebago and Fort Dodge.

The excess of the warming influence on the east side of Lake Michigan is most apparent. The winter mean of Chicago is 24½°, while that of New Buffalo, in the same latitude, is 28°. The winter mean of Milwaukie is 22°, while that of its vis-a-vis, Grand Haven, is 26°. The winter mean of Fort Howard is 20° and of Appleton, 19° ; while that of Traverse City, farther north than either, is 23½°. These contrasts illustrate again the effect of the prevalence, during the cold season, of winds from the west of the meridian.

As to the isothermals for the spring and autumn, it might be expected that they would suffer little deflection under the influence of the lakes. Comparatively speaking, this is the case ; but it will be noticed, nevertheless, that a marked cooling influence is exerted in the spring ; since the isotherm of 43°, for instance, is deflected southward one hundred and fifty miles. It is worthy of remark, at the same time, that the maximum deflection takes place on the west side of Lake Michigan. On the east side, the deflection of the same isotherm amounts to no more than twenty miles. In general, we find the mean spring temperature of the eastern side of Lake Michigan to be about three degrees higher than the mean spring temperature of the western side. As this excess is accumulated in April and May,— especially in May—it is at once apparent that the circumstance has a most important bearing upon the growth of spring crops on the opposite sides of the lake. The effect is such that the temperature of Grand Haven, March 15, is equal to that of Milwaukie, March 21 ; that of Grand Haven, April 15, is equal to that of Milwaukie, April 24 ; that of Grand Haven, May 15, is equal to that of

Milwaukie, May 26. These contrasts relate to *mean* temperatures. They show that vegetation on the east side secures a start of six to thirteen days. Add to this, protection from *exceptional* cold, in the form of spring frosts, and, to this, the effects of a drier and lighter soil, and we get a clear and demonstrative explanation of the difference of the agricultural and pomological products of the opposite sides of the lake.

This contrast of temperatures in spring is explained, as before, by the predominance, during the cold month of March, of winds from the west of the meridian, and, during the warmer months of April and May, of winds from the east of the meridian. Thus, at Manitowoc, in March, the winds from the west of the meridian are to those from the east, as 43 : 24=1.8; at Milwaukie, they are as 44 : 32=1.4; at Chicago, as 57 : 20=2.85. On the contrary, the preponderance of winds from the east of the meridian, during May, is, at Manitowoc, as 37 : 26=1.42; at Milwaukie, as 62 : 24=2.58; and in April, as 52 : 33=1.6. At Chicago, including north winds, which are here lake winds, the ratio of lake and land winds, in May, is as 44 : 40=1.1.

In autumn, the resultant of the lake influences on the west side is almost zero; while, on the east of Lake Michigan, a warming effect is experienced, amounting, along the southern half of the lake, to one or two degrees, and, along the northern half of the lake, to three or four degrees. This, as before, is caused by a preponderance, during each of the autumn months, of winds from the west of the meridian. This preponderance is shown, for Chicago, by the ratio of 151 : 70=2.16; for Milwaukie, by the ratio of 147 : 94=1.56, and for Manitowoc, by the ratio of 160 : 60=2.67.

The advantages thus secured to vegetation along the east side of the lake are not less in autumn than in spring. These singular facts depend upon a shifting of the prevalent winds at the end of the cold season, toward the close of March, and again at the end of the mild season near the close of November. An investigation of the monthly means on the opposite sides of the lake, during autumn, shows that the temperature attained at Milwaukie, October 15, is not reached at Grand Haven until October 20. The Milwaukie temperature of November 15 is only reached at Grand Haven, November 23. Comparing Chicago and New Buffalo, we find the Chicago temperature of September 15 is the same as the New Buffalo temperature of September 21. The October and November temperatures seem to be nearly coincident. These comparisons show that the warm season is lengthened on the east side, about six to eight days in the autumn. This, added to the time gained in the spring, makes the growing season, on the east side of Lake Michigan, from twelve to twenty-one days longer than on the west side—to say nothing about exemption from unseasonable frosts and a much warmer constitution of the soil upon the east side.

Turning our attention, now, to the chart of isothermals for the year, we might anticipate that the warming and cooling influences of the lakes would exactly neutralize each other, so that the isothermals would experience no deflection. We find, however, that on the western side the resultant influence is slightly cooling, and on the eastern side, decidedly warming. The resultant of these two influences gives a final resultant of a warming character exerted upon the eastern side. This final resultant has a value of one-half to two degrees. In other words, Lake Michigan elevates the mean annual temperature of the contiguous region nearly two degrees above the norm. This results, of course, from the fact that the mean temperature of the lake waters is higher than that of the land. This excess must be considerably greater than the resultant warming influence upon the land. Its explanation is a curious and interesting subject of inquiry. It cannot be caused, as in the case of the Gulf Stream, by great currents moving from tropical regions. Nor can we attribute it to a large volume of river water poured into the lake from regions lying to the southward. Some more occult cause operates to raise the mean temperature of the lake above the normal temperature of the land. Some suggestions as to the nature of that cause have been offered by the writer on a former occasion, but it would be foreign to our purpose to introduce the discussion in this place.

In studying the influence of the great lakes upon the climate of the contiguous regions, we should especially note its presence under circumstances of exceptional cold or heat upon the land. For the purpose of illustrating these relations, we have constructed two isothermal charts for minimum temperatures. One of these is a chart for *mean minima*, and the other a chart for *extreme minima*. By the "mean minimum" of a locality, is meant the *average* of the yearly minima for a series of years; and by the "extreme minimum," the *lowest point* attained during that series of years. These charts present results which are truly striking. The isotherms in the vicinity of lakes Huron and Michigan, trend literally north and south. In the chart of mean minima, the isotherm of —15° strikes from Mackinac through Manitowoc, Milwaukie, and New Buffalo, to Fort Riley, in Kansas, near the parallel of 39°. Here is a deflection over nearly seven degrees of latitude, or about 480 miles in a straight line. The meaning of this is, that the most excessive cold at Mackinac, for a period of 28 years, is not, on the average greater than at Fort Riley, 480 miles further south. It is one degree less than at Chicago for a term of eleven years. By a glance at the chart of extreme minima, we perceive, that the lowest point reached at Mackinac is but two degrees lower than the extreme minimum of St. Louis. Extreme weather of Chicago is twelve degrees colder than at New Buffalo. The lowest extreme of Milwaukie is fourteen degrees below the extreme minimum of Grand Haven, while the extreme of Fort

Howard is twenty degrees below that of Northport. In general, while the mean minimum along the west side of Lake Michigan is —16°; that along the east side is —6°; while the extreme minimum on the west side is —22° to —30°, that of the east side is —10° to —16°.

It is proper to direct attention to the important bearing of these additional facts upon the results of soil-cultivation. It will be remembered that it is not the severity of the winter mean, but that of the winter *extremes* which conditions the immunity of exotic plants from destructive frost. One killing freeze is as fatal as thirty. That one killing freeze is as likely to occur at Fort Riley, or Leavenworth, or Peoria, or even at St. Louis, as at Mackinac. The whole east shore of Lake Michigan is 15° to 20° more secure than any of the places just named. As grapes and peach trees require for their destruction, a temperature of —20°, it is apparent that peach orchards and vineyards are perfectly secure along the whole extent of the eastern shore of Lake Michigan.[*]

The *rationale* of these climatic effects is not difficult to discover. It lies in the comparatively low capacity of watery surfaces for absorbing and radiating heat. The mean temperature of the land, in the middle latitude of Lake Michigan, is about 44½°, and that of the lake, a few degrees higher. In July, the temperature of the land rises to 74° while that of the lake is not above 51° or 52°. This difference is partly due to the fact that upon the land the heat from the solar rays is accumulated near the surface, while upon the water it is disseminated through the whole mass, at least to a considerable extent, by the action of waves and currents. In January, the mean temperature of the land sinks to 19°, while that of the water does not, probably fall below 40°. The atmosphere in contact with the water must partake, to some extent, of the temperature of the water, and, when moving from the water to the land, must transfer to the land, some portion of the heat or cold proper to the lake. The effect is a tendency to equalize the land temperatures in summer and winter. This tendency is most distinctly felt in case of extreme weather. On occasion of our coldest weather, the wind blows generally from the southwest, and, passing diagonally over Lake Michigan for a distance of 100 to 200 miles must necessarily experience a great degree of amelioration.

In this connection, it is worth while to point out the fact that the arcuation of the longitudinal axis of Lake Michigan is such that a southwest wind striking the Grand Traverse region, must have passed over a much greater breadth of lake-surface than the same wind, in striking the region of St. Joseph; and hence the amelioration of winter extremes must be more marked in the

former region than in the latter. It is further obvious that in the rare case of absolute calm or a southerly wind at a time of extreme cold, no portion of the peninsula would experience the warming influence of the lake.

The foregoing generalizations from the numerical data of the science of meteorology are abundantly confirmed by the results of the attempts made during a few years past to introduce the cultivation of peaches, grapes and other fruits along the entire belt from St. Joseph to Grand Traverse Bay. These results are so much a success that it is now generally acknowledged that scarcely a superior fruit-producing region exists within the United States.

The influence of the sea in equalizing temperatures has long been understood. The immunity from unseasonable frosts secured by bodies of fresh water to localities in their immediate vicinity, has also been universally observed; but the fact that inland lakes, of the size of Lake Michigan, exert an ameliorating agency quite comparable with that of the Atlantic Ocean, is something which has only been brought to light by recent thorough discussions of a wide range of meteorological data. On general principles, it has, indeed, been asserted by Professor Henry and by Blodget, and, at an earlier period, by Humboldt, that the great lakes of North America must exert some influence in deflecting the isothermal lines; but when we come to examine any of the charts which have been published to represent existing knowledge or conceptions, we fail to detect any marked inflection of these lines in passing the region of the great lakes. In fact, the thermometric observations from the fifty-five meteorological stations in Michigan have not heretofore been employed in tracing out the remarkable tortuosities of the isothermals of the lower peninsula of Michigan. These disclosures are destined to take their place among the most interesting phenomena of climatological science.[*]

We do not deem it expedient to extend this paper by the introduction of barometrical and psychrometrical results; but the distribution of rain and snow is a climatic element of such paramount economical importance that we think a summarized table may be acceptable. We have, accordingly, selected from our voluminous records of results the following condensed view of the aqueous precipitation at a series of representative localities.

[*] The foregoing general results were embodied in a popular paper published (with reduced isothermal charts for July and January) in Harper's Magazine for July, 1871. This paper, with the charts, has been reproduced in Der Michigan Wegweiser, in Hamburg, and also in the Zeitschrift der oesterreichischen Gesellschaft für Meteorologie in Vienna, Vol. viii. p. 40, et seq. (February 1, 1873.) It seems a suggestive commentary on the intelligence of American state governments that, while these results, though thus meagrely set forth, possess such interest as to be published and republished at home and abroad, by newspaper and magazine managers, emigration agencies, learned societies, medical journals and horticultural associations, the public authorities of Michigan have neither instigated, aided nor endorsed their publication; but, incredible as it may seem, have actually declined, with expressions of derision, to publish them to their own citizens and the world. [See Michigan Legislative Proceedings, March and April, 1871.]

Precipitation of Rain and Snow.

This Table is based on observations extended, generally, to the year 1870, inclusive. Since the results were worked out, the volume of Tables and Results of the Precipitation in Rain and Snow, in the United States, compiled and discussed by Charles A. Schott of the U. S. Coast Survey, has been published by the Smithsonian Institution. Some slight discrepancies with our determinations may, undoubtedly, be attributed to the fact that Mr. Schott's data do not, generally, extend beyond 1866 or 1867. This Report, like everything which emanates from Mr. Schott's hands, is a masterly work. The country is deeply indebted to the Smithsonian Institution for meteorological data and discussions unsurpassed in volume and value by the productions of any country.

The mean annual precipitation over the whole State is 31 inches; in the Upper Peninsula, 30 inches, and in the Lower, 32 inches. This is about the average for Wisconsin, Minnesota, Iowa, Nebraska and Kansas. In the states south and east of Michigan, the annual fall of rain and snow reaches 40 to 44 inches. Further south, and along the Atlantic border, it rises still higher. The total precipitation throughout the lake-region sustains no discoverable relation to the great lakes. Aside from the varying influence of the great current of moisture from the Gulf of Mexico, the precipitation seems to vary with the topography and surface of the country. It is singular, however, that, in this State, the four localities receiving the lowest mean annual precipitation, are situated upon the lake shores. These are Tawas, Ontonagon, Mackinac, and Grand Haven. On the contrary, however, two other localities, Copper Falls and Holland, situated in close proximity to the lakes, are exceeded only by Grand Rapids.

The mode of distribution of the precipitation through the year is a question which has an important bearing on the ability of a region to sustain an agricultural industry. The Table referred to has columns headed "Ratio," in which is placed, for each season, the ratio of the precipitation for that season to the whole annual precipitation at the same place. These ratios are expressed in the form of percentages. From these percentages we have calculated the following generalized Table.

DISTRIBUTION OF PRECIPITATION THROUGH THE SEASONS.
(In percentages of Total Precipitation.)

	SPRING.	SUMMER.	AUTUMN.	WINTER.
Upper Peninsula,	19	27	25.8	22
Lower Peninsula,	23.8	28.7	27.3	19.1
Whole State,	23.6	28.3	27.7	20

In the State at large, we have, as appears, considerably less precipitation during winter than during any other season. The Lower Peninsula presents this deficiency to a marked extent, while, in the Upper Peninsula, the spring is the period of minimum precipitation, though Copper Falls has a

marked winter excess. In the whole State, and in the Lower Peninsula, the summer season is marked by the greatest amount of rain; in the Upper Peninsula, the autumn. In the Lower Peninsula the three seasons of vegetable growth together receive nearly 82 per cent. of the whole precipitation. That is, the rain-fall, during the growing months, is as great as in other states having a total precipitation of 35 inches distributed equally through the seasons.

The liability of a region to occasional excessive droughts is not indicated by the total mean annual precipitation, nor, indeed, by the mean seasonal precipitation. An occasional prolonged and destructive period of dryness may occur without materially disturbing the annual or seasonal means. We have, accordingly, selected from the annual and seasonal means for a series of years, the ones which are lowest for each locality, and introduced them in our Table, in the columns headed "minima." From the column of minima for the year, we observe that the extreme minimum at Sault Ste. Marie is 12.11 inches, which is only 40 per cent. of the annual amount, and at Mackinac it is only 48 per cent. of the amount at that place. These numbers represent years of extreme scantiness of rain and snow. Had we the data, it would probably appear that the year 1871 was a year of remarkable dryness throughout the State. Generally, the extreme minimum of annual precipitation does not fall excessively below the normal annual mean. At Detroit, it is 60 per cent. of the annual mean; at Lansing, 81 per cent.; at Ann Arbor and Monroe, 82 per cent.; at Ontonagon, 83 per cent.; at Tawas, 84 per cent.; at Grand Haven, 87 per cent.; at Grand Rapids, 92 per cent., and at Marquette and Holland, 93 per cent., showing a remarkably uniform distribution through a series of years.

The extreme minima of the seasons exhibit a much greater departure from the normal seasonal means. For instance, in spring, the extreme minimum precipitation at Mack-

inac is only 33 per cent. of the norm; at Sault Ste. Marie, 34 per cent.; at Marquette, 43; at Ontonagon, 50; at Battle Creek and Ann Arbor, 54; at Detroit, 55; at Monroe, 56; at Grand Rapids, 60; at Thunder Bay I., 61; at Lansing, 81; at Holland, 86 per cent. Thus extreme dryness in spring is less severe in the lower peninsula than in the upper.

In summer, the extreme minimum precipitation at Mackinac is 34 per cent. of the norm; at Tawas, 38 per cent; at Sault Ste. Marie, 39; at Detroit, 41; at Marquette, 45; at Battle Creek and Ann Arbor, 52; at Lansing and Grand Rapids, 58; at Monroe, 62; at Ontonagon, Holland and Flint, 68; at Grand Haven, 90 per cent. This means that the liability to extreme dryness throughout the summer is greater at Tawas, Sault Ste. Marie, Detroit and Marquette than at the other places; and that at Grand Haven, the normal supply is never diminished more than one tenth. The trustworthiness of those generalizations, however, is only in proportion to the length of the period of observations at the several places.

In autumn, the extreme minimum of precipitation at Mackinac is only 22 per cent. of the normal precipitation for that season; at Tawas, it is 38 per cent.; at Marquette, 39; at Lansing, 40; at Detroit, 43; at Monroe, 47; at Battle Creek, 51; at Sault Ste. Marie, 52;

at Grand Haven, 53; at Grand Rapids 60; at Flint, 67; at Ann Arbor, 71; at Ontonagon, 75; and at Holland, 97 per cent. of the norm.

In winter, the extreme minimum precipitation at Detroit is 31 per cent. of the normal amount; at Mackinac, it is 38 per cent.; at Sault Ste. Marie, 49; at Monroe, 56; at Ann Arbor, 60; at Battle Creek, 62; at Marquette, 64; at Ontonagon, 66; at Lansing, 69; at Tawas, 74; at Grand Haven, 76; at Holland, 90 per cent.

From the foregoing generalizations, it appears that the northern localities experience a somewhat greater liability to dryness in all the seasons. It must be borne in mind, however, that the percentages given are percentages of the seasonal means at the several localities. But this mean may be comparatively low. Thus, when we state extreme winter dryness at Ann Arbor as 60 per cent of the normal precipitation, it will be remembered that the normal precipitation, in winter, is only 15 per cent of the whole annual precipitation.

It is apparent that the seasonal minima are more excessive than the annual minima. It follows from this, that a deficiency of precipitation in one season is followed, within twelve months, by an excess in another season. This accords with popular belief.*

* The foregoing results are liable to be changed by further ob-

We append, finally, a condensed Table of the Winds of the State. The numbers in the columns denote the number of tri-daily observations, in each season and during the year, at which the wind, at the several localities, was from the directions indicated at the heads of the columns. Thus, at Ontonagon, in the spring, as the average result of three years' observations, the wind was found from the north 39 times, from the northeast, 45 times, and so on. The column headed "Ca" denotes the number of times a calm prevailed. Some observers report no calm—deciding always that there exists some determinable movement of the air, however slight. Hence the blanks in this column. Many interesting generalizations might be based upon the Table, some of which have already been presented in connection with the discussion of isothermals, but we forbear to extend this paper.

The foregoing popularized abstract of meteorological results is but a meagre exhibit of the amount of information in our possession, but the presentation is probably sufficiently full for the present purpose.

servations—the most so, at localities where the series of observations has not extended over a number of years. Of all the results, the extreme minima are most liable to undergo change. It will be noticed that the minima given are generally most extreme at those localities where the series of observations is most extended.

WINDS.

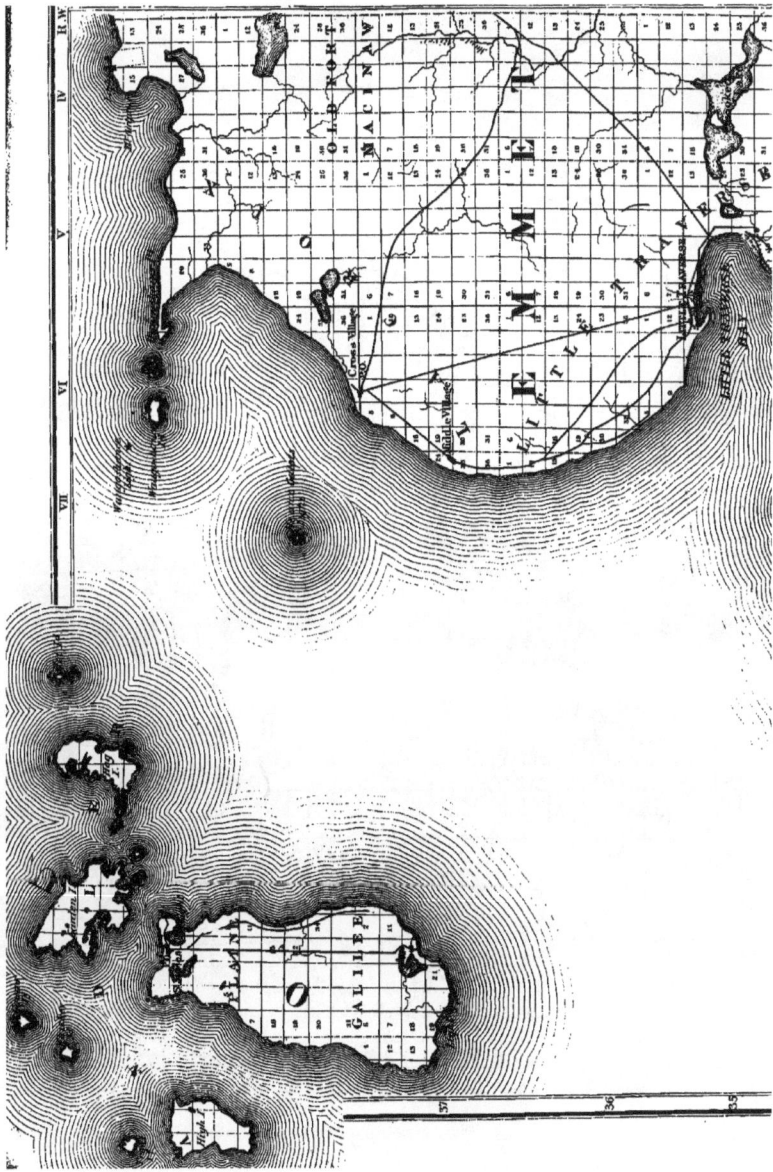

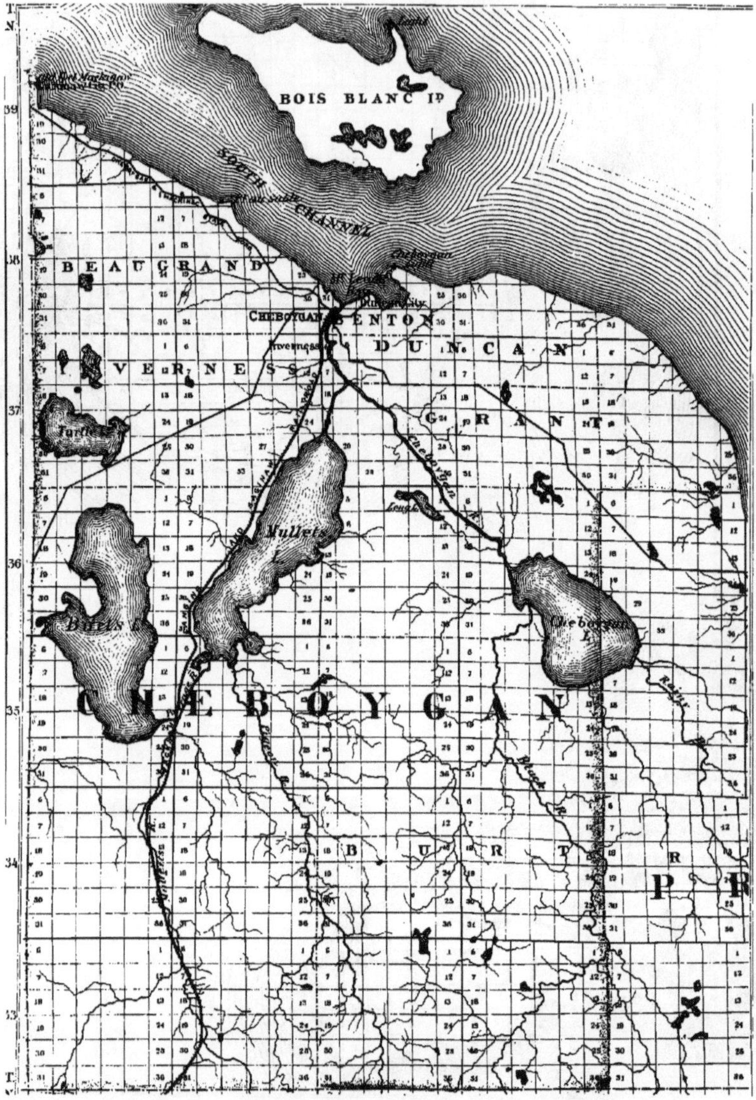
BOIS BLANC ID
SOUTH CHANNEL
BEAUGRAND
CHEBOYGAN
BENTON
DUNCAN
INVERNESS
GRANT
Mullets
Burts L.
Cheboygan L.
CHEBOYGAN
BURT
Cheboygan R.
Black R.
Rainy R.
Cheboygan Light
Duncan City

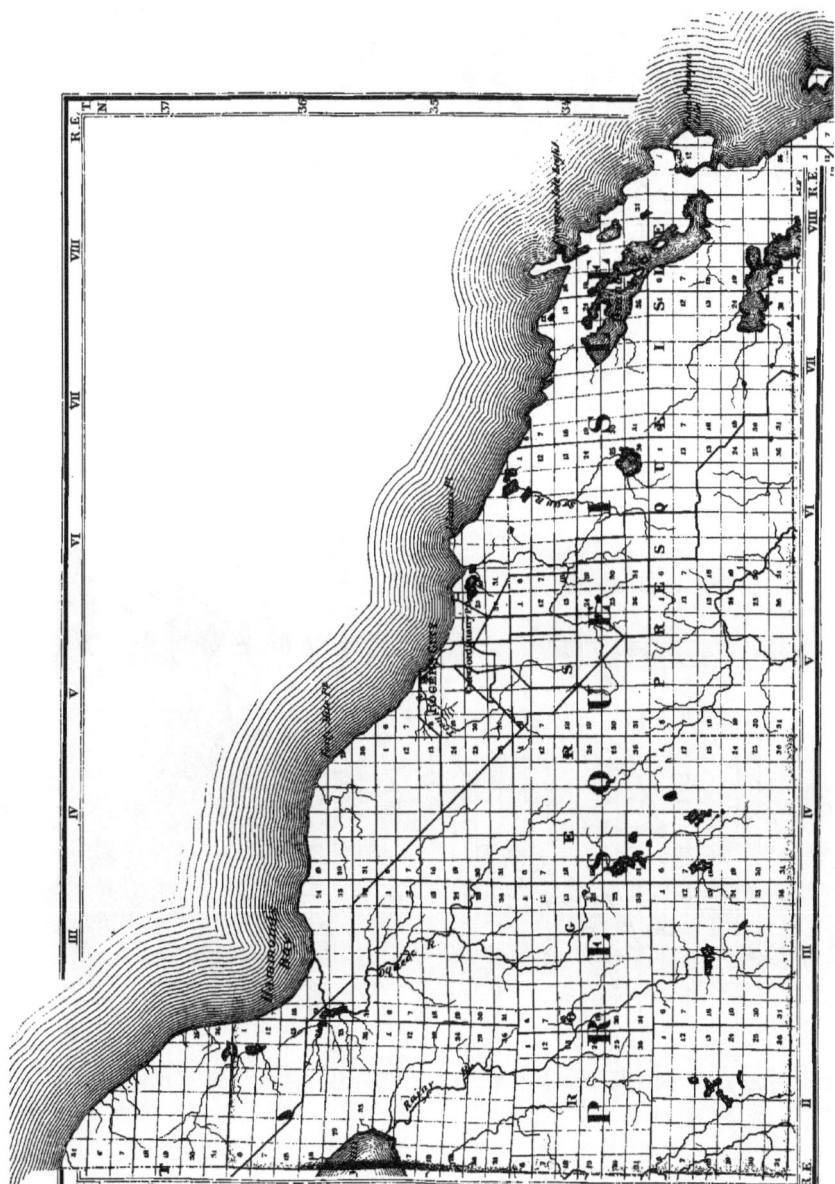

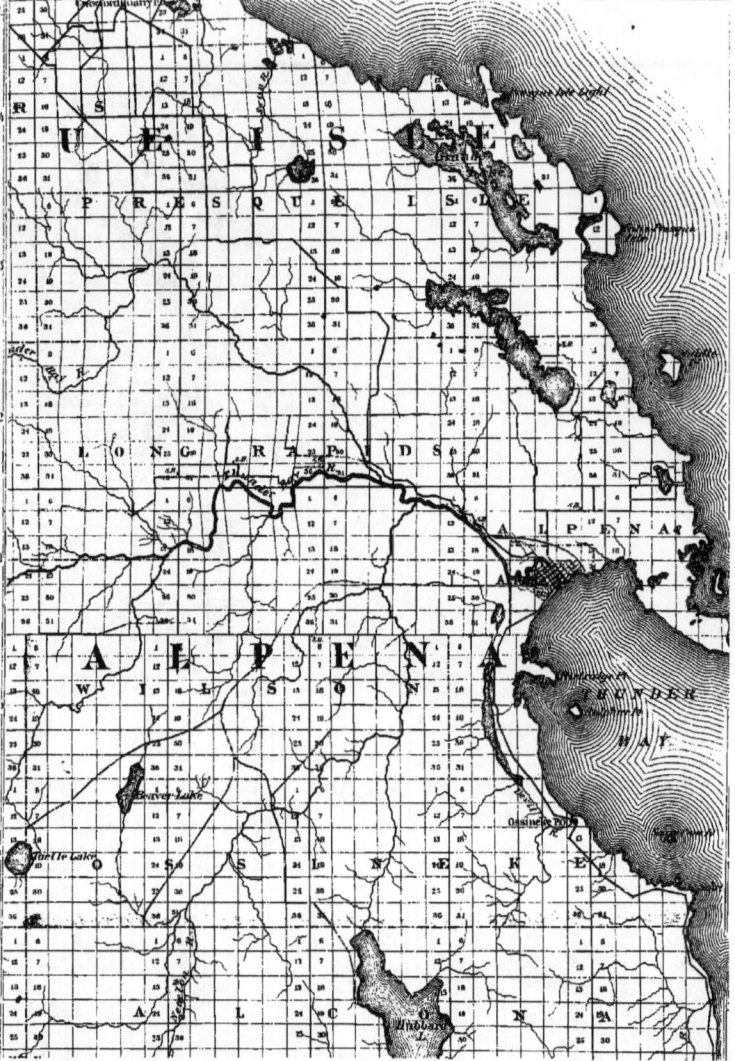

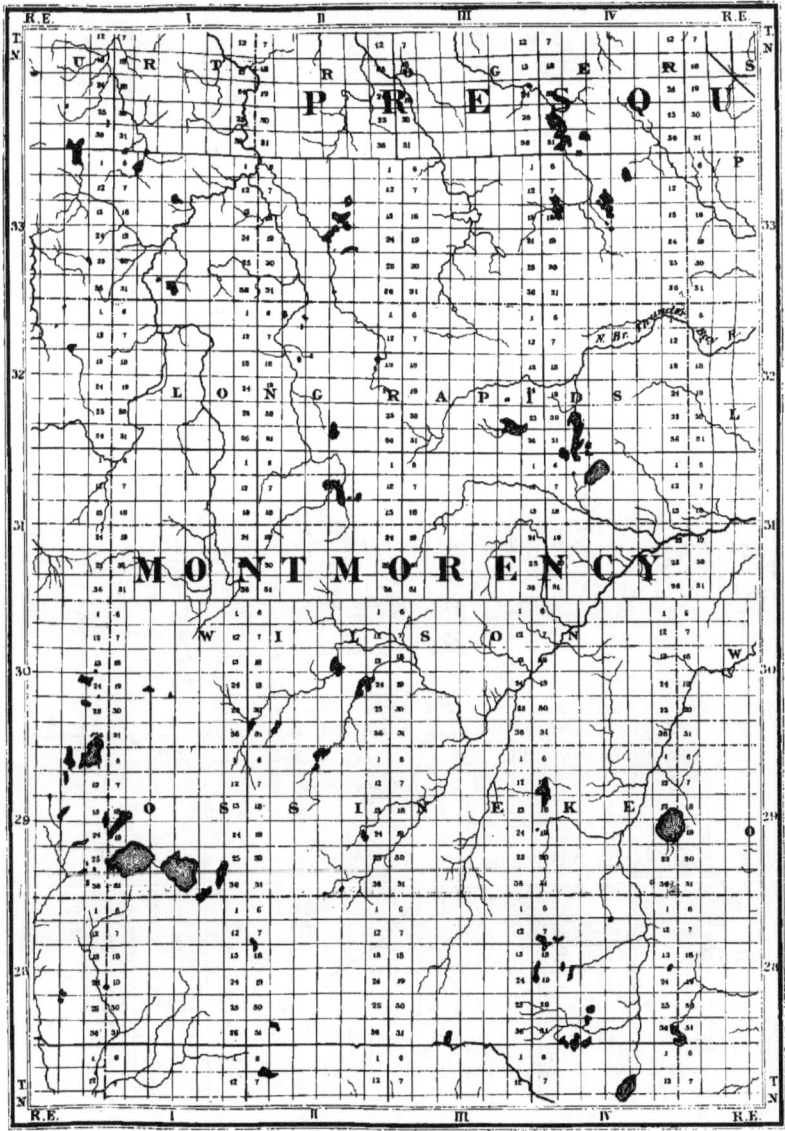

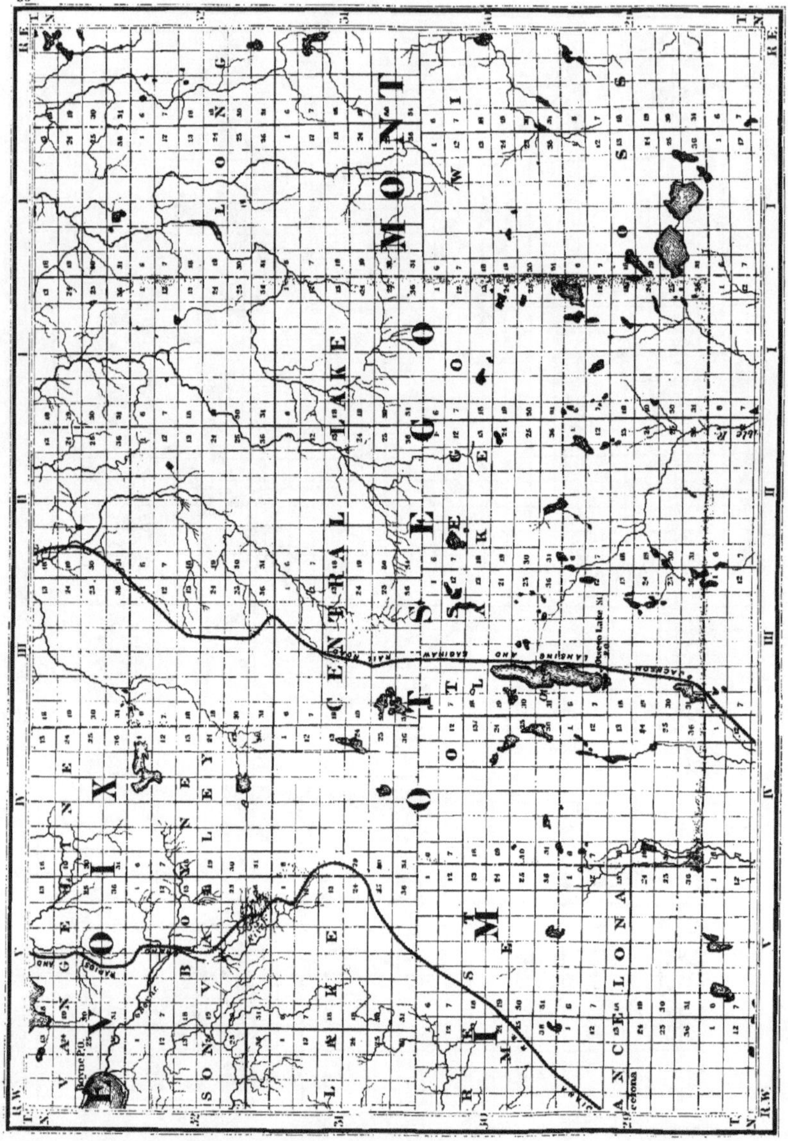
CENTRAL LAKE
Boyne P.O.
Osceola Lake

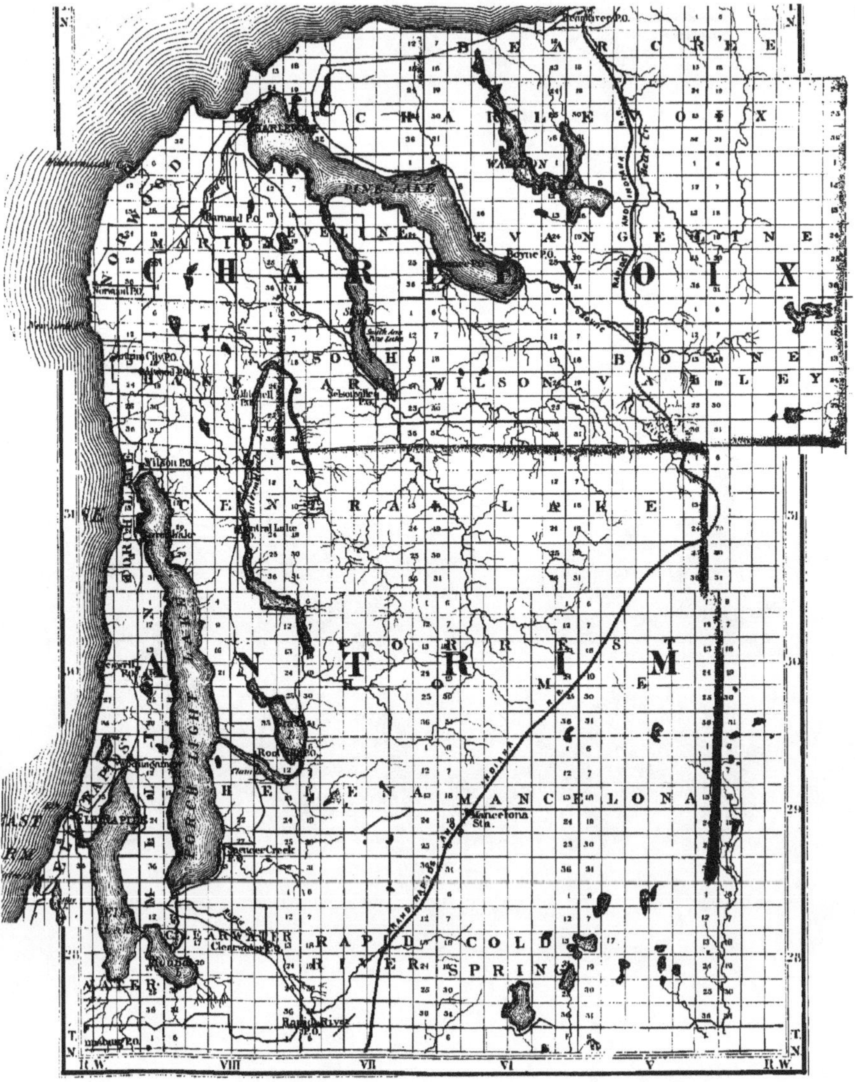

CHARLEVOIX
ANTRIM
CHARLEVOIX
EVANGELINE
EVELINE
MARION
NORWOOD
SOUTH ARM
WILSON
BOYNE VALLEY
CENTRAL LAKE
FOREST HOME
HELENA
MANCELONA
CLEARWATER
RAPID RIVER
COLD SPRING
PINE LAKE
TORCH LIGHT LAKE
Boyne P.O.
Barnard P.O.
Norwood P.O.
Wilson P.O.
Central Lake
Mancelona Sta.
Spencer Creek
Clearwater P.O.
Rapid River P.O.
Elk Rapids
EAST ARM
R.W.
VIII
VII
VI
V
R.W.

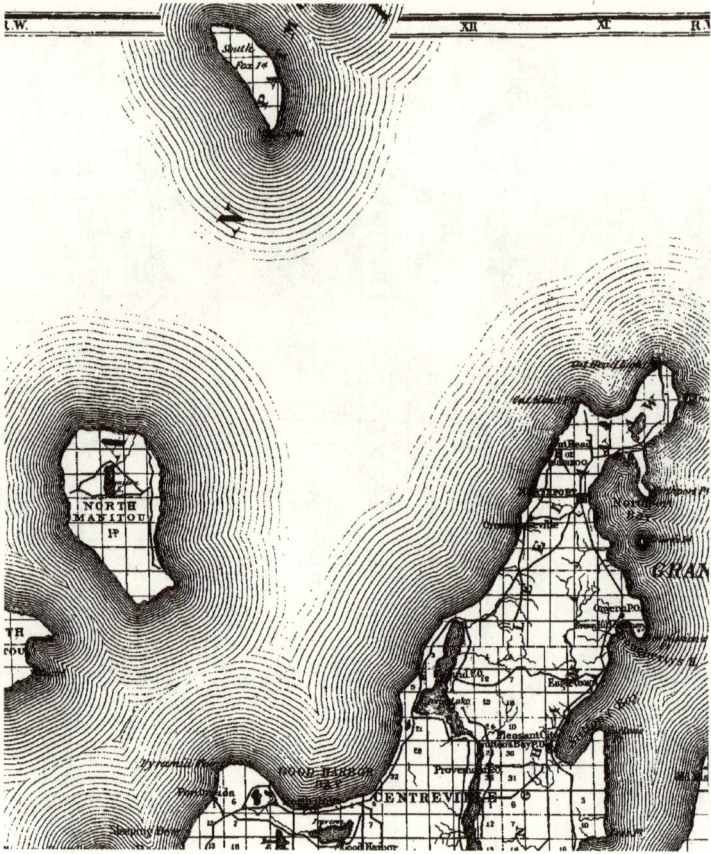

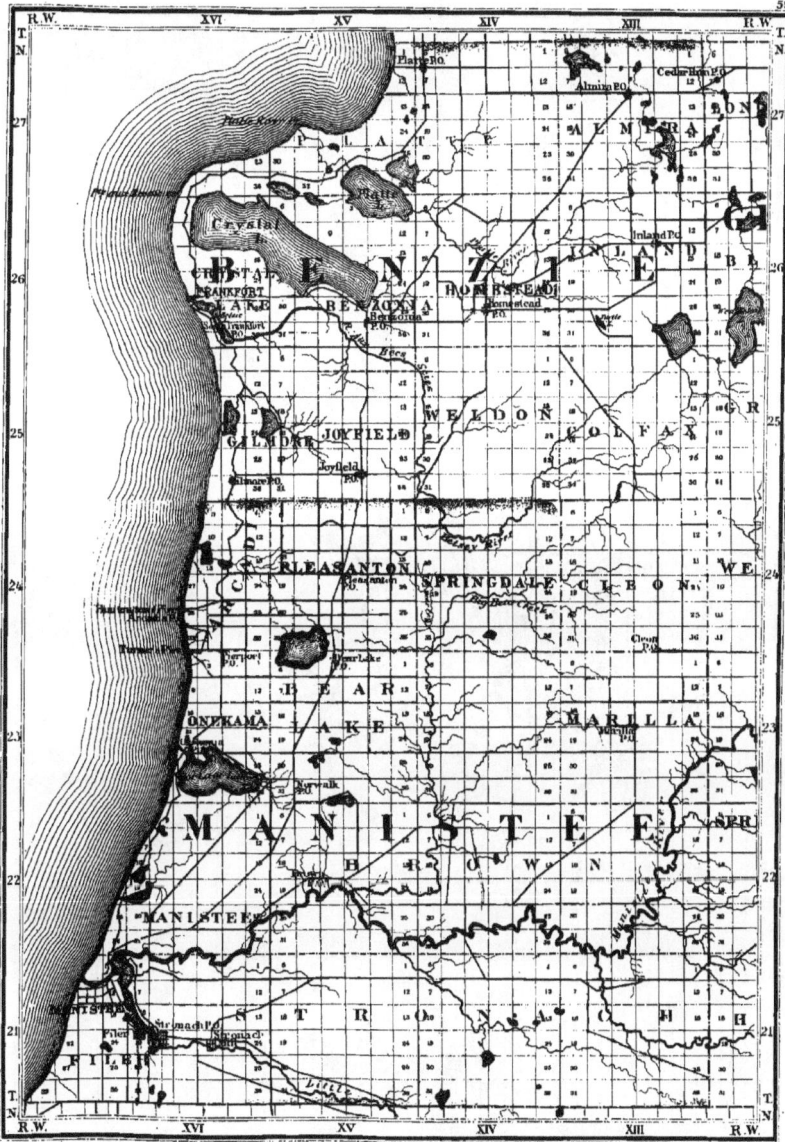

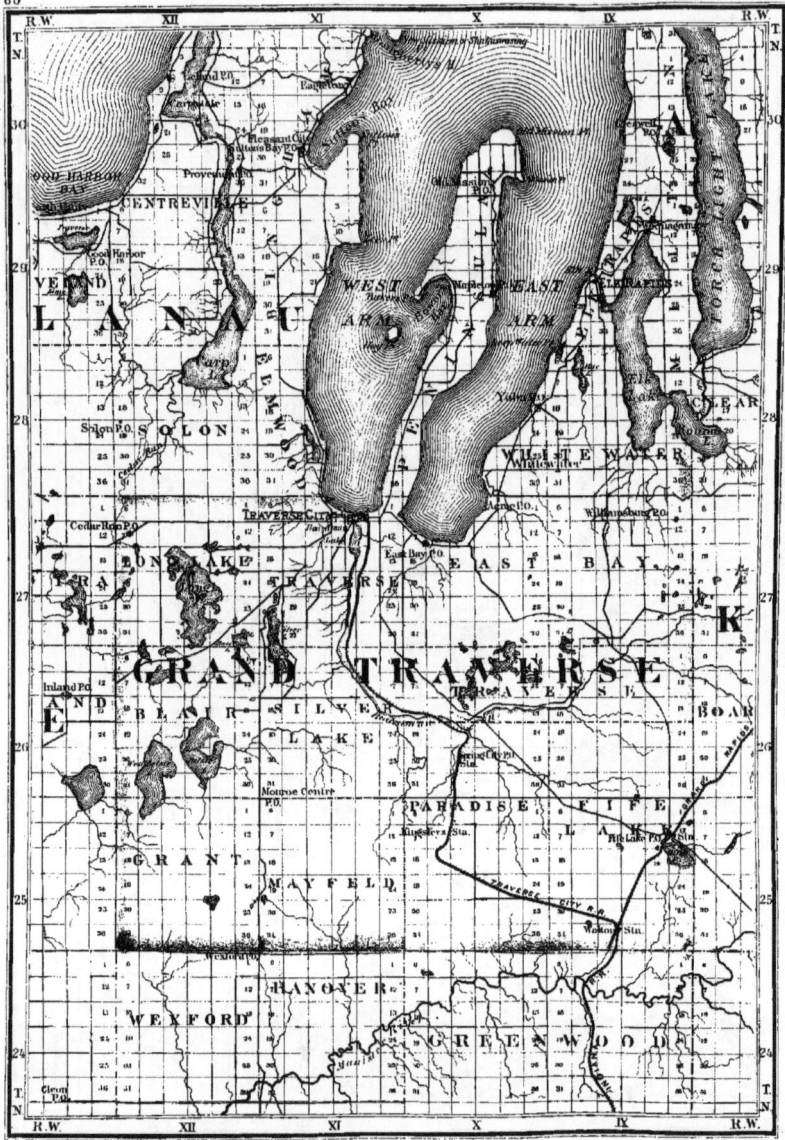

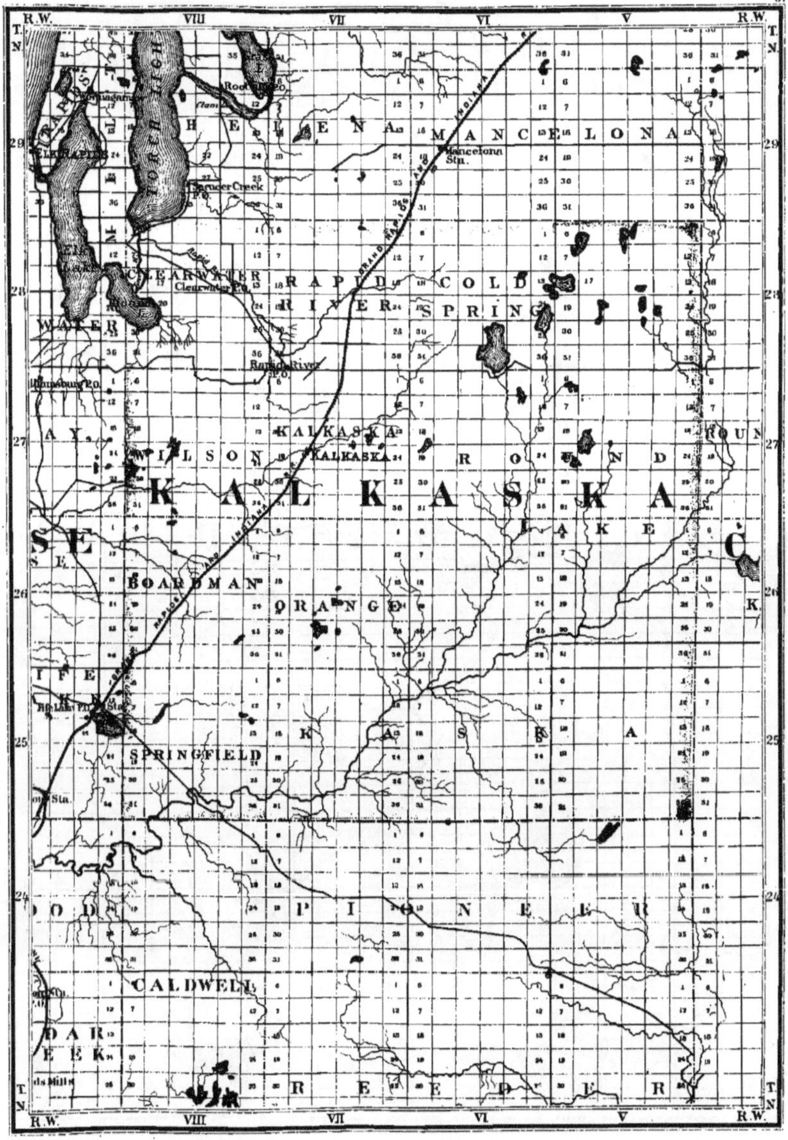
R.W.
VIII
VII
VI
V
T.
N.
29
28
27
26
25
24
HELENA
MANCELONA
Mancelona Stn.
Spencer Creek P.O.
CLEARWATER
Clearwater P.O.
RAPID
RIVER
COLD
SPRINGS
Rapid River P.O.
GRAND RAPIDS AND INDIANA
KALKASKA
WILSON
ROUND
KALKASKA
LAKE
BOARDMAN
ORANGE
SPRINGFIELD
PIONEER
CALDWELL
REEDER

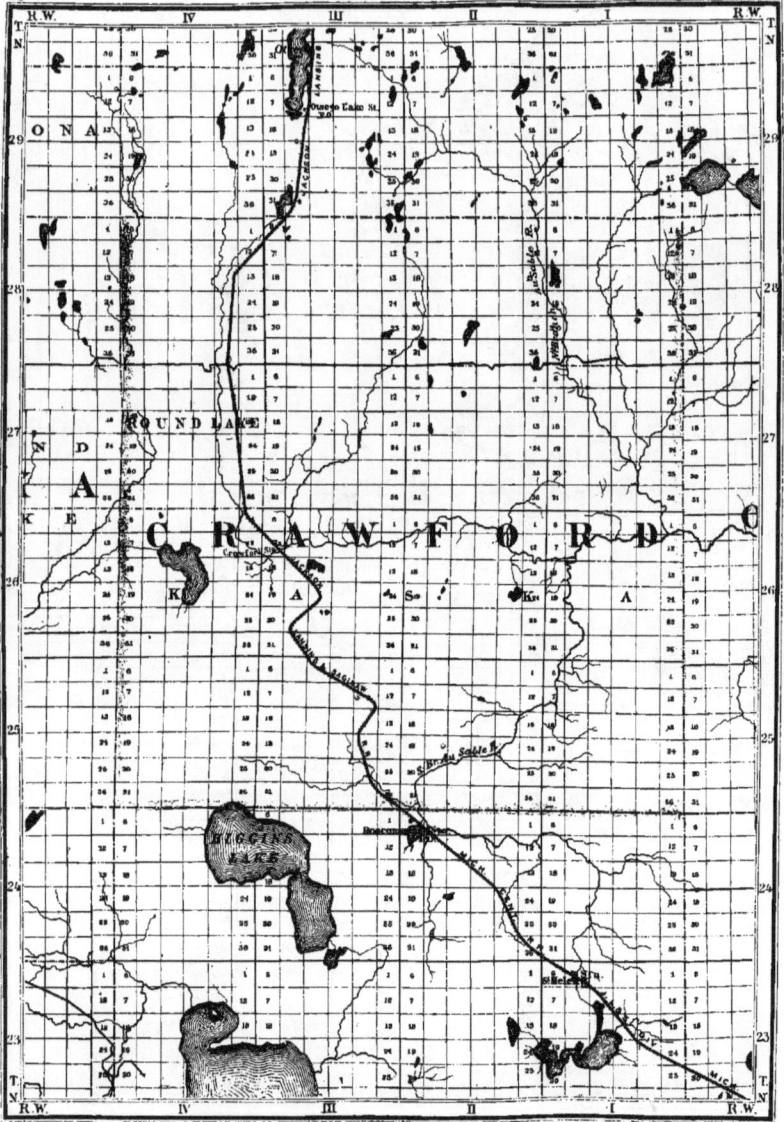

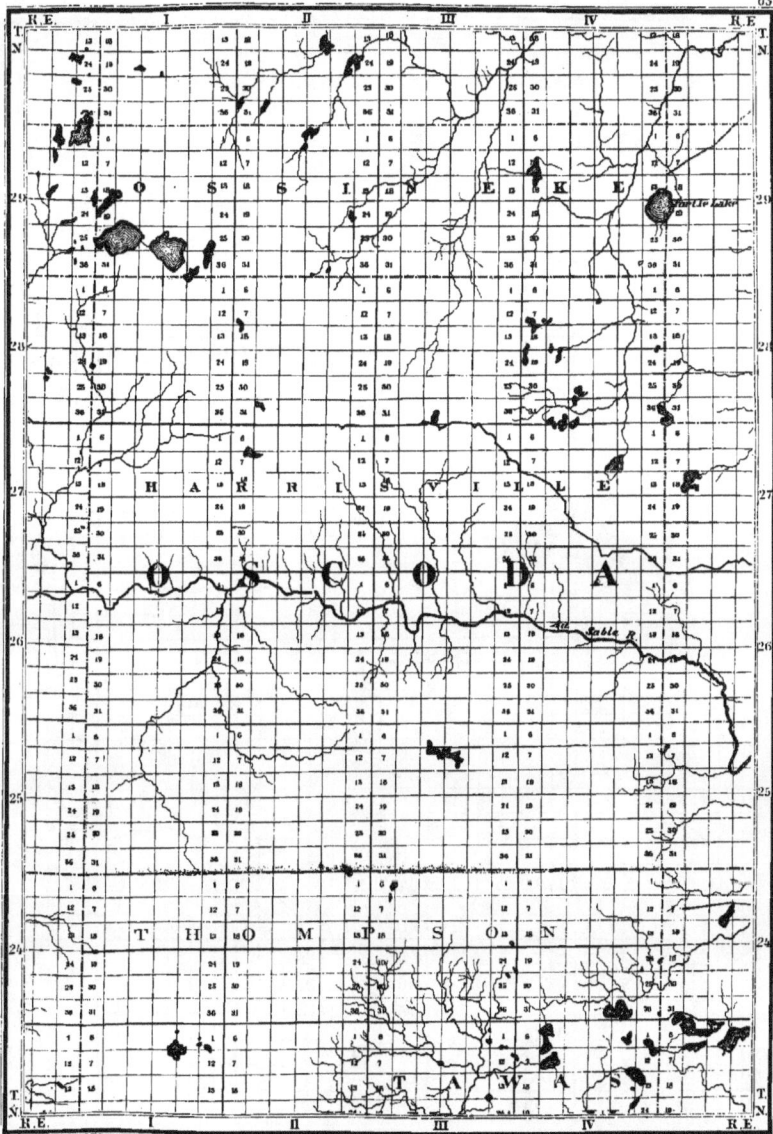

R.E.   I   II   III   IV   R.E.

T. N.   T. N.

29   O S S I N E K E   *Turtle Lake*   29

28   28

27   H A R R I S V I L L E   27

     O S C O D A

26   *Au Sable R.*   26

25   25

24   T H O M P S O N   24

T. N.   T A W A S   T. N.

R.E.   I   II   III   IV   R.E.

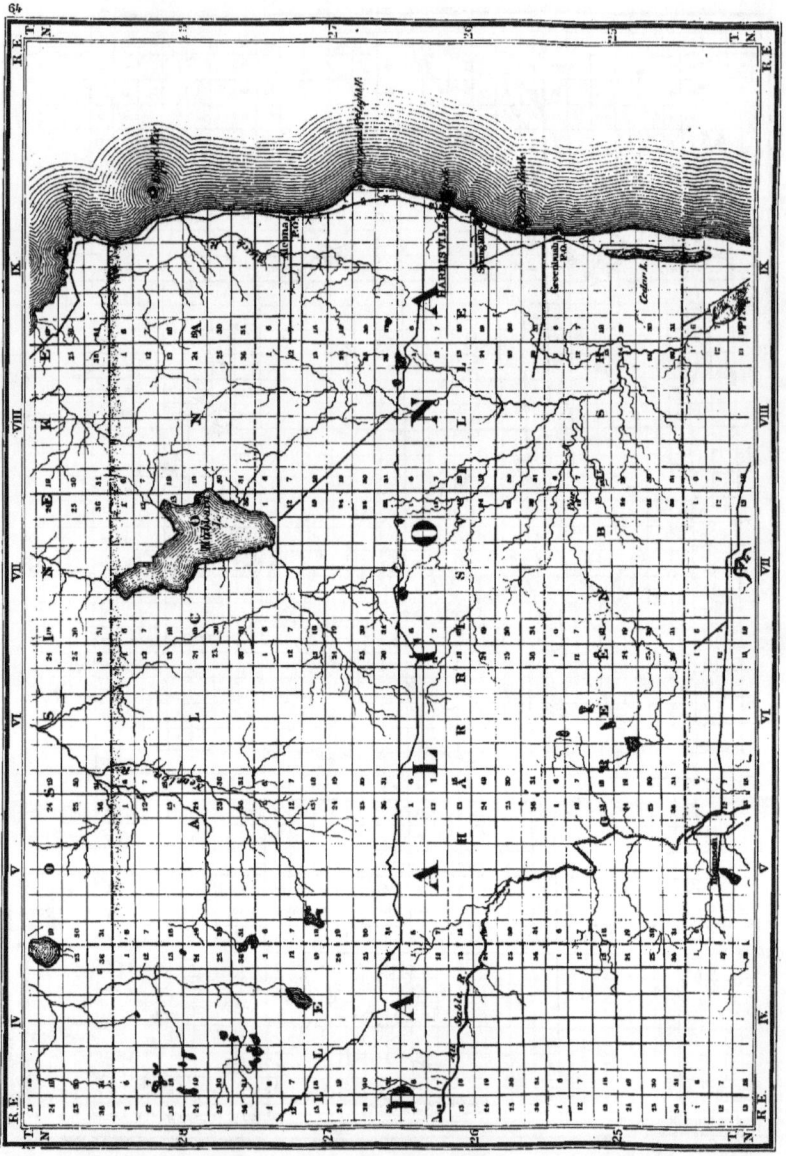

R.E. V VI VII VIII IX R.E.

T.N. | T.N.

O G E M A W   B U S H

THOMPSON

24 | S C O D A 24

PLAINFIELD

23 | S A B L E 23

Cedar I.

Au Sable P.O.

Pinora

I O S C O

Ogemaw P.O.

22 | T A W A S 22

GRANT

TAWAS CITY

A L A B A S T E R

21 | 21

Alabaster P.O.

20 | 20

A U G R E S

ARENAC

19 | 19

Little River P.O.

Omer P.O.

T.N. | T.N.

R.E. V VI VII VIII IX R.E.

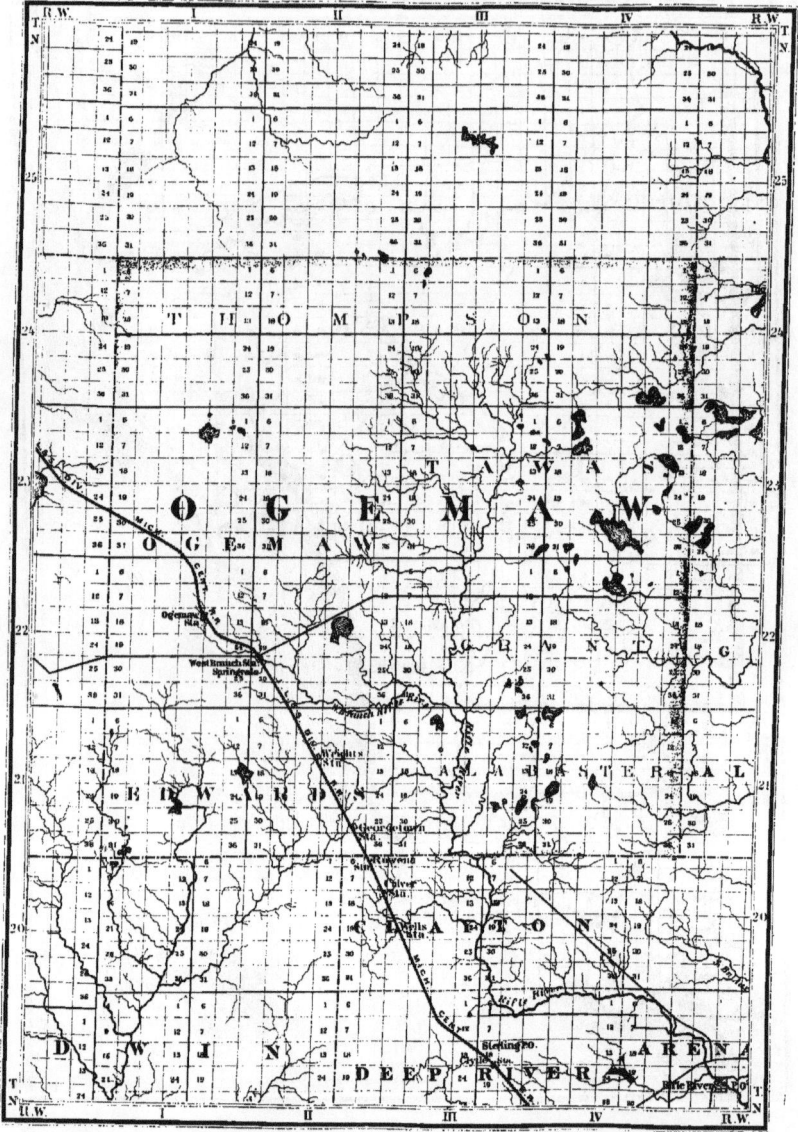

R.W.   I   II   III   IV   R.W.

T H O M P S O N

O G E M A W

T A W A S

OGEMAW

G R A N T

E D W A R D S

A L A B A S T E R A L

Ogemaw Sta.

West Branch Sta.
Springville

Georgetown

Oliver Mill

C L A Y T O N

D W I N

DEEP RIVER   A R E N

Sterling P.O.

Rifle River Co.

R.W.   I   II   III   IV   R.W.

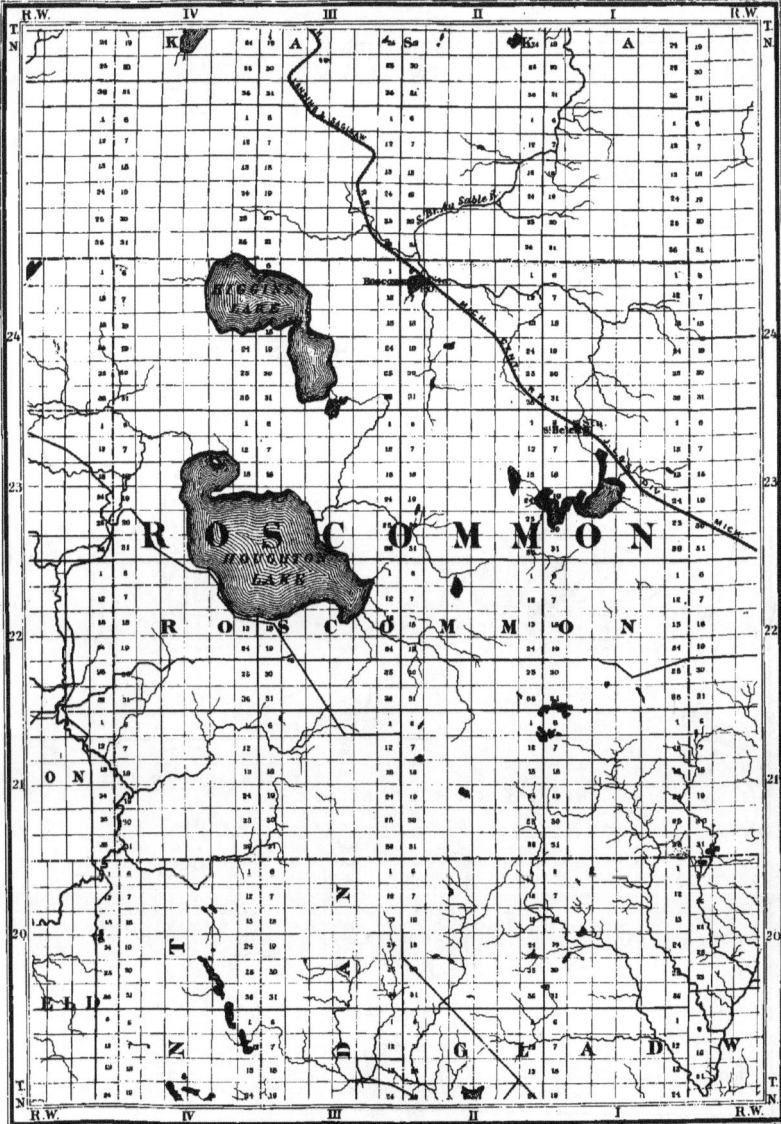

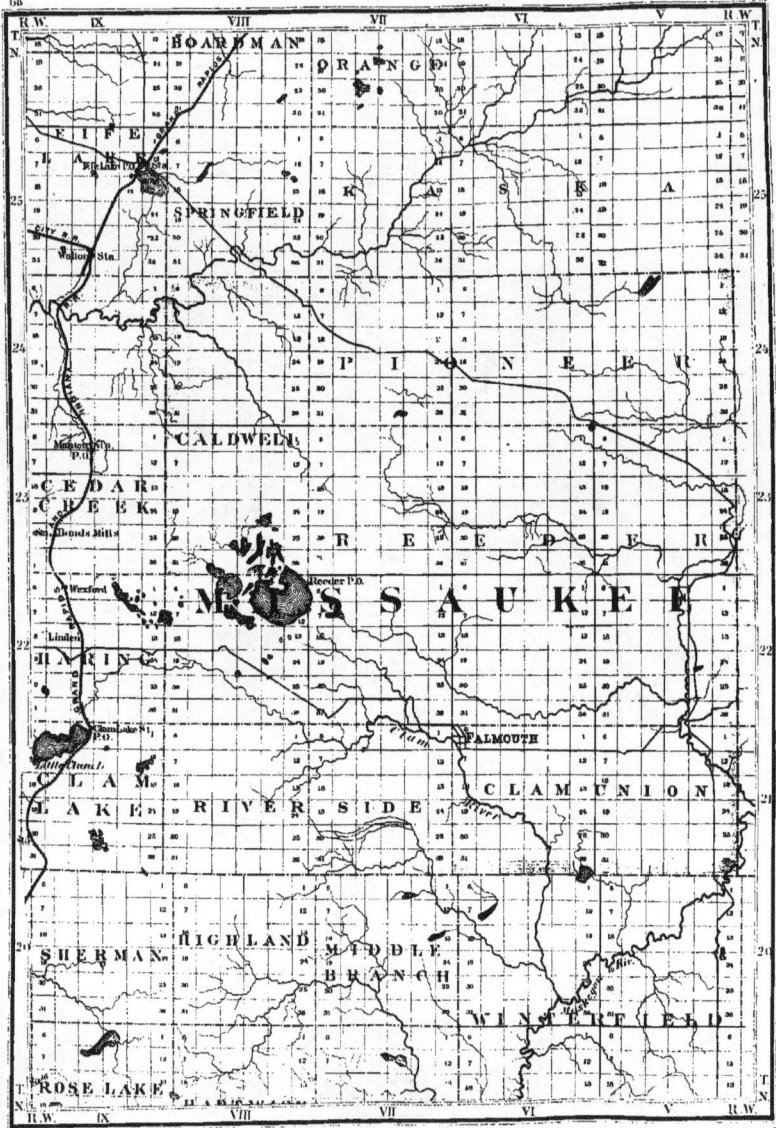

R.W.   IX   VIII   VII   VI   V   R.W.
T.N.

BOARDMAN

ORANGE

FIFE

K   A   S   K   A

Big Lake P.O.

SPRINGFIELD

Walton Sta.

PIONEER

CALDWELL

Manton Sta. P.O.

CEDAR CREEK

McClouds Mills

REEDER

Reeder P.O.

Wexford

MISSAUKEE

Linden

LAKE

Clam Lake P.O.

FALMOUTH

Little Clam L.

CLAM

CLAM UNION

LAKE   RIVER SIDE

SHERMAN

HIGHLAND

MIDDLE BRANCH

WINTERFIELD

ROSE LAKE

T.N. R.W.   IX   VIII   VII   VI   V   R.W.

R.W. XII XI X IX R.W.

LAKE

Monroe Centre P.O.

Spring City P.O. Sta.

PARADISE FIFE

Kingsleys Sta. Ala. P.O. Sta.

GRANT MAYFELD

FAX

Walton's Sta.

Wexford P.O.

HANOVER

WEXFORD

GREENWOOD

CLEON

Clam P.O.

SHERMAN P.O.

Manton Sta. P.O.

Wheatland P.O. CEDAR CREEK

LLA COLFAX Bennis Mills

WEXFORD

ANTIOCH Manton ulake P.O.

SPRINGVILLE Wexford

SELMA Linden

HARIN

Clay Hill P.O.

Big Clam Lake Round Lake St. CHERRY Clam Lake P.O.

HENDERSON GROVE CLAM LAKE

H

Summit St.

BUCK BURDELL SHERMAN

IL Pine River Tustins Sta.

River Ellsworth P.O. ROSE LAKE

LLSWORTH LEROY

R.W. XII XI X IX R.W.

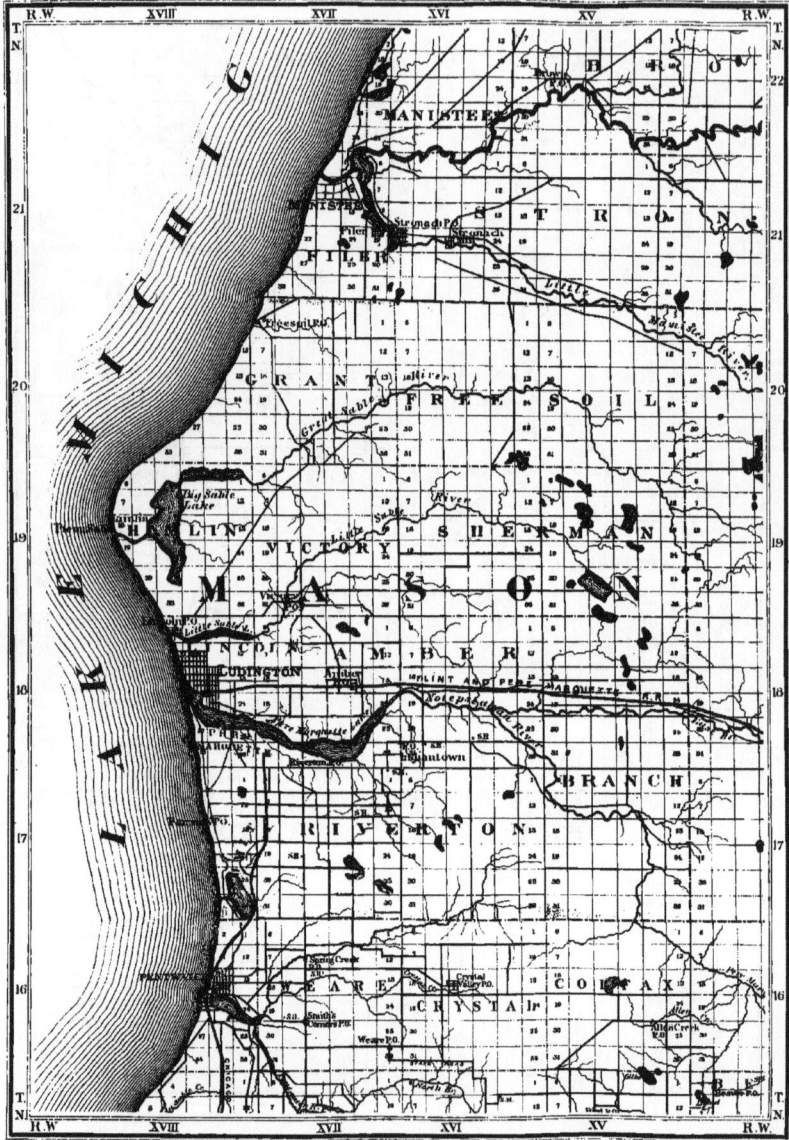

R.W. XVIII XVII XVI XV R.W.

T.N.

MICHIGAN

LAKE

MANISTEE

STRONACH

FILER

GRANT

FREE SOIL

Big Sable Lake

HAMLIN

VICTORY

SHERMAN

MASON

Little Sable River

LINCOLN AMBER

LUDINGTON

FLINT & PERE MARQUETTE R.R.

Pere Marquette

RIVERTON

BRANCH

Spring Creek

WEARE

CRYSTAL

COLFAX

Smith's Corners P.O.

Weare P.O.

T.N.

R.W. XVIII XVII XVI XV R.W.

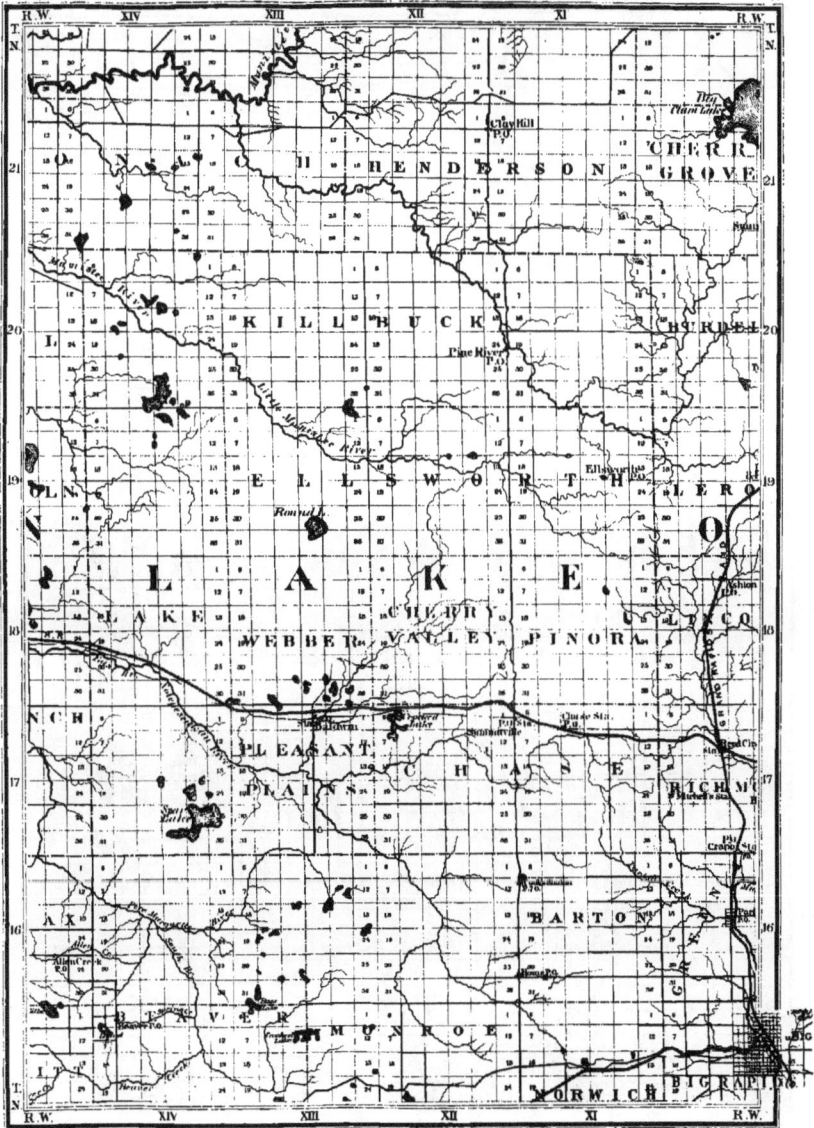

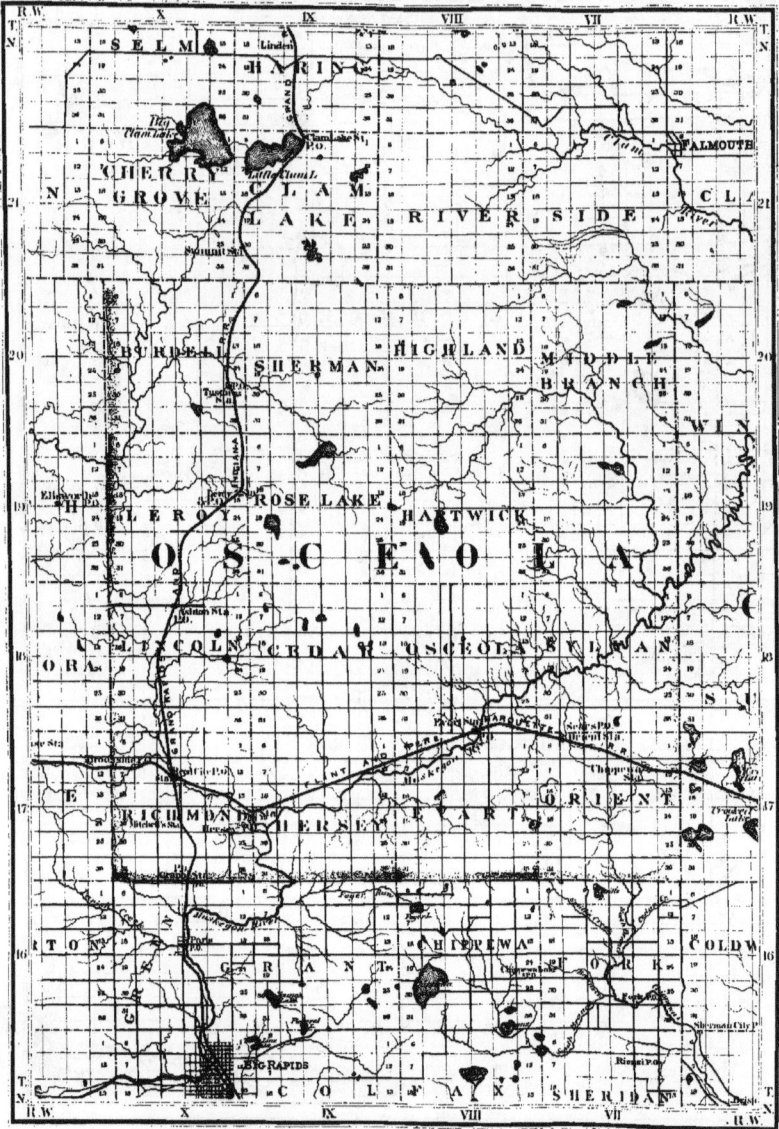

72

R.W.   X   IX   VIII   VII   R.W.

SELMA   MARION   Linden

CHERRY GROVE   CLAM LAKE   RIVER-SIDE   CLAM   FALMOUTH

Big Clam Lake   Little Clam L.   Summit Sta.

BURDELL   SHERMAN   HIGHLAND   MIDDLE BRANCH   WIN

Paris Sta.

Ellsworth   LEROY   ROSE LAKE   HARTWICK

O S C E O L A

Ashton Sta.

LINCOLN   CEDAR   OSCEOLA   SYLVAN   SU

ORA

Reed City P.O.   FLINT AND PERE MARQUETTE R.R.   ORIENT

RICHMOND   HERSEY   EVART   Hersey   Evart Sta.

Orange Sta.

TON   GRANT   CHIPPEWA   YORK   COLDW

Chippewa Lake

BIG RAPIDS   Rose Lake

R.W.   X   COLFAX   IX   VIII   SHERIDAN   VII   R.W.

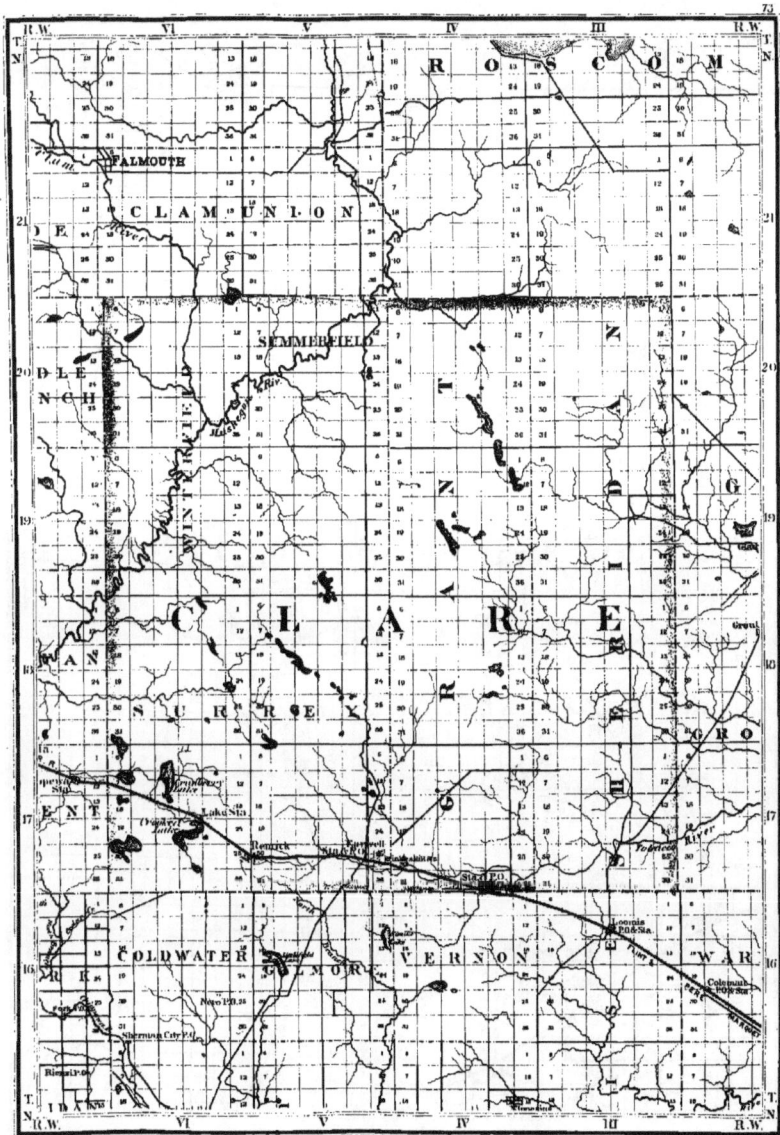

R.W. | VI | V | IV | III | R.W.

T. N.

R O S C O M M

FALMOUTH

C L A M U N I O N

21

D E

20 D L E N C H

SEMMERFIELD

Z

D

G

19

C L A R E

S U R R E Y

GRO

E N T

Cranberry Lake

Lake Sta.

Dodge Lake

Renick

Sixth Mile

Tobacco River

St. P.O.

Loomis P.O. & Sta.

WAR

COLDWATER

GILMORE

VERNON

Coleman P.O. & Sta.

Sherman City P.O.

Rienzi P.O.

T. N.

R.W. | VI | V | IV | II | R.W.

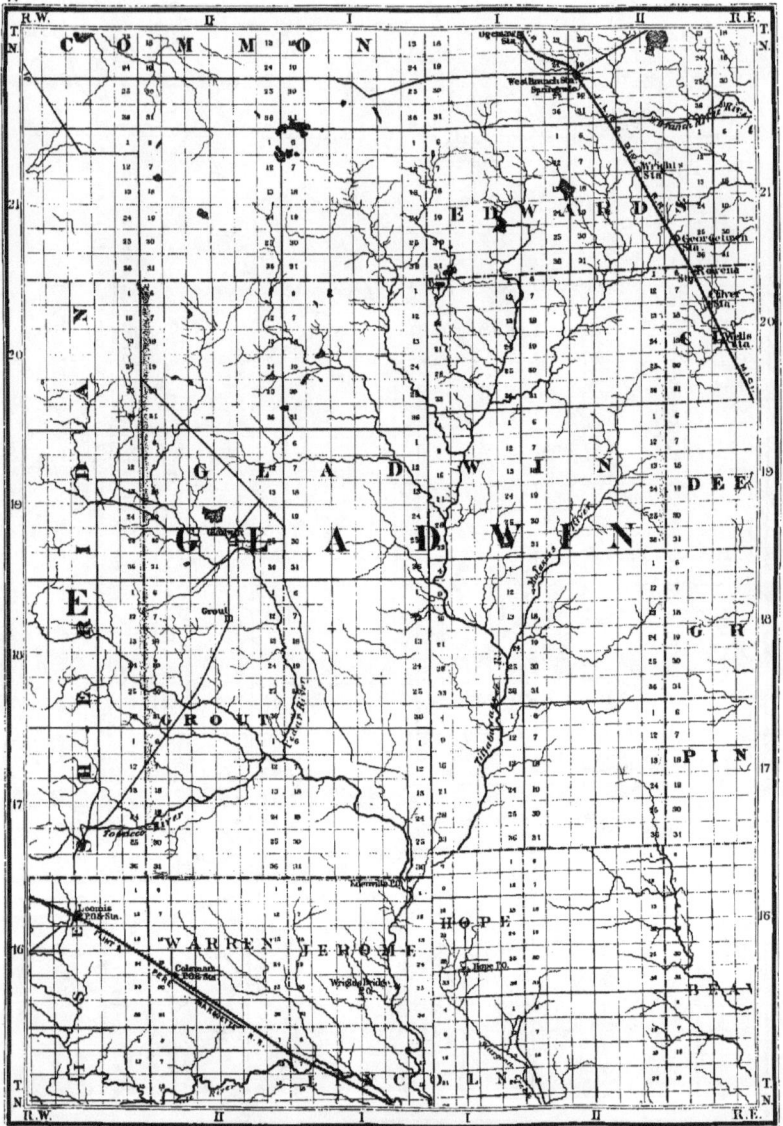

GLADWIN

COMMON

EDWARDS

GLADWIN

GROUT

WARREN JEROME HOPE

LINCOLN

West Branch Sta.

Georgetown Sta.

Ravenna

Oliver Sta.

Beaverton

Coleman P.O.& Sta.

Loomis P.O.& Sta.

R.W. II I I II R.E.
T.N.

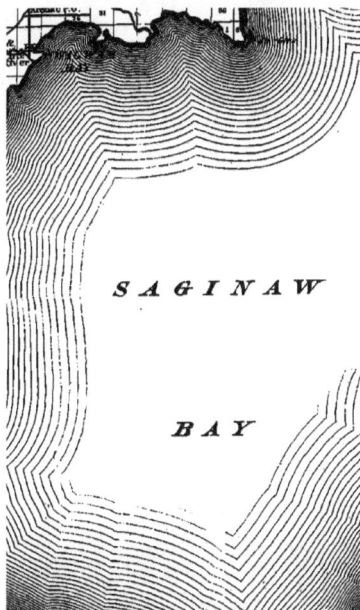

SAGINAW

BAY

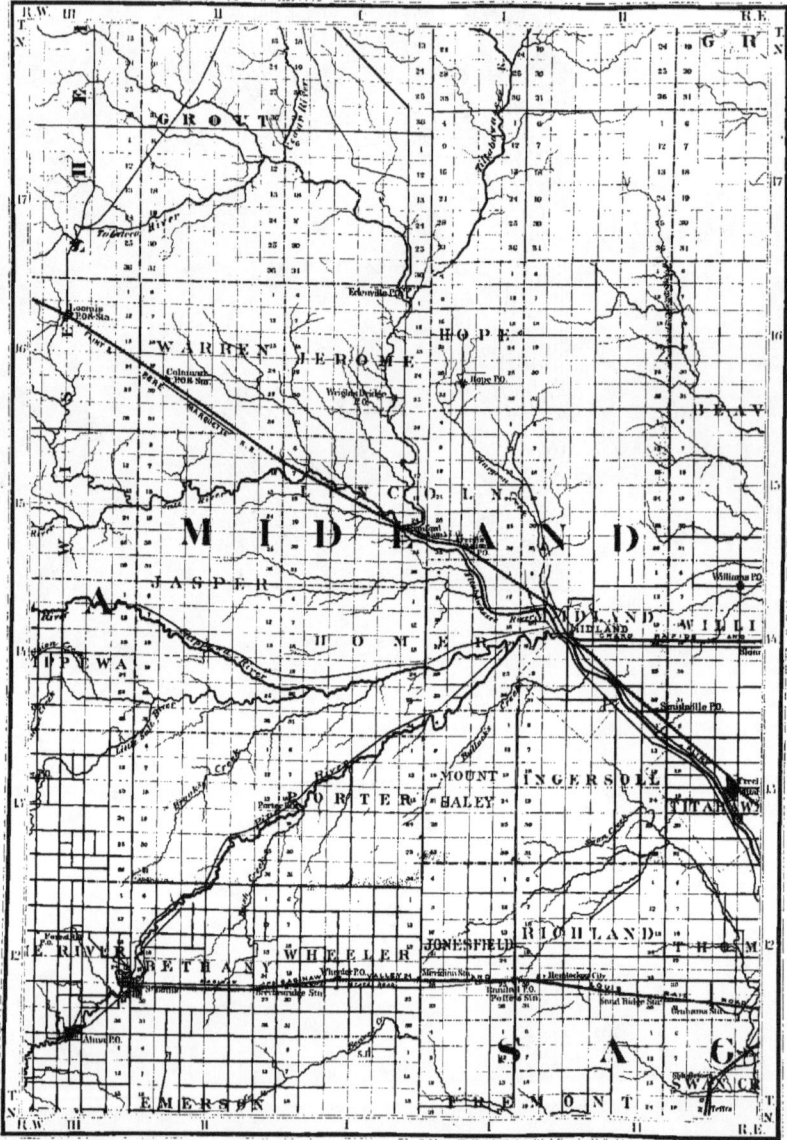

R.W. III | II | I | I | II | R.E.
T. N.

G R O U T

GR

WARREN JEROME HOPE

BAY

L I N C O L N

M I D L A N D

JASPER

WILLIAMS P.O.

HOMER

MIDLAND

WILLI

Smithville P.O.

CHIPPEWA

MOUNT INGERSOLL

PORTER HALEY

TITTA

RICHLAND

BETHANY WHEELER JONESFIELD

E. RIVER

EMERSON FREMONT SWAN CR

T. N.
R.W. III | II | I | I | II | R.E.

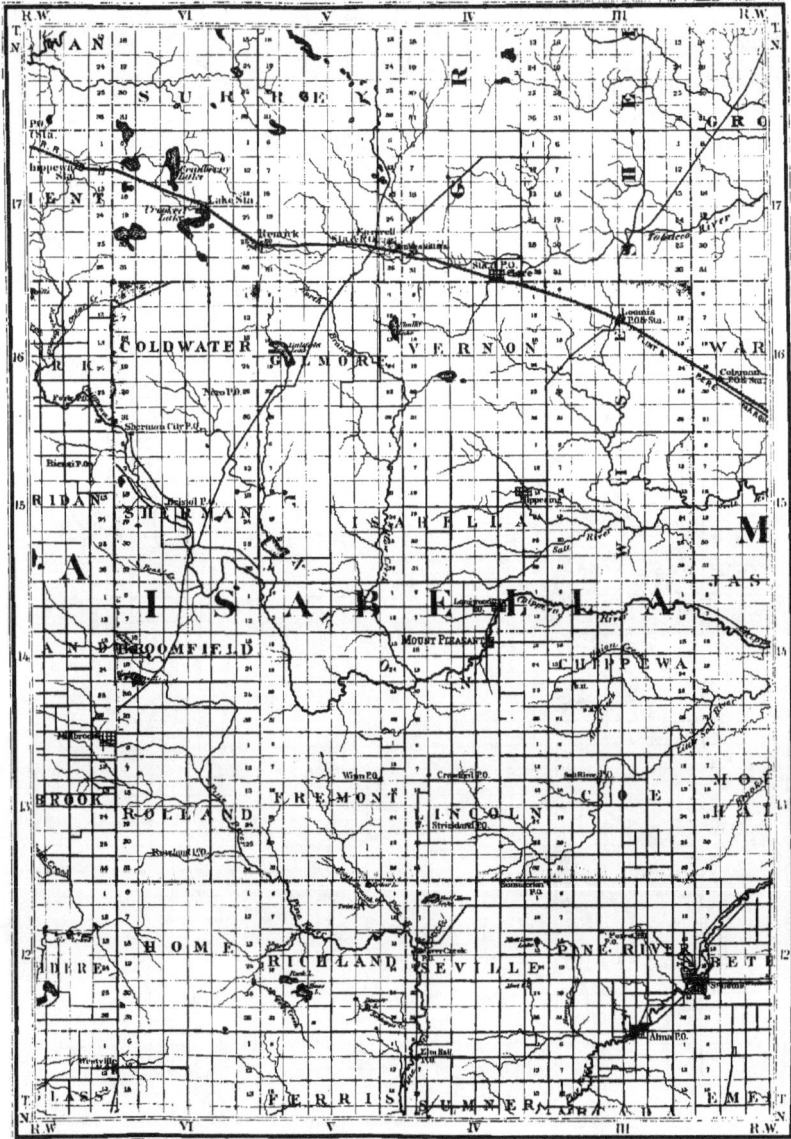

R.W. | VI | V | IV | III | R.W.
T. N.

WAN ... SURGEY ... R ... GRO

LENT ... Lake Sta.

Remark ... SIX P.O. ... Tobacco River

Leonis P.O. Sta.

COLDWATER GILMORE VERNON WAR

New P.O. Coleman P.O. Sta.

Sherman City P.O.

RIDAN SHERMAN ISABELLA M

Salt River

I S A B E L L A JAS

BROOMFIELD MOUNT PLEASANT CHIPPEWA

Millbrook

BROOK ROLLAND FREMONT LINCOLN COE MO

Roseland P.O. Strickland P.O.

Summerfret P.O.

DERE HOME RICHLAND SEVILLE PINE RIVER BET

Alma P.O.

LAS FERRIS SUMNER

R.W. | VI | V | IV | III | R.W.
T. N.

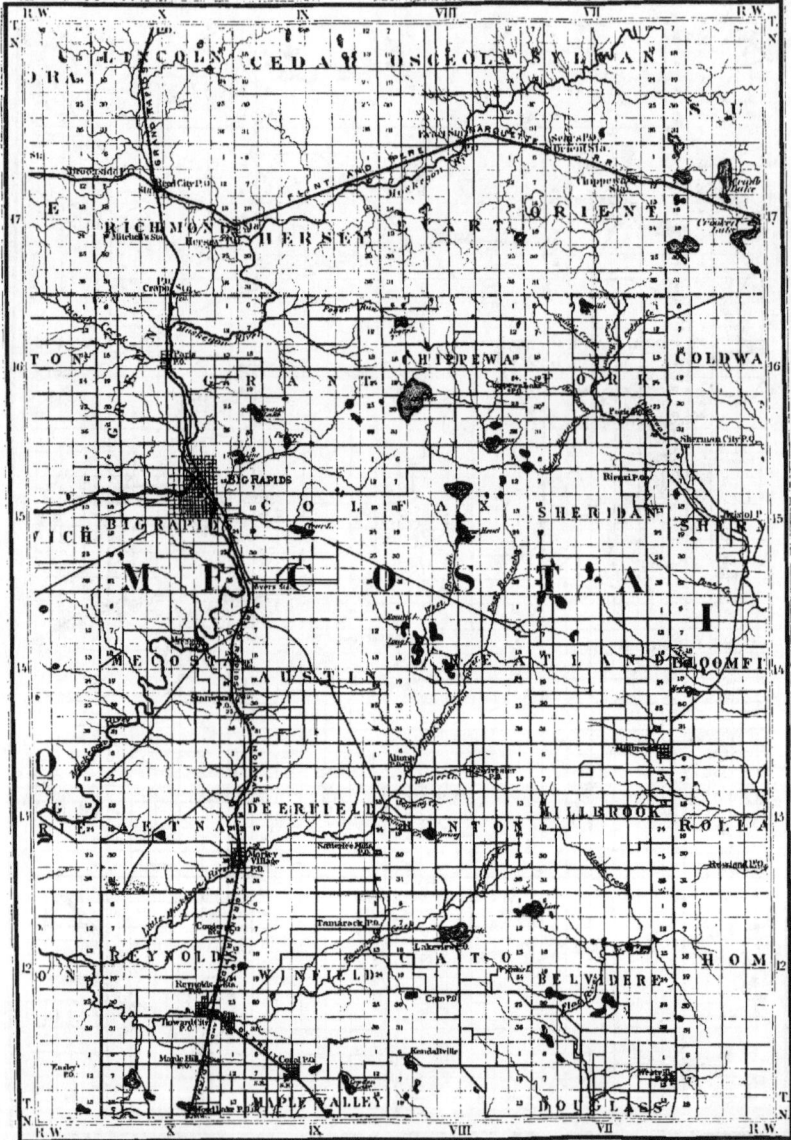

78

LINCOLN CEDAR OSCEOLA SYLVAN

RICHMOND HERSEY ORIENT

Crockery Lake

GRANT CHIPPEWA FORK COLDWA

Sherman City P.O.

BIG RAPIDS COLFAX SHERIDAN

MECOSTA

MECOSTA AUSTIN GRANT LAND BLOOMFI

AETNA DEERFIELD MILLBROOK ROLLA

REYNOLDS WINFIELD CATO BELVIDERE HO M

Maple Hill Kendallville

MAPLE VALLEY DOUGLASS

R.W. X IX VIII VII R.W.

PLAINS CHASE RICH...

BARTON

BEAVER MONROE

NORWICH BIG...

MECO...

FIELD BEAVER

NEWAYGO

...NWOOD DAYTON SHERMAN EVERETT ...PRAIRIE

TO... SHERIDAN BROOKS COLTON LYNX

D... BRIDGETON ...LAND GRANT ENSLEY M...

E...GON

...STON MOORLAND CASNOVIA TYRONE SOLON NELS...

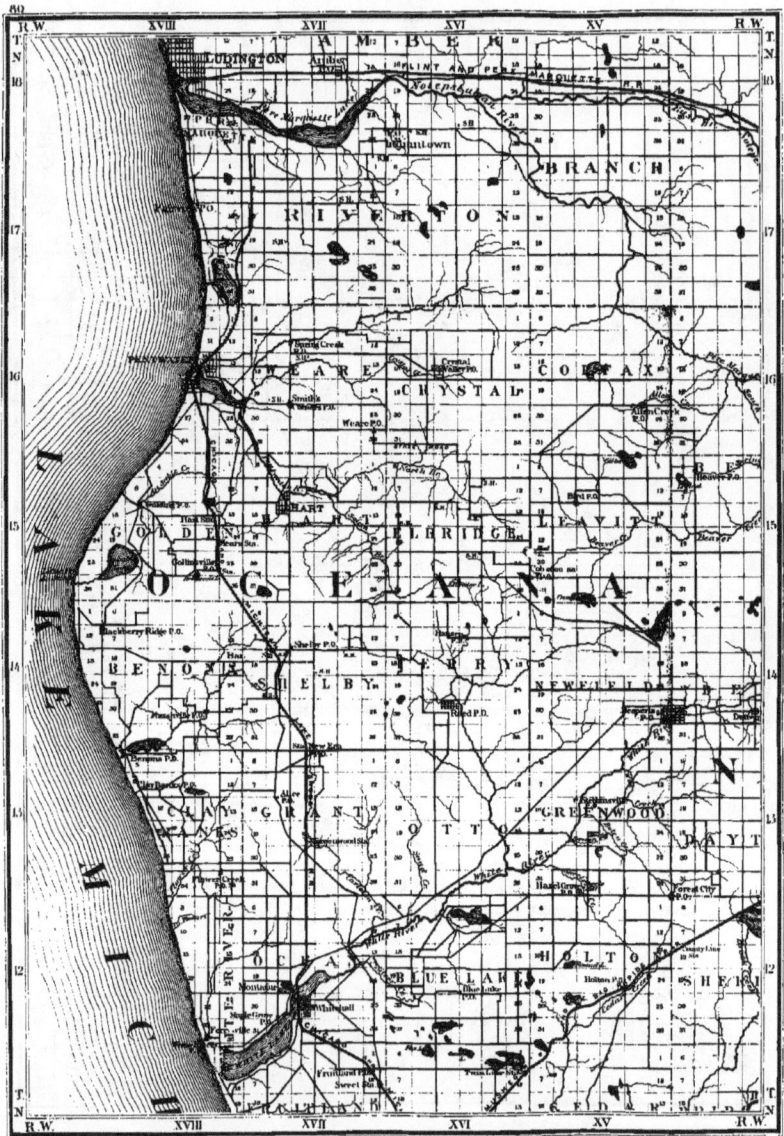

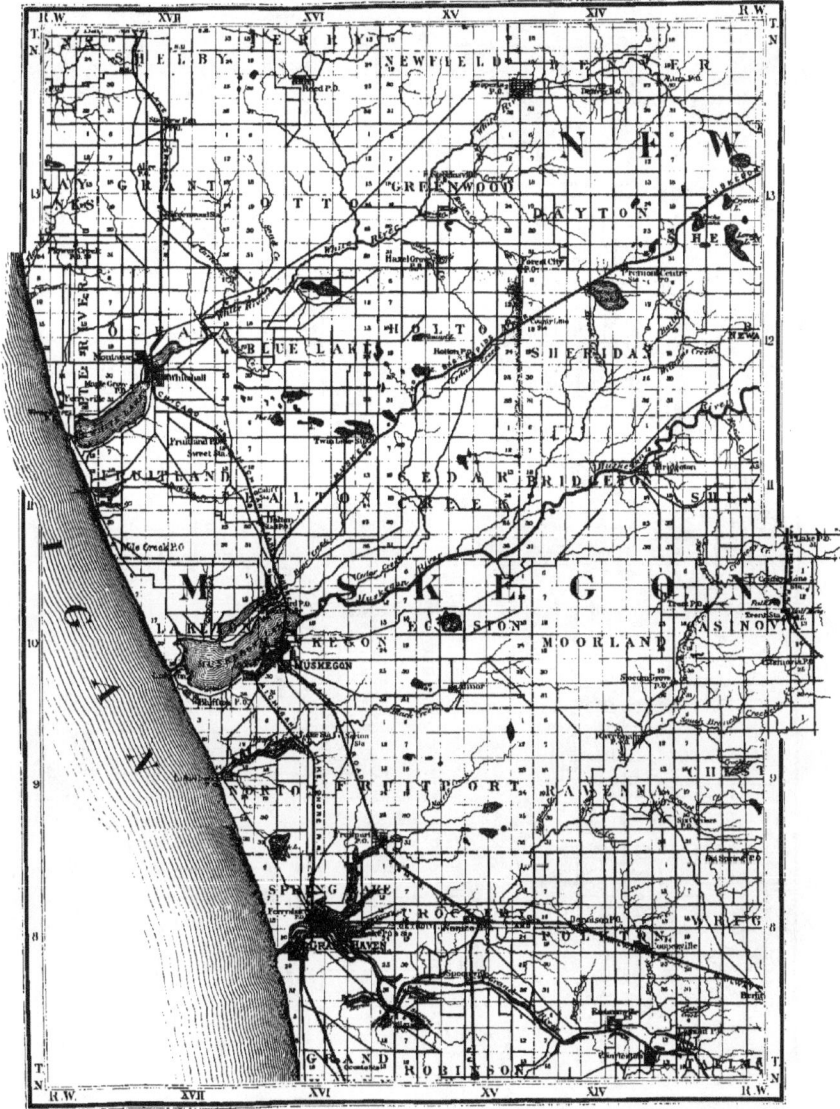

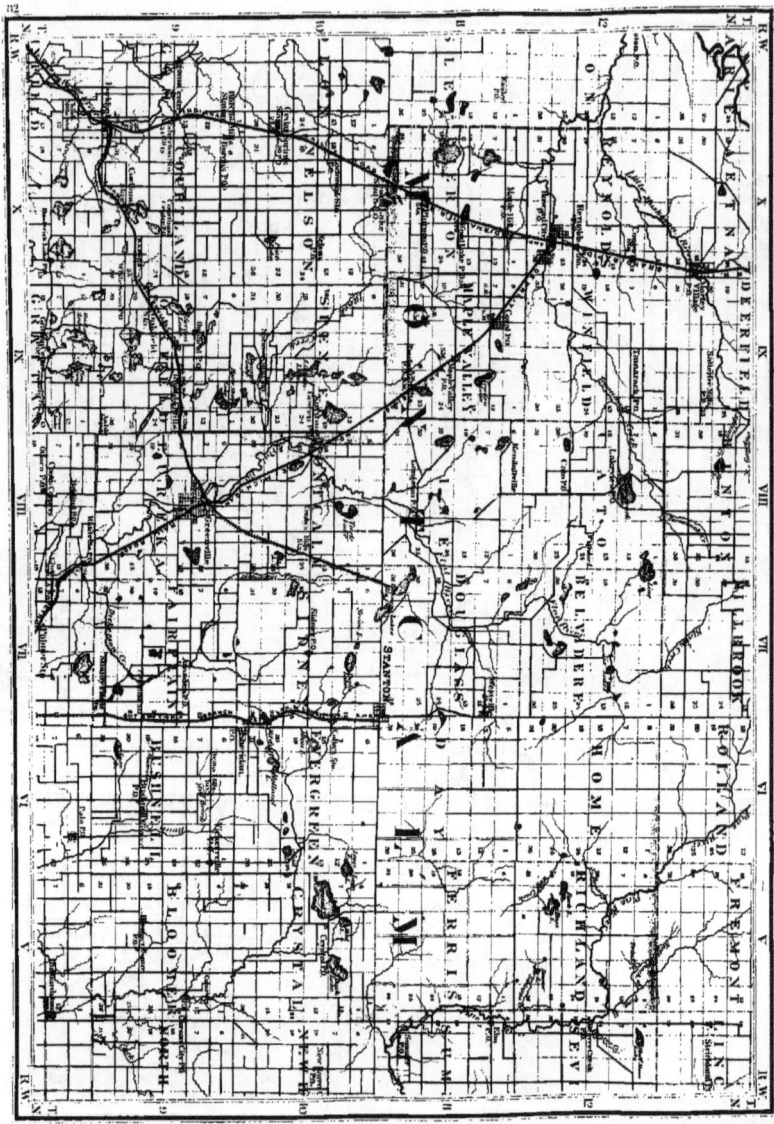

Map of Gratiot County, Michigan

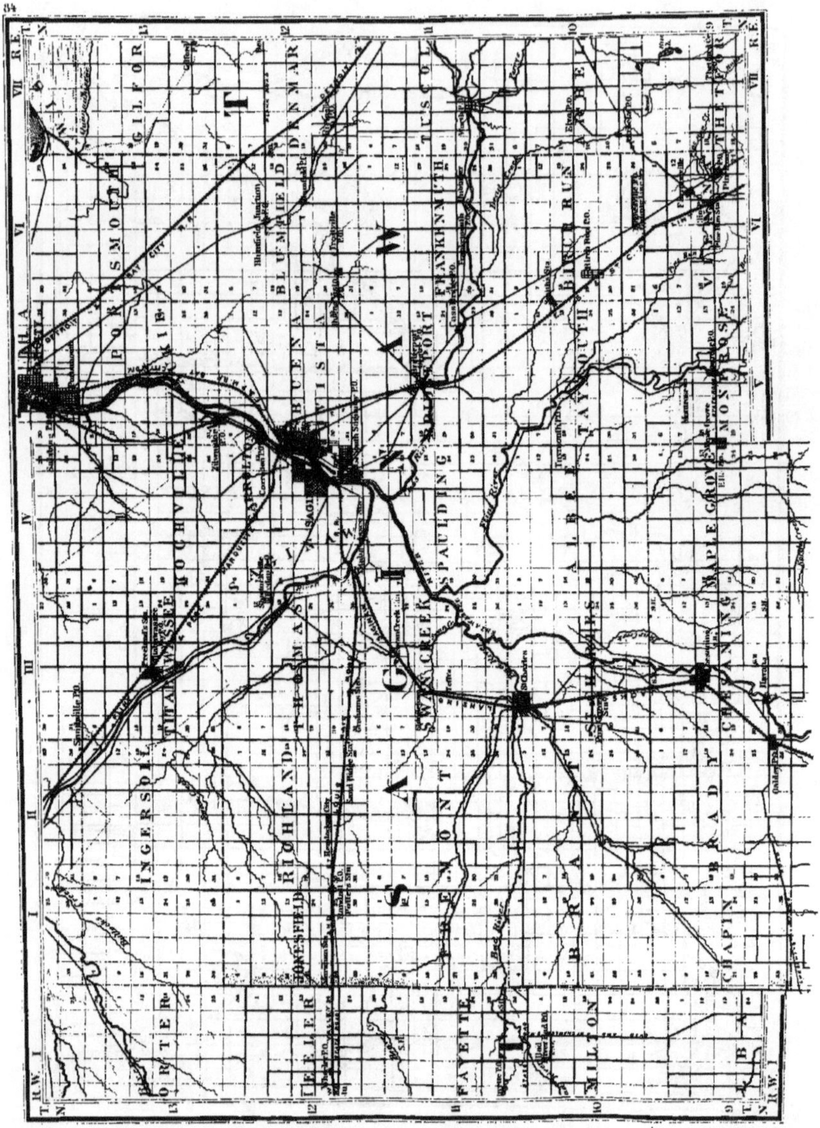

TUSCOLA

R.E. VII VIII IX X XI R.E.

SEBEWAING P.O.
SEBEWAING
GENEVA
BROOKFIELD
GRANT
Caroll
Saroll
ELKLAND
COLUMBIA
ELMWOOD
Good Governor
Elkton
Gagetownville
Aldozale
Case City P.O.
Johnsville
Ellington
GILFORD
FAIRGROVE
VASSAR
ELLINGTON
NOVESTA
Valley Center
White Creek
Gilford
CARO
TUSCOLA
DENMARK
JUNIATA
VAN FIELDS
WELLS
KINGSTON
Watrousville
Watrousville
Kingston P.O.
Newbury
Harris Corners
(East Dayton P.O.)
VASSAR
FREMONT
DAYTON
KOYLTON
Perisville
Clarks L.
TUSCOLA
VASSAR
Marville
May P.O.
Watertown
ARBELA
MILLINGTON
WATERTOWN
RICH
BURLINGTON
Elva P.O.
Gifford P.O.
Millington
Watrous P.O.
Vassar
North Branch P.O.
Fostoria
Shabbville
THETFORD
FOREST
MARATHON
DEERFIELD
BRANCH
Amalie
Mayville
Millington P.O.

R.E. VII VIII IX X XI R.E.

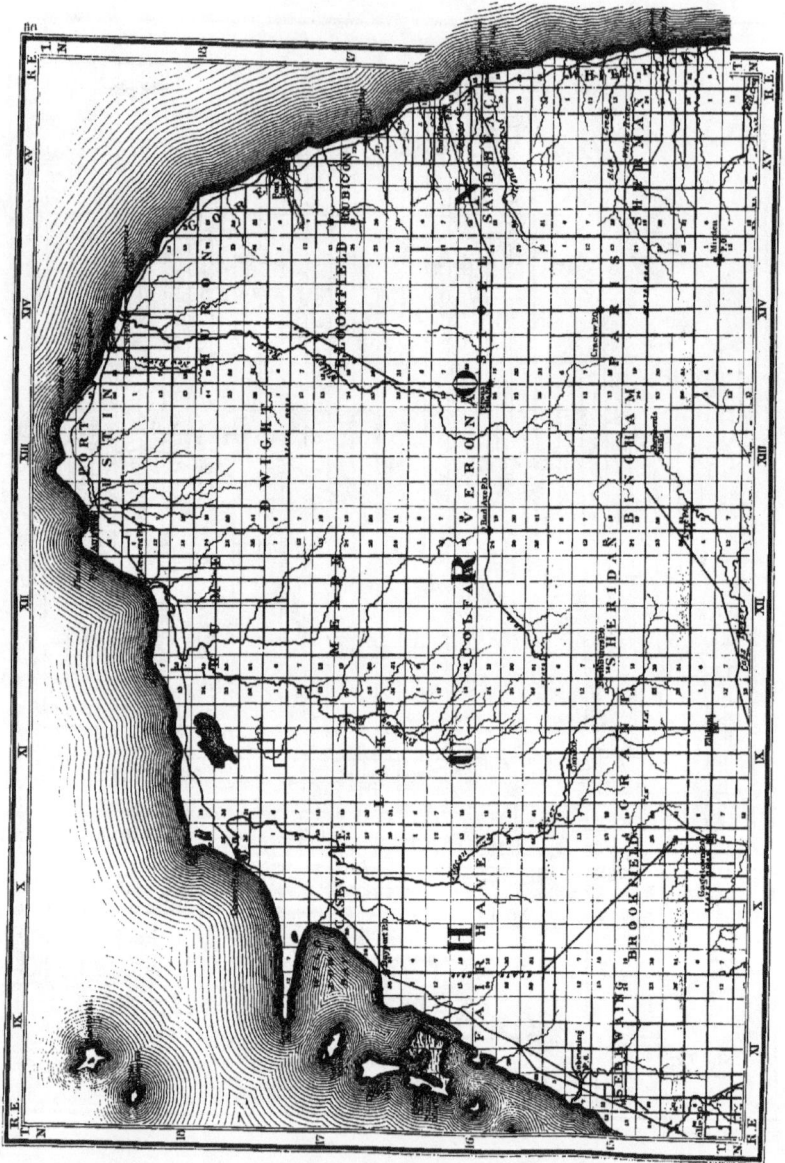

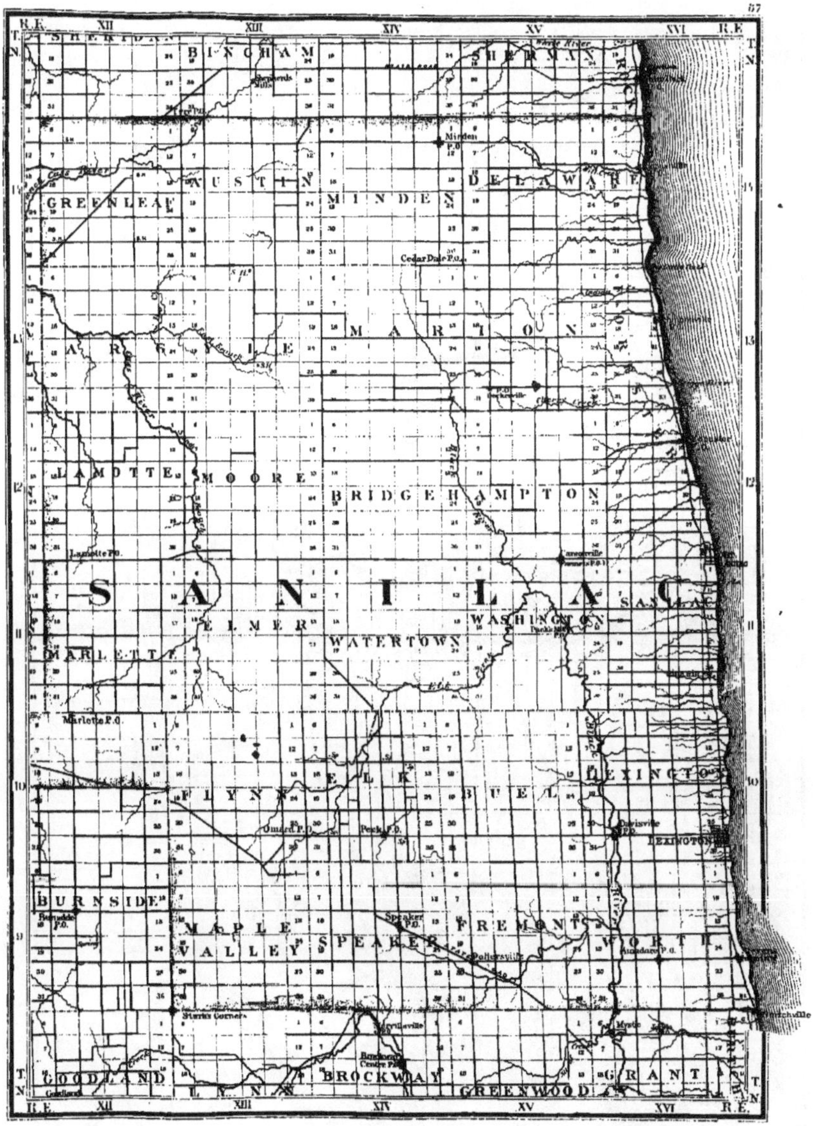
R.E.
XII
XIII
XIV
XV
XVI
T.N.
BINGHAM
SHERMAN
Minden P.O.
AUSTIN
GREENLEAF
DELAWARE
MINDEN
Cedar Dale P.O.
MARION
ARGYLE
LAMOTTE
MOORE
BRIDGEHAMPTON
Lamotte P.O.
SANILAC
ELMER
WASHINGTON
WATERTOWN
MARLETTE
Marlette P.O.
ELK
FLYNN
BUEL
LEXINGTON
Davisville P.O.
Omard P.O.
Peck P.O.
BURNSIDE
Burnside P.O.
MAPLE VALLEY
SPEAKER
Speaker P.O.
FREMONT
WORTH
Sturts Corners
Mystic
GOODLAND
LYNN
BROCKWAY
Brockway Centre P.O.
GREENWOOD
GRANT

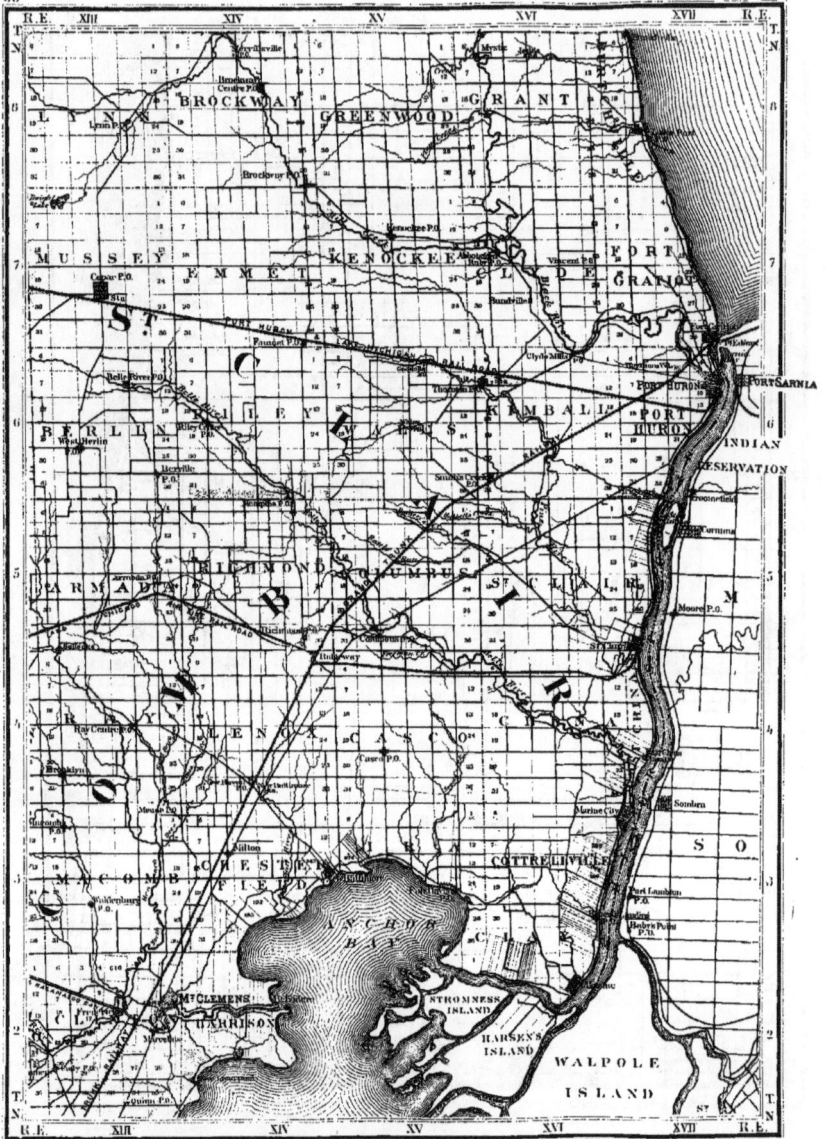

98

R.E. XIII   XIV   XV   XVI   XVII   R.E.

BROCKWAY   GREENWOOD   GRANT

LYNN   Lynn P.O.   Brockway Centre P.O.   Brockway P.O.

MUSSEY   EMMET   KENOCKEE   CLYDE   FORT GRATIOT

Cuba P.O.

ST. CLAIR

PORT HURON   Fargo P.O.

Belle River P.O.   Clyde Mills P.O.

BERLIN   West Berlin   Riley Centre   KIMBALL   PORT HURON   PORT SARNIA

Berville P.O.   Smiths Creek   INDIAN RESERVATION

RICHMOND   COLUMBUS   ST. CLAIR   Marysville   Cornunna

ARMADA   Moore P.O.   M

COLUMBUS   Ridgeway   Columbus P.O.

RAY   Ray Centre P.O.   LENOX   CASCO   Casco P.O.   C   SO

Memphis   New Haven   Marine City   Souden

MACOMB   CHESTER   FIELD   COTTRELLVILLE   Port Lambton P.O.   Harber Point P.O.

ANCHOR BAY   STROMNESS ISLAND   HARSEN'S ISLAND

Mt. CLEMENS   HARRISON   WALPOLE ISLAND

Quinn P.O.

R.E. XIII   XIV   XV   XVI   XVII   R.E.

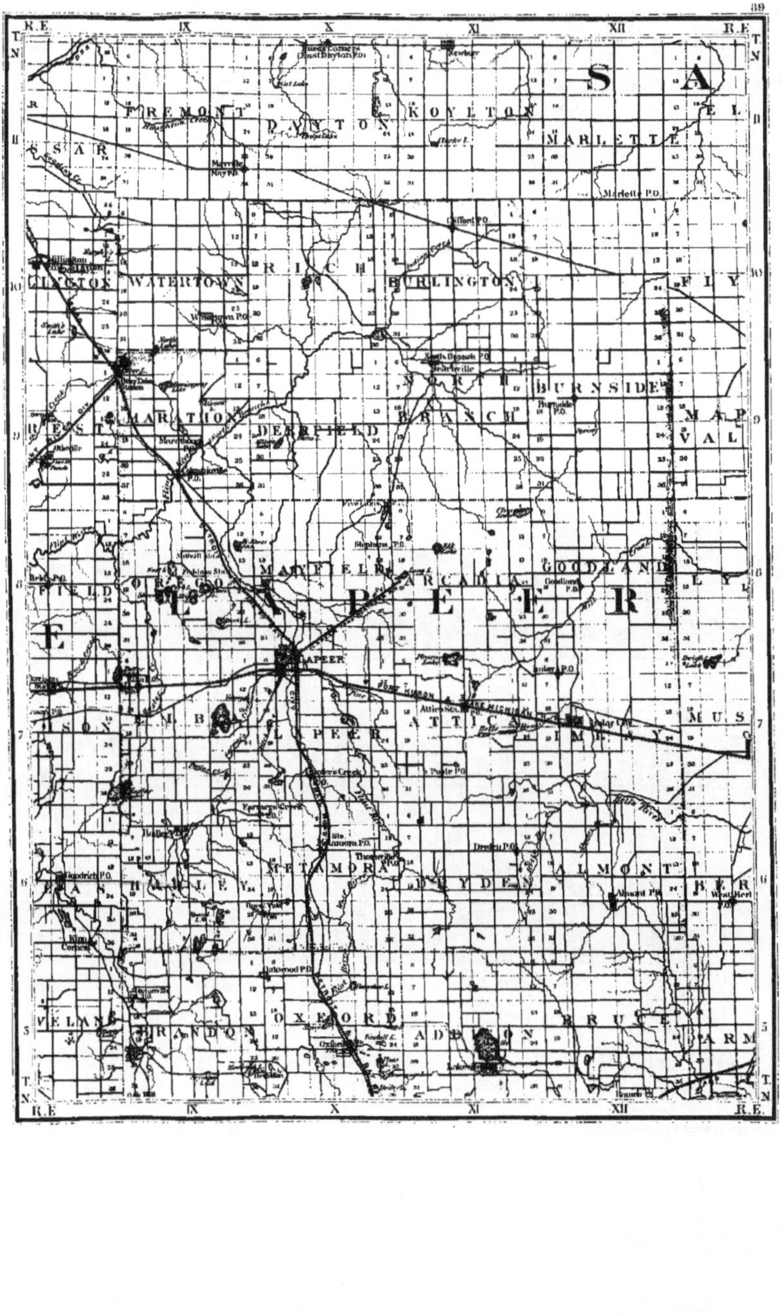
R.E.
IX
X
XI
XII
T.
N
FREMONT
DAYTON
KOYLTON
MARLETTE
Newbury
Marlette P.O.
Clifford P.O.
RICH
BURLINGTON
WATERTOWN
Watertown P.O.
NORTH
BRANCH
BURNSIDE
Burnside P.O.
MARATHON
DEERFIELD
MAYFIELD
ARCADIA
GOODLAND
Goodland P.O.
OREGON
LAPEER
Lapeer
ATTICA
IMLAY
Attica Sta.
ELBA
METAMORA
DRYDEN
ALMONT
Almont P.O.
Dryden P.O.
HADLEY
Goodrich P.O.
OXFORD
ADDISON
BRUCE
BRANDON
Oxford
Oakwood P.O.
Farmers Creek
Columbiaville P.O.
Stephens P.O.
Five Lakes
Hadley
Thornville

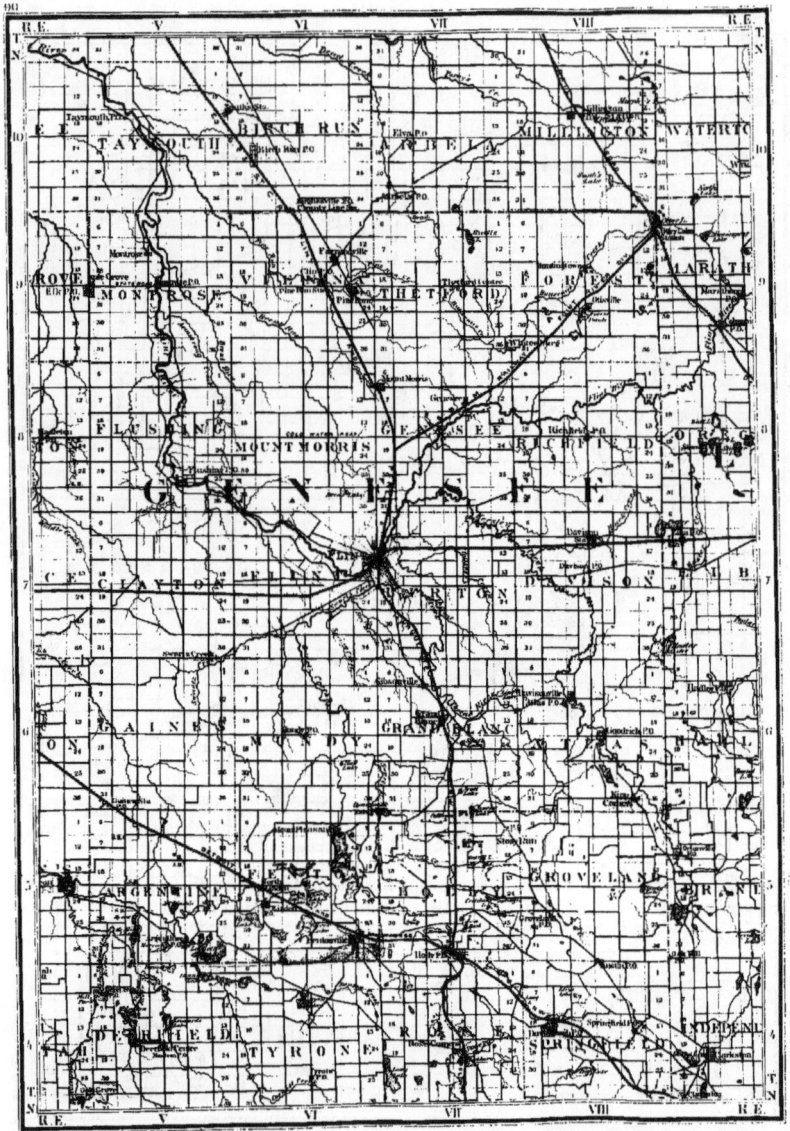

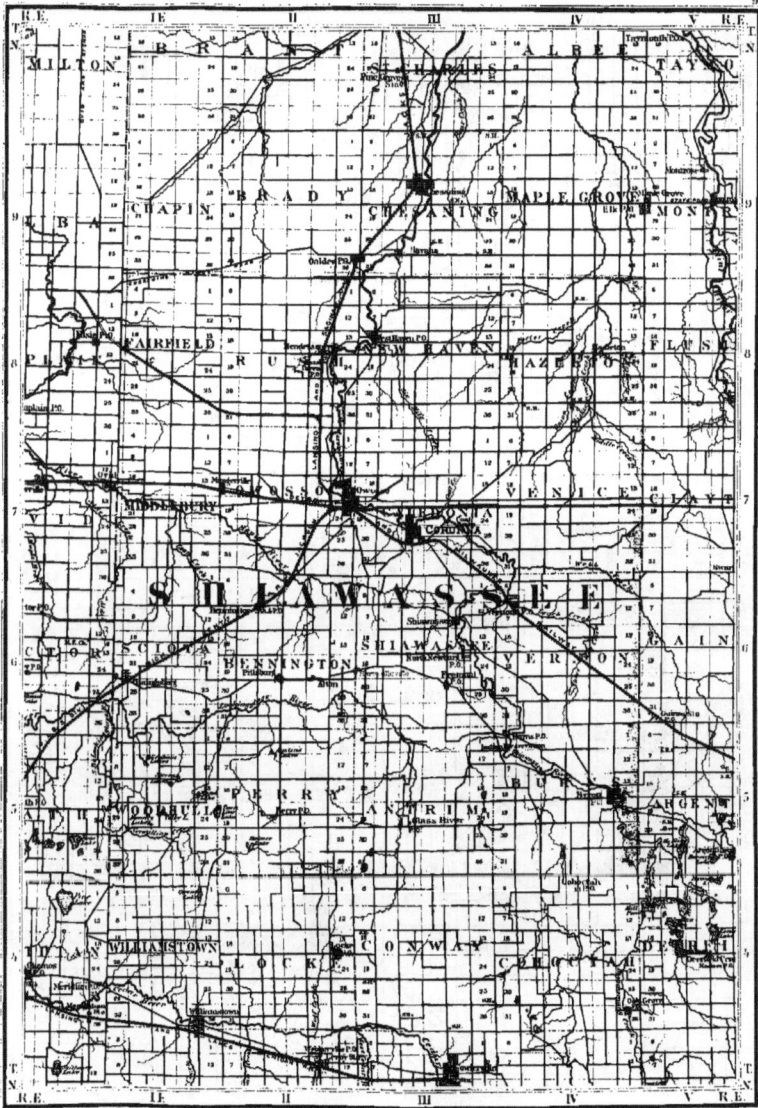

SHIAWASSEE

MILTON BRANT ST. CHARLES ALBEE TAYMO

CHAPIN BRADY CHESANING MAPLE GROVE MONROE

FAIRFIELD RUSH NEW HAVEN HAZELTON FLUSH

MIDDLEBURY CAR SON CORUNNA VENICE CLAY T

SHIAWASSEE BENNINGTON SHIAWASSEE VERNON GAIN

WOODHULL PERRY ANTRIM BU AGEN

WILLIAMSTOWN LOCKE CONWAY OO DE UTT

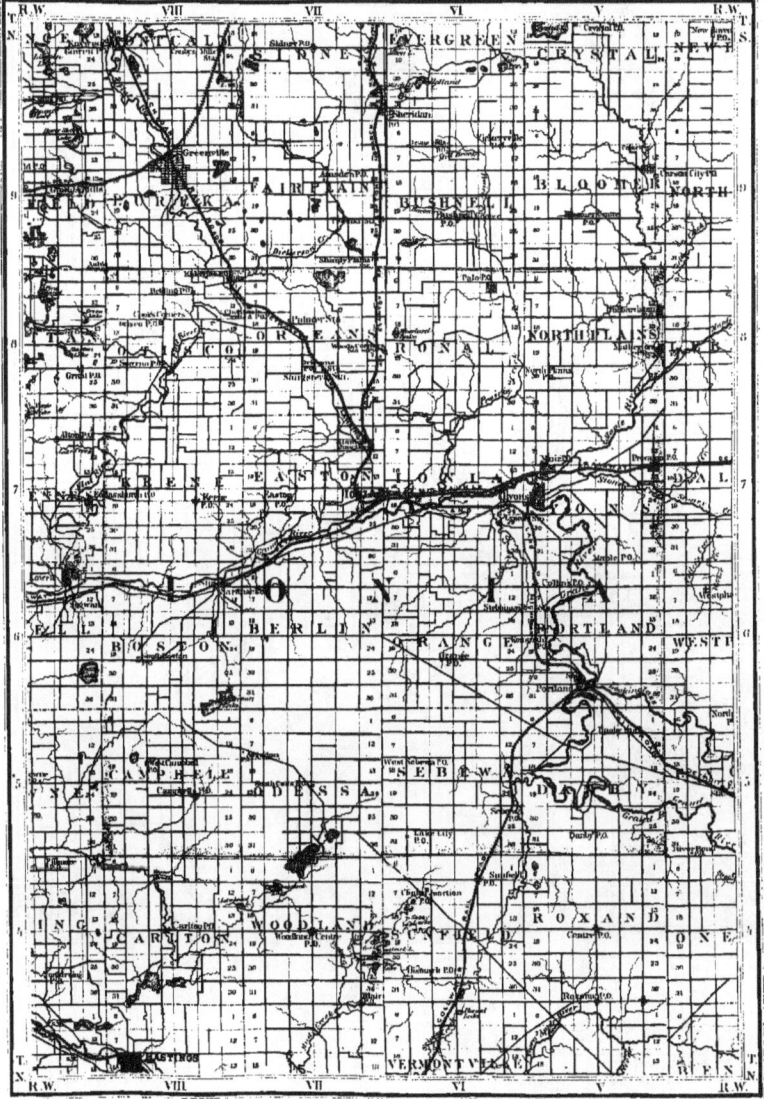

IONIA

MONTCALM   SIDNEY   EVERGREEN   CRYSTAL   NEW

Greenville

FAIRPLAIN   BUSHNELL   BLOOMER   NORTH

EUREKA   Palo P.O.

ORLEANS   IONIA   NORTH PLAINS

EASTON   Ionia   LYONS   DANBY

Portland

BERLIN   ORANGE   PORTLAND   WEST

BOSTON

CAMPBELL   ODESSA   SEBEWA   DANBY

CARLTON   WOODLAND   OXFORD   ROXAND   ONE

HASTINGS   VERMONTVILLE

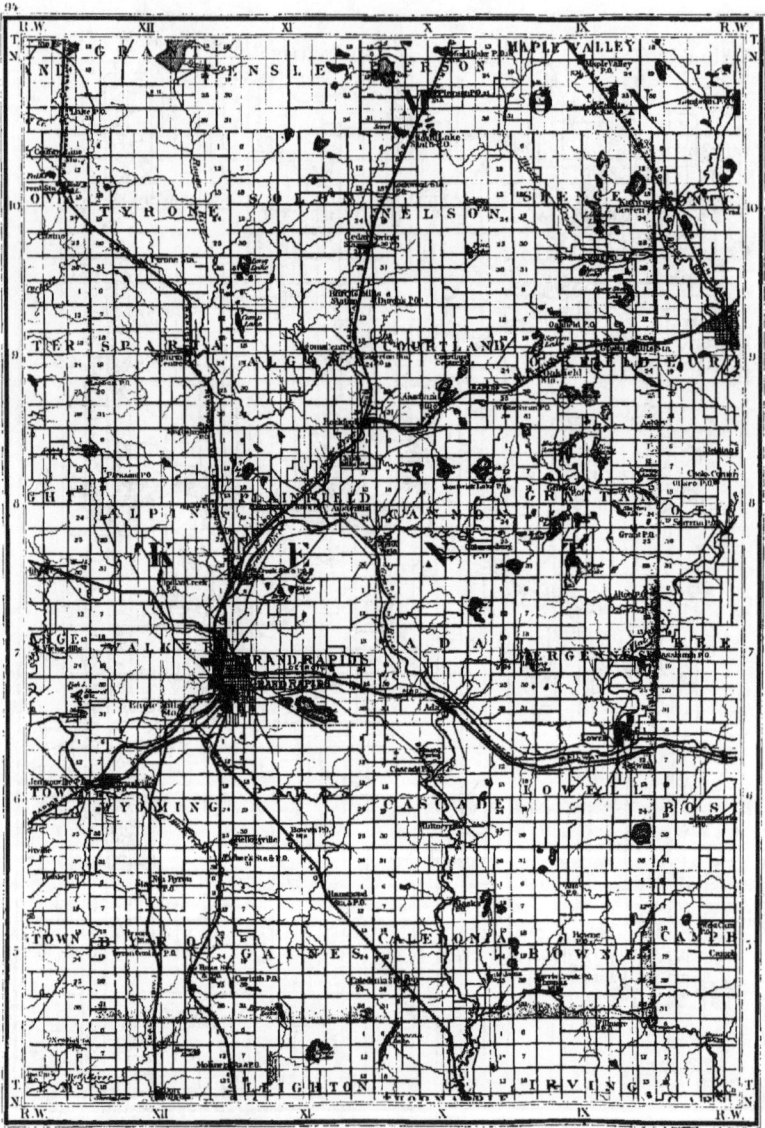

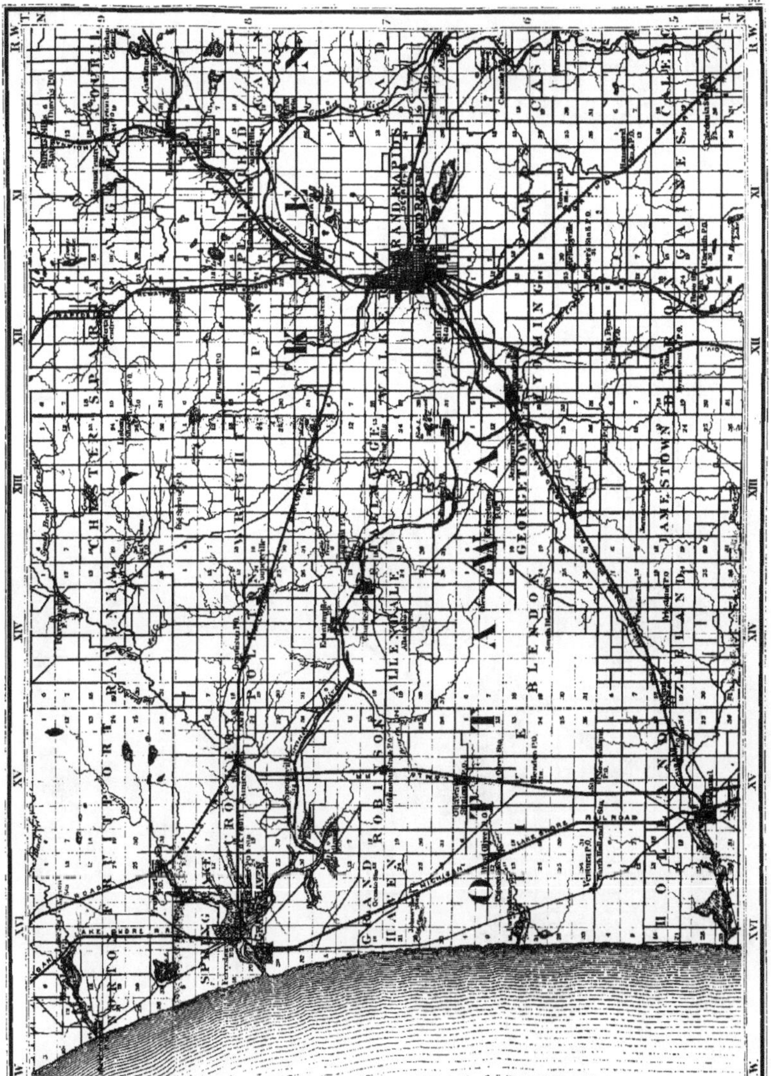
GRAND RAPIDS
WALKER
GEORGETOWN
JAMESTOWN
ALLENDALE
BLENDON
ROBINSON

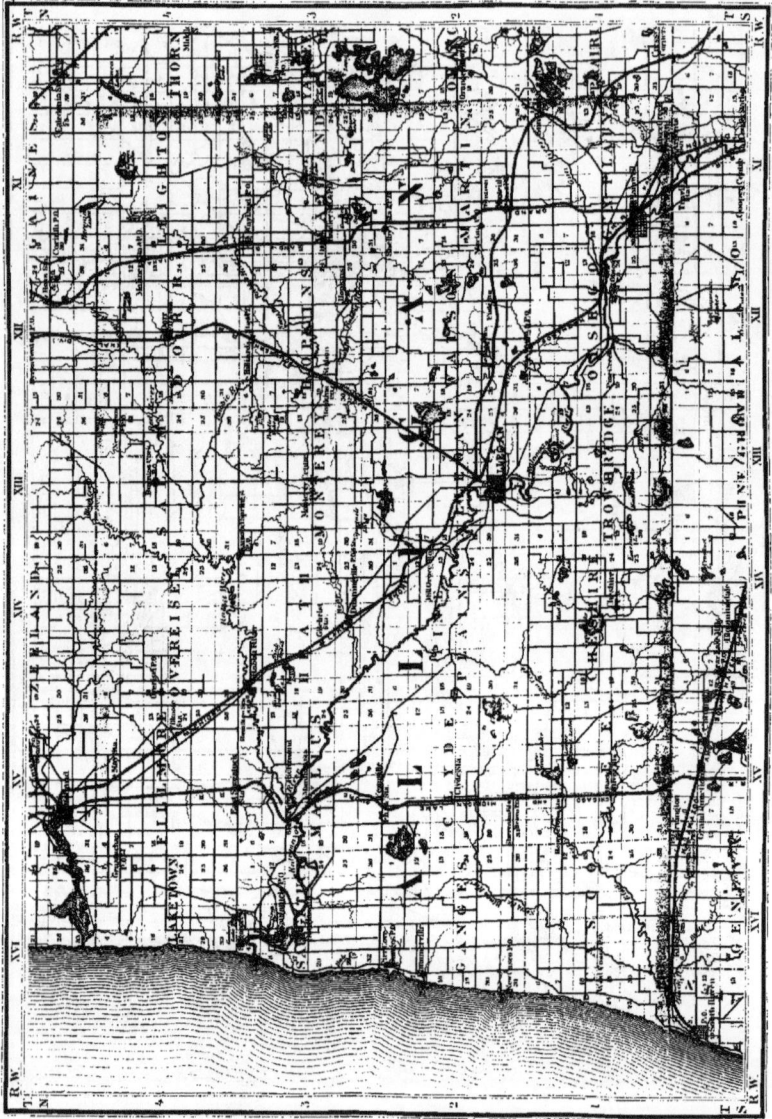

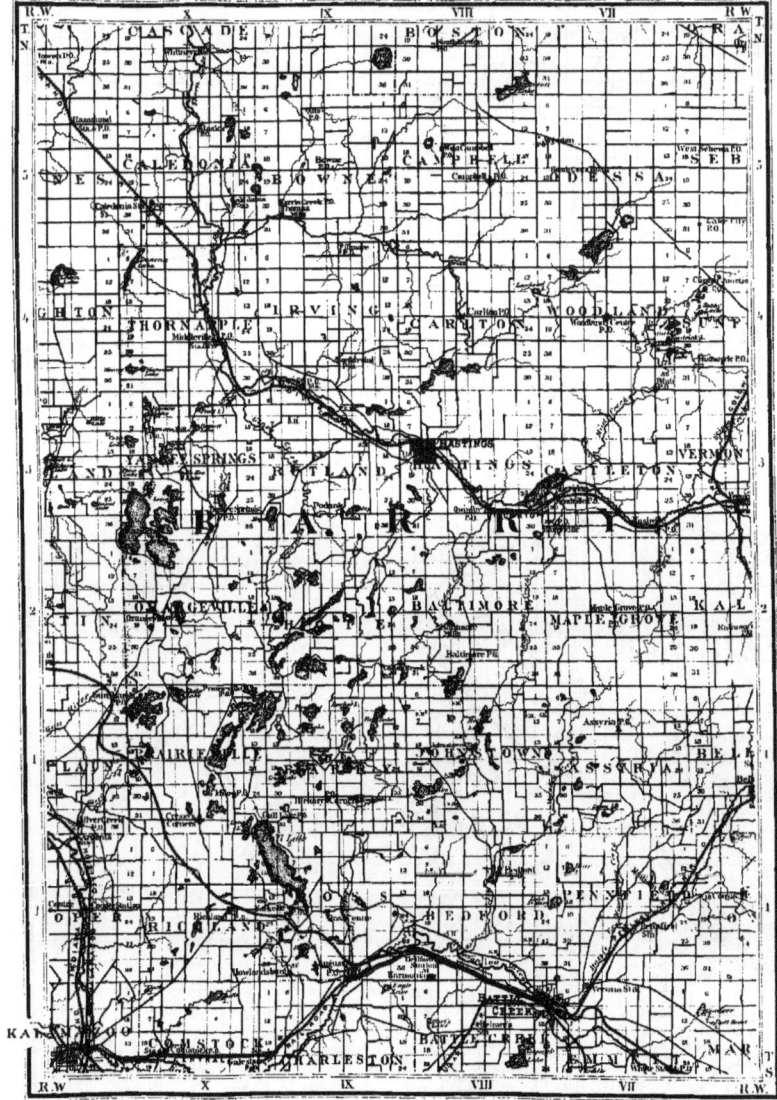

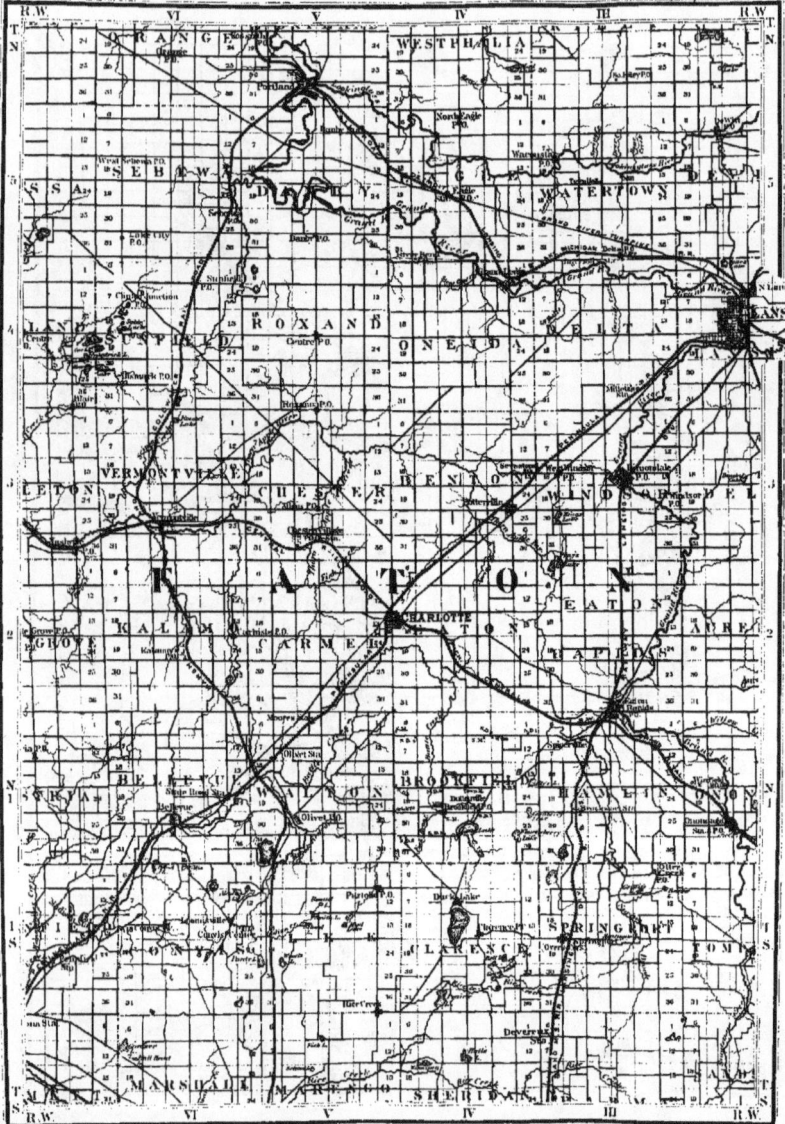

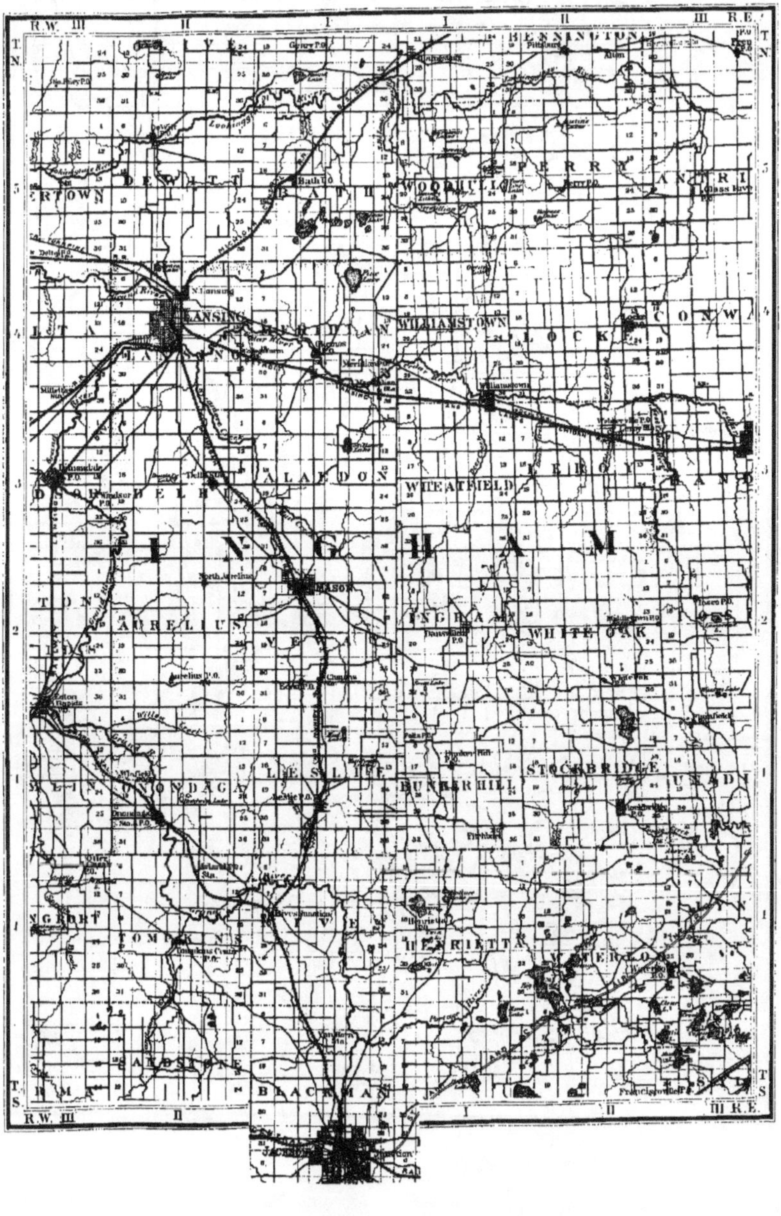
R.W. III
II
I
I
II
III R.E.
T. N.
T. S.
INGHAM
LANSING
N. Lansing
MERIDIAN
WILLIAMSTOWN
Williamstown
LOCKE
WHEATFIELD
LEROY
ALAIEDON
DELHI
Holt
MASON
North Aurelius
AURELIUS
Aurelius P.O.
VEVAY
Eden
INGHAM
Dansville
WHITE OAK
STOCKBRIDGE
BUNKER HILL
LESLIE
ONONDAGA
Eaton Rapids
DE WITT
BATH
Bath P.O.
WOODHULL
PERRY
Perry P.O.
BENNINGTON
Pittsburg
TOMPKINS
HENRIETTA
WATERLOO
SANDSTONE
BLACKMAN
JACKSON
Francisco P.O.

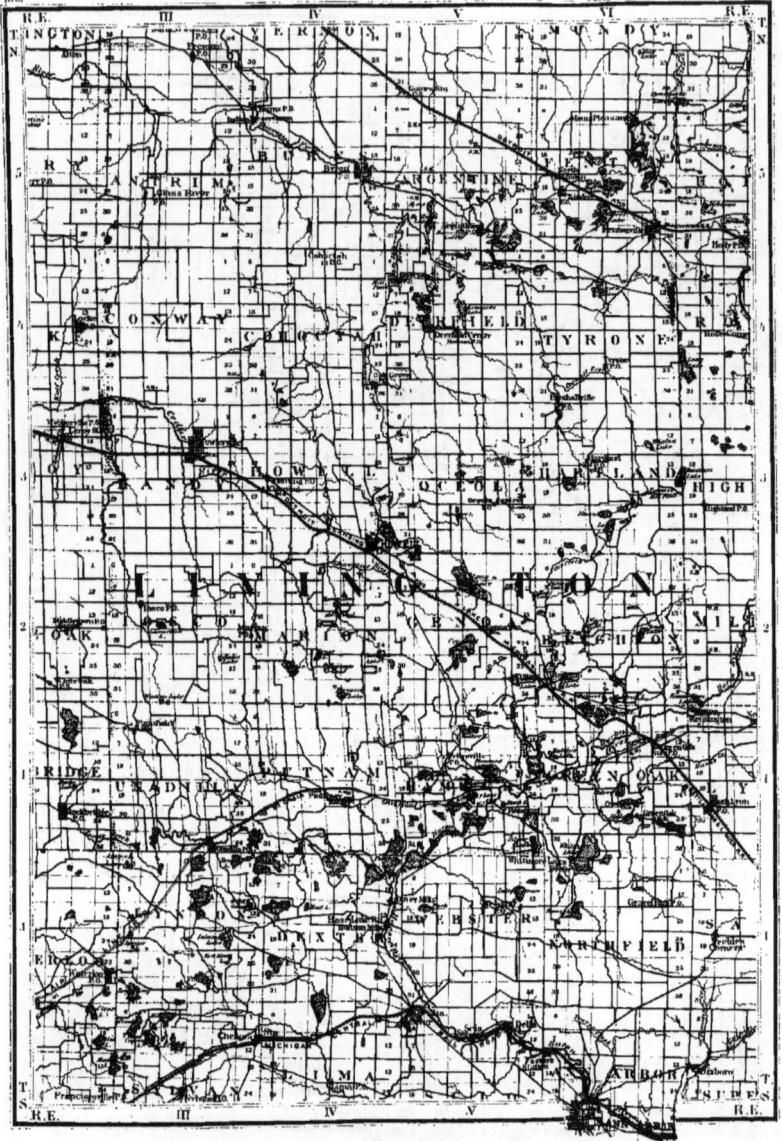

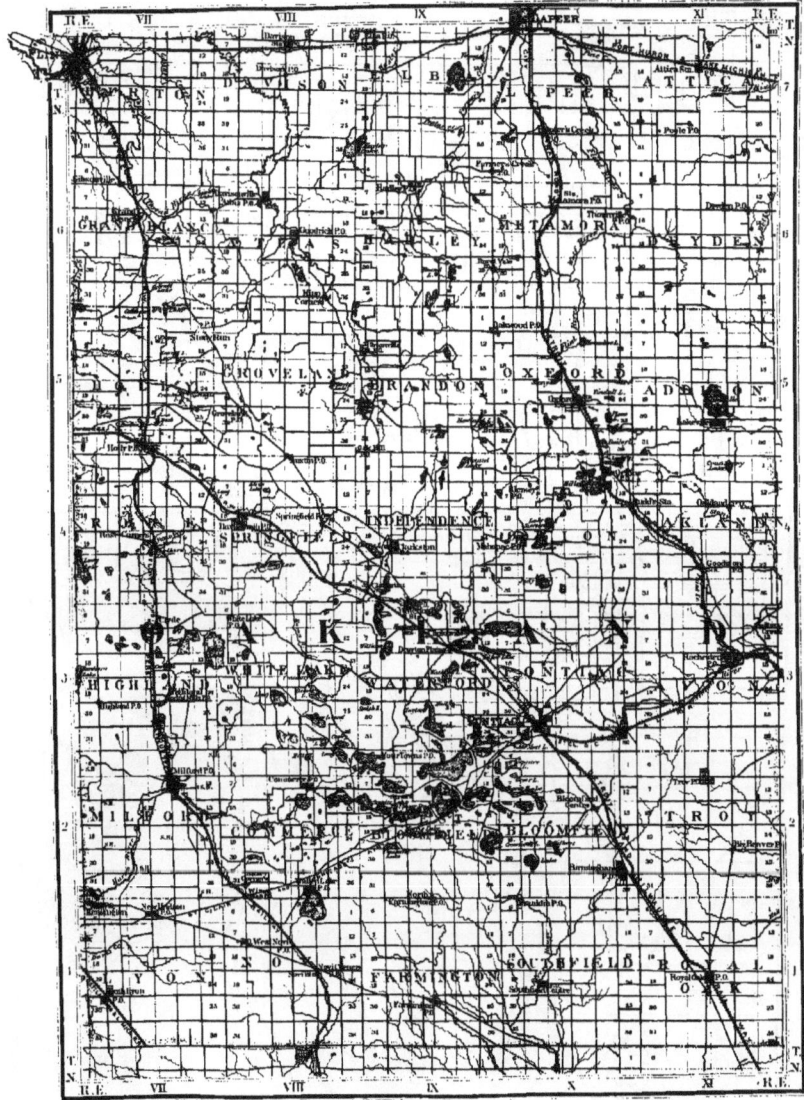

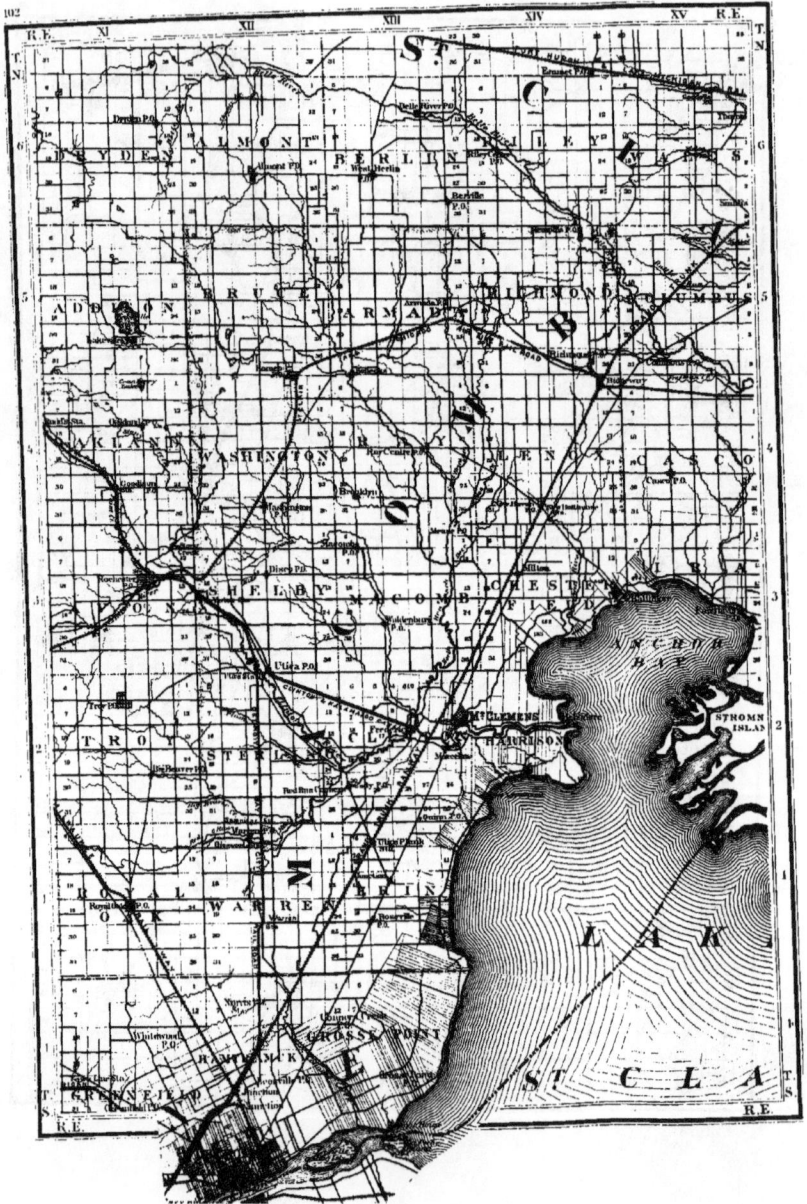

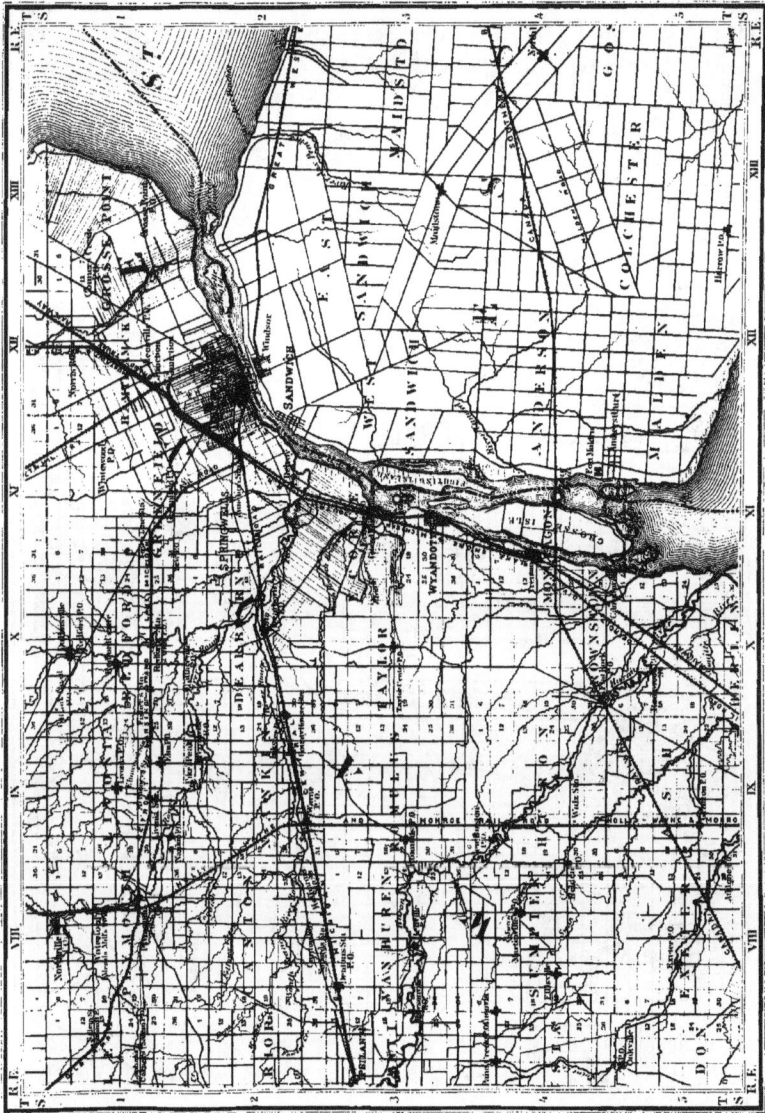

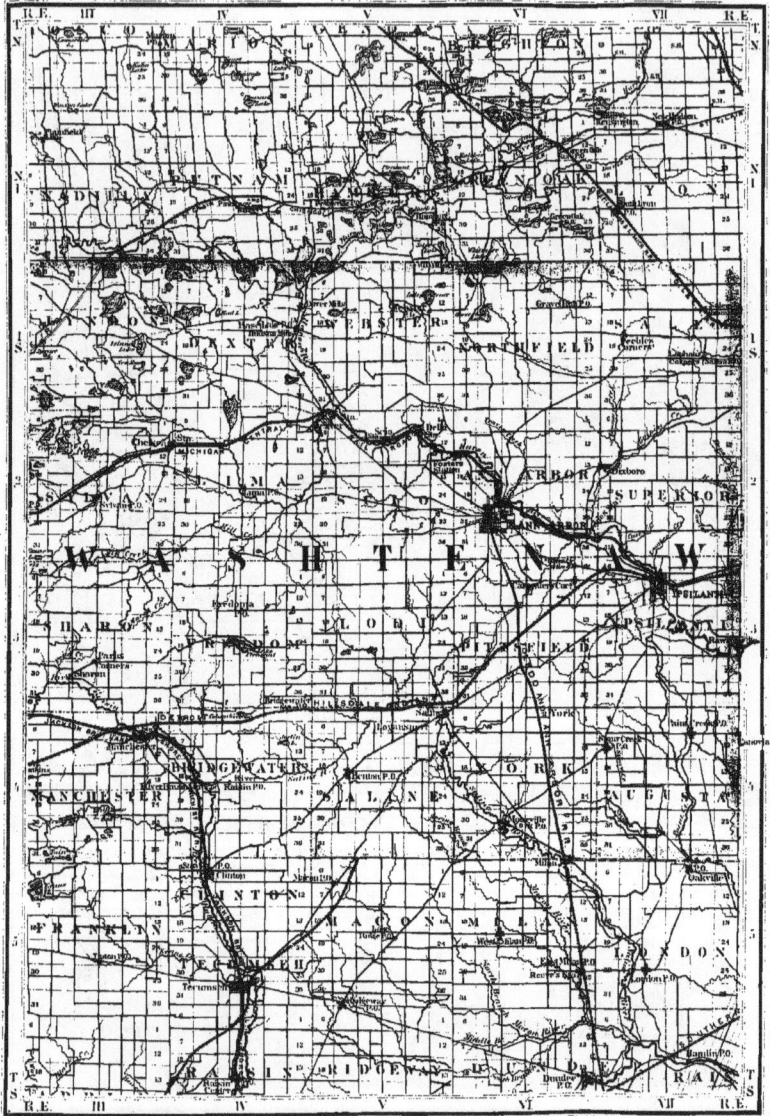

Map of Washtenaw County, Michigan

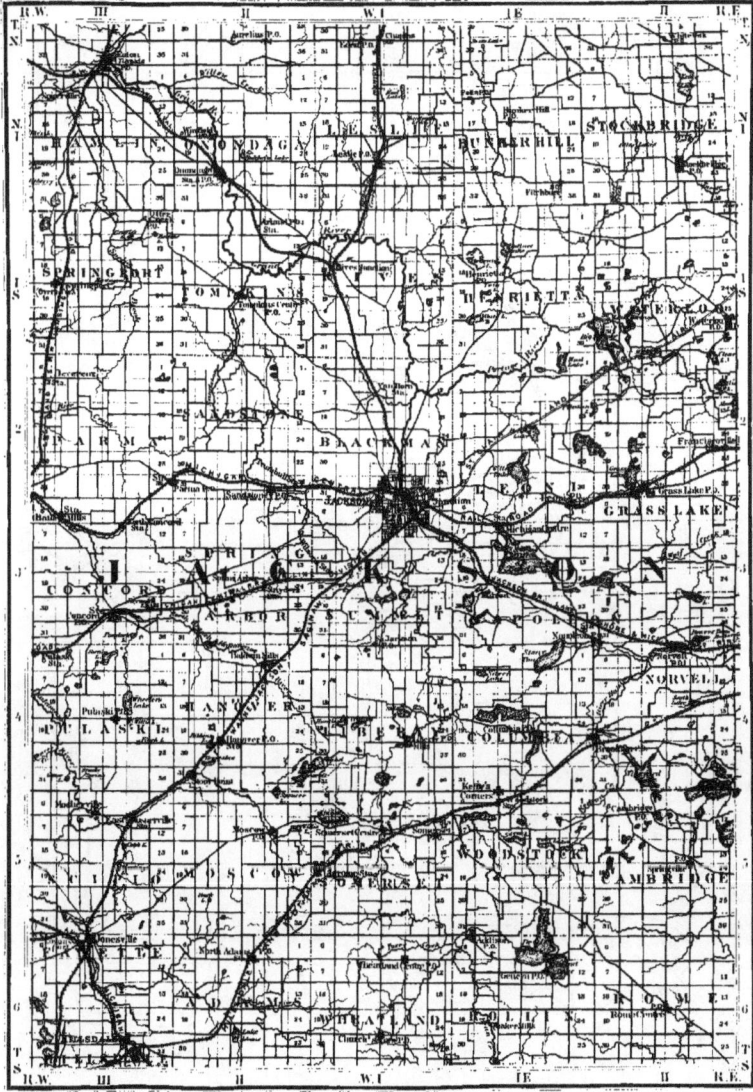

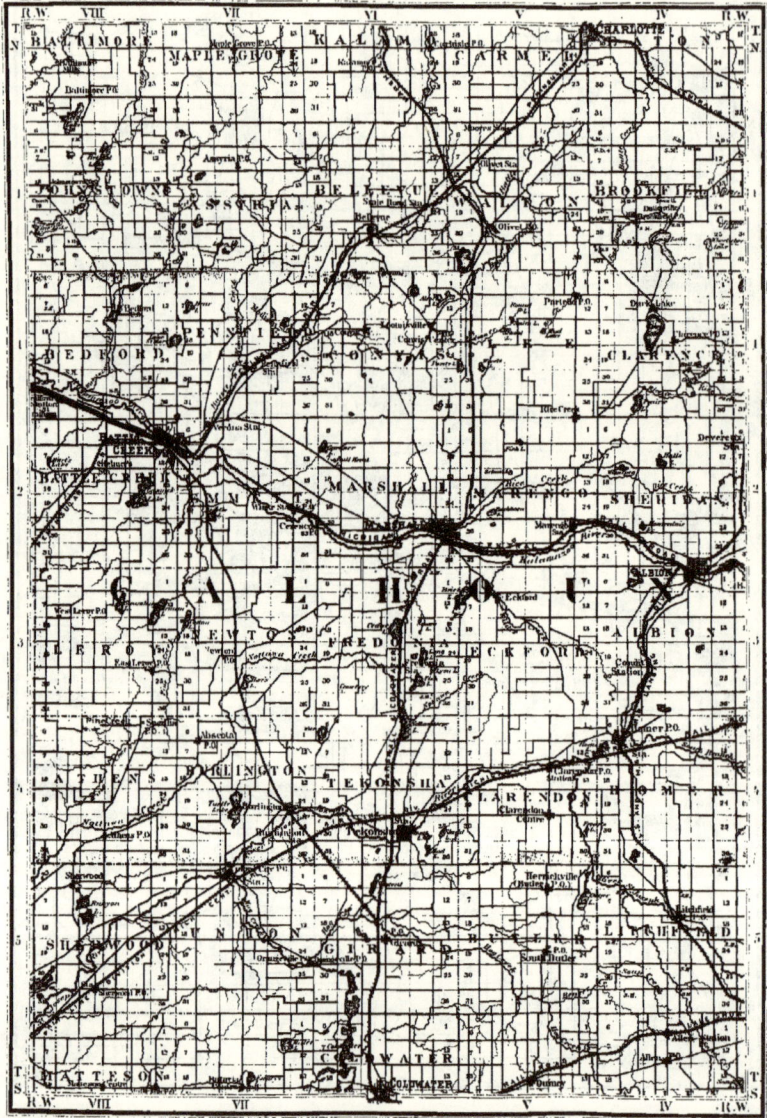

R.W. VIII VII VI V IV R.W.

BALTIMORE · MAPLE GROVE · KALAM · CARMEL · CHARLOTTE

JOHNSTOWN · ASSYRIA · BELLEVUE · WALTON · BROOKFIELD

BEDFORD · PENNFIELD · CONVIS · LEE · CLARENCE

BATTLE CREEK · MARSHALL · MARENGO · SHERIDAN

C A L H O U N

LEROY · NEWTON · FREDONIA · ECKFORD · ALBION

ATHENS · BURLINGTON · TEKONSHA · CLARENDON · HOMER

SHERWOOD · GIRARD · BUTLER · LITCHFIELD

MATTESON · COLDWATER

R.W. VIII VII V IV R.W.

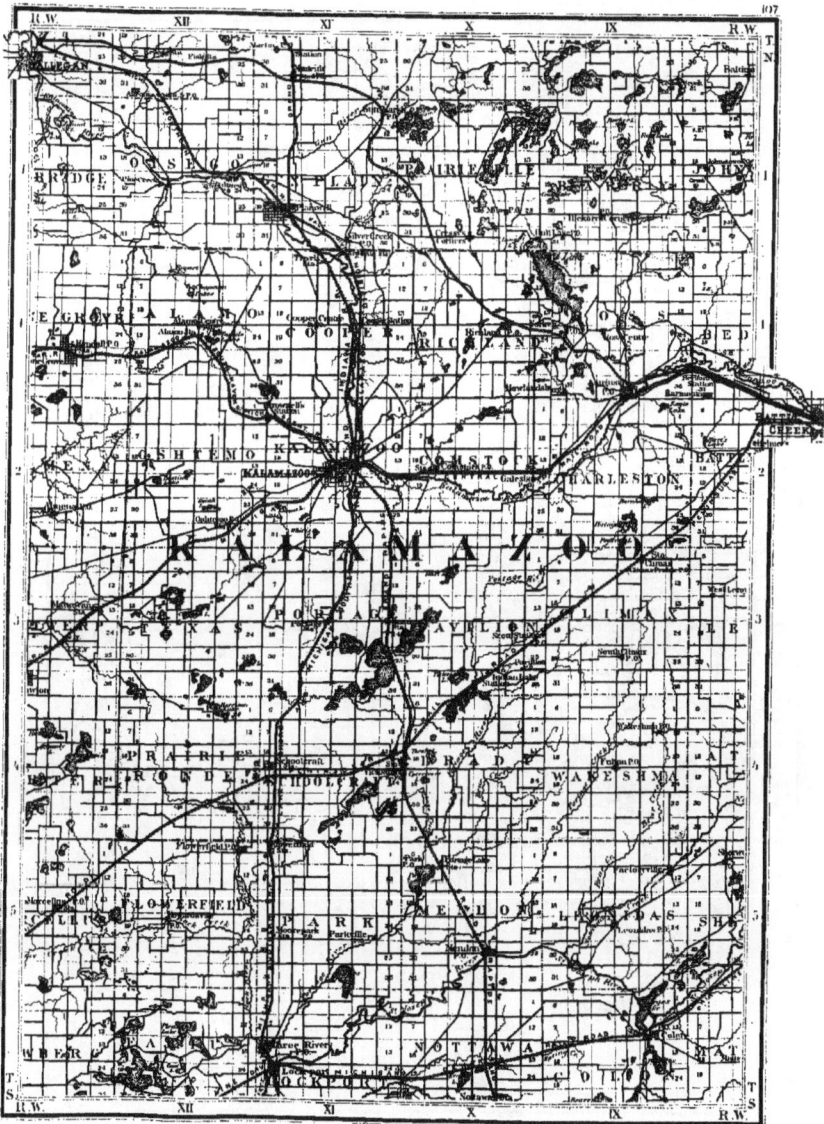

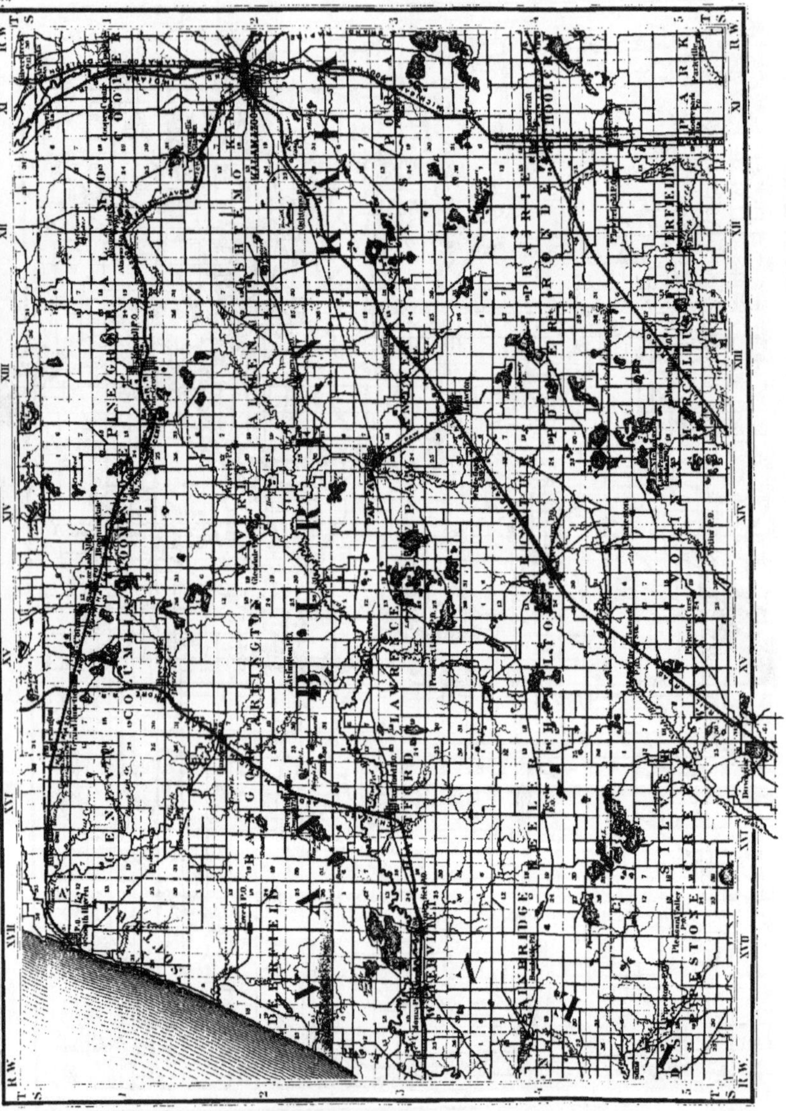

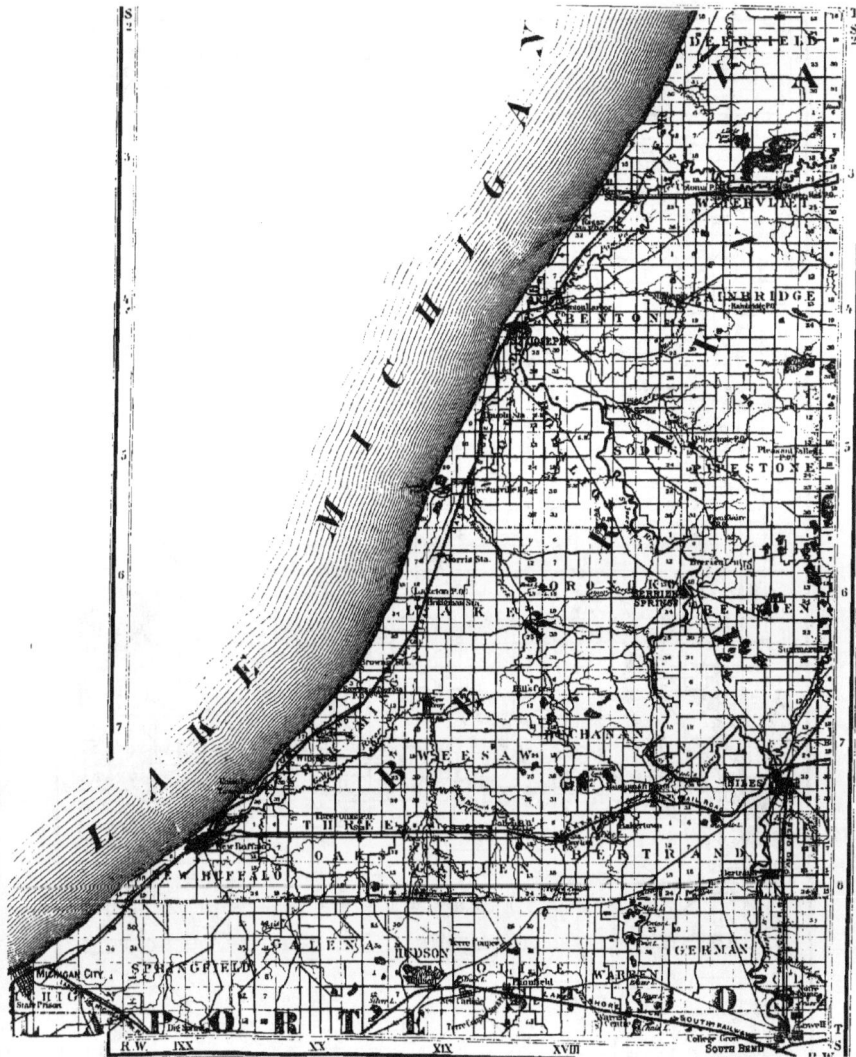

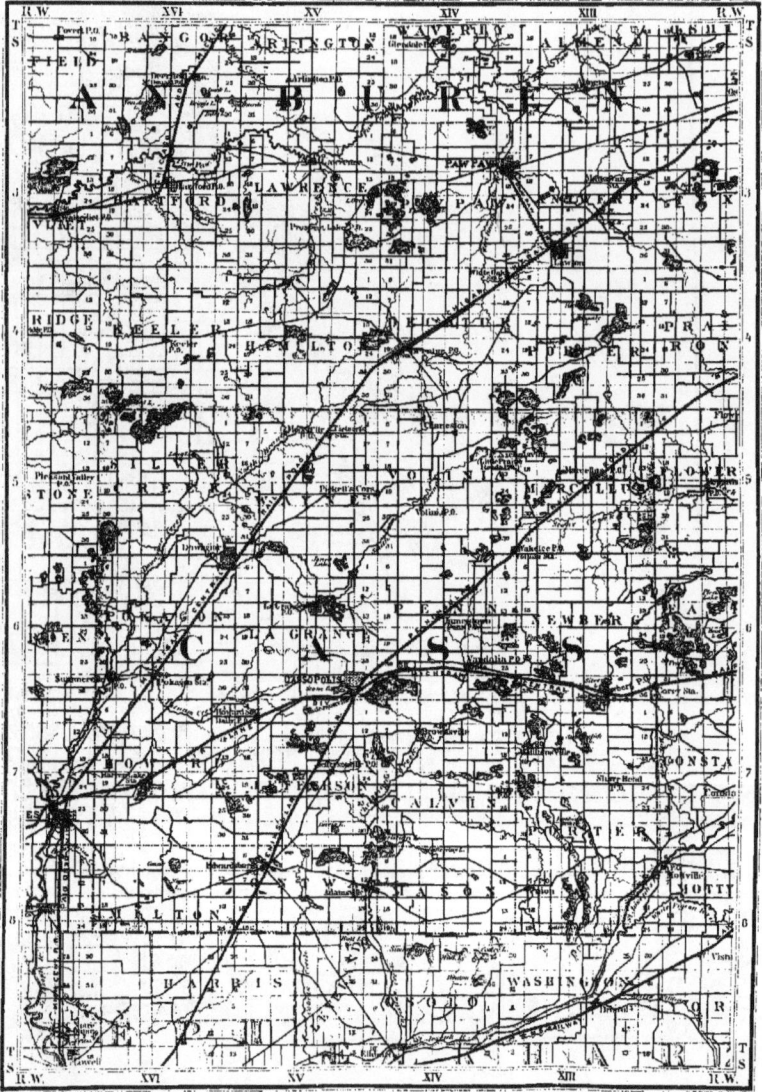

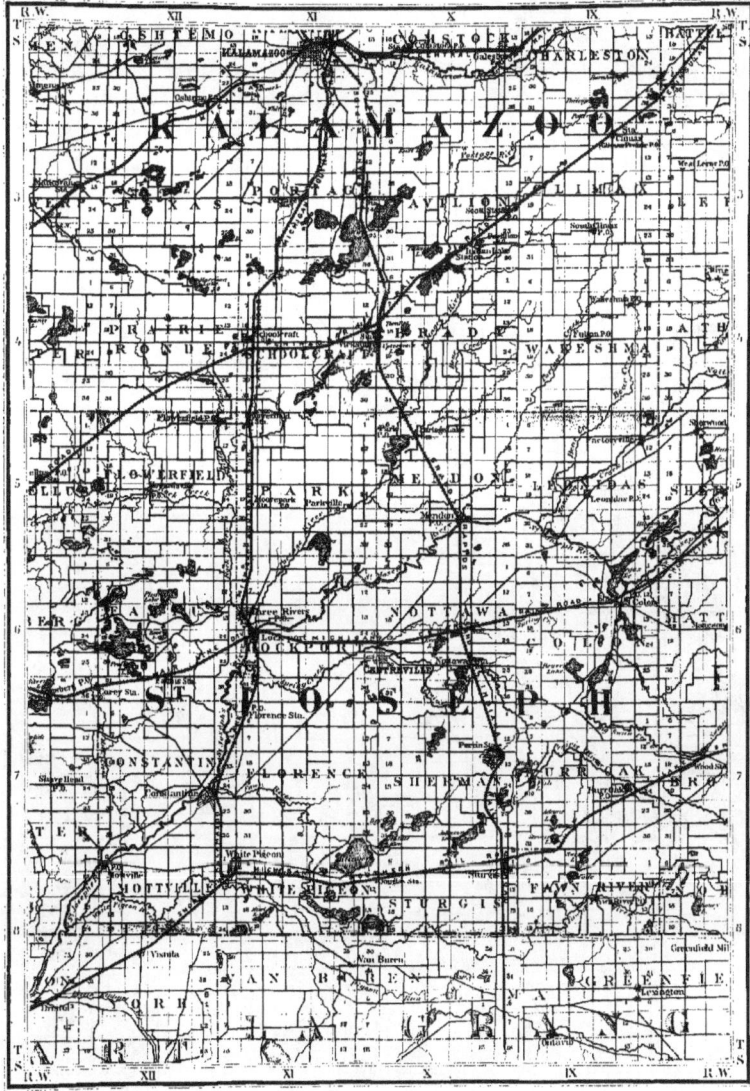

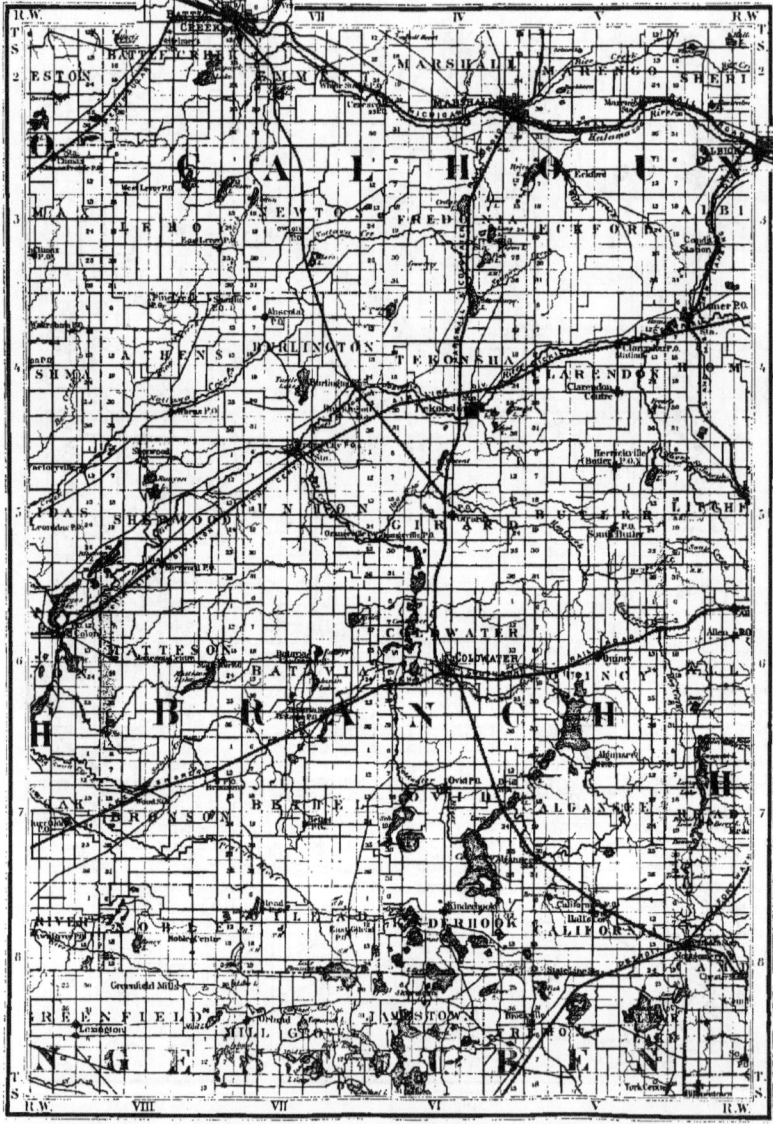

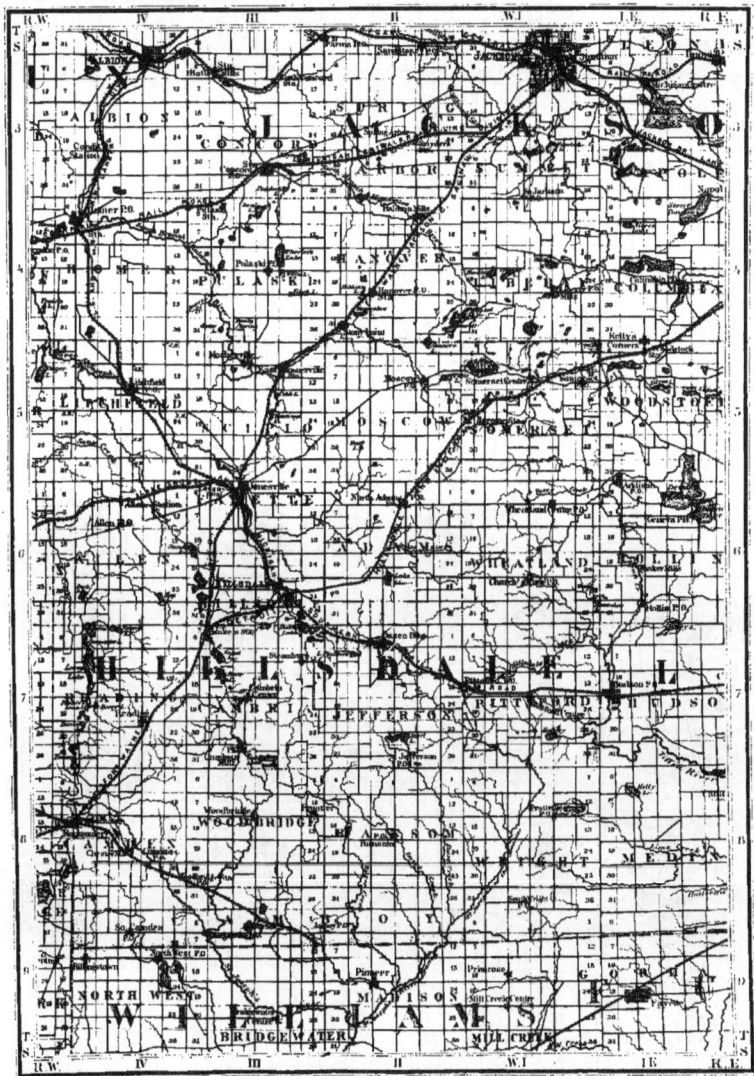

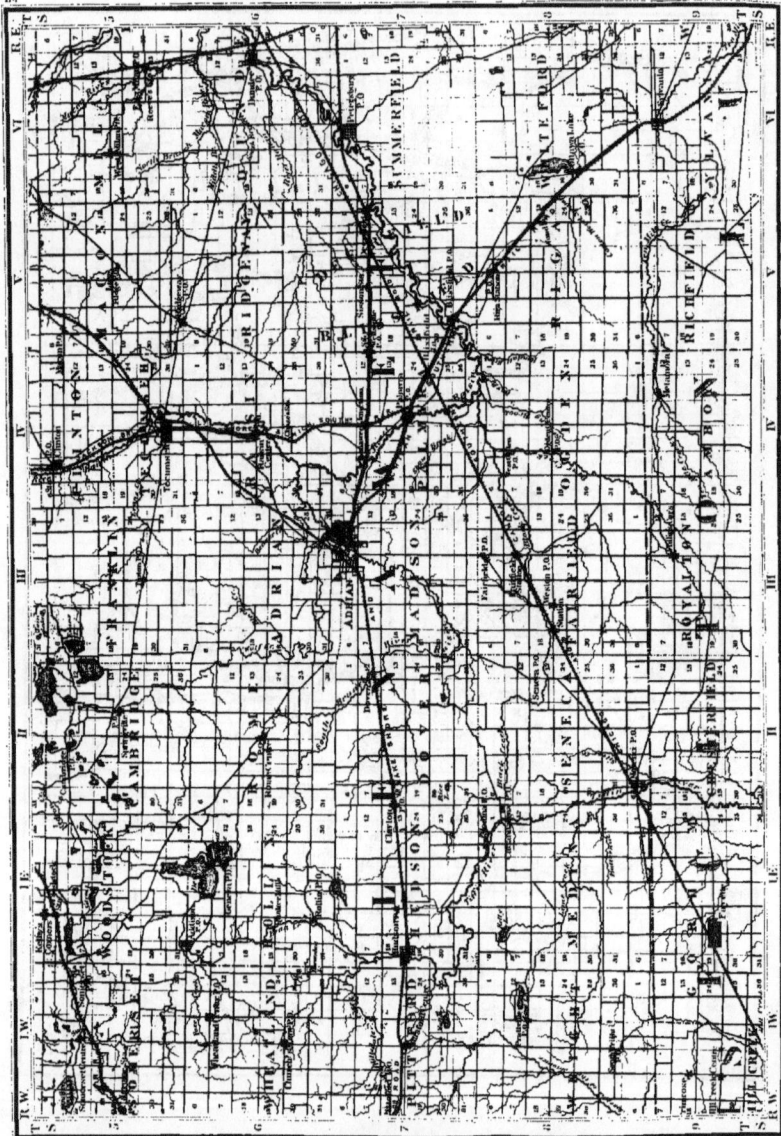

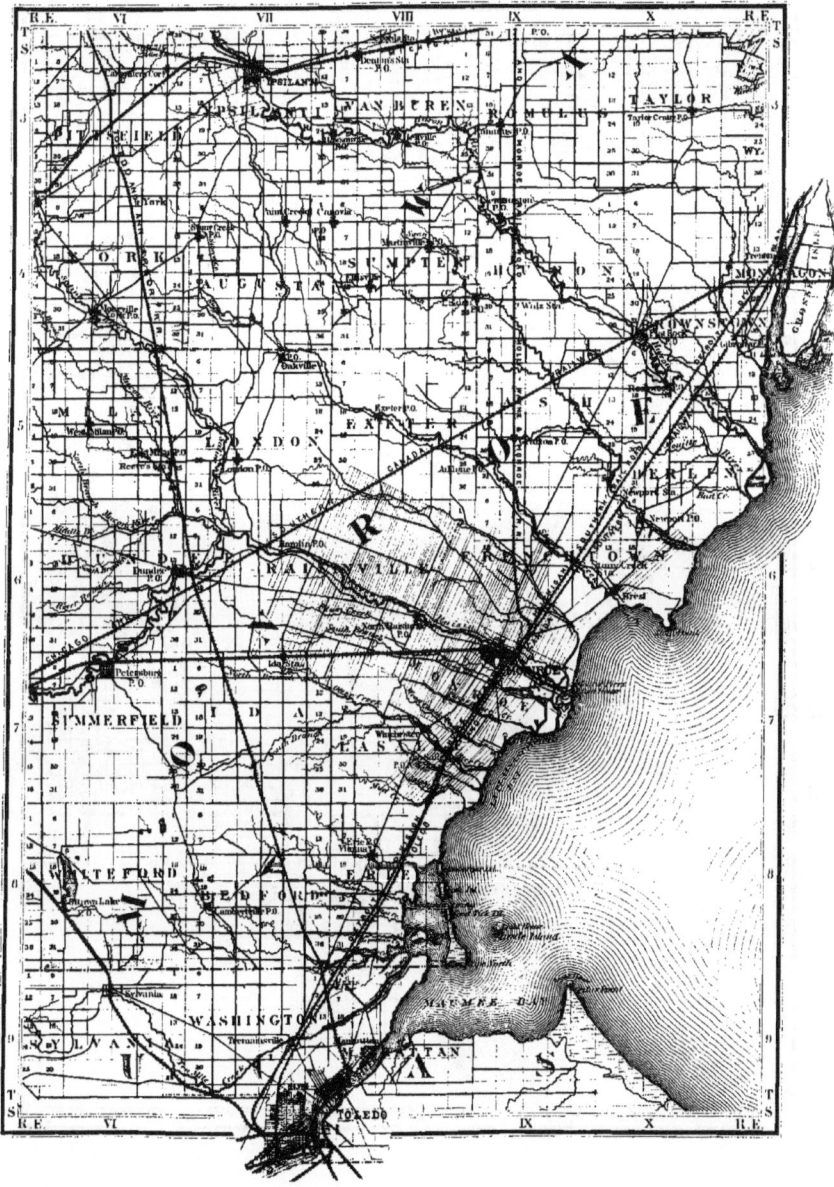

116

UPPER PENINSULA. SCALE SIX MILES TO AN INCH

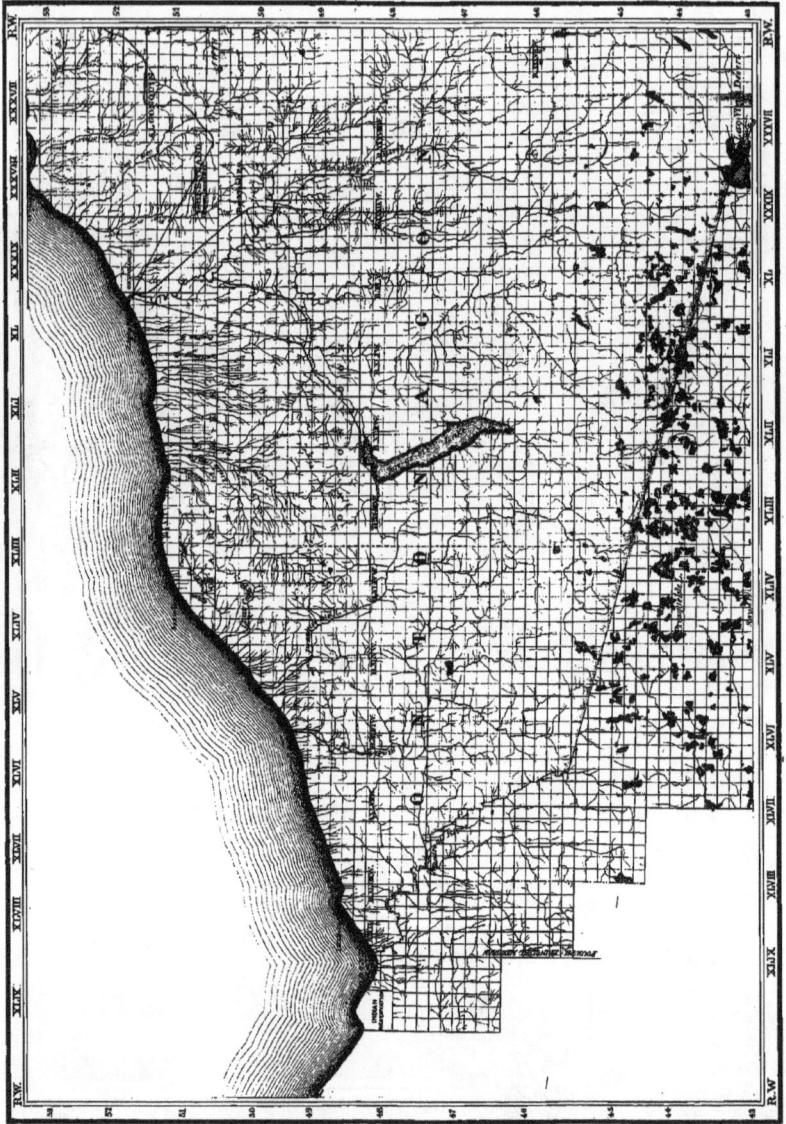

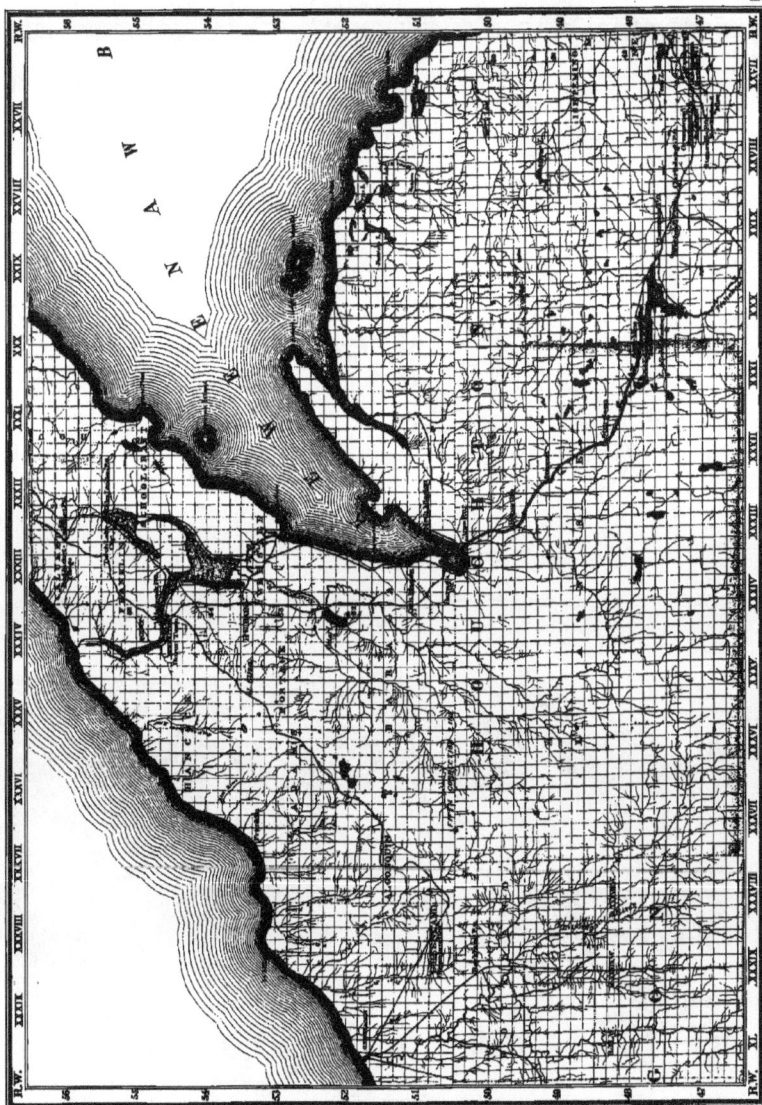

UPPER PENINSULA SCALE SIX MILES TO AN INCH

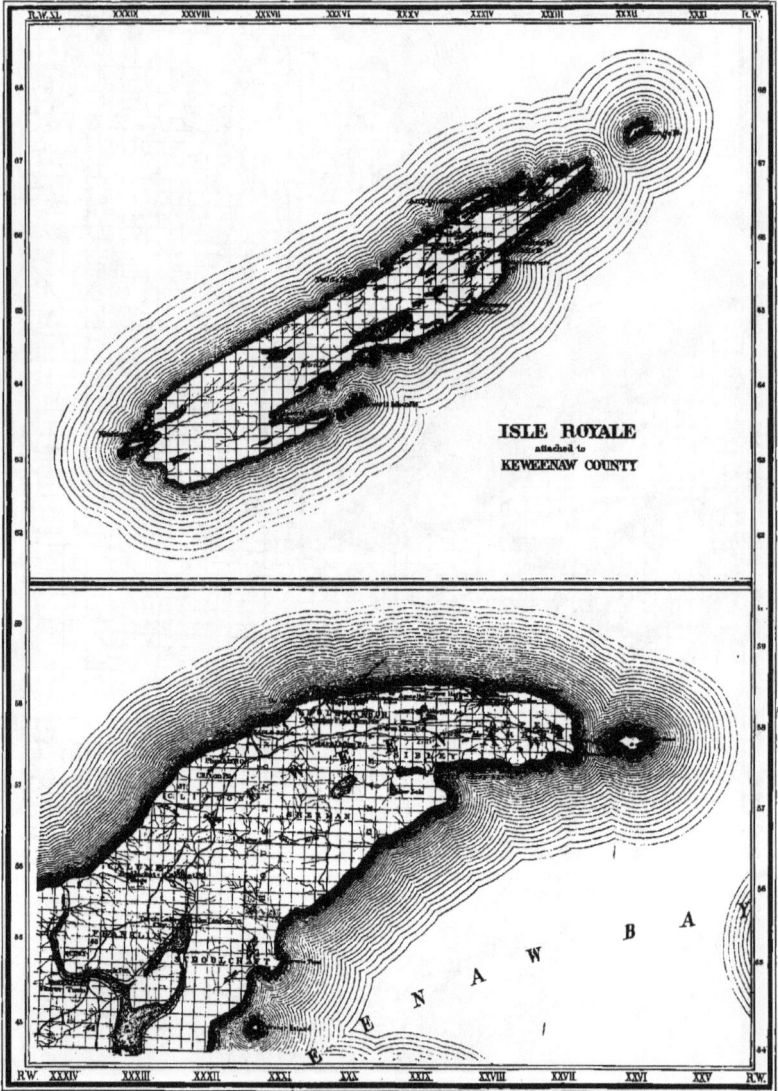

ISLE ROYALE
attached to
KEWEENAW COUNTY

UPPER PENINSULA. SCALE SIX MILES TO AN INCH

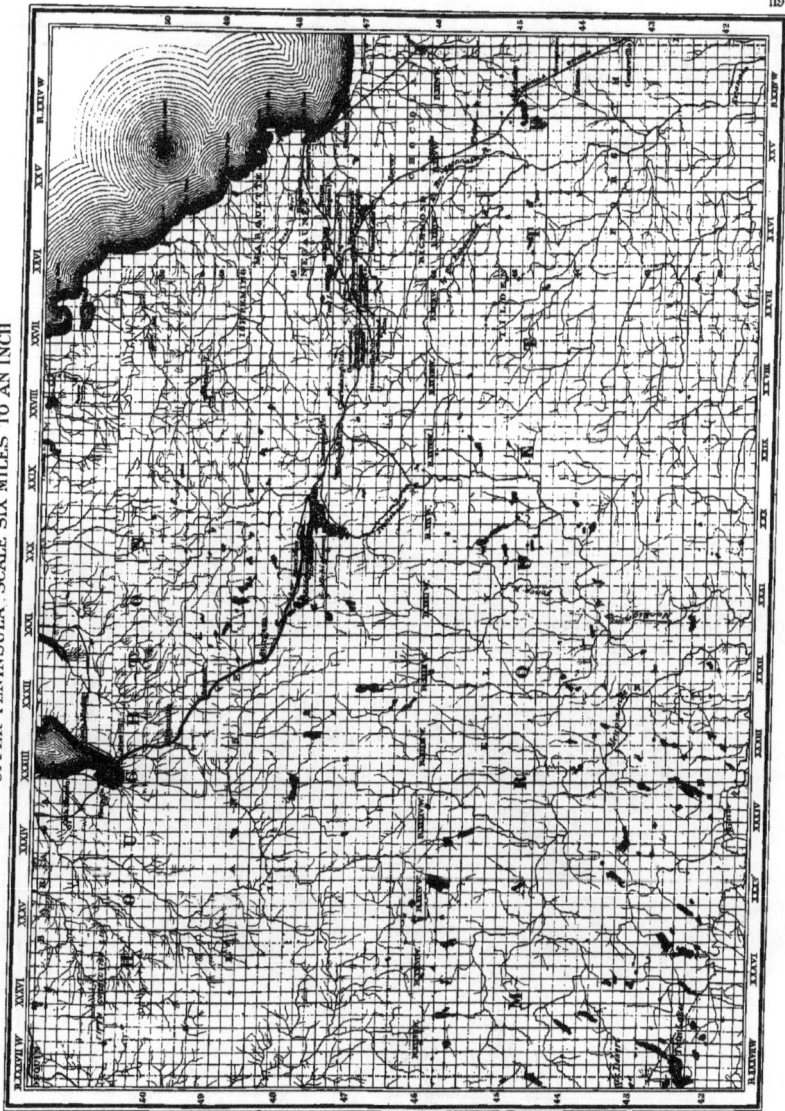

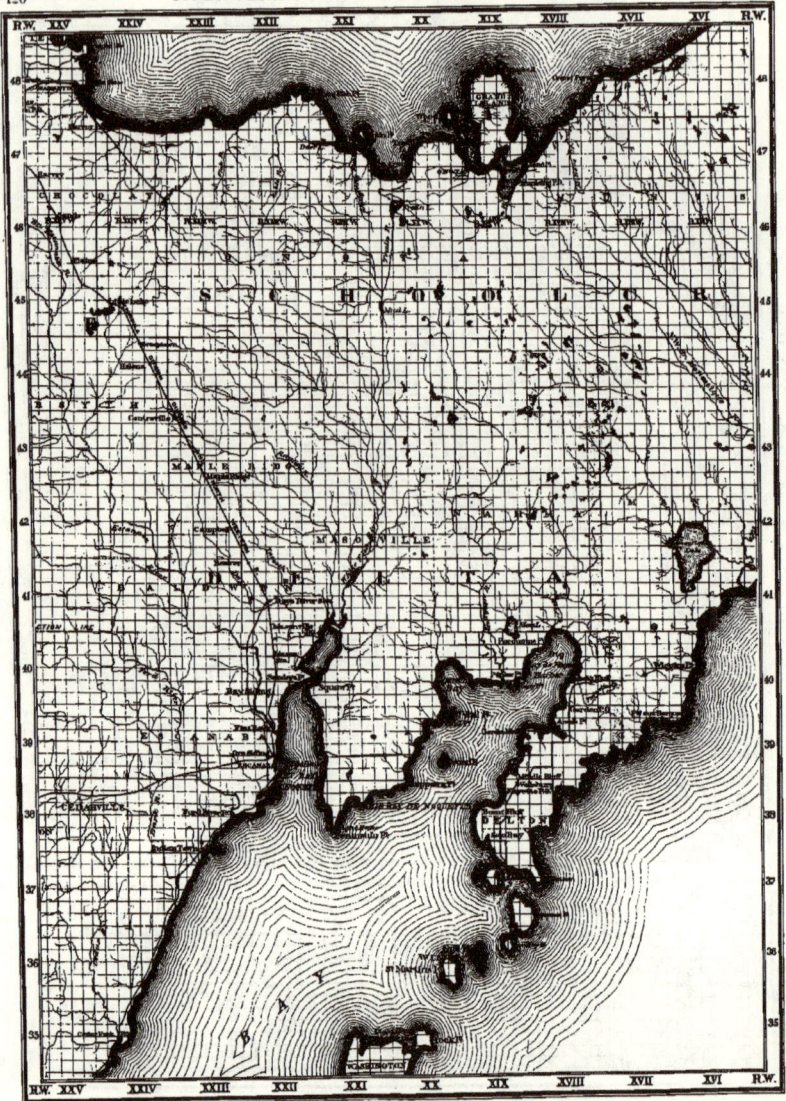

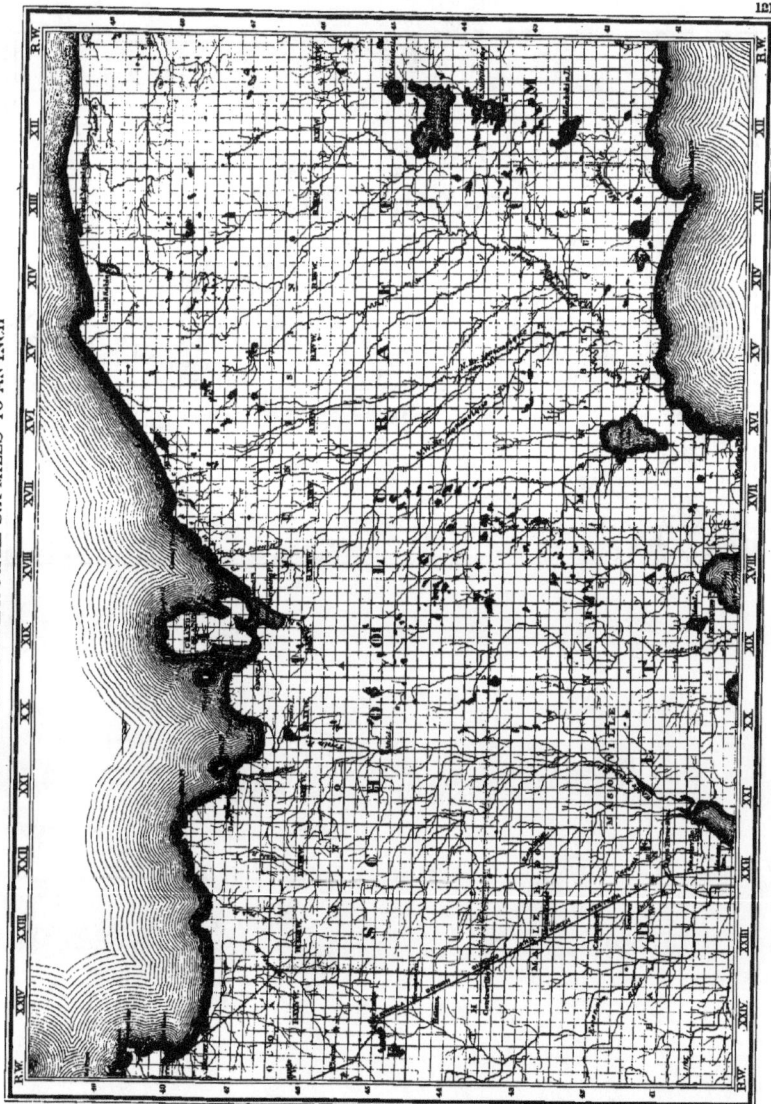

UPPER PENINSULA. SCALE SIX MILES TO AN INCH

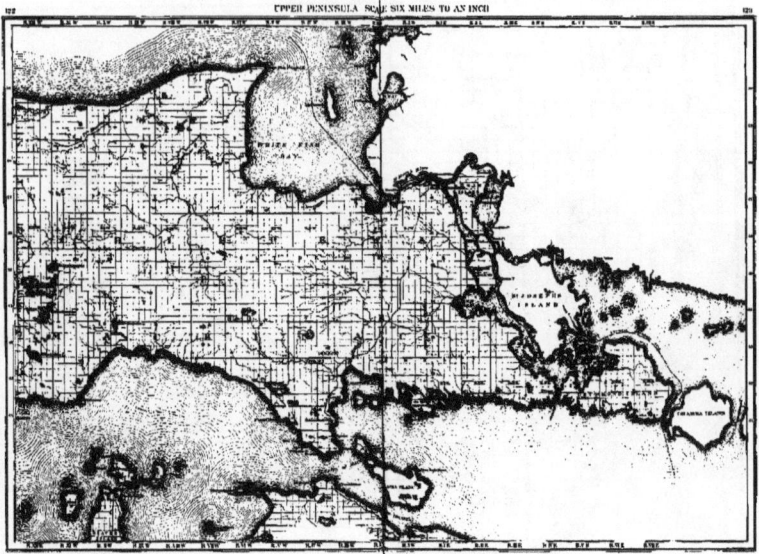

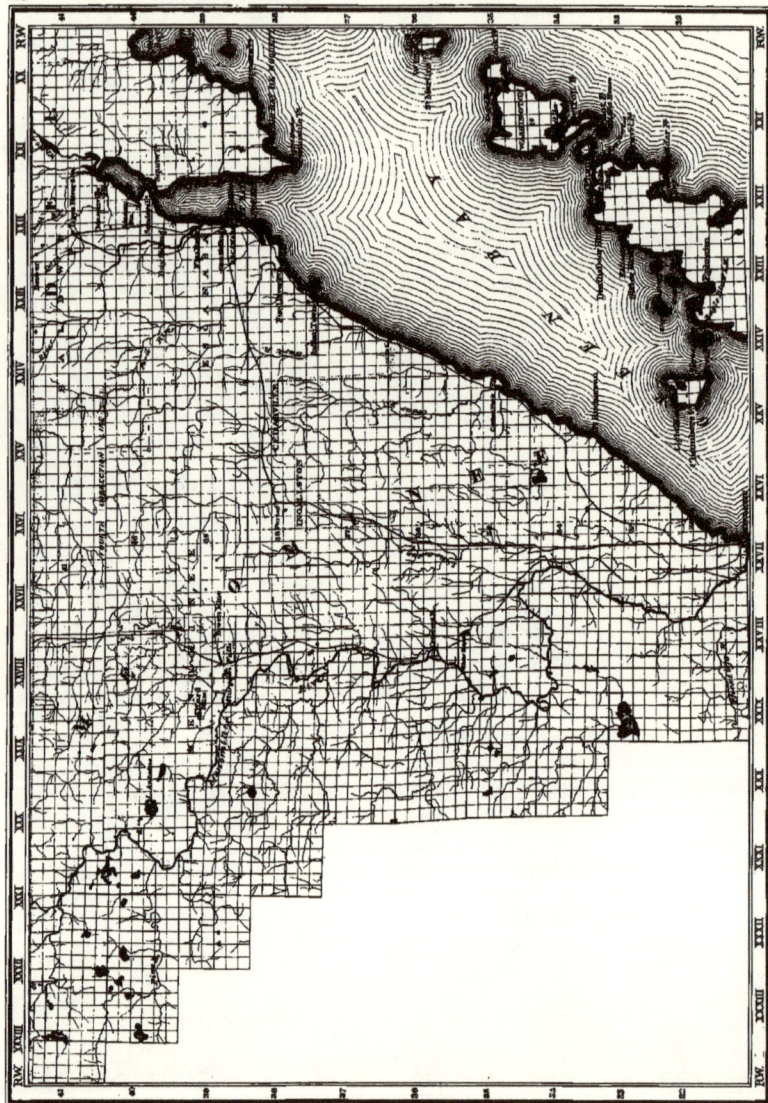

UPPER PENINSULA. SCALE SIX MILES TO AN INCH

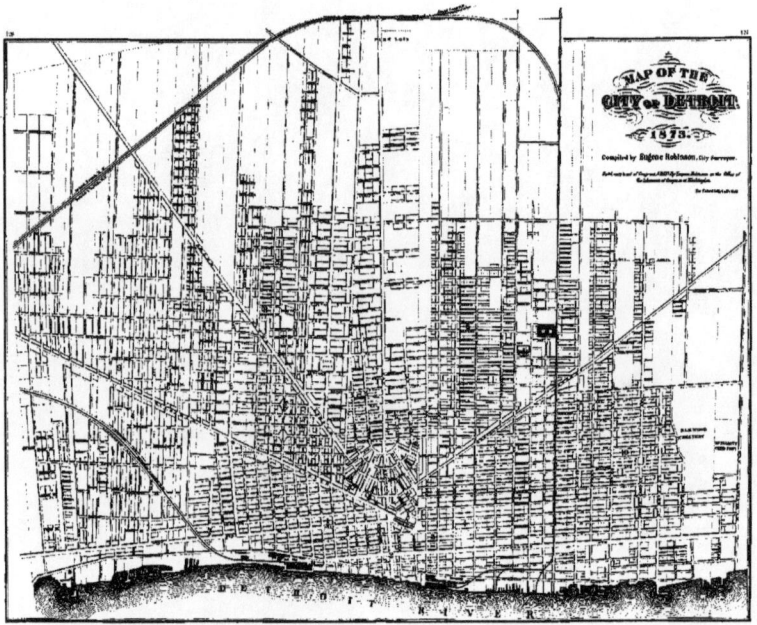

DETROIT RIVER

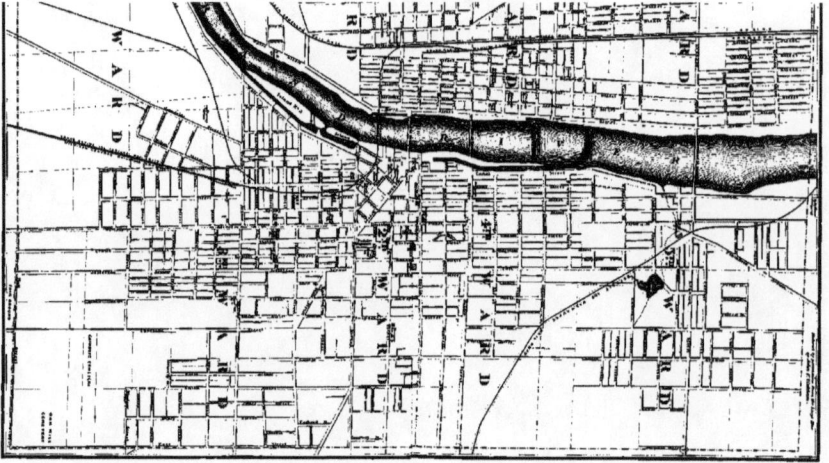

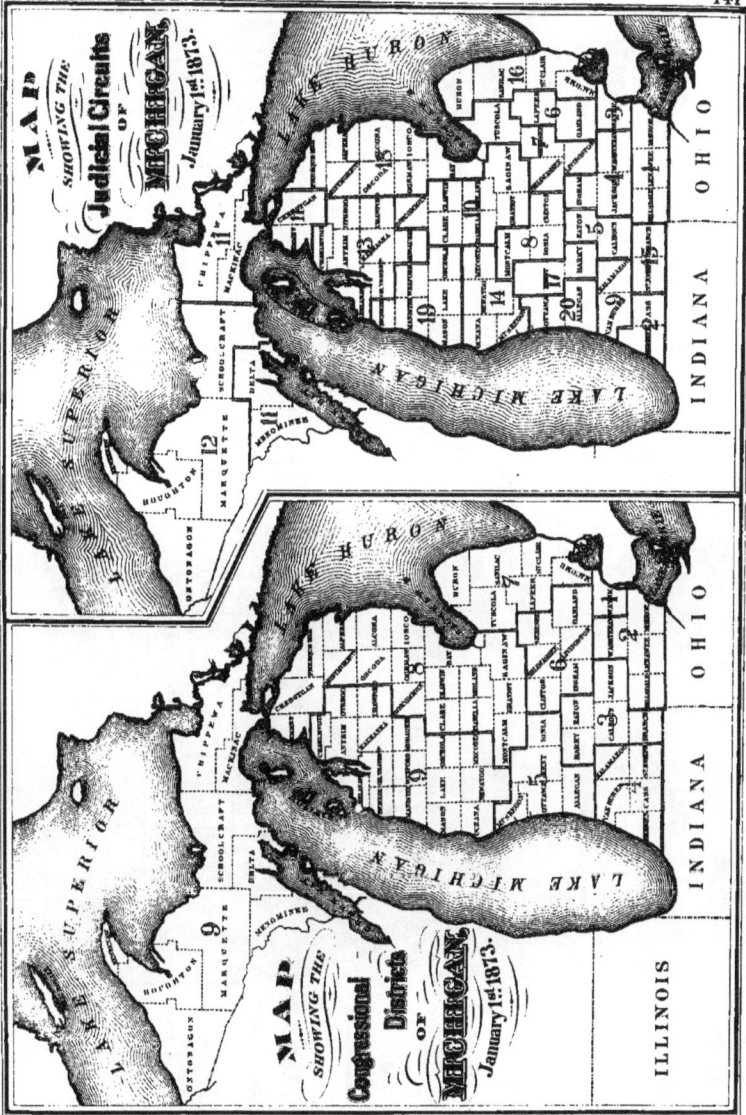

MAP SHOWING THE Judicial Circuits OF MICHIGAN, January 1st 1873.

MAP SHOWING THE Congressional Districts OF MICHIGAN, January 1st 1873.

MAP
SHOWING THE
Representative Districts
OF
MICHIGAN,
January 1st, 1873.

MAP
SHOWING THE
Senatorial Districts
OF
MICHIGAN,
January 1st, 1873.

POPULATION OF THE UNITED STATES AND TERRITORIES, BY COUNTIES.

From the United States Censuses of 1860 and 1870.

ALABAMA.

	1860.	1870.
Autauga	16,739	11,623
Baker	....	6,194
Baldwin	7,530	6,004
Barbour	30,812	29,309
Bibb	11,894	7,469
Blount	10,865	9,945
Bullock	....	24,474
Butler	18,122	14,981
Calhoun	21,539	13,980
Chambers	23,214	17,562
Cherokee	18,360	11,132
Choctaw	13,877	12,676
Clarke	15,049	14,663
Clay	....	9,560
Cleburne	....	8,017
Coffee	9,623	6,171
Colbert	....	12,537
Conecuh	11,311	9,574
Coosa	19,273	11,945
Covington	6,469	4,868
Crenshaw	....	11,156
Dale	12,197	11,325
Dallas	33,625	40,705
De Kalb	10,705	7,126
Elmore	....	14,477
Escambia	....	4,041
Etowah	....	10,109
Fayette	12,850	7,136
Franklin	18,627	8,006
Geneva	....	2,959
Greene	30,859	18,399
Hale	....	21,792
Henry	14,918	14,191
Jackson	18,283	19,410
Jefferson	11,746	12,345
Lauderdale	17,420	15,091
Lawrence	13,975	16,658
Lee	....	21,750
Limestone	15,306	15,017
Lowndes	27,716	25,719
Macon	26,802	17,727
Madison	26,451	31,267
Marengo	31,171	26,151
Marion	11,182	6,059
Marshall	11,472	9,871
Mobile	41,131	49,311
Monroe	15,667	14,214
Montgomery	35,904	43,704
Morgan	11,335	12,187
Perry	27,724	24,975
Pickens	22,316	17,690
Pike	24,435	17,423
Randolph	20,059	12,006
Russell	26,592	21,636
Sanford	....	8,893
Shelby	12,618	12,218
St. Clair	11,013	9,360
Sumpter	24,035	24,109
Talladega	23,520	18,064
Tallapoosa	23,827	16,963
Tuscaloosa	23,200	20,081
Walker	7,980	6,543
Washington	4,669	3,912
Wilcox	24,818	28,377
Winston	3,576	4,155
Total	964,201	996,992

(435,080 *slaves included in the total population for* 1860.)

ARKANSAS.

	1860.	1870.
Arkansas	8,844	8,268
Ashley	8,590	8,042
Benton	9,306	13,831
Boone	....	7,032
Bradley	8,388	8,646
Calhoun	4,103	3,853
Carroll	9,383	5,780
Chicot	9,234	7,214
Clarke	9,735	11,953
Columbia	12,449	11,397
Conway	6,697	8,112
Craighead	3,066	4,577
Crawford	7,850	8,957
Crittenden	4,920	3,831
Cross	....	3,915
Dallas	8,283	5,707
Desha	6,459	6,125
Drew	9,078	9,960
Franklin	7,298	9,627
Fulton	4,024	4,843
Grant	....	3,943
Greene	5,843	7,573
Hempstead	13,989	13,768
Hot Springs	5,635	5,877
Independence	14,307	14,566
Izard	7,215	6,806
Jackson	10,493	7,268
Jefferson	14,971	15,733
Johnson	7,612	9,152
Lafayette	8,464	9,139
Lawrence	9,372	5,981
Little River	....	3,236
Madison	7,740	8,231
Marion	6,192	3,979
Mississippi	3,895	3,633
Monroe	5,657	8,336
Montgomery	3,633	2,984
Newton	3,393	4,374
Ouachita	12,936	12,975
Perry	2,465	2,685
Phillips	14,877	15,372
Pike	4,025	3,788
Poinsett	3,621	1,720
Polk	4,262	3,376
Pope	7,883	8,386
Prairie	8,854	5,604
Pulaski	11,699	32,066
Randolph	6,261	7,466
St. Francis	8,672	6,714
Saline	6,640	3,911
Scott	5,145	7,483
Searcy	5,271	5,614
Sebastian	9,238	12,940
Sevier	10,516	4,492
Sharpe	....	5,400
Union	12,288	10,571
Van Buren	5,357	5,107
Washington	14,673	17,266
White	8,316	10,347
Woodruff	....	6,891
Yell	6,333	8,048
Total	435,450	484,471

(111,115 *slaves included in the total population for* 1860.)

CALIFORNIA.

	1860.	1870.
Alameda	8,927	24,237
Alpine	....	685
Amador	10,930	9,582
Butte	12,106	11,403
Calaveras	16,299	8,895
Colusa	2,274	6,165
Contra Costa	5,328	8,461
Del Norte	1,993	2,022
El Dorado	20,562	10,309
Fresno	4,605	6,336
Humboldt	2,694	6,140
Inyo	....	1,956
Kern	....	2,925
Klamath	1,803	1,686
Lake	....	2,969
Lassen	....	1,327
Los Angeles	11,333	15,309
Marin	3,334	6,903
Mariposa	6,243	4,572
Mendocino	3,969	7,545
Merced	1,141	2,807
Mono	....	430
Monterey	4,739	9,876
Napa	5,521	7,163
Nevada	16,446	19,134
Placer	13,270	11,357
Plumas	4,363	4,489
Sacramento	24,142	26,830
San Bernardino	5,551	3,988
San Diego	4,324	4,951
San Francisco	56,802	149,473
San Joaquin	9,435	21,050
San Luis Obispo	1,782	4,772
San Mateo	3,214	6,635
Santa Barbara	3,543	7,784
Santa Clara	11,912	26,246
Santa Cruz	4,944	8,743
Shasta	4,360	4,173
Sierra	11,387	5,619
Siskiyou	7,629	6,848
Solano	7,169	16,871
Sonoma	11,867	19,819
Stanislaus	2,245	6,499
Sutter	3,390	5,030
Tehama	4,044	3,587
Trinity	5,125	3,213
Tulare	4,638	4,533
Tuolumne	16,229	8,150
Yolo	4,716	9,899
Yuba	13,668	10,851
Total	379,994	560,247

CONNECTICUT.

	1860.	1870.
Fairfield	77,476	95,276
Hartford	89,962	109,007
Litchfield	47,318	48,727
Middlesex	30,859	36,099
New Haven	97,345	121,257
New London	61,731	66,570
Tolland	21,177	22,000
Windham	34,279	38,518
Total	460,147	537,454

DELAWARE.

	1860.	1870.
Kent	27,804	29,804
New Castle	54,797	63,515
Sussex	29,615	31,696
Total	112,216	125,015

(1,798 *slaves included in the total population for* 1860.)

FLORIDA.

	1860.	1870.
Alachua	8,232	17,328
Baker	....	1,325
Bradford	....	3,671
Brevard	246	1,216
Calhoun	1,446	998
Clay	1,914	2,098
Columbia	4,646	7,335
Dade	83	85
Duval	5,074	11,921
Escambia	5,768	7,817
Franklin	1,904	1,256
Gadsden	9,396	9,802
Hamilton	4,154	5,749
Hernando	1,200	2,938
Hillsborough	2,981	3,216
Holmes	1,386	1,572
Jackson	10,209	9,528
Jefferson	9,876	13,398
Lafayette	2,068	1,783
Leon	12,343	15,236
Levy	1,781	2,018
Liberty	1,457	1,050
Madison	7,779	11,121
Manatee	854	1,931
Marion	8,609	10,804
Monroe	2,913	5,657
Nassau	3,644	4,247
New River	3,820	....
Orange	987	2,195
Polk	....	3,169
Putnam	2,712	3,821
Santa Rosa	5,480	3,312
St. John's	3,038	2,618
Sumter	1,549	2,952
Suwannee	2,303	3,556
Taylor	1,384	1,453
Volusia	1,158	1,723
Wakulla	2,839	2,506
Walton	3,037	3,041
Washington	2,154	2,302
Total	140,424	187,748

(61,745 *slaves included in the total population for* 1860.)

GEORGIA.

	1860.	1870.
Appling	4,190	5,086
Baker	4,985	6,843
Baldwin	9,078	10,618
Banks	4,707	4,973
Bartow	....	16,566
Berrien	3,475	4,518
Bibb	16,291	21,255
Brooks	6,356	8,342
Bryan	4,015	5,252
Bulloch	5,668	5,610
Burke	17,165	17,679
Butts	6,455	6,941
Calhoun	4,913	5,503
Camden	5,420	4,615
Campbell	8,301	9,176
Carroll	11,991	11,782
Cass	15,724	....
Catoosa	5,082	4,409
Charlton	1,780	1,897
Chatham	31,043	41,279
Chattahoochee	5,797	6,059
Chattooga	7,165	6,902
Cherokee	11,291	10,399
Clarke	11,218	12,941
Clay	4,893	5,493
Clayton	4,466	5,477
Clinch	3,063	3,945
Cobb	14,242	13,814
Coffee	2,879	3,192
Colquitt	1,316	1,654
Columbia	11,860	13,529
Coweta	14,703	15,875
Crawford	7,693	7,557
Dade	3,069	3,033
Dawson	3,856	4,369
Decatur	11,922	15,183
De Kalb	7,806	10,014
Dooly	8,917	9,790
Dougherty	8,295	11,517
Early	6,149	6,998
Echols	1,491	1,978
Effingham	4,755	4,214
Elbert	10,433	9,249
Emanuel	5,081	6,134
Fannin	5,139	5,429
Fayette	7,047	8,221
Floyd	15,195	17,230
Forsyth	7,749	7,983
Franklin	7,893	7,893
Fulton	14,427	33,446
Gilmer	6,724	6,644
Glascock	2,437	2,736
Glynn	3,889	5,376
Gordon	10,146	9,268
Greene	12,652	12,454
Gwinnett	12,940	12,431
Habersham	5,966	6,322
Hall	9,366	9,607
Hancock	12,044	11,317
Haralson	3,039	4,004
Harris	13,736	13,284
Hart	6,137	6,783
Heard	7,805	7,866
Henry	10,702	10,102
Houston	15,611	20,406
Irwin	1,699	1,837
Jackson	10,605	11,181
Jasper	10,743	10,439
Jefferson	10,219	12,190
Johnson	2,919	2,964
Jones	9,107	9,436
Laurens	6,998	7,834
Lee	7,196	9,567
Liberty	8,367	7,688
Lincoln	5,466	5,413
Lowndes	5,249	8,321
Lumpkin	4,626	5,161
Macon	8,449	11,458
Madison	5,933	5,227
Marion	7,390	8,000
McIntosh	5,546	4,491
Meriwether	15,330	13,756
Miller	1,791	3,091
Milton	4,602	4,284
Mitchell	4,308	6,633
Monroe	15,953	17,213
Montgomery	2,997	3,586
Morgan	9,997	10,696
Murray	7,083	6,500
Muscogee	16,584	16,663
Newton	14,320	14,615
Oglethorpe	11,549	11,782
Paulding	7,038	7,639
Pickens	4,951	5,317
Pierce	1,973	2,778
Pike	10,078	10,905
Polk	6,295	7,822
Pulaski	8,744	11,940
Putnam	10,125	10,461
Quitman	3,499	4,150
Rabun	3,271	3,256
Randolph	9,571	10,561
Richmond	21,284	25,724
Schley	4,633	5,129
Screven	8,274	9,175
Spalding	8,699	10,205
Stewart	13,422	14,204
Sumter	9,428	16,559
Talbot	13,616	11,913
Taliaferro	4,583	4,796
Tattnall	4,352	4,860
Taylor	5,998	7,143
Telfair	2,713	3,245
Terrell	6,232	9,053
Thomas	10,766	14,523
Towns	2,459	2,780
Troup	16,262	17,632
Twiggs	8,320	8,545
Union	4,413	5,267
Upson	9,910	9,430
Walker	10,082	9,925
Walton	11,074	11,038
Ware	2,200	2,286
Warren	9,820	10,545
Washington	12,698	15,842
Wayne	2,268	2,177
Webster	5,030	4,677
White	3,315	4,606
Whitfield	10,047	10,117
Wilcox	2,115	2,439
Wilkes	11,420	11,796
Wilkinson	9,376	9,383
Worth	2,763	3,778
Total	1,057,286	1,184,109

(462,198 *slaves included in the total population for* 1860.)

ILLINOIS.

	1860.	1870.
Adams	41,323	56,367
Alexander	4,707	10,564
Bond	9,815	13,152
Boone	11,678	12,942
Brown	9,938	12,205
Bureau	26,426	32,415
Calhoun	5,144	6,562
Carroll	11,733	16,705
Cass	11,325	11,580
Champaign	14,629	32,737
Christian	10,492	20,363
Clark	14,987	18,719
Clay	9,336	15,875
Clinton	10,941	16,285
Coles	14,203	25,235
Cook	144,954	349,966
Crawford	11,551	13,889
Cumberland	8,311	12,223
De Kalb	19,086	23,265
De Witt	10,820	14,768
Douglas	7,140	13,484
Du Page	14,701	16,685
Edgar	16,925	21,450
Edwards	5,454	7,565
Effingham	7,816	15,653
Fayette	11,189	19,638
Ford	1,979	9,103
Franklin	9,393	12,652
Fulton	33,338	38,291
Gallatin	8,055	11,134
Greene	16,093	20,277
Grundy	10,379	14,938
Hamilton	9,915	13,014
Hancock	29,061	35,935
Hardin	3,759	5,113
Henderson	9,501	12,582
Henry	20,660	35,506
Iroquois	12,325	25,782
Jackson	9,589	19,634
Jasper	8,364	11,234
Jefferson	12,965	17,864
Jersey	12,051	15,054
Jo Daviess	27,325	27,820
Johnson	9,342	11,248
Kane	30,062	39,091
Kankakee	15,412	24,352
Kendall	13,074	12,399
Knox	28,663	39,522
Lake	18,257	21,014
La Salle	48,332	60,792
Lawrence	9,214	12,533
Lee	17,651	27,171
Livingston	11,637	31,471
Logan	14,272	23,053
Macon	13,738	26,481
Macoupin	24,602	32,726
Madison	31,251	44,131
Marion	12,739	20,622
Marshall	13,437	16,956
Mason	10,931	16,184
Massac	6,213	9,581
McDonough	20,069	26,509
McHenry	22,089	23,762
McLean	28,772	53,988
Menard	9,584	11,735
Mercer	15,042	18,769
Monroe	12,832	12,982
Montgomery	13,979	25,314
Morgan	22,112	28,463
Moultrie	6,385	10,385
Ogle	22,888	27,492
Peoria	36,601	47,540
Perry	9,552	13,723
Piatt	6,127	10,953
Pike	27,249	30,768
Pope	6,742	11,437
Pulaski	3,943	8,752
Putnam	5,587	6,280
Randolph	17,205	20,859
Richland	9,711	12,803
Rock Island	21,005	29,783
Saline	9,331	12,714
Sangamon	32,274	46,352
Schuyler	14,684	17,419
Scott	9,069	10,530
Shelby	14,613	25,476
Stark	9,004	10,751
St. Clair	37,694	51,068
Stephenson	25,112	30,608
Tazewell	21,470	27,903
Union	11,181	16,518
Vermilion	19,800	30,388
Wabash	7,313	8,841
Warren	18,336	23,174
Washington	13,731	17,599
Wayne	12,223	19,758
White	12,403	16,846
Whiteside	18,737	27,503
Will	29,321	43,013
Williamson	12,205	17,329
Winnebago	24,491	29,301
Woodford	13,282	18,956
Total	1,711,951	2,539,891

INDIANA.

	1860.	1870.
Adams	9,252	11,382
Allen	29,328	43,494
Bartholomew	17,865	21,133
Benton	2,809	5,615
Blackford	4,122	6,272
Boone	16,753	22,593
Brown	6,507	8,681
Carroll	13,489	16,152
Cass	16,843	24,193
Clarke	20,502	24,770
Clay	12,161	19,084
Clinton	14,505	17,330
Crawford	8,226	9,851
Daviess	13,323	16,747
Dearborn	24,406	24,116
Decatur	17,294	19,053
De Kalb	13,880	17,167
Delaware	15,753	19,030
Dubois	10,394	12,597
Elkhart	20,986	26,026
Fayette	10,225	10,476
Floyd	20,183	23,300
Fountain	15,566	16,389
Franklin	19,549	20,223
Fulton	9,422	12,726
Gibson	14,532	17,371
Grant	15,797	18,487
Greene	16,041	19,514
Hamilton	17,310	20,882
Hancock	12,802	15,123
Harrison	18,521	19,913
Hendricks	16,953	20,277
Henry	20,119	22,986
Howard	12,524	15,847
Huntington	14,867	19,036
Jackson	16,286	18,974
Jasper	4,291	6,354
Jay	11,399	15,000
Jefferson	25,036	29,741
Jennings	14,749	16,218
Johnson	14,854	18,366
Knox	16,056	21,562
Kosciusko	17,418	23,531
La Grange	11,366	14,148
Lake	9,145	12,339
La Porte	22,919	27,062
Lawrence	13,692	14,628
Madison	16,518	22,770
Marion	39,855	71,939
Marshall	12,722	20,211
Martin	8,975	11,103
Miami	16,851	21,052
Monroe	12,847	14,168
Montgomery	20,888	23,765
Morgan	16,110	17,528
Newton	2,360	5,829
Noble	14,915	20,389
Ohio	5,462	5,837
Orange	12,076	13,497
Owen	14,376	16,137
Parke	15,538	18,166
Perry	11,847	14,801
Pike	10,078	13,779
Porter	10,313	13,942
Posey	16,167	19,185
Pulaski	5,711	7,801
Putnam	20,681	21,514
Randolph	18,997	22,862
Ripley	19,054	20,977
Rush	16,193	17,626
Scott	7,303	7,873
Shelby	19,569	21,892
Spencer	14,556	17,998
Starke	2,195	3,888
Steuben	10,374	12,854
St. Joseph	18,455	25,322
Sullivan	15,064	18,453
Switzerland	12,698	12,134
Tippecanoe	25,726	33,515
Tipton	8,170	11,953
Union	7,109	6,341
Vanderburgh	20,552	33,145
Vermillion	9,422	10,840
Vigo	22,517	33,549
Wabash	17,547	21,305
Warren	10,057	10,204
Warrick	13,261	17,653
Washington	17,909	18,495
Wayne	29,558	34,048
Wells	10,844	13,585
White	8,258	10,554
Whitley	10,730	14,399
Total	1,350,428	1,680,637

IOWA.

	1860.	1870.
Adair	984	3,982
Adams	1,533	4,614
Allamakee	12,237	17,868
Appanoose	11,931	16,456
Audubon	454	1,212
Benton	8,496	22,454
Black Hawk	8,244	21,706
Boone	4,232	14,584
Bremer	4,915	12,528
Buchanan	7,906	17,034
Buena Vista	57	1,585
Butler	3,724	9,951
Calhoun	147	1,602
Carroll	281	2,451
Cass	1,612	5,464
Cedar	12,949	19,731
Cerro Gordo	940	4,722
Cherokee	58	1,967
Chickasaw	4,336	10,180
Clarke	5,427	8,735
Clay	52	1,523
Clayton	20,728	27,771
Clinton	18,938	35,357
Crawford	383	2,530
Dallas	5,244	12,019
Davis	13,764	15,565
Decatur	8,677	12,018
Delaware	11,024	17,432
Des Moines	19,611	27,256
Dickinson	180	1,389
Dubuque	31,164	38,969
Emmett	105	1,392
Fayette	12,073	16,973
Floyd	3,744	10,768
Franklin	1,309	4,738
Fremont	5,074	11,174
Greene	1,374	4,627
Grundy	793	6,399
Guthrie	3,058	7,061
Hamilton	1,699	6,055
Hancock	179	999
Hardin	5,440	13,684
Harrison	3,621	8,931
Henry	18,701	21,463
Howard	3,168	6,282
Humboldt	332	2,596
Ida	43	226
Iowa	8,029	16,644
Jackson	18,493	22,619
Jasper	9,883	22,116
Jefferson	15,038	17,839
Johnson	17,573	24,898
Jones	13,306	19,731
Keokuk	13,271	19,434
Kossuth	416	3,351
Lee	29,232	37,210
Linn	18,947	28,852
Louisa	10,370	12,877
Lucas	5,766	10,388
Lyon	....	221
Madison	7,339	13,884
Mahaska	14,816	22,508
Marion	16,813	24,436
Marshall	6,015	17,576
Mills	4,481	8,718
Mitchell	3,409	9,582
Monona	832	3,654
Monroe	8,612	12,724
Montgomery	1,256	5,934
Muscatine	16,444	21,688
O'Brien	8	715
Osceola	....	....
Page	4,419	9,975
Palo Alto	132	1,336
Plymouth	148	2,199
Pocahontas	103	1,446
Polk	11,625	27,857
Pottawattamie	4,968	16,893
Poweshiek	5,668	15,581
Ringgold	2,923	5,691
Sac	246	1,411
Scott	25,959	38,599
Shelby	818	2,540
Sioux	10	576
Story	4,051	11,651
Tama	5,285	16,131
Taylor	3,590	6,989
Union	2,012	5,986
Van Buren	17,081	17,672
Wapello	14,518	22,346
Warren	10,281	17,980
Washington	14,235	18,952
Wayne	6,409	11,287
Webster	2,504	10,484
Winnebago	168	1,562
Winneshiek	13,942	23,570
Woodbury	1,119	6,172
Worth	756	2,892
Wright	653	2,392
Total	674,913	1,191,792

KANSAS.

	1860.	1870.
Allen	3,082	7,022
Anderson	2,400	5,220
Atchison	7,729	15,507
Barton	....	2
Bourbon	6,101	15,076
Breckenridge	3,197	....
Brown	2,607	6,823
Butler	437	3,035
Chase	808	1,975
Cherokee	....	11,038
Clay	163	2,942
Cloud	....	2,323
Coffey	2,842	6,201
Cowley	....	1,175
Crawford	....	8,160
Davis	1,163	5,526
Dickinson	378	3,043
Doniphan	8,083	13,969
Dorn	88	....
Douglas	8,637	20,592
Ellis	....	1,336
Ellsworth	....	1,185
Ford	....	427
Franklin	3,030	10,385
Godfrey	19	....
Greenwood	760	3,484
Howard	....	2,794
Hunter	152	....
Jackson	1,936	6,053
Jefferson	4,459	12,526
Jewell	....	207
Johnson	4,364	13,684
Labette	....	9,973
Leavenworth	12,606	32,444
Lincoln	....	516
Linn	6,336	12,174
Lykins	4,980	....
Lyon	....	8,014
Madison	636	....
Marion	74	768
Marshall	2,280	6,901
McGhee	1,501	....
McPherson	....	738
Miami	....	11,725
Mitchell	....	485
Montgomery	....	7,564
Morris	770	2,225
Nemaha	2,436	7,339
Neosho	....	10,206
Ness	....	2
Osage	1,113	7,648
Osborne	....	33
Otoe	238	....
Ottawa	....	2,127
Pawnee	....	179

	1860.	1870.

KENTUCKY.

LOUISIANA.

MAINE.

MARYLAND.

MASSACHUSETTS.

MICHIGAN.

MINNESOTA.

MISSISSIPPI.

MISSOURI.

NEBRASKA.

NEVADA.

NEW HAMPSHIRE.

NEW JERSEY.

NEW YORK.

	1880.	1870.

NORTH CAROLINA.

OHIO.

OREGON.

PENNSYLVANIA.

RHODE ISLAND.

SOUTH CAROLINA.

TENNESSEE.

TEXAS.

VERMONT.

VIRGINIA.

WEST VIRGINIA.*

WISCONSIN.

*In 1863 organized from Virginia.

POPULATION OF THE PRINCIPAL TOWNS AND CITIES OF THE UNITED STATES AND TERRITORIES.

EXPLANATION:—State Capitals thus, as **Harrisburg**. Other cities, as Philadelphia. Towns in Italics, as *Easton*.

LIST OF

CITIES, TOWNS AND VILLAGES IN MICHIGAN,

STATING MEANS OF ACCESS, APPROXIMATE NUMBERS OF POPULATION, ETC.

EXPLANATION.

Names of County Seats are given in full-faced type, thus,—**Adrian.** If a City, the word City is added. Cities which are *not* County Seats in small caps, thus,—BATTLE CREEK. P. O. denotes Post Office. Money Order Post Office, thus,—P. O. R. R. Sta. denotes Railroad Station. Tel. Sta., Telegraph Station. Ldg. Landing. In the second column will be found the abbreviated name of the most accessible Railroad, or the full name of the nearest Lake or navigable River, in case there is no railroad within convenient distance. The third column gives the nearest Railroad Station or Landing with its distance in miles (m.) The fourth and fifth columns give the Township and County in which the place is located, and the sixth column the estimated population, taken, by permission, from the new State Directory. The seventh column indicates the page where the place will be found in the Atlas. Names of Railroads are abbreviated as follows:

Chicago and Canada Southern Railroad,	Chi. & Can. So. R. R.
Chicago and Michigan Lake Shore Railroad,	Chi. & Mich. L. Shore R. R.
Grand Rapids Division,	Gr. R. Div.
Chicago and Northwestern Railroad	Chi. & N. W. R. R.
Detroit and Bay City Railroad,	Det. & B. City R. R.
Detroit, Hillsdale and Indiana Railroad,	Det., Hill. and Ind. R. R.
Detroit, Lansing and Lake Michigan Railroad,	Det., L. & L. M. R. R.
Ionia and Stanton Branch,	I. & S. Br.
Detroit and Milwaukee Railroad,	Det. & Mil. R. R.
Flint & Pere Marquette R.W. (including Ludg, Wayne & Sta.)	F. & P. M. R. W.
Bay City Division,	B. City Div.
Otter Lake Branch,	Ot. Lake Br.
Fort Wayne, Jackson and Saginaw Railroad,	Ft. W., J. & S. R. R.
Grand Rapids and Indiana Railroad,	Gr. R. and Ind. R. R.
Traverse City Branch,	Trav. City Br.
Grand Rapids, Greenville and Alpena Railroad,	Gr. Rap., G. & A. R. R.
Grand Rapids, Newaygo and Lake Shore Railroad,	Gr. Rap. N. & L. S. R. R.
Grand Trunk Railway,	G. T. R. W.
Lake Shore and Michigan Southern Railway,	L. S. & M. S. R. W.
Detroit Division,	Det. Div.
Kalamazoo Division,	Kal. Div.
Jackson Branch,	Jack. Br.
Lansing Division,	
Lapeer and Northern Railroad	Lap. & N. R. R.
Mansfield, Coldwater and Lake Michigan Railroad,	M., Cold. & L. M. R. R.
Marshall and Coldwater Railroad,	Mar. & Cold. R. R.
Marquette, Houghton and Ontonagon Railroad,	Marq., H. & Ont. R. R.
Michigan Air Line Railroad,	Mich. Air L. R. R.
Michigan Central Railroad,	Mich. Cent. R. R.
Grand River Valley Division,	Gr. R. Val. Div.
Jackson Landing and Saginaw Division,	J. L. & S. Div.
Air Line Division,	Air L. Div.
Kalamazoo and South Haven Division,	Kal. & S. Hav. Div.
South Bend Division,	S. Bend Div.
Michigan and Lake Shore Railroad,	Mich. L. Sh. R. R.
Muskegon and Big Rapids Railroad,	Mus. & Big Rap. R. R.
Owosso and Northwestern Railroad,	Ow. & N. W. R. R.
Paw Paw Railroad,	Paw Paw R. R.
Peninsular Railway,	Penin. R. W.
Port Huron and Lake Michigan Railroad,	P. H. & L. M. R. R.
Saginaw Valley and Saint Louis Railroad,	Sag. Val. & St. L. R. R.
Saint Clair and Chicago Air Line Railroad,	St. Cl. & C. Air L. R. R.
Toledo and Ann Arbor Railroad,	Tol. & Ann Ar. R. R.
Toledo, Canada Southern and Detroit Railway,	Tol., Can. S. & Det. R. W.
Lans. Div.	
Lap. & N. R. R.	

Name of Village.	Railroad, Lake or River.	Nearest Station or Landing.	Township.	County.	Pop.	Page.
Abronia, P. O. & R. R. Sta.,	L. S. & M. S. R. R., (Kal. Div.,)		Watson,	Allegan,	50	96
Abbotsford, (Ibsby P. O.,)	P. H. & L. M. R. R.,	Thornton, 5 m.,	Clyde,	St. Clair,		88
Abscota, P. O.,	Mass., Cold. & L. Mich. R. R.,	Burlington, 5 m.,	Burlington,	Calhoun,		106
Acme, P. O. & Landing,	Gr. Rap. & Ind. (Trav. City Br.,)	Traverse City, 7 m.,	East Bay, Whitewater,	G'd Traverse,	50	60
Ada, P. O. & R. R. Sta.,	Det. & Mil. R. R.,		Ada,	Kent,	800	94
Adamsville, P. O.,	Peninsular R. W.,	Edwardsburg, 4 m.,	Ontwa,	Cass,		110
Addison, P. O.,	Det., Hills. & Ind. R. R.,	Woodstock, 9 m.,	Rollin & Woodstock,	Lenawee,	400	114
Adrian, P. O., R. R. & Tel. Sta.,			Adrian & Madison,	Lenawee,	10,072	114
Advance, P. O.,	Gr. Rap. & Ind. R. R.,		Evangeline,	Charlevoix,		57
Ætna, P. O.,	Mus. & Big Rap. R. R.,	Fremont, 10 m.,	Denver,	Newaygo,	80	79
Agate Harbor,	Lake Superior,		Sibley,	Keweenaw,		118
Akron, P. O.,	Saginaw Bay,	Wisner, 8 m.,	Akron,	Tuscola,		85
Alabaster, P. O., Tel. Sta. & Landing,	Lake Huron,		Alabaster,	Iosco,	400	65
Alamo, R. R. Sta.,	Mich. Cent. R. R., (Kal. & S. Hav. Div.,)		Alamo,	Kalamazoo,	50	107
Alamo Centre, P. O.,	Mich. Cent. R. R. (Kal. & S. Hav. Div.,)	Alamo, 1 m.,	Alamo,	Kalamazoo,		107
Alaska, P. O.,	Mich. Cent. R. R., (G'd Riv. Val. Div.,)	Caledonia, 5 m.,	Caledonia,	Kent,	400	94
Albion, P. O., R. R. & Tel. Sta.,	Mich. Cent. R. R., L. S. & M. S., (Lans. Div.,)		Sheridan, Albion,	Calhoun,	2,100	106
Alcona, P. O., Tel. Sta. & Landing,	Lake Huron,		Alcona,	Alcona,	200	64
Alganee, P. O.,	L. S. & M. S. R. W.,	Quincy, 4 m.,	Algansee,	Branch,		112
Algansee, R. R. Sta.,	M., Cold. & L. M R R		Algansee,	Branch,		112
Algodon, P. O.,	Det. & Mil. R. R.,	Saranac, 7 m.,	Odessa,	Ionia,		98
Algoma Centre,	Gr. Rap. & Ind. R. R.,	Edgerton, 1 m.,	Algoma,	Kent,		94
Algonac, P. O., Tel. Sta. & Landing,	River St. Clair,		Clay,	St. Clair,	700	68
Alice, P. O.,	Chi. & Mich. L. Shore R. R.,	Greenwood, 2 m.,	Grant,	Oceana,		80
Allegan, P. O., R. R. & Tel. Sta.,	L. S. & M. S. (Kal. Div.) Kal. L. S. & M. S. R. R.,		Allegan,	Allegan,	2,500	96
Allen, P. O.,	L. S. & M. S. R. W.,	Allen, 1 m.,	Allen,	Hillsdale,	600	113
Allen Creek, P. O.,	Chi. & Mich. L. S., Flint & Pere Marquette R.W.,	Pentwater, 19 m.,	Colfax,	Oceana,	72	80
Allendale, P. O.,	Chi. & Mich. L. S. R. R.,	Robinson, 7 m.,	Allendale,	Ottawa,		95
Allens, P. O.,	Mich. Cent. R. R. (G. R. Val. Div.,)		Chester,	Eaton,		98
Allen Station, R. R. & Tel. Sta.,	L. S. & M. S. R. W.,		Allen,	Hillsdale,		113
Alleytown, R. R. Sta.,	Mus. & Big Rap. R. R.,		Everett,	Newaygo,		79
Alma, P. O.,	Sag. Val. & St. L. R. R.,		Pine River, Arcada,	Gratiot,		89
Almar,	Chi. & Mich. L. S. R. R.,	Norton, 5 m.,	Egelston,	Muskegon,		81
Almena, P. O.,	Mich. Cent. R. R.,	Paw Paw, 5 m.,	Almena,	Van Buren,	500	108
Almira, P. O.,	Gr. R. & Ind. R. R. (Trav. City Br.,)	Traverse City, 14 m.,	Almira,	Benzie,	500	59
Almont, P. O.,	St. C. & C. Air L. R. R.,	Romeo, 6 m.,	Almont,	Lapeer,	1,000	69
Alpena, P. O., R. R. Sta. & Landing,	Lake Huron,		Alpena,	Alpena,	3,500	54
Alpine, P. O.,	Gr. Rap., R. & L. S. R. R.,		Alpine,	Kent,	500	94
Alto, P. O.,	Det. & Mil. R. R.,	Lowell, 6 m.,	Bowne,	Kent,		94
Alton, P. O.,	Det. & Mil. R. R.,	Lowell, 6 m.,	Vergennes,	Kent,		94
Alton,	Mich. Cent. R. R. (J. L. & S. Div.,)	Bennington, 5 m.,	Bennington,	Shiawassee,		91
Altona, P. O.,	Gr. Rap. & Ind. R. R.,	Stanwood, 9 m.,	Hinton,	Mecosta,	75	78

Name of Village.	Railroad, Lake or River.	Nearest Station or Landing.	Township.	County.	Pop.	Pop.
Alverson, P. O.,	Det. L. & L. M. R. R.,	Williamstown, 6 m.,	Williamstown,	Ingham,		96
Amadore, P. O.,	Lake Huron,	Stevens's Landing, 4 m.,	Worth,	Sanilac,		87
Amber, P. O. & R. R. Sta.,	F. & P. M. R. W.,		Amber,	Mason,		70
Amboy, P. O.,	M., Cold. & L. M. R. R.,	Pioneer, 2 m.,	Amboy,	Hillsdale,		113
Amsden, P. O.,	Det., L. & L. Mich. R. R., (L. & S. Br.,)	Fenwicks, 3 m.,	Fair Plain,	Montcalm,	100	82
Anderson's Settlement,	Det. & Mil. R. R.,	Davisburgh, 3 m.,	Springfield,	Oakland,		101
Andersonville,	Penin. R. R., Mich. Cent. R. R., (Air Line Div.,)	Cassopolis, 1 m.,	La Grange,	Cass,		110
Ann Arbor City, P. O., R. R. & Tel. Sta.,	Mich. Cent. R. R.,		Ann Arbor,	Washtenaw,	8,500	104
Antrim City, P. O. & Landing,	Lake Michigan,		Banks,	Antrim,	200	87
Arbela, P. O.,	F. & P. M. R. W.,	County Line Sta., 5 m.,	Arbela,	Tuscola,		85
Arenac, P. O. & Tel. Sta.,	Mich. Cent. R. R. (J. L. & S. Div.,)	Sodus, 4 m.,	Arenac,	Bay,		75
Argenta Sta. Silver Creek P. O.,	L. Shore & Mich. Southern. R. W., (Kal. Div.,)		Cooper,	Kalamazoo,		
Argentine, P. O.,	Det. & Mil. R. R.,	Linden, 4 m.,	Argentine,	Genesee,	200	90
Arland, P. O. & R. R. Sta.,	Mich. Cent. R. R., (Gr. Riv. Val. Div.,)		Jackson,	Jackson,		105
Arlington, P. O.,	Chi. & Mich. Lake Shore R. R.,	Deerfield, 4 m.,	Arlington,	Van Buren,		108
Armada, P. O., R. R. & Tel. Sta.,	Gr. Bap. & Ind. R. R.,		Armada,	Macomb,	500	102
Ashland, R. R. Sta.,	Gr. Rap., New. & Lake Shore R. R.,		Ashland,	Newaygo,		75
Ashley, P. O.,	Gr. Rap., Greenville & Alpena R. R.,	Gould's Mills, 4 m.,	Oatfield, Gratiot,	Kent,		94
Ashton, P. O. & R. R. Sta.,	Gr. Rap. & Ind. R. R.,		Lincoln,	Osceola,	100	72
Assyria, P. O.,	Peninsular R. R.,	Bellevue, 5 m.,	Assyria,	Barry,	50	97
Athens, P. O.,	Mich. Cent. R. R., (Air Line Div.,)	Union, 5 m.,	Calhoun,	Calhoun,	800	108
Atbison, P. O.,	F. & P. M. R. W.,	Grafton, 3 m.,	Ash,	Monroe,		115
Atlas, P. O.,	F. & P. M. R. W.,	Grand Blanc, 5 m.,	Atlas,	Genesee,	200	90
Attica, P. O., R. R. & Tel. Sta.,	F. H. & L. M. R. R.,		Attica,	Lapeer,	600	89
Atwood, P. O.,	Lake Michigan,	Antrim City, 1 m.,	Banks,	Antrim,		87
Auburn, R. R. Sta.,	St. C. & Co., Air Line R. R.,		Pontiac,	Oakland,		101
Au Gres, P. O. & Landing,	Saginaw Bay,		Au Gres,	Bay,	200	75
Augusta, P. O., R. R. & Tel. Sta.,	Mich. Cent. & Mass. & Cold. & L. Mich. R. R.,		Ross,	Kalamazoo,	608	107
Aurelius, P. O.,	Mich. Cent. R. R., (J. L. & S. Div.,)	Chapin's, 5 m.,	Aurelius,	Ingham,	300	99
Au Sable, P. O., Tel. Sta. & Landing,	Lake Huron,		Sable,	Iosco,	2,000	65
Austerlitz, P. O.,	Gr. Rap. & 2nd. R. R.,	Belmont, 2 m.,	Plainfield,	Kent,	200	94
Austin, R. R. Sta.,	Gr. Rap. & 2nd. R. R.,		Portage,	Kalamazoo,		107
Austin, P. O.,	Det. & Mil. R. R.,	Davisburg, 3 m.,	Springfield, Oakland,	Oakland,	100	101
Averill, R. R. & Tel. Sta., (Averill's Sta. P. O.,)	Flint & P. M. R. W.,		Lincoln,	Midland,	150	76
Avery, P. O. & R. R. Sta.,	Mich. Cent. R. R.,		Galien,	Berrien,	150	109
Bad Axe, P. O.,	Lake Huron,	Port Crescent, 15 m.,	Verona, Colfax,	Huron,	87	86
Bad River, P. O.,	Saginaw Val. & St. Louis R. R.,	Wheeler, 12 m.,	Hamilton,	Gratiot,		83
Bailey, P. O.,				Muskegon,		81
Bainbridge, P. O.,	Chi. & Mich. Lake Shore R. R.,	Watervliet, 6 m.,	Bainbridge,	Berrien,		109
Bakerstown,	Mich. Cent. R. R.,	Buchanan, 3 m.,	Bertrand,	Berrien,		109
Baldwin, P. O. & R. R. Sta.,	F. & P. M. R. W.,		Pleasant Plains,	Lake,		71
Baldwin Mills, P. O., R. R. & Tel. Sta.,	Fl. W., J. & S. R. R.,		Hanover,	Jackson,	250	105
Baltimore, P. O.,	Mich. Cent. R. R., (Gr. Riv. Val. Div.,)	Quincy, 7 m.,	Baltimore,	Barry,		97
Baltimore Mills,	Mich. Cent. R. R. (Gr. Riv. Val. Div.,)	Quincy, 6 m.,	Baltimore,	Barry,		97
Bancroft, R. R. S.,	Marq., H. & Ont. R. R.,		Marquette,	Marquette,		119
Bangor, P. O., R. R. & Tel. Sta.,	Chi. & Mich. L. Shore R. R.,	Bangor, ,	Bangor,	Van Buren,	450	108
Banker Sta., P. O., R. R. & Tel. Sta.,	Det., Hills. & Ind. R. R. & Ft. W., J. & S. R. R.,		Cambria,	Hillsdale,	75	114
Banks, P. O., (Bangor)	Mich. Cent. R. R., (J. L. & S. Div.,)	Wenona, 3 m.,	Bangor,	Bay,		75
Baraga, P. O.,	Marq., H. & Ont. R. R.,	L'Anse, 2 m.,	Baraga,	Houghton,	75	117
Barnard, P. O.,	Lake Michigan,	Charlevoix, 6 m.,	Marion,	Charlevoix,		57
Barton Lake, R. R. Sta.,	Mich. Cent. R. R., (Air Line Div.,)		Howard,	Cass,		110
Barrett, R. R. Sta.,	Chi. & Mich. L. Shore R. R.,		Shelby,	Oceana,		80
Barryville, P. O.,	Mich. Cent. R. R., (Gr. Riv. Val. Div.,)	Sheridan, 1 m.,	Castleton,	Barry,	100	97
Base Lake, P. O., (Hudson Mills)	Mich. Cent. R. R.,	Dexter, 4 m.,	Dexter,	Washtenaw,	75	104
Batavia, P. O. & R. R. Sta.,	L. Shore & Mich. Southern R. W.,		Batavia,	Branch,		112
Batavia Centre, P. O.,	L. Shore & Mich. Southern R. W.,	Batavia, 3 m.,	Batavia,	Branch,		112
Bath, P. O. & R. R. Sta.,	Mich. Cent. R. R.,		Bath,	Clinton,	205	93
Bath Mills, R. R. Sta.,	Mich. Cent. R. R.,		Concord,	Jackson,		92
Battle Creek, P. O., R. R. & Tel. Sta.,	Mich. Cent. R. R., L. Col. & L. S. R. R., Peila. R. R.,		Battle Creek, Bedford,	Calhoun,	6,000	106
Bay City, P. O., R. R. & Tel. Sta.,	Det. & Bay City R. R.,		Bay City,	Bay,	10,000	75
Bayport, P. O. & Landing,	Saginaw Bay,	Caseville, Fair Haven,	Hamilton,	Huron,	90	86
Bay Siding, R. R. Sta.,	Ch. & N. W. R. W., (Pen. Div.,)		Escanaba,	Delta,		120
Beechville, North Branch P. O.,	Lapeer & Northern R. R.,	Fish Lake, 10 m.,	North Branch,	Lapeer,		89
Bear Lake, P. O.,	Lake Michigan,	Pierport, 6 m.,	Bear Lake,	Manistee,		59
Bear Lake Mills, P. O. & R. R. Sta.,	Mich. Cent. R. R., (K. & S. H. Div.,)		Columbia, Bloomingdale,	Van Buren,	100	108
Bear River, P. O. & R. R. Sta.,	Gr. Rapids & Ind. R. R.,		Bear Creek,	Emmet,	50	51
Beaver, R. R. Sta.,	Ch. & N. W. R. W., (Pen. Div.,)		Baldwin,	Delta,		120
Beaver, P. O.,	Musk. & Big Rap. R. R.,	Fremont, 20 m.,	Denver,	Newaygo,		79
Beaver Creek, P. O.,	Sag. Val. & St. Louis R. R.,	St. Louis, 12 m.,	Seville,	Gratiot,	100	82
Bedford, P. O.,	Mich. Cent. R. R., L. Col. & L. S. R. R., Peila. R. R.,	Bedford, 5 m.,	Bedford,	Calhoun,	300	106
Bedford, R. R. Sta.,	Mich. Cent., R. R., Mass., Cold. & L. Mich. R. R.,		Bedford,	Calhoun,		106
Beech, P. O., (Fisher's Sta.),	Det., L. & L. Mich. R. R.,		Bedford,	Wayne,	50	103
Beldeo, P. O.,	F. & P. M. R. W.,	Walz, 2 m.,	Sumpter, Huron,	Wayne,		103
Belding, P. O.,	Det., Lans. & L. Mich. R. R.,	Kiddville, 2 m.,	Otisco,	Ionia,		93
Belle River, P. O.,	F. H. & L. M. R. R.,	Capac, 4 m.,	Berlin,	St. Clair,		88
Bellevue, P. O. & R. R. & Tel. Sta.,	Peninsular R. W.,		Bellevue,	Eaton,	700	98
Bellville, P. O.,	Mich. Cent. R. R.,	Denton, 4 m.,	Van Buren,	Wayne,	500	103
Belmont, P. O. & R. R. Sta.,	Gr. Rap. & Ind. R. R.,		Plainfield,	Kent,	100	94
Belvidere,	Grand Trunk R. W.,	Mt. Clemens, 6 m.,	Harrison,	Macomb,		102
Bengal, P. O.,	Det. & Mil. R. R.,	Fowler, 4 m.,	Bengal,	Clinton,		92
Bennington, P. O. & R. R. Sta.,	Mich. Cent. R. R., (J. L. & S. Div.,)		Bennington,	Shiawassee,	100	91
Benona, P. O.,	Chi. & Mich. L. Shore R. R.,	New Era, 6 m.,	Benona,	Oceana,	200	80
Benson, P. O.,	Det., Hills. & Ind. R. R.,	Salina, 4 m.,	Salina,	Washtenaw,		104
Benton Harbor, P. O., R. R. & Tel. Sta.,	Chi. & Mich. L. Shore R. R.,		Benton,	Berrien,	1,200	109
Benzonia, P. O.,	Lake Michigan,	Frankfort, 7 m.,	Benzonia,	Benzie,	250	59
Berlin, P. O., R. R. & Tel. Sta.,	Det. & Mil. R. R.,		Wright,	Ottawa,	300	95
Berrien Centre, P. O.,	Mich. Cent. R. R.,	Niles, 9 m.,	Berrien,	Berrien,		109
Berrien Springs, P. O. & Tel. Sta.,	Mich. Cent. R. R.,	Niles, 12 m.,	Oronoko,	Berrien,	800	109
Bertrand, P. O., R. R. & Tel. Sta.,	Mich. Cent. R. R., (South Bend Div.,)		Bertrand,	Berrien,	300	109
Berville, P. O., (Baker's Corner,)	F. H. & L. M. R. R.,	Capac, 9 m.,	Berlin,	St. Clair,	50	88
Bethel, P. O.,	L. Shore & Mich. Southern R. W.,	Batavia, 5 m.,	Bethel,	Branch,		112
Big Beaver, P. O.,	Det. & Mil. R. R.,	Birmingham, 5 m.,	Troy,	Oakland,		101
Big Prairie, P. O.,	Musk. & Big Rap. R. R.,	Morganville, 4 m.,	Big Prairie,	Newaygo,		79
Big Rapids P. O., R. R. & Tel. Sta.,	Gr. Rap. & Ind. R. R., Musk. & Big Rap. R. R.,		Big Rapids,	Mecosta,	3,000	78
Big Springs, P. O.,	Det. & Mil. R. R.,	Berlin, 3 m.,	Wright,	Ottawa,		95
Birch Run, P. O., R. R. & Tel. Sta.,	Flint & P. M. R. W.,		Birch Run,	Saginaw,	200	84
Bird, P. O.,	Chi. & Mich. L. Shore R. R.,	Hart Sta., 15 m.,	Leavitt,	Oceana,		80
Birmingham, P. O., R. R. & Tel. Sta.,	Det. & Mil. R. R.,	Bloomfield,	Birmingham,	Oakland,	700	101
Bismarck, P. O.,	Mass., Cold. & L. Mich. R. R.,		Sunfield,	Eaton,		98
Blackberry Ridge, P. O.,	Chi. & Mich. L. Shore R. R.,	Collins, 6 m.,	Benona,	Oceana,		80
Black Lake, P. O., (Lake Sta.,)	Mich. L. Shore R. R.,		Norton,	Muskegon,		81
Black River R. R. Sta.,	Chi. & Mich. L. Shore R. R.,		Lee,	Allegan,		96

Name of Village.	Railroad, Lake or River.	Nearest Station or Landing.	Township.	County.	Pop.	Page
Blair, P. O.,	Mich. Cent. R. R., (Gr. Riv. Val. Div.),	Nashville, 6 m.,	Woodland, Castleton,	Barry,		97
Blendon, P. O.,	Chi. & Mich. L. & R. R., (Gr. Rap. Div.),	Hudson, 6 m.,	Blendon,	Ottawa,		95
Blendon Station, P. O. & D. R. Sta.,	Chi. & Mich. L. & R. R.,		Olive,	Ottawa,		95
Blissfield, P. O., R. R. & Tel. Sta.,	L. S. & Mich. Southern R. W.,		Blissfield,	Lenawee,	1,000	114
Bloomer Centre, P. O.,	Det., Lans. & L. Mich. R. R., (Stanton Br.,)	Fenwicks, 9 m.,	Bloomer,	Montcalm,		92
Bloomfield Centre,	Det. & Mil. R. R.,	Birmingham, 3 m.,	Bloomfield,	Oakland,		101
Bloomingdale, P. O., R. R. & Tel. Sta.,	Mich. Cent. R. R., (K. & S. H. Div.,)		Bloomingdale,	Van Buren,	300	108
Blufton, P. O.,	Chi. & Mich. L. S. R. R., Mich. L. S. R. R.,	Muskegon, 4 m.,	Laketon,	Muskegon,	500	91
Blumfield, P. O.,	Det. & Bay City R. R.,	Reese, 6 m.,	Blumfield,	Saginaw,		84
Blumfield Junction, P. O.,	Det. & Bay City R. R.,	Reese, 7 m.,	Blumfield,	Saginaw,		84
Bond's Mills, P. O. & R. R. Sta.,	Gr. Rap. & Ind. R. R.,		Cedar Creek,	Wexford,		99
Bostwick Lake, P. O.,	Gr. Rap., Greenville & Alpena R. R.,	Cortland Sta., 5 m.,	Cannon,	Kent,		94
Bowen, (Bowen Sta. P. O.,) R. R. Sta.,	Mich. Cent. R. R., (Gr. Riv. Val. Div.,)		Paris,	Kent,		94
Bowen's Mills, P. O.,	Mich. Cent. R. R., (Gr. Riv. Val. Div.,)	Middleville, 6 m.,	Yankee Springs,	Barry,		97
Bowne, P. O.,	Det. & Mill R. R.,	Lowell, 7 m.,	Bowne,	Kent,		94
Boyne, P. O.,	Gr. Rap. & Ind. R. R.,		Evangeline,	Charlevoix,	200	57
Boynton Village,	Grand Trunk R. W.,		Port Huron,	St. Clair,		88
Bradley, P. O. & R. R. Sta.,	Gr. Rap. & Ind. R. R.,		Wayland,	Allegan,	500	96
Brady, R. R. & Tel. Sta.,	Peninsular R. W.,		Brady,	Kalamazoo,		107
Brandon, P. O.,	Det. & Bay City R. R.,	Oxford, 5 m.,	Brandon,	Oakland,		101
Bravo, P. O., Sherman Sta.,	Chi. & Mich. L. Shore R. R.,		Clyde,	Allegan,		96
Breckenridge, R. R. Sta.,	Sag. Val. & St. Louis R. R.,		Wheeler,	Gratiot,		88
Breedsville, P. O. & R. R. Sta.,	Chi. & Mich. L. Shore R. R.,		Columbia,	Van Buren,	450	108
Brest,	L. S. & M. S. R. W. (St. Br.,) Mi, Ca. & I. Ind. R. W.,	Stony Creek, 2 m.,	Frenchtown,	Monroe,		115
Bridgeport Centre, P. O., R. R. & Tel. Sta.,	Flint & P. M. R. W.,		Bridgeport,	Saginaw,	600	84
Bridgeton, P. O.,	Gr. Rap., New. & L. Shore R. R.,	Ashland, 5 m.,	Bridgeton,	Newaygo,	200	70
Bridgeville, P. O.,	Det. & Mil. R. R.,	St. Johns, 11 m.,	Washington,	Gratiot,		88
Bridgewater, P. O. & R. R. Sta.,	Det., Hills. & Ind. R. R.,		Bridgewater,	Washtenaw,		104
Bridgman, R. R. & Tel. Sta., (Laketon P. O.,)	Chi. & Mich. L. Shore R. R.,		Lake,	Berrien,		100
Brighton, P. O., R. R. & Tel. Sta.,	Det. L. & L. M. R. R.,		Brighton,	Livingston,		100
Bristol, P. O.,	Flint & P. M. R. W.,	Remick, 12 m.,	Sherman,	Isabella,		77
Brockway,	P. H. & I. M. R. R.,	Emmet, 6 m.,	Brockway,	St. Clair,	118	88
Brockway, R. R. Sta.,	L. S. & M. S. R. W. (Lansing Div.,)		Hamlin,	Eaton,		88
Brockway Centre, P. O.,	P. H. & I. M. R. Rap.,	Capac, 14 m.,	Brockway,	St. Clair,	600	88
Bronson, P. O., R. R. & Tel. Sta.,	L. Shore & Mich. Southern R. W.,		Bronson,	Branch,	800	112
Brookfield, P. O., Duttonville,	L. S. & M. S. R. W., (Lansing Div.,)	Brockway, 6 m.,	Brookfield,	Eaton,		88
Brooklyn,	Sa. Cl. & C. Air Line R. W.,	Washington, 4 m.,	Ray,	Macomb,		102
Brooklyn, P. O. & R. R. Sta.,	Det., Hills. & Ind. R. R.,		Columbia,	Jackson,	800	105
Broomfield, P. O.,	Flint & P. M. R. W.,	Remick, 18 m.,	Sherman,	Isabella,		77
Brown, P. O.,	Lake Michigan R. R.,	Manistee, 11 m.,	Brown,	Manistee,		59
Brownell's,	Mich. Cent. R. R., (Kal. & S. Hav. Div.,)		Kalmo & Liberman,	Kalamazoo,		107
Brown's P. O.,	Chi. & Mich. L. Shore R. R.,		Lake & Chickering,	Berrien,		100
Brownsville, P. O.,	Mich. Cent. R. R., (Air Line Div.,)	Vandalia, 4 m.,	Calvin,	Cass,	200	110
Bruce, R. R. Sta.,	M. R. & C. R. R.,		Negaunee,	Marquette,		110
Buchanan, P. O., R. R. & Tel. Sta.,	Mich. Cent. R. R.,		Buchanan,	Berrien,	2,000	109
Buena Vista,	Gr. Rap. & Ind. R. R.,	Belmont, 4 m.,	Cannon, Plainfield,	Kent,		94
Buena Vista, P. O.,	Flint & P. M. R. W.,	Bridgeport, 6 m.,	Blumfield,	Saginaw,		84
Bundville,	F. K. & L. M. R. R.,	Thornton, 4 m.,	Clyde,	St. Clair,		88
Bunker Hill, P. O.,	Mich. Cent. R. R., (J. L. & S. Div.,)	Leslie, 6 m.,	Bunker Hill,	Ingham,		99
Burch's Mill, R. R. Sta., (Burch's P. O.,)	Gr. Rap. & Ind. R. R.,		Algoma,	Kent,	300	94
Burlickville, P. O.,	Lake Michigan R. R.,	Glen Arbor, 6 m.,	Empire,	Leelanaw,		58
Burlington, P. O. & R. R. Sta.,	Bit. Cel. & I. (Air Line R.,) Bat. Cel. & I. Rck. R. R.,		Burlington,	Calhoun,	400	106
Burnips Corners, P. O.,	L. S. & M. S. R. W., (Kal. Div.,)	Dorr, 5 m.,	Salem,	Allegan,		96
Burns, P. O.,	Det. & Mil. R. R.,	Vernon, 5 m.,	Burns,	Shiawassee,		91
Burnside, P. O.,	P. H. & I. M. R. R.,	Imlay City, 13 m.,	Burnside,	Lapeer,		89
Burr Oak, P. O., R. R. & Tel. Sta.,	L. Shore & Mich. Southern R. R.,		Burr Oak,	St. Joseph,	900	111
Burtchville,	Lake Huron R. R.,		Burtchville,	St. Clair,		88
Bushnell Centre, P. O.,	Det., Lans. & L. Mich. R. R., (Stanton Dr.,)	Fenwicks, 3 m.,	Bushnell,	Montcalm,		92
Butler, P. O., (Herrickville Sta.)	Mich. Cent. R. R., (Air Line Div.,)		Butler,	Branch,		112
Byers, R. R. Sta.,	Gr. Rap. & Ind. R. R.,		Colfax,	Mecosta,		78
Byron, P. O.,	D. & M. R. R.,	Gaines, 5 m.,	Burns,	Shiawassee,	500	91
Byron, R. R. Sta., (Byron Centre P. O.,)	L. S. & M. S. R. R., (Kal. Div.,)		Byron,	Kent,		94
Cady, P. O., (Red Run Corners,)	G. T. R. W.,	Utica Plank, 2½ m.,	Clinton,	Macomb,		102
Caledonia, P. O.,	Mich. Cent. R. R., (Gr. Riv. Val. Div.,)	Caledonia, 4 m.,	Caledonia,	Kent,		94
Caledonia Station, P. O. & R. R. Sta.,	Mich. Cent. R. R., (G'd Riv. Val. Div.,)		Caledonia,	Kent,	70	94
Califf, R. R. Sta.,	Chi. & Mich. L. Shore R. R.,		Dalton,	Muskegon,		91
California, P. O. & R. R. Sta., (Hall's Corners,)	Mans. & Cold. & L. Mich. R. R.,		California,	Branch,		112
Calumet, P. O., R. R. & Tel. S., (Red Jacket Vill.,)	Hecla & Torch Lake R. R.,		Calumet,	Houghton,	8,800	117
Calvin, P. O.,	Mich. Cent. R. R., (Air Line Div.,)	Vandalia, 7 m.,	Calvin,	Cass,		110
Cambria Centre,	Det., Hills. & Ind., L. S. & M. S. R. R.,	Hillsdale, 5 m.,	Cambria,	Hillsdale,		113
Cambria Mills, P. O.,	Ft. Wayne, Jack. & Sag. R. R.,	Reading, 5 m.,	Cambria,	Hillsdale,	250	113
Cambridge, P. O.,	Det., Hills. & Ind. R. R.,	Brooklyn, 6 m.,	Cambridge,	Lenawee,		114
Camden, P. O. & R. R. Sta., (Chester Sta.,)	Mans., Cold. & L. Mich. R. R.,		Camden,	Hillsdale,	150	113
Campbell, P. O.,	Det. & Mil. R. R.,	Saranac, 9 m.,	Campbell,	Ionia,		93
Campbell, R. R. Sta.,	Chi. & N. W. R. R., (Pen. Div.,)		Baldwin,	Delta,		122
Can, P. O.,	Saginaw Bay.,	Bayport, 12 m.,	Grant,	Huron,		86
Canandaigua, P. O.,	L. S. & M. Southern R. R.,	Clayton, 4 m.,	Medina & Seneca,	Lenawee,	250	114
Cannonsburg, P. O.,	Gr. Rap., Greenville & Alpena R. R.,	Cortland Sta., 5 m.,	Cannon,	Kent,	300	94
Canovia,	Mich. Cent. R. R.,	Denton's, 7 m.,	Sumpter,	Wayne,		103
Canton, P. O.,	Mich. Cent. R. R.,	Sowell's, 7 m.,	Canton,	Wayne,		103
Capac, P. O. & R. R. & Tel. Sta.,	P. H. & I. M. R. R.,	Kalamo, 2 m.,	Mussey,	St. Clair,	500	88
Carlisle, P. O.,	Marsh. & Cold. R. R.,	Hastings, 6 m.,	Kalamo,	Eaton,		88
Carlson, P. O.,	Mich. Cent. R. R., (Gr. Riv. Val. Div.,)	Vassar, 18 m.,	Carlton,	Barry,		97
Caro, P. O.,	Det. & Bay City R. R.,		Indian Fields,	Tuscola,	700	85
Carpenter's Corners,	Mich. Cent. R. R., Det. Hills. & Ind. R. R.,	Ypsilanti, 3 m.,	Pittsfield,	Washtenaw,		104
Carrolton, P. O. & R. R. Sta.,	Flint & P. M., (J. L. & S. Div.,)		Carrolton,	Saginaw,	500	84
Carson City, P. O.,	Det. & Mil. R. R.,	Pewamo, 12 m.,	Bloomer,	Montcalm,	600	92
Carsonville, (Farmers P. O.,)	Lake Huron.,	Port Sanilac, 6 m.,	Bridgehampton, Washington,	Sanilac,		87
Cascade, P. O.,	Det. & Mil. R. R.,	Ada, 3 m.,	Cascade,	Kent,		94
Casco, P. O.,	G. Trunk R. W., St. C. & C. R. R.,	Ridgeway, 5 m.,	Casco,	St. Clair,		88
Caseville, P. O., Tel. Sta. & Landing,	Saginaw Bay,		Caseville,	Huron,		86
Cassovia, P. O. & R. R. Sta.,	Gr. Rap., New. & L. S. R. R.,		Tyrone,	Saginaw,	200	84
Cass Bridge, P. O.,	Flint & P. M. R. R.,	Bridgeport, 3 m.,	Bridgeport,	Saginaw,		94
Cass City, P. O.,	Saginaw Bay.,	Sebewaing, 18 m.,	Elkland,	Tuscola,		85
Cassopolis, P. O., Tel. & R. R. Sta.,	Mich. Cent. (Air L. Div.,) Penin. R. W.,		La Grange,	Cass,	1,000	110
Cat Head Landing (Waukazoo,)	Lake Michigan,		Leelanaw,	Leelanaw,		58
Catholic Mission, Landing,	M. H. & O. R. R., Keweenaw Bay.,	L'Anse, 4 m.,	Baraga,	Houghton,		117
Cato, P. O.,	Gr. Rap. & Ind. R. R., Det. L. & L. Mich. R. R.,	Howards, 10 m., Ord. Sta.,	Cato,	Montcalm,		93
Cedar Creek, P. O.,	Mich. Cent. R. R., (Gr. Riv. Val. Div.,)	Quimby, 10 m.,	Hope,	Barry,		97
Cedar Dale, P. O.,	Mich. Cent. R. R.,	Forestville, 3 m.,	Minden, Delaware,	Sanilac,		87
Cedar Fork, P. O. & Landing,	Green Bay.,		Cedarville,	Menominee,	124	
Cedar Run. P. O.,	Gr. Rap. & Ind. R. R., (Trav. City Br.,)	Traverse City, 10 m.,	Long Lake,	Grand Traverse,		60

☞ For Explanations, names of Railroads abbreviated, etc., see page 147.

Name of Village.	Railroad, Lake or River.	Nearest Station or Landing.	Township.	County.	Pop.	Pge.
Cedar Springs, P. O., R. R. & Tel. Sta.,.....	Gr. Rapids & Ind. R. R.,.....		Solon,	Kent,	1800	94
Central Lake. P. O.,.....	Grand Traverse Bay, ...	Torch Lake, 5 m., ...	Central Lake,	Antrim,		57
Central Mine, P. O.,.....	Lake Superior,.....	Eagle River, 5 m., ...	Sherman,	Keweenaw,	1000	118
Centre, P. O.,.....	Mar. & Cold. R. R.,.....		Rozana,	Eaton,		98
Centre Harbor, L'd'g, (Rock Falls P. O.)....	Lake Huron,.....		Sand Beach,	Huron,	200	86
Centreville, R. R. & Tel. Sta.,.....	Ch. & N. W. R. R., (Penin. Div.,)		Maple Ridge,	Delta,	800	120
Centreville, P. O., R. R. & Tel. Sta.,.....	Mich. Cent. R. R., (Air Line Div.,)		Nottawa & Lockport,	St. Joseph,		111
Cereaco, P. O. & R. R. Sta.,.....	Mich. Cent. R. R.,.....		Marshall, Emmett,	Calhoun,	500	106
Chadwick. P. O. & R. R. Sta.,.....	Det., L. & L. M. R. R.,.....		Orleans,	Ionia,		98
Chamberlain. P. O.,.....	Penin. R. W.,.....		Flowerfield,	St. Joseph,		111
Champion, P. O. & R. R. Sta.,.....	Marq., H. & Ont. R. R.,.....		Ely,	Marquette,	800	110
Champion & Chippewa Mine, H. R. & Tel. Sta.,..	Branch of Marq., H. & Ont. R. R.,.....		Ely,	Marquette,		119
Chapin's, R. R. Sta.,.....	Mich. Cent. R. R., (J. L. & S. Div.,)	Cooperville, 5 m.,..	Vevay,	Ingham,		96
Charleston,.....	Det. & Mil. R. R.,.....	Tietsorta, 5 m.,.....	Albenisle,	Ottawa,		95
Charleston, P. O.,.....	Mich. Cent. R. R.,.....		Volinia,	Cass,		110
Charleston, P. O.,.....				Satliae,		67
Charlevoix, P. O. & Landing,.....	Lake Michigan,.....		Charlevoix,	Charlevoix,	500	57
Charlotte, P. O., R. R. & Tel. Sta.,.....	Mich. Cent. R. R., (Gr. Riv. Val. Div.,) Pain. R. W.,		Eaton & Carmel,	Eaton,	3017	98
Chase, P. O. & R. R. Sta.,.....	F. & P. M. R. W.,.....		Chase,	Lake,		71
Chase's, R. R. Sta.,.....	L. S. & M. S. R. W., (Jack. Div.,)		Raisin,	Lenawee,		114
Cheboygan, P. O., R. R. Sta. & Ldg.,.....	Mich. Cent. R. R., (J. L. & S. Div.,) L. Huron,..		Beaugrand,	Cheboygan,	1,200	62
Chelsea, P. O., R. R. & Tel. Sta.,.....	Mich. Cent. R. R.,.....		Sylvan,	Washtenaw,	1,000	104
Chesaning, P. O., R. R. & Tel. Sta.,.....	Mich. Cent. R. R., (J. L. & S. Div.,)		Chesaning,	Saginaw,		64
Cheshire, P. O.,.....	L. S. & M. S., (Kal. Div.,) Tol. L. S. & M. & ...	Allegan, 8 m.,...	Cheshire,	Allegan,		96
Chester, P. O. & R. R. Sta.,.....	Mich. Cent. R. R., (Gr. Riv. Val. Div.,)		Chester,	Eaton,		98
Chester, R. R. Sta., (Camden P. O.,)....	Mayc. Cold. & L. Mich. R. R.,.....		Camden,	Hillsdale,	1,500	118
Chickaming, P. O.,.....	Chi. & Mich. L. Shore R. R.,.....		Chickaming,	Berrien,		109
Child's Mills, R. R. Sta.,.....	Gr. Rap. & Ind. R. R.,.....		Plainfield,	Kent,		94
China, P. O. & Ldg.,.....	St. Clair River,.....		East China,	St. Clair,	800	88
Chippewa, R. R. & Tel. Sta.,.....	F. & P. M. R. W.,.....		Orient,	Osceola,		72
Chippewa Lake, P. O.,.....	F. & P. M. R. W.,.....	Orient, 10 m.,.....	Chippewa,	Mecosta,	800	78
Christiana,.....	Penin. R. W.,.....	Edwardsburg, 4 m.,..	Ontwa, Mason,	Cass,		110
Church's Corners, P. O.,.....	L. Shore & Mich. Southern R. W.,.....	Pittsford, 7 m.,.....	Wheatland,	Hillsdale,		113
Churchville Landing,.....	St. Mary's River & Lake George,.....			Chippewa,		122
Clam Lake, P. O., R. R. & Tel. Sta.,.....	Gr. Rap. & Ind. R. R.,.....		Clam Lake,	Wexford,	600	69
Clare, P. O., R. R. & Tel. Sta.,.....	Flint & P. M. R. W.,.....		Grant,	Clare,		78
Clarence, P. O.,.....	L. S. & M. S. R. W., (Lansing Div.,)	Springport, 4 m.,..	Clarence,	Calhoun,		106
Clarenceville, (Plank Road P. O.,)....	Det., L. & L. M. R. R.,.....	Fisher's, 5 m.,.....	Redford,	Wayne,		108
Clarendon, P. O. & R. R. Sta.,.....	Mich. Cent. R. R., (Air Line Div.,)		Clarendon,	Calhoun,		104
Clarksburgh, P. O., R. R. & Tel. Sta.,.....	Marq., H. & Ont. R. R.,.....		Ely,	Marquette,	500	110
Clarkston, P. O.,.....	Det. & Mil. R. R.,.....	Clarkston Sta., 2 m.,..	Independence,	Oakland,	600	101
Clarkston Station, R. R. & Tel. Sta.,.....	Det. & Mil. R. R.,.....		Independence,	Oakland,		101
Clay Banks, P. O.,.....	Chi. & Mich. L. Shore R. R.,.....	New Era, 7 m.,.....	Clay Banks,	Oceana,		60
Clay Hill, P. O.,.....	Gr. Rap. & Ind. R. R.,.....	West Summit, 13 m.,..	Henderson,	Wexford,		69
Clayton, P. O., R. R. & Tel. Sta.,.....	L. Shore & Mich. Southern R. W.,.....		Hudson & Dover,	Lenawee,	600	114
Clear Water, P. O.,.....	Gr. Rap. & Ind. R. R.,.....	Kalkaska, 7 m.,.....	Clear Water,	Kalkaska,	60	61
Cleon, P. O.,.....	Gr. Rap. & Ind. R. R.,.....	Manton, 25 m.,.....	Cleon,	Wexford,	150	80
Clifford, P. O.,.....	Lapeer & Northern R. R.,.....	Fish Lake,.....	Burlington,	Lapeer,	75	80
Clifton, P. O.,.....	Lake Superior,.....	Eagle River, 4 m.,..	Clifton,	Keweenaw,	400	118
Climax, R. R. & Tel. Sta., (Climax Prairie P. O.,)	Peninsular R. W.,.....		Climax,	Kalamazoo,	250	107
Climax Prairie, P. O., (Climax Sta.,)....	Peninsular R. W.,.....		Climax,	Kalamazoo,		107
Clinton, P. O., R. R. & Tel. Sta.,.....	L. S. & M. S. R. W., (Jackson Div.,)		Clinton,	Lenawee,	850	114
Clinton Junction, P. O.,.....	Mar. & Cold. R. R.,.....		Sanfield,	Eaton,		98
Clintonville,.....	Det. & Mil. R. R.,.....	Drayton Plains, 2m.,..	Waterford,	Oakland,		101
Clio, P. O., (Pine Run Sta.,)....	F. & P. M. R. W.,.....		Vienna,	Genesee,		90
Clyde, P. O. & R. R. Sta.,.....	F. & P. M. R. W.,.....		Highland,	Oakland,		101
Clyde, R. R. Sta., (Sterling P O.,)....	Mich. Cent. R. R., (J. L. & S. Div.,)		Deep River,	Bay,		78
Clyde Mills, P. O.,.....	P. H. & L. M. R. R.,.....	Thornton, 3 m.,.....	Kimball,	St. Clair,		88
Cob-Mo-Sa, P. O.,.....	Chi. & Mich. Lake Shore R. R.,.....	Barnet, 12 m.,.....	Leavitt,	Oceana,		80
Cohoctah, P. O.,.....	Det. & Mil. R. R.,.....	Gaines, 10 m.,.....	Cohoctah,	Livingston,		100
Colby, R. R. Sta.,.....	Det., L. & L. M. R. R., (Stanton Br.,)		Sidney,	Montcalm,		92
Coldwater City, P. O., R. R. & Tel. Sta.,.....	L. S. & M. S. R. R., M., Cold. & L. Mich. R. R.,..		Coldwater,	Branch,	6,000	112
Coleman, P. O., R. R. & Tel. Sta.,.....	F. & P. M. R. W.,.....		Warren,	Midland,		78
College Farm, R. R. Sta.,.....	Det., L. & L. Mich. R. R.,.....		Lansing,	Ingham,		96
Collins, P. O.,.....	Det., L. & L. Mich. R. R.,.....	Stebbinsville, 1 m.,..	Portland,	Ionia,		80
Collinsville, P. O., (Collins Sta.,)....	Chi. & Mich. L. Shore R. R.,.....		Golden,	Oceana,	250	109
Coloma, P. O., R. R. & Tel. Sta.,.....	Chi. & Mich. L. Shore R. R.,.....		Watervliet,	Berrien,	450	111
Colon, P. O., R. R. & Tel. Sta.,.....	Mich. Cent. R. R., (Air L. Div.,)		Colon,	St. Joseph,	150	105
Columbia, P. O.,.....	Det., Hills. & Ind. R. R.,.....	Brooklyn, 3 m.,.....	Columbia,	Jackson,		105
Columbia, R. R. Sta.,.....	Mich. Cent. R. R., (Kal. & S. H. Div.,)		Columbia,	Van Buren,		108
Columbiaville, P. O. & R. R. Sta.,.....	Det. & Bay City R. R.,.....		Marathon,	Lapeer,	200	80
Columbus, P. O.,.....	Grand Trunk R. W. & St. Cl. & C. Air L. R. R.,	Ridgeway, 3 m.,..	Columbus,	St. Clair,		88
Commerce, P. O.,.....	Flint & P. M. R. W.,.....	Milford, 6 m.,.....	Commerce,	Oakland,	200	101
Comstock, P. O. & R. R. Sta.,.....	Mich. Cent. R. R.,.....		Comstock,	Kalamazoo,	175	107
Concord, P. O., R. R. & Tel. Sta.,.....	Mich. Cent. R. R., (Air L. Div.,)		Concord,	Jackson,	500	105
Condit, R. R. Sta.,.....	L. S. & M. S. R. W., (Lansing Div.,)		Albion,	Calhoun,		106
Conger, P. O. & R. R. Sta.,.....	Gr. Rap. & Ind. R. R.,.....		Reynolds,	Montcalm,		82
Conner's Creek, P. O.,.....	Det. & B. City R. R.,.....	Norris, 2 m.,.....	Grosse Point,	Wayne,		108
Constantine, P. O., R. R. & Tel. Sta.,.....	L. S. & M. S. R. W., (Kal. Div.,)		Constantine,	St. Joseph,	1,000	111
Coovis,.....	Penin. R. W.,.....	Madison, 3 m.,.....	Convis,	Calhoun,		106
Convis Centre, P. O.,.....	Penin. R. W.,.....	Madison, 6 m.,.....	Convis,	Calhoun,		106
Cook's Corners, (Olisco P. O.,)....	Det., L. & L. M. R. R.,.....	Kiddville, 3 m.,.....	Olisco,	Ionia,		79
Cook's Station. P. O.,.....	Musk. & Big Rap. R. R.,.....	Monroeville, 9 m.,..	Barton, Monroe,	Newaygo,		107
Cooper, R. R. Sta.,.....	Gr. R. & Ind. R. R., L. S. & M. S. R.W. (Kal. Div.,)		Cooper,	Kalamazoo,		107
Cooper Centre, P. O.,.....	Gr. R. & Ind. R. R., L. S. & M. S. R. W. (Kal. Div.)	Cooper, 2 m.,.....	Cooper,	Kalamazoo,	200	107
Coopersville, P. O., R. R. & Tel. Sta.,.....	Det. & Mil. R. R.,.....		Pottastown,	Ottawa,	500	95
Copper Falls Mine, P. O. & Tel. Sta.,.....	Lake Superior,.....	Eagle Harbor, 2 m.,..	Eagle Harbor,	Keweenaw,	400	118
Copper Harbor, P. O.,.....	Lake Superior,.....		Copper Harbor,	Keweenaw,	200	118
Coral, P. O., R. R. & Tel. Sta.,.....	Det., L. & L. M. R. R.,.....		Maple Valley,	Montcalm,		82
Corey. P. O. & R. R. Sta.,.....	Mich. Cent. R. R., (Air L. Div.,)		Fabius,	St. Joseph,	100	111
Corinth, P. O.,.....	Gr. Rap. & Ind. R. R.,.....	Ross, 2 m.,.....	Byron, Gaines,	Kent,		94
Cortland, R. R. Sta.,.....	Gr. Rap., Greenville & Alpena R. R.,.....		Cortland,	Kent,		94
Cortland Centre, P. O.,.....	Gr. Rap., Greenville & Alpena R. R.,.....	Cortland Sta., 3 m.,..	Cortland,	Kent,		94
Corunna City, P. O., R. R. & Tel. Sta.,.....	Det. & Mil. R. R.,.....		Caledonia,	Shiawassee,	2,000	108
County Horse, R. R. Sta.,.....	Mich. Cent. R. R.,.....		Nankin,	Wayne,		108
County Line, R. R. Sta.,.....	Gr. Rap. & Ind. R. R.,.....		Sheridan, Holton,	Newaygo & Muskegon,		78&81
County Line, R. R. Sta.,.....	Mus. & Big Rap. R. R.,.....		Casinovia,	Muskegon,		81
County Line Sta., (Hughesville P. O.,)....	Gr. Rap., New. & L. Shore. R. R.,.....		Birch Run,	Saginaw,		84
Covert, P. O.,.....	F. & P. M. R. W.,.....		Covert,	Van Buren,		114
Cracow, P. O.,.....	Chi. & Mich. L. Shore R. R.,.....	Bangor, 8 m.,.....	Deerfield,	Huron,		86
Crapo, P. O. & R. R. Sta.,.....	Gr. Rap. & Ind. R. R.,.....	White Rock, 11 m.,..	Paris,	Green,	100	72&73
Crawford, P. O.,.....	Sag. Val. & St L. R. R.,.....	St. Louis 12 m.,...	Lincoln,	Isabella,		77

LIST OF CITIES, TOWNS, &C.

Name of Village.	Railroad, Lake or River.	Nearest Station or Landing.	Township.	County.	Pop.	Page.
Crawford, R. R. Sta.,	Mich. Cent. R. R., (J. L. & S. Div.),		Kaska,	Crawford,		62
Crawford, P. O.,	Sag. Val. & St. Louis R. R.,	St. Louis, 17 m.,	Lincoln,	Isabella,		77
Crawford's Quarry, P. O., Landing & Tel. Sta.,	Lake Huron,		Rogers,	Presque Isle,	200	53
Creasy's Corners,	Mass. & Cold. & L. Mich. R. R.,	Gun Marsh, 7 m.,	Prairieville,	Barry,		97
Creswell, P. O.,	Gr. Traverse Bay,		Milton,	Antrim,		87
Crosby's Mills, R. R. Sta.,	Gr. Rap., Greenville & Alpena R. R.,		Montcalm,	Montcalm,		82
Cross Village, P. O. & Landing,	Lake Michigan,		La Croix,	Emmet,		51
Croton, P. O.,	Gr. Rap., New. & L. Shore R. R.,	Newago, 8 m.,	Croton,	Newaygo,	400	70
Crystal, P. O.,	Det., Lane & L. Mich. R. R., (Stanton Br.,)	Stanton, 10 m.,	Crystal,	Montcalm,		82
Crystal Valley, P. O.,	Chi. & Mich. L. Shore R. R.,	Pentwater, 10 m.,	Crystal,	Oceana,	100	80
Culver, R. R. Sta.,	Mich. Cent. R. R., (J. L. & S. Div.,)		Clayton,	Bay,		75
Dailey, P. O., (Howard Sta.,)	Mich. Cent. R. R. (Air Line Div.,)		Jefferson,	Cass,		110
Dalton, P. O. & R. R. Sta.,	Chi. & Mich. L. Shore R. R.,		Dalton,	Muskegon,	200	81
Dana, R. R. Sta.,	Det. L. & L. M. R. R.,		Leroy,	Ingham,		99
Danby, P. O.,	Marsh. & Cold. R. R.,	Schewa, 4 m.,	Danby,	Ionia,		93
Danby, R. R. Sta.,	Det., L. & L. M. R. R.,		Danby,	Ionia,		93
Danville, P. O.,	Mich. Cent. (J. L. & S. Div.)	Mason, 7 m.,	Ingham,	Ingham,	600	99
Davisburgh, P. O., R. R. & Tel. Sta.,	Det. & Mil. R. R.,		Springfield,	Oakland,	600	101
Davison, P. O.,	P. H. & L. M. R. R.,	Davison Sta., 1½ m.,	Davison,	Genesee,		90
Davison Station, P. O., R. R. & Tel. Sta.,	P. H. & L. M. R. R.,		Davison,	Genesee,	125	90
Davisonville, (Atlas P. O.,)	Flint & P. M. R. R.,	Grand Diane, 5 m.,	Atlas,	Genesee,		90
Davisville, P. O.,	Lake Huron,	Lexington, 5 m.,	Lexington,	Sanilac,	400	87
Day's River, R. R. Sta.,	Chi. & N. W. R. R., (Pen. Div.,)		Baldwin,	Delta,		120
Dayton, P. O., R. R. & Tel. Sta.,	Mich. Cent. R. R.,		Bertrand,	Berrien,	400	109
Dean's Mills, P. O.,	Det., Lana. & L. Mich. R. R., (Stanton Br.,)	Sheridan, 4 m.,	Bushnell,	Montcalm,		82
Dearborn, P. O., R. R. & Tel. Sta.,	Mich. Cent. R. R.,		Dearborn,	Wayne,	600	108
Decater, P. O., R. R. & Tel. Sta.,	Mich. Cent. R. R.,		Decatur,	Van Buren,	600	108
Deckerville, P. O.,	Lake Huron,	Forester, 9 m.,	Marion,	Sanilac,		87
Deep River, P. O. & R. R. Sta.,	Mich. Cent., (J. L. & S. Div.,)		Deep River,	Bay,		75
Deer Creek, P. O.,	Det. & Mil. R. R.,	Gaines, 8 m.,	Deerfield,	Livingston,	200	100
Deerfield, P. O.,	L. Shore & Mich. Southern R. W.,		Deerfield,	Lenawee,	800	114
Deerfield, R. R. Sta., (McDonald P. O.,)	Chi. & Mich. L. Shore R. R.,		Bangor,	Van Buren,		108
Deerfield Centre, Madison P. O.,	Det. & Mil. R. R.,	Linden, 10 m.,	Deerfield,	Livingston,		100
Delhi, R. R. Sta., (Holt P. O.,)	Mich. Cent., (J. L. & S. Div.,)		Delhi,	Ingham,		99
Delhi, R. R. & Tel. Sta.,	Mich. Cent. R. R.,		Scio,	Washtenaw,		104
Delray, P. O.,	L. S. & M. S. R. W. (bet. Riv.) Tol. Can. St. & Det. R. W.,	Detroit Junct., 2 m.,	Springwells,	Wayne,	150	108
Delta, P. O. & R. R. Sta.,	Det., L. & L. M. R. R.,		Delta,	Eaton,		93
Denmark, P. O.,	Det. & Bay City R. R.,	Reese, 3 m.,	Denmark,	Tuscola,		85
Dennison, P. O. & R. R. Sta.,	Det. & Mil. R. R.,		Polktown,	Ottawa,		95
Denton, P. O., R. R. & Tel. Sta.,	Mich. Cent. R. R.,		Van Buren,	Wayne,		103
Denver, P. O.,	Mus. & Big Rapids R. R.,	Fremont, 8 m.,	Denver,	Newaygo,		79
Detour, P. O. & Landing,	Detour Passage,		Chippewa,			122
Detroit City, P. O., R. R. & Tel. Sta.,	Mich. Cent., L. S. & M. S., (Det. Div.) Det., L. & L. M., Gr. Trunk, Det. & Mil., Det. & Bay City, Great Western R. W.,		Detroit,	Wayne,	90,000	108
Deverenx, R. R. Sta.,	L. S. & M. S. R. W., (Lansing Div.,)		Parma,	Jackson,		105
De Witt, P. O.,	Det., L. & L. M. & Mich Cent. R. R., (J. L. & I. Sta.,)	North Lansing, 6 m.,	De Witt,	Clinton,	300	92
Dexter, P. O., R. R. & Tel. Sta.,	Mich. Cent. R. R.,		Scio,	Washtenaw,	1,800	104
Diamond Spring, P. O.,	Gr. Rap., Greenville & Alpena R. R.,	Hamilton, 8 m.,	Monterey,	Allegan,	200	95
Dickerson's Lake, R. R. Sta.,	L. S. & M. S. R. W., (Lansing Div.,)		Douglass,	Montcalm,	-	82
Dimondale, P. O., R. R. & Tel. Sta.,	St. Cl. & Cr. Air Line R. R., Det. & B. City R. R.,		Windsor,	Eaton,		98
Disco, P. O.,	Mich. Cent. R. R.,	Yates' & Washington 3m.,	Shelby,	Macomb,	125	102
Disboro',	L. S. & M. S. R. W., (Kal. Div.,)	Geddes, 3 m.,	Superior,	Washtenaw,		104
Dorr, P. O., R. R. & Tel. Sta.,	Chi. & Mich. L. Shore R. R.,	New Richmond, 6 m.,	Dorr,	Allegan,	300	96
Douglass, P. O.,	L. S. & M. S. R. W.,		Saugatuck,	Allegan,	75	96
Douglass, R. R. Sta.,	L. S. & M. S. R. W.,		White Pigeon,	St. Joseph,		111
Dovar, R. R. Sta.,	L. S. & M. S. R. W.,		Dover,	Lenawee,		114
Dover Mills,	Mich. Cent. R. R.,	Dexter, 5 m.,	Dexter,	Washtenaw,		104
Dowagiac, P. O., R. R. & Tel. Sta.,	Mich. Cent. R. R.,		Silver Creek, Nuga,	Cass,	2,100	110
Drayton Plains, P. O., R. R. & Tel. Sta.,	Det. & Mil. R. R.,		Waterford,	Oakland,	600	101
Dryden, P. O.,	P. H. & L. M. R. R.,	Imlay City, 7 m.,	Dryden,	Lapeer,	850	89
Da Boisville, (Redford P. O.,)	Det., L. & L. M. R. R.,	Redford, 4 m.,	Redford,	Wayne,		103
Duck Lake,	L. S. & M. S. R. W., (Lansing Div.,)	Springport, 6 m.,	Clarence,	Calhoun,		106
Duncan City, Landing & Tel. Sta.,	Lake Huron,		Benton,	Cheboygan,		93
Dundee, P. O. & R. R. Sta.,	Tol. & Ann Ar. R. R.,		Dundee,	Monroe,	600	115
Dunningsville, P. O. & R. R. Sta.,	Mich. L. Sh. R. R.,		Heath,	Allegan,		96
Duplain, P. O.,	L. S. & M. S. R. W., (Lansing Div.,)	Shepherdsville, 8 m.,	Duplain,	Clinton,	150	92
Duttonville, (Brookfield P. O.,)	L. S. & M. S. R. W., (Lansing Div.,)	Brockway, 6 m.,	Brookfield,	Eaton,		98
Eagle, P. O. & R. R. Sta.,	Det., L. & L. M. R. R.,		Eagle,	Clinton,	400	92
Eagle Harbor, P. O. & Landing,	Lake Superior,		Eagle Harbor,	Keweenaw,		118
Eagle Mill, R. R. Sta.,	Marq., H. & Ont. R. R.,		Negaunee,	Marquette,		119
Eagle Mills, R. R. Sta.,	L. S. & M. S. R. W., (Kal. Div.,)		Walker,	Kent,		65
Eagle River, P. O., Tel. Sta. & Landing,	Lake Superior,		Clifton & Houghton,	Keweenaw,	600	118
Eagletown Landing,	Grand Traverse Bay,		Dingham,	Leelanaw,		58
East Bay, Landing, (East Traverse Bay P. O.,),	Gr. R. & Ind. R. R., (Trav. City Br.,) & Int. Bay,	Traverse City, 3 m.,	East Bay,	G'd Traverse,		50
East China Ldg., (China P. O.,),	River St. Clair,		St. Clair,	St. Clair,		88
East Dayton, P. O., (Hurd's Corner,),	Det. & Bay City R. R.,	Vassar, 14 m.,	Wells, Dayton,	Tuscola,		85
East Gilead, P. O.,	L. S. & M. S. R. W.,	Batavia, 10 m.,	Gilead,	Branch,		112
East Leroy, P. O.,	Mass., Cold. & L. Mich. R. R.,	Newton, 3 m.,	Leroy,	Calhoun,		106
Eastmanville, P. O.,	Det. & Mil. R. R.,	Coopersville, 4 m.,	Polkton,	Ottawa,	450	95
East Milan, P. O., (Reeves Sta.,)	Tol. & Ann Ar. R. R.,		Milan,	Monroe,	100	115
East Mosherville, (Mosherville Sta.,)	Ft. Wayne, Jack. & Sag. R. R.,		Scipio,	Hillsdale,		113
Easton, P. O.,	Det., L. & L. M. & Det. & Mil. R. R.,	Ionia, 5 m.,	Easton,	Ionia,		93
East Saginaw, P. O., R. R. & Tel. Sta.,	Flint & P. M. R. W.,		East Saginaw,	Saginaw,	17,000	84
East Saugatuck, R. R. Sta.,	Chi. & Mich. L. Shore R. R.,		Manlius,	Allegan,		96
East Tawas, P. O., Tel. Sta. & Landing,	Lake Huron,		Tawas,	Iosco,	900	65
Eaton Rapids, P. O., R. R. & Tel. Sta.,	I. S. & M. S. (Lan. Div.) E. Cen. & St. Cl. (A. V. R.)		Eaton Rapids,	Eaton,	2,000	98
Eau Claire, P. O.,	Mich. Cent. R. R.,	Dowagiac, 11 m.,	Pipestone,	Berrien,		109
Eckford,	Mich. Cent. R. R., Mar. & Cold. R. R.,	Marshville, 3 m.,	Eckford,	Calhoun,		106
Ecorce, P. O. & R. R. Sta., (Grand Point,)	L. S. & M. S. R. R., Tol., Can. S. & Det. R. R.,		Ecorce,	Wayne,	600	103
Eden, P. O.,	Mich. Cent. R. R., (J. L. & S. Div.,)	Chapin's, 1 m.,	Vevay,	Ingham,		99
Edenville, P. O.,	Flint & P. M. R. R.,	Sanford, 10 m.,	Jerome,	Midland,		76
Edgerton, P. O. & R. R. Sta.,	Gr. Rap. & Ind. R. R.,		Algoma,	Kent,	200	94
Edwardsburg, P. O., R. R. & Tel. Sta.,	Peninsular R. W.,		Ontwa,	Cass,	750	110
Elba, P. O., R. R. & Tel. Sta.,	P. H. & L. M. R. R.,		Elba,	Lapeer,		80
Eldred, R. R. Sta.,	L. S. & M. S. R. W., (Jack. Div.,)		Napoleon,	Jackson,		105
Elk, P. O., (Maple Grove,),	Flint & P. M. R. W.,	Olin, 10 m.,	Maple Grove,	Saginaw,		84
Elkland, P. O.,	Saginaw Bay,	Sebewaing, 17 m.,	Elkland,	Tuscola,		85
Elk Rapids, P. O. & Landing,	Grand Traverse Bay,		Elk Rapids,	Antrim,	600	57
Ellington, P. O.,	Det. & Bay City R. R.,	Vassar, 19 m.,	Ellington,	Tuscola,		85
Ellisville,	Holly, Wayne & Monroe R. R.,	Wala, 5 m.,	Hampter,	Wayne,		103
Elsworth, P. O.,	Gr. Rap. & Ind. R. R.,	Ashton, 6 m.,	Ellsworth,	Lake,		71

☞ For Explanations, names of Railroads abbreviated, etc., see page 147.

Name of Village.	Railroad, Lake or River.	Nearest Station or Landing.	Township.	County.	Pop.	Pop.
Elm, P. O.,	Det., L. & L. M. R. R.,	Mc Kinney, 1 m.,	Livonia,	Wayne,		108
Elm Hall, P. O.,	Sag. Val. & St. L. R. R.,	St. Louis, 12 m.,	Sumner,	Gratiot,	800	88
Elmwood, P. O.,	Saginaw Bay.,	Sebewaing, 15 m.,	Elmwood, Ellington,	Tuscola,		85
Elmwood, R. R. Sta.,	Det., L. & L. M. R. R.,		Livonia,	Wayne,		108
Elsie, P. O.,	Owosso & North-Western R. R.,	(R. R. unfinished,)	Duplain,	Clinton,	400	92
Elm, P. O.,	Det. & D. City R. R.,	Millington, 7 m.,	Arbela,	Tuscola,		85
Eomel, P. O., R. R. & Tel. Sta.,	P. H. & L. M. R. R.,		Emmet,	St. Clair,	100	88
Empire, P. O. & Ldg.,	Lake Michigan,		Empire,	Leelanan,	200	58
Englishville, P. O. & R. R. Sta.,	Gr. Rap. Now. & I. Shore R. R.,		Alpine, Sparta,	Kent,	150	94
Ensley, P. O.,	Gr. Rap. & Ind. R. R.,	Maple Hill, 5 m.,	Ensley,	Newaygo,		79
Eric, P. O., (Vienna Sta.,)	Tol., Can. S. & Det., & L. S. & M. S. R. W., (Mt St.)		Erie,	Monroe,		115
Escanaba, P. O., R. R. & Tel. Sta.,	Ch. & N. W. R. R., (Penin. Div.,)		Escanaba,	Delta,	2,000	120
Essex, P. O.,	Det. & Mil. R. R.,	St. Johns, 7 m.,	Essex,	Clinton,		92
Essexville, P. O.,	Det. & B. City R. R.,	Bay City, 1 m.,	Bay City,	Bay,	500	75
Eureka, P. O.,	Det. & Mil. R. R.,	St. Johns, 8 m.,	Greenbush,	Clinton,	108	92
Evart, P. O. R. R. & Tel. Sta.,	F. & P. M. R. W.,		Evart, Osceola,	Osceola,	800	72
Exeter, P. O.,	Chi. & Can. So. R. R.,		Exeter,	Monroe,		115
Fabius, R. R. Sta.,	Mich. Cent. R. R., (Air Line Div.,)		Fabius,	St. Joseph,		111
Factoryville, P. O.,	Mich. Cent. R. R., (Air Line Div.,)	Colon, 7 m.,	Leonidas,	St. Joseph,		111
Fairfield, P. O.,	Chi. & Can. So. R. R.,	Fairfield, 2m.,	Fairfield,	Lenawee,	400	114
Fairfield, R. R. Sta.,	Chi. & Can. So. R. R.,		Fairfield,	Lenawee,		114
Fair Grove, P. O.,	Det. & Bay City R. R.,	Reese, 11 m.,	Fair Grove,	Tuscola,		85
Fair Haven, P. O. & Ldg.,	Lake St. Clair.,		Ira,	St. Clair,	500	88
Fairview, P. O. & Ldg.,	F. & P. M. R. W.,	Ludington, 8 m.,	Summit,	Mason,	250	70
Fallasvirg, P. O.,	Det. & Mil. R. R.,	Lowell, 4 m.,	Vergennes,	Kent,	100	94
Falmouth, P. O.,	Gr. Rap. & Ind. R. R.,	Clam Lake, 10 m.,	Clam Union,	Missaukee,	200	68
Farmers, P. O., (Carsonville,)	Lake Huron.,		Bridgehampton, Washington,	Sanilac,		87
Farmers' Creek, P. O.,	Det. & Bay City R. R.,	Metamora, 4 m.,	Hadley, Metamora,	Lapeer,		80
Farmington, P. O.,	Flint & P. M. R. W.,	Novi, 5 m.,	Farmington,	Oakland,	450	101
Farrandville,	F. & P. M. R. W.,	Pine Run Sta., 1 m.,	Vienna,	Genesee,		90
Farwell, P. O., R. R. & Tel. Sta.,	F. & P. M. R. W.,		Surrey,	Clare,		78
Fawn River, P. O.,	L. S. & M. S. R. R., Gr. Rap. & Ind. R. R.,	Sturgis, 4 m.,	Fawn River,	St. Joseph,	200	111
Fawn River P. O.,	L. Shore & Mich. Southern R. W.,	Burr Oak, 5 m.,	Fawn River,	St. Joseph,		111
Fayette, P. O. & Ldg.,	Big Bay de Noquette,		Delta,	Delta,		120
Felt's, P. O.,	Mich. Cent. R. R., (J. L. & S. Div.,)	Leslie, 8 m.,	Bunker Hill,	Ingham,		99
Fennville, P. O. & R. R. Sta.,	Chi. & Mich. L. Shore R. R.,		Manlius, Clyde,	Allegan,		96
Fentonville, P. O., R. R. & Tel. Sta.,	Det. & Mil. R. R.,		Fenton,	Genesee,	3,000	90
Fenwicks, R. R. Sta.,	Det. L. & M R. R., (Stanton Br.,)		Fairplain,	Montcalm,		82
Ferris, P. O.,	Det., L. & L. M. R. R., (Stanton Branch,)	Stanton, 12 m.,	Ferris,	Montcalm,		82
Ferry, P. O. (Reed,),	Chi. & Mich. Lake Shore R. R.,	New Era, 7 m.,	Ferry,	Oceana,		80
Ferrysburg, P. O., R. R. & Tel. Sta.,	Det. & Mil. R. R. & Mich. L. S. R. R.,		Spring Lake,	Ottawa,	860	95
Ferryville,	Chi. & Mich. L. S. R. R.,	Montague, 4 m.,	White River,	Muskegon,		81
Fife Lake, P. O. & R. R. Sta.,			Fife Lake,	Grand Traverse		60
Filer City,	Lake Michigan,	Manistee, 3 m.,	Filer,	Manistee,		59
Fillmore, P. O.,	Mich. Cent. R. R., (Gr. Riv. Val. Div.,)	Irving, 6 m.,	Irving,	Barry,		97
Fillmore, R. R. Sta.,	Mich. L. S R. R.,		Fillmore,	Allegan,		96
Fisher's, Fisher's Sta. P. O.,)	Gr. Rapids & Ind. R. R.,		Wyoming,	Kent,		94
Fisher's Sta., (Beach P. O.,)	Det., L. & L. M. R. R.,		Redford,	Wayne,		108
Fish Lake, R. R. Sta.,	Det. & Bay City R. R.,		Oregon,	Lapeer,		89
Fish Lake, R. R. Sta.,	Lapeer & Northern R. R.,		Mayfield,	Lapeer,		89
Fisk, R. R. Sta.,	Mem. Cold & L. Mich. R. R.,		Allegan,	Allegan,		96
Fitchburg, P. O.,	Mich. Cent. R. R. (J. L. & S. Div.,)	Leslie, 8 m.,	Bunker Hill,	Ingham,		99
Five Lakes, P. O.,	Lapeer & Northern R. R.,	Fish Lake, 4 m.,	Mayfield,	Lapeer,	100	89
Flat Rock, P. O. & R. R. Sta.,	Chi. & Can. So. R. R.,		Brownstown,	Wayne,		103
Flat Rock. R. R. & Tel. Sta.,	Ch. & N. W. R. R., (Pen. Div.)		Escanaba,	Delta,	500	120
Fleming, P. O. & R. R. Sta.,	Det., L. & L. Mich. R. R.,		Howell,	Livingston,	125	100
Flint City, P. O., R. R. & Tel. Sta.,	Flint & P. M. R. W., P. H. & L. M. R. R.,		Flint & Burton,	Genesee,	7,000	90
Florence, P. O. & R. R. Sta.,	L. S. & M. S. R. W., (Kal. Div.,)		Florence,	St. Joseph,		111
Flower Creek, P. O.,	Chi. & Mich. L. Shore R. R.,	Greenwood, 4 m.,	Clay Banks,	Oceana,		80
Flowerfield, P. O.,	L. S. & M. S. R. W., (Kal. Div.,)	Flowerfield, 1 m.,	Flowerfield,	St. Joseph,	230	111
Flowerfield, R. R. Sta.,	L. S. & M. S. R. W, (Kal. Div.,)		Park,	St. Joseph,		111
Flushing, P. O.,	F. & P. M. R. W., P. H. & L. M. R. R.,	Flint, 9 m.,	Flushing,	Genesee,	900	90
Foul River, P. O. & Ldg.,	Green Day,		Escanaba,	Delta,		120
Forest, R. R. Sta.,	Mich. Cent. R. R., (J. L. & S. Div.,)		Kocka,	Crawford,		00
Forest Bay, P. O. & Ldg.,	Lake Huron,		Rubicon,	Huron,		86
Forest City, P. O.,	Musk. & Big Rap. R. R.,	County Line Sta., 2 m.,	Holton,	Muskegon,		81
Forester, P. O., Tel. Sta. & Ldg.,	Lake Huron,		Forester,	Sanilac,	600	87
Forest Hill, P. O.,	Sag. Val. & St. L R. R.,	St. Louis, 5 m.,	Pine River,	Gratiot,		88
Forestville, P. O. Tel. Sta. & Ldg.,	Lake Huron,		Delaware,	Sanilac,	200	87
Fork, P. O.,	F. & P. M. R. W.,	Lake Station, 10 m.,	Fork,	Mecosta,		78
Fort Gratiot, P. O., R. R. Sta. & Ldg.,	Grand Trunk R. W.,		Fort Gratiot,	St. Clair,	852	88
Foster's, R. R. Sta.,	Mich. Cent. R. R.,		Ann Arbor,	Washtenaw,		104
Four Towns, P. O.,	Det. & Mil R. R.,	Pontiac, 7 m.,	West Bloomfield, Waterford,	Oakland,		101
Fowler, P. O., R. R. & Tel. Sta.,	Det. & Mil. R. R.,		Dallas,	Clinton,	200	92
Fowlerville, P. O., R. R. & Tel. Sta.,	Det., L. & L. M. R. R.,		Handy,	Livingston,	800	100
Francisco, P. O.,	Mich. Cent. R. R.,		Grass Lake,	Jackson,		105
Francisco Sta., Francisco P. O., R. R. & Tel. Sta.,	Mich. Cent. R. R., (J. L. & S. Div.,)	Salzburg, 3 m.,	Monitor,	Bay,	380	75
Frankenlust, P. O.,	Mich. Cent. R. R. (J. L. & S. Div.,)	Bridgeport, 8 m.,	Frankenmuth,	Saginaw,	200	94
Frankenmuth, P. O.,	Flint & P. M. R. W.,		Crystal Lake,	Benzie,	1,500	50
Frankfort, P. O. & Ldg.,	Lake Michigan,		Algonquin,	Ontonagon,		116
Franklin Landing,	Lake Superior,		Southfield,	Oakland,	200	101
Franklin, P. O.,	Det. & Mil R. R.,	Birmingham, 5 m.,	Erin,	Macomb,	600	102
Frazer, P. O.,	Grand Trunk R. W.,	Utica Plank 1 m.,	Clinton,	Macomb,		102
Fredrick,	Grand Trunk R. W.,	Mt. Clemens, 1 m.,	Freedom,	Washtenaw,		104
Fredonia, P. O.,	Det., Hills. & Ind. R. R.,	Bridgewater, 6 m.,	Fredonia,	Calhoun,		106
Fredonia, R. R. Sta.,	Mar. & Cold. R. R.,		Tittabawassee,	Saginaw,		86
Freeland's Sta., (Jay P. O.,) R. R. & Tel. Sta.,	F. & P. M. R. W.,		Grant,	Mason,		70
Fremont, P. O.,	Lake Michigan,		Shiawassee,	Shiawassee,		91
Fremont, P. O.,	Det. & Mil R. R.,	Vernon, 8 m.,	Dayton, Sheridan,	Newaygo,	200	79
Fremont Centre, P. O. & R. R. Sta.,	Musk. & Big Rapids R. R.,		Woodbridge,	Hillsdale,	400	112
Frontier, P. O.,	Mars., C. & L. M. R. R.,	Amboy, 5 m.,	Fruitland,	Muskegon,		81
Fruitland, P. O.,	Chi. & Mich. L. Shore R. R.,	Sweets, 1 m.,	Fruitport,	Muskegon,	400	81
Fruitport, P. O. & R. R. Sta.,	Chi. & Mich. L. Shore R. R.,		Wakeshma,	Kalamazoo,		107
Fulton, P. O.,	Peninsular R. W., Grand Rap. & Ind. R. R.,	Vicksburg, 3 m.,	Elmwood,	Tuscola,		85
Gagetown, P. O.,	Saginaw Bay,		Gaines,	Genesee,	800	90
Gaines Station, P. O., R. R. & Tel. Sta.,	Det. & Mil R. R.,		Comstock,	Kalamazoo,	800	107
Galesburg. P. O., R. R. & Tel. Sta.,	Mich. Cent. R. R.,		Iosrier,	Lapeer,	400	109
Galien, P. O., R. R. & Tel. Sta.,	Mich. Cent. R. R.,		Ganges,	Allegan,	200	96
Ganges, P. O., (Pier Cove,)	Chi. & Mich. L. S. R. R.,	Fennville, 7 m.,	Nahma,	Delta,		120
Garden. P. O. & Ldg.,	Big Bay de Noquette,		Denmark,	Tuscola,	150	85
Gates, P. O.,	Det. & Bay City R. R.,		Victor,	Clinton,	400	92
Geary, P. O.,	Mich. Cent. R. R., (J. L. & S. Div.,)	Laingsburg, 5 m.,	Ann Arbor,	Washtenaw,		104
Oedrics, R. R. Sta.,	Mich. Cent. R. R.,					

For Explanations, names of Railroads abbreviated, etc., see page 147.

Name of Village.	Railroad, Lake or River.	Nearest Station or Landing.	Township.	County.	Pop.	Pag.
Genesee, R. R. Sta., (Genesee Village P. O.,)	F. & P. M. R. W., (Ot. Lake Dr.,)	....	Genesee,	Genesee,	200	90
Geneva, P. O.,	Det., Hill. & Ind. R. R.,	Woodstock, 9 m.,	Rollin,	Lenawee,		114
Geneva, R. R. Sta., (West Geneva P. O.,)	Mich. Cent. R. R., (Kal. & S. Hav. Div.,)	....	Geneva,	Van Buren,		108
Genoa, P. O. & R. R. Sta.,	Det., L. & L. M. R. R.,	....	Genoa,	Livingston,		100
Georgetown, P. O.,	Chi. & Mich. L. Shore R. R., (Gr. Rap. Div.,)	Jenison's, 3 m.,	Georgetown,	Ottawa,		93
Georgetown, R. R. Sta.,	Mich. Cent. R. R., (J. L. & S. Div.,)	....	Edwards,	Ottawa,		96
Gibraltar, P. O. & Tel. Sta.,	L. S. & M. S. R. R., Chi. & Can. So. R.,	Newton, 3 m.,	Brownstown,	Wayne,	400	103
Gibsonville,	F. & P. M. R. W.,	Grand Blanc, 2 m.,	Grand Blanc,	Genesee,		90
Gilchrist, R. R. Sta.,	Mich. L. Sh. R. R.,	....	Heath,	Allegan,		96
Gilead, P. O.,	L. S. & M. S. R. W.,	Bronson, 6 m.,	Gilead,	Branch,		112
Gilford, P. O.,	Det. & D. City R. R.,	Reese, 7 m.,	Gilford,	Tuscola,		85
Gilmore, P. O.,	Lake Michigan,	S: Frankfort, 6 m.,	Gilmore,	Benzie,		90
Girard, P. O. & R. R. Sta.,	M., Cold. & L. M. R. R.,	....	Girard,	Branch,	200	112
Gladwin,	F. & P. M. R. W.,	Loomis, 17 m.,	Gladwin,	Gladwin,		74
Glass River, P. O.,	Det., L. & L. M. R. R.,	Fowlerville, 10 m.,	Antrim,	Shiawassee,		91
Glen Arbor, P. O. & Ldg.,	Lake Michigan,	....	Glen Arbor,	Leelanaw,		58
Glendale, P. O.,	Mich. Cent. R. R., (Kal. & S. Hav. Div.,)	Bloomingdale, 6 m.,	Waverly,	Van Buren,	100	108
Glen Haven, P. O. & Ldg.,	Lake Michigan,	....	Glen Arbor,	Leelanaw,		58
Glenwood, R. R. Sta., (Warren P. O.,)	Det. & B. City R. R.,	....	Warren,	Macomb,		102
Goble, P. O. & R. R. Sta.,	Mich. Cent. R. R., (Kal. & S. Hav. Div.,)	....	Bloomingdale,	Van Buren,	300	108
Golding, P. O.,	Chi. & Mich. L. Shore R. R.,	Hart Sta., 3 m.,	Golden,	Oceana,		80
Goodell's, P. O. & R. R. Sta.,	P. H. & L. M. R. R.,	....	Wales,	St. Clair,		98
Good Harbor, P. O.,	Lake Michigan,	....	Cleveland,	Leelanaw,		58
Goodison's Station, P. O.,	Det. & D. City R. R.,	North Unity, 4 m.,	Oakland,	Oakland,		101
Goodland, P. O.,	P. H. & L. M. R. R.,	Imlay City, 6 m.,	Goodland,	Lapeer,		89
Goodrich, P. O.,	F. & P. M. R. W.,	Grand Blanc, 7 m.,	Atlas,	Genesee,	350	90
Goose Lake, R. R. Sta.,	Chi. & N. W. R. R., (Penin. Div.,)	....	Richmond,	Marquette,		119
Gould's Mills, R. R. Sta.,	Gr. Rap. Greenville & Alpena R. R.,	....	Oakfield,	Kent,		94
Gowen, P. O., (Kaywood Sta.,)	Det., L. & L. M. R. R.,	....	Montcalm,	Montcalm,		82
Graafschap, P. O.,	Chi. & Mich. L. Shore R. R., Mich. L. Sh. R. R.,	Holland, 6 m.,	Fillmore,	Allegan,		96
Grafton, P. O. & R. R. Sta.,	F. & P. M. R. W.,	....	Ash,	Monroe,		116
Graham's Sta.,	Sag. Val. & St. L. R. R.,	....	Thomas,	Saginaw,		84
Grand Blanc, P. O., R. R. & Tel. Sta.,	F. & P. M. R. W.,	....	Grand Blanc,	Genesee,	200	90
Grand Haven City, P. O., R. R. & Tel. Sta.,	Mich. L. Sh. R. R., Det. & Mil. R. R.,	....	Grand Haven,	Ottawa,	5,000	95
Grand Junction, P. O., R. R. & Tel. Sta.,	Mich. Cent. R. R.,(K.& S Hv.,)Chi.& M. L. S. R. R.,	....	Columbia,	Van Buren,	400	108
Grand Ledge, P. O., R. R. & Tel. Sta.,	Det., L. & L. M. R. R.,	....	Oneida,	Eaton,		98
Grand Point, (Bourne P. O. & Sta.,)	L. S. & M. S. R., Tol, Can S. & Det. R. W.,	....	Kearce,	Wayne,		103
Grand Rapids City, P. O., R. R. & Tel. Sta.,	Det. & Mil R.R., Gr.Rap.& Ind.R.R., Gr.Rap.,N. & L. S. R. R., Mich. Cent. R. R., (Gr.& Val. Div.,) Chi. & Mich. L. Shore R. R., (Gr.Rap.Div.,) L. S. R. R. (Id. br.,)	....	Grand Rapids,	Kent,	20,000	94
Grandville, P. O. & R. R. Sta.,	Chi. & Mich. L. Shore R. R., (Gr. Rap Div.,)	....	Wyoming,	Kent,	400	94
Grant, P. O.,	Det., L. & L. M. R. R.,	Chadwick, 9 m.,	Grattan,	Kent,		94
Granton or Standish, P. O. & R. R. Sta.,	Mich. Cent. R. R., (J. L. & S. Div.,)	....	Standish,	Bay,		75
Grass Lake, P. O., R. R. & Tel. Sta.,	Mich. Cent. R. R.,	....	Grass Lake,	Jackson,	1,000	105
Grattan, P. O.,	Gr. Rap., Greenville & Alpena R. R.,	Oakfield Sta., 6 m.,	Grattan,	Kent,		94
Gravel Run, P. O.,	Det., L. & L. M. R. R.,	Salem 6 m.,	Northfield,	Washtenaw,		104
Greenbush, P. O., Tel. Sta. & Ldg.,	Lake Huron,	....	Greenbush,	Alcona,	200	94
Greenfield, P. O.,	Det. L. & L. M. R. R.,	....	Greenfield,	Wayne,		108
Greenland, P. O. & Tel. Sta.,	Lake Superior,	Ontonagon, 12 m.,	Greenland,	Ontonagon,		116
Green Oak, P. O.,	Det., L. & L. M. R. R.,	Green Oak Sta., 3 m.,	Green Oak,	Livingston,		100
Green Oak Station, P. O. & R. R. Sta.,	Det., L. & L. M. R. R.,	....	Green Oak,	Livingston,		100
Greenville, P. O., R. R. & Tel. Sta.,	Det., L. & L. M. R. R., Gr. Rap., G. & A. R. R.,	....	Eureka,	Montcalm,	3,000	82
Greenwood, R. R. Sta.,	Chi. & Mich. L. Shore R. R.,	....	Grant,	Oceana,		80
Greenwood Furnace, P. O. & R. R. Sta., (Greenwood R. R. Sta.,)	Marq., H. & Ont. R. R.,	....	Ely,	Marquette,		119
Grindstone City, P. O., Tel. Sta. & Ldg.,	Lake Huron,	....	Port Austin,	Huron,	200	85
Groningen, P. O.,	Chi. & Mich. L. Shore R. R., (Gr. Rap. Div.,)	Zeeland, 1 m.,	Holland,	Ottawa,	100	95
Grosse Point, P. O.,	....	Detroit, 6 m.,	Grosse Point,	Wayne,	900	103
Grost,	Flint & P. M. R. W.,	Loomis, 14 m.,	Grost,	Gladwin,		74
Groveland, P. O.,	Det. & Mil. R. R., F. & P. M. R. W.,	Holly, 5 m.,	Groveland,	Oakland,		101
Gull Lake, P. O.,	Mich. Cent. R. R.,	Augusta, 9 m.,	Prairieville,	Barry,		97
Gun Marsh, P. O. & R. R. Sta.,	M., Cold. & L. M. R. R.,	....	Gun Plain,	Allegan,		96
Hadley, P. O.,	Det. & Bay City R. R.,	Metamora, 7 m.,	Hadley,	Lapeer,	200	89
Hagar, P. O. & R. R. Sta.,	Chi. & Mich. L. Shore R. R.,	....	Hagar,	Berrien,		100
Hamburg, P. O.,	St. Cl. & Cr. Air Line R. R.,	....	Hamburg,	Livingston,	100	100
Hamilton, P. O. & R. R. Sta., (Rabbit River,)	Mich. L. Sh. R. R.,	....	Heath,	Allegan,	250	96
Hamlin Landing,	Lake Michigan,	....	Hamlin,	Mason,		70
Hamlin, P. O. & R. R. Sta.,	Chi. & Can. So. R. R.,	....	Raisinville,	Monroe,		115
Hammond, P. O. & R. R. Sta.,	Mich. Cent. R. R., (Gr. Riv. Val. Div.,)	....	Union,	Kent,		94
Hancock, P. O., Tel. Sta. & Ldg.,	Portage Lake,	....	Quincy,	Houghton,	2,000	117
Hanley, P. O.,	Chi. & Mich. L. Shore R. R., (Gr. Rap. Div.,)	Jenison's, 4 m.,	Jamestown,	Ottawa,		95
Hanover, P. O., R. R. & Tel. Sta.,	Ft. Wayne, Jack. & Sag. R. R.,	....	Hanover,	Jackson,	150	105
Hanses, P. O.,	Chi. & Mich. L. Shore R. R.,	Barrett's, 9 m.,	Ferry,	Oceana,		80
Harmonia,	Mich. Cent. R. R., (Gr. Riv. Val. Div.,)	Bedford, 1 m.,	Bedford,	Calhoun,		106
Harris Creek, P. O.,	Mich. Cent. R. R., (Gr. Riv. Val. Div.,)	Caledonia, 6 m.,	Bowne,	Kent,		94
Harrietville, P. O., Tel. Sta. & Ldg.,	Lake Huron,	....	Harrisville,	Alcona,	500	94
Hart, P. O.,	Chi. & Mich. L. Shore R. R.,	Hart Sta., 3 m.,	Hart,	Oceana,	600	80
Hart Station,	Chi. & Mich. L. Shore R. R.,	....	Golden,	Oceana,		80
Hartford, P. O., R. R. & Tel. Sta.,	Chi. & Mich. L. Shore R. R.	....	Hartford,	Van Buren,		108
Hartland, P. O.,	Flint & P. M. R. W.,	Clyde, 8 m.,	Hartland,	Livingston,	250	100
Hartsuffville, P. O.,	Mich. Cent. R. R., (J. L. & S. Div.,)	Bennington, 6 m.,	Bennington, Shiawassee,	Shiawassee,		91
Harvey, P. O. & Ldg.,	Lake Superior, Marq., H. & Ont. R. R.,	Marquette, 5 m.,	Chocolay,	Marquette,		119
Harvey Station, R. R. Sta.,	Chi. & N. W. R. R., (Pen. Div.,)	....	Chocolay,	Marquette,		119
Hasler, P. O.,	....	....	....	Lapeer,		89
Hastings, P. O., R. R. & Tel. Sta.,	Mich. Cent. R. R., (Gr. Riv. Val. Div.,)	....	Hastings,	Barry,	2,000	97
Havanna,	Mich. Cent. R. R., (J. L. & S. Div.,)	Oakley, 2 m.,	Chesaning,	Saginaw,		84
Hazel Green, P. O., (Hendersonville Sta.,)	Mich. Cent. R. R., (J. L. & S. Div.,)	....	Bush,	Shiawassee,		91
Hazel Green, P. O.,	Mus. & Big Rapids R. R.,	Holton, 5 m.,	Greenwood,	Oceana,		80
Hazelton, P. O.,	P. H. & L. M. R. R.,	(R. R. unfinished,)	Hazleton,	Shiawassee,		91
Hecla, R. R. Sta.,	Hecla & Torch Lake R. R.,	....	Calumet & Schoolcraft,	Houghton,		117
Helena, R. R. Sta.,	Chi. & N. W. R. R., (Penin. Div.,)	....	Forsyth,	Marquette,		119
Helmer's, R. R. Sta.,	Peninsular R. W.,	....	Battle Creek,	Calhoun,		106
Hemphill, P. O.,	Marq., H. & Ont. R. R.,	....	....	Houghton,		117
Hemlock City, P. O. & R. R. Sta.,	Sag. Val. & St. Louis R. R.,	....	Richland,	Saginaw,	200	84
Hendersonville, R. R. Sta., (Hazel Green P. O.,)	Mich. Cent. R. R., (J. L. & S. Div.,)	....	Bush,	Shiawassee,		91
Henrietta, P. O.,	Mich. Cent. R. R., (L & S. Hv. & G. & Vl. Dv.,)	Rives Junction, 6 m.,	Henrietta,	Jackson,		105
Herrickville, (Butler P. O.,)	Mich. Cent. R. R., (Air Line Div.,)	Clarendon, 5 m.,	Butler,	Branch,		112
Hersey, P. O., R. R. & Tel. Sta.,	Flint & P. M. R. W.,	....	Hersey, Richmond,	Osceola,	500	72
Hesperia, P. O.,	Mus. & Big Rap. R. R.,	....	Denver, Newfield,	Newaygo & Oceana,	300	78,80
Hickory Corners, P. O.,	Mich. Cent. R. R.,	Augusta, 6 m.,	Barry,	Barry,		97
Highland, P. O.,	Flint & P. M. R. W.,	Highland Sta., 3 m.,	Highland,	Oakland,		101
Highland Sta., R. R. & Tel. Sta., (Spring Mill's P. O.,)	F. & P. M. R. W.,	....	Highland,	Oakland,		101
Hilliard's, P. O. & R. R. Sta.,	L. S. & M. S. R. W., (Kal. Div.,)	....	Hopkins,	Allegan,		96

☞ For Explanations, names of Railroads abbreviated, etc., see page 147.

Name of Village.	Railroad, Lake or River.	Nearest Station or Landing.	Township.	County.	Pop.	Page
Hill's Corners, (Weesaw P. O.,)	Mich. Cent. R. R.,	Galien, 7 m.,	Weesaw,	Berrien,		109
Hillsdale, P. O., R. R. & Tel. Sta.,	L. S. & M. S. R. W., Det., Hill. & Ind. R. R.,		Hillsdale,	Hillsdale,	3,600	113
Hinkle's Mill, R. R. Sta.,	F. & P. M. R. W.,		Grant,	Clare,		78
Heffigan's, R. R. Sta.,	Mich. Cent. R. R.,		Canton,	Wayne,		103
Holland, P. O., R. R. & Tel. Sta.,	Mich. L. Sh. R. R., Chi. & Mich. L. Shore R. R. & Gr. Riv.,		Holland,	Ottawa,	3,000	95
Holly, P. O., R. R. & Tel. Sta.,	Det. & Mil., & F. & P. M. R. W.,		Holly,	Oakland,	2,200	101
Holt, P. O., (Delhi Sta.,)	Mich. Cent. R. R., (J. L. & S. Div.,)		Delhi,	Ingham,	200	99
Holton, P. O. & R. R. Sta.,	Mus. & Big Rap. R. R.,		Holton,	Muskegon,	200	81
Home, P. O.,	Mus. & Big Rap. R. R.,		Newaygo,	Cass,		70
Homer, P. O., R. R. & Tel. Sta.,	Mich. Cent. L. S. & M. S. R. W. (Lans. Div.)	Monroeville, 5 m.,	Monroe, Barton,	Homer,		70
Homestead, P. O.,	Gr. Rap. & Ind. R. R. (Trav. City Dr.,)		Homer,	Calhoun,	1,100	106
Hocker, P. O.,	Chi. & Mich. L. Shore R. R.,	Traverse City, 23 m.,	Homestead,	Benzie,		50
Hope, P. O.,	F. & P. M. R. W.,	Bangor, 5 m.,	Geneva,	Van Buren,		108
Hopkins, P. O.,	L. S. & M. S. R. W., (Kal. Div.)	Averill, 6 m.,	Hope,	Midland,		76
Hopkins Station, P. O. & R. R. Sta.,	L. S. & M. S. R. W., (Kal. Div.)	Hopkins, 3 m.,	Hopkins,	Allegan,		96
Hoppertown, R. R. Sta.,	Chi. & Mich. L. Shore R. R.,		Hopkins,	Allegan,		96
Houghton, P. O., Tel. Sta. & Ldg.,	Portage Lake,		Lee,	Allegan,		96
Houghton Falls, R. R. Sta.,	Hecla & Torch Lake R. R.,		Portage,	Houghton,	2,000	117
Howard, P. O., (Hoodsville,)	Chi. & Mich. L. Shore R. R.,	Muskegon, 2 m.,	Schoolcraft,	Houghton,		117
Howard, R. R. Sta., (Daily P. O.)	Mich. Cent. R. R., (Air L. Div.,)		Muskegon,	Muskegon,		81
Howard City, P. O., R. R. & Tel. Sta.,	Gr. Rap. & Ind. & Det. L. & L. M. R. R.,		Jefferson,	Cass,	600	150
Howardville, P. O.,	L. S. & M. S. R. W., (Kal. Div.,)	Moorepark, 5 m.,	Reynolds,	Montcalm,		82
Howell, P. O., R. R. & Tel. Sta.,	Det., L. & L. M. R. R.,		Florerfield,	St. Joseph,		111
Howlardsburg,	Det., L. & M., & Cold. & L. M. R. R.,	Augusta, 2 m.,	Howell,	Livingston,	2,200	100
Hubbardston, P. O.,	Det. & Mil. R. R.,	Pewamo, 5 m.,	Ross,	Kalamazoo,		107
Hubinger, (Frankenmuth P. O.,)	F. & P. M. R. W.,	Bridgeport, 8 m.,	North Plains,	Ionia,	750	98
Hudson, P. O., R. R. & Tel. Sta.,	L. S. & M. S. R. W.,		Frankenmuth,	Saginaw,		84
Hudson Mills, (Bear Lake P. O.,)	Mich. Cent. R. R.,	Dexter, 4 m.,	Hudson,	Lenawee,	3,000	114
Hudsonville, P. O., (Hudson Sta.,)	Chi. & Mich. L. Shore R. R., (Gr. Rap. Div.,)		Dexter,	Washtenaw,		104
Hughesville, P. O., (County Line Sta.,)	F. & P. M. R. W.,		Georgetown,	Ottawa,		95
Humboldt, P. O. & R. R. Sta.,	Marq., H. & Ont. R. R.,		Brick Run,	Saginaw,		83
Hunter's Creek, P. O. & R. R. Sta.,	Det. & D. City R. R.,		Ely,	Marquette,	2,000	119
Huntingdown,	F. & P. M. R. W., (Ot. Lake Br.)	Oisville, 1 m.,	Lapeer,	Lapeer,		89
Hurd's Corners, (East Dayton P. O.)	Det. & Bay City R. R.,	Vassar, 15 m.,	Forest,	Genesee,		90
Huron City, P. O., Tel. Sta. & Ldg.,	Lake Huron,		Wells, Dayton,	Tuscola,		85
Ida, P. O. & R. R. Sta.,	L. S. & M. S. R. W., (Det. Div.)		Huron,	Huron,		86
Imlay, P. O.,	P. H. & L. M. R. R.,	Imlay City, 2 m.,	Ida,	Monroe,	100	115
Imlay City, P. O., R. R. & Tel. Sta.,	P. H. & L. M. R. R.,		Imlay,	Lapeer,	700	89
Indian Creek, P. O.,	Det. & Mil., & Gr. Rap. & Ind. R. R.,	Grand Rapids, 4 m.,	Imlay,	Lapeer,	*	89
Indian Lake, R. R. Sta.,	Penin. R. W.,		Walker,	Kent,		94
Indian Town, Ldg.,	Green Bay,		Pavilion,	Kalamazoo,		107
Indiantown, P. O.,	F. & P. M. R. W.,	Amber, 3 m.,	Escanaba,	Delta,		120
Ingersoll, R. R. Sta.,	Det., L. & L. M. R. R.,		Riverton,	Mason,		70
Inkster, P. O. & R. R. Sta.,	Mich. Cent. R. R.,		Watertown,	Clinton,		92
Inland, P. O.,	Gr. Rap. & Ind R. R., (Traverse City Dr.,)	Traverse City, 15 m.,	Kankin, Dearborn,	Wayne,	800	103
Inverness, R. R. Sta.,	Mich. Cent. R. R., (J. L. & S. Div.,)		Inland,	Benzie,		52
Ionia, P. O., R. R. & Tel. Sta.,	Det., L. & L. M., & Det. & Mil. R. R.,	Fowlerville, 8 m.,	Inverness,	Cheboygan,	3,700	98
Iosco, P. O.,	Det., L. & L. M. R. R.,		Easton, Ionia,	Ionia,		100
Irving, P. O. & R. R. Sta.,	Mich. Cent. R. R., (Gr. Riv. Val. Div.)	Geneva,	Iosco,	Livingston,		97
Irvington, (West Geneva P. O.,)	Mich. Cent. R. R., (Kal. & S. Hav. Div.)		Irving,	Barry,		106
Ishpeming, P. O., R. R. & Tel. Sta.,	M., H. & O., & Chi. & N. W. R. R. (Pen. Div.,)		Genera,	Van Buren,	4,000	110
Ithaca, P. O.,	Sag. Val. & St. L. R. R.,	St. Louis, 8 m.,	Ishpeming,	Marquette,	600	89
Jackson City, P. O., R. R. & Tel. Sta.,	Mich. Cent. (&c. J. L. & S. Div. & Air. L. Div.)		Arcada, Loren, Kennel,	Gratiot,	15,000	103
	L. S. & M. S. (Jack. Br.) Ft. W., J. & S R. R.,		Blackman, Summit,	Jackson,		
Jamestown, P. O.,	Chi. & Mich. L. Shore R. R., (Gr. Rap. Div.,)	Hudson, 4 m.,	Jamestown,	Ottawa,		95
Jamestown, R. R. Sta., (Penn. P. O.,)	Penin. R. W.,		Penn,	Cass,		110
Jay, P. O., (Freeland's Sta.,)	F. & P. M. R. W.,	Thornton, 13 m.,	Tittabawassee,	Saginaw,		84
Jeddo, P. O.,	P. H. & L. M. R. R.,	Pittsford, 4 m.,	Grant,	St. Clair,		88
Jefferson, P. O.,	L. S. & M. S. R. W.,		Jefferson,	Hillsdale,		113
Jeffersonville, P. O.,	Mich. Cent. R. R., (Air L. Div.,) & Penin. R. W.,	Cassopolis, 3 m.,	Jefferson,	Cass,		110
Jennisonville, P. O., (Jenison's, R. R. Sta.,	Chi. & Mich. L. Shore R. R., (Gr. R. Div.,)		Georgetown,	Ottawa,		95
Jericho, P. O.,	Mich. Cent. R. R., (Kal. & S. Hav. Div.,)	Kibbs, 5 m.,	Geneva,	Van Buren,		108
Jerome, R. R. Sta.,	Det., Hill. & Ind. R. R.,		Somerset,	Hillsdale,	100	113
Jersey, P. O.,	Det. & Bay City R. R.,	Orion, 5 m.,	Orion,	Oakland,		101
Johnstown, P. O.,	Mich. Cent. R. R., (Gr. Riv. Val. Div.,)	Quimby, 10 m.,	Johnstown,	Barry,		97
Johnsville, P. O. & R. R. Sta.,	Mich. L. Sh. R. R.,		Grand Haven,	Ottawa,		95
Johnsville,	Det. & B. City R. R.,	Reese, 12 m.,	Fair Grove,	Tuscola,		85
Jonas, R. R. Sta., (Newberg P. O.,)	Mich. Cent. R. R.,		Newberg,	Cass,		110
Jonesville, P. O., R. R. & Tel. Sta.,	Ft. W., J. & S. R. R., L. S. & M. S. R. W.,		Fayette,	Hillsdale,	2,600	113
Joyfield, P. O.,	Lake Michigan,	S. Frankfort, 11 m.,	Joyfield,	Benzie,	100	50
Junction,	Grand Trunk R. W.,	Utica Plank, 1½ m.,	Erin,	Macomb,		102
Kalamazoo, P. O., R. R. & Tel. Sta.,	Mich. Cent. (&c., Kal. & S. Hav. Div.,) L. S. & M. S. (Kal. Div.,) Gr. Rap. & Ind R. R.,		Kalamazoo,	Kalamazoo,	10,500	107
Kalamo, P. O. & R. R. Sta.,	Mar. & Cold. R. R.,		Kalamo,	Eaton,	100	96
Kalkaska, R. R. Sta.,	Gr. Rap. & Ind. R. R.,		Kalkaska,	Kalkaska,		61
Kasson, P. O.,	Gr. Rapids & Ind. R. R., (Trav. City Dr.,)	Traverse City, 15 m.,	Kasson,	Leelanaw,		58
Kawkawlin, P. O. R. R. & Tel Sta.,	Mich. Cent. R. R. (J. L. & S. Div.)		Kawkawlin,	Bay,	500	75
Kaywood, R. R. Sta., (Gowen, P. O.,)	Det., L. & L. Mich. R. R.,		Montcalm,	Montcalm,		82
Keelersville, P. O.,	Chi. & Mich. L. Shore R. R.,	Hartford, 7 m.,	Keeler,	Van Buren,	200	108
Keene, P. O.,	Det. & Mil. R. R.,	Saranac, 4 m.,	Keene,	Ionia,		98
Kellogg, R. R. Sta.,	Mann, Cold. & L. Mich. R. R.,		Watson,	Allegan,		96
Kelloggville,	Gr. Rap. & Ind. R. R.,	Fisburn, 1 m.,	Wyoming, Paris,	Kent,		94
Kelly's Corners P. O., (Woodstock Sta.,)	Det., Hills. & Ind. R. R.,		Wyoming, Jackson,	Lenawee, Jackson,	100	114
Kendall, P. O., R. R. & Tel Sta.,	Mich Cent. R. R., (Kal. & S. Hav. Div.,)		Pine Grove,	Van Buren,	400	108
Kendallville,	Det., L. & L. M. R. R.,	Maple Valley, 5 m.,	Pine,	Montcalm,		82
Kenockee, P. O.,	F. H. & L. M. R. R.,	Goodell's, 5 m.,	Kenockee,	St. Clair,		88
Kensington, P. O.,	Det., L. & L. M. R. R., So. Cl. & C. Air L. R. R.	Green Oak, 8 m.,	Lyon,	Oakland,		101
Kibbe, P. O., R. R. & Tel. Sta.,	Mich. Cent. R. R. (Kal. & S. Hav. Div.,)		Geneva,	Van Buren,		108
Kidville, P. O. & R. R. Sta.,	Det. L. & L. M. R. R.,		Otisco,	Ionia,	200	98
Kinderhook, P. O.,	M., Cold. & L. M. R. R.,	California, 6 m.,	Kinderhook,	Branch,	200	112
Kingsley's R. R. Sta.,	Gr. R. & Ind. R. R., (Trav. City Br.,)		Paradise,	G'd Traverse,		60
Kingston, P. O., (Newburg,)	Det. & Bay City R. R.,	Vassar, 20 m.,	Kingston, Koylton,	Tuscola,	80	86
Kipp Corners,	F. & P. M. R. W.,	Grand Blanc, 10 m.,	Atlas,	Genesee,		90
Kossuth, P. O.,	Det., L. & L. M. R. R.,	Stubbinsville, 1 m.,	Portland,	Ionia,		98
Lafayette, P. O.,	Sag. Val. & St. L. R. R.,	Wheeler, 7 m.,	Lafayette,	Gratiot,	150	110
La Grange, P. O.,	Mich. Cent. R. R., (Air Line Div.,) & Penin. R. W.,	Cassopolis, 4 m.,	Lagrange,	Cass,		110
Lainsburg, P. O., R. R. & Tel. Sta.,	Mich. Cent. R. R., (J. L. & S. Div.,)	Pelota,	Sciota,	Shiawassee,	600	91
Lake, P. O.,	Gr. Rap., New & L. Shore R. R.,	County Line, 2 m.,	Ashland,	Newaygo,		79
Lake, R. R. & Tel. Sta.,	Flint & P. M. R. W.,		Surrey,	Clare,		78
Lake, R. R. Sta., (Black Lake P. O.,)	Mich. L. Sh. R. R.,		Norton,	Muskegon,		81
Lake City, P. O.,	Mar. & Cold. R. R.,	Sunfield, 4 m.,	Sebewa,	Ionia,		95
Lake Harbor, P. O.,	Mich. L. Sh. R. R.,	Black Lake, 8 m.,	Norton,	Muskegon,	800	81

☞ For Explanations, names of Railroads abbreviated, etc., see page 147.

Name of Village.	Railroad, Lake or River.	Nearest Station or Landing.	Township.	County.	Pop.	Page.
Lake Linden, P. O., (Torch Lake Mills, R. R. Sta.,)	Hecla & Torch Lake H. R.,		Schoolcraft,	Houghton,	500	117
Lake Mills, P. O.,	Mich. Cent. R. R., (Kal. & S. Hav. Div.,)		B ooningsdale,	Van Buren,		108
Lakeport, P. O., Tel. Sta. & Ldg.,	Lake Huron,		Butlerville,	St. Clair,	300	88
Lake Ridge, P. O.,	L. S. & M. S. R. W., (Jackson Br.,)	Tecumseh, 8 m.,	Macon,	Lenawee,		114
Laketon, P. O., (Bridgman Sta.,)	Chi. & Mich. L. Shore R. R.,		Lake,	Berrien,		100
Laketon,	Chi. & Mich. L. Shore, & Mich. L. Sh. R. R.,	Muskegon, 5 m.,	Laketon,	Muskegon,		81
Lakeview, P. O.,	Gr. R. & Ind. R. R.,	Cenger, 9 m.,	Coto,	Montcalm,	300	82
Lakeville, P. O.,	Det. & B. City R. R.,	Oxford, 6 m.,	Addison,	Oakland,	150	101
Lamberville, P. O.,	Tol. & Ann Ar. R. R.,		Bedford,	Monroe,		115
Lamont, P. O.,	Det. & Mil. R. R.,	Cooperville, 4 m.,	Tallmadge,	Ottawa,	250	95
Lamotte, P. O.,	P. H. & L. M. R. R.,	Imlay, 20 m.,	Lamotte,	Sanilac,		87
Langston, P. O.,	Det., L. & L. M. R. R.,	Trufant, 6 m.,	Pine,	Montcalm,	800	82
L'Anse, P. O., R. R. & Tel. Sta.,	Marq., H. & Ont. R. R.,		L'Anse,	Houghton,	300	117
Lansing, State Capital, P. O., R. R. & Tel Sta.,	Mich. Cent. (J. L. & S. Div.,) Det., L. & L. M., Penin.; L. S. & M. S. R. W. (Lansing Div.,)		Lansing,	Ingham,	6,500	90
Lapeer, P. O., R. R. & Tel. Sta.,	Det. & B. City; P. H. & L. M. R. R.,		Lapeer,	Lapeer,	3,500	89
Lapham's Corners, (Salem P. O.,)	Det., L. & L. M. R. R.,	Salem, 2 m.,	Salem,	Washtenaw,		104
La Salle, P. O. & R. R. Sta.,	L. S. & M. S. R. W., (St. Nt.,) Na. Cor. S. & St. L V.,		La Salle,	Monroe,		115
Lawrence, P. O.,	Chi. & Mich. L. Shore R. R.,	Hartford, 6 m.,	Lawrence,	Van Buren,	600	108
Lawton, P. O., R. R. & Tel. Sta.,	Mich. Cent. R. R.,		Antwerp,	Van Buren,	1,500	108
Leesville. P. O.,		Det. Junction, 3 m.,	Hamtramck,	Wayne,		103
Leland, P. O. & Ldg.,	Lake Michigan,		Centreville,	Leelanaw,	420	58
Lenawee Junction, R. R. & Tel. Sta.,	L. S. & M. S. R. W. & Do. (Det. Div. & Jack. Br.,)		Palmyra,	Lenawee,		114
Leoni, P. O. & R. R. Sta.,	Mich. Cent. R. R.,		Leoni,	Jackson,	900	105
Leonidas, P. O.,	Mich. Cent. R. R., (Air L. Div.,)	Colon, 5 m.,	Leonidas,	St. Joseph,	290	111
Leslie, P. O. R. R. & Tel. Sta.,	Mich. Cent. R. R., (J. L. & S. Div.,)		Leslie,	Ingham,	1,200	99
Leroy, P. O. R. R. & Tel. Sta.,	Gr. Rap. & Ind. R. R.,		Leroy,	Osceola,		72
Leroy, R. R. & Tel Sta., (Webberville P. O.,)	Det., L. & L. M. R. R.,		Leroy,	Ingham,		99
Lexington, P. O., Tel. Sta. & Ldg.,	Lake Huron,		Lexington,	Sanilac,	1,000	87
Liberty Mills, (Liberty P. O.,)	Det., Hill. & Ind. R. R.,	Somerset, 4 m.,	Liberty,	Jackson,	300	105
Lima, P. O.,	Mich. Cent. R. R.,	Chelsea, 4 m.,	Lima,	Washtenaw,	140	104
Lincoln, P. O. & Ldg.,	F. & P. M. R. W., Lake Michigan,	Ludington, 2 m.,	Lincoln,	Mason,	100	70
Lincoln, R. R. Sta.,	Chi. & Mich. L. Shore R. R.,		Lincoln,	Berrien,		109
Linden, P. O.,	Det. & Mil. R. R.,		Fenton,	Genesee,	800	90
Linden, R. R. & Tel. Sta.,	Gr. Rap. & Ind. R. R.,	Linden Sta., 1 m.,	Haring,	Wexford,		69
Lisbon, P. O.,	Gr. Rap., New. & L. Shore R. R.,	Sparta, 5 m.,	Chester, Sparta,	Ottawa, Kent,	93, 94	
Litchfield, P. O. & R. R. Sta.,	L. S. & M. S. R. W., (Lansing Div.,)		Litchfield,	Hillsdale,	750	113
Little Lake, R. R. Sta.,	Chi. & N. W. R. R., (Penin. Div.,)		Forsyth,	Marquette,		119
Little Prairie Ronds, P. O., (Nicholesville,)	Penin. R. W.,	Volinia, 5 m.,	Volinia,	Cass,		110
Little Traverse, P. O. & Ldg.,	Lake Michigan,		Little Traverse,	Emmet,	812	51
Livonia, P. O.,	Det., L. & L. M. R. R.,	Livonia, 2 m.,	Livonia,	Wayne,		103
Livonia, R. R. Sta.,	Det., L. & L. M. R. R.,		Livonia,	Wayne,		103
Locke, P. O.,	Det. L. & L. M. R. R.,	Leroy, 5 m.,	Locke,	Ingham,		99
Lockport, R. R. Sta.,	Mich. Cent. R. R., (Air Line Br.,) L. S. & M. S. R. W., (Air Br.,)		Lockport,	St. Joseph,		111
Lockwood, P. O. & R. R. Sta.,	Gr. R. & Ind. R. R.,		Nelson,	Kent,		94
London, P. O.,	Tol. & Ann Ar. R. R.,	Bueren, 3 m.,	London,	Monroe,		115
Longwood, P. O.,	F. & P. M. R. W.,		Isabella,	Isabella,	100	77
Loomis, P. O. R. R. & Tel. Sta.,	F. & P. M. R. W.,		Wise,	Isabella,	300	77
Loomisville,	Pedimeter R. W.,	Madison, 6 m.,	Ceuvre,	Calhoun,		106
Lowell, P. O., R. R. & Tel. Sta.,	Det. & Mil. R. R.,		Lowell,	Kent,	2,000	94
Lower Big Rapids, R. R. & Tel. Sta.,	Gr. R. & Ind. R. R.,		Big Rapids,	Mecosta,		78
Ludington, P. O., R. R. & Tel. Sta. & Ldg.,	F. & P. M. R. W. & Lake Michigan,		Ludington,	Mason,	2,500	70
Lynn, P. O.,	F. H. & L. M. R. R.,	Capac, 7 m.,	Lynn,	St. Clair,		88
Lyons, P. O. & R R Sta.,	Det., L. & L. M. R. R.,		Lyons,	Ionia,	1,000	93
Lyons Mill, P. O.,	Det. & Mil. R. R.,	St. Johns, 4 m.,	Bengal,	Clinton,		90
Mc Donald, P. O., (Deerfield Sta.,)	Chi. & Mich. L. Shore R. R.,		Bangor,	Van Buren,		108
Mackinaw, P. O., Tel. Sta. & Ldg.,	Straits of Mackinac,		Mackinac,	Cheboygan,	1,000	122?
Mackinaw City, P. O. & Ldg.,	Lake Huron,		Beaugrand,	Cheboygan,		52
Mc Kinney's, R. R. Sta.,	Det., L. & L. M. R. R.,		Livonia,	Wayne,		103
Macomb, P. O.,	St. Cl. & C. Air L. R. R.,	Washington, 6 m.,	Macomb,	Macomb,		102
Macon, P. O.,	L. S. & M. S. R. W., (Jack. Dr.,)	Clinton, 5 m.,	Macon,	Lenawee,	300	114
Madison, P. O., (Deerfield Centre,)	Det. & Mil. R. R.,	Linden, 10 m.,	Deerfield,	Livingston,		102
Madison, R. R. Sta.,	Penin. R. W.,		Prairfield,	Calhoun,		106
Mahopac, P. O.,	Det. & B. City R. R.,	Rudds, 6 m.,	Orion,	Oakland,		101
Mancelona, R. R. Sta.,	Gr. Rap. & Ind. R. R.,		Mancelona,	Antrim,		57
Manchester, P. O., R. R. & Tel. Sta.,	L. S. & M. S. R. W., (Jack. Dr.,) Det., Hill. & Ind. R. R.,		Manchester,	Washtenaw,	2,000	104
Manistee City, P. O., Tel. Sta. & Ldg.,	Lake Michigan,		Manistee City,	Manistee,	4,000	50
Manlius, R. R. Sta.,	Chi. & Mich. L. Shore R. R.,		Manlius,	Allegan,		98
Manton, P. O. & R. R. Sta.,	Gr. Rap. & Ind R. R.,		Cedar Creek,	Wexford,		69
Manwataze, P. O.,	Gr. Rap. & Ind. R. R.,	Wexford Sta., 5 m.,	Colfax & Selma,	Wexford,		69
Maple, P. O.,	Det., L. & L. M. R. R.,	Lyons, 4 m.,	Portland,	Ionia,		93
Maple Grove, P. O.,	Mich. Cent. R. R., (Gr. Riv. Val. Div.,)	Nashville, 5 m.,	Maple Valley,	Barry,		92
Maple Grove, (Elk P. O.,)	F. & P. M. R. W.,	Clio, 10 m.,	Maple Grove, Reirow,	Saginaw, Genes,		84
Maple Hill, P. O. & R. R. Sta.,	Gr. Rap. & Ind. R. R.,		Pierson,	Montcalm,		82
Maple Rapids, P. O.,	Det. & Mil. R. R.,	Fowler, 8 m.,	Essex,	Clinton,	600	92
Maple Ridge, R. R. Sta.,	Gr. R. & W. R. R., (Penin. Div.,)		Alegle Ridge,	Delta,		120
Mapleton, P. O. & Ldg.,	Grand Traverse Bay,		Peninsula,	Grand Traverse,		60
Maple Valley, P. O. & R R Sta.,	Det., L. & L. M. R. R.,		Maple Valley,	Montcalm,	200	82
Marathon, P. O.,	Det. & Bay City R. R.,	Columbiaville, 2 m.,	Marathon,	Lapeer,		89
Marcellus, P. O., R. R. & Tel. Sta.,	Penin. R. W.,		Marcellus,	Cass,	150	110
Marcellus,	Grand Trunk R. W.,	Mt. Clemens, 4 m.,	Clinton,	Macomb,		102
Marengo, P. O. & R R Sta.,	Mich. Cent. R. R.,		Marengo,	Calhoun,		106
Marilla, P. O.,	Gr. Rap. & Ind. R. R.,	Wexford, 23 m.,	Marilla,	Manistee,		50
Marine City, P. O., Tel. Sta. & Ldg.,	River St. Clair,		Cottrellville,	St. Clair,	1,800	88
Marion, P. O.,	Det. L. & L. M. R. R.,	Howell, 7 m.,	Marion,	Livingston,		100
Marlette, P. O.,	P. H. & L. M. R. R.,	Imlay, 21 m.,	Marlette,	Sanilac,	250	87
Marquette City, P. O., R. R. & Tel. Sta.,	Marq., H. & Ont. R. R.,		Marquette City,	Marquette City,	7,000	119
Marshall City, P. O., R. R. & Tel. Sta.,	Mich. Cent. R. R. Mar. & Cold R.,		Marshall,	Calhoun,	6,000	106
Marshville, P. O.,	Chi. & Mich. L. Shore R. R.,	Barrett, 5 m.,	Benona,	Oceana,		82
Martin, P. O. & R R Sta.,	Gr. Rap. & Ind. R. R.,		Martin,	Allegan,	200	98
Martinsville, P. O.,	F. & P. M. R. W.,	Wait, 5 m.,	Sumpter,	Wayne,		103
Marysville, P. O. & Ldg., (Vicksburg,)	River St. Clair,		Port Huron,	St. Clair,	250	88
Mason, P. O., R. R. & Tel. Sta.,	Mich. Cent. R. R., (J. L. & S. Div.,)		Vevay,	Ingham,	1,050	99
Mason, R. R. Sta.,	Chi. & N. W. R. R., (Pen. Div.,)		Escanaba,	Delta,		120
Masonville, P. O.,	Chi. & N. W. R. R., (Penin. Div.,)	Mason Sta., 4 m.,	Masonville,	Delta,	150	120
Matherton, P. O.,	Det. & Mil. R. R.,	Pewamo, 5 m.,	North Plains,	Ionia,	250	93
Mattawan, P. O., R. R. & Tel. Sta.,	Mich. Cent. R. R.,		Antwerp,	Van Buren,	500	108
Mattesoo, P. O.,	L. S. & M. S. R. W.,	Bronson, 5 m.,	Branch,	Branch,	500	112
Mattison Centre,	Mich. Cent. R. R., (Air L. Div.,)	Colon, 5 m.,	Matteson,	Branch,		112
Max Station, R. R. Sta.,	F. & P. M. R. W., (Ot. Lake Br.,)		Richfield,	Genesee,		90
May P. O., (Mayville,)	Det. & B. City R. R.,	Millington, 10 m.,	Fremont,	Tuscola,	300	85
Mayfield, P. O. & R R Sta.,	Gr. R. & Ind. R. R., (Traverse City Br.,)		Paradise,	Grand Traverse,	150	60

☞ For Explanations, names of Railroads abbreviated, etc., see page 147.

Name of Village.	Railroad, Lake or River.	Nearest Station or Landing.	Township.	County.	Pop.	Page.
May, R. R. Sta.,	Mich. L. Sh. R. R.,		Fillmore,	Allegan,		96
Meade, P. O.,	Grand Trunk R. W.,	New Baltimore Sta., 5 m.,	Macomb, Ray,	Macomb,	100	102
Mead's Mill, P. O. & R. R. Sta., (Waterford,)	F. & P. M. R. W.,		Plymouth,	Wayne,	250	103
Meadville, P. O., (Castleton Sta.,)	Mich. Cent. R. R. (Gr. Riv. Val. Div.,)		Castleton,	Barry,		97
Mears, R. R. Sta.,	Chi. & Mich. L. Shore R. R.,		Golden,	Oceana,		80
Mecosta, P. O.,	Gr. Rap. & Ind. R. R.,	Rust, 2 m.,	Mecosta,	Mecosta,		78
Medina, P. O.,	L. S. & M. S. R. W.,	Clayton, 4 m.,	Medina,	Lenawee,	200	114
Memphis, P. O.,	St. Cl. & C. Air L. R. R., Grand Trunk R. W.,	Ridgeway, 6 m.,	Richmond, Riley,	Macomb, St. Clair.	1,000	102, 53
Mendon, P. O., R. R. & Tel. Sta.,	Gr. Rap. & Ind. R. R.,		Mendon,	St. Joseph,	800	111
Menekaunee, Ldg.,	White Fish Bay, Lake Superior,			Chippewa,		122
Menominee, P. O., Tel. Sta. & Ldg.,	Green Bay,		Menomonee,	Menomonee,	8,000	124
Meridian, P. O.,	Det., L. & L. M. R. R.	Meridian. 2 m.,	Meridian,	Ingham,		99
Meridian, R. R. Sta.,	Det., L. & L. M. R. R.,		Meridian,	Ingham,		99
Meridian, R. R. Sta.,	Sag. Val. & St. L. R. R.,		Wheeler,	Gratiot,		83
Merrillville, P. O.,	P. M. & L. M. R. R.,	Capac, 14 m.,	Brockway,	St. Clair,		88
Metamora, P. O., R. R. & Tel. Sta.,	Det. & B. City R. R.,		Metamora,	Lapeer,		89
Methodist Mission, Ldg.,	Keweenaw Bay, Mary., R. & Ont. R. R.,	L'Anse, 8 m.,	L'Anse,	Houghton,		117
Michigamni, P. O. & R. R. Sta.,	Marq., H. & Ont. R. R.,		Ely,	Marquette,		119
Michigan Centre, P. O. & R. R. Sta.,	Mich. Cent. R. R.,		Leoni,	Jackson,		105
Middletown, P. O.,	Det., L. & L. M. R. R.,	Leroy, 9 m.,	White Oak,	Ingham,		99
Middle Village, Ldg.,	Lake Michigan,		La Croix,	Emmet,		81
Middleville, P. O., R. R. & Tel. Sta.,	Mich. Cent. R. R. (Gr. Riv. Val. Div.,)		Thornapple,	Barry,	1,000	97
Midland City, P. O., R. R. & Tel. Sta.,	F. & P. M. R. W.,		Midland,	Midland,	2,000	76
Milan, P. O. & R. R. Sta.,	Det. & Ann Ar. R. R.,		Milan, York,	Bears, Washtenaw,	197	115
Mile Creek, P. O.,	Chi. & Mich. L. Shore R. R.,	Dalton, 6 m.,	Fruitland,	Muskegon,		81
Milford, P. O., R. R. & Tel. Sta.,	Flint & P. M. R. W.,		Milford,	Oakland,	1,500	101
Millbrook, P. O.,	Gr. Rap. & Ind. R. R.,	Stanwood, 19 m.,	Millbrook,	Mecosta,	300	78
Millburgh, P. O.,	Chi. & Mich. L. Shore R. R.,	Benton Harbor, 3 m.,	Benton,	Berrien,	180	109
Mill Creek, P. O. & R. R. Sta., (Plumb's Mills,)	Gr. R. & Ind. R. R.,		Plainfield,	Kent,		94
Millett's, R. R. Sta.,	Penin. R. W.,		Delta,	Eaton,		98
Mill Grove, R. R. Sta.,	Mich. L. Sh. R. R.,		Allegan,	Allegan,		96
Millington, P. O. & R. R. Sta.,	Det. & Bay City R. R.,		Millington,	Tuscola,	200	85
Millville, R. R. Sta.,	Det. & Bay City R. R.,		Oregon,	Lapeer,		89
Milo, P. O.,	M., Cold. & L. M. R. R.,	Gun Marsh, 7 m.,	Prairieville,	Barry,		97
Milton, P. O.,	Grand Trunk R. W.,	New Baltimore Sta., 3 m.,	Chesterfield,	Macomb,		102
Minden, P. O.,	Lake Huron,	Forestville, 8 m.,	Minden,	Sanilac,	120	87
Mineral Branch, R. R. Sta.,	Chi. & N. W. R. R., (Penin. Div.,)		Negaunee,	Marquette,		119
Mission, Ldg.,	Head of St. Mary's River,			Chippewa,		122
Mitchell, P. O.,	Lake Michigan,	Antrim City, 6 m.,	Banks,	Antrim,		57
Mitchell's, R. R. Sta.,	Gr. Rapids & Ind. R. R.,		Richmond,	Osceola,		72
Model City, P. O., (Tietcorts Sta.,)	Mich. Cent. R. R.,		Wayne,	Cass,		110
Moline, P. O. & R. R. Sta.,	Gr. Rap. & Ind. R. R.,		Dorr,	Allegan,	500	96
Montaigue, P. O.,				Schoolcraft,	200	121
Monroe City, P. O., R. R. & Tel. Sta.,	F. & P. M. R. W., L. S. & M. S. (Det. Div.,) Tol., Can. S. & Det. R. W.,		Monroe,	Monroe,	6,500	115
Monroe Centre, P. O.,	Gr. Rap. & Ind. R. R., (Traverse City Br.,)	Kingsley Sta., 9 m.,	Mayfield & Grant,	Grand Traverse		60
Monroe Junction, R. R. Sta.,	Huds. & Torch Lake R. R.,		Schoolcraft,	Houghton,		117
Monroeville, R. R. Sta.,	Mus. & Big Rap. R. R.,		Monroe,	Newaygo,		79
Montague, P. O., R. R. & Tel. Sta.,	Chi. & Mich. L. Shore R. R.,		Oceana,	Muskegon,	800	81
Monteith, P. O., R. R. & Tel. Sta.,	Gr. R. & Ind. R. R., M., Cold. & L. M. R. R.,		Martin,	Allegan,		96
Monterey, P. O.,	L. S. & M. S. R. W., (Kal. Div.,)	Hopkins, 4 m.,	Monterey,	Allegan,	175	95
Montgomery, P. O. & Tel. Sta., (Cades Sta.,)	M., Cold. & L. M., Ft. W. J. & S. R. R.,		Camden,	Hillsdale,	200	113
Montrose, P. O.,	F. & P. M. R. W.,	Pine Run Sta., 7 m.,	Montrose,	Genesee,		90
Montrose,	F. & P. M. R. W.,	Pine Run Sta., 9 m.,	Montrose,	Genesee,		90
Mooreyark, P. O. & R. R. Sta.,	L. S. & M. S. R. W., (Kal. Div.,)		Park,	St. Joseph,		111
Moore's, R. R. Sta.,	Peninsular R. W.,		Walton,	Eaton,		98
Mooreville, (York P. O.,)	Det. & Ann Ar. R. R.,	Milan, 3 m.,	York,	Washtenaw,		104
Morenci, P. O., R. R. & Tel. Sta.,	Chi. & Can. So. R. R.,		Seneca,	Lenawee,	1,500	114
Morgan, P. O., R. R. & Tel. Sta., (Bryan Furnace,)	Marq., H. & Ont. R. R.,		Negaunee,	Marquette,		119
Morganville, R. R. Sta.,	Mus. & Big Rap. R. R.,		Everett,	Newaygo,		79
Morganville,	M., Cold. & L. M. R. R.,	Woodbridge, 8 m.,	Amboy,	Hillsdale,		113
Morley, P. O., R. R. & Tel. Sta.,	Gr. Rap. & Ind. R. R.,		Æina,	Mecosta,	600	78
Morris, R. R. Sta.,	Chi. & Mich. L. Shore R. R.,		Lake,	Berrien,		109
Moscow, P. O.,	Det., Hill. & Ind. R. R.,	Jerome, 4 m.,	Moscow,	Hillsdale,		113
Mosherville, P. O.,	Ft. W., J. & S. R. R.,	Mosherville Sta., 2 m.,	Scipio,	Hillsdale,	150	113
Mottville, P. O.,	L. S. & M. S. R. W.,	White Pigeon, 6 m.,	Mottville,	St. Joseph,	150	111
Mt. Clemens, P. O., R. R. & Tel. Sta.,	Grand Trunk R. W.,		Clinton,	Macomb,	2,000	102
Mount Morris Sta., P. O., R. R. & Tel. Sta.,	F. & P. M. R. W.,		Mt. Morris & Genesee,	Genesee,	600	90
Mount Pleasant,	Det. & Mil. R. R.,	Fenton, 5 m.,	Fenton,	Genesee,	500	90
Mount Pleasant, P. O.,	F. & P. M. R. W.,	Loomis, 17 m.,	Union,	Isabella,		77
Mount Vernon, P. O.,	Det. & B. City R. R., St. Cl. & C. Air L. R. R.,	Emden, 4 m., Washington, 4 m.,	Washington,	Macomb,		102
Moir, P. O., R. R. & Tel. Sta.,	Det. & Mil. R. R.,		Lyons,	Ionia,	1,200	93
Mundy, P. O.,	Flint & P. M. R. W.,	Grand Blanc, 6 m.,	Mundy,	Genesee,		90
Mungerville, P. O.,	Det. & Mil. R. R.,		Owasso,	Shiawassee,		91
Munwing, P. O. & Ldg.,	Lake Superior,		Munising,	Schoolcraft,		121
Muskegon City, P. O., R. R. & Tel. Sta.,	Chi. & Mich. L. Shore R. R., Mich. L. Sh. R. R.,		Muskegon,	Muskegon,	6,000	81
Mystic, P. O.,	Det. & L. M. R. R.,	Thornton, 13 m.,	Grant,	St. Clair,		88
Nahma, P. O. & Landing,	Big Bay de Noquette,		Nahma,	Delta,		120
Nankin, P. O.,	Det., L. & L. M. R. R.,	Livonia, 3 m.,	Livonia,	Wayne,		103
Napoleon, P. O., R. R. & Tel. Sta.,	L. S. & M. S. R. W., (Jack. Br.,)		Napoleon,	Jackson,	500	105
Nashville, P. O., R. R. Sta.,	Mich. Cent. R. R., (Gr. Riv. Val. Div.,)		Castleton,	Barry,	900	97
Negaunee, P. O., R. R. & Tel. Sta.,	Chi. & Ont. Chi. & N. W. R. R (Pen. Br.,)		Negaunee,	Marquette,	3,200	119
Nelson P. O.,	Gr. Rap. & Ind. R. R.,	Lockwood, 4 m.,	Nelson,	Kent,		94
Nelsonville, P. O.,	Gr. R. & Ind. R. R.,		South Arm,	Charlevoix,		57
Neto, P. O.,	F. & P. M. R. W.,	Remick, 9 m.,	Coldwater,	Isabella,		77
Newark, P. O.,	Sag. Val. & St. L. R. R.,	St. Louis, 12 m.,	Newark,	Gratiot,		83
Newaygo, P. O., & R. R. Sta.,	Gr. Rap., New. & L. Shore R. R.,		Brook,	Newaygo,	1,000	79
New Baltimore, P. O., & R. R. Sta.,	Grand Trunk R. W.,	New Baltimore Sta., 4 m.,	Chesterfield,	Macomb,	1,360	102
Newburg, P. O., (Jones Sta.,)	Mich. Cent. R. R., (Air Line Div.,)		Newberg,	Cass,		110
New Boston, P. O., R. R. & Tel. Sta.,	F. & P. M. R. W.,		Huron,	Wayne,	800	103
New Buffalo, P. O., R. R. & Tel. Sta.,	Mich. Cent. R. R., Chi. & Mich. L. Shore R. R.,		New Buffalo,	Berrien,	800	109
Newbury, (Kingston P. O.,)	Det. & Bay City R. R.,	Vassar, 20 m.,	Kingston, Koylton,	Tuscola,		85
New Casco, P. O.,	Chi. & Mich. L. Shore R. R.,	Sherman, 7 m.,	Gange,	Allegan,		95
New England Mine, R. R. Sta.,	Branch of Marq, H. & Ont. R. R.,		Ishpeming, Tilden,	Marquette,		119
New Era, P. O. & R. R. Sta.,	Chi. & Mich. L. Shore R. R.,		Shelby, Grant,	Oceana,		80
New Groningen, (Groningen P. O.,)	Chi. & Mich. L. Shore R. R., (Gr. Rap. Div.,)	Zeeland, 3 m.,	Holland,	Ottawa,	100	95
New Hart. P. O. & Tel. Sta., (New Baltimore Sta.,)	Grand Trunk R. W.,		Lenox,	Macomb,	500	102
New Haven Centre, P. O.,	Sag. Val. & St. L. R. R.,	St. Louis, 18 m.,	New Haven,	Gratiot,		84
New Holland, P. O., & R. R. Sta.,	Chi. & Mich. L. Shore R. R.,		Holland, Olive,	Ottawa,		95
New Hudson, P. O.,	F. & P. M.; Det. L. & L. M., R. & C. Mr L. R. R.,	Wixom, 4 m., Grand Oak, 4 m.,	Lyon,	Oakland,	200	101
Newaut, P. O.,				Sanilac,		87
Newport, P. O.,	L. S. & M. S. W., (Det. Div.,)	Newport Sta., 2 m.,	Berlin,	Monroe,	400	115

☞For Explanations, names of Railroads abbreviated, etc., see page 147.

Name of Village.	Railroad, Lake or River.	Nearest Station or Landing.	Township.	County.	Pop.	Page.
Newport Sta.,	L. S. & M. S. (M. N.); Tol., Can. S. & Det. R. W.,		Berlin,	Monroe,		115
New Richmond, P. O. & R. R. Sta.,	Chi. & Mich. L. Shore R. R.,		Manlius,	Allegan,		26
New River, Ldg.,	Lake Huron,		Huron,	Huron,		86
New Salem, P. O.	L. S. & M. S. R. W., (Kal. Div.,)	Durr, 5 m.,	Salem,	Allegan,		96
Newton, P. O. & R. R.,	M., Cold. & L. M. R. R.,		Newton,	Calhoun,		106
New Troy, P. O.,	Chi. & Mich. L. Shore R. R.,	Troy, 3 m.,	Weesaw,	Berrien,		107
New York Mine, R. R. Sta.,	Chi & N. W. R. R., (Penin. Div.,)		Ishpeming,	Marquette,		119
Nicholsville, (Little Prairie Ronde P. O.,)	Penin. R. W.,	Volinia, 4 m.,	Volinia,	Cass,		110
Niles, P. O., R. R. & Tel. Sta.,	Mich. Cent. R. R.,		Niles,	Berrien,	5,000	100
Nippersing,	F. & P. M. R. W.,	Loomis, 8 m.,	Isabella,	Isabella,		77
Noble Centre, P. O.,	L. S. & M. S. R. W.,	Bronson, 7 m.,	Noble,	Branch,		112
Norris, P. O. & R. R. Sta.,	Det. & Bay City R. R.,		Hamtramck,	Wayne,		108
North Adams, P. O., R. R. & Tel. Sta.,	Det., Hill. & Ind. R. R.,		Adams,	Hillsdale,		113
North Aurelius,	Mich. Cent. R. R., (J. L. & S. Div.,)	Mason, 4 m.,	Aurelius,	Ingham,		99
North Branch, P. O., (Beachville,)	Lapeer & Northern R. R.,	Fish Lake,	North Branch,	Lapeer,	800	89
North Burns, P. O.,	Saginaw Bay,	Bayport, 16 m.,	Sheridan,	Huron,		86
North Byron, P. O. & R. R. Sta.,	L. S. & M. S. R. W., (Kal. Div.,)		Byron,	Kent,		94
North Concord, R. R. Sta.,	Mich. Cent. R. R.,		Concord,	Jackson,		105
North Eagle, P. O.,	Det., L. & L. M. R. R.,	Eagle, 8 m.,	Eagle,	Clinton,		93
North Farmington, P. O.,	Flint & P. M. R. W.,	Novi, 8 m.,	South Bendel Farmington,	Oakland,		101
North Holland, R. R. Sta.,	Mich. L. Sh. R. R.,		Holland,	Ottawa,		95
North Irving, P. O.,	Mich. Cent. R. R., (Gr. Riv. Val. Div.,)	Irving, 2 m.,	Irving,	Barry,		98
North Lansing, R. R. & Tel. Sta.,	Mich. Cent. (L L & R.); Det., L. & L. M. R. R.,		Landing,	Ingham,		99
North Linden, R. R. & Tel. Sta., (Linden Sta.,)	Det. & Mil. R. R.,		Fenton,	Genesee,		90
North Newburgh P.O.,	Det. & Mil. R. R.,	Vernon, 8 m.,	Shiawassee,	Shiawassee,	250	91
North Plains, P. O.,	Det. & Mil. R. R.,	Muir, 5 m.,	North Plains,	Ionia,		88
Northport, P. O. & Landing,	Grand Traverse Bay,		Leelanau,	Leelanau,	800	58
North Raisinville, P. O.,	L. S. & M. S. R. W. (Det. Div.,)	Monroe, 4 m.,	Raisinville,	Monroe,		115
North Shade, P. O.,			North Shade,	Gratiot,		103
North Star, P. O.,	Sag. Val. & St. Louis R. R.,	Breckenridge, 10 m.,	North Star,	Gratiot,		83
North Unity, P. O. & Landing,	Lake Michigan,		Cleveland,	Leelanau,		58
Northville, P. O., R. R. & Tel. Sta.,	F. & P. M. R. W.,		Plymouth,	Wayne,	700	103
Norton, R. R. Sta.,	Chi. & Mich. L. Shore R. R.,		Fruitport,	Muskegon,		81
Nortonville, P. O.,	Det. & Mil. R. R.,		Spring Lake,	Ottawa,		95
Norvell, P. O., R. R. & Tel. Sta.,	L. S. & M. S. R. W., (Jack. Br.,)	Spring Lake, 1 m.,	Norvell,	Jackson,	800	105
Norwalk, P. O.,	Lake Michigan,	Onekama, 5 m.,	Bear Lake,	Manistee,		60
Norwood, P. O. & Landing,	Lake Michigan,		Norwood,	Charlevoix,	150	67
Nottawa, R. R. Sta.,	Mich. Cent. R. R., (Air L. Div.,)		Nottawa,	St. Joseph,		111
Nottawa, P. O. & R. R. Sta.,	Gr. R. & Ind. R. R.,		Nottawa,	St. Joseph,		111
Novi, P. O., R. R. & Tel. Sta.,	Flint & P. M. R. W.,		Novi,	Oakland,	800	101
Nunica, P. O., R. R. & Tel. Sta.,	Det. & Mil.; Chi. & Mich. L. Shore R. R.,		Crockery,	Ottawa,		95
Oak, P. O., (Redford Sta.,)	Det., L. & L. M. R. R.,		Redford,	Wayne,		103
Oakfield, P. O.,	Gr. Rap., Greenville & Alpena R. R.,	Oakfield Sta., 2 m.,	Oakfield,	Kent,		94
Oakfield, R. R. Sta.,	Gr. Rap., Greenville & Alpena R. R.,		Oakfield,	Kent,		94
Oak Grove, P. O.,	Det. L. & L. M. R. R.,	Howell, 7 m.,	Cohoctah,	Livingston,	200	100
Oak Hill, P. O.,	Det. & Mil. R. R.,	Davisburgh, 6 m.,	Brandon, Independence,	Oakland,		101
Oakland, P. O.,	Det. & B. City R. R.,	Rudd's Sta., 4 m.,	Oakland,	Oakland,		101
Oakley, P. O., R. R. & Tel. Sta.,	Mich. Cent. R. R., (J. L. & S. Div.,)		Brady, Chesaning,	Saginaw,	150	84
Oakville, P. O.,	Tol. & Ann Ar. R. R.,	Milan, 5 m.,	London,	Monroe,	70	115
Oakwood P. O.,	Det. & Bay City R. R.,	Oxford, 6 m.,	Oxford, Brandon,	Oakland,	800	101
Oceola, R. R. Sta.,	Mich. L. Sh. R. R.,		Grand Haven,	Ottawa,		95
Ogden Centre, P. O.,	Chi. & Can. So. R. R.,	Weston, 7 m.,	Ogden,	Lenawee,	200	114
Ogemaw, P. O.,	Lake Huron,	Tawas City, 8 m.,	Grant,	Iosco,		66
Ogemaw, R. R. Sta.,	Mich. Cent. R. R., (J. L. & S. Div.,)		Ogemaw,	Ogemaw,		65
Okemos, P. O., R. R. & Tel. Sta.,	Det., L. & L. M. R. R.,		Meridian,	Ingham,	800	99
Old Mission, P. O. & Landing.,	Gr. Trav. Bay, Gr. R. & Ind. R. R., (Trav. City Br.,)	Traverse City, 15 m.,	Peninsular,	Grand Traverse		59
Olive, P. O.,	Det. & Mil R. R.,	St. Johns, 6 m.,	Olive,	Clinton,		92
Olive, R. R. Sta.,	Chi. & Mich. L. Shore R. R.,		Olive,	Ottawa,		95
Olivet, P. O., R. R. & Tel. Sta.,	Mar. & Cold. R. R.,		Walton,	Eaton,	500	98
Olivet Sta. R. R. Sta.,	Penin R. W.,		Walton,	Eaton,		98
Onsted, P. O.,	P. H. & L. M. R. R.,	Cadet, 21 m.,	Flynn,	Sanilac,		87
Onena, P. O. & Landing,	Grand Traverse Bay,		Leelanau,	Leelanau,	100	58
Onekama, P. O. & Landing,	Lake Michigan,		Onekama,	Manistee,	150	60
Onondaga, P. O., R. R. & Tel. Sta.,	Mich. Cent. R. R., (Gr. Riv. Val. Div.,)		Onondaga,	Ingham,	700	99
Onota, P. O. & Landing,	Lake Superior,		Onota,	Schoolcraft,	600	121
Ontonagon, P. O. & Landing.,	Lake Superior,		Ontonagon,	Ontonagon,	600	116
Ontonagon Junction,	Marq. H. & Ont. R. R.,		Ishpeming,	Marquette,		119
Onusnemeeville,	Lake Michigan,		Leelanau,	Leelanau,		58
Orange, P. O.,	Det., L. & L. M. R. R.,	Stebbinsville, 6 m.,	Orange,	Ionia,		93
Orangeville, P. O.,	Mich. Cent. R. R., (Air Line Div.,)	Union City, 4 m.,	Branch,	Branch,		112
Orangeville Mills, P. O.,	M., Cold. & L. M. R. R.,	Gun Marsh, 4 m.,	Orangeville,	Barry,	800	97
Orchard Lake,	Det. & Mil. R. R.,	Pontiac, 4½ m.,	West Bloomfield,	Oakland,		101
Ore Siding, R. R. Sta.,	Chi. & N. W. R. R., (Penin. Div.,)		Escanaba,	Delta,		120
Orient, R. R. & Tel. Sta., (Sears P. O.,)	F. & P. M. R. W.,		Osceola, Sylvan,	Osceola,		72
Orion, P. O. & R. R. Sta.,	Det. & B. City R. R.,		Orion,	Oakland,	500	101
Orleans, P. O., (Sangstern Sta.,)	Det., L. & L. M. R. R.,		Orleans,	Ionia,		93
Oronoville, P. O.,	Det. & B. City; Det. & Mil. R. R.,	Rdwd. 10 m. Pntiasbrgh, 10 m.,	Brandon,	Oakland,	800	101
Osceola Centre, P. O.,	Det., L. & L. M. R. R.,	Howell, 6 m.,	Osceola,	Livingston,		100
Oshtemo, P. O., R. R. & Tel. Sta.,	Mich. Cent. R. R.,		Oshtemo,	Kalamazoo,	800	108
Osseo, P. O., R. R. & Tel. Sta.,	L. S. & M. S. R. W.,		Jefferson,	Hillsdale,	800	113
Ossineke, P. O., Tel. Sta. & Landing,	Lake Huron,		Ossineke,	Alpena,	800	54
Otisco, P. O., (Cook's Corners,)	Det., L. & L. M. R. R.,	Kiddville, 8 m.,	Otisco,	Ionia,	500	93
Otisville, P. O., R. R. & Tel. Sta.,	F. & P. M. R. W. (Flint River Div.,)		Forest,	Genesee,		90
Otsego, P. O., R. R. & Tel. Sta.,	L. S. & M. S. R. W., (Kal. Div.,)		Otsego,	Allegan,	1,500	96
Otsego Lake, P. O. & R. R. Sta.,	Mich. Cent. R. R., (J. L. & S. Div.,)		Otsego Lake,	Otsego,		65
Ottawa Lake, P. O., R. R. & Tel. Sta.,	L. S. & M. S. R. W.,		Whiteford,	Monroe,		115
Ottawa Sta., P. O. & R. R. Sta.,	Chi. & Mich. L. Shore R. R.,		Olive,	Ottawa,		95
Otter Creek, P. O.,	L. S. & M. S. R. W., (Lansing Div.,)	Springport, 6 m.,	Springport,	Jackson,		105
Otter Lake, R. R. & Tel. Sta.,	Det. & B. City; F & P. M. R. W., (Flint R. Div.,)		Arathen,	Lapeer,	850	90
Overisel, P. O.,	Mich. L. Sh. R. R.,	Fillmore, 2 m.,	Overisel,	Allegan,		96
Owen Corners, (Springport P. O.,)	L. S. & M. S. R. W., (Lans. Div.,)		Springport,	Jackson,		105
Ovid, P. O. & R. R. Sta.,	Det. & Mil. R. R.,		Ovid,	Clinton,	1,500	92
Ovid,	M., Cold. & L. M. R. R.,	Ovid, 2 m.,	Ovid,	Branch,		112
Ovid, R. R. Sta.,	M., Cold. & L. M. R. R.,		Ovid,	Branch,		112
Owosso, P. O., R. R. & Tel. Sta.,	Det. & Mil.; f. & h. h. R., Kch. Cen. R. R. (L L & S Br.,)		Owosso, Caledonia,	Shiawassee,	3,000	91
Oxford, P. O. & R. R. Sta.,	Det. & B. City R. R.,		Oxford,	Oakland,		101
Pack's Mills, P. O.,	Lake Huron,	Port Sanilac, 7 m.,	Washington,	Sanilac,		87
Paint Creek, P. O.,	Mich. Cent. R. R.,	Ypsilanti, 6 m.,	Augusta,	Washtenaw,		104
Palmere, R. R. Sta.,	Det. L. & L. M. R.,		Orleans,	Ionia,		114
Palmyra, P. O. & R. R. Sta.,	L. S. & M. S. R. W.,		Palmyra,	Lenawee,	200	114
Palo, P. O.,	Det. & Mil. R. R.,	Muir, 9 m.,	Ronald,	Ionia,	500	93
Paris, P. O., R. R. & Tel Sta.	Gr. Rap. & Ind. R. R.,		Green,	Mecosta,	800	78

☞ For Explanations, names of Railroads abbreviated, etc., see page 147.

Name of Village.	Railroad, Lake or River.	Nearest Station or Landing.	Township.	County.	Pop.	Pop?
Park, P. O.,	Gr. Rap. & Ind. R. R.,	Portage Lake, 2 m.,	Mendon,	St. Joseph,		111
Park's Corners,	L. S. & M. S. (Jack. Br.) Det., Hill. & Ind. R. R.,	Manchester, 8 m.,	Sharon,	Washtenaw,		104
Parkville, P. O.,	L. S. & M. S. R. W., (Kal. Div.)	Moorepark, 4 m.,	Park,	St. Joseph,	160	111
Parma, P. O., R. R. & Tel. Sta.,	Mich. Cent. R. R.,		Sandstone, Parma,	Jackson,	500	105
Parshallville, P. O.,	F. & P. M. R. W.,	Clyde, 3 m.,	Hartland,	Livingston,	150	100
Partello, P. O.,	Mar. & Cold. R. R., Mich. Cent. R. R.,	Marengo, 9 m.,	Lee,	Calhoun,		106
Partridge, R. R. Sta.,	Chi. & N. W. R. R., (Penin. Div.)		Negaunee,	Marquette,		119
Pavilion, P. O.,	Penin. R. W.,	Scott, 1 m.,	Pavilion,	Kalamazoo,		107
Paw Paw, P. O., R. R. & Tel. Sta.,	Mich. Cent. R. R., (Paw Paw Br.,)		Paw Paw,	Van Buren,	1,500	109
Peck, P. O.,	P. H. & L. M. R. R.,	Emmett's 21 m.,	Elk,	Sanilac,		87
Peebles Corners,	Det., L. & L. M. R. R.,	Salem, 4 m.,	Salem,	Washtenaw,		104
Penn, P. O., (Jamestown Sta.,),	Penin. R. W.,		Penn,	Cass,	100	110
Pennfield, R. R. Sta.,	Penin. R. W.,		Pennfield,	Calhoun,		108
Penn Mine, P. O.,	Lake Superior,	Eagle Harbor, 8 m.,	Grant,	Keweenaw,		118
Pentwater, P. O., R. R. & Tel. Sta.,	Chi. & Mich. L. Shore R. R.,		Pentwater,	Oceana,	2,000	80
Perkins, P. O. & R. R. Sta.,	Mich. Cent. R. R., (J. L. & S. Div.,)		Deep River,	Bay,		75
Perrin, R. R. Sta.,	Gr. Rap. & Ind. R. R.,		Sherman,	St. Joseph,		108
Perrinville, P. O.	Det., L. & L. M. R. R.,	McKinney's, 2 m.,	Nankin,	Wayne,	250	103
Perry, P. O.,	Mich. Cent. R. R., (J. L. & S. Div.)	Laingsburg, 10m.,	Perry,	Shiawassee,	100	91
Petersburg, P. O., R. R. & Tel. Sta.,	L. S. & M. S. R. W., (Det. Div.)		Summerfield,	Monroe,	700	115
Petysville, P. O.,	St. Cl. & C. Air Line R. R.,		Hamburg,	Livingston,	50	100
Pewamo, P. O., R. R. & Tel. Sta.,	Det. & Mil. R. R.,		Lyons,	Ionia,	500	98
Phenix, P. O.,	Lake Superior,	Eagle River, 2 m.,	Clifton,	Keweenaw,	500	118
Pickett's Corners,	Mich. Cent. R. R.,	Trentaroa, 4 m.,	Volinia, Wayne,	Cass,		110
Pier Cove, (Ganges P. O.,)	Chi. & Mich. L. Shore R. R.	Fennville, 7 m.,	Ganges,	Allegan,		96
Pierport, P. O. & Landing,	Lake Michigan,		Onekama,	Manistee,		50
Pierson, P. O. R. R. & Tel. Sta.,	Gr. Rap. & Ind R. R.,		Pierson,	Montcalm,	500	82
Pigeon, R. R. Sta., (West Olive, P. O.,)	Mich. L. Sh. R. R.,		Olive,	Ottawa,		95
Pike's Peak,	Det., L. & L. M. R. R.,	Livonia, 2 m.,	Nankin,	Wayne,		103
Pinckney, P. O. & R. R. Sta.,	St. Cl. & C. Air Line R. R.,		Putnam,	Livingston,	500	100
Pinconning, R. R. & Tel. Sta.,	Mich. Cent. R. R., (J. L. & S. Div.)		Pinconning,	Bay,		73
Pine Creek,	L. S. & M. S. R. W., (Kal. Div.)	Otsego, 2 m.,	Otsego,	Allegan,		96
Pine Creek, P. O.,	M., Cold. & L. M. R. R.,		Athens,	Calhoun,		99
Pine Grove, P. O.,				Tuscola,		85
Pine Grove R. R. Sta., (Pine Grove Mills, P. O.,)	Mich. Cent. R. R., (Kal. & S. Hav. Div.,)		Pine Grove,	Van Buren,	100	108
Pine Grove, R. R. Sta.,	Mich. Cent. R. R., (J. L. & S. Div.)		St. Charles,	Saginaw,		84
Pine Hill, P. O. & Ldg.,	Lake Huron,		Sanilac,	Sanilac,		87
Pine River, Landing,	Saginaw Bay, Mich. Cent. R. R., (J. L. & S. Div.,)	Standish, 5 m.,	Standish,	Bay,		73
Pine Run, P. O. & Tel. Sta.,	Gr. R. & Ind R. R.,	Tustin, 11 m.,	Killbuck,	Lake,		71
Pine Run, P. O. & Tel. Sta.,	F. & P. M. R. W.,	Pine Run Sta., 1 m.,	Vienna,	Genesee,	300	90
Pipestone, P. O.,	Chi. & Mich. L. Shore R. R.,	St. Joseph, 9 m.,	Pipestone,	Berrien,		109
Pittsburg, P. O.,	Mich. Cent. R. R., (J. L. & S. Div.)	Bennington, 4 m.,	Bennington,	Shiawassee,	500	91
Pittsford, P. O., R. R. & Tel. Sta.,	L. S. & M. S. R. W.,		Pittsford,	Hillsdale,	800	112
Pittsford Centre,	L. S. & M. S. R. W.,	Pittsford, 3 m.,	Pittsford,	Hillsdale,		113
Plainfield, P. O.,	St. Cl. & C. Air Line R. R.,	Unadilla, 6 m.,	Unadilla,	Livingston,	500	100
Plains, R. R. Sta.,	Chi. & N. W. R. R., (Penin. Div.)		Chocolay, Forsyth,	Marquette,		119
Plainwell, P. O., R. R. & Tel. Sta.,	Gr. Rap. & Ind.; L. S. & M. S. R. W. (Kal. Div.)		Gun Plain,	Allegan,	1,500	96
Plank Road, P. O.,	Det., L. & L. M. R. R.,	Fisher's, 3 m.,	Redford,	Wayne,		103
Platte, P. O.,	Lake Michigan,	Empire Landing, 8 m.,	Platte,	Benzie,		59
Pleasant, P. O.,	Gr. Rap., N. & L. S. R. R.,	Alpine, 9 m.,	Alpine,	Kent,		94
Pleasant City, Landing, (Sutton's Bay P. O.,	Grand Traverse Bay,		Bingham,	Leelanaw,		58
Pleasanton, P. O.,	Lake Michigan,	Pierport, 7 m.,	Pleasanton,	Manistee,	350	59
Pleasant Valley, P. O.,	Mich. Cent. R. R.,	Dowagiac, 10 m.,	Pipestone,	Berrien,		109
Plumb's Mills, (Mill Creek, P. O. & R. R. Sta.,)	Gr. Rap. & Ind. R. R.,		Plainfield,	Kent,		94
Plummerville,	Chi. & Mich. L. Shore R. R.,	Fennville, 8 m.,	Ganges,	Allegan,		96
Plymouth, P. O., R. R. & Tel. Sta.,	F. & P. M. R. W., Det., L. & L. M. R. R.,		Plymouth,	Wayne,	1,500	103
Podunk,	Mich. Cent. R. R., (Gr. Riv. Val. Div.,)	Hastings, 6 m.,	Rutland,	Barry,		97
Podunk,	Det., L. & L. Mich. R. R.,	Dana, 1 m.,	Leroy,	Ingham,		99
Pokagon, P. O. & R. R. Sta.,	Mich. Cent. R. R.,		Pokagon,	Cass,	300	110
Pompeii, P. O.,	Sag. Val. & St. L. R. R.,	St. Louis, 2½ m.,	Washington,	Gratiot,	40	83
Pontiac, P. O., R. R. & Tel. Sta.,	Det. & Mil. R. R., St. Cl. & C. Air L. R. R.,		Pontiac,	Oakland,	5,000	101
Poole, P. O.,	P. H. & L. M. R. R.,	Attica, 4 m.,	Attica,	Lapeer,		89
Portage, P. O. & R. R. Sta.,	L. S. & M. S. R. W., (Kal. Div.)		Portage,	Kalamazoo,		107
Portage Lake, R. R. Sta.,	Gr. Rap. & Ind. R. R.,		Mendon,	St. Joseph,		111
Port Austin, P. O., Ldg., Tel. Sta.,	Lake Huron,		Port Austin,	Huron,	1,000	86
Port Crescent, P. O., Ldg. & Tel. Sta.,	Lake Huron,		Hume,	Huron,	800	86
Porter, P. O.,	Green Bay,	Escanaba, 22 m., Indian Town, 16 m.,	Ingallston,	Menominee,		124
Porter, P. O.,	Sag. Val. & St. L. R. R.,	Breckenridge, 8 m.,	Porter,	Midland,		76
Porter's R. R. Sta., (Randall P. O.,)	Sag. Val. & St. L. R. R.,		Jonesfield, Richland,	Saginaw,		84
Port Hope, P. O., Ldg. & Tel. Sta., (Stafford,)	Lake Huron,		Rubicon,	Huron,	400	99
Port Huron City, P. O., R. R. & Tel. Sta.,	P. H. & L. M. R. R., Grand Trunk R. W.,		Port Huron,	St. Clair,	7,500	88
Portland, P. O., R. R. & Tel. Sta.,	Det., L. & L. M. R. R., Mar. & Cold. R. R.,		Portland,	Ionia,	2,500	98
Port Oneida, Landing,	Lake Michigan,		Glen Arbor,	Leelanaw,		58
Port Sanilac, P. O., Ldg. & Tel. Sta.,	Lake Huron,		Sanilac,	Sanilac,	600	87
Port Sheldon, P. O.,	Mich. L. Sh. R. R.,	Pigeon Sta., 3½ m.,	Olive,	Ottawa,		95
Portsmouth, P. O., (Part of Bay City,)	Det. & B. City R. R.,	Bay City, 2 m.,	Bay City,	Bay,	2,500	73
Pottawic, P. O.,	Mich. L. Sh. R. R., Det. & Mil. R. R.,	Grand Haven, 4 m.,	Robinson,	Ottawa,		95
Pottersville,	Lake Huron,	Steven's Landing, 10 m.,	Fremont,	Sanilac,		97
Potterville, P. O., R. R. & Tel. Sta.,	Peninsular R. W.,		Benton,	Eaton,	640	98
Prairieville, P. O.,	M., Cold. & L. M. R. R.,	Gun Marsh, 8 m.,	Prairieville,	Barry,		97
Prattville, P. O.,	L. S. & M. S. R. W.,	Hudson, 8 m.,	Wright,	Hillsdale,		113
Prospect Lake, P. O.,	Mich. Cent. R. R.,	Decatur, 7 m.,	Lawrence,	Van Buren,		108
Provemont, P. O.,	Grand Traverse Bay,	Pleasant City, 8 m.,	Centreville,	Leelanaw,		58
Pulaski, P. O.,	Ft. W., J. & S.; Mich. Cent. R. R., (Air Line Br.,)	Berry Road, 4 m., Concord, 4 m.,	Pulaski,	Jackson,		105
Pulaski Station,	Mich. Cent. R. R., (Air Line Div.)		Pulaski,	Jackson,		106
Quaker Mills,	L. S. & M. S. R. W.,	Hudson, 6 m.,	Rollin,	Lenawee,		114
Quincy, P. O. & R. R. Sta.,	Mich. Cent. R. R., (Gr. Riv. Val. Div.,)		Hastings,	Barry,	100	97
Quincy, P. O., R. R. & Tel. Sta.,	L. S. & M. S. R. W.,		Quincy,	Branch,	1,200	112
Quinn, P. O.,	Grand Trunk R. W.,	Utica Plank, 2 m.,	Clinton,	Macomb,		102
Rabbit River, (Hamilton, P. O. & R. R. Sta.,)	Mich. L. Sh. R. R.,		Heath,	Allegan,		96
Raisin Centre, P. O., & R. R. Sta.,	L. S. & M. S. R. W., (Jack. Br.)		Raisin,	Lenawee,		114
Randall, P. O., (Porter's Sta.,)	Sag. Val. & St. L. R. R.,		Jonesfield, Richland,	Saginaw,		84
Ransom, P. O.,	M., Cold. & L. M. R. R.,	Pioneer, 7 m.,	Ransom,	Hillsdale,		61
Rapid River, P. O.,	Gr. Rap. & Ind. R. R.,	Kalkaska, 8 m.,	Rapid River,	Kalkaska,		61
Ravenna, P. O.,	Gr. Rap., New. & L. Shore R. R.,	Casicovia, 9 m.,	Ravenna,	Muskegon,	400	81
Rawsonville, P. O.,	Mich. Cent. R. R.,	Ypsilanti, 4 m.,	Ypsilanti, In Save,	Wayne,	150	103
Ray Centre P. O.,	Grand Trunk R. W.,	New Baltimore, 8 m., 5 m.,	Ray,	Macomb,		102
Reynolds, P. O., (See Reynolds.),				Montcalm,		82
Reading, P. O., R. R. & Tel. Sta.,	Ft. W., J. & R. R.,		Reading,	Hillsdale,	600	118
Redan, P. O., (De Doleville,),	Mich. Cent. R. R., (J. L. & S. Div.,)	Saginaw, 6 m.,	Saginaw,	Saginaw,		84
Redford, P. O.,	Det., L. & L. M. R. R.,	Redford, 4 m.,	Redford,	Wayne,		103
Redford Sta., (Oak P. O.,),	Det., L. & L. M. R. R.,		Redford,	Wayne,		103

☞ For Explanations, names of Railroads abbreviated, etc., see page 147.

Name of Village.	Railroad, Lake or River.	Nearest Station or Landing.	Township.	County.	Pop.	Page.
Redford Centre,	Det., L. & L. M. R. R.,	Redford, 2 m.,	Redford,	Wayne,		102
Red Run Corners, (Cady P. O.,)	Grand Trunk R. W.,	Utica Plank, 2½ m.,	Clinton,	Macomb,		102
Reed, P. O.,	Chi. & Mich. L. Shore R. R.,	New Era, 7 m.,	Ferry,	Oceana,	100	90
Reed City, P. O., R. R. & Tel. Sta.,	Gr. Rap. & Ind. R. R., F. & P. M. R. W.,		Richmond,	Osceola,	500	72
Reeder, P. O.,	Gr. Rap. & Ind. R. R.,	Linden, 11 m.,	Reeder,	Missaukee,	500	68
Reedsville, (Howard P. O.,)	Chi. & Mich. L. Shore R. R.,	Muskegon, 2 m.,	Muskegon,	Muskegon,		81
Reese, R. R. Sta.,	Det. & Bay City R. R.,		Denmark,	Tuscola,		85
Reeves, R. R. Sta., (East Milan P. O.,)	Tol. & Ann Ar. R. R.,		Milan,	Monroe,		115
Remick, R. R. Sta.,	F. & P. M. R. W.,		Surrey,	Clare,		12
Republic Mine, R. R. Sta.,	Branch of Marq., Id. & Ont. R. R.,		Ely,	Marquette,		110
Reynolds, P. O. & R. R. Sta.,	Gr. Rap. & Ind. R. R.,		Reynolds,	Montcalm,		92
Rice Creek,	Mar. & Cold. R. R., Mich. Cent. R. R.,	Marengo, 4 m.,	Lee, Marengo,	Calhoun,		106
Richfield, P. O.,	P. H. & L. M. R. R.,	Davison, 4 m.,	Richfield,	Genesee,		90
Richland, P. O. & R. R. Sta.,	M., Cold. & L. M. R. R.,		Richland,	Kalamazoo,	200	107
Richmond, P. O. & Tel. Sta.,	St. Cl. & C. Air L. R. R., Grand Trunk R. W.,	Ridgeway, 1 m.,	Richmond,	Macomb,	1,000	102
Richmond, R. R. Sta., (New Richmond P. O.,)	Chi. & Mich. L. Shore R. R.,		Manlius,	Allegan,		96
Richmondville, P. O., Tel. Sta. & Ldg.,	Lake Huron,		Forester,	Sanilac,	200	87
Richville, P. O.,	Det. & Bay City R. R.,	Reese, 8 m.,	Denmark,	Tuscola,	200	85
Ridgeville, P. O.,				Gladwin,		74
Ridgeway, P. O.,	L. S. & M. S. R. W., (Jack. Br.),	Tecumseh, 5 m.,	Ridgeway,	Lenawee,	800	114
Ridgeway, R. R. & Tel. Sta., (Richmond P. O.,)	Grand Trunk R. W., St. Cl. & C. Air L. R. R.,		Lenox,	Macomb,		102
Riensi, P. O.,	Flint & P. M. R. W.,	Lake Sta., 17 m.,	Sheridan,	Mecosta,		78
Rife River, P. O. & Tel. Sta.,	Mich. Cent. R. R., (J. L. & S. Div.),	Standish, 7 m.,	Arenac,	Bay,		75
Riga, P. O. & R. R. Sta.,	L. S. & M. S. R. W.,		Riga,	Lenawee,	400	114
Riley, P. O.,	Det. & Mil. R. R.,	Fowler, 7 m.,	Riley,	Clinton,		92
Riley Centre, P. O.,	P. H. & L. M. R. R.,	Emmet, 6 m.,	Riley,	St. Clair,		88
River Bend, P. O.,	Det., L. & L. M. R. R.,	Eagle, 4 m.,	Eagle,	Clinton,		92
River Raisin, P. O.,	L. S. & M. S. R. W., (Jack. Br.),	River Raisin Sta., 2 m.,	Bridgewater,	Washtenaw,		104
River Raisin, R. R. Sta.,	L. S. & M. S. R. W., (Jack. Br.),		Bridgewater,	Washtenaw,		104
Riverside, P. O. & R. R. Sta.,	Chi. & Mich. L. Shore R. R.,		Berrien,	Berrien,		100
Riverton, P. O.,	F. & P. M. R. W., Lake Michigan,	Ludington, 6 m.,	Riverton,	Mason,		70
River Junction, P. O., R. R. & Tel. Sta.,	Mich. Cent. R. R., (L & J. S. & M. S. R.),		River,	Jackson,		105
Roberts' Landing, P. O. & Ldg.,	River St. Clair,		Cottrellville,	St. Clair,		88
Robinson, P. O., R. R. & Tel. Sta.,	Chi. & Mich. L. Shore R. R.,		Robinson,	Ottawa,		95
Rochester, P. O., R. R. & Tel. Sta.,	Det. & D. City R. R., St. Cl. & C. Air L. R. R.,		Avon,	Oakland,	700	101
Rock Falls, P. O. & Tel. Sta., (Ormie Harbor Ldg.,)	Lake Huron,		Sand Beach,	Huron,	200	86
Rockford, P. O., R. R. & Tel. Sta.,	Gr. R. & Ind. R. R., Gr. Rap., G. & A. R. R.,		Algoma,	Kent,	1,200	94
Rockland, P. O. & Tel. Sta.,	Lake Superior,	Ontonagon, 12 m.,	Rockland,	Ontonagon,		116
Rockwood, P. O. & R. R. Sta.,	L. S. & M. S. (Det. Jct.), Tol., Can. S. & Det. R. W.,		Berlin, Brownstown,	Monroe, Wayne,	500	115
Rogers City, P. O. & Ldg.,	Lake Huron,		Rogers,	Presque Isle,	500	68
Rollin, P. O.,	L. S. & M. S. R. W.,	Hudson 4 m.,	Rollin,	Lenawee,		114
Rome, P. O.,	L. S. & M. S. R. W.,	Dover, 7 m.,	Rome,	Lenawee,		114
Romeo, P. O., R. R. & Tel. Sta.,	St. Cl. & C. Air L. R. R.,		Bruce, Washington,	Macomb,	2,500	102
Romulus, P. O. & R. R. Sta.,	F. & P. M. R. W.,		Romulus,	Wayne,	90	102
Roseville, P. O.,	Gr. Rapids & Ind. R. R.,	Muscoloca, 10 m.,	Helena,	Antrim,		57
Roscommon, P. O. & R. R. Sta.,	Mich. Cent. R. R., (J. L. & S. Div.),		Roscommon,	Roscommon,		62
Rose, P. O. & R. R. Sta.,	F. & P. M. R. W.,		Rose,	Oakland,		101
Rose Corners,	F. & P. M. R. W.,	Rose, 1 m.,	Rose,	Oakland,		101
Roseville, P. O.,	Grand Trunk R. W.,	Utica Plank, 8m.,	Erin,	Macomb,	500	102
Rose, P. O. & R. R. Sta.,	Gr. Rap. & Ind. R. R.,		Rose,	Kent,		94
Ross Centre,	Mich. Cent. R. R., M., Cold. & L. M. R. R.,	Augusta, 2 m.,	Ross,	Kalamazoo,		107
Round Lake, P. O.,	L. S. & M. S. R. W.,	Burr Oak, 5 m.,	Noble,	Branch,		112
Rowena, R. R. Sta.,	Mich. Cent. R. R., (J. L. & S. Div.),		Clayton,	Bay,		75
Rowland, P. O.,	Sag. Val. & St. Louis R. R.,	St. Louis, 21 m.,	Holland,	Isabella,		77
Roxanna, P. O.,	Mich. Cent. R. R., (Gr. Riv. Val. Div.,)	Chester, 5 m.,	Roxand,	Eaton,		98
Royal Oak, P. O., R. R. & Tel. Sta.,	Det. & Mil. R. R.,		Royal Oak,	Oakland,	400	101
Ruby, P. O.,	P. H. & L. M. R. R.,	Thornton, 5 m.,	Clyde,	St. Clair,		88
Rudd's Station,	Det. & Bay City R. R.,		Orion,	Oakland,		101
Rural Vale, P. O.,	Det. & Bay City R. R.,	Metamora 5 m.,	Metamora, Hadley,	Lapeer,		89
Rust, R. R. Sta.,	Gr. Rap. & Ind. R. R.,		Mecosta,	Mecosta,		78
Sac Bay, Ldg.,	Lake Michigan,		Delta,	Delta,		120
Saganin Ldg.,	Saginaw Bay, Mich. Cent. R. R. (J L & S Br.),	Saginin Sta., 3 m.,	Standish,	Bay,		75
Saganin Station, R. R. Sta.,	Mich. Cent. R. R., (J. L. & S. Div.),		Standish,	Bay,		75
Saginaw, P. O., R. R. & Tel. Sta.,	Mich. Cent. R. R. (J. L. & S. Div.),		Saginaw,	Saginaw,	10,000	84
Saginaw, R. R. Sta.,	Marq., H. & Ont. R. R.,		Ishpeming,	Marquette,		110
Saginaw Mine, R. R. Sta., (Stoneville P. O.,)	Branch of Marq., H. & Ont. R. R.,		Ishpeming,	Marquette,		110
St. Charles, P. O., R. R. & Tel. Sta.,	Mich. Cent. R. R., (J. L. & S. Div.),		St. Charles,	Saginaw,	500	84
St. Clair, P. O., R. R. & Tel. Sta.,	St. Cl. & C. Air L. R. R.,		St. Clair,	St. Clair,	2,700	88
St. Helen's, R. R. & Tel. Sta.,	Mich. Cent. R. R., (J. L. & S. Div.),		Roscommon,	Roscommon,		67
St. Ignace, Ldg.,	Lake Huron,		St. Ignace,	Mackinac,		122
St. James, P. O. & Ldg.,	Lake Michigan,		Chandler,	Manitou,		51
St. Johns, P. O., R. R. & Tel. Sta.,	Det. & Mil. R. R.,		Bingham,	Clinton,	2,500	92
St. Joseph, P. O., R. R. & Tel. Sta.,	Chi. & Mich. L. Shore R. R.,		St. Joseph,	Berrien,	3,500	100
St. Louis, P. O., R. R. & Tel. Sta.,	Sag. Val. & St. L. R. R.,		Pine River, Bethany,	Gratiot,	1,300	93
Salem, P. O., (Lapham's Corners,)	Det., L. & L. M. R. R.,	Salem, 2 m.,	Salem,	Washtenaw,		104
Salem, R. R. Sta., (Summit P. O.,)	Det. L. & L. M. R. R.,		Salem,	Washtenaw,		104
Saline, P. O., R. R. & Tel. Sta.,	Det., Hill & Ind. R. R.,		Saline,	Washtenaw,	700	104
Salt River, P. O.,	Sag. Val. & St. L. R. R.,	St. Louis, 16 m.,	Coe,	Isabella,	150	77
Saltzburg, P. O. & R. R. Sta.,	Mich. Cent. R. R., (J. L. & S. Div.,)		Bangor,	Bay,		75
Sand Beach, P. O. & Ldg.,	Lake Huron,		Sand Beach,	Huron,	150	86
Sand Lake, P. O., R. R. & Tel. Sta.,	Gr. R. & Ind. R. R.,		Nelson, Pierson,	Kent, Isabella,	600	94
Sand Ridge, R. R. Sta.,	Sag. Val. & St. L. R. R.,		Richland, Thomas,	Saginaw,		84
Sand's, R. R. Sta.,	Chi. & N. W. R. R., (Penin. Div.,)		Chocolay,	Marquette,		110
Sandstone, P. O. & R. R. Sta.,	Mich. Cent. R. R.,		Sandstone,	Jackson,		105
Sanford, P. O. R. R. & Tel. Sta.,	F. & P. M. R. W.,		Lincoln,	Midland,	100	70
Sangatuck, R. R. Sta., (Orleans P. O.,)	Det., L. & L. M. R. R.,		Orleans,	Ionia,		93
Saranac, P. O., R. R. & Tel. Sta.,	Det. & Mil. R. R.,		Boston,	Ionia,	1,200	93
Satterlee's Milk, P. O.,	Gr. Rap. & Ind. R. R.,	Morley, 6 m.,	Deerfield,	Mecosta,		78
Saugatuck, P. O. & Tel. Sta.,	Chi. & Mich. L. Shore R. R.,	New Richmond, 5 m.,	Saugatuck,	Allegan,	1,200	96
Sault de St. Marie, P. O. & Ldg.,	St. Mary's River,		Chichaming,	Chippewa,	500	122
Sawyer, P. O., (Troy Sta.,)	Chi. & Mich. L. Shore R. R.,		Chichaming,	Berrien,		100
Scholcraft, P. O., R. R. & Tel. Sta.,	L. S. & M. S. R. W., (Kal. Div.), Penin. R. W.,		Schoolcraft,	Kalamazoo,	1,000	107
Scio, P. O., R. R. & Tel. Sta.,	Mich. Cent. R. R.,		Scio,	Washtenaw,	200	104
Scott, P. O. & R. R. Sta.,	Penin. R. W.,		Pavilion,	Kalamazoo,		107
Sears, P. O., (Orient R. R. Sta.,)	F. & P. M. R. W.,		Orient, Sylvan,	Osceola,	100	72
Sebewa, P. O. & R. R. Sta.,	Mar. & Cold. R. R.,		Sebewa,	Ionia,		93
Sebewaing, P. O.,	Saginaw Bay,		Sebewaing,	Huron,	600	86
Sedilia, P. O.,	M., Cold. & L. M. R. R.,		Athens,	Calhoun,		106
Second's, R. R. Sta.,	Mich. Cent. R. R.,		Van Buren,	Wayne,		102
Sec. Nine, R. R. Sta.,	Branch of Marq., H. & Ont. R. R.,			Houghton,		110
Segwun, (Lowell Sta.,)	Det. & Mil. R. R.,		Lowell,	Kent,		94
S olecka,	St. Cl. & C. Air L. R. R.,	Romeo, 2 ½ m.,	Armada, Ray,	Macomb,		102

For Explanations, names of Railroads abbreviated, etc., see page 147.

Name of Village.	Railroad, Lake or River.	Nearest Station or Landing.	Township.	County.	Pop.	Page.
Seneca, P. O.,	Chi. & Can. So. R. R.,	Weston, 3 m.,	Seneca,	Lenawee,		114
Settlement, Ldg.,	Lake Michigan,		Morse,	Mackinac,		123
Sevastopol, R. R. Sta.,	Penin R. W.,		Benton, Windsor,	Eaton,		98
Shanty Plains, R. R. Sta.,	Det., L. & L. M. R. R., (Stanton Br.,)		Fair Plain,	Montcalm,		92
Sharon,	L. S. & M. S. (Jack. Br.); Det. Hill. & Ind. R. R.,	Manchester, 3 m.,	Sharon,	Washtenaw,		104
Stattuckville, (Redan P. O.,)	Mich. Cent. R. R., (J. L. & S. Div.,)	Saginaw, 6 m.,	Saginaw,	Saginaw,		84
Shave Head, P. O.,	Mich. Cent. R. R., (Air L. Div.,)	Jones, 4 m.,	Porter,	Cass,		110
Shelby, P. O.,	Chi. & Mich. L. Shore R. R.,	Barrett, 1 m.,	Shelby,	Oceana,	200	80
Shelby, R. R. Sta., (Shelbyville P. O.,)	Gr. R. & Ind. R. R.,		Wayland, Martin,	Allegan,		96
Shepardsville, P. O. & R. R. Sta.,	Det. & Mil. R. R.,		Ovid,	Clinton,	200	92
Shepherd's Mills,	Lake Huron,	White Rock, 17 m.,	Bingham,	Huron,		93
Sheridan P. O. & R. R. Sta.,	Det., L. & L. M. R. R., (Stanton Br.)		Sidney, Evergreen,	Montcalm,	350	82
Sheridan, Sta., (Meadville P. O.,)	Mich. Cent. R. R., (Gr. Riv. Val. Div.,)		Castleton,	Barry,		97
Sherman, P. O.,	Gr. Rap. & Ind. R. R.,	Manton, 15 m.,	Weizel, General, Springville,	Wexford,	400	69
Sherman, Sta., (Bravo P. O.,)	Chi. & Mich. L. Shore R. R.,		Clyde,	Allegan,		96
Sherman City, P. O.,	F. & P. M. R. W.,	Remick 9 m.,	Sherman, Coldwater,	Isabella,	150	77
Sherwood, P. O.,	Mich. Cent. R. R., (Air L. Div.,)	Sherwood, 5 m.,	Sherwood,	Branch,		112
Sherwood, P. O., & R. R. Sta.,	Mich. Cent. R. R., (Air L. Div.,)		Sherwood,	Branch,		112
Shiawassee,	Det. & Mil. R. R.,	Vernon 2 m.,	Shiawassee,	Shiawassee,		91
Shingletown,	Mich. Cent. R. R., (J. L. & S. Div.,)	Swan Creek, 2 m.,	Swan Creek,	Saginaw,		84
Sibley Corners,	Flint & P. M. R. W.,	Wixom, 4 m.,	Commerce,	Oakland,		77
Sidney, P. O.,	Gr. R., G. & A.; Det., L. & L. M. R. R., (Stanton Br.)	Sidney Sta. 1 m., Sidney, 4 m.,	Sidney,	Montcalm,	200	82
Silver Creek, P. O., (Argenta, R. R. Sta.,)	L. S. & M. S. R. W., (Kal. Div.,)	Plainwell, 2 m.,	Gun Plain,	Allegan,		96
Singapore,	Chi. & Mich. L. Shore R. R.,	East Saugatuck, 8 m.,	Saugatuck,	Allegan,		96
Sisson, R. R. Sta.,	L. S. & M. S. R. W., (Det. Div.,)		Deerfield,	Lenawee,		114
Six Corners, P. O.,	Det. & Mil. R. R.,	Coopersville, 6 m.,	Chester,	Ottawa,		95
Skinner, P. O.,	Gr. Rap. & Bay City R. R.,		Williams,	Bay,	200	75
Slocum Grove, P. O.,	Gr. Rap., N. & L. S. R. R.,	Casnovia, 7 m.,	Casnovia,	Muskegon,		81
Smith's R. R. Sta.,	F. & P. M. R. W.,		Taymouth,	Saginaw,		84
Smith's Corners, P. O.,	Chi. & Mich. L. Shore R. R.,	Pentwater, 4 m.,	Weare,	Oceana,		80
Smith's Creek, P. O., R. R. & Tel. Sta.,	Grand Trunk R. W.,		Kimball,	St. Clair,		88
Smithville, P. O. & R. R. Sta.,	F. & P. M. R. W.,		Midland, Ingersoll,	Midland,		78
Smyrna, P. O.,	Det. L. & L. M. R. R.,	Chadwick, 5 m.,	Otisco,	Ionia,	600	93
Snyder's, R. R. Sta.,	Mich. Cent., (Air L. Div.,)		Spring Arbor,	Jackson,		105
Sodus, P. O.,	Chi. & Mich. L. Shore R. R.,	St. Joseph, 6 m.,	Sodus,	Berrien,		109
Solon, P. O.,	Gr. Rap. & Ind. R. R., (Trav. City Br.,)	Traverse City, 12 m.,	Solon,	Leelanau,		58
Somerset, P. O., R. R. & Tel. Sta.,	Det., Hill. & Ind. R. R.,		Somerset,	Hillsdale,	100	113
Somerset Centre, P. O.,	Det., Hill. & Ind. R. R.,	Somerset Sta., 3 m.,	Somerset,	Hillsdale,	100	113
South Blendon, P. O.,	Chi. & Mich. L. Shore R. R., (Gr. Rap. Div.,)	Vriesland, 4 m.,	Blendon,	Ottawa,		95
South Boston, P. O.,	Det. & Mil. R. R.,	Saranac, 4 m.,	Boston,	Ionia,		93
South Butler, P. O.,	L. S. & M. S. R. W.,	Quincy, 5 m.,	Butler,	Branch,		112
South Camden, P. O.,	M., Cold. & L. M. R. R.,	Camden, 8 m.,	Camden,	Hillsdale,		113
South Cass, P. O.,	Mar. & Cold. R. R.,	Sunfield, 8 m.,	Odessa,	Ionia,		93
South Climax, P. O.,	Penin. R. W.,	Scott, 5 m.,	Climax,	Kalamazoo,		107
Southfield, P. O.,	Det. & Mil. R. R.,	Royal Oak, 6 m.,	Southfield,	Oakland,	150	101
South Frankport, P. O. & Ldg.,	Lake Michigan,		Gilmore,	Benzie,	200	59
South Haven, P. O., R. R. & Tel. Sta.,	Mich. Cent. R. R., (Kal. & S. Hav. Div.,)		South Haven,	Van Buren,	1,700	106
South Jackson, P. O.,	Ft. W., J. & S.; Mich Cent. (Air L. Div.,)	Wilcox, 4 m.,	Summit,	Jackson,		105
South Lyon, P. O., & R. R. Sta.,	Det., L. & L. M. R. R.,		Lyon,	Oakland,	400	101
South Riley, P. O.,	Det., L. & L. M. R. R.,	Dello, 7 m.,	Riley,	Clinton,		92
South Saginaw, P. O. & Tel. Sta.,	Mich. Cent. R. R., (J. L. & S. Div.,)	Saginaw, 2 m.,	East Saginaw,	Saginaw,	2,500	84
South Wright,	L. S. & M. S. R. W.,	Hudson, 12 m.,	Wright,	Hillsdale,		113
Sparta, R. R. Sta., (Sparta Centre P. O.,)	Gr. Rap., N. & L. S. R. R.,		Sparta,	Kent,		94
Speaker, P. O.,	F. H. & L. M. R. R.,	Emmet, 17 m.,		Sanilac,		87
Spencer Creek, P. O.,	Gr. Rap. & Ind. R. R.,	Mancelona, 11 m.,	Helena,	Antrim,		57
Spencer's Mill,	Lake Huron,	Tawas City, 8 m.,	Plainfield,	Iosco,		65
Spencer's Mills, P. O.,	Gr. Rap., G. & A. R. R.,	Gould's Mills, 4 m.,	Spencer,	Kent,		94
Spicerville,	Mich. Cent., (Gr. Val. Br.); L. & S. L. R. Y. (Lan. Br.)	Eaton Rapids, 2 m.,	Sterling, Warren,	Macomb,		98
Spinnings, R. R. Sta.,	Det. & D. City R. R.,		Crockery,	Ottawa,		102
Spoonville, R. R. Sta.,	Chi. & Mich. L. Shore R. R.,		Crockery,	Ottawa,		95
Spring Arbor, P. O.,	Mich. Cent. R. R., (Air Line Div.,)	Snyder's, 2 m.,	Spring Arbor,	Jackson,		105
Spring Brook, P. O.,	Det. & Mil. R. R.,	St. John's, 12 m.,	Fulton,	Gratiot,		83
Spring City, P. O., & R. R. Sta.,	Gr. Rap. & Ind R. R., (Trav. City Br.,)		Paradise,	Grand Traverse		60
Spring Creek, P. O.,	Chi. & Mich. L. Shore R. R.,	Pentwater, 4 m.,	Weare,	Oceana,		80
Springfield, P. O.,	Det. & Mil. R. R.,	Davisburgh, 4 m.,	Springfield,	Oakland,		101
Spring Lake, P. O., R. R. & Tel. Sta.,	Det. & Mil. R. R.,		Spring Lake,	Ottawa,	2,000	95
Spring Mill Landing,	Lake Huron,		Harrisville,	Alcona,		64
Spring Mills, P. O., (Highland Station,)	F. & P. M. R. W.,		Highland,	Oakland,		101
Springport, P. O. & Tel. Sta., (Over's Corners,)	L. S. & M. S. R. W., (Lansing Div.,)		Springport,	Jackson,	275	105
Springvale, (West Branch R. R. Sta.,)	Mich. Cent. R. R., (J. L. & S. Div.,)		Ogemaw,	Ogemaw,		66
Springville, P. O.,	Det., Hill. & Ind. R. R.,	Brooklyn, 5 m.,	Cambridge,	Lenawee,	100	114
Spurr Mine, R. R. Sta.,	Marq., H. & Ont. R. R.,		Houghton,	Houghton,		117
Stafford, (Port Hope P. O., Tel. Sta. & Ldg.,)	Lake Huron,		Rubicon,	Huron,	400	93
Standish or Greaton, P. O., R. R. & Tel. Sta.,	Mich. Cent. R. R., (J. L. & S. Div.,)		Standish,	Bay,	375	75
Stanton, P. O. & R. R. Sta.,	Det., L. & L. M. R. R., (Stanton Dir.,)		Douglas, Sidney,	Montcalm,	700	82
Stanton Junction, R. R. Sta.,	Det., L. & L. M. R. R.,		Easton,	Ionia,		93
Starwood, P. O., R. R. & Tel. Sta.,	Gr. Rap. & Ind. R. R.,		Mecosta,	Mecosta,	400	78
State Line, R. R. Sta.,	Ft. W., J. & S. R. R.,		California,	Branch,		112
State Road, R. R. Sta.,	Penin. R. W.,		Bellevue,	Kalco,		98
State Road, R. R. Sta.,	Mich. Cent. R. R., (J. L. & S. Div.,)		Kawkawlin,	Bay,		75
Stannburg,	Det., Hill. & Ind. R. R., L. S. & M. S. R. W.,	Hillsdale, 5 m.,	Cambria,	Hillsdale,		113
Stebbinsville, P. O.,	Mus. & Big Rap. R. R.,	Holton, 6 m.,	Greenwood,	Oceana,		80
Stebbinsville, R. R. Sta.,	Det., L. & L. M. R. R.,		Portland,	Ionia,		93
Stella, P. O.,	Sag. Val. & St. L. R. R.,	Brockenridge, 12 m.,	Hamilton,	Gratiot,	400	93
Stephens, P. O.,	Lapeer & Northern R. R.,	Fish Lake, 2 m.,	Mayfield,	Lapeer,	250	89
Sterling, P. O., (Clyde R. R. Sta.,)	Mich. Cent. R. R., (J. L. & S. Div.,)		Deep River,	Bay,		75
Stevens Landing,	Lake Huron,		Worth,	Sanilac,		87
Stevensville, P. O., R. R. & Tel. Sta.,	Chi. & Mich. L. Shore R. R.,		Lincoln,	Berrien,		109
Stockbridge, P. O.,	Mich. Cent. R. R., (J. L. & S. Div.,)	Leslie, 14 m.,	Stockbridge,	Ingham,		99
Stoneville, P. O., (Saginaw Mine, R. R. Sta.,)	Branch of Marq., H. & Ont. R. R.,		Ishpeming,	Marquette,		119
Stony Creek,	Det. & B. City; Ch. Cl. & O. Air L. R. R.,	Rochester, 2 m.,	Avon,	Oakland,		101
Stony Creek, P. O.,	Tol. & Ann Ar. R. R.,	York, 4 m.,	Augusta,	Washtenaw,		104
Stony Creek, R. R. Sta.,	L. S. & M. S. (Det. Div.), Tol., Can. S. & Det. R. W.,		Frenchtown,	Monroe,		115
Stony Point, P. O. & R. R. Sta.,	Ft. W., J. & S. R. R.,		Hanover,	Jackson,		105
Stony Run, P. O.,	F. & P. M. R. W.,	Grand Blanc, 5 m.,	Holly,	Oakland,	100	101
Strait's Lake, P. O.,	Det. & Mil.; F. & P. M.; St. Cl. & C. Air L. R. R.,	Wixom, 7 m., Walled, 7 m.,	West Bloomfield,	Oakland,		101
Strickland, P. O.,	Sag. Val. & St. L. R. R.,	St. Louis, 13 m.,		Isabelle,		77
Stronach Mill,	Lake Michigan,	Manistee, 6 m.,	Stronach,	Manistee,		66
Stronach, P. O. & Tel. Sta.,	Lake Michigan,	Manistee, 4 m.,	Stronach,	Manistee,	850	59
Sturgeon, R. R. Sta.,	Marq., H. & Ont. R. R.,			Houghton,		117
Sturgis, P. O., R. R. & Tel. Sta.,	L. S. & M. S. R. W., Gr. R. & Ind. R. R.,		Sturgis,	St. Joseph,	2,000	111
Summerton, P. O.,	Sag. Val. & St. L. R. R.,	St. Louis, 6 m.,	Seville,	Gratiot,		83

☞ For Explanations, names of Railroads abbreviated, etc., see page 147.

Name of Village.	Railroad, Lake or River.	Nearest Station or Landing.	Township.	County.	Pop.	Dept.
Summerville, P. O.,	Mich. Cent. R. R.,	Pokagon, 2 m.,	Pokagon,	Cass,	200	110
Summit, P. O., (Salem Sta.,)	Det., L. & L. M. R. R.,		Salem,	Washtenaw,		104
Summit, R. R. Sta.,	Mary., H. & Ont. R. R.,			Houghton,		117
Summitville, P. O. & R. R. Sta.,	Flint & P. M. R. W.,		Chase,	Lake,		71
Sumner, P. O.,	Sag. Val. & St. L. R. R.,	St. Louis, 14 m.,	Sumner,	Gratiot,	200	83
Sunfield, P. O.,	Mar. & Cold. R. R.,		Sunfield,	Eaton,		96
Sutton's Bay, P. O., (Pleasant City, Landing,)	Grand Traverse Bay,		Bingham,	Leelanau,		56
Swan Creek, P. O. & R. R. Sta.,	Mich. Cent. R. R., (J. L. & S. Div.,)		Swan Creek,	Saginaw,		84
Swan Creek R. R. Sta.,	Sag. Val. & St. Louis R. R.,		Thomas,	Saginaw,		84
Swartz Creek, P. O.,	P. M. & L. M. R. R.,	R. R. unfinished,	Clayton, Gaines,	Genesee,	200	90
Sweet's, R. R. Sta.,	Chi. & Mich. L. Shore R. R.,		Fruitland,	Muskegon,		81
Sylvan, P. O.,	Mich. Cent. R. R.,	Chelsea, 3m	Sylvan,	Washtenaw,		104
Sylvester, P. O.,	Gr. Rap. & Ind. R. R.,	Stanwood, 11 m.,	Hinton,	Mecosta,	70	78
Tallmadge, P. O.,	Chi. & Mich. L. Shore R. R., (Gr. Rap. Div.,)	Jenrison's, 4 m.,	Tallmadge,	Ottawa,		98
Tamarack, P. O.,	Gr. Rap. & Ind. R. R.,	Conger, 8 m.,	Winfield,	Montcalm,		82
Tawas City, P. O., Tel. Sta. & Ldg.,	Lake Huron,		Tawas,	Iosco,	700	65
Taylor Centre, P. O.,	Mich. Cent. R. R.,	Dearborn, 6 m.,	Taylor,	Wayne,		102
Taymouth, P. O.,	F. & P. M. R. W.,	Smith's, 5 m.,	Taymouth,	Saginaw,		84
Tecumseh, P. O., Tel. & R. R. Sta.,	L. S. & M. S., R. W., (Jack. Br.),		Tecumseh,	Lenawee,	3,000	114
Teffi's,	Mich. Cent. R. R., (J. L. & S. Div.,)	Swan Creek, 3 m.,	Swan Creek,	Saginaw,		84
Tekonsha, P. O., R. R. & Tel. Sta.,	Mich. Cent. (Air L. Div.,) Mar. & Cold. R. R.,		Tekonsha,	Calhoun,	500	108
Terry Station, P. O., Tel. & R. R. Sta.,	Mich. Cent. R. R., (J. L. & S. Div.,)		Kawkawlin,	Bay,	100	75
Thetford Centre, P. O.,	F. & P. M. R. W.,	Pine Run Sta., 5 m.,	Thetford,	Genesee,		90
Thomas Mills, (Harris Creek P. O.,)	Mich. Cent. R. R., (Gr. Riv. Val. Div.,)	Caledonia, 6 m.,	Bowne,	Kent,		94
Thompson,	Mich. Cent. R. R., (J. L. & S. Div.,)	West Branch, 27 m.,	Thompson,	Iosco,		65
Thornton, P. O. & R. R. Sta.,	P. H. & L. M. R. R.,		Kimball,	St. Clair,		83
Thornville, P. O.,	Det. & B. City R. R.,	Metamora, 3 m.,	Metamora,	Lapeer,	400	89
Three Oaks, P. O., R. R. & Tel. Sta.,	Mich. Cent. R. R.,		Three Oaks,	Berrien,	600	109
Three Rivers, P. O., R. R. & Tel Sta.,	L. S. & M. S. R. W., (Kal. Div.,)		Lockport,	St. Joseph,	3,000	111
Tietsorts, R. R. Sta., (Model City P. O.,)	Mich. Cent. R. R.,		Wayne,	Cass,		110
Tipton, P. O.,	L. S. & M. S. R. W., (Jack. Br.,)	Tecumseh, 6 m.,	Franklin,	Lenawee,		114
Titabawassee, (Freeland's Sta., Jay P. O.,)	F. & P. M. R. W.,		Tittabawassee,	Saginaw,		84
Tittabawassee, R. R. Sta.,	Mich. Cent. (L. & S. Br.), Sag. Val. & St. L. R. R.,		Spaulding,	Saginaw,		84
Tompkins, P. O., (Tompkins Centre,)	Mich. Cent. R. R., (L. & S. Br. & L. Riv. Val. Br.),	Rives Junction, 3 m.,	Tompkins,	Jackson,		105
Torch Lake, P. O.,	Grand Traverse Bay,		Torch Lake,	Antrim,	150	57
Torch Lake Mills, R. R. Sta., (Lake Linden P. O.)	Hecla & Torch Lake R. R.,		Schoolcraft,	Houghton,		117
Town Line, R. R. Sta.,	Det., L. & L. M. R. R.,		Redford, Greenfield,	Wayne,		102
Traverse City, P. O., R. R. & Tel. Sta. & Ldg.,	Gr. R. & Ind. R. R. (for. City br.,) Gr. Traverse Bay,		Traverse,	Grand Traverse	1,200	60
Travis, R. R. Sta.,	Gr. Rapids & Ind. R. R.,		Cooper,	Kalamazoo,		107
Trent, P. O.,	Gr. Riv., N. & L. R. R.,	Trent Sta., 3 m.,	Casnovia,	Muskegon,		81
Trent, R. R. Sta.,	Gr. Rap., N. & L. S. R. R.,		Casnovia,	Muskegon,		81
Trenton, P. O., R. R. & Tel. Sta.,	L. S. & M. S. R. W., Chi. & Can. So. R. R.,		Monguagon,	Wayne,	500	103
Trostville, P. O.,	Det. & Bay City R. R.,	Bridgeport, 7 m.,	Blumfield,	Saginaw,	200	84
Troy, P. O.,	Det. & Mil. R. R., Det. & B. City R. R.,	Birmingham, 7 Rochester, 6 m.	Troy,	Oakland,		101
Troy, R. R. Sta., (sawyer P. O.,)	Chi. & Mich. L. Shore R. R.,		Chickaming,	Berrien,		109
Troy, P. O. & R. R. Sta.,	Det., L. & L. M. R. R.,		Maple Valley,	Montcalm,	250	82
Trumbull, R. R. Sta.,	Mich. Cent. R. R.,		Sandstone,	Jackson,		105
Tustin, P. O. & R. R. Sta.,	Gr. Rap. & Ind. R. R.,		Burdell,	Osceola,		72
Twin Lake, R. R. Sta.,	Mus. & Big Rap. R. R.,		Dalton,	Muskegon,		81
Tyre, P. O.,	Lake Huron,	Forestville, 16 m.,	Austin, Bingham,	Sanilac, Barns	37, 55	
Tyrone, P. O.,	Det. & Mil. R. R.,	Fentonville, 5 m.,	Tyrone,	Livingston,		100
Tyrone, R. R. Sta.,	Gr. Rap., N. & L. S. R. R.,		Tyrone,	Kent,		94
Unadilla, P. O. & R. R. Sta.,	St. Cl. & C. Air L. R. R.,		Unadilla,	Livingston,	300	100
Union, P. O.,	Mich. Cent. R. R., (Air L. Div.,)	Jones, 9 m.,	Porter,	Cass,		110
Union City, P. O., R. R. & Tel. Sta.,	Mich. Cent. R. R., (Air L. Div.,)		Union,	Branch,	1,200	112
Union Home, P. O.,			Greenbush,	Clinton,		92
Union Pier, P. O., (Town Line Sta.,)	Chi. & Mich. L. Shore R. R.,	St. Johns, 8 m.,	Chickaming, New Buffalo,	Berrien,		109
Unionville, P. O.,	Saginaw Bay,	Sebewaing, 6 m.,	Gasto, Akron, Columbia,	Tuscola,	150	85
Uties, P. O., R. R. & Tel. Sta.,	Det. & B. City R. R.,		Shelby, Sterling,	Macomb,	650	102
Utica Plank, R. R. & Tel. Sta.,	Grand Trunk R. W.,		Erie,	Macomb,		102
Vandalia, P. O. R. R. & Tel. Sta.,	Mich. Cent. R. R., (Air L. Div.,)		Penn,	Cass,	850	110
Van Horn, R. R. Sta.,	Mich. Cent. R. R., (J. L. & S. Div.,)		Blackman,	Jackson,		105
Vassar, P. O. & R. R. Sta.,	Det. & Bay City R. R.,		Vassar,	Tuscola,	1,000	85
Ventura,	Mich. L. Sh. R.,	North Holland, 3 m.,	Olive, Holland,	Ottawa,	300	95
Vermontville, P. O., R. R. & Tel. Sta.,	Mich. Cent. (Gr. Riv. Val. Br.), Mar. & Cold. R. R.,		Vermontville,	Eaton,	600	98
Vernon, P. O., R. R. & Tel. Sta.,	Det. & Mil. R. R.,		Vernon,	Shiawassee,	600	91
Verona, R. R. Sta.,	Penin. R. W.,		Emmet,	Calhoun,		102
Verona Falls, P. O.,	Lake Huron,	Sand Reach, 12 m.,	Verona, Sigel,	Huron,		102
Vickeryville, P. O.,	Det., L. & L. M. R. R., (Stanton Br.,)	Sheridan, 7 m.,	Evergreen,	Montcalm,		82
Vicksburg, Ldg., (Marysville P. O.,)	River St. Clair,		Port Huron,	St. Clair,		83
Vicksburg, P. O., R. R. & Tel Sta.,	Gr. R. & Ind. R. R., Penin. R. W.,		Brady, Schoolcraft,	Kalamazoo,	1,000	107
Victor, P. O.,	Det. & Mil. R. R.,	Shepardsville, 5 m.,	Victor,	Clinton,		92
Victor Mills,	Det. & Mil. R. R.,	Berlin, 3 m.,	Tallmadge,	Ottawa,		95
Victory, P. O.,	F. & P. M. R. W.,	Amber, 4 m.,	Victory,	Mason,	100	70
Vienna, R. R. & Tel. Sta., (Erie, P. O.,)	Tol., Can. S. & Det.; L. S. & M. S. R. W. (Bel. Br.,)		Erie,	Monroe,		115
Vincent, P. O.,	Grand Trunk R. W.,	Fort Gratiot, 6 m.,	Clyde,	St. Clair,		110
Volinia, P. O.,	Penin. R. W.,	Volinia, 5 m.,	Cass,	Cass,		110
Volinia, R. R. Sta., (Wakelee, P. O.,)	Penin. R. W.,		Volinia,	Cass,		110
Vriesland, P. O.,	Chi. & Mich. L. Shore R. R., (Gr. Rap. Div.,)	Vriesland Sta., 2 m.,	Zeeland,	Ottawa,		95
Vriesland Sta., R. R. Sta.,	Chi. & Mich. L. Shore R. R., (Gr. Rap. Div.,)		Zeeland,	Ottawa,		95
Waccasta, P. O.,	Det., L. & L. M. R. R.,	Ingersoll's, 4 m.,	Watertown,	Clinton,	200	92
Wahjamega, P. O.,	Det. & Bay City R. R.,	Vassar, 9 m.,	Indian Fields,	Tuscola,	100	85
Wakelee, P. O., (Volinia R. R. Sta.,)	Penin. R. W.,		Volinia,	Cass,		110
Wakeshma, P. O.,		Indian Lake, 8 m.,	Wakeshma,	Kalamazoo,		107
Walblushurg, P. O.,	Grand Trunk R. W.,	Mt. Clemens, 6 m.,	Macomb,	Macomb,		102
Wales, P. O.,	P. H. & L. M. R. R.,	Goodell's, 2 m.,	Wales,	St. Clair,		109
Walkerville, P. O.,	Det., L. & L. M. R. R.,	Fishers, 2 m.,	Dearborn,	Wayne,		103
Walled Lake, P. O.,	F. & P. M. R. W., St. Cl. & C. Air L. R. R.,	Wixom, 5 m.,	Commerce,	Oakland,	200	101
Walton, R. R. & Tel. Sta.,	Gr. Rap. & Ind. R. R., & do., Trav. City Dr.,		Fife Lake,	Grand Traverse		60
Walz, R. R. & Tel. Sta.,	F. & P. M. R. W.,		Warren,	Wayne,		102
Warren, P. O., (Glenwood R. R. Sta.,)	Det. & B. City R. R.,		Warren,	Macomb,	150	102
Warren, R. R. Sta.,	Det. & B. City R. R.,		Warren,	Macomb,		102
Washington, P. O. & R. R. Sta.,	St. Cl. & C. Air L. R. R.,		Washington,	Macomb,	200	102
Waterford, P. O. & R. R. Sta.,	Det. & Mil. R. R.,		Waterford,	Oakland,	350	101
Waterford, R. R. Sta., (Mund's Mills, P. O.,)	Det. & Mil. R. R.,		Plymouth,	Wayne,		102
Waterloo, P. O.,	Mich. Cent. R. R.,	Francisco, 6 m.,	Waterloo,	Jackson,	500	105
Watertown, P. O.,	Det. & Bay City R. R.,	Otter Lake, 5 m.,	Watertown,	Tuscola,		85
Watervliet, P. O., R. R. & Tel. Sta.,	Mich. Cent., L. Shore R. R.,		Watervliet,	Berrien,	800	109
Watkins, R. R. Sta.,	Det., Hill & Ind. R. R.,		Norvell,	Jackson,		105
Watromville, P. O.,	Det. & B. City R. R.,		Juniata,	Tuscola,	300	85
Waukazoo, (Cat Head,)	Lake Michigan,	Vassar, 7 m.,	Leelanau,	Leelanau,		56
Waverly, P. O.,	Mich. Cent. R. R., (Kal. & S. Hav. Div.,)	Goble, 4 m.,	Waverly,	Van Buren,		108

☞ For Explanations, names of Railroads abbreviated, etc., see page 147.

Name of Village.	Railroad, Lake or River.	Nearest Station or Landing.	Township.	County.	Pop.	Page.
Wayland, P. O., R. R. & Tel. Sta.,	Gr. Rap. & Ind. R. R.,		Wayland,	Allegan,	700	96
Wayne, P. O., R. R. Tel. Sta.,	Mich. Cent. R. R., F. & P. M. R. W.,		Nankin,	Wayne,	1,200	103
Weare, P. O.,	Chi. & Mich. L. Shore R. R.,	Pentwater, 8 m.,	Weare,	Oceana,		80
Webberville, P. O., (Leroy Sta.,)	Det., L. & L. M. R. R.,		Leroy,	Ingham,		99
Webster, P. O.,	Mich. Cent. R. R.,	Delhi, 5 m.,	Webster,	Washtenaw,		104
Weesaw, P. O.,	Mich. Cent. R. R.,	Galien, 7 m.,	Weesaw,	Berrien,		109
Wells, R. R. & Tel. Sta.,	Mich. Cent. R. R., (J. L. & S. Div.,)		Clayton,	Bay,		75
Wellsburg, Ldg.,	Lake Michigan,		Dalton,	Delta,		120
Wellsville, P. O. & R. R. Sta.,	L. S. & M. S. R. W., (Det. Div.,)		Blissfield, Palmyra,	Lenawee,		114
Wenona, P. O., R. R. & Tel. Sta.,	Mich. Cent. R. R., (J. L. & S. Div.,)		Bangor,	Bay,	2,100	75
Wequagamaw's,	Grand Traverse Bay,		Elk Rapids,	Antrim,		57
West Berlin, P. O.,	P. H. & L. M. R. R.,	Capac, 5 m.,	Berlin,	St. Clair,		88
West Branch, R. R. & Tel. Sta., (Springvale,)	Mich. Cent. (J. L. & S. Div.,)		Ogemaw,	Ogemaw,		66
West Campbell, P. O.,	Det. & Mil. R. R.,	Saranac, 9 m.,	Campbell,	Ionia,		93
West Casco, P. O.,	Mich. Cent. R. R., (Kal. & S. Hav. Div.,)	South Haven, 4 m.,	Casco,	Allegan,		96
West Geneva, P. O., (Irvington, Geneva Sta.,)	Mich. Cent. R. R., (Kal. & S. Hav. Div.,)		Geneva,	Van Buren,	150	108
West Haven, P. O.,	Mich. Cent. R. R., (J. L. & S. Div.,)	Hendersonville, 2 m.,	New Haven,	Shiawassee,	800	91
West Leroy, P. O.,	Penin. R. W.,	Climax, 4 m.,	Leroy,	Calhoun,		108
West Milan, P. O.,	Tol. & Ann Ar. R. R.,	Reeves, 5 m.,	Milan,	Monroe,		115
West Novi, P. O.,	F. & P. M. R. W.,	Wixom, 2 m.,	Novi,	Oakland,		101
West Ogden, P. O.,	Chi. & Can. So. R. R.,	Fairfield, 4 m.,	Ogden,	Lenawee,		114
West Olive, P. O., (Pigeon Sta.,)	Mich. L. Sh. R. R.,		Olive,	Ottawa,		95
Weston, P. O. & R. R. Sta.,	Chi. & Can. So. R. R.,		Fairfield,	Lenawee,		114
Westphalia, P. O.,	Det. & Mil. R. R.,	Fowler, 6 m.,	Westphalia,	Clinton,		92
West Sebewa, P. O.,	Mar. & Cold. R. R.,	Sebewa, 7 m.,	Sebewa,	Ionia,		93
West Summit, R. R. Sta.,	Gr. Rap. & Ind. R. R.,		Clam Lake,	Wexford,		69
Westville, P. O.,	Det., L. & L. M. R. R. (Stanton Br.,)	Stanton, 4 m.,	Douglass,	Montcalm,		82
West Windsor, P. O.,	Penin. R. W.,	Sevastopol, 1 m.,	Windsor,	Eaton,		98
Wexford, P. O.,	Gr. Rap. & Ind. R. R.,	Walton, 15 m.,	Wexford,	Wexford,		69
Wexford, Sta. R. R. Sta.,	Gr. Rap. & Ind. R. R.,		Haring,	Wexford,		69
Wheatland, P. O.,	Gr. Rap. & Ind. R. R.,		Colfax,	Wexford,		69
Wheatland Centre, P. O.,	Det., Hill & Ind. R. R.,	North Adams, 7 m.,	Wheatland,	Hillsdale,		113
Wheeler, P. O. & R. R. Sta.,	Sag. Val. & St. L. R. R.,		Wheeler,	Gratiot,		83
White, P. O. & R. R. Sta.,	M., Cold. & L. M. R. R.,		Woodbridge,	Hillsdale,		113
Whiteford Centre, P. O.,	L. S. & M. S. R. W.,		Whiteford,	Monroe,		115
Whitehall, P. O., R. R. & Tel. Sta.,	Chi. & Mich. L. Shore R. R.,	Ottawa Lake, 4 m.,	Oceana,	Muskegon,	2,000	91
White Lake, P. O.,	Flint & P. M. R. W.,	Clyde, 3 m.,	White Lake,	Oakland,		101
White Oak, P. O.,	Det. L. & L. M. R. R.,	Leroy, 11 m.,	White Oak,	Ingham,		99
White Oak, R. R. Sta.,	Mich. Cent. R. R.,		Decatur,	Van Buren,		108
White Pigeon, P. O., R. R. & Tel. Sta.,	L. S. & M. S., R. W.,		Mottville, White Pigeon,	St. Joseph,	1,200	111
White River, P. O.,	Chi. & Mich. L. Shore R. R.,	Montague, 4 m.,	White River,	Muskegon,	200	91
White Rock, P. O. & Tel. Sta.,	Lake Huron,		White Rock,	Huron,	250	90
Whitesburg, P. O.,	F. & P. M. R. W., (Ot. Lake Dr.,)	Max Sta., 1 m.,	Thetford,	Genesee,		90
White's Sta., P. O., R. R. & Tel. Sta.,	Mich. Cent. R. R.,		Emmet,	Calhoun,		109
White Swan, P. O.,	Gr. Rap., Greenville & Alpena R. R.,	Oakfield Sta., 1 m.,	Oakfield,	Kent,		94
Whitewater, P. O.,	Gr. Rap. & Ind. R. R., (Trav. City Br.,)	Traverse City, 10 m.,	Whitewater,	Grand Traverse		94
Whitewood, P. O.,	Det. & Mil. R. R.,	Detroit, 2 m.,	Greenfield,	Wayne,		103
Whitmore Lake, P. O.,	Mich. Cent. R.,	Delhi, 7 m.,	Northfield,	Washtenaw,	200	104
Whitneyville,	Det. & Mil. R. R.,	Ada, 5 m.,	Cascade,	Kent,		94
Wilkinson, R. R. Sta.,	Chi. & Mich. L. Shore R. R.,		Chickaming,	Berrien,		109
Williams, P. O.,	Gr. Rap. & Bay City R. R.,		Williams,	Bay,		75
Williamsburg, P. O.,	Gr. Rap. & Ind. R. R., (Trav. City Br.,)	Traverse City, 11 m.,	East Bay,	G'd Traverse,		60
Williamstown, P. O., R. R. & Tel. Sta.,	Det., L. & L. M. R. R.,		Williamston, Westfield,	Ingham,		99
Williamsville, P. O.,	Mich. Cent. R. R., (Air L. Div.,)	Jones, 5 m.,	Porter,	Cass,	200	110
Wilson, P. O.,	Grand Traverse Bay,		Torch Lake, Central Lake,	Antrim,		57
Wilson's, R. R. Sta.,	Mich. Cent. (Air L. Div.,) Pt. W., J. & S. R. R.,		Summit,	Jackson,		105
Winchester,	L. S. & M. S. (Det. Br.,) Tol., Can. S. & Det. R. W.,	La Salle, 1 m.,	La Salle, Monroe,	Monroe,		115
Windsor, P. O.,	L. S. & M. S. R. W., (Lansing Div.,)	Dimondale, 2 m.,	Windsor,	Eaton,		98
Winfield, P. O.,	Mich. Cent. R. R., (Gr. Riv. Val. Div.,)	Onondaga, 1½ m.,	Onondaga,	Ingham,		99
Wise, P. O.,	Sag. Val. & St. L. R. R.,	St. Louis, 10 m.,	Fremont,	Isabella,	200	77
Wisner, P. O. & Ldg.,	Saginaw Bay,		Wisner,	Tuscola,	191	85
Wixom, P. O., R. R. & Tel. Sta.,	F. & P. M. R. W., St. Cl. & C. Air L. R. R.,		Commerce,	Oakland,	50	101
Wood, R. R. Sta.,	L. S. & M. S. R. W.,		Bronson,	Branch,		113
Wood, R. R. Sta.,	L. S. & M. S. R. W.,		Riga,	Lenawee,		114
Woodbridge,	M., Cold. & L. M. R. R.,	Woodbridge, 8 m.,	Woodbridge,	Hillsdale,		113
Woodbridge, P. O., R. R. & Tel. Sta.,	M., Cold. & L. M. R. R.,		Woodbridge,	Hillsdale,		113
Wood Lake, P. O. & R. R. Sta.,	Gr. Rap. & Ind. R. R.,		Pierson,	Montcalm,	100	84
Woodland, P. O.,	Mich. Cent. R. R. (Gr. Riv. Val. Div.,)	Sheridan, 8 m.,	Woodland,	Barry,	200	97
Wood's Corners, P. O. & R. R.,	Det., L. & L. M. R. R. (Stanton Br.,)		Orleans,	Ionia,		93
Woodstock, (Kelly's Corners P. O.,)	Det., Hill & Ind. R. R.,		Woodstock,	Lenawee,		114
Worth, P. O.,	Det. & B. City R. R.,	Vassar, 5 m.,	Tuscola,	Tuscola,	800	85
Wright's, R. R. Sta.,	Mich. Cent. R. R., (J. L. & S. Div.,)		Edwards,	Ogemaw,		66
Wright's Bridge, P. O.,	F. & P. M. R. W.,	Sanford, 6 m.,	Jerome,	Midland,		76
Wyandotte, Tel. Sta. & Ldg.,	L. S. & M. S. R. W. Tol., Can. S. & Det. R. W.,		Ecorce,	Wayne,	4,000	103
Yankee Springs, P. O.,	Mich. Cent. R. R., (Gr. Riv. Val. Div.,)	Irving, 7 m.,	Yankee Springs,	Barry,		97
Yates, R. R. Sta.,	Det. & B. City R. R.,		Shelby, Avon,	Macomb, Oakland,		102
Yew, P. O.,	Det., L. & L. M. R. R.,	Town Line, 1 m.,	Greenfield,	Wayne,		103
York, P. O., (Mooreville,)	Tol. & Ann Ar. R. R.,	Milan, 3 m.,	York,	Washtenaw,		104
York, R. R. Sta.,	Tol. & Ann Ar. R. R.,		York,	Washtenaw,		104
Yorkville, P. O.,	M., Cold. & L. M. R. R.,	Richland, 3 m.,	Ross,	Kalamazoo,	115	107
Ypsilanti, P. O., R. R. & Tel. Sta.,	Mich. Cent. R. R., Det., Hill. & Ind. R. R.,		Ypsilanti,	Washtenaw,	6,500	104
Yuba, P. O. & Ldg.,	Gr. Trav. Bay, Gr. R. & Ind. R. R. (Tra. City Br.,)	Traverse City, 11 m.,	Whitewater,	Grand Traverse	113	60
Zeeland, P. O. & R. R. Sta.,	Chi. & Mich. L. Shore R. R., (J. L. & S. Div.,)		Zeeland,	Ottawa,	400	95
Zilwaukee, P. O. & R. R.,	Mich. Cent. R. R., (J. L. & S. Div.,)		Zilwaukee,	Saginaw,	1,400	84

For Explanations, names of Railroads abbreviated, etc., see page 147.

BUSINESS CARDS
OF
PATRONS IN DETROIT.

ATTORNEYS.

Alfred Russell,
Attorney at Law,
91 Griswold St.   Rooms 48 & 49.

Geo. V. N. Lothrop,
Attorney at Law,
86 Seitz Block.

C. I. Walker,
Attorney at Law,
Moffat Block.

E. W. Meddaugh,
Attorney at Law.

E. Y. Swift,
Attorney at Law,
102 Woodward Avenue.

H. M. Duffield,
Attorney at Law,
Seitz Block.

John G. Hawley,
Attorney at Law,
Seitz Block.

F. G. Russell,
Attorney at Law,
Moffat Block.

Geo. H. Penniman,
Attorney at Law,
15 Telegraph Block.

Marcus G. B. Swift,
Attorney at Law,
Rooms 18 & 19,   Bank Block.

Kane & Hibbard,
Law and Collection Office,
Moffat Block.

Pond & Brown,
Attorneys and Counselors,
Bank Block.

Wilkinson & Post,
Attorneys at Law,
Bank Block.

Cleaveland & Firnane,
War claim Agents,
Moffat Block.

C. J. O'Flynn,
Lawyer,
Room 19,   Telegraph Block.

Samuel T. Douglass,
Counselor at Law,
68 Seitz Block.

R. P. Toms,
Lawyer,
Moffat Block.

James J. Brown,
Lawyer.

George S. Swift,
Judge Recorder's Court,
Office 12,   City Hall.

James A. Randall,
Attorney at Law,
Telegraph Block.

Wm. E. Cheever,
Attorney at Law,
Telegraph Block.

A. F. Wilcox,
Attorney at Law,
Bank Block.

C. J. Reilly,
Counselor at Law,
149 Jefferson Avenue.

Wm. Jennison,
Counselor at Law,
No. 46 Seitz Block.

L. S. Trowbridge,
Counselor at Law,
Moffat Block.

Robinson & Flinn,
Lawyers,
Moffat Block.

D. C. Holbrook,
Attorney at Law,
Moffat Block.

Wm. C. Hoyt,
Attorney at Law,
Telegraph Block.

Wm. P. Wells,
Attorney at Law,
Moffat Block.

Levi T. Griffin,
Attorney at Law,
Moffat Block.

Samuel J. Kelso,
Attorney at Law,
Seitz Block.

Alex. D. Fowler,
Attorney at Law,
Moffat Block.

Albert J. Chapman,
Counselor at Law.

Julien Williams,
Attorney,
Seitz Block.

Walker & Kent,
Attorneys,   Moffat Block.
E. C. WALKER.   C. A. KENT.

T. C. Owen,
Attorney,
Foot of Wayne St.

J. Logan Chipman,
Counselor at Law,
12 Kanter's Block.

John T. McKeown,
Law & Real Estate,
Moffat Block.

Eugene C. Skinner,
Abstract of Land Titles of Detroit
and Wayne County.

ADVERTISING AGENTS.

Walter T. Dwight & Co.,
Advertising Agents,
25 Rotunda Buildings.

AGENTS.

H. A. Howe,
Business Agent of Burt Manuf'g. Co. and General Supt. of Agencies of Wyandotte Agricultural Works, 25 Woodward Avenue.

F. A. Whitbeck,
Agent for Buhl, Ducharme & Co.

AGRICULTURAL IMPLEMENTS.

W. S. Penfield,
Agricultural Ware House & Seed
Store.   Field & Garden Seeds.
121 Woodward Ave.

Edwin Jerome & Co.,
Agricultural Implements
Wholesale & Retail.
185 Woodward Ave.

C. F. Swain,
State Agent Farm Machinery,
21 Jefferson Ave.

ALE & PORTER BREWERS.

Davis & Newbury,
Ale & Porter Brewers.

Edward Johnson & Son,
Ale & Porter Brewers.

ARCHITECTS.

J. V. Smith,
Architect & Supt.,
10 Merrill Block.

Gordon W. Lloyd,
Architect,
101 Griswold St.

Julius Hess,
Architect,
99 Griswold St.

James Anderson,
Architect,
Buhl Block, Griswold St.

Mortimer L. Smith,
Architect,
Telegraph Block, Griswold St.

Porter & Watkins,
Architects,
Nos. 10 & 11 Telegraph Block,
Also Bay City, Bank Block.

ARTIFICIAL LIMBS.

James A. Foster,
Manufacturer of Artificial Limbs,
Detroit, Mich., Cincinnati, O.,
and Phila., Pa.

BANKS.

American National Bank.
Alex. H. Dey, Pres.
John G. Bagley, Vice Pres.
Geo. D. Sartwell, Cashier.

German American Bank.
C. Kanter, President.
H. L. Kanter, Cashier.

First National Bank.
J. S. Farrand, President.
Emory Wendell, Cashier.

Second National Bank.
H. P. Baldwin, President.
C. M. Davidson, Cashier.

Detroit Savings Bank.
Elon Farnsworth, President.
A. H. Adams, Cashier.

Wayne County Savings Bank.
Wm. B. Wesson, President.
Dr. H. Kiefer, Vice President.
S. D. Elwood, Sec'y and Treas.
Wm. A. Moore, Attorney.

David Preston & Co.,
Bankers.

Mechanic's Bank.
Wm. A. Butler, President.
E. H. Butler, Cashier.

A. Ives & Sons,
Bankers.

Peoples Savings Bank.
Francis Palms, President.
M. W. O'Brien, Cashier.

Vincent N. Scott,
Banker,
and Dealer in Foreign Exchange.

City Bank.
S. C. Kannady, President.
N. T. Taylor, Cashier.

Fisher, Booth & Co.,
Bankers.

W. D. Morton & Co.,
Bankers & Brokers,
cor. 2d and Woodbridge Sts.

BARREL MANUFACTURERS.

Philip Kling,
Cooper, and Manufacturer of Barrels,
Tubs, Casks &c.

Meinrad Roth,
Manuf'r. of Wine & Beer Casks; also
Beer, Pork & Whisky Barrels.
205 Mullet St.

BEER BREWERS.

B. Stroh,
Brewer.

Henry Miller,
Brewer.

P. Kling & Co.,
Brewers.

Charles Endrias,
Brewer.

Milwaukee Brewery,
E. W. Voight, Brewer of the famous
Milwaukee Lager Beer,
Grand River Avenue.

Joseph Yoelkel,
Brewer.

J. Mann,
Lager Beer Brewer,
28 & 30 Maple St.

Augustus Ruoff,
Lager Beer Brewer,
Gratiot Avenue.

Anton Michenfelder,
Lager Beer Brewer,
61 Sherman, cor. Rivard.

Edward H. Vogel,
Lager Beer Brewer,
cor. Clinton & Elmwood Avenues.

Adam Oehsenhirt,
Lager Beer Brewer,
142 to 148 Sherman St.

G. F. Endris,
Celebrated Bottled Lager Beer,
352 Rivard St.

BELT MANUFACTURER.

Thomas Parker,
Belt Manufacturer,
29 Monroe Avenue.

Billiard Table Manufacturer.

George Smith,
Billiard Table Manufacturer,
Patent Steel Band-Cushions,
Nos. 69 & 71 Larned St. East.

BLACKSMITHS.

Wm. Wade,
Practical Horse shoeing,
Nos. 9 LaFayette Ave.
and 78 Larned St. West.

L. Whittle,
250 & 252 Cass Ave.
All lameness remedied, and all work
done to order.

P. J. Hickey & Co.,
General Horse shoeing,
98 Larned St. West.

Richard Lars,
Carriage Manufactory & Horse shoeing,
No. 9 Middle St.

Block Manufacturers.

Detroit Block Works,
Manufacturers of Iron & Rope Strap Blocks, Mast
Hoops, Sheaves, Dead Eyes &c.
Jas. A. Duncan, Proprietor,
30 & 32 Atwater St. East.

BOOKSELLERS & STATIONERS.

E. B. Smith & Co.,
Booksellers,
Moffat Block.

J. M. Arnold & Co.,
Booksellers & Stationers,
289 Woodward Ave.

Richmond & Backus,
Stationers, and Blank Book Manuf'rs,
188 Jefferson Avenue.

Wm. Suckert,
Stationer, Printer & Book Binder,
46 Larned St. West.

Boot & Shoe Manufacturers.

H. P. Baldwin & Co.,
Wholesale Boots & Shoes.

Pingree & Smith,
Ladies' Fine Shoes.

G. M. Holbrook & Co.,
Ladies Fine Shoes.

Cotharin & Colvin.,
Dealers in Boots & shoes,
163 Woodward Avenue.

BRASS FOUNDER.

I. D. Burt,
Proprietor Detroit Brass Works.

Brackets & Parlor Ornaments.

Patterson & Allen,
Manufacturers of Parlor and
Ornamental Brackets.
195 Cass St.

BRICK & TILE MANF'RS.

Geo. B. & Richard M. Hall,
Brick & Tile Manufacturers,
147 Griswold St.

John Greusel & Sons,
Brick & Tile Manufactory,
237 Third St.

BRIDGE MANUFACTURERS.

Mich. Bridge & Car Co.,
Manuf'rs. of Bridges, Roofs, &c.,
Wight St., above Marion Hospital.

BROOM MANUFACTORIES.

Detroit Broom Co.,
J. McEldowney & Sons,
Manufacturers of Brooms & Brushes,
820 Jefferson Ave.

BRUSH MANUFACTURERS.

Laitner Brothers,
Manufacturers of all kinds of Brushes,
86 Monroe Avenue.

BUILDERS.

Felix Julien & E. Carbonneau,
Boat, House & Stair Builders.
Cor. Second & Larned Sts.

Candler Bros.,
Builders,
276 Atwater St.

Morehouse, Mitchell & Byram,
Builders.

Robert Seaton,
Builder,
193 & 195 Cass St. cor. Spencer

Alex. Chapoton,
Builder,
126 East Congress St.

W. H. Langley,
Builder,
153 Bates St.

Mackey & Dee,
Mason Builders,
181 Congress St. West.

BUSINESS COLLEGES.

Mayhew's Business College,
Conducted by the author of Mayhew's
series of Book Keeping, cor. Congress
& Randolph Sts. Ira Mayhew, Pres.

Goldsmith's Bryant & Stratton
Business University,
Next to the Post Office.

Webster's Educational Institute,
Open Day & Evening
throughout the year.

CARPENTERS & BUILDERS.

W. G. Vinton,
Jobber & Builder,
169 Cass St.

I. W. Ingersoll,
Builder, and Manufacturer of
Sash, Doors & Blinds.
72 & 74 Fort St. East.

William Whyte,
Carpenter, Joiner, Builder
and Pattern Maker.
40 Orchard St. Cor. 2nd,

Underwood Armstrong,
Carpenter & Builder, bet. Woodward
& Washington Ave's. on Clifford St.

John Waterfall,
Carpenter & Builder.

Shefferly Brothers,
Builders, and Manuf'rs. of Doors,
Sash, Blinds, Moulding, Flooring &c.
Croghan St., bet. Hastings & Rivard Sts.

John Bieber,
Carpenter & Builder.
279 Fort St. East.

E. A. Candler,
Builder & Jobber.

CARRIAGE MANUFACTURERS.

Theut & Korte,
Carriage & Wagon Shop,
49, 51 & 53 Croghan St.

Charles Lempke,
Blacksmith & Wagon Maker,
571 Gratiot St.

E. Chope & Son,
Spring Wagon Factory,
106, 108 Randolph St.

John Patton & Son,
Carriage Manufacturers.

William Danz,
Wagon Making and Blacksmithing,
396, 398 Gratiot.

Joseph Kengel,
Carriage Manufactory,
55 Gratiot St.

Nicholson & Van Syckle,
Carriage & Wagon Manufactory.

J. C. Neubroner,
Carriage & Wagon Shop,
83 Fort St.

F. Reichle,
Carriage Manufactory.

Hugh Johnson,
Carriage Maker.

BUSINESS CARDS OF PATRONS IN DETROIT.

William Hartman,
Wagon Maker.

Thomas A. Clifford,
Carriage Maker.

Caspar Dreher,
Carriage Manufactory.

Longprey & Peters,
Manuf'rs of Top and Open Buggies. Special attention paid to repairing, painting, trimming &c.
40 & 42 Larned St., East.

Joseph Bushway,
Carriage & Wagon Shop,
57 State, & Park Place.

Oswald H. Voigt,
Manufacturer of Carriages & Wagons,
239 Griswold St.

F. R. Bruner,
Manufacturer of Carriages & Sleighs.

Carriage Repositories.

Alonzo Rolfe,
Great Western Carriage, Harness and
Sleigh Depot,
288, 290 & 292 Jefferson Avenue.

CARRIAGE TRIMMERS.

John Ulrich,
Carriage Trimmer, & Dealer in
Carriages & Buggies.
71 Larned St. East.

William Christoph,
Carriage Trimmer, & Dealer in Carriages, Buggies &c.
38 Larned St. East.

F. R. Bruner,
Carriage Trimmer

CAR MANUFAFACTURERS.

Detroit Car Manuf'g Co., Manuf'rs of
Pullman Palace Cars,
Croghan St.

CARVERS.

Schmitz & Martins,
Designers, Carvers, Sculptors,
Modelers, and Stucco Workers.

CATHOLIC BOOK STORE.

Wm. Mackay Lomasney,
Catholic Book Store and Stationer.
Bibles, Prayer Books and Catholic
Articles generally.   98 Mich. Ave.

CHAIR MANUFCATURERS.

Detroit Chair Factory,
Corner of Fourth & Porter Sts.
Henry Smith, Treasurer.

CHEMIST.

H. C. Parke,
Manufacturing Chemist,
18 High St.

CIVIL ENGINEERS.

Wm. Scott,
Civil Engineer and Architect,
Rooms 73 & 74
Seitz New Building.

Edward Molitor,
Civil Engineer
United States Lake Survey.

John F. Munro.
Surveyor & Civil Engineer.

CLERGYMEN.

PROTESTANT.
Rt. Rev. Sam'l A. McCoskry,
D. D., D. C. L., Oxon.,
Bishop of Michigan.

Rev. Thos. C. Pitkin, D. D.,
Rector of St. Paul's Church.

Rev. Geo. Worthington,
Rector of St. John's Church.

Rev. John W. Brown,
Rector of Christ Church.

W. Hogarth.
Pastor Jefferson Avenue Pres. Church.

Geo. D. Baker,
Pastor First Pres. Church.

Rev. M. C. Lightner,
Rector Grace Church.

Leo M. Woodruff,
Pastor 1st Baptist Church.

J. A. Huegli,
Pastor German Lutheran Church.

Arthur Tappan Pierson,
Pastor of Fort St. Pres. Church.

John Mc Eldewney,
Pastor LaFayette Ave. M. E. Church.

Chas. Haass,
Pastor of German St. John's Church.

Rev. A. M. Lewis,
Rector Mariners' Free Church.

CATHOLIC
Rt. Rev. C. H. Borgess,
Bishop of Detroit.

Rev. Ernest Van Dyk,
Cathedral.

James Savage,
116 Carter St.

Rev. A. F. Bleyenbergh,
Trinity Church.

Rev. J. A. Hennessy
St. Patrick's Church.

T. Anciaux,
St. Ann's Church.

Rev. John Friedland,
St. Joseph's Church.

Rev. G. Limpins,
Our Lady of Help.

Rev. A. Kullmann,
St. Boniface's Church.

COAL

C. R. Letis & Co.,
Dealers in Coal & Pig Iron,
685 Woodbridge St. West

Viger Brothers,
Coal Dealers,
44 Atwater Street.

COMMERCIAL AGENCY.

The Commercial Agency,
Tappan, Mc Killop & Co.,
157 Jefferson Avenue.
Established 1842.

CONTRACTORS.

Hendrie & Co.,
Contractors,
Office D, & M. R'y. Depot.

COPPER WORKS.

**Detroit & Lake Superior
Copper Smelting Works,**
John R. Grout, Superintendent.

CORNICE MANUFACTURERS.

Eagle Cornice Works,
Manufacturers of all kinds of Galvanized Iron Cornices.
Gustave Bergman, Proprietor.

Crockery & Glass Ware.

L. Selling,
Crockery & Glass Ware,
Jefferson Avenue.

R. W. King,
Crockery, China & Glass Ware,
Cor. Jeff. Ave. & Wayne St.

Fiske & Jenness,
Crockery, China & Glass Ware,
86 Jeff. Ave.

F. Wetmore & Co.,
Crockery, China & Glass Ware,
Lamps, Gas Fixtures &c.,
100 Woodward Ave.

John B. Shefferly,
Crockery, China & Glass Ware,
140 Woodward Ave.

V. M. Hyde,
Lamps & Lamp Fixtures,
183 Woodward Ave.

Anton Koehler,
Crockery & Glass Ware,
232 Randolph St.

DENTISTS.

G. R. Thomas,
Dentist,
Opera House Block.

Joseph Lathrop,
Dentist,
148 Woodward Ave.

H. H. Smith,
Dentist,
159 Woodward Ave.

Wm. C. Brittan,
Dentist,
114 Woodward Ave.

H. Benedict,
Dentist,
156 Jeff. Ave.

DISTILLER.

Smith R. Woolley,
Distiller of Alcohol & Cologne
Spirits, and Manufacturer of Pure
Cider Vinegar.

DRUGGISTS. Wholesale.

H. P. Swift & Co.,
Druggists.

J. H. Hinchman & Son,
Wholesale Druggists, Oil Dealers and
Grocers.

Frederick Stearns,
Wholesale Druggist.

John H. Griffith,
Drugs, Chemicals, Liquors & Cigars.
104 Jeff. Ave.

DRUGGISTS. Retail.

Kermott & Balleray,
Dr. Kermott's Family Medicines,
208 Woodward Ave.

John H. Griffith,
Drugs, Chemicals, Liquors and Cigars,
104 Jefferson Avenue.

BUSINESS CARDS OF PATRONS IN DETROIT.

Mathews & Wilson,
Cigars and Leaf Tobacco,
216 Jefferson Ave.

Wm. Wilmot,
Cigars and Tobacco,
247 Jefferson Ave.

Jelsch & Co.,
Cigar Manufacturers,
No. 1 Michigan Grand Avenue.

J. D. Carter,
Tobacconist,
Cor. Beaubien & La Fayette Sts.

A. Schuneman & Co.,
Cigar Manufacturers,
228 Jefferson Ave.

Burk & Moebs,
Leaf Tobacco and Cigars,
76 Congress St. East.

L. Michaels,
Cigars.

Tea Caddy & Cigar Box Manf'r.

T. A. Wadsworth,
Manufacturer of Cigar and Tea Boxes,
269 Croghan St.

TRUNKS.

L. H. Wolff & Co.,
Trunk Manufacturers,
215 Jeff. Avenue.

Martin Maier,
Trunk Manufacturer,
55 Monroe Ave.

UNDERTAKER.

R. Bronson,
Undertaker,
92 & 94 Larned St. West.

UNITED STATES OFFICIALS.

Mark Flannigan,
Internal Revenue Assessor.

F. W. Swift,
Postmaster.

Geo. I. Betts,
U. S. Indian Agent.

VARNISH & GLUES.

Berry Brothers,
Manufacturers of Varnish and Glues,
Wright St.

WAYNE CO. OFFICERS.

Geo. C. Codd,
Sheriff of Wayne Co.,

Ray Haddock,
County Clerk.

WINES.

Jacob Beller,
Dealer in Catawba Wines,
and Canandaigua Stock Ales.
11 State St.

C. F. Allen,
Manuf'r and Dealer in Native Wines.
Paw Paw, Van Buren County.

WIRE MANUFACTURERS.

Sam'l Adams,
Manuf'r of Brass & Iron Wire Cloth,
Cheese Safes, and Rat Traps.
9 & 11 Spruce St.

Snow & Bolles,
Wire Manufacturers.
62 Jeff. Ave.

E. T. Barnum,
Manuf'r of Wire Cloth, Wire Railing & Fencing,
Cheese Safes, Wire & Wire Goods generally.
118 Woodward Ave.

T. W. Smith & Son,
Peninsular Diamond Wire Works,
Manuf'rs of all kinds of Wire Work.
352 Gratiot St.

Detroit Cement Sewer Pipe Co.,
E. W. Carr, Ag't,
Manuf'r of Patent Compressed Hydraulic Cement,
Drain & Sewer Pipe of every Description, with
Elbows, Connections Stench Traps, Chimney Caps &c.

WOOD YARDS.

Jas. McGonegal,
Dealer in Wood,
37 Larned St. and Foot of Wayne, on
Dock.

Chas. Koch & Co.,
Coal and Wood Yard, on Dock.
Foot of Rivard St.

WOODEN WARE.

J. W. Sutton,
M'f'r. Tubs, Pails & Tobacco Packages,
478 & 480 Fort St. West.

Wool Commission Merchants.

Thos. McGraw & Co.,
Wool Commission Merchants.

Woolens and Tailors Trimmings.

Hitchcock, Esselyn & Co.,
Importers and Jobbers
of Woolens and Tailors Trimmings.
100 Jeff. Ave.

Elliot & Brother,
Imported and American Woolens and
Tailors Trimmings.
128 Woodward Avenue.

YEAST.

Waterloo Yeast Co.,
M'f'rs of Twin Bros., Dry Hop Yeast.
208 Mich. Ave.

BUSINESS CARDS OF PATRONS IN GRAND RAPIDS.

ARCHITECTS.

D. Sprague Hopkins,
Architect,
26 Canal Street.

W. G. Robinson & Co.,
Architects,
No. 1 Justice St.,
W. G. Robinson,   F. B. Barnaby.

D. H. Cottrell,
Architect,
Monroe Street.

F. B. Hynes,
Designer and Builder, and Manuf'r.
of Church Furniture.

ATTORNEYS AT LAW.

Eggleston & Kleinhans,
Attorneys at Law,
McReynolds' Block.

Jas. W. Ransom,
Attorney at Law,
McReynolds' Block.

Eben Smith,
Attorney at Law,
McReynolds' Block.

Jas. B. Willson,
Attorney at Law,
McReynolds' Block.

D. E. Corbitt,
Attorney at Law,
McReynolds' Block.

Taylor & Eddy,
Attorneys at Law,
Phœnix Block.

Eugene E. Allen,
Attorney at Law,
Phœnix Block.

Wm. Ashley,
Attorney at Law,
City National Bank Building.

T. B. Church,
Attorney at Law,
McReynolds' Block.

Ball & McKee,
Attorneys at Law,
Luce's Block.

G. Chase Godwin,
Attorney at Law,
Fremont Block.

L. W. Wolcott,
Attorney at Law,
Ball's Block, 48 Canal St.

Benjamin F. Sliter,
Lawyer and Land Agent,
40 Canal St.

L. A. Miller,
Attorney at Law,
40 Canal St.

Emil A. Dapper,
Attorney at Law,
Foot of Monroe St.

Benjamin A. Harlan,
Attorney at Law, and Judge of
Probate.

A. J. McReynolds,
Attorney at Law,
McReynolds' Block.

BANKS.

First National Bank
of Grand Rapids.

City National Bank,
of Grand Rapids,
No. 1, Monroe St.

Grand Rapids Savings Bank.

BARREL MANUFACTURERS.

Willard & Colgrove,
Manu'f'rs of Willard's Double-Stave
Barrels.

Michigan Barrel Company,
Waters' Improved Barrels, and all kinds
of Improved Rim and Bent Work.

H. Willard,
Patentee of the Willard Double-Stave
Barrel.

BOOTS & SHOES.

L. J. Rindge & Co.,
Wholesale Manufacturers of Boots
and Shoes,
14 Canal Street.

Godfry Kulmbach,
Retail Boots and Shoes,
26 Monroe St.

Patrick McMahan,
Dealer in Boots and Shoes,
36 Monroe St.

BUSINESS CARDS OF PATRONS IN JACKSON COUNTY.

CARPENTER & JOINER.

Frank E. Deming,
Carpenter and Joiner,
Waterloo, Grass Lake P. O.

CLERGYMAN.

J. B. Russel,
Minister, Methodist Episcopal Church,
Henrietta, Fitchburg P. O.

DOCTOR.

L. S. Conant,
Physician and Surgeon,
Henrietta.

FARMERS.

Charles Ahin,
Farmer and Hotel keeper,
Sec. 25, 124 acres,
Brooklyn.

J. P. Dresser,
Farmer,
Sec. 28, 160 acres,
Brooklyn, Norvell P. O.

Philip S. Howland,
Farmer,
Sec. 21, 115 acres,
Brooklyn, Norvell P. O.

David Brown,
Farmer,
Sec. 23, 160 acres,
Brooklyn, Norvell P. O.

S. M. Dewey,
Farmer,
80 acres, S. E. Sec. 15,
Henrietta.

Miles B. Snyder,
Farmer,
300 acres, N. W. Sec. 29,
Henrietta.

J. H. Olney,
Farmer,
124 acres, S. W. Sec. 29,
Henrietta, Jackson P. O.

Robert Ridge,
Farmer,
155 acres, S. W. Sec. 6,
Henrietta, Jackson P. O.

Eli Stillson,
Farmer,
60 acres, S. W. Sec. 27,
Henrietta.

Daniel Fellows,
Farmer,
80 acres, S.W. Sec. 18,
Henrietta.

Cha's. H. Glean,
Farmer,
Henrietta.

Eugene Haley,
Farmer,
960 acres, S. W. Sec. 21,
Henrietta.

James Fox,
Farmer, 97 acres, S. E. Sec. 5,
Henrietta.

H. Taber,
Farmer,
100 acres, N. E. Sec. 21,
Jackson.

Samuel D. Eldred,
Farmer,
Leoni, Michigan Center P. O.

S. C. Crafts,
Farmer,
274 acres, N. W. Sec. 19,
Leoni, Jackson P. O.

Almon Cain,
Farmer, 180 acres, S. W. Sec. 26,
Leoni.

Horton S. Maxon,
Farmer,
S. E. Sec. 19,
Leoni, Jackson P. O.

Daniel Johnson,
Farmer,
200 acres, S. E. Sec. 17,
Leoni, Jackson P. O.

Frank D. Maxon,
Farmer,
22 acres, S. E. Sec. 19,
Leoni, Jackson P. O.

W. Watt,
Farmer,
100 acres, S. E. Sec. 18,
Leoni, Jackson P. O.,
Manufacturer of Buggies and Light Wagons.

Ed. Greenwood,
Farmer,
188 acres, N. E. Sec. 23,
Leoni, Grass Lake P. O.

Chester Dubois,
Farmer,
225 acres, N. E. Sec. 24,
Leoni, Grass Lake P. O.

Wm. Glenn,
Farmer,
80 acres, S. W. Sec. 13,
Leoni, Grass Lake P. O.

E. Holloway,
Farmer,
80 acres, S. W. Sec. 23,
Leoni.

C. H. Smith,
Farmer,
150 acres, N. E. Sec. 14,
Leoni.

Margaret S. Stearns,
Farmer,
80 acres, S. E. Sec. 27,
Leoni.

Calvin Cooper,
Farmer,
100 acres, N. E. Sec. 14,
Leoni.

Lorenzo Badgley,
Farmer,
90 acres, N. W. Sec. 24,
Leoni.

John Quick,
Farmer,
192 acres, S. E. Sec. 1,
Leoni.

D. H. Lockwood,
Farmer,
200 acres, S. E. Sec. 14,
Leoni.

E. Hewlet,
Farmer,
140 acres, N. W. Sec. 14,
Leoni.

S. A. Updike,
Farmer,
400 acres, N. 1-2. Sec. 13,
Leoni, Grass Lake P. O.

V. D. Thurston,
Farmer,
165 acres, N. E. Sec. 12,
Leoni, Grass Lake P. O.

T. L. Garred,
Farmer,
120 acres, S. W. Sec. 11,
Leoni, Jackson P. O.

J. L. Rockwell,
Farmer,
120 acres, S. W. Sec. 2,
Leoni, Jackson P. O.

Edwin Stearns,
Farmer,
60 acres, N. E. Sec. 27,
Leoni.

Daniel Boynton,
Farmer,
160 acres, N. W. Sec. 28,
Leoni.

John Scofield,
Farmer,
140 acres, S. W. Sec. 23,
Leoni.

Joel Parks,
Farmer,
205 acres, N. E. Sec. 25,
Leoni.

A. W. Morey,
Farmer,
160 acres, N. E. Sec. 20,
Waterloo, Grass Lake P. O.

Jacob Call,
Farmer,
170 acres, S. W. Sec. 7,
Waterloo, Fitchburg P. O.

James Scylandt,
Farmer,
200 acres, S. W. Sec. 8,
Waterloo, Stockbridge P. O.

Lorenzo Dewey,
Farmer,
120 acres, N. W. Sec. 8,
Waterloo, Stockbridge P. O.

Mrs. N. V. Preston,
Farmer,
87 acres, N. E. Sec. 8,
Waterloo, Stockbridge P. O.

Samuel E. Dewey,
Farmer,
111 acres, N. E. Sec. 5,
Waterloo, Stockbridge P. O.

Thomas Willmore,
Farmer,
847 acres, N. E. Sec. 4,
Waterloo, Stockbridge P. O.

Abram Croman,
Farmer,
100 acres, N. W. Sec. 10,
Waterloo, Stockbridge P. O.

F. D. Maxon,
Farmer,
147 acres, N. E. Sec. 7,
Waterloo, Stockbridge P. O.

Cyrel Adams,
Farmer,
185 acres, N. E. Sec. 7,
Waterloo, Fitchburg P. O.

Michael Ryan,
Farmer,
222 acres, N. W. Sec. 5,
Waterloo, Stockbridge P. O.

Nathan Hall,
Farmer,
80 acres, N. E. Sec. 4,
Waterloo, Stockbridge P. O.

A. McCloy,
Farmer,
280 acres, N. E. Sec. 3,
Waterloo, Stockbridge P. O.

J. M. Berry,
Farmer,
150 acres, N. W. Sec. 2,
Waterloo, Stockbridge P. O.

Ezekiel Bevier,
Farmer,
N. E. Sec. 2,
Waterloo, Stockbridge P. O.,
Cider and Vinegar Manufacturer.

J. C. Brininstool,
Farmer,
40 acres, N. W. Sec. 2,
Waterloo, Stockbridge P. O.

B. W. Sweet,
Farmer,
201 acres, N. E. Sec. 2,
Waterloo, Stockbridge P. O.

John A. Collins,
Farmer,
60 acres, N. W. Sec. 1,
Waterloo, Stockbridge P. O.

Mary Rockwall,
Farmer,
560 acres, S. W. Sec. 12,
Waterloo.

A. T. Gorton,
Farmer,
280 acres, S. E. Sec. 24,
Waterloo.

Geo. Croman,
Farmer,
200 acres, N. W. Sec. 25,
Waterloo.

Frederick Arts,
Farmer,
250 acres, S. W. Sec. 23,
Waterloo.

S. R. West,
Farmer,
Waterloo.

A. A. Quigley,
Farmer,
220 acres, N. W. Sec. 36,
Waterloo.

Wm. H. Showerman,
Farmer,
200 acres, S. E. Sec. 36,
Waterloo.

Phil. Mc Kernen,
Farmer,
200 acres, S. W. Sec. 35,
Waterloo.

J. T. Quigley,
Farmer,
200 acres, S. E. Sec. 34,
Waterloo.

Nelson Hoyt,
Farmer,
100 acres, S. W. Sec. 19,
Waterloo, Grass Lake P. O.,
Carpenter and Joiner.

Wm. Randolph,
Farmer,
175 acres, N. E. Sec. 19,
Waterloo, Grass Lake P. O.

John A. Baldwin,
Farmer,
260 acres, S. E. Sec. 4,
Waterloo, Grass Lake P. O.

Matthew J. Hudler,
Farmer,
211 acres, N. E. Sec. 4,
Waterloo, Grass Lake P. O.

E. S. Robinson,
Farmer,
165 acres, N. E. Sec. 8,
Waterloo, Grass Lake P. O.

Benj. Cook,
Farmer,
160 acres, N. E. Sec. 8,
Waterloo, Grass Lake P. O.

LUMBER.

Benjamin Blaisdell,
Saw-mill, N. E. Sec. 7,
Waterloo, Grass Lake P. O.

BUSINESS CARDS OF PATRONS IN KALAMAZOO COUNTY.

ATTORNEYS AT LAW.

H. G. Wells,
Attorney at Law,
Kalamazoo Village.

Hawes & Edson,
Attorneys and Counsellors at law,
J. L. Hawes.   R. F. Edson.
Kalamazoo Village.

CARRIAGE MAKER.

Mark Worthington,
Carriage Maker,
Vicksburg.

DRY GOODS, CLOTHING &c.

C. H. Gainsley,
Dry Goods, Clothing, Boots & Shoes,
Hats, Caps &c.,
Schoolcraft.

ENGINEER.

Francis Smith,
Engineer,
Prairie Ronde,

FARMERS.

Henry A. Tallman,
Farmer,
Alamo.

E. Tallman,
Farmer,
Alamo.

Z. Sanford,
Farmer,
Alamo.

S. D. Barbour,
Farmer,
Alamo.

Jacob Lemon,
Farmer,
Brady.

Seymour Richardson,
Farmer,
Brady.

Leander Canon,
Brady.

Wm. Worthington,
Brady.

Peter Oakley,
Farmer,
Charleston, Galesburg P. O.

George W. Hawar,
Farmer,
Charleston, Galesburg P. O.

Elias Bayle,
Farmer,
Charleston, Galesburg P. O.

John W. Kirby,
Farmer,
Charleston, Galesburg P. O.

Samuel Carson,
Farmer,
Charleston, Galesburg P. O.

L. S. Evans,
Farmer,
Charleston, Galesburg P. O.

Jeremiah Harrison,
Farmer,
Charleston, Battle Creek P. O.

Orsemus Barnam,
Farmer,
Charleston, Climax P. O.

Walter C. Smith,
Farmer,
Charleston, Climax P. O.

O. A. Morgan,
Farmer,
Charleston, Climax P. O.

Col. H. Gifford,
Farmer,
Charleston, Augusta P. O.

Joseph Whitford,
Farmer,
Charleston, Augusta P. O.

George W. Bristol,
Farmer,
Charleston, Augusta P. O.

A. Kent,
Farmer,
Charleston, Augusta P. O.

J. W. Parkhurst,
Farmer,
Charleston, Augusta P. O.

Stephen Eldred,
Farmer,
Climax.

L. W. Lovell,
Farmer,
Climax.

J. D. Adams,
Farmer,
Climax.

J. N. Le Ferre,
Farmer,
Climax.

A. N. Le Ferre,
Farmer,
Climax.

Isaac Pierce,
Farmer,
Climax.

J. B. Milliman,
Farmer,
Climax.

J. T. Retalick,
Farmer,
Climax.

Enos T. Lovell,
Farmer,
Climax.

Phebe Haviland,
Farmer,
Climax.

E. M. Clapp,
Farmer,
Comstock, Galesburg P. O.

James Milham,
Farmer,
Comstock, Galesburg P. O.

Leverett Crooks,
Farmer,
Comstock.

Thomas B. Lord,
Farmer,
Comstock.

R. A. Ingersoll,
Farmer,
Comstock.

A. W. Wolcott,
Farmer,
Comstock, Galesburg P. O.

J. D. Lord,
Farmer,
Comstock, Galesburg P. O.

E. N. Flanders,
Farmer,
Comstock, Galesburg P. O.

E. S. Knapp,
Farmer,
Comstock, Kalamazoo P. O.

Calvin B. Mitchell,
Farmer,
Comstock, Kalamazoo P. O.

Henry S. Sleeper,
Farmer,
Comstock, Kalamazoo P. O.

F. D. Austin,
Farmer,
Comstock, Kalamazoo P. O.

W. W. Russell,
Farmer,
Comstock, Kalamazoo P. O.

O. F. Campbell,
Farmer,
Comstock, Kalamazoo P. O.

H. Dale Adams,
Farmer,
Comstock, Kalamazoo P. O.

Wm. S. Delano,
Farmer,
Cooper.

Levi B. Fisher,
Farmer,
Cooper.

James Armstrong,
Farmer,
Cooper.

Wm. Skinner,
Farmer,
Cooper.

John Walker,
Farmer,
Cooper.

S. M. Nichols,
Farmer,
Kalamazoo.

Noah Briggs,
Farmer,
Kalamazoo.

G. W. Parker,
Farmer,
Kalamazoo.

Hiram Arnold,
Farmer,
Kalamazoo.

Hiram Lewis,
Farmer,
Kalamazoo.

M. Parks,
Farmer, Kalamazoo.

John A. Kendall,
Farmer, Kalamazoo.

M. B. Tainter,
Farmer, Kalamazoo.

C. C. Curtenius,
Farmer, Kalamazoo.

Cha's. F. Glenn,
Farmer, Kalamazoo.

Thomas Murphy,
Farmer, Kalamazoo.

J. R. Warren,
Farmer, Kalamazoo.

J. W. Rosbrook,
Farmer,
Oshtemo.

A. A. Phillips,
Farmer,
Oshtemo.

J. J. Lusk,
Farmer,
Oshtemo.

D. H. Hill,
Farmer,
Oshtemo.

Joseph Lockwood,
Farmer,
Oshtemo.

Cha's. S. King,
Farmer,
Oshtemo.

Mrs. D. M. Tuttle, Farmer, Oshtemo.	Azel N. Chipman, Farmer, Pavillion.	D. R. Finley, Farmer, Schoolcraft.	Samuel Virgo, Farmer, Texas.
John H. Bushnell, Farmer, Oshtemo.	Thos. Nesbitt, Farmer, Prairie Ronde.	E. L. Brown, Farmer, Schoolcraft.	Joseph R. Virgo, Farmer, Texas.
Daniel Chamberlain, Farmer, Oshtemo.	George G. Crose, Jr., Farmer, Prairie Ronde.	A. Finley, Farmer, Schoolcraft.	Hugh Campbell, Farmer, Texas.
Sarah A. Smith, Portage.	George G. Crose, Farmer, Prairie Ronde.	M. F. Woodward, Farmer, Schoolcraft.	E. Hope, Farmer, Texas.
Francis Downey, Portage, Box 1149, Kalamazoo P. O.	Wilbur Hackett, Farmer, Prairie Ronde.	Gilbert Stewart, Farmer, Schoolcraft.	S. M. Wells, Farmer, Texas.
James Campbell, Portage, Box 972, Kalamazoo P. O.	Charles C. Duncan, Farmer, Prairie Ronde.	E. F. Duncan, Farmer, Schoolcraft.	Jerome Clark, Farmer, Texas.
Henry Nesbitt, Farmer, Portage, Kalamazoo P. O.	Truman Hunt, Farmer, Prairie Ronde.	H. W. Fellows, Farmer, Schoolcraft.	Albert Wajar, Farmer, Texas.
Joseph Beckley, Farmer, Portage, Kalamazoo P. O.	George Munger, Farmer, Prairie Ronde.	Robert Frakes, Farmer, Schoolcraft.	Newton Luce, Farmer, Texas.
Geo. Sutherland, Farmer, Portage, Kalamazoo P. O.	Return Mack, Farmer, Prairie Ronde.	Stephen Smith, Farmer, Schoolcraft.	Wm. Kinney, Farmer, Texas.
Harvey S. Booth, Farmer, Portage, Kalamazoo P. O.	W. L. Curtiss, Farmer, Richland P. O.	W. E. McComsey, Farmer, Schoolcraft.	Jacob Mc Lin, Farmer, Texas.
Mrs. A. F. Fox, Farmer, Portage, Kalamazoo P. O.	E. A. Bissell, Farmer, Richland P. O.	David B. Stuart, Farmer, Schoolcraft.	H. B. Douglass, Farmer, Texas.
R. A. Axtell, Farmer, Portage, Kalamazoo P. O.	C. P. Hale, Farmer, Richland P. O.	George P. Stuart, Farmer, Schoolcraft.	Lewis Johnson, Farmer, Texas.
John M. Shandy, Farmer, Portage, Kalamazoo P. O.	T. Kirkland, Farmer, Richland P. O.	Ramsey Bidleman, Farmer, Schoolcraft.	R. A. Towers, Farmer, Texas.
Levi Blackmer, Farmer, Portage, Kalamazoo P. O.	J. F. Gilky, Farmer, Richland P. O.	Bruce Deatler, Farmer, Schoolcraft.	Cha's. S. Whipple, Farmer, Texas.
Isaac Weeks, Farmer, Portage, Kalamazoo P. O.	Geo. F Reed, Farmer, Richland P. O.	J. L. Brown, Farmer, Schoolcraft.	Steven Morgan, Farmer, Texas.
Wm. Campbill, Farmer, Portage, Kalamazoo P. O.	A. Dawson, Farmer, Schoolcraft.	Chauncey Boufeoy, Farmer, Texas.	Cha's. F. Abbott, Farmer, Texas.
John E. Woodard, Farmer, Portage, Kalamazoo P. O.	A. K. Burson, Farmer, Schoolcraft.	O. P. Morton, Farmer, Texas.	Lafayette Hill, Farmer, Texas.
F. Van Housen, Farmer, Portage.	S. F. Brown, Farmer, Schoolcraft.	Geo. B. Bix, Farmer, Texas.	**HOTEL.**
Dwight C. Pierce, Farmer, Portage.	J. M. Neasmith, Farmer, Schoolcraft.	O. M. Stevens, Farmer, Texas.	J. H. McElvain, Proprietor of McElvain House, Vicksburg.
Ebenezer Pike, Farmer, Portage.	Thomas Wright, Farmer, Schoolcraft.	D. K. Bix, Farmer, Texas.	**INSURANCE AGENT.**
Nathan Pike, Farmer, Portage.	H. T. Holmes, Farmer, Schoolcraft.	Wm. H. McCormick, Farmer, Texas.	D. T. Dell, Special Ag't. Phenix Life Insu. Co., Vicksburg.
L. R. Cooley, Farmer, Pavillion.	J. C. Fraser, Farmer, Schoolcraft.	George Gage, Farmer, Texas.	**MANUFACTURERS.**
D. C. Powers, Farmer, Pavillion.	Elias H. Rawson, Farmer, Schoolcraft.	Orange Stevens, Farmer, Texas.	Kellogg & Sawyer, Manufacturers of Lumber, Leroy Station, Oceola Co.

BUSINESS CARDS OF PATRONS IN KALAMAZOO COUNTY.

Ward Air Brake Company,
Manuf'rs. of the Ward Pat. Compressed Air Brake
Office 127, Main St. Kalamazoo,
B KENDALL, Pres.   T. S. COBB, Sec. & Treas.

Ja's. N. Cooley,
Inventor & Dealer in Adjustable Steel
Plow Points,
Portage, Kalamazoo P. O.

Dewing & Son,
Manuf'rs. of Doors, Sash, & Blinds,
Wholesale & Retail Dealers, Kalamazoo.

Kellogg & Holtenhouse,
Wholesale and Retail Dealers in
Lumber, Shingles, Lath, Doors, Blinds, & Sash,
Kalamazoo Village.

MERCHANTS.

A. B. Eldred,
ELDRED & SINCLAIR,
Dealers in Dry Goods & Groceries,
Climax.

Wm. Marsh,
General dealer in Dry Goods,
Groceries etc.,
Henrietta, Jackson Co.

Pursel & Co.,
Merchant Millers.
Manf'rs. of "Pursel & Co's. Best,"
"Earl's Standard," & "Ward's Extra,"
Schoolcraft.

NURSERY.

L. G. Bragg & Co.,
General Nursery Stock,
" Union Nurseries," Asylum Avenue. Kalamazoo.

PHYSICIANS.

N. A. Hill,
Physician & Surgeon, Brady.

Nathan M. Thomas, M. D.,
Schoolcraft.

SURVEYOR & CIVIL ENGINEER.

F. Hodgman,
Will do Leveling for Water Powers or Railroads,
and Furnish Estimates for Bridges,
Galesburg.

TEACHERS.

D. D. Dorrance,
Teacher, Pavilion.

Nancy E. Parks,
Teacher,
Waterloo, Jackson Co.

WAGON MAKER.

A. M. Barber,
Wagon Maker,
Michigan Center P. O., Jackson Co.

BUSINESS CARDS OF PATRONS IN WENONA.

BARBER.

M. L. Fowler,
Barber & Dealer in Gents' Furnishing
Goods.

BOOTS & SHOES.

George Nickel,
Manuf'r. & Dealer in Boots & Shoes.

DRUGGIST.

John Davis,
Druggist.

FURNITURE.

Wm. Loose,
Manuf'r. and Dealer in Furniture, also
Undertaker and Upholsterer.

GROCERS.

T. P. Hawkins,
Grocer.

Geo. A. Allen,
Dealer in Groceries & Provisions.

Travis & Bebe,
Grocery Dealers.

HARNESS & SADDLES.

Wm. H. Merritt,
Manuf'r. & Dealer in Harness, Saddles,
Whips and Horse Clothing.

HOTELS.

M. A. Rouech,
Proprietor of Rouech House.

P. Irwin,

Proprietor of Irwin House.

T. Toohey,
Proprietor of Toohey House.

LUMBER & SALT.

Taylor & Moulthrop,
Manuf'rs. of Lumber and Salt.

Moore, Smith & Co.,
Manuf'rs. of Lumber and Salt,
Mill at Banks,
PETER SMITH, Banks, HENRY C. MOORE, Bay City.

MERCHANTS.

H. G. Ingersoll,
General Merchant.

H. W. Sage & Co.,

General Merchants.

PRINTER.

Ed. D. Cowles,
Proprietor of Herald Printing House.

SEWING MACHINES.

H. H. Aplin,
Post Master, & Sewing Machine Ag't.

TANNERY.

John Bourn,
Proprietor Wenona Tannery.

WATCHES.

J. S. Huckins,
Agent for all American Watch Co's.

BUSINESS CARDS OF PATRONS IN BARRY COUNTY.

ATTORNEYS AT LAW.

Sweezey & Wood,
Attorneys & Counsellors at Law,
Hastings.
Ja's. A SWEEZEY.   Cha's. B. WOOD.

Wright & Holbrook,
Attorneys & Solicitors,
Hastings.
HARVEY WRIGHT.   E. A. HOLBROOK.

Cha's. G. Holbrook,
Attorney and Counsellor at Law,
Hastings.

Geo. C. Worth,
Lawyer, Hastings.

Isaac A. Holbrook,
Attorney at Law & Solicitor
in Chancery,
Hastings.

Jno. R. Van Velsor,
Lawyer,
Hastings.

Daniel Striker,
Collection Lawyer,
Hastings.

Clement Smith,
Attorney at Law,
Nashville.

Ray Streeter,

Lawyer, Nashville.

John R. Eastman,
Attorney, Real Estate & Ins. Agent,
Woodland.

BANKERS.

Bowne, Combs & Co.,
Bankers,
Middleville.

BARBER.

Delos Hinman,
Barber, Nashville.

BARREL HOOPS.

F. W. Kirtland,
Manuf'r. of Hard and Soft Wood Headings,
Shingles, and Rock Elm Flour Barrel Hoops,
Nashville.

BOOTS & SHOES.

Chauncey Priest,
Dealer in Boots & Shoes, and Farmer,
Sec. 26, 40 acres, Woodland.

CARPENTER.

Horace S. Larkin,
Carpenter and Joiner, and
Mail Contractor,
Woodland.

CLERGYMAN.

Charles Chick,
Pastor, Methodist Episcopal Church,
Woodland.

DRUGGIST.

C. B. Richardson,
Dealer in Drugs, Medicines
and Groceries,
Nashville.

FARMERS.

Richard Jones,
Farmer, Assyria.

Thomas Blasdel,
Breeder of Pure Blood Cotswold Sheep.
Producer of Wool, Stock, Grains and Fruits,
Assyria.

J. L. Wotring,
Sec. 11, Castleton,
Stock, Hay, Grains, Fruits and Maple Sugar,
Assyria.

R. Carlton,

Grain, Fruit and Wool Farmer,
Sec. 23, 80 acres, Castleton.

John Keagle,
Farmer,
Sec. 19, 200 acres, Castleton.

Wm. H. Dodge,
Farmer, Castleton.

J. H. Wickwier,
Farmer, Johnstown.

J. H. Munroe,
Farmer, Johnston.

Danforth Fisher,
Farmer, 240 acres, Sec. 36,
Johnstown.

Frank Bullis,
Farmer, Johnstown.

S. J. Badock,
Farmer, 110 acres, Sec. 5,
Maple Grove.

Levi Elliott,
Stock, Grain, Wool & Fruit Farmer,
122 acres, Maple Grove.

BUSINESS CARDS OF PATRONS IN BARRY COUNTY.

Charles Baker,
General Farmer,
Sec. 2, 80 acres, Assyria.

C. G. Baker,
General Farmer, Sec. 2, 150 acres,
Assyria.

John F. Holbrook,
Farmer and Hotel Keeper,
Sec. 14, 80 acres, Assyria.

E. D. Betzood,
Farmer & Hotel Keeper,
Sec. 16, Assyria Center.

John Heckathorn,
Stock, Wool & Grain Farmer,
Sec. 25, 80 acres,
Caseton, Nashville P. O.

Alexander Price,
Stock, Wool & Grain Farmer,
Sec. 23, 160 acres,
Caseton, Nashville P. O.

Christopher Hill,
Stock, Grain, Fruit & Wool Farmer,
200 acres, Caseton, Nashville P. O.

J. F. Woodwing,
Stock, Wool and Grain Farmer,
Sec. 22, 75 acres,
Caseton, Nashville P. O.

James H. Harper,
Stock and Grain,
Sec. 16, 60 acres,
Caseton, Nashville P. O.

David F. Irland,
Stock, Wool and Grain Farmer,
Sec. 15, 110 acres,
Carleton, Nashville P. O.

James Hurd,
Farmer, Caseltion, Nashville P. O.

V. S. Skinner,
Farmer and Miller,
40 acres, Caseton, Nashville P. O.

Benjamin Park,
Stock, Grain and Fruit Farmer,
40 acres, Caseton, Nashville P. O.

Job K. Wilcox,
Grain, Wool and Maple Sugar,
Sec. 37, 50 acres, Maple Grove.

Agnes Barker,
Grain, Wool and Stock Farmer,
Sec. 32, 80 acres, Maple Grove.

Thomas & Edward Moody,
Grain, Wool and Stock Farmers,
Sec. 31, 80 acres, Maple Grove.

Russel Slade,
Grain and Wool Farmer,
Sec. 26, 160 acres, Maple Grove.

John J. Potter,
Stock and Grain Farmer,
Sec. 35, Maple Grove.

James G. Barnes,
Grain, Wool and Stock Farmer,
Sec. 26, 180 acres, Maple Grove.

Daniel Jackson,
Grain, Fruit and Stock,
Sec. 26, 120 acres, Maple Grove.

John Wilkinson,
Grain, Fruit and Wool Farmer,
Sec. 34, 155 acres, Maple Grove.

Charles Fowler,
Stock, Wool and Grain Farmer and
Justice of Peace,
Maple Grove.

O. Z. Woodward,
Stock and Wool Farmer,
Sec. 15, 80 acres, Maple Grove.

A. J. Culp,
Stock, Grain and Wool Farmer,
Sec. 16, 80 acres, Maple Grove.

George Balls,
Farmer and Blacksmith,
Maple Grove.

Leander Lapham,
Farmer and Merchant,
140 acres, Maple Grove.

Gilbert Lapham,
Stock, Grain and Wool, Farmer,
Sec. 27, 100 acres, Maple Grove.

Philander K. Hyde,
Stock, Wool, Grain and Fruit,
Sec. 27, 70 acres, Maple Grove.

Albert Eno,
Fruit Farmer,
80 acres, Maple Grove.

Wm. Anderson,
Stock, Grain and Fruit Farmer,
Sec. 22, 66 acres, Maple Grove.

Horace Dean,
Stock, Fruit and Grain Farmer,
Sec. 36, 60 acres, Maple Grove.

Wm. Sanford,
Farmer,
Sec. 11, 40 acres, Maple Grove.

Isaac McCrea,
Stock, Grain and Fruit,
Sec. 14, 60 acres, Maple Grove.

S. T. Hagerman,
Farmer,
Sec. 24, 160 acres, Maple Grove.

James McKelver,
Grain, Fruit, Wool & Stock Farmer,
Sec. 24, 160 acres, Maple Grove.

Henry Demaray,
Grain, Fruit and Stock Farmer,
Sec. 36, 60 acres, Maple Grove.

Lucien B. Potter,
Grain, Wool, Fruit & Stock,
Sec. 35, 160 acres, Maple Grove.

M. W. Cooper,
Grain, Fruit and Wool,
Sec. 27, 40 acres, Maple Grove.

Pliny McCumber,
Grain, Fruit and Wool Farmer,
Sec's. 22 & 28, 280 acres,
Maple Grove.

Elbridge G. Potter,
Stock, Fruit and Grain Farmer and
Town Treasurer,
Maple Grove.

C. W. Taylor,
Stock, Grain, Wool and Honey,
Sec. 33, 205 acres, Maple Grove.

J. W. Glenn,
Grain and Fruit Farmer, & Agri'l. Im.,
Sec. 15, 840 acres, Nashville.

T. B. Lamond,
County Supt. of Schools, & Farmer,
Sec. 24, 111 acres, Orangeville.

Wm. R. Blanchard,
General Farmer,
Sec. 17, 80 acres, Rutland.

G. M. Davenport,
Farmer, 160 acres, Sec. 27,
Wool, Stock, Grain and Fruit,
Woodland.

Merrill Haight,
Wheat, Wool and Stock Farmer,
Sec. 15, 140 acres, Woodland.

Morgan Huff,
Wool, Stock & Grain Farmer,
Sec. 4, 50 acres, Woodland.

Josie S. Valentine & Brother,
Grain, Stock and Wool Farmer,
Sec. 10, 160 acres, Woodland.

B. F. Dennemore,
Wheat, Stock and Wool Farmer,
Sec. 27, 40 acres, Woodland.

A. P. & W. P. Holly,
Farmers and Machinists,
Woodland.

J. G. Jordan,
Stock, Grain, Wool & Fruit Farmer,
Sec. 18, 80 acres, Woodland.

J. W. Stinchcomb,
Stock, Grain & Wool Farmer,
Sec. 9315, 240 acres, Woodland.

Alfred Bolton,
Farmer, 10 acres,
Woodland.

Patrick Cunningham,
Wheat, Stock & Wool Farmer,
Sec. 6, 120 acres, Woodland.

HARDWARE.

H. A. Goodyear,
Hardware, Stoves, Iron &c.,
Hastings.

Charles C. Wolcott,
Hardware & Agricultural Implements,
Nashville.

C. M. Haller,
Hardware, Nashville.

Albert A. Selleck,
Tinsmith, Nashville.

HOTELS.

Hastings House,
J. H. Taylor, Proprietor,
Good Sample Rooms on first Floor,
Hastings.

Capt. G. W. McCormick,
Prop. Nashville House & Livery Stable,
Nashville.

Union House,
Wm. H. Beadle, Proprietor,
Nashville.

JUSTICE.

Abel Simonds,
Justice of the Peace,
Maple Grove.

LUMBER.

A. W. Olds & Co.,
Manufr's. of Hardwood Lumber,
Nashville.

W. F. Bert & Co.,
Dealers in all kinds of Soft and Hardwood Lumber,
Broom and Fork Handles,
Woodland.

MANUFACTURERS.

J. W. & C. G. Bentley,
Manuf'rs. Sash, Doors, Blinds and Moulding,
Dealers in Lumber &c.,
Hastings.

MARBLE DEALER.

S. W. D. Conway,
Marble Dealer,
Nashville.

MECHANIC.

R. W. Shiner,
Mechanic, Woodland.

MERCHANTS.

Russell & Nevins,
Dry Goods, Boots & Shoes, Hats, Caps &c.,
Julius Russell.   John M. Nevins
Hastings.

Geo. W. Hakes,
Speculator, Hastings.

Browne, Coombs & Storms,
General Merchants, also Agents for C. F. Light's
Celebrated Pianos.
Middleville.

John G. Myers,
Merchant, Woodland.

MILLERS.

David Purchis,
Miller and Stone Dresser,
Nashville.

John C. Stous,
Miller and Stone Dresser,
Nashville.

MINISTERS.

M. W. Tuck,
Pastor first Christian Church
of Nashville.

J. M. Atkin,
Pastor of first M. E. Church,
Nashville.

NEWSPAPER.

Hastings Republican Banner,
E. B. Dewey, G. M. Dewey,
G. H. Brooks, Proprietors,
Hastings.

Barry County Republican,
P. W. Niskorn, Proprietor,
Middleville.

POST MASTER.

H. H. Wood,
Postmaster, Nashville.

PHYSICIAN.

A. P. Drake, M. D.,
Hastings.

W. M. Young,
Physician and Surgeon,
Nashville.

REAL ESTATE.

Cook & Sheldon,
Abstract Office, Land & Tax Agency. Money
to Loan on Real Estate.
D. R. Cook,   P. A. Sheldon
Hastings.

BUSINESS CARDS OF PATRONS IN BARRY COUNTY.

REGISTER OF DEEDS.

John Hotchkiss,
Register of Deeds, Hastings.

SHERIFFS.

J. W. Vrooman,
Sheriff of Barry County,
Hastings.

James Fleming,
Deputy Sheriff, Nashville.

STATION AGENT.

Lewis Durkle,
Station Agent,
Nashville.

TEACHERS.

Mary D. Palmer,
Teacher, Assyria.

Mary C. Parker,
Teacher, Caselton.

Ada M. Mc Clelland,
Teacher, Hastings.

Curtis G. Miner,
Teacher, Hastings.

Miss. Minnie Rowley,
Teacher, Hastings.

Wm. H. Carveth,
Teacher of High School,
Woodland.

Henry N. Lovewell,
Teacher, Woodland.

WAGON MAKER.

T. T. Dewey,
Wagon Maker and Town Clerk,
Maple Grove.

BUSINESS CARDS OF PATRONS IN EATON COUNTY.

ARCHITECT.

L. V. Carpenter,
Architect & Builder,
Eaton Rapids.

ATTORNEYS.

M. S. Brackett,
Attorney & Solicitor,
Bellevue.

P. T. Van Zile,
Attorney at Law,
Charlotte.

E. A. Foote,
Attorney at Law,
Charlotte.

J. Wesley Nichols,
Attorney at Law,
Charlotte.

D. P. Sagendorph,
Attorney at Law,
Office in Musson & Sagendorph, Arcade Block,
Charlotte.

I. H. Corbin,
Attorney at Law & Real Estate Dealer,
Eaton Rapids.

Isaac M. Crane,
Attorney at Law,
Eaton Rapids.

Shearer & Pennington,
Attorneys at Law,
Eaton Rapids & Charlotte.

John M. Corbin,
Attorney at Law,
Eaton Rapids.

J. L. Mc Peek,
Real Estate Agent & Attorney at Law,
Grand Ledge.

Charles A. Swine,
Attorney at Law,
Vermontville.

Henry F. Higgins,
Attorney at Law,
Insurance and Collection Ag't. & Notary Public,
Vermontville.

A. J. Porter,
Attorney at Law & Collecting Agent,
Vermontville.

E. J. Ryman,
Att'y. at Law & Justice of the Peace,
Vermontville.

BANKS & BANKERS.

First National Bank,
J. Musgrave, Pres.   E. S. Lacey, Cash.
Charlotte.

Morgan Yaugh,
Banker & Real Estate Broker.
Collections attended to,
Ellsson Osborn, Cash., Eaton Rapids.

Geo. W. Keyes,
Banker & Dealer in Books
& Stationery,
Olivet.

Barber & Martin,
Bankers and General Merchants,
Vermontville.

BARBER.

L. D. Crosby,
Barber and Hair Dresser,
Olivet.

BLACKSMITHS.

Charles G. Belnap,
General Blacksmith and Carriage
Ironer,
Eaton Rapids.

J. Briggs,
Blacksmith,
Eaton Rapids.

Henry Woodruff,
Blacksmith & Horseshoer,
Eaton Rapids.

D. A. Babcock,
Buggy and Wagon Ironing,
Potterville.

BOOTS & SHOES.

Isaiah Ferris,
Boot and Shoe Maker,
Eaton Rapids.

Horace Dunbar,
Boots and Shoes,
Eaton Rapids.

James Ennis,
Man'r. of Boots & Shoes,
Eaton Rapids.

L. Bentley & Co.,
General Dealer in Boots and Shoes
And Rubber Goods,
Eaton Rapids.

BRICK MAKER.

A. H. Mason,
Brickmaker,
Sec. 16, Kalamo.

John York,
Mason and Bricklayer,
Kalamo.

BUILDER.

Wilson M. Holmes,
Builder, Grand Ledge.

BUTCHERS.

Wm. Rossman,
Meat Market,
Grand Ledge.

S. J. Kirkpatrick,
Butcher and Dealer in Cattle,
Olivet.

CABINET MAKER.

L. L. Davis,
Cabinet Maker, & Fancy Workman,
Eaton Rapids.

CARPENTERS & JOINERS.

Eli D. Heffner,
Carpenter & Joiner,
Charlotte.

John H. Chase,
Carpenter & Joiner,
Olivet.

D. Kester,
Carpenter,
Olivet.

CARRIAGE MAKERS.

A. W. Ridd,
Carriage Builder,
Eaton Rapids.

Geo. Riemer,
Body & Sleigh Maker,
Eaton Rapids.

A. G. Morrill,
Carriage Trimmer,
Eaton Rapids.

James Strawn,
General Wagon, Carriage and Sleigh
Manufacturer,
Eaton Rapids.

Joseph Mason,
Carriage Maker,
Olivet.

CHEESE FACTORY.

J. H. Mc Cotter,
Prop. Vermontville Cheese Factory,
Vermontville.

CHEMIST.

J. Newton Newman,
Pharmaceutical & Consulting Ana-
lytical Chemist,
Charlotte.

CLERGYMEN.

D. R. Shoop,
Pastor Congregational Church,
Bellevue.

P. Van Winkle,
Pastor Baptist Church,
Eaton Rapids.

A. Hunsberger,
Pastor M. E. Olivet Church,
Olivet.

J. E. Riesdorph,
Pastor United Brethren in Christ,
Potterville.

James Nixon,
Pastor United Brethren in Christ and Farmer,
80 acres, on Sec. 25, Stock, Grain, Wool & Fruit,
Potterville.

J. Gulick,
Pastor M. E. Church,
Vermontville.

CLOTHING.

Geo. Bull,
Dealer in Clothing and Gents'
Furnishing Goods,
Eaton Rapids.

CONSTABLE.

Albert Houghton,
Constable and Collector,
Eaton Rapids.

CONTRACTORS & BUILDERS.

Edward Marshall,
Contractor and Builder,
Potterville.

Charles H. Gallusha,
Contractor & Builder & Notary Public,
Olivet.

DENTIST.

H. Cole,
Dentist, Grand Ledge.

DRUGGISTS.

G. Y. Collins,
Dealer in Drugs and Medicines,
Charlotte.

Isaac R. Jameson,
Druggist and Grocer,
Dimondale.

Jackson & Hodges,
Druggist and Chemists,
Eaton Rapids.

Truman Johnson,
Druggist, Grand Ledge.

Edw. H. Hammond,
Drugs & Medicines, Groceries, Paints,
Oils etc., Grand Ledge.

BUSINESS CARDS OF PATRONS IN EATON COUNTY.

S. A. Andrus,
Druggist, Olivet.

Chs's. Hall,
Druggist & Dealer in Boots & Shoes,
Vermontville.

ENGINEERS.

E. F. Grant,
Engineer, Kalamo.

J. R. Woodin,
Mechanical Engineer,
Vermontville.

Frank P. Davis,
Surveyor and Civil Engineer,
and Contractor for Iron Bridges,
Vermontville.

FARMERS.

Geo. Martins,
General Farmer,
Sec. 5, 220 acres,
Bellevue.

William Farlin,
160 acres, Wool, Stock, Grains &c.,
Bellevue.

Horatio Hall,
Wool, Stock, Grains & Fruits,
400 acres, Sec. 24,
Bellevue.

Phillip H. Jarvis,
Grain, Stock, and Fruit,
80 acres, Sec. 13,
Bellevue.

E. E. Owen,
Grain, Stock, Wool &c.,
200 acres, Sec. 23,
Bellevue.

P. G. Heminway,
Wool, Stock, Grains and Fruit,
82 acres, Sec. 22,
Bellevue.

Henry Judd,
Stock, Grain, Fruit &c.,
80 acres, Sec. 23,
Bellevue.

Vedder Sprague,
Wool, Stock, Grains and Fruit,
80 acres, Sec. 23,
Bellevue.

Willard Follett & Oliver S. Follett,
Wool, Stock, Grains, Fruits. Dealers in Live Stock,
236 acres, Sec. 9,
Bellevue.

Edwin Osmun,
Wool, Stock, Grains &c.,
123 acres, Sec. 27,
Bellevue.

Norman P. Shumway,
Wool, Stock, Grains & Fruits,
85 acres, Sec. 26,
Bellevue.

Watt Gregg,
Stock, Grain, Wool and Fruit,
80 acres, Sec. 24,
Benton, Potterville P. O.

J. F. Carman,
Stock, Grain, Wool and Fruit,
120 acres, Sec. 24,
Benton, Potterville P. O.

Amos N. Fox,
Stock, Wool, Grain and Fruit,
240 acres, Sec. 28,
Benton.

Lorenzo Hatch,
Stock, Wool, Grain and Fruit,
140 acres, Sec. 29,
Benton.

Rowland Paine,
Stock, Wool, Grain and Fruit,
170 acres, Sec. 28,
Benton.

B. Landers,
Stock, Grain, Wool and Fruit,
110 acres, Sec. 28,
Benton.

A. L. Bingham,
Sec. 21, 87 acres,
Brookfield.

Almon C. Ells,
Farmer and Justice of Peace,
Sec. 15, 130 acres,
Carmel.

James M. D. Davis,
Farmer and Carpenter and Joiner,
Sec. 20, 40 acres,
Carmel.

Wesley Houck,
General Farmer,
Sec. 19, 80 acres,
Carmel.

Amos Dillin,
Farmer and Clergyman,
Carmel.

J. D. & D. C. Cole,
Farmers,
Sec. 29, 124 acres,
Carmel.

Ira Hitchcock,
Farmer,
Sec. 29, 80 acres,
Carmel.

Mrs. F. Taft,
General Farming,
Sec. 18, 120 acres,
Carmel.

Pearl Rogers,
Stock, Wool and Grain,
240 acres, Sec. 6,
Chester.

W. J. Moyer,
Stock, Grain, Wool and Fruit,
249 acres, Sec. 3,
Chester.

Orrin Clapper,
Wool, Stock, Grain &c.,
75 acres, Sec. 30, Chester.

Wm. Crocker,
Wool, Stock, Grain &c.,
90 acres, Sec. 29, Chester.

Anson Scott,
Wool, Stock, Lumber, Grains &c.,
420 acres, Sec. 17, Chester.

J. C. Williams,
Wool, Stock, Grains and Fruits,
76 acres, Sec. 21, Chester.

W. A. Rogers,
Stock, Grains, Fruits,
120 acres, Sec. 7, Chester.

Edwin Boyer,
Grains, Stock and Fruits,
190 acres, Sec. 10, Chester.

Jorum Boyer,
Stock, Grains, Fruits,
110 acres, Sec. 10, Chester.

Edward R. Martin,
Stock, Wool, Fruits &c.,
185 acres, Sec. 14, Chester.

Wm. Phelps,
Grains, Stock, Fruits,
80 acres, Sec. 11, Chester.

G. H. Beeman,
Stock, Grains, Fruits &c.,
240 acres, Sec. 1, Chester.

Asa W. Mitchell,
Wool, Stock, Grains and Fruits,
120 acres, Sec. 1, Chester.

W. H. H. Rowley,
Wool, Stock, Grains,
80 acres, Sec. 11, Chester.

R. M. Wheaton,
Grains, Stock and Fruits,
160 acres, Sec. 23, Chester.

Philo P. Moore,
Wool, Stock, Grains, Fruits & Honey,
100 acres, Sec. 24, Chester.

James Lipsey,
Stock, Grains and Fruit,
160 acres, Sec. 13, Chester.

Henry C. Wheaton,
Stock and Grains,
Chester.

Fred. Phelps,
Wool, Stock, Grains &c.,
40 acres, Sec. 22, Chester.

Hiram Hutchings,
Wool, Stock, Grains and Fruits,
280 acres, Sec. 35, Chester.

B. Polhamus,
Stock, Grains &c.,
120 acres, Sec. 23, Chester.

James Hubbard,
Wool, Stock, Grains and Fruit,
120 acres, Sec. 27, Chester.

James McConnell,
Wool, Stock, Grains &c.,
120 acres, Sec. 27, Chester.

John W. Shaw,
Stock, Grains &c.,
95 acres, Sec. 27, Chester.

William Willson,
Woo., Stock, Grains & Fruit,
80 acres, Sec. 22, Chester.

John R. Kingman,
Wool, Stock, Grains &c.,
60 acres, Chester.

J. W. McMillan,
160 acres, Sec. 26,
Stock, Grain, Wool and Fruit,
Farm in Eagle tp. Clinton Co.

James Bryan,
Stock, Grain, Fruit and Wool,
120 acres, Sec. 1,
Eaton, Charlotte P. O.

Patrick H. Garvey,
Stock, Grain, Wool and Fruit,
70 acres, Sec. 22,
Eaton, Charlotte P. O.

P. E. Pennington,
Stock, Grain, Wool and Fruit,
162 acres, Sec. 10,
Eaton, Charlotte P. O.

Samuel Linsley,
Stock, Grain, Wool and Fruit,
300 acres, Sec. 1,
Eaton, Potterville P. O.

Wm. Wall,
Fruit, Stock, and Grain,
Sec. 25, 165 acres,
Eaton Rapids.

A. D. Saxton,
Wheat, Stock and Wool,
Sec. 14, 100 acres, Eaton Rapids.

Norman Rose,
Grain and Stock,
20 acres, Eaton Rapids.

J. M. Hale,
Fruit and Stock, 80 acres,
Eaton Rapids.

Benjamin Covey,
Grain, Stock and Wool,
100 acres, Eaton Rapids.

Jared Kulp,
Grain, Fruit and Stock,
40 acres, Eaton Rapids.

I. P. Rogers,
Wool, Stock, Grain, Sheep Fruit,
66 acres, Sec. 1,
Grand Ledge.

A. W. Reynolds,
120 acres, Grand Ledge.

G. W. Jones, Jr.,
Farmer, Grand Ledge.

S. D. Trobridge,
Stock, Grain and Wool,
Sec. 10, 80 acres,
Kalamo.

Wm. Wright,
Stock, Grain and Wool,
40 acres, Kalamo.

Oliver J. Stall,
Stock and Grain,
Sec. 3, 80 acres, Kalamo.

James A. Grant,
Farmer and Carpenter, Sec. 27,
Kalamo.

Mary A. Hunter,
Grain, Fruit and Stock,
Sec. 28, 40 acres,
Kalamo.

Robert W. Willis,
Stock, Grain and Wool,
Sec. 29, 120 acres,
Kalamo.

Sarah Shutt,
Stock, Grain and Wool,
Sec. 17, 40 acres,
Kalamo.

John Fowler,
Stock, Grain and Wool,
Sec. 17, 200 acres,
Kalamo.

Lucy Ann Welch,
Grain, Stock and Wool,
Sec. 8, 40 acres, Kalamo.

Wm. Karcher,
Grain Farmer, and Musician,
Sec. 4, 40 acres, Kalamo.

Wesley Andrews,
Grain, Fruit, and Stock,
and Teacher, Sec. 27, 40 acres,
Kalamo.

Warren H. King,
Stock & Grain Farmer & Millwright,
Sec. 17, 90 acres, Kalamo.

Susan M. Smith,
Farmer and Dress maker,
Sec. 18, 7 acres, Kalamo.

L. Barnes & Son,
Stock, Grain, Fruit and Wool,
Sec. 5, 100 acres, Kalamo.

Elijah Pope,
Stock, Grain and Fruit,
Sec. 4, 40 acres, Kalamo.

Daniel Townsend,
Grain, Stock and Fruit,
Sec. 16, 40 acres, Kalamo.

James Fairweather,
Stock, Grain and Fruit,
Sec. 7, 40 acres, Kalamo.

Gilman O. Stone,
Stock, Grain and Fruit Farmer,
Sec. 18, 10 acres, Kalamo.

A. B. Tyler,
Farmer and Carpenter,
Kalamo.

A. J. Larawig,
Fruit and Stock Farm,
Sec. 11, 120 acres, Kalamo.

Gideon Cogsdill,
Stock, Grain and Fruit Farmer,
Sec. 11 & 12, 187 acres, Kalamo.

P. Vanderhoof,
Farmer, and Proprietor of the
Vanderhoof Sawmill,
Sec's. 12 & 13, 44 acres, Kalamo.

Jacob Treeber,
Stock, Grain and Wool Farmer,
Sec. 12, 80 acres, Kalamo.

Peter Sears,
Stock Raiser, Sheep a speciality,
Sec. 12 & 13, 280 acres, Kalamo.

C. W. & L. P. Tubbs,
Stock, Grain and Fruit Farmer,
Sec. 14, 120 acres, Kalamo.

G. W. Herring,
Grain, Stock and Wool,
Sec. 9, 40 acres, Kalamo.

Mrs Fanny Wilson,
Stock, Grain and Wool Farmer,
Sec. 20, 80 acres, Kalamo.

H. & M. Pope,
Stock, Grain and Wool,
Sec. 24, 120 acres, Kalamo.

Miles Alexander,
Stock, Grain and Wool,
Sec. 24, 40 acres, Kalamo.

T. U. Bradley,
General Farmer and Thresher,
Sec. 36, 200 acres, Kalamo.

Geo. Wilson,
General Farmer,
Sec. 33, 120 acres, Kalamo.

Addison G. Brace,
Stock, Grain and Wool,
Sec. 31, 85 acres, Kalamo.

C. H. Conklin,
General Farmer, Sec. 32, 80 acres,
Kalamo.

Emanuel E. Tieck,
Stock, Grain and Fruit,
Sec. 18, 60 acres, Kalamo.

S. A. Shepard,
Stock, Grain, and Fruit,
Sec. 18, 40 acres, Kalamo.

Wm. Griffin,
Stock, Grain and Wool,
Sec. 20, 200 acres, Kalamo.

E. S. Kennedy,
Stock & Grain Farmer & Grafter,
Sec. 18, 40 acres, Kalamo.

Benjamin Evans,
Grain, Wool and Fruit,
Sec. 31, 160 acres, Kalamo.

Wm. Kohlmeyer,
Farmer and Engineer,
Sec. 26, 40 acres, Kalamo.

Henry Davis,
Grain, Wool, Fruit and Stock,
Sec. 26, 40 acres, Kalamo.

Henry Barly,
Grain, Wool and Stock,
Sec. 27, 38 acres, Kalamo.

Eliza A. Webb,
General Farmer,
Kalamo.

J. D. & Wm. Campbell,
Stock, Grain and Fruit,
Sec. 36, 120 acres, Kalamo.

D. Hart & Wife,
Teachers and Farmers, Grain
Fruit and Wool,
Sec's. 32 & 33, 80 acres, Olivet.

Melintas Bowen,
Fruit Grain and Wool,
Sec. 1, 80 acres, Olivet.

L. Shepard,
80 acres, Olivet.

N. Stone,
Grain, Wool and Dairy Farmer,
Sec. 28, 100 acres, Olivet.

Nelson Whitback,
Grain, Wool and Fruit,
Sec. 14, 40 acres, Olivet.

John Burrows,
General Farmer, 120 acres,
Olivet.

B. C. Hammond,
General Farmer, 60 acres,
Olivet.

F. L. Reed,
Wool, Stock Grains &c.,
280 acres, Sec. 29, Olivet.

N. Hobart,
Grains, Stock &c.,
120 acres, Sec. 21, Olivet.

Martin Nichols,
Stock, Grain and Fruit,
114 acres, Sec. 36, Oneida.

Christopher Glenn,
Stock, Grain and Fruit,
100 acres, Sec. 35, Oneida.

John Barker,
Grain, Stock, Wool and Fruit,
80 acres, Sec. 10, Oneida.

F. W. Place,
Stock, Wool, Grain & Fruit,
120 acres, Sec. 9, Oneida.

A. Bowen,
Stock, Wool, Grain & Fruit,
120 acres, Sec. 7, Oneida.

Jos. S. Holmes,
Grain, Stock and Fruit,
40 acres, Sec. 28, Oneida.

Geo. W. Nichols,
Stock, Wool, Grain & Fruit,
240 acres, Sec. 25, Oneida.

C. M. Preston,
Commission Agent for Agricultural Implements,
40 acres, Sec. 36, Oneida.

J. K. Fuller,
Farmer and Teacher,
Sec. 13, Oneida.

R. Nixon,
Farmer, 300 acres, Sec. 85,
Stock, Grain and Fruit, Oneida.

Edwin Nixon,
Stock, Grain & Wool,
100 acres, Sec. 35, Oneida.

A. Hancock,
Farmer and Teacher,
Stock, Grain & Fruit,
80 acres, Sec. 32, Oneida.

Henry Earl,
Stock, Grain and Fruit,
400 acres, Sec. 31, Oneida.

Geo. Jones,
Farmer & Supervisor, Stock, Wool,
Grain and Fruit, 80 acres, Sec. 9,
Oneida.

Wm. Henry,
Wool, Stock, Grain & Fruit,
185 acres, Sec. 10, Oneida.

P. D. Phelps,
Grain Stock, Wool, Fruit, and
Livery Stable,
115 acres, Potterville.

Wm. Parmenter,
Grain Stock, and Wool,
40 acres, Potterville.

Zulila Moyer,
Stock, Wool & Grain,
120 acres, Sec. 34, Roxand.

Edwin Tyler,
Stock, Grain and Wool,
Sec. 33, 150 acres, Vermontville.

Robert Muir,
Stock, Wheat and Wool,
Sec. 33, 80 acres, Vermontville.

Miron Belding,
Farmer and School Teacher,
Sec. 34, 40 acres, Vermontville.

Elmer Ellis,
Stock, Grain and Fruit,
Sec. 37, 210 acres, Vermontville.

W. J. French,
Grain, Stock and Wool,
Sec. 34, 120 acres, Vermontville.

Cha's. S. Demond,
Vermontville.

John L. Howell,
Grain, Fruit and Stock,
Sec. 31, 47 acres, Vermontville.

J. B. Williams,
Stock, Grain and Fruit,
190 acres, Sec. 24, Vermontville.

Rufus Haner,
Wool, Stock, Grains, Fruits,
320 acres, Sec. 13, Vermontville.

M. W. Squier,
Wool, Stock, Grains, Fruits,
163 acres, Sec. 26, Vermontville.

J. H. Squier,
Wool, Stock, Grains &c.,
150 acres, Sec. 25, Vermontville.

Perry Fox,
General Farmer,
67 acres, Sec. 28, Vermontville.

Levi C. Sprague,
General Farming, 97 acres,
Sec. 14, Vermontville.

A. D. Lake,
Stock, Dairying, Grains &c.,
80 acres, Sec. 11, Vermontville.

A. P. Denton,
Stock and Grains, 80 acres,
Sec. 11, Vermontville.

Jacob Moore,
Stock, Wool, Grains and Fruit,
160 acres, Sec. 26, Vermontville.

W. C. Frost,
Grain, Wool and Fruit,
Sec's. 31 & 32, 114 acres, Walton.

Matthew Willis,
Farmer and Shoemaker,
Sec. 27, 80 acres, Walton.

J. S. Stone,
Stock, Grain and Wool and Surveyor,
Sec. 27, 100 acres, Walton.

Ezra Willis,
Stock, Grain and Fruit,
Sec. 21, 180 acres, Walton.

Rhoanna Galusha,
Stock, Grain and Wool
Sec. 35, 40 acres, Walton.

Jacob Reasoner,
Farmer, and Agent for Fruit and
Ornamental Trees,
Sec. 35, 80 acres, Walton.

Wm. Rogers,
Farmer, Sec. 26,
Walton.

Richard Carver,
Stock, Grain and Fruit,
Sec's. 27 & 116, Walton.

Nathan Hendekson,
Farmer, Walton.

C. C. Mitchell,
Grain and Fruit, 40 acres,
Sec. 16, Walton.

T. P. Meker,
Stock, Grain and Wool,
Walton.

J. Cole,
Sec. 6, 150 acres,
Walton.

John E. Courter,
Stock, Grain and Fruit,
120 acres, Sec. 21, Windsor.

John D. Skinner,
Stock, Grain, Wool and Fruit,
160 acres, Sec. 26, Windsor.

James S. Skinner,
Farmer, Fruit Grower, & Retired
Physician, 12 acres & Nursery of
1000 Trees, Windsor.

Charles B. Hawk,
Grain, Wool and Fruit,
230 acres, Sec. 25,
Windsor, Dimondale P. O.

Esek, Pray,
Stock, Wool, Grain and Fruit,
160 acres, Sec. 29, Windsor, Dimondale P. O.

B. O. Carlton,
Stock, Grain and Fruit,
76½ acres, Windsor.

S. L. Streeter,
Stock, Grain and Fruit,
43 1-2 acres, Sec. 29, Windsor, Dimondale P. O.

BUSINESS CARDS OF PATRONS IN EATON COUNTY.

John E. Woodworth,
120 acres, Sec. 8,
Benton.

Willard E. Mitchell,
220 acres, Sec. 20,
Benton.

Wm. Quantrell,
Farmer and Brick Maker, 188 acres,
Sec. 30, Benton.

Alvah Blanchard,
40 acres, Sec. 7,
Benton.

Clark Wetmore,
120 acres, Sec. 16,
Benton.

H. V. Hamill,
40 acres, Sec. 5,
Benton.

Geo. J. Vrunm,
60 acres, Sec. 20,
Benton.

Charles Decoo,
Agricultural Agt. for Colby's Washer & Wringer,
40 acres, Sec. 5,
Benton, Potterville P. O.

T. M. Brown,
Farmer and Justice of the Peace,
280 acres, Sec. 28, Benton.

Joseph Cupit,
Farmer and Miller,
160 acres, Sec. 1, Delta.

H. E. Porter,
Farmer & Dealer in Fruit, Stock, Wool and Grain.
120 acres. Sec 21, Delta.

R. W. Choate,
Farmer and Teacher,
80 acres, Sec 9, Delta.

John Cupit,
Farmer and Miller 180 acres.
Sec. 82 Watertown.

B. F. Bailey,
Farmer and Manf'r of Lumber,
360 acres, Sec. 4, Windsor.

L. L. Shotwell,
Farmer and Lumber dealer. 127 acres,
Sec. 18, Windsor.

Abram Van Wie,

Sec. 12, Windsor.

Rollin P. Ward,
Stock, Grain and Fruit,
50 acres, Sec. 7, Windsor.

Samuel Martin,
Stock, Wool, Grain and Fruit,
80 acres, Sec. 20, Windsor.

Joseph P. Lewis,
General Farming,
125 acres, Sec. 18, Windsor.

Robert M. Redfield,
Stock, Grain, Fruit and Wool,
Windsor, Dimondale P. O.

C. Sloan,
64 acres, Windsor, West Windsor P. O.

Geo. P. Carman,
Stock, Wool, Grain and Fruit,
275 acres, Sec. 18, West Windsor P. O.

H. M. Carman,
Stock, Wool, Grain and Fruit,
200 acres, Sec. 18, Windsor, West Windsor P. O.

Austin Cunningham,
200 acres, Stock, Grain and Fruit,
Windsor, West Windsor P. O.

John M. King,
Stock, Wool, Grain and Fruit,
146.33 acres, Sec. 3, Windsor, Dimondale P. O.

N. R. Albro,
15½ acres, Sec. 17, Mechan'l. Carpenter,
Windsor, West Windsor P. O.

FARRIER.

J. A. Ogden,
Horse Farrier, Sec 20,
Kalamo.

FURNITURE.

A. D. Baker & Co.,
Dealers in Furniture, Collins, Wall Paper
and Upholstery.
Eaton Rapids.

R. B. Morritt,
Manufacturer of all kinds of Small Furniture,
Children's Toy Carts, Sleighs, &c.,
Eaton Rapids.

GROCERS.

J. L. Anderson,
Grocery, Fruit, Oysters, Restaurant,
Eaton Rapids.

W. D. Brainard,
Gen'l Grocery, Provisions, and Feed Store,
Eaton Rapids.

F. Rogers,
General Grocery and Produce Store,
Eaton Rapids.

M. Pettit,
Grocery, and Bakery, Flour, and Feed,
Eaton Rapids.

J. C. Shearer,
Grocery and Provisions, Crockery, and Glass,
Eaton Rapids.

C. A. Coller,
Grocery and Provision Store,
Eaton Rapids.

Wm. Resmequin,
Groceries and Produce,
Grand Ledge.

C. I. Scott,
Groceries and Produce,
Grand Ledge.

Geo. A. Lewis,
Dry Goods, Groceries, Boots & Shoes,
Grand Ledge.

J. S. Holmes,
Postmaster, Groceries and Stationery,
Grand Ledge.

W. H. Benedict,
General Grocer, Proprietor of Elevator and
Shipper of Grain and Produce,
Vermontville.

GUNSMITH

Nelson Edgett,
Gunsmith and Machinist,
Eaton Rapids.

HARDWARE.

Foreman, Ketchum & Co.,
General Dealers in Hardware,
Charlotte.

J. F. Knapp,
General Dealer in Hardware, Tin and
Pedlers' Goods,
Eaton Rapids.

Ja'n Winnie,
Hardware,
Grand Ledge.

HARNESS & SADDLE MAKERS.

C. T. Hartsen,
General Dealer in Harness, Saddles, Trunks,
and Horse Furnishing Goods,
Main St., Eaton Rapids.

Geer & Vansickle,
Manufacturer of Harness & Saddles,
Main St., Eaton Rapids.

Bennona B. Booth,
Harness Maker,
Eaton Rapids.

W. H. Furgeson,
Saddle and Harness Maker,
Eaton Rapids.

HOTELS.

A. M. Olmsted,
Proprietor of Olmstead House,
Dimondale.

S. D. Hayward,
Proprietor of Anderson House.
Eaton Rapids.

Joseph Stretch,
Proprietor of Mineral House,
Grand Ledge.

Olivet House,
H. Shallier, Prop.   Meat Market attached,
Olivet.

Jno. Gladding,
Proprietor of Gladding House, and agent for
Colby's Little Washer and Wringer,
Potterville.

Geo. H. Potter,
Proprietor of Potter House, Manufacturer of
Lumber, 1500 acres, Sec. 23, Stock, Grain and
Fruit Raising, Potterville.

JEWELERS.

D. Lewis,
Dealer in all kinds of Jewelry, Clocks, Watches, &c.
Eaton Rapids.,

L. W. Ross,
Jeweler,
Grand Ledge.

A. E. Sherman,
Jewelry and Millinery,
Vermontville.

Justice of the Peace.

S. Chadwick,
Justice of the Peace and Claim Agt.,
Grand Ledge.

LABORER.

Andrew McQuoun,
Laborer,
Windsor.

LIVERY STABLE.

Birney Brothers,
Livery Stable and Omnibus Line,
Eaton Rapids.

LUMBERMEN.

N. I. Griest & Bro.,
Manufacturers of Lumber,
Chester.

Henry Hibbard,
Lumber Dealer,
Chester.

Alexander Oliver,
Lumber Dealer,
Dimondale.

Wm. C. Bodine,
Manufacturer and dealer in Hardwood Lumber,
Vermontville.

P. J. Bryan;
Manufacturer of Lumber,
Vermontville.

Henry J. Martin,
Dealer in Hardwood Lumber,
Vermontville.

MACHINIST.

Wm. A. Stryker,
Machinist and Engineer,
Vermontville.

MAGNETIC SPRINGS.

E. B. Frost,
Proprietor of the first Magnetic Spring discovered
at Eaton Rapids. Good Bath-rooms in connection.
1st door south of Frost House.
Eaton Rapids.

MANUFACTURERS.

Francis M. Potter,
Manf'r of Staves, Shingles and Lath,
Bellevue.

J. W. H. Smith & Co.,
Manuf're. of Handles and Lumber,
Charlotte.

Hart & Richardson,
Manuf'rs of Doors, Sash and Blinds; & Dealers in
Lumber, Shingles, Lath, Lime, &c.,
Charlotte.

Elisha H. Hudson,
Manuf'r of Hand, Hay, and Grain Rakes, and
General Merchandise,
Dimondale.

Garret Vedder,
Manuf'r of Sash and Door Blinds,
Grand Ledge.

Myron Slaton,
Manuf'rs. Shingles and Rakes,
Olivet.

J. J. Higby,
Dealer in Staves & Heading. Agt. Peninsular R.W.
Potterville.

M. M. Wakeman,
Manuf'r. of Wagons, Carriages &c.,
Vermontville.

MARBLE DEALER.

F. X. Lewis,
Marble Dealer,
Grand Ledge.

MASON.

Joseph W. Call,
Brick and Stone Mason, Plastering, etc.,
West Windsor P. O.

MECHANICS.

B. W. Cove,
Carpenter,
Sec. 4, Eaton.

G. H. Hatch,
Sec. 26.
Oneida, Grand Ledge P. O.

MERCHANTS.

Evans, Avery & Co.,
Dealers in Dry Goods, Groceries, and General
Merchandise,
Bellevue.

Enos Boughton.
Dry Goods, Groceries, Boots and Shoes,
Bellevue.

B. Hutges,
General Merchant & Manuf'r of Lime,
Bellevue.

BUSINESS CARDS OF PATRONS IN EATON COUNTY.

Evans, Avery & Co.,
Dealers in General Merchandise,
Bellevue.

Clark Sloan,
General Merchant Dealer in Stock, Grain, etc.
Dimondale.

Stuart Hutt,
Dealer in Dry goods, Groceries, Grain and Wool,
Dimondale.

I. N. Reynolds,
Groceries, Boots Shoes, and Produce,
Eaton Rapids.

B. T Esler,
Dealer in General Merchandise,
Grand Ledge.

O. Johnson,
Merchant,
Grand Ledge.

M. A. Collins,
General Store Keeper, and Post Master,
Kalamo.

E. L. Sargent,
Merchant,
Olivet.

J. W. Potter & Co.,
General Dealers. Postmaster.
Potterville.

H. O. Merritt,
Merchant,
Potterville.

W. H. Wilmont,
Dealer in Fancy Goods,
Walton.

MILLERS.

Gardiner, Warren & Co.,
Merchant and Custom Millers,
Bellevue.

E. W. Hunt,
Dealer in grain, Dimondale Mills,
Dimondale.

Aaron Mest,
Miller and Stone Cutter,
Eaton Rapids.

K. C. Wright,
Miller and Dealer in Agricultural Implements,
Eaton Rapids.

Wm. Kite,
Proprietor of Carlisle Grist Mill,
Kalamo.

B. H. Rose,
Planing Mill, Shingles, etc.
Grand Ledge.

Joseph C. Dutcher,
Miller,
Grand Ledge.

E. F. Kent,
Grand Ledge Mills, (Kent, Hixson & Co.)
Grand Ledge.

A. L. Green,
Merchant Miller and Lumberman,
Olivet.

MILLINERS.

Mrs. M Dyer,
General Millinery and Fancy Goods,
Eaton Rapids.

T. L. & L. L. Emmerson,
Milliners,
Olivet.

MINISTER.

Gustavus Ellis,
Pastor M. E. Church,
Potterville.

NEWSPAPERS & PRINTERS.

J. V. Johnson & Co.,
Steam Job Printers, and Publishers of
the Democratic Leader,
Charlotte.

Joseph Saunders & Co.,
Job Printers and Publishers of the Charlotte
Republican,
Charlotte.

Wm. S. Trask,
Printer,
Charlotte

Frank C. Culley,
Steam Book and Job Printer, and Publisher of
Eaton Rapids Journal.
Eaton Rapids.

B. W. Blanchard,
Printer, Grand Ledge Independent,
Grand Ledge.

NURSERYMEN.

A. F. Gaylord,
Nurseryman. All kinds of Fruit and Ornamental
Trees. Eaton Rapids.

L. S. Benham & Bros.,
Nurserymen and Florists,
Olivet.

PHOTOGRAPHERS.

A. P. Ball,
Photographer,
Eaton Rapids.

J. B. DeLamater,
Photographer,
Grand Ledge.

PHYSICIANS.

P. F. Taylor,
Physician and Druggist,
Bellevue.

S. W. Sleater,
Physician and Surgeon,
Charlotte.

Amos Knight, M. D.,
Physician and Surgeon,
Eaton Rapids,

Jas. H. Wellings,
Grand Ledge.

G. S. Messenger, M. D,
Grand Ledge,

C. J. Corey, M. D.,
Grand Ledge.

Dr. L. P. Huxen & Griswold,
Homeopathic Physicians,
Olivet.

E. C. Palmer,
Physician and Surgeon,
Potterville.

L. J. Ford, M. D.,
Special Agent for Electric Life Ins. Co., N. Y.,
Potterville.

C. J. Lane,
Eclectic and Homeopathic Physician and Surgeon,
Vermontville.

Wm. Parmenter,
Physician and Surgeon,
Vermontville.

L. Dewey,
Botanic Physician and Surgeon,
Vermontville.

PICTURE DEALER.

B. W. Pinch,
Dealer in Pictures,
Olivet.

PHRENOLOGIST.

M. S. Kibby,
Professor of Phrenology,
West Windsor.

PROVISION DEALERS.

S. Drake & Curtis,
Dealers in all kinds of Salt and Fresh Meats,
Eaton Rapids.

Real Estate, R. R., and other Agts.

Mills & Dwinell,
Real Estate, Insurance and Loan Agents,
Charlotte.

Wm. I. McMaster,
Agent, D. L. & L. M. R R.,
Grand Ledge.

J. H. Golden,
R. R. Agent,
Vermontville.

Jesse Chance,
Agt. for Canton Wrought Iron Bridge Co.,
Vermontville.

RETIRED.

Levi D. Mitchell,
Grand Ledge.

SAWYER.

George Thompson,
Sawyer,
Eaton Rapids.

SEWING MACHINES, &C.

H. S. Cassidy,
Supervising Agent for the Elias Howe Machine
Company for Eaton County,
Charlotte.

James T. Sargent,
Agent for Sewing Machines, Organs, Pianos, &c.,
Eaton Rapids.

J. M. Lampman,
Agent for the Elias Howe Sewing Machine,
Vermontville.

TAILOR.

J. T. Wellman,
Fashionable Tailor.
Cutting and Fitting neatly done, on short notice,
Grand Ledge.

TEACHERS.

William Follett,
Teacher,
Bellevue.

Salvia Rider,
Section 6,
Chester.

Wm. H. Simpson,
Teacher,
Grand Ledge.

Wm. P. Tinker,
Teacher,
Sec. 35, Kalamo.

O. Hosford,
Professor of Mathematics in Olivet College,
Olivet.

A. B. Brown,
Professor of Music in Olivet College.
General Dealer in Music and Musical Instruments
Olivet.

Miss H. P. Dennis,
Principal Ladies' Department, Olivet College,
Olivet.

Joseph L. Daniels,
Professor of Greek in Olivet College,
Olivet.

Misses Dell & Nell Galusha,
Teachers,
Olivet.

Miss Mary Weddel,
Teacher,
Olivet.

Leroy A. Jackson,
Teacher,
Potterville.

W. D. Southworth,
Teacher,
Potterville,

Magley Ashley,
School Teacher,
Windsor.

Leonidas H. McQueen,
Teacher,
40 acres, Sec. 7, Windsor.

D. R. Hall,
Principal of Vermontville High School.
Vermontville.

Miss Lizzie McCotter,
Teacher,
Vermontville.

TIN SMITH.

H. L. Curtis,
Tin Smith,
Vermontville.

WAGONS.

A. G. Wright,
Dealer in Wagons and Agricultural Implements,
Olivet.

WELL DIGGER.

A. Ketchum,
Well Digger,
Olivet.

ATTORNEYS.

M. M. Atwood,
Attorney at Law,
Ingham tp., Dansville P. O.

Cornelius Calkins,
Counselor at Law and General Collecting Agent,
Leslie.

BANK

H. T. Allen & Son,
Banking and Exchange Office,
Leslie.

BLACKSMITHS.

John A. Curtis,
Blacksmith, Sec. 15,
Bunker Hill.

H. J. Wilson,
General Blacksmith, and Manuf'r of Wilson's Patent Wagon Jack. Country and State Rights for sale on reasonable terms.
Mason.

J. Bevier,
Blacksmith,
Stockbridge.

CARPENTERS.

M. D. Sumner,
Carpenter, and Agent for Dr. Clark Johnson's Indian Blood Syrup,
Sec. 17, Bath.

James G. Sewell,
Carpenter and Joiner,
Whiteoak.

CARRIAGE MAKERS.

Vandercook & Sanderson,
General Carriage Making, and Jobbing of all kinds,
Mason.

CLERGYMEN.

Byron S. Pratt,
Pastor M. E. Church,
Bath.

L. D. Bruce,
Missionary, Ogemos,
Bunker Hill.

E. K. Grout,
Pastor of Baptist Church,
Leslie.

COOPERS.

Edwin E. Barker,
Cooper,
Leslie.

C. C. Dubois,
Cooper,
Whiteoak.

ENGINEER.

John Forster,
Civil and Mining Engineer,
Meridian.

FARMERS.

John Read,
Farmer and Supervisor, 160 acres, Sec. 21,
Bath.

Isaac M. Dryer,
Farmer, 160 acres, Sec. 20,
Bath.

Hugh Blakely,
General Farmer, 150 acres, Sec. 5,
Bunker Hill tp., Felts P. O.

E. H. Angel,
General Farmer and
County Drain Commissioner, 235 acres, Sec. 16,
Bunker Hill.

J. Dubois,
General Farmer, 160 acres, Sec. 6,
Bunker Hill tp., Felts P. O.

Amasa Dubois,
General Farmer, 140 acres, Sec. 7
Bunker Hill tp., Felts P. O.

D. C. Olds,
Gen'l Farmer, 64 acres, Sec. 22,
Bunker Hill.

Charles Lebar,
General Farmer, 240 acres, Sec. 22,
Bunker Hill tp., Fitchburg P. O.

Wm. Clark,
General Farmer, 84 acres, Sec. 26,
Bunker Hill tp., Fitchburg P. O.

A. D. Beers,
General Farmer, 50 acres, Sec. 16,
Bunker Hill tp., Fitchburg P. O.

George Lord,
General Farmer, 80 acres, Sec. 23,
Bunker Hill tp., Fitchburg P. O.

John C. Shaw,
General Farmer, Sec. 24,
Bunker Hill tp., Fitchburg P. O.

W. H. Whelan & Brothers,
General Farmers, 160 acres, Sec. 26,
Bunker Hill tp., Fitchburg P. O.

G. P. Bailey,
General Farmer, 120 acres, Sec. 16,
Bunker Hill.

A. C. Lawrence,
Farmer, 171 acres, Sec. 36,
Bunker Hill tp., Fitchburg P. O.

Oscar Earl,
Dealer in Lightning Rods,
80 acres, Sec. 36,
Bunker Hill tp., Fitchburg P. O.

A. J. Rayner,
General Farmer, 396 acres, Sec. 21,
Bunker Hill.

S. W. Archer,
General Farmer, 230 acres, Sec. 20,
Bunker Hill tp., Leslie. P. O.

A. B. Angell,
Farmer & Lightning Rod Dealer, 194 acres, Sec. 21,
Bunker Hill tp., Fitchburg P. O.

Isaac Davis,
Bunker Hill

Nelson Everett,
Supervisor of Onondaga,
and Farmer, Sec. 9, 80 acres,
Bunker Hill.

John Ferguson,
Farmer, 80 acres, Sec. 15,
Delhi.

Thomas J. Brown,
County Surveyor and Farmer 40 acres, Sec 18,
Delhi.

Samuel Skadan,
General Farmer, 175 acres, Sec. 13,
Ingham tp., Dansville P. O.

J. C. Marshall,
General Farmer, 160 acres, Sec. 12,
Ingham tp., Dansville P. O.

W. W. Raymond,
General Farmer, 100 acres, Sec. 2,
Ingham tp., Dansville P. O.

J. H. Hatch,
General Farmer, 114 acres, Sec. 2,
Ingham tp., Dansville P. O.

J. C. Steves,
Farmer and Dealer in all kinds
of Agricultural Implements, 124 acres, Sec. 28,
Ingham tp., Dansville P. O.

A. Phillips,
Farmer and Dealer in Organs
and Agricultural Implements, 140 acres, Sec. 2,
Ingham tp., Dansville P. O.

Charles H. James,
Farmer, Carpenter & Joiner, Sec. 11,
Ingham tp., Dansville P. O.

D. F. Sawyer,
Farmer, 175 acres, Sec. 11,
Ingham tp., Dansville P. O.

James Royston,
Farmer, Sec. 18, S. E. ¼,
Leslie.

Wheaton Saunders,
Sec. 7, N. E. ¼,
Leslie.

Coan C. King,
Sec. 11, S. E. ¼,
Leslie tp., Onondaga P. O.

Geo. W. Cantrell,
Farmer,
Leslie.

John H. Mullett,
Farmer & Surveyor, Sec. 25,
Meridian.

O. F. Smith,
Farmer,
Meridian tp., Perry P. O.

Phebe Hicks,
Farmer, 160 acres, Sec. 24,
Meridian tp., Bell Oak P. O.

Edmund Alchin,
General Farmer, 160 acres, Sec. 28,
Meridian tp., Webberville P. O.

Robert Reid,
160 acres, S. W. Sec. 13,
Stockbridge.

G. Asquith,
Stockbridge.

Robert Mc Kenzey,
155 acres, S. W. Sec. 13,
Stockbridge.

O. S. Gregory,
160 acres, S. W. Sec. 12,
Stockbridge.

Daniel Mc Kenzey,
140 acres, S. W. Sec. 12,
Stockbridge.

Rensselaer Ramsdill,
200 acres, S. W. Sec. 15,
Stockbridge.

John Howell,
120 acres, N. E. Sec. 12,
Stockbridge tp., Plainfield P. O.

Asher G. Miller,
240 acres, S. W. Sec. 1,
Stockbridge.

S. C. Proctor,
99 acres, N. W. Sec. 1,
Stockbridge.

Geo. H. Proctor,
68 acres, N. W. Sec. 2,
Stockbridge.

Wm. Cobb,
200 acres, N. W. Sec. 35,
Stockbridge.

Hugh A. McColl,
100 acres, N. W. Sec. 35,
Stockbridge.

Joshua Whitney,
160 acres, S. W. Sec. 28,
Stockbridge.

Benjamin Judson,
200 acres, S. W. Sec. 33,
Stockbridge.

Hugh H. McCloy,
200 acres, N. E. Sec. 36,
Stockbridge.

Wm. B. Craig,
120 acres, N. E. Sec. 25,
Stockbridge.

John Farmer,
40 acres, N. E. Sec. 25,
Stockbridge.

Geo. M. Westfall,
120 acres, S. E. Sec. 24,
Stockbridge.

S. P. Reynolds,
40 acres, N. W. Sec. 25,
Stockbridge.

Wm. C. Nichols,
180 acres, N. E. Sec. 23,
Stockbridge.

Chester Field,
75 acres, S. E. Sec. 6,
Stockbridge tp., Dansville P. O.

Charles H. Wood,
120 acres, S. E. Sec. 7,
Stockbridge.

Gershom M. Lyon,
80 acres, S. W. Sec. 16,
Stockbridge.

J. W. Doud,
147 acres, S. E. Sec. 11,
Stockbridge.

William Crossley,
53 acres, S. E. Sec. 11,
Stockbridge.

Wheeler Gaylord,
160 acres, S. E. Sec. 1,
Stockbridge tp., Plainfield P. O.

R. J. Townsend,
157 acres, N. E. Sec. 1,
Stockbridge.

Machagur Otis,
General Farmer 84 acres, Sec. 36,
Wheatfield tp., Dansville P. O.

M. J. Pollok,
Farmer & Dealer in Star Organs, 100 acres, Sec. 29,
Wheatfield tp., Dansville P. O.

Geo. M. Edgerton,
80 acres, Sec. 20,
Wheatfield tp., Dansville P. O.

BUSINESS CARDS OF PATRONS IN EATON COUNTY.

Evans, Avery & Co.,
Dealers in General Merchandise,
Bellevue.

Clark Sloan,
General Merchant Dealer in Stock, Grain, etc.
Dimondale.

Stuart Hutt,
Dealer in Dry goods, Groceries, Grain and Wool,
Dimondale.

I. N. Reynolds,
Groceries, Boots Shoes, and Produce,
Eaton Rapids.

B. T Esler,
Dealer in General Merchandise,
Grand Ledge.

O. Johnson,
Merchant,
Grand Ledge.

M. A. Collins,
General Store Keeper, and Post Master,
Kalamo.

E. L. Sargent,
Merchant,
Olivet.

J. W. Potter & Co.,
General Dealers. Postmaster.
Potterville.

H. O. Merritt,
Merchant,
Potterville.

W. H. Wilmont,
Dealer in Fancy Goods,
Walton.

MILLERS.

Gardiner, Warren & Co.,
Merchant and Custom Millers,
Bellevue.

E. W. Hunt,
Dealer in grain, Dimondale Mills,
Dimondale.

Aaron Nest,
Miller and Stone Cutter,
Eaton Rapids.

K. C. Wright,
Miller and Dealer in Agricultural Implements.
Eaton Rapids.

Wm. Kite,
Proprietor of Carlisle Grist Mill,
Kalamo.

B. H. Rose,
Planing Mill, Shingles, etc.
Grand Ledge.

Joseph C. Dutcher,
Miller,
Grand Ledge.

E. F. Kent,
Grand Ledge Mills, (Kent, Hixson & Co.)
Grand Ledge.

A. L. Green,
Merchant Miller and Lumberman,
Olivet.

MILLINERS.

Mrs. M Dyer,
General Millinery and Fancy Goods,
Eaton Rapids.

T. L. & L. L. Emmerson,
Milliners,
Olivet.

MINISTER.

Gustarus Ellis,
Pastor M. E. Church,
Potterville.

NEWSPAPERS & PRINTERS.

J. V. Johnson & Co.,
Steam Job Printers, and Publishers of
the Democratic Leader,
Charlotte.

Joseph Saunders & Co.,
Job Printers and Publishers of the Charlotte
Republican.
Charlotte.

Wm. S. Trask,
Printer,
Charlotte

Frank C. Culley,
Steam Book and Job Printer, and Publisher of
Eaton Rapids Journal.
Eaton Rapids.

B. W. Blanchard,
Printer, Grand Ledge Independent,
Grand Ledge.

NURSERYMEN.

A. F. Gaylord,
Nurseryman. All kinds of Fruit and Ornamental
Trees. Eaton Rapids.

L. S. Benham & Bros.,
Nurserymen and Florists,
Olivet.

PHOTOGRAPHERS.

A. P. Rall,
Photographer,
Eaton Rapids.

J. B. DeLamater,
Photographer,
Grand Ledge.

PHYSICIANS.

P. F. Taylor,
Physician and Druggist,
Bellevue.

S. W. Sleater,
Physician and Surgeon,
Charlotte.

Amos Knight, M. D.,
Physician and Surgeon,
Eaton Rapids.

Jas. H. Wellings,
Grand Ledge.

G. S. Messenger, M. D,
Grand Ledge,

C. J. Covey, M. D.,
Grand Ledge.

Dr. L. P. Huzen & Griswold,
Homœopathic Physicians,
Olivet.

E. C. Palmer,
Physician and Surgeon,
Potterville.

L. J. Ford, M. D.,
Special Agent for Electric Life Ins. Co., N. Y.,
Potterville.

C. J. Lane,
Eclectic and Homoeopathic Physician and Surgeon.
Vermontville.

Wm. Parmenter,
Physician and Surgeon,
Vermontville.

L. Dewey,
Botanic Physician and Surgeon,
Vermontville.

PICTURE DEALER.

B. W. Pinch,
Dealer in Pictures,
Olivet.

PHRENOLOGIST.

M. S. Kibby,
Professor of Phrenology,
West Windsor.

PROVISION DEALERS.

S. Drake & Curtis,
Dealers in all kinds of Salt and Fresh Meats,
Eaton Rapids.

Real Estate, R. R., and other Agts.

Mills & Dwinell,
Real Estate, Insurance and Loan Agents,
Charlotte.

Wm. I. McMaster,
Agent, D. L. & L. M. R. R.,
Grand Ledge.

J. H. Golden,
R. R. Agent,
Vermontville.

Jesse Chance,
Agt. for Canton Wrought Iron Bridge Co.,
Vermontville.

RETIRED.

Levi D. Mitchell,
Grand Ledge.

SAWYER.

George Thompson,
Sawyer,
Eaton Rapids.

SEWING MACHINES, &C.

H. S. Cassidy,
Supervising Agent for the Elias Howe Machine
Company for Eaton County,
Charlotte.

James T. Sargent,
Agent for Sewing Machines, Organs, Pianos, &c.,
Eaton Rapids.

J. M. Lampman,
Agent for the Elias Howe Sewing Machine,
Vermontville.

TAILOR.

J. T. Wellman,
Fashionable Tailor.
Cutting and Fitting neatly done, on short notice.
Grand Ledge.

TEACHERS.

William Follett,
Teacher,
Bellevue.

Salvia Rider,
Section 6,
Chester.

Wm. H. Simpson,
Teacher,
Grand Ledge.

Wm. P. Tinker,
Teacher,
Sec. 35, Kalamo.

O. Hosford,
Professor of Mathematics in Olivet College,
Olivet.

A. B. Brown,
Professor of Music in Olivet College,
General Dealer in Music and Musical Instruments
Olivet.

Miss H. P. Dennis,
Principal Ladies' Department, Olivet College,
Olivet.

Joseph L. Daniels,
Professor of Greek in Olivet College,
Olivet.

Nimon Dell & Nell Galusha,
Teachers,
Olivet.

Miss Mary Weddel,
Teacher,
Olivet.

Leroy A. Jackson,
Teacher,
Potterville.

W. D. Southworth,
Teacher,
Potterville,

Magley Ashley,
School Teacher,
Windsor.

Leonidas H. McQuoun,
Teacher,
40 acres, Sec. 7, Windsor.

D. B. Hall,
Principal of Vermontville High School.
Vermontville.

Miss Lizzie McCotter,
Teacher,
Vermontville.

TIN SMITH.

H. L. Curtis,
Tin Smith,
Vermontville.

WAGONS.

A. G. Wright,
Dealer in Wagons and Agricultural Implements,
Olivet.

WELL DIGGER.

A. Ketchum,
Well Digger,
Olivet.

BUSINESS CARDS OF PATRONS IN IONIA COUNTY.

AGENT.

D. M. Howie,
Ag't. D. & M. R. R. and Telegraph Operator,
Pewamo.

H. P. Taylor,
Real Estate and Insurance Agent,
Montcalm, Kenosha, Clara, Lake, Maxon, Osceola, Vevay, &c.,
Ransomers, Sherwicks, Ionia and Wexford Counties,
Ionia City.

H. M. Goodwin,
Insurance,
Ionia and Montcalm Counties,
Ionia City.

AGRICULTURAL IMPLEMENTS.

R. K. Smith,
Agent for Mowing Machines
and Agricultural Implements. Farmer, 50 acres,
Hubbardston.

Willett & Yates,
Agricultural Warehouse,
Ionia.

ARCHITECT.

Henry B. W. Vanzallingen,
Architect and Builder,
Ionia.

ATTORNEYS.

Oscar F. Wisner,
Attorney at Law,
Solicitor in Chancery and Notary Public,
Hubbardston.

Seneca Woolfen,
Attorney at Law and Solicitor in Chancery.
Hubbardston.

Alexander W. Dodge,
Attorney, Solicitor and Counsellor,
Ionia.

A. Williams,
Attorney at Law,
Ionia.

J. S. Bennett,
Attorney at Law,
Ionia.

F. S. Hutchinson,
Attorney at Law,
Ionia.

Wm. Oliver Webster,
Attorney at Law,
Ionia.

Wm. B. Thomas,
Attorney at Law and Justice of the Peace,
Ionia City.

G. W. Beelman,
Attorney at Law and Solicitor in Chancery,
Ionia.

Benjamin Vospar,
Attorney at Law and City Clerk,
Ionia City.

A. F. Bell,
Attorney at Law,
Ionia City.

A. B. N. Morse,
Attorney at Law,
Ionia City.

B. F. Spencer,
Attorney at Law,
Ionia City.

Albert K. Roof,
Attorney at Law.
Lyons.

A. J. Southard,
Justice of the Peace and Attorney at Law,
Portland.

A. D. McCabe,
Attorney at Law, &c.,
Portland.

T. D. Scofield,
Attorney at Law,
Portland.

Wilson & Stickland,
Attorneys and Solicitors,
Saranac.

B. D. Hudson,
Attorney at Law,
Saranac.

AUCTIONEER.

J. A. Brokaw,
Auctioneer and Restaurant,
Portland.

BANKS & BANKERS.

Hubbardston Exchange Bank,
E. B. Perceval, Cashier,
Hubbardston.

N. B. Hayes & Co.,
N. B. Hayes, Wm. H. Freeman, S. W. Webber,
Bankers,
Hubbardston.

A. F. Carr,
Cashier First National Bank,
Ionia City.

Geo. W. Webber,
Vice Pres. Second National Bank.
Ionia City.

Amasa Lee,
Banker & Farmer, 135 acres, Sec. 23,
Keene.

John A. Weber,
Banker,
Portland.

S. W. Webber & Co.,
Bankers and Brokers,
Lyons.

S. W. Webber,
Vice President First National Bank,
Muir.

BLACKSMITHS.

James A. Anderson,
Blacksmithing and Carriage Maker,
Muir.

N. R. Shults,
Blacksmith,
Wood's Corner.

Duncan Kennedy,
Blacksmith,
Portland.

W. T. Smith,
Blacksmith,
Portland.

BUTCHER.

Sylvanus Goff,
Meat Market,
Portland.

CARPENTERS.

H. S. Babcock,
Carpenter,
Berlin.

George L. Allen,
Carpenter,
Berlin.

CLERGYMEN.

Rev. C. G. Bolte,
Pastor St. Peter's Church,
Ionia.

D. F. Barnes,
Presiding Elder of Ionia Dist.,
Mich. Annual Conference,
Ionia City.

Rev. J. Pierson,
Pastor First Pres. Church,
Ionia City.

A. B. Hicks,
Pastor 1st Baptist Church,
Lyons.

A. Cornell,
Pastor of Baptist Church,
Portland.

A. P. Moors,
Pastor of M. E. Church,
Portland,

Augustus Marsh,
Pastor of Presbyterian Church,
Portland.

L. P. Spelman,
Pastor of Congregational Church,
Portland.

A. M. Sowle,
Pastor of Universalist Church,
Portland.

COUNTY OFFICERS.

E. F. Gifford,
Sheriff of Ionia County,
Ionia City.

Amasa Sessions,
Dept. County Clerk,
Ionia City.

A. H. Heath,
Register of Deeds,
Ionia.

H. C. Sessions,
County Clerk,
Ionia.

DRUGGISTS.

Kelly & Son,
Druggists,
Lyons.

Tremayne & Webster,
Druggist,
Portland.

Ross & Ewing,
Drug and Book Store,
Portland.

ENGINEER.

B. Flint,
Ronald.

FARMERS.

Peleg Eddy,
120 acres, Sec. 10,
Berlin.

Wm. C. Reed,
120 acres, Sec's. 10 & 15,
Berlin.

Wm. Doty,
85 acres,
Berlin.

Alonzo Sessions,
800 acres, Sec's. 32, 33 & 34,
Berlin.

L. J. Barnard,
220 acres, Sec's. 14 & 23,
Berlin.

C. D. Mitchell,
120 acres, Sec. 23,
Berlin.

Wm. Letts,
85 acres, Sec. 24,
Berlin.

George Hosford,
Grape Grower, and Wine Manufacturer,
80 acres, Sec. 25,
Berlin.

Lyman Simmons,
160 acres, Sec. 11,
Berlin.

David O. Branson,
110 acres, Sec's. 4 & 5,
Berlin.

H. P. Gates,
80 acres, Sec. 5,
Berlin.

Zephaniah Gates,
40 acres, Sec. 4 & 5,
Berlin.

D. R. Hartwell,
175 acres, Sec. 8 & 8,
Berlin.

T. D. Hartwell,
320 acres Sec's. 8 & 9,
Berlin.

G. S. Bryant,
Boston.

J. H. Allen,
240 acres,
Boston.

N. K. Farmer,
70 acres,
Boston.

A. S. Stannard,
400 acres, Sec's. 29 & 32,
South Boston.

Sanford A. Yeomans,
450 acres, Sec. 28,
Easton.

Curtis Merifield,
Retired farmer and money loaner, Sec. 13.
Easton.

Ezra W. North,
160 acres, Sec. 16,
Easton.

J. Snell,
216 acres, Sec. 8,
Easton.

J. C. Snell,
125 acres, Sec. 6,
Easton.

Wm. H. Annable,
360 acres, Sec. 26 & 27,
Easton.

A. A. Kellogg,
Easton.

Silas Sprague,
120 acres, Sec. 21,
Easton.

W. A. Inman,
190 acres, Sec's. 23, 25 & 26,
Easton.

Henry Jackson,
80 acres, Sec. 1,
Easton.

Jerry Spaulding,
240 acres, Sec. 10,
Ionia.

Alonzo Rice,
120 acres, Sec's. 4 & 32,
Ionia.

James L. Fowler,
120 acres, Sec. 33,
Ionia.

J. B. Welch,
807 acres, Sec's. 9, 10 & 4,
Ionia.

B. H. Bentley,
120 acres, Sec's. 8 & 5,
Ionia.

Wm. Sessions,
200 acres,
Ionia.

B. J. Green,
200 acres, Sec's. 1 & 2,
Ionia.

John A. Sessions,
160 acres,
Ionia.

L. Burdick,
296 acres, Sec's. 1 & 3,
Ionia.

A. G. Benedict,
160 acres, Sec. 2,
Ionia.

Eva Levalley,
104 acres, Sec's. 7 & 12,
Ionia.

Darius Stone,
200 acres, Sec's 11 & 12,
Ionia.

John B. Chase,
196 acres, Sec. 2,
Ionia.

G. J. Hayes,
121 acres, Sec. 11,
Ionia.

Darius Stone,
200 acres, Sec. 12,
Ionia.

Thomas Cornell,
Farmer and Surveyor,
Sec's. 24 & 25,
Ionia City.

W. E. Hall,
95 acres, Sec. 10,
Keene tp., Saranac P. O.

Vine Welch,
240 acres, Sec. 22,
Keene.

G. R. Sayles,
160 acres, Sec. 27,
Keene tp., Lowell P. O.

Adam L. Roof,
Stock, Grain, Fruit and Hay,
400 acres, Sec's. 24 & 19,
Lyons.

Patrick M. Fox,
Lumberman & Farmer, 431 acres,
Lyons.

W. H. Fox,
Farmer & Money Loaner, 350 acres,
Lyons.

A. Y. Sessions,
160 acres, Sec's. 23 & 26,
North Plains tp., Matherton P. O.

E. R. Williams,
240 acres, Sec's. 15 & 16,
North Plains.

J. O. Williams,
166 acres, Sec. 16,
North Plains.

N. B. Hayes,
Farmer & Lumberman, Stock, Grain Wool, and
Fruit, 980 acres, Sec. 31,
North Plains.

S. O. Hosford,
Farmer and Tradesman, 80 acres, Sec. 13,
Odessa tp., South Cass P. O.

Sam'l B. Chipman,
Gen'l Farming, 160 acres, Sec. 38,
Odessa tp., South Cass P. O.

E. Stephen Russell,
Gen'l Farmer, Sec. 27,
Odessa tp., South Cass P. O.

E. Cramer,
Gen'l Farmer, 106 acres, Sec. 35,
Odessa tp., South Cass P. O.

Solomon Foght,
Gen'l Farmer, 240 acres,
Odessa tp., South Cass P. O.

Volentine Bretz,
Gen'l Farmer, 120 acres, Sec. 35,
Odessa tp., South Cass P. O.

David Crapo,
General Farmer, Land Selector, 200 acres, Sec. 36,
Odessa tp., Lake City P. O.

D. W. Godard,
General Farmer, 144 acres, Sec. 31,
Odessa tp., Lake City P. O.

Asa Houghton,
100 acres, Sec's. 25 & 26,
Orleans.

A. G. Hubbell,
57 acres, Sec. 25,
Orleans.

Elisha Cheney,
155 acres, Sec's. 25 & 26,
Orleans.

Joshua J. Hall,
240 acres, Sec. 86,
Orleans.

Henry Hall,
120 acres, Sec's. 25 & 36,
Orleans.

Daniel Hoyt,
120 acres, Sec. 21,
Orleans.

Charles Hurd,
200 acres, Sec's. 15 & 16,
Orleans, Palmer Sta.

Albert Dorr,
Farmer and Station Agent, 140 acres, Sec's. 8 & 9,
Orleans, Chadwick Sta.

L. P. Beddington,
40 acres, Sec. 24,
Orleans.

Russel Wood,
120 acres, Sec. 24,
Orleans, tp. Wood's Corners.

Samuel Long,
80 acres, Sec's. 2 & 3,
Otisco.

B. R. Cook,
500 acres,
Otisco tp., Cooks Corners,

Freeman Killborn,
80 acres, Sec. 26,
Otisco.

Abijah Rich,
120 acres, Sec. 26,
Otisco.

Wm. R. Douglass,
80 acres, Sec. 30,
Otisco.

E. D. Purdy,
80 acres, Sec. 19,
Otisco.

Wm. Gardner,
Hotel Keeper, and Farmer,
Otisco tp. Smyrna.

Albert Van Vleck,
1,250 acres, Sec's. 1, 2, 10, 11 & 12,
Palo.

Wm. H. Woodworth,
Judge of Probate and Farmer, 360 acres, Sec. 14,
Pewamo P. O., Lyons tp.

J. M. Benedict,
Stock, Wool, Grain and Fruit,
130 acres, Sec. 18,
Portland.

Josiah Dilley,
Stock, Grain Wool and Fruit, Dealer in Real Estate
and all kind of Staves, 160 acres, Sec. 14,
Portland.

H. Bartow,
Dealer in Real Estate, 230 acres, Sec. 33,
Portland.

N. P. Shuert,
Stock, Wool, Grain and Fruit,
Ag't Weed's Sewing Machines, 120 acres, Sec. 33,
Portland.

George A. Dow,
Grain, Fruit, and Stock, 37 acres, Sec. 27,
Portland.

M. J. Taylor,
Grain, Wool, Stock and Fruit,
207 acres, Sec. 18,
Portland.

L. A. Smith,
480 acres Sec. 10,
Portland.

S. K. Welch,
316 acres, Sec. 10,
Portland.

Henry Hubbell,
140 acres, Sec. 81,
Ronald.

N. R. Brooks,
140 acres, Sec. 32,
Ronald.

Alonzo Hubbell,
155 acres, Sec. 31,
Ronald.

Allen J. Mattison,
300 acres, Sec. 35,
Ronald.

Peter Van Vleck,
400 acres, Sec's. 2 & 3,
Ronald.

Oscar Talcot,
80 acres, Sec. 27,
Ronald.

Seth Burk,
120 acres, Sec. 21,
Ronald.

J. P. Powell,
400 acres, Sec's. 33 & 34,
Ronald.

Eli T. Conkey,
240 acres, Sec. 17,
Ronald.

Harvey Dye,
160 acres, Sec. 7,
Ronald.

George Frey,
Farmer and Physician, 335 acres, Sec. 7,
Ronald.

H. J. Allen,
160 acres, Sec. 5,
Ronald.

J. C. Jennings,
200 acres, Sec. 16,
Ronald.

Myron Shauker,
Ronald.

L. J. Mosher,
240 acres, Sec. 20,
Ronald.

Melvin Allen,
171 acres,
Ronald, North Plains P. O.

Wm. H. Bentley,
140 acres, Sec. 13,
Ronald, North Plains.

W. M. Steere,
200 acres, Sec. 10,
Ronald.

George J. Story,
75 acres, Sec. 18,
South Boston.

HOTELS.

George C. Baker,
Proprietor of Hotel,
Boston.

A. J. Van Slyke,
Proprietor Sherman House,
Ionia.

Olmsted House,
Jay Olmsted, Proprietor,
Muir.

W. B. Stannard,
Exchange Hotel,
Pewamo.

BUSINESS CARDS OF PATRONS IN IONIA COUNTY.

E. C. Marcy,
Proprietor of Portland House,
Portland.

A. J. Dean,
Proprietor of Hotel,
Wood's Corners.

INSURANCE.

F. S. Freeman,
Insurance,
Ionia.

C. L. Smith,
Life Insurance Agent,
Ionia.

Justice of the Peace.

Sylvestus Taylor,
Justice of the Peace,
Ionia.

LIVERY.

George Borden & Co.,
Livery,
Ionia City.

Wm. Moore,
Portland Livery and Sale Stable,
Portland.

Chas. E. Allen,
Livery,
Portland.

LUMBER.

A. R. Covey,
Lumberman,
Belding.

Hubbardston Lumber Company,
N. Rogers, Secretary & Treas.,
Hubbardston.

Joseph Dunn,
Gratiot, Montcalm, Ogemaw, Ionia,
Otsego, Gladwin and Isabella Counties,
Ionia City.

Wm. C. Niles,
Lumberman,
Ionia City.

C. W. Colby,
Manufacturer of Lumber,
Ionia City.

E. H. Stanton & Co.,
Manuf'rs & Dealers in Lumber,
Ionia.

Noah Bean,
Lumberman,
Muir.

E. H. Dakin,
Stock and Lumber Dealer,
Muir.

Geo. W. French,
Dealer in Lumber, Lath & Shingles,
Muir.

W. P. Hewitt,
Manuf'r of Lumber & Shingles,
Muir.

Asaph Mather,
Lumberman, 400 acres, Sec. 24,
North Plains.

Taylor & Benedict,
Lumber, Lath & Ag'l. Implements,
Portland.

MACHINISTS.

Stuck & Palmer,
Foundrymen and Machinists,
Hubbardston.

Thomas S. Tew,
Founder and Machinist,
Ionia.

E. A. Chuble,
Founder and Machinist,
Ionia.

James H. Burgess,
Sawyer and Machinist,
Muir.

James A. Sage,
Foundryman and Machinist,
Smyrna.

MANUFACTURERS.

R. Hearsey,
Manuf'rs. Sash, Doors & Blinds,
Ionia City.

H. C. Morse,
Sash, Doors and Blinds,
Ionia City.

C. Waterbury,
Sash, Doors & Blinds,
Ionia City.

W. H. Vanderhayden,
Manuf'r of Brick and Drawn Tile,
Ionia City.

Robinson & Turner,
Manuf'rs of Pumps & Plows. Foundry,
Lyons.

Londal Engalls,
Carriage and Wagon Manufacturer,
Lyons.

Fosmir & Sherman,
Carriage and Wagon Manuf'rs,
Lyons.

C. Swarthart,
Furniture Manufacturer,
Muir.

W. V. Weeden,
Dealer in Staves,
Pewamo.

C. W. Bailey,
Stave and Heading Factory,
Portland.

Portland Woolen Mill Co.,
Manuf'rs of Woolen Goods, Yarn, &c.,
Portland.

Charles Storm,
Manuf'r and Dealer in Harness, &c.,
Portland.

Goss & Porter,
Manuf'rs & Dealers in the Duckere Force Pumps,
Portland.

C. H. Gilden,
Manuf'r of Wagons and Carriages,
Portland.

Bowser, Griffin & Co.,
Sash, Door & Blind Factory,
Portland.

T. J. Bandfield,
Manuf'r and Dealer in Rich and Plain Furniture,
Portland.

Bice & Blanchard,
Undertakers and Furniture Dealers,
Portland.

Thos. J. Hitchcock,
Foreman School Furniture Factory,
Portland.

S. K. Gates,
Foundrymen,
also Supervisor and Justice of the Peace,
Portland.

Hill & Storm,
Iron Works and Machine Shop,
Manuf'rs of Newman's Turbine Water Wheel,
Portland.

W. T. S. Cardy,
Handle Manufacturer,
Saranac.

W. Fox,
Manufacturer and Dealer in Staves,
Saranac.

MARBLE DEALERS.

James L. Dearin,
Dealer in all kind of American & Foreign Marble
For Monuments and Tomb Stones,
Portland.

E. M. Van Antwerp,
Marble Cutter,
Portland.

MASONS.

Perry Hawry,
Mason,
Portland.

Harvey Howe,
Bricklayer &c.,
Portland.

MERCHANTS.

D. S. Bennett,
Groceries, Provisions and Yankee Notions,
Hubbardston.

H. W. Hitchcock,
Hardware Dealer,
Hubbardston.

A. M. Drake,
Dealer in Boots, Shoes & Groceries,
Hubbardston.

A. J. Welch,
Grocer & Drover & Dealer in Stock,
Ionia City.

Smith & Lowe,
Booksellers & Newsdealers,
Ionia City.

F. J. Lemon,
Wholesale Grocery Merchant,
Ionia.

E. L. Irish,
Drug Store,
Ionia.

G. S. Cooper,
Cooper & Thayer, Dry Goods,
Ionia.

L. H. Thayer,
Cooper & Thayor, Dry Goods,
Ionia.

H. Rich,
Dry Goods,
Ionia.

Cooper, Wilson & Wood,
Wholesale and Retail Dealers in Dry Goods,
Ionia.

William H. L. Smoke,
Dealer in Lime, Coal, Salt, Hair, &c.,
Ionia.

Charles Dean & Co.,
Dealer in Grain, Salt, Coal, Lime, &c.,
Ionia.

Benjamin Harter,
Merchant,
Ionia.

O. & O. S. Tower,
Hardware,
Ionia.

W. S. Barnard,
Books, Stationery, Notions, &c.,
Lyons.

J. O. Probasco,
Hardware Merchant,
Muir.

Abbey, French & Co.,
General Merchandise, Dry Goods, Groceries.
Boots & Shoes, Hats Caps & Ready-made Clothing
Muir.

Charles Chadwick,
Dry Goods & Groceries. Station and Wood Agen'
on D. L. & M. R. R.,
Orleans tp., Chadwick Sta.

Jno. Pennington,
Merchant,
Dry Goods, Groceries, Notions &c. Postmaster,
Pewamo.

J. J. Ludwick,
Merchant,
Dry Goods, Groceries, Boots & Shoes,
Pewamo.

A. S. Pettinger,
Flour and Feed Store,
Pewamo.

Bowser Bros.,
General Grocers and Dealers in Groceries.
Crockery, Glassware, &c.,
Portland.

Harvey Knox,
Grocer,
Portland.

A. C. Cadwell & Co.,
Merchants,
Portland.

John D. Woodbury,
General Merchant,
Portland.

F. M. Critcheon,
Boots, Shoes and Book Store,
Portland.

Delos G. Smith,
Dry Goods and Clothing,
Portland.

C. H. Hunter & Co.,
Dry Goods and Clothing,
Portland.

H. G. Stevens,
Hardware Dealer,
Portland.

J. C. Catharin,
Hardware Dealer,
Portland.

Weld & Halladay,
Dry Goods and Groceries,
Portland.

J. J. Young,
Dealer in Dry Goods,
Saranac.

A. H. Northway,
Merchant,
Smyrna.

MILLERS.

G. M. Jones,
Miller,
Hubbardston.

S. S. Millard,
Miller,
Ionia.

John Hale,
Proprietor "Gothic Mills,"
Lyons.

Olmstead & Gardner,
Milling and Produce,
Muir.

George B. Fish,
Miller,
Otisco.

Robert Boyce,
Proprietor Pewamo Grist and Flour Mills,
Pewamo.

R. B Smith,
Miller,
Portland.

Newman Hixon & Co.,
Millers & Dealers in Grain, Flour & Feed,
Portland.

Joseph D. Sterns,
Saw Mill and Sash Factory,
Smyrna.

NEWSPAPERS.

A. V. Phister,
Proprietor of Advertiser,
Hubbardston.

T. G. Stevenson & Co.,
Publishers Ionia Sentinel,
Ionia.

B. Bement,
Grand-River Herald,
Muir.

Joseph W. Bailey,
Editor of Portland Observer,
Portland.

PAINTER.

H. L. Cumming,
Painter and Glazier,
Ronald.

PATTERN MAKER.

W. R. White,
Pattern Maker,
Ionia City.

PHYSICIANS.

F. R. Allen M. D.,
Homœopathic Physician,
Ionia City.

S. M. Bayard,
Physician and Surgeon.
Ionia City.

T. George Ranney M. D.,
Operating Surgeon,
Ionia City.

D. C. Spalding,
Physician and Surgeon,
Lyons.

James M. Barnard,
Physician and Surgeon,
Portland.

M. B. Beers,
Physician and Surgeon,
Portland.

Chester Smith,
Physician and Surgeon,
Portland.

H. H. Power,
Physician,
Saranac.

A. P. C. Jones,
Physician and Surgeon,
Saranac.

Charles Wunch,
Surgeon,
Saranac.

C. W. Dolley,
Physician and Surgeon,
Smyrna.

POSTMASTER.

Wm. Root,
Postmaster,
Portland.

RAILROADMEN.

F. G. Compton,
Train Dispatcher,
Mill Creek P. O., Kent Co.

Hiram B. Harrington,
Railroadman,
Portland.

REAL ESTATE.

John E. Morrison,
Real Estate,
Ionia.

Frederick Hall,
Real Estate,
Ionia.

SEWING MACHINES.

S. E. Whitney,
Agent Wilson Sewing Machine,
Portland.

SPORTSMAN.

L. W. Van Hood,
American Sportsman,
Portland.

SURVEYOR.

S. C. Alderman,
Surveyor,
Ionia City.

TAILOR.

Hiram A. Dow,
Tailor, Sec. 27,
Portland.

TEACHERS.

J. W. Ewing,
Principal Ionia Union School,
Ionia City.

Mary C. Davenport,
Teacher,
Keene.

John McQuillin,
Teacher,
Lyons.

W. H. Stone,
Principal Public Schools of Portland,
Portland.

O. C. Browning,
Music Teacher,
Portland.

Anna M. Woolridge,
Teacher,
Sebewa.

C. F. Braden,
Teacher,
Sebewa.

WAGONS & CARRIAGES.

D. A. Dimll,
Wagons and Carriages,
Ionia City.

WATCH MAKER.

D. A. Simmons,
Watch Maker & Jeweler,
Portland.

UNITED STATES LAND OFFICE.

J. S. Jennings,
Receiver,
Ionia City.

ADDITIONAL BUSINESS CARDS OF PATRONS IN JACKSON COUNTY.

BANKING.

Orren Gillett,
Banking Office,
Palmer.

BLACKSMITHS.

Swezey & Moulton,
Carriage Ironing and General Blacksmithing.
Grass Lake.

E. M. Covert,
General Blacksmithing,
All kind of Repairs promptly done,
Napoleon.

Charles G. Calkins,
Wagon Maker and General Blacksmith.
All kind of Repairs promptly done,
Napoleon.

BUTCHER.

Russell Talmage,
Butcher,
Napoleon.

CLERGYMEN.

Rev. George Williams,
Pastor 1st Congregational Church,
Grass Lake.

Rev. R. S. Pardington,
Pastor M. E. Church,
Grass Lake.

Otis Saxton,
Pastor Baptist Church,
Grass Lake.

O. F. A. Spinning,
State S. S. Missionary of Baptist S. S. Association,
Grass Lake.

FARMERS.

S. W. Cooper,
Sec. 25, S. E.,
Franciscoville.

Gilbert Rowe,
Sec. 25, S. W.,
Franciscoville.

Dorman Felt,
Sec. 25, S. W.,
Franciscoville.

John Notten,
Sec. 24, N. E.,
Franciscoville.

Samuel Updike,
Sec. 31, N. W.,
Grass Lake.

M. K. Crafts,
Sec. 31, N. W.,
Franciscoville.

Mrs. A. W. Palmer,
Sec. 28, S. W.,
Grass Lake.

Samuel Bunker,
Sec. 29, N. W.,
Grass Lake.

John Bunker,
Sec. 30, N. E.,
Grass Lake.

Henry H. Hobart,
Sec. 32, S. W.,
Grass Lake.

John C. Phelps,
Sec. 33, N. W.
Grass Lake.

I. M. Sanford,
Sec. 28, N. E.,
Grass Lake.

O. F Pease,
Sec. 33, S. W.,
Grass Lake.

H. D. Raymond,
Sec. 33, S. W.,
Grass Lake.

Jerome Watkins,
Sec. 34, S. E.,
Grass Lake.

Enos C. Osborn,
Sec. 33, S. W.
Grass Lake.

James Clark,
Sec. 8, N. W. ¼,
Grass Lake.

Peter Haynes,
Sec. 17,
Grass Lake.

BUSINESS CARDS OF PATRONS IN JACKSON COUNTY.

John C. Love,
120 acres, Sec. 12, S. W.,
Brooklyn tp., Columbia P. O.

S. S. Barstow,
160 acres, Sec. 24, S. W.,
Brooklyn tp., Columbia P. O.

Hiram Crego,
162 acres, Sec. 32, N. W.,
Brooklyn tp., Columbia P. O.

A. H. De Lamater,
Columbia.

Jackson De Lamater,
160 acres, Sec. 21, N. W.,
Columbia.

Charles De Lamater,
160 acres, Sec. 21, N. W.,
Columbia.

Asa Charles,
200 acres, Sec. 9, S. E.,
Columbia.

John Russell,
91 acres, Sec. 16,
Columbia.

Wm. J. Cary,
40 acres, Sec. 17, N. E.,
Columbia.

Gordon Hitt,
100 acres, Sec. 17, S. E.,
Columbia.

Alphonso Nash,
90 acres, Sec. 17, N. E.,
Columbia.

Harvey Pierce,
270 acres, Sec. 28, N. W.,
Columbia.

E. Pratt,
68 acres, Sec. 14, N. E.,
Columbia.

E. Robinson,
Sec. 3, N. E.,
Franciscoville.

L. Cady,
Sec. 18, N. W. ¼.
Grass Lake.

S. S. Clark,
Sec. 5,
Grass Lake.

Elisha E. Swift,
Sec. 8,
Grass Lake.

E. W. Clark,
Sec. 8, N. W., ¼
Grass Lake.

H. M. Bunnell,
Sec. 8, S. W.,
Grass Lake.

Girard Cady,
Sec. 10, N. W.,
Grass Lake.

Osband T. Bush,
Sec. 8, N. W.,
Grass Lake.

Jacob Preston,
Sec. 2, N. W.,
Grass Lake.

William Preston,
Sec. 35, S. E.,
Grass Lake.

Isaac Wiborn,
Sec. 12, N. E.,
Grass Lake.

S. T. Smith,
Sec. 34, N. E.
Grass Lake.

H. E. Francisco,
Sec. 3, N. E.,
Grass Lake.

James Irwin,
Sec. 4, N. E.,
Grass Lake.

Horace Gifford,
75 acres, Sec. 2, S. W.,
Hanover tp., Baldwin P. O.,

A. G. Ayers,
240 acres, Sec. 10, N. E.,
Hanover tp., Baldwin P. O.,

Cornelius Sloat,
130 acres, Sec. 8, N. E.,
Liberty tp., S. Jackson P. O.

Wm. H. Foot,
240 acres, Sec. 28, N. E.
Liberty.

Philetus Lewis,
160 acres, Sec. 21, S. W.,
Liberty.

H. J. Crouch,
81 acres, Sec. 10, N. E.,
Liberty tp., S. Jackson P. O.

S. P. Angevine,
80 acres, Sec. 4, S. E.,
Liberty tp., S. Jackson P. O.

Richard Crouch,
210 acres, Sec. 3, S. W.,
Liberty tp., S. Jackson P. O.

Perry Wetherby,
120 acres, Sec. 12, N. E.,
Liberty.

G. G. Pond,
120 acres, Sec. 28, N. W.
Liberty.

Hiram Scott,
116 acres, Sec. 31,
Liberty.

Henry J. Crego,
200 acres, Sec. 10, S. E.
Liberty.

Prentes Palmer,
402 acres, Sec. 15, S. W.,
Liberty.

J. B. Hoagland,
80 acres, Sec. 11, N. W.,
Napoleon tp., Columbia P. O.,

B. F. Van Slyke,
Napoleon.

B. F. Ordiway,
Napoleon.

D. D. Morse,
Farmer and Wagon Maker, Sec. 25,
Napoleon.

D. D. Clark,
Napoleon.

J. Freeman,
Napoleon.

C. B. Palmer,
Sec. 1, 4 South, 1 East,
Napoleon.

C. B. Blackmar,
Sec. 1, 4 South, 2 East,
Napoleon.

Horace Dean,
Napoleon.

H. Pelham,
Sec. 35, 3 South, 1 East,
Napoleon.

E. A. Fuller,
Farmer and Joiner,
Napoleon.

Irvine Wood,
Sec. 1, 4 South, 2 East,
Napoleon.

J. R. Godfrey,
Sec. 24, N. E.,
Parma.

Lewis Brown,
Sec. 12, N. E.,
Parma.

Oliver R. Munn,
Sec 19, N. W.,
Sandstone tp., Parma P. O.

Edmund Upton,
Sec. 18, N. W.,
Sandstone tp., Parma P. O.

Jeff Smith,
Sec. 29,
Sandstone tp., Parma P. O.

Azariah Townsend,
Sec. 13, S. W.,
Sandstone tp., Parma P. O.,

J. C. Burchard,
239 acres, Sec. 22, N. W.,
Summit tp., Jackson P. O.,

George Facey,
172 acres, Sec. 22, S. W.,
Summit tp., Jackson P. O.,

Elisha Locke,
100 acres, Sec. 27, S. W.,
Summit tp., Jackson P. O.

John Scott,
82 acres, Sec. 14, N. W.,
Summit tp., Jackson P. O.

T. Boldrey,
240 acres, Sec. 35, N. W.,
Summit tp., S. Jackson P. O.,

D. B. Walworth,
80 acres, Sec. 23, N. E.,
Summit tp., Jackson P. O.

Abram Lee,
193 acres, Sec. 26, N. E.,
Summit tp., Jackson P. O.

Isaac Storm,
140 acres, Sec. 26, N. W.
Summit tp., Jackson P. O.

M. Van Gelson,
200 acres, Sec. 28, N. E.,
Summit tp., Jackson P. O.

J. C. Ives,
102 acres, Sec. 33, N. E.,
Summit tp., S. Jackson P. O.

E. B. Walworth,
77 acres, Sec. 34, S. W.,
Summit tp., S. Jackson P. O.,

Horace Webster,
80 acres, Sec. 32, N. W.,
Summit tp., Jackson P. O.,

Peter Lowe,
480 acres, Sec. 20, N. E.,
Summit tp., Jackson P. O.

A. M. Latimer,
80 acres, Sec. 9 S. W.,
Summit tp., Jackson P. O.

W. W. Rogers,
70 acres, Sec. 14, S. W.,
Summit tp., Jackson P. O.

James Draper,
115 acres, Sec. 24, S. W.
Summit tp., Jackson P. O.

G. C. Draper,
80 acres, Sec. 25, N. E.,
Summit tp., Jackson P. O.

L. G. Perry,
200 acres, Sec. 21, N. E.
Summit tp., Jackson P. O.

FURNITURE.

Henry Vinkle, Jr.,
Furniture Dealer,
Grass Lake.

HOTELS.

E. L. Lewis,
Proprietor Eagle Hotel,
Parma.

Updike & Longyear,
Union Hotel and Water Cure,
Grass Lake.

JOINERS.

William Hastings,
Joiner,
Napoleon.

A. J. Van Winkle,
Joiner,
Napoleon.

Justice of the Peace.

Lewis J. Pickett,
Justice of the Peace,
Columbia.

LAWYERS.

N. G. King,
Lawyer,
Brooklyn.

G. R. Palmer,
Law, Loan and Collecting Office,
Manchester.

MASON.

S. P. Hoskins,
Mason,
Napoleon.

MERCHANTS.

W. B. Ghenman,
Produce Commission,
Brooklyn.

A. P. Cook,
General Merchandise & Land Dealer,
Brooklyn.

BUSINESS CARDS OF PATRONS IN JACKSON COUNTY.

Dwelle & Raymond,
Druggist,
Grass Lake.

Smith G. Ray,
Grocery and Crockery Store,
Grass Lake.

Fargo, Lord & Co.,
Millers and Drovers,
Also Dealers in Dry Goods and Groceries,
Ready-made Clothing, Hats, Caps, Boots & Shoes,
Yankee Notions, &c.,
Salt, Water Lime, and Plaster, kept constantly
on hand. Cash paid for Wheat, Wool, Oats,
Dressed Pork, Hides & Pelts, and all kinds of
Country Produce. Also Banking Office for the Sale
of Eastern Exchange.
Grass Lake.

Wesley Burchard,
Dealer in Dry Goods, Groceries, Hats, Caps, Clothing,
Boots & Shoes, Notions, &c.,
also in all kinds of Country Produce,
Grass Lake.

J. C. Branch,
Dealer in General Merchandise,
Grass Lake.

George R. Chapman,
Dealer in Yankee Notions,
Books, Stationery and General News,
Grass Lake.

Edmond L. Cooper,
General Merchandise,
Grass Lake.

W. J. Weeks,
Dealer in Dry Goods, Groceries, Boots and Shoes,
Ready-made Clothing, Millinery Goods, Drugs & Medicines,
Hanover tp., Baldwin's P O.

L. B. Thorne,
Dealer in Dry Goods, Groceries,
Hardware, Notions, Patent Medicines, &c.,
Hanover tp., Baldwin's P. O.

Julius E. Lyon,
Merchant and Custom Miller,
Hanover tp., Baldwin P. O.

Dean & Peabody,
Dealers in Dry Goods, Hats, Caps, Boots & Shoes,
Ready-made Clothing, Hardware, Crockery, Groceries, &c.,
Hanover.

Nelson K. Elliott,
Merchant and Custom Miller,
Lake Mills.

Wm. M. Haynes,
Dry Goods & Groceries,
Liberty.

H. C. Greene,
Dealer in Groceries, Boots & Shoes,
Napoleon.

Jones Brothers,
General Merchants,
Napoleon.

Dr. Manley,
Druggist,
Napoleon.

J. Coldwell,
Hardware,
Napoleon.

Mark Miller,
Drugs and Groceries,
Parma.

Fargo & Lord,
Dealer in Dry Goods, General Merchandise
and Produce, Parma.

NOTARY PUBLIC.

Harmon M. Ford,
Conveyancer and War Claim Agent,
Ag't for Watertown & Agricultural Fire Ins. Co's,
Grass Lake.

PAINTERS.

Geo. W. Gallup,
House Painter,
Napoleon.

John Killeen,
Practical Painter and Grainer,
Napoleon.

George Killeen,
Practical Painter and Grainer,
Napoleon.

Jesse S. Brown,
Grainer,
Napoleon.

PHYSICIANS.

L. M. Jones,
Physician,
Brooklyn.

E. B. Chapin,
Physician and Surgeon,
Grass Lake.

Dr. McColl,
Physician &c.,
Napoleon.

D. A. Davis,
Homeopathic Physician.
Parma.

TAILORS.

John Malsieght,
Merchant Tailor,
Grass Lake.

Daniel Hedden,
Merchant Tailor,
Parma.

TEACHERS.

J. H. Coonradt,
Principal Public School.
Napoleon.

D. E. Haskin,
Principal Public School,
Parma.

BUSINESS CARDS OF PATRONS IN MOUNT CLEMENS.

ATTORNEYS.

Hubbard & Crocker,
Attorneys at Law,
Particular Attention given to Collections.

Edgar Weeks,
Attorney at Law.

B. P. & J. P. Eldridge,
Attorney at Law.

Joseph Chubb,
Attorney and Counsellor at Law.

BANKERS.

Daniel C. Tilden & Co.,
Bankers.

BLACKSMITHS.

W. S. Donelson,
Blacksmithing.

Parke & Bracey,
Blacksmithing and Horse Shoeing.

Andrew Donaldson,
Blacksmith and Iron Founder.

BOOKS & STATIONERY.

Jas. K. Snooks,
P. M. & Dealer in Books & Stationery.

BUILDERS.

H. O. Conner,
Builder.

George B. Walker,
Builder.

BUTCHER.

T. W. Newton,
Butcher and Pork Packer.

COUNTY OFFICIALS.

F. G. Hendrick,
Sheriff Macomb County.

C. S. Groesbeck.
County Clerk.

A. M. Keeler,
Abstract Office.

DENTIST.

George A. Rockham,
Dentist.

DRUGGIST.

H. W. Babcock,
Druggist.

FARMERS.

Campbell & Sackett,
900 acres.

A. Stewart,
Grain and Fruit Farmer,
105 acres, Sec. 24.

George Bacon,
Stock, Wool and Grain,
80 acres, Sec. 3.

C. D. Crittenden,
Ag't for sale of Farming Implements,
105 acres, Sec. 18.

Samuel Whitney,
Stock, Grain and Wool Farmer,
200 acres.

MANUFACTURERS.

Calvin Bush,
Lumber and Sash.

E. I. Tucker,
Pine Lumber and Shingles.

E. C. Gallop,
Dealer in Wool.

MERCHANTS.

T. Traver,
General Merchant.

T. W. Snook & Co.,
Merchants.

Hess, Kellogg & Co.,
Proprietors Mt. Clemens City Mills,
Merchant Millers & Grain Purchasers.

S. S. Gale,
Hardware and Stoves.

Robertson & Daley,
General Hardware Dealers.

Rooker & Lungershausen,
Hardware and Stoves.

J. W. Shook,
Produce Dealer.

MINISTERS.

H. N. Bissell,
Pastor Presbyterian Church.

J. T. Hankinson,
Pastor M. E. Church.

Sidney H. Woodford,
Rector Grace Church.

G. C. Tripp,
Pastor Baptist Church.

C. Ryckaert,
Pastor St. Peter's Church.

MONEY LOANER.

Robert Weltz,
Money Lender.

NEWSPAPERS.

W. T. Lee,
Editor Mt. Clemens Monitor.

John Trevidick,
Publisher of Press.

PHYSICIANS.

T. W. Hitchcock,
Physician and Surgeon.

H. Taylor, Jr.,
Physician.

H. R. Babcock,
Physician and Surgeon.

/

BUSINESS CARDS OF PATRONS IN MOUNT CLEMENS.

A. Hayward,
Homeopathic Physician & Surgeon.

Dr. N. Garand,
Physician and Surgeon.

PIANOS &C.

Otto Rasch,
Dealer in Pianos, Organs, Musical
Merchandise & Sewing Machines.

RAIL ROAD OFFICIALS.

W. H. Morgan,
Station Master.

W. H. Higgins,
Freight Agent.

REAL ESTATE.

J. B. Dickinson,
Dealer in Real Estate.

TEACHERS.

J. E. Bissell,
Principal Union School.

Carrie E. Richardson,
Teacher.

G. H. Snook,
Teacher.

Mahala A. Williams,
Teacher,

Sarah Bowman,
Teacher.

UNDERTAKER.

F. F. Chappell,
Undertaker.

WAGON MAKERS.

E. B. Drake,
Wagon, Carriage and
Sleigh Maker.

Joseph Chubb,
Carriage Maker and
Iron Founder.

WATCHMAKER.

F. H. Bentley,
Watch Maker,
and Jeweler. Fancy Goods,

BUSINESS CARDS OF PATRONS IN ROMEO.

ATTORNEYS.

Irving D. Hanscom,
Attorney at Law.

Dwight N. Lowell,
Attorney at Law.

ASSESSOR.

C. P. Dake,
Assessor Internal Revenue,
Fifth District.

BANKS.

First National Bank,
Capital $100,000.

Giddings & Moore,
Bankers.

BARBER.

J. K. L. Barbershop,
D. J. Harris, Proprietor,

BLACKSMITHS.

Edward Shipley,
Blacksmith.

J. F. Amsdan,
Blacksmith.

T. Lyon,
Blacksmith.

Carriage Manufacturers.

James H. Boden,
Carriage Manufacturer.

Ketcham Brothers,
Carriage Manufacturers.

Horace Bogart,
Manufacturer of Carriages.

A. H. Shelp,
Manufacturer of Buggies, Wagons
and Agricultural Implements.

CIGARS & TOBACCO.

H. W. Bradley,
Manuf'r of Cigars
and Dealer in Tobacco.

DENTIST.

S. J. Hayes,
Dentist.

DRUGGISTS.

Holland & Reade,
Druggists.

C. Y. Durand,
Dealer in Perfumes & Toilet Articles.

ENGINEERS.

Eugene Predmore,
Civil Engineer.

C. Fessenden,
Civil Engineer and Surveyor.

FARMERS.

Hon. D. S. Prest,
Farmer.

S. B. Cannon,
Tile Manuf'r and Farmer.

L. S. Edson,
Farmer and Stock Dealer,
1½ miles North East of Romeo.

J. L. Proctor,
Farmer,
¼ mile from Romeo.

S. A. Colby,
Farmer and Stock Raiser,
4½ miles from Romeo.

Thomas Dawson,
Farmer.

S. B. Cooley,
Farmer.

P. C. Killam,
Farmer and Lumber Dealer.

Harvey B. Dewey,
3½ miles West of Romeo.

Jacob H. Hosmer,
Farmer and Stock Raiser,
5 miles from Romeo.

M. L. Turrell,
Farmer.

George G. Hartung,
Farmer.

James J. Warner,
4 miles N. W. of Romeo.

T. S. Crisman,
4½ miles S. W. Romeo.

G. N. Brabb,
Farmer.

G. E. Graves,
Wheat and Wool Farmer,
160 acres, Sec. 32.

FURNITURE.

A. E. Palmer,
Undertaker
and Dealer in Furniture.

HOTELS.

Perry House,
Perry Brothers, Proprietors.

American Hotel,
J. D. Ellott, Proprietor.

IRON FOUNDERS.

Selfridge Brothers,
New York Shoeing Shop and Foundry.
All kinds fancy Job Work in Wrought or Cast Iron,
done with neatness.

JUSTICES.

Martin Buzzell,
Justice of the Peace
and General Insurance Agent.

E. S. Snover,
Justice of the Peace.

LIVERY.

Nathan H. Lee,
Livery.

MASON.

John Harrop,
Mason.

MARBLE WORKS.

Phillip P. Jersey,
Marble Works.

MANUFACTURERS.

Wm. F. McMullin,
Harness Manufacturer.

Hon. John N. Mellen,
Grain and Lumber Merchant.

Harvey Mellen,
Grain and Lumber.

A. Kennedy Waycott,
Sash, Doors and Blinds.

MERCHANTS.

W. R. Owen,
Jeweller and Bookseller.

N. Larzeller,
Grocer.

C. F. Mallory & Co.,
Shelf and Heavy
Hardware.

A. B. Rawles' Sons,
Hardware & Stoves.

Fred Engel,
Hardware and Stoves.

A. & J. Tillman,
Boots and Shoes.

P. H. McFarland.
Manuf'r of
Boots and Shoes.

J. L. Benjamin,
Produce Dealer.

H. J. Mann,
Dealer in Produce.

BUSINESS CARDS OF PATRONS IN ROMEO.

MILLERS.

James Gray,
Proprietor Clifton Mills.

Dexter Mussey,
Miller.

MINISTERS.

Horatio O. Ladd,
Pastor Congregational Church.

A. Martell,
Pastor
Baptist Church.

A. M. Lewis,
Rector
Episcopal Church.

J. S. Smart,
Pastor
M. E. Church.

MONEY LOANERS.

H. C. Grey,
Miller and Money Loaner.

John H. Brabb,
Money Loaner.

NEWSPAPER.

Samuel H. Ewell,
Editor
Romeo Observer.

PAINTER.

Wm. Keyes,
Carriage Painter.

PATTERN MAKER.

Schuyler Vandar,
Pattern Maker.

PHYSICIANS.

Philo Tillotson,
Practicing Physician.

Chamberlin & Clark,
Electic and Botanic
Physicians.

A. E. Leet,
Physician.

T. W. Stilt,
Physician and Surgeon,

Seth L. Andrew,
Physician and Surgeon.

Isaac Douglass D. D. S.,
Office at his Residence,
Opposite Gray's Block.

PENSION AGENT.

Daniel Wood,
Notary Public, Pension and
Insurance Agent.

PHOTOGRAPHERS.

Benjamin Cuyler,
Photographic Artist.

PIANOS.

L. G. Norton,
Dealer in Pianos, Organs
and Musical Merchandise,

PRINTER.

Jno. O. Hopkins,
Printer.

RAIL ROAD OFFICIALS.

P. H. Jamp,
Agent St. C. & C. R. R. A. L.

Thomas Roff,
Conductor.

J. W. Leighton,
Railroad Contractor.

REAL ESTATE.

Dwight N. Lowell,
Real Estate Dealer.

RESTAURANT.

A. J. Parker,
Restaurant.

SCHOOLS &c.

D. B. Briggs,
State Superintendent of Schools.

E. Barton Wood,
Principal of Public Schools.

John H. Gatzky,
Teacher of Music.

STEAM ENGINES.

Morton & Hamblin,
Proprietors
of Romeo Steam Engine Works.

SURVEYOR.

Milton Nye,
Surveyor.

TAILOR.

John Ford,
Merchant Tailor
and Furnishing Goods.

BUSINESS CARDS OF PATRONS IN UTICA.

ATTORNEY.

Seth K. Shetterly,
Attorney at Law and Justice.

BLACKSMITH.

A. T. Sopher,
Blacksmith.

BREWER.

Nicolaus Priemer,
Brewer.

BUILDER.

Marcus B. Vanhusen,
Builder.

BUTCHER.

Samuel D. De Kay,
Butcher and Livery.

CLERGYMEN.

B. S. Taylor,
Pastor M. E. Church.

D. Payson Breed,
Pastor Congregational Church.

CONSTABLE.

F. O. Crocker,
Constable.

DROVER.

James Foley,
Drover.

DRUGGIST.

Wm. W. Andrews,
Drugs and Medicines,

ENGINEERS.

A. G. Mullen,
Engineer D. B. & C.

George E. Adair,
Surveyor and Engineer.

L. F. Lintz,
Railroad Engineer.

FARMERS.

Frederick Sticker,
Grain Farmer,
154 acres, Sec. 33.

Addison Green,
100 acres, Sec. 22.

Charles E. Whitney,
120 acres, Sec. 29.

Mary Phillips,
Grain Farmer,
98 acres, Sec. 29.

Lyman Fuller,
Sec. 22.

Jas. C. Cheney,
General Farmer,
80 acres, Sec. 20.

L. C. Russell,
General Farmer,
188 acres.

George Switzer,
Stock, Wool and Grain Farmer,
188 acres, Sec. 21.

Joel Lewis,
Stock, Wool and Fruit Farming,
120 acres, Sec. 24.

Harmon Vosburg,
Wheat Corn and Fruit,
100 acres, Sec. 21.

John D. Merchant,
General Farmer,
Sec. 18.

Wm. W. Blouch,
Farmer.

John Crow,
Wool, Stock and Grain Farmer,
180 acres, Sec. 26.

F. Selleck,
70 acres.

Wm. K. Payne,
810 acres.

Thomas F. Summers,
Farmer and Stock Raiser,
157 acres, Sec. 31.

Ira G. Chapman,
221 acres.

Wm. F. Postal,
100 acres.

Charles D. Hutchins,
100 acres,

J. H. Boughton,
Stock and Grain Farmer,
195 acres, Sec. 32.

George W. Summer,
187 acres, Sec. 31.

John B. St. John,
105 acres.

W. S. Wise,
Farmer and Grain Raiser,
140 acres.

M. D. L. Howell,
186 acres.

Samuel Ladd,
105 acres, Sec. 31.

Payne K. Leech,
Farmer and Raiser of Devon Cattle,
860 acres, Sec. 31.

BUSINESS CARDS OF PATRONS IN UTICA.

P. H. Child, Farmer and School Teacher, 80 acres.	**Philip Price,** 100 acres, Sec. 27.	**M. Abenathy,** Boots and Shoes.	**PHYSICIANS.** **Joseph C. Davis,** Physician.
J. D. Summers, 60 acres, Sec. 19.	**George B. Wright,** 150 acres, Sec. 28.	**Dennis Rowley,** Shoe Manufacturer.	**Wm. Brownell.** Physician and Surgeon.
Joseph D. Cougle, 120 acres, Sec. 30.	**Richard Wright,** 117 acres, Sec. 28.	**D. Chapion,** Boots and Shoes.	**POSTMASTER.** **W. M. Scott,** Postmaster.
H. W. Haines, 190 acres, Sec. 30.	**Christian Blouch,** 175 acres, Sec. 21.	**Young & Wilcox,** Dry Goods, Clothing, Carpets, &c.	**STATION AGENT.** **W. H. Dack,** Station Agent D. & B. C. R. R.
Peter D. Lerich, 880 acres, Sec. 29.	**Joseph Crow,** 62 acres, Sec. 21.	**Firman & Mitchell,** Dry Goods, Groceries, &c.	
Miss Mary Harris, 120 acres.	**Joseph Crow,** General Farmer, Sec. 21.	**S. P. St. Johns,** Dry Goods, Groceries, &c.	**TEACHERS.** **Sarah E. Gunn,** Teacher.
Julius B. McLallen, 80 acres, Sec. 36.	**FURNITURE.** **S. S. Merrill,** Furniture Dealer and Undertaker.	**Sumner Leech,** Grocer.	**F. L. Tiffany,** Principal of Union School.
H. A. McLallen, Grain Farmer, 80 acres, Sec. 36,		**John Ruby,** Grocer.	**Clara Selleck,** Teacher.
James McLallen, Farmer and Stock Raiser, 120 acres, Sec. 36.	**IRON FOUNDER &c.** **George Wilkins,** Foundryman and Blacksmith.	**Marshall Summers,** Dealer in Hardware.	**Alice V. Adair,** Teacher of High School.
S. M. Ruby, Grain Farmer, Sec. 25.	**LECTURER.** **G. A. Brown,** Lecturer.	**R. H. Sliter,** Hardware Merchant.	**Nellie L. Lewis,** Teacher.
John W. Hayes, Grain Farmer, 80 acres, Sec. 25.	**LIVERY.** **J. T. B. Skillman,** Livery.	**MILLERS &c.** **Chapel & Robinson,** Proprietors Canal Mills.	**TELEGRAPH.** **Thomas Welch,** Telegraph Builder.
Seymour Brownell, Farmer and Lumberman.		**A. J. Runyan,** Millwright.	**F. R. Andrews,** Telegraph Operator.
Wm. M. Marsay, Farmer and Raiser of Cotswold Sheep, Shipping to Chicago and Lake Superior Ports, 556 acres.	**LUMBER.** **B. S. Lawrence & Co.,** Manufacturer of Lumber.	**NEWSPAPER.** **Gordon D. Deshon,** Knight of the Tin Whistle.	**Roswell Goff,** Telegraph Builder.
John Eames. 40 acres, Sec. 38.	**MERCHANT.** **T. B. Knapp,** Merchant.	**NURSERYMAN.** **R. T. St. John,** Nurseryman, 100 acres, Sec. 33.	**WATCHES CLOCKS &c.** **P. Monfort,** Clocks, Watches, Jewelry and Fancy Articles.
R. T. Burgess, Sec. 28.			

BUSINESS CARDS OF PATRONS IN MACOMB COUNTY.

ARCHITECT & BUILDER.	CARPENTER.	FARMERS.	
David G. Stewart, Architect and Builder, Washington.	**James Daly,** Hamtramck.	**Josiah Sanburn,** Farmer, Almont, Lapeer County.	**Richard Welts,** Grain, Stock and Wool Farmer, 260 acres, Sec. 5, Macomb.
ATTORNEYS. **Wm. H. Clark, Jr.,** Attorney at Law. Armada.	**CLERGYMEN.** **Robert G. Braid,** Pastor Congregational Church and County Supt. Schools Armada.	**Charles Andrews,** Stock and Wool Farmer, 260 acres. Armada.	**Calvin Davis,** Grain, Stock and Wool Farmer, 155 acres, Sec. 8. Macomb.
T. K. Crocker, Attorney at Law. Mount Clemens.	**H. Hood,** Pastor M. E. Church. Armada.	**Chas. A. Lathrop,** Farmer, Armada.	**James Crandall,** Wool, Stock and Grain Farmer, 120 acres, Sec. 12, Mead.
T. L. Sackett, Judge of Probate. Mount Clemens.	**John Wesley,** Pastor M. E. Church. Ray.	**Nathaniel Carter,** Farmer and Proprietor of Saw-mill. Armada.	**J. H. C. Garvin,** 160 acres, Sec. 2. Mead.
BLACKSMITH. **H. N. Orcutt,** Blacksmith, Sec. 16, Utica tp., Disco P O.	**John Cannon,** Pastor Christian Church. Washington.	**H. Garlick,** Farmer, Armada.	**Joel Hart,** Wool, Stock and Grain Farmer, 160 acres, Sec. 7. Milton.
		Wm. H. Yates, 87 acres, Avon, Oakland Co.	**Haswell Church,** Stock and Grain Farmer, 80 acres, Ray.

BUSINESS CARDS OF PATRONS IN MACOMB COUNTY.

Elisha Briggs,
Fruit Raiser and Farmer,
Ray.

Jesse Grover,
Fruit Farmer, 40 acres,
Ray.

Homer Davis,
Stock, Grain and Wool Farmer, 103 acres,
Ray.

Bela R. Davis,
Stock, Wool and Grain Farmer, 100 acres,
Ray.

Sidney M. Whitcomb,
Farmer and Teacher, 120 acres,
Ray.

M. Jane Taft,
80 acres, Sec. 29,
Ray.

Geo. W. Gass,
Farmer, Stock and Grain, 200 acres, Sec. 29,
Ray.

Geo. W. Garvin,
Farmer, Grain and Stock, 100 acres, Sec. 21.
Ray.

Ruth Corey,
Fruit and Grain Farmer, 74 acres, Sec. 16,
Ray.

A. B. Shelden,
Grain, Dairy and Wool Farmer, 138 acres, Sec. 12,
Ray.

Elvira Freeman,
Grain, Stock and Fruit Farm, 95 acres, Sec. 16,
Ray.

Harriet Sutherland,
Grain, Stock and Fruit Farm, 177 acres, Sec. 9,
Ray.

Ezra Nye,
Fruit Farmer, 20 acres, Sec. 21,
Ray.

George Whiting,
Grain and Wool Farmer, 120 acres, Sec. 8,
Ray.

George W. Brown,
Farmer and Mechanic, Sec. 4,
Washington.

Hiram Wethy,
General Farmer, Sec. 4,
Washington.

G. A. Graves,
Wheat and Wool Farmer, 160 acres Sec. 32,
Washington.

Jessie Gillett,
Fruit Farmer, 66 acres, Sec. 5,
Washington.

Daniel Wilson,
Stock & Wool Farmer, 80 acres, Sec. 33,
Washington.

Geo. H. Cannon,
Farmer & Surveyor, 800 acres, Sec. 4,
Washington.

Willet Wilcox,
General Farmer, 60 acres, Sec. 2,
Washington.

T. S. Warren,
200 acres.
Washington.

Timothy Lockwood,
240 acres,
Washington.

J. Whitmore,
101 acres, Sec. 33,
Washington.

Luther Proctor,
84 acres, Sec. 1,
Washington.

Una Miller,
68 acres, Stock Raising,
Washington.

Emulous Stone,
127 acres, Stock and Grain,
Washington.

Wm. A. Stone,
246 acres, Stock, Grain and Wool,
Washington.

Mary J. Keeler,
160 acres, Stock and Grain,
Washington.

William Delaney,
80 acres, Stock and Grain,
Washington.

Samuel F. Warren,
Farmer, Peach, Grain and Wool Raiser,
104 acres, Sec. 5,
Shelby.

INSURANCE.

J. W. Vaughan,
Fire, Life and Insurance Agent,
Washington.

MANUFACTURER.

Cyrus Farrar,
Staves, Handles, &c.,
Armada.

MERCHANTS.

M. Barrows,
Merchant,
Armada.

L. Granger,
Merchant,
Armada.

A. E. Collins,
Merchant and Postmaster,
Mead.

William Wellsted,
Dealer in Boots and Shoes,
Ray.

Wm. P. Evrett,
Merchant,
Ray.

T. B. Knapp,
Merchant,
Washington.

MILLERS.

Oliver M. Patterson,
Proprietor Silver Creek Mills,
Ray.

Alonzo H. Cole,
Proprietor Steam Saw-mill,
Washington.

Thomas Battenbury,
Proprietor Steam Saw-mill,
Washington tp., Romeo P. O.

MONEY LOANER.

Thomas Brabb,
Money Loaning,
Washington.

PAINTER.

Wallace Whittemore,
House and Sign Painter, Sec. 3,
Washington.

PHYSICIANS.

F. M. Garlick,
Physician,
Armada.

R. N. Harris,
Physician,
Armada.

S. T. Beardsley,
Physician,
Armada.

J. M. Stotkinson,
Physician and Surgeon,
Washington.

STATION AGENT.

E. F. Sibley,
Station Ag't, St. C. & C. Air Line,
Armada.

TEACHERS.

Seth Frost,
Teacher,
Armada.

S. E. Whitney,
Principal Union School,
Armada.

A. J. Grout,
Teacher,
Armada Village.

F. R. Payne,
Teacher,
Disco.

Miss Carrie Underwood,
Teacher,
Oakland, Oakland County.

Miss Ella Cannon,
Teacher, Sec. 3,
Washington.

Olive Bacon,
Teacher, Sec. 8,
Washington tp., Disco P. O.

BUSINESS CARDS OF PATRONS IN GRAND HAVEN.

ATTORNEYS.

Akeley & Stewart,
Attorneys and Counsellors.

R. W. Duncan,
Attorney at Law.

B. F. Curtiss,
Attorney at Law.

Edwin Baxter,
Attorney at Law.

Stephen L. Lowing,
Attorney at Law.

Boynton & Pratt,
Attorneys at Law.

Wm. N. Angel,
Attorney at Law.

Lowing, Cross & Angell,
Attorneys at Law.

E. G. Parsons,
Attorney at Law, &c.

Samuel L. Tate,
Attorney at Law.

BANK.

First National Bank,
Edward C. Ferry, Pres.,
Geo. Stickney, Cash.

CARPENTER.

J. W. Cook,
Carpenter

DENTISTS.

E. P. Cumings D. D. S.,
Dentist.

J. E. Storrs,
Dentist.

FARM IMPLEMENTS.

J. B. Wait & Co.,
Manuf'r of Farm Implements.

FURNITURE.

A. Kiel,
Dealer in Furniture and Coffins.

HOTELS.

Cutler House,
D. F. Starr, Proprietor.

Union Hotel,
A. M. Sprague, Proprietor.

Rice House,
J. A. Rice, Proprietor.

City Hotel,
L. Van Drezer, Proprietor.

Ernest Andres,
Hotel.

BUSINESS CARDS OF PATRONS IN GRAND HAVEN.

LEATHER.

C. B. Albee,
Manufacturer of Leather.

LIVERY.

Killean & Chase,
Livery Stable.

LUMBER.

Cutler & Savidge,
Dealers and Manuf'rs of Lumber.

Ferry & Brother,
Lumber Dealers.

N. H. White,
Manu'f'r of Shingles.

Charles Reynolds,
Manuf'r of and Dealer in Lumber.

George Parks & Co.,
Manuf'rs of Shingles.

C. L. Storrs & Co.,
Manuf'rs of and Dealers in Lumber, Lath and Pickets.

George Shippey,
Manuf'r and Dealer in Lumber, Lath and Pickets.

John W. Hopkins,
Lumberman.

Loomis & Storrs,
Manuf'rs of and Dealers in Lumber.

Wyman, Buswell & Co.,
Manufacturers of Lumber, Lath and Pickets.

R. H. Sinclair,
Lumber Inspector.

W. F. Storrs,
Lumberman.

Sherman M. Boyce,
Lumber Dealer.

Frank E. Kearney,
Lumber Dealer.

Friant & Hall,
Lumber Manufacturers.

H. Rysdorff & Co.,
Manufacturers of Lumber.

P. A. Wooley,
Lumberman.

J. L. Taylor,
Lumber Inspector.

MERCHANTS.

George E. Hubbard,
General Dealer in Hardware and Mill Furnishing Goods.

G. D. Sanford & Co.,
Merchant Tailor and Dealer in Gents Furnishing Goods.

Julius Radcke,
Wholesale and Retail Dealer in Wines, Liquors, Tobacco and Cigars.

S. Gale,
General Dealer in Drugs and Fancy Goods.

NEWSPAPERS.

Grand Haven Weekly Herald, & Northern Agriculturist,
Published by Cha's. N. Dickinson.

John H. Mitchell,
Publisher Grand Haven News.
Book and Job Office attached.

OFFICERS.

A. A. Tracy,
County Clerk.

Chas. T. Pagelson,
Consul for Sweden and Norway, Gen'l European Passage Ag't, Notary Public & Real Estate Agent.

Chas. J. Pfaff,
Chief of Police, Marshal and Harbor Master.

Ann Reynolds,
Postmaster.

PUBLIC HALL.

Music Hall,
Cor. Second and Franklin Sts.

REAL ESTATE.

Galen Eastman,
Real Estate Office Grand Haven. Eastman & Mowly, Lumberman in Robinson, Mich.

E. D. Blair,
Real Estate and Proprietor of Abstracts of Ottawa Co.

J. A. Leggat,
Real Estate Dealer.

BUSINESS CARDS OF PATRONS IN LENAWEE COUNTY.

ATTORNEYS.

L. R. Peirson,
Attorney and Counsellor at Law, Hudson.

J. & G. W. Whitbeck,
Attorneys and Counsellors, Hudson.

James J. Hogaboom,
Att'y at Law and Justice of the Peace, Hudson.

BANK.

Exchange Bank,
Boies, Rude & Co., Proprietors, Hudson.

CLERGYMAN.

B. D. Conkling,
Pastor Congregational Church, Hudson.

FARMERS.

Phineas Price,
Sec. 8, N. E. ¼, Madison tp., Adrian P. O.

E. P. Allis,
Sec. 8, N. E. & N. W. ¼, Madison tp., Adrian P. O.

George S. Webster,
Sec. 6, S. W. ¼, Madison tp., Adrian P. O.

David Dutcher,
Sec. 12, N. E. ¼, Dover tp., Adrian P. O.

David Gander,
Sec. 16, N. W. ¼, Madison tp., Adrian P. O.

Alfred Crane,
Sec. 17, S. E. ¼, Madison tp., Adrian P. O.

M. C. Bradish,
Sec. 17, S. E. ¼, Madison tp., Adrian P. O.

George W. Jordan,
Sec. 29, N. E. ¼, Madison tp., Adrian P. O.

Josiah Putman,
Sec. 29, N. W. ¼, Madison tp., Adrian P. O.

Charles A. Wilcox,
Sec. 29, N. W. ¼, Madison tp., Adrian P. O.

N. D. Wilson,
Sec. 29, N. E. ¼, Madison tp., Adrian P. O.

J. W. Woolsey,
Sec. 21, N. E. ¼, Madison tp., Adrian P. O.

Hiram D. Smith,
Sec. 9, N. E. ¼, Madison tp., Adrian P. O.

Allen Warren,
Sec. 18, N. E. ¼, Madison tp., Adrian P. O.

Edwin P. Graham,
Sec. 19, N. E. ¼, Madison tp., Adrian P. O.

A. Bradish,
Sec. 23, N. W. ¼, Madison tp., Adrian P. O.

Mrs. S. N. Donaldson,
Sec. 22, S. W. ¼, Madison tp., Adrian P. O.

Levi Baker,
Sec. 34, S. E. ¼, Madison tp., Fairfield P. O.

L. C. Drake,
Sec. 33, S. W. ¼, Madison tp., Fairfield P. O.

G. Livesay,
Sec. 32, N. E. ¼, Madison tp., Adrian P. O.

JOBBERS.

C. C. Bloomfield,
Jobber of Oil and Glassware, 71 Jackson St., Jackson.

George Lake & Sons,
Jobbers of Ohio and Jackson White Lime, Portland Louisville & Akron Cement, Stucco & Superior Salt, Calcined Plaster, Hair and Dairy Salt, Jackson.

LIVERY.

A. E. Sutton,
Livery, Sale and Boarding Stables, Jackson.

MANUFACTURERS.

Jacob Beiber,
Manufacturer of Buggies, Wagons, Sleighs, &c., 33 Mill Street, Jackson.

M. B. Sandborn,
Hudson Carriage Manufactory and Trimming Establishment, Hudson.

G. W. Carter,
Manufacturer of Telegraph Insulators, Hudson.

G. A. Brown,
Turning, Scroll Sawing and Manufacturer of wooden Screws, Hudson.

F. F. Palmer & Son,
M'f'rs of Sheet Iron & Tin Ware, and Dealers in Stoves, House Trimmings and General Hardware, Hudson.

H. Montgomery,
Saddle and Harness Maker, Hudson.

James De Colyer & Co,
Manuf'rs of Spokes, Hubs, Bent Work &c., Hudson.

Standish Brothers,
Dealers in Lumber, Sash, Doors and Blinds, Hudson.

MERCHANT.

Orrison Kelly,
Dealer in Dry Goods, Boots & Shoes, Drugs, &c., Woodstock tp., Kelly's Corners P. O.

NEWSPAPERS.

James M. Scarritt,
Editor & Proprietor Hudson Post Newspaper, and Job Printing Establishment, Hudson.

W. T. B. Schermerhorn,
Editor and Publisher of Hudson Gazette, Hudson.

POST MASTER.

E. J. Southworth,
Postmaster, Hudson.

BUSINESS CARDS OF PATRONS IN HOLLAND CITY.

Agricultural Implements.

R. K. Heald,
Manufacturer of Agricultural Implements,
Sash, Doors & Blinds,
Planing Matching & Sawing done.

G. J. Haverkate & Son,
Dealers in General Hardware and
Agricultural Implements.

Wm. J. Scott,
Planing, Matching and Jobbing.

ATTORNEY.

Henry D. Post,
Law and Collection Office,
U. S. Commissioner, Notary Public & Conveyancer.

CLERGYMAN.

W. A. Bronson,
M. E. Church.

HOTEL.

E. Kellogg & Son,
Proprietors of City Hotel,
A New and First Class House.

Justice of the Peace.

G. Van Schelven,
Justice of the Peace.

MANUFACTURERS.

Panels Van Putten & Co.,
Lumber Manufacturers
also Flour, Feed and Pearl Barley.

Edward Cole,
Lumber Dealer.

J. Van Dyk & Co.,
Lumber Dealers.

R. B. Ferris,
Dealer in and Manufacturer of
Lumber.

Cappon Bertsch & Co.,
Manuf'rs of all kinds of Leather.

MERCHANTS.

Ernst Herold.
Boots and Shoes.

J. Binnekant,
Dealer in Books, Stationery,
Confectionary &c. A Fine Bakery in Connection.

Daniel Bertsch,
Dry Goods, Ladies & Gents.
Furnishing Goods, Hats and Caps.

D. DeVries,
General Merchandise.

Henry D. Werkman,
Dealer in Choice Family Groceries,
Provisions & Crockery, Gents Furnishing Goods &c.

C. B. Wynne,
Watchmaker and Jeweler.

Arend Cloetingh,
Dealer in Books and Stationery.
Book Binding in every style.

J. W. Bosman,
Merchant Tailor, Dealer in Hats, Caps,
Ready-made Clothing,
and Gents. Furnishing Goods.

J. E. Higgins,
Gen'l Dealer in Farm Produce, Coal, &c.,
Hay House and Hay Press
at M. L. S. R. R.

PHOTOGRAPHER

George Lauder,
Photographer.

COLLEGE FACULTY.

Philip Phelps, D. D.,
President of Hope College.

Cornelius E. Crispell, D. D.,
Professor of Didactic Polemic History
at Hope College.

J. Romeyn Beck,
Professor Latin and Greek,
Hope College.

P. Moerdyk,
Assistant Prof. Latin and Greek,
Hope College.

Charles Scott,
Prof. of Chemistry &c.,
Hope College.

PUBLISHERS.

Wm. Benjaminse,
Publisher "De Hollander."

Morgensteger & Muller,
Pub. of the "Groundwet".

C. Vorst,
Publisher of "De Wachter"
Agent of the Jansen Line Ocean Steamers,
Between N. Y. and Rotterdam

RAILROAD AGENT.

H. C. Matron,
Agent C. & M. L. S. R. R.

REAL ESTATE.

M. D. Howard,
Real Estate.

SALOON KEEPER.

John Stevens,
Saloon Keeper.

TEACHERS.

L. C. Miller,
Supt. Union School.

Addie March,
Assistant Teacher U. S.

WAGON MAKERS.

Peter Gunst & Co.,
Wagon Makers.

BUSINESS CARDS OF PATRONS IN SPRING LAKE.

ATTORNEY.

Levi M. Comstock,
Attorney at Law.

CLERGYMAN.

W. M. Blair,
Pastor Presbyterian Church.

CONTRACTORS,

Squier & White,
General Contractors.

Wm. R. Lake,
Builder and Contractor.

FRUIT GROWERS.

J. B. Soule,
Fruit Grower.

J. S. Sessions,
Fruit Grower.

Geo. G. Lovell,
Fruit Grower.

Chas. E. Soule,
Fruit Grower.

A. L. Soule,
Fruit Grower.

Thomas Petty,
Fruit Grower.

Francis Hall,
Fruit Grower.

D. R. Waters,
Fruit Grower.

Lyman Hall,
Fruit Grower.

John S. Dewey,
Fruit Grower.

David G. Alston,
Fruit Grower.

H. G. Smith,
Fruit Grower.

HOTELS.

W. S. Hammond,
Proprietor American House.

L. S. Barnum,
Barnum House.

Geo. D. Sisson,
Spring Lake House,
and Magnetic Mineral Spring.

LUMBERMEN.

Haire, Savidge & Cutler,
Manufacturers & Dealers in Lumber,
Lath and Pickets.

Cutler & Savidge,
Manuf'rs and Dealers in Lumber.

Wm. H. Bell, & Co.,
Manufacturers of Lumber,
Lath and Pickets.

David Patterson,
Lumber Dealer.

L. D. Heath,
Lumberman.

John Thompson,
Dealer & Manufacturer of Lumber.

Magnetic Mineral Springs.

Magnetic Mineral Springs.
W. G. Sinclair Secretary.

MANUFACTURERS.

R. Stitt & Co.,
Manuf'rs of Wagons and Carriages.

MERCHANTS.

Cliff & Bro.,
Wholesale & Retail Dealers in Hardware &
Furniture, & Manuf'rs of Tin, Copper, and
Sheet Iron work.

Chas. M. Mellor,
Merchant Tailor and dealer in
Gents. Furnishing Goods.

Perham & Adsit,
Dry Goods Groceries, Boots & Shoes.

Martin Walsh.
Dry Goods, Groceries, Boots & Shoes.

A. Bilz,
Manufacturer & Dealer in Hardware
and Furniture, and Insurance Agent.

R. H. Lee,
Jeweler and Dealer in Watches, Clocks
and Jewelry.

PHYSICIANS.

J. O. Bates,
Physician and Surgeon.

C. B. Brown,
Physician and Surgeon.

PUBLISHER.

John Lee,
Publisher of the Independent.
Book and Job Printer.

TEACHER.

A. W. Taylor,
Principal High School.

ATTORNEY.

James Cilley,
Attorney at Law and Manuf'r of
Sash, Doors & Blinds,
Lamont.

BOILER MAKER.

J. W. Johnston,
Boiler Maker,
Ferrysburg.

CARPENTERS.

Bernard Lauer,
Carpenter and Joiner,
Cooperville, P. O. Polkton.

John H. Westover,
Carpenter and Joiner,
Nunica.

C. M. Brown,
Carpenter and Joiner,
Nunica.

CONTRACTOR.

Jonathan G. Westover,
Contractor and General Builder,
Nunica.

CITIZEN.

Wm. Mines,
Citizen,
Nunica.

ENGINEERS.

John Kelley,
Mechanical Engineer,
Ferrysburg.

Donald Mc Millon,
Engineer,
Nunica.

W. F. Mitchell,
Engineer and Machinist,
Nunica.

FARMERS.

John EcKoff,
Hay, Stock, and Grain, 80 acres, Sec. 20,
Crockery.

Andrew Roth,
Hay, Grain, Stock and Fruit,
80 acres, Sec. 30,
Crockery.

Martin Viebrock,
Hay, Grain, Stock, Fruit & Bees, 70 acres, Sec. 21,
Crockery.

Wm. Thompson,
Farmer and Lumberman,
Crockery.

F. French & Son,
Farmer and Lumberman,
Crockery.

Wm. H. Bond,
Farmer, 160 acres, Sec. 11,
Crockery.

T. F. Hunter.
Hay, Grain, Stock, & Fruit, Butter & Cheese,
160 acres, Sec. 25,
Crockery.

Edmund Rainonard,
Hay, Stock and Grain, 30 acres, Sec. 34,
Eastmanville, Polkton.

John Vine,
Hay, Grain, Stock, Wool, Beef, Pork, Fruit & Bees,
120 acres, Sec. 34,
Eastmanville, Polkton.

D. K. Spencer,
Hay, Grain, Stock, Beef & Pork, Butter & Fruit,
80 acres, Sec. 36,
Eastmanville, Polkton.

George M. Wells,
Hay, Grain, Stock, Beef and Pork Butter, Cheese & Fruit,
160 acres, Sec. 7,
Eastmanville, Polkton.

L. Slngter,
Hay, Grain, Beef & Pork, Fruit, & Cattle Dealer,
50 acres, Sec. 3,
Eastmanville Polkton.

Wm. Vander Made,
Hay, Grain, Stock, Beef, Pork, Butter, Cheese and Fruit,
40 acres, Sec. 5,
Eastmanville, Polkton.

Albert F. Gus,
Wagon Maker and Farmer, 60 acres, Sec. 3,
Eastmanville, Polkton.

John Spencer,
Wagon Maker,
Eastmanville, Polkton.

L. K. Lull,
Hay, Grain, Beef, Pork, Butter and Fruit,
70 acres, Sec. 1,
Eastmanville, Polkton.

Wm. H. Nilon,
Hay, Grain, Fruit, Butter, Beef, Pork and Bees,
45 acres, Secs. 3-7-14,
Eastmanville, Polkton.

B. F. Earns,
Fruit Grower,
Ferrysburg.

Simeon Hazelton,
Hay, Grain, Fruit & extensive Strawberry Grower,
80 acres, Sec. 24,
Nunica tp., Cooperville, P. O.

Alexander Cooper,
Hay, Grain, Stock, Beef, Pork, Butter & Fruit,
43 acres,
Nunica tp., Cooperville P. O.

Charles Q. Chadwick,
Hay, Grain, Stock, & Fruit 160 acres, Sec. 22,
Nunica tp., Cooperville P. O.

R. Toothaker,
Hay, Grain, Stock, Fruit, Beef & Pork,
160 acres Sec. 27,
Nunica tp., Cooperville P. O.

Henry Reynolds,
Hay, Grain, Stock, Fruit, Beef, Pork, Butter
& Cheese, 105 acres, Sec's 33 & 34.
Nunica tp., Cooperville P. O.

L. Barringer,
Stock, Grain, Fruit, Butter, Cheese & Bees,
90 acres, Sec. 36,
Nunica.

Mrs. Sarah Griswold,
Stock, Grain, Fruit, Butter & Cheese,
120 acres, Sec. 36,
Nunica.

Nathan Griswold,
Stock, Hay, Grain, Butter, Cheese & Fruit,
40 acres, Sec. 31,
Nunica.

Sidney Lawrence,
Lumberman and Farmer,
280 acres, Sec. 1,
Nunica.

Lukas Elbers,
Stock, Hay, Grain, Wool, Beef, Pork, Butter
and Cheese, 140 acres, Sec. 35,
Polkton tp., Cooperville P. O.

Mark Richards,
Hay, Grain, Stock, Wool, Butter, Cheese, Beef,
Pork & Fruit, 160 acres, Sec's 8, 9,
Polkton tp., Dealsea P. O.

Simeon Hazelton,
Hay, Grain, Fruit and Strawberries, 40 acres Sec. 24,
Polkton.

James Foogett,
Hay, Grain, & Stock, 40 acres, Sec. 31,
Polkton.

Wm. A. Simpson,
Farmer and Lumberman, 120 acres, Sec. 1,
Polkton.

A. L. Taylor,
General Farmer, 76 acres, Sec. 6,
Polkton.

Benjamin Luther,
Stock, Hay, and Grain 80 acres, Sec. 36,
Polkton.

John Johnson,
Hay, Grain, Stock and Fruit, 160 acres, Sec. 13,
Polkton.

Walter S. Cole,
Hay, Grain, and Stock, 60 acres Sec.12,
Polkton.

H. C. Durphy,
Mixed Husbandry, 160 acres, Sec. 22,
Polkton.

A. C. Ellis,
Hay, Grain, Stock, and extensive Strawberry
Grower, 170 acres, Sec. 23.
Polkton.

Wm. Bateman,
Hay, Grain, Stock and Fruit,
130 a, Sec. 6.
Talimadge.

Wm. Babcock,
Hay, Grain, Stock and Fruit,
70 acres, Sec. 19,
Talimadge.

Palmer Church,
Farmer and Lumberman
120 acres,
Talimadge.

Francis Lord,
General Farmer,
66 acres, Sec. 34,
Talimadge.

Chas. Deunas,
General Farmer, 40 acres, Sec. 28,
Talimadge.

L. S. Lawton,
General Farmer, 76 acres, Sec. 6,
Talimadge.

M. De Witt,
Farmer and Manuf'r of Churns, 110 acres, Sec. 6,
Talimadge.

Myron Harris,
Wool Grower, 1600 acres Sec. 27,
Talimadge.

E. Sheldon,
Hay, Stock, Grain, and Fruit, 100 acres, Sec. 26,
Wright.

Lois B. Hatch,
Hay, Grain and Fruit, 80 acres Sec. 27,
Wright.

James I. Cramer,
Hay, Grain and Fruit, 80 acres, Sec 20,
Wright.

Benjamin Loubeck,
Mixed Husbandry, 220 acres, Sec.12,
Wright.

S. D. Covey,
General Farmer 80 acres, Sec. 20,
Wright.

Henry W. Gerden,
General Farmer, 74 acres, Sec. 16,
Wright.

W. T. Warren, Jr.,
General Farmer, 240 acres, Sec. 17,
Wright.

Thomas Wilde,
General Farmer and extensive Strawberry Grower
120 acres, Sec. 20,
Wright.

Benjamin Lillie,
General Husbandry, 140 acres, Sec. 30,
Wright.

HOTELS.

O. G. Maxfield,
Hotel Keeper,
Eastmanville, Polkton.

Mary A. Bales.

E. S. Richmond,
Hotel Keeper,
Nunica.

IRON FOUNDERY.

Wm. M. Ferry & Co.,
Prop'r's. of Ottawa Iron Works, Manuf'rs of
General Saw Mill & Steam Machinery, Patent
Parallel Edgers, Log Turners, &c.,
Ferrysburg.

LABORER.

Willis M. Stoup,
Laborer,
Polkton.

LUMBERMEN.

Geo. Eastman,
Lumber Merchant,
Eastmanville, Polkton.

Thomas Heffernan,
Lumberman,
Eastmanville, Polkton.

White, Glover & Co.,
Manuf'rs & Dealers in Lumber, Lath, & Pickets,
Ferrysburg.

E. Babcock,
Lumberman,
Lamont.

John Spoon,
Spoon & Thompson, Spoonville, Manuf'rs of
Lumber, Lath, Shingles, & General Merchandise,
Nunica.

Daniel Spoon,
Foreman at Spoonville,
Nunica.

MERCHANTS.

Chas. Stroebe,
Grocer and Post Master,
Ferrysburgh.

B. Oosterhoff,
Dry, Goods, and Groceries,
Ferrysburg.

S. W. Clark,
Drugs and Medicines,
Nunica.

E. A. Carpenter,
Groceries, Drugs, Boots & Shoes, Agent of Z. Misner,
Nunica.

Cha's W. Rose,
Grocer,
Nunica.

BUSINESS CARDS OF PATRONS IN OTTAWA COUNTY.

Scott & Walling,
Dealers in Drugs, Groceries & Furniture,
Lamont.

Geo. Luther,
General Merchant,
Lamont.

Henry Furgerson,
Merchant,
Nunica tp., Coopersville P. O.

Wm. G. & J. Watson,
Dry Goods, Groceries, Boots & Shoes,
Nunica.

Wm. M. Wilson,
Groceries & Provisions, Boots & Shoes,
Nunica tp., Coopersville P. O.

F. A. Coleman & Bros.,
Dealers in Drugs, Medicines, Paints, Oils & Choice
Family Groceries,
Polkton.

MILLERS.

George Macey,
Miller,
Berlin.

I. Griffith,
Custom Merchant Miller,
Dealer in Grain,
Polkton.

PHYSICIANS.

J. T. Dayton,
Physician,
Berlin.

Ezra Walling,
Physician, and Surgeon,
Berlin.

J. J. Austin,
Physician and Surgeon,
Polkton tp., Coopersville P. O.

POSTMASTER.

Wm. T. Per Lee,
Post Master,
Lamont.

RAILROAD AGENT.

Geo. M. Read,
Agent D. & M. R. Road,
Nunica.

REAL ESTATE.

James C. Christenson,
Real Estate,
Nunica.

RESTAURANT.

R. B. Jennings,
R. R. Eating House,
Nunica.

SALOON KEEPER.

Ban's. Robinson,
Saloon Keeper,
Nunica.

SHIP BUILDER.

M. C. Pearsons,
Ship Builder.
Tugs, Yachts, and Schooners, built and repaired,
Ferrysburg.

TEACHERS.

Roxina M. Fonger,
Teacher,
Ottawa Centre.

Wm. D. Alverson,
Principal Union School,
Ottawa Centre.

Sarah & Mary Smith,
Teachers,
Ottawa Centre.

E. M. Luce,
Teacher,
Polkton.

BUSINESS CARDS OF PATRONS IN YPSILANTI.

ATTORNEYS.

Cutcheon & Allen,
Attorneys at Law.
S. M. Cutcheon.   E. P. Allen.

Chauncey Joslin,
Attorney at Law.

J. Willard Babbitt,
Attorney at Law and Collecting
and Insurance Agent.

Edwin F. Uhl,
Attorney at Law,
Collections promptly attended to.

BANKS.

First National Bank,
Capital $75,000.   Surplus $25,000.
E. Boganus, Pres.   F. P. Boganus, Cash.

Cornwell, Hemphill & Co.,
Bankers.

BLACKSMITH.

David Peins,
General Blacksmithing & Man'f'r of Agricultural
Implements & Farming Tools of all kinds.

BREWERY.

A. Foerster, Bro. & Co.,
Grove Brewery,
Brewers of Lager Beer.

CLERGYMAN.

M. Willgun,
Pastor St John's Church.

DENTISTS.

Watling & Tremper,
Dentists.
J. A. Watling.   W. D. Tremper.

A. F. Barr,
Dentist.

Engineer and Surveyor.

George S. Caswell,
Engineer & Surveyor of
Washtenaw Co.

FARMERS.

E. F. Alexander,
Farmer & Brick Manufacturer.

Alonzo Bennett,
Grain and Grazing,
160. acres.

Lyman Ward,
Grain, Fruit, Grazing, and
Vinegar Manufacturer.
200 acres.

Alonzo Bennett,
Grain & Grazing,
160 acres.

E. F. Alexander,
Farmer & Brick Manufacturer.

Wm. T. Sweet,
Grain Farmer,
60 acres.

D. P. Patten,
Grain and Dairy Farmer,
140 acres.

J. Evart Smith,
Stock, Fruit and Grain,
190 acres.

Alverson Drury,
General Farmer,
185 acres.

Leander Stiles,
General Farmer,
160 acres, Sec. 31.

Charles Howlett,
General Farmer,
62 acres, Sec. 32.

R. L. Hall,
General Farmer,
80 acres, Sec. 29.

Evan Begole,
General Farmer and Breeder of Fine Sheep.
120 acres, Sec. 18.

Peter D. Martin,
General Farmer,
60 acres, Sec. 18.

Fountain Watling,
General Farmer,
840 acres, Sec. 18.

Nathan Reed,
General Farmer,
180 acres, Sec. 31.

L. A. McBain,
General Farmer,
Sec. 31.

N. E. Crittenden,
General Farmer,
350 acres, Sec. 32.

A. M. Benham,
General Farmer,
160 acres, Sec. 29.

W. K. Brock,
General Farmer,
145 acres, Sec. 23.

J. W. Tuttle,
General Farmer,
280 acres, Sec. 23.

N. B. Tuttle,
General Farmer,
80 acres Sec. 22.

H. S. Boutwell,
Farmer & Traveling Ag't for Mowry & Co., Detroit,
140 acres, Sec. 26.

Edwin Vorce,
General Farmer,
80 acres.

Perry Vorce,
General Farmer,
140 acres, Sec. 18.

G. D. Ward,
Farmer & Man'f'r Cider & Cider Vinegar.
282 acres, Sec. 12.

W. H. Willings,
General Farmer,
60 acres, Sec. 35.

Albert Stockdale & Bros.,
General Farmers,
160 acres, Sec. 21.

Edward King,
General Farmer,
180 acres, Sec. 15.

Wm. H. Lay,
General Farmer,
175 acres, Sec. 2.

Benjamin S. Covert,
General Farmer,
200 acres, Sec. 18.

F. A. Graves,
General Farmer, 205 acres, Sec. 28,
Augusta P. O.

Jessie Hewens,
General Farmer, 196 acres, Soc. 4,
Augusta P. O.

W. B. Smith,
General Farmer, 125 acres Sec. 24,
Rawsonville P. O.

Isaac Amerman,
General Farmer. 346 acres Sec. 25,
Rawsonville P. O.

G. L. Warner,
Farmer, and Dealer in Dry Goods, and Groceries,
Rawsonville P. O.

L. R. Brown,
General Farmer, & First Co. Supt. of Schools.
80 acres, Sec. 31. Rawsonville, P. O.

FLOURING MILLS.

T. C. Owen,
Proprietor Ypsilanti Flouring Mills.

N. Follett,
Proprietor Huron Flouring Mills.

C. Cook & Co.,
Propr's Ransomville Flouring Mills,
Ransomville.

BUSINESS CARDS OF PATRONS IN YPSILANTI.

GARDENER.

P. Hendricks,
Gardener & grower of Small
Fruits, Plants, &c.

HOTELS.

Follett House,

J. M. Cutler, Proprietor.

Ypsilanti House,

W. H. Young, Proprietor.

Schade's Hotel,

Leopold Schade, Proprietor.

LIVERY STABLE.

A. M. Nobt.

Livery, Sale & Feed Stable.

MANUFACTURER.

E. R. Forsyth,

Broom and Brush Manufactory.

MERCHANTS.

J. H. Sampson,

Dealer in Heavy and Shelf Hardware.

Daniel B. Greene,
Successor to Bickford & Camp.
Dealer in Clothing, Gents, Furnishing Goods,
Hats, Caps, and Straw Goods.

H. C. Camp,
Successor to Bickford & Camp.
Dealer in Shelf Hardware, Iron, Nails,
Agricultural Implements, & Man'fr. of Tin,
Copper, & Sheet Iron ware.

NEWSPAPERS.

Ypsilanti Commercial,

. C. R. Patterson, Proprietor.

Ypsilanti Sentinel,
Saturday Edition. Paper, Book
and Job Printing.

NORMAL SCHOOL.

Normal School,

J. Estabrook, Principal.

PHOTOGRAPHER.

A. J. Clark,
Photo-Artist, Porcelain, Ink, and Oil
Pictures made in the best style.

PHYSICIANS.

A. F. Klune,

Physician and Surgeon.

H. W. Brazie,

Homœopathic Physician & Surgeon.

Edward Batwell,

Physician & Surgeon.

R. E. Knapp,

Homœopathic Physician.

Planing Mills and Lumber Yards.

Edwards, Mc Kinstry & Van Clerc,
Manufacturers of Sash, Doors, Blinds, & Moldings;
and Dealers in Lumber, Paints, Oils, Varnish,
Window Glass, &c.

Fallmer & Scoville,
Planing Mill & Lumber Yard,
and Dealer in Lath, Shingles, &c.

Real Estate & Insurance Agent.

Charles Holmes, Jr.,

Real Estate & Insurance Agent.

SEGAR MANUFACTORY.

A. Guild & Son,
Manufacturers of choice brands of Cigars,
and Dealers in Smokers Goods, of all kinds.

SALOONS.

Lithauser & Vought,
Prop'rs. of Orchestrion & American
& German Hall, Congress St.

TEACHERS.

M. W. Smith,

Teacher.

Miss A. L. Dickerson,

Teacher.

BUSINESS CARDS OF PATRONS IN ALPENA CITY.

BANKERS.

Bewick, Comstock & Co.,
Transact a general Banking & Exchange business.
Special attention given to collections.
A. W. Comstock, Cash.   Chas. Bewick, Pres.

Exchange Bank,

of Alpena, Michigan.

Geo. L. Maltz & Co.,
Bankers,
Correspondents American National Bank, Detroit,
Howes and Macy, New York.

BAKERY.

Eagle Bakery,
George Masters, Proprietor.
Baker, & Dealer in all kinds of Confectionaries.

BLACKSMITHS.

A. Mc Callum,

Blacksmith & Machinist.

Crippen Brothers,
Blacksmiths, Machinists,
Iron and Brass Founders.

BREWERIES.

A. Leins,

Proprietor of Leins' Brewery.

Lake Shore Brewery,

Robert Keiser & Bro., Proprietors.

BUTCHER.

Geo. D. Bradford,
Wholesale & Retail Butcher. All kinds of meats
on hand. Poultry & Game a specialty.

CARPENTERS & BUILDERS.

Ira Stout,

Carpenter and Builder.

James M. Johnston,

Carpenter, Joiner & Mill-Wright.

A. T. Gibson,

Carpenter and Joiner,

James Reid,

Carpenter and Builder.

Alex. Campbell,

Carpenter and Builder.

John Dumford,

Carpenter and Joiner.

CLERGYMAN.

W. W. Rafter,

Rector of Trinity Church.

Commission Dealer.

Geo. W. Hawkins,
Commission Dealer & Inspector
of Lumber.

County Officers

James A. Case,

Supt. Co. Poor, and Notary Public.

Chas. N. Cornell,

County Clerk.

Alex. Mc Donald,

Register of Deeds.

Wm. Kirre,

County & City Surveyor & Architect.

DRUGGISTS.

Blewend & Golling,

Druggists & Chemists.

J. T. Bostwick,
Ag't. Prescription Drug Store,
Sign of the Red Mortar.

FARMERS.

A. R. Richardson,
Farmer, Sec. 20. Town 31 north.
Range 6 east.

Joseph Heustis,

Fruit and Produce Dealer.

HOTELS.

Alpena House,

Julius Potvin, Proprietor.

Denton House,

J. E. Denton, Proprietor.

INSURANCE.

J. F. Mc Sween,

General Insurance Agent.

JEWELER.

Fred S. Goodrich,
Jeweler & Dealer in American Watches, Clocks
Silver & Silver Plated Ware, Books & Stationery.

LAWYERS.

A. R. Mc Donald,

Attorney at Law.

Victor C. Burham,

Attorney and Counsellor.

Lumber Manufacturers & Dealers.

Bewick, Comstock & Co.,
Manuf'rs of Gang Sawed Pine Lumber, Lath,
Pickets, Cedar Posts.
also of the celebrated B. C. & Co's. Pine Shingles.
Office at Detroit, Mills at Alpena

F. W. Gilchrist,
Manufacturer of and Dealer in
Lumber & Lath.

E. Harrington,
Manufacturer & Dealer in Lumber,
and Lath.

Campbell, Potter & Co.,
Manuf'rs. and Dealers in Lumber,
Lath &c.

B. Cushman & Co.,
Manuf'rs & Dealers in Lumber,
Shingles and Clapboards.

Mason, Luce & Co.,
Manuf'rs of Lumber, Shingles,
and R. R. Timber.

F. D. Spratt,

Manuf'r of Shingles.

J. S. Miner,

Manuf'r. of Lumber &c.

G. H. Davis & Co.,

Manuf'rs of Shingles.

Lyman J. Sylvester,

Dealer in Logs, and Country Produce.

Thomas G. Spratt,

Lumberman and Dealer in Logs.

Albert Pack & Co.,
Dealers in White and Norway Pine,
Saw-Logs and Lumber.

Land Hunter,

F. H. Dyer,
Land Hunter. Pine Lands examined & carefully
estimated. Minutes of good farm lands on hand.
References, Geo. N. Fletcher, Detroit,
Hugh Hilliard & Co., Chicago.

MERCHANTS.

Crowell & Godfrey,
Manuf'rs & Dealers in Boots & Shoes, &c.
Also agents for the buying & selling of Pine Lands.
Reliable estimates of Lands furnished.

J. W. Creighton,
Manuf'r. of & Dealer in Boots & Shoes.

Warner Purdy & Co.,
Dealers in Domestic & Fancy Dry
Goods, Gents Furnishing Goods, &c.
Lumbermen's Supplies.

A. Hopper & Co.,
Dealers in General Dry Goods,
and Millinery.

Julius Myers,
Dealer in Staple & Fancy Dry Goods, Clothing
Gents Furnishing Goods, Hats, Caps,
Boots, Shoes, &c.

J. Gillett & Co.,
Dealer in Groceries & Provisions, Boots & Shoes,
Clothing, Hats, Caps, &c.

G. N. Benton,
Dealer in Groceries & Provisions,
Flour, Feed, Hay &c.

Henry Beebe,
Dealer in Groceries & Provisions, Flour, Feed,
Fruit and Vegetables.

Potter & Brother,
Dealers in Hardware.

A. Harshaw,
Dealer in Hardware.

B. Richards & Co.,
Dealers in Hardware.

NEWSPAPERS.

Alpena Argus,
J. C. Viall, Editor. The only
Democratic Journal on Lake Huron.

Alpena County Pioneer,
A. C. Teft, Editor & Proprietor.
First Class Job Office in connection.

PHYSICIANS.

Wm. P. Maiden,
Physician, Surgeon &c.

J. McTavish,
Physician & Surgeon.

A. Jayte,
Physician & Surgeon.

REAL ESTATE.

S. E. Hitchcock,
Real Estate Dealer.

SCHOOLS.

Philip O. Farrell,
Sup't. Catholic Schools.

WAGON MAKERS.

Harvey Edwards & Co.,
Wagon & Carriage Shop, & General
Jobbers in all kinds of Blacksmithing.

WELLS.

D. D. Haggerty,
Artesian, & Salt Well Contractor.

BUSINESS CARDS OF PATRONS IN CHELSEA.

ATTORNEYS.

G. W. Turn Bull,
Attorney at Law,
Chelsea.

James M. Martin,
Attorney at Law,
Chelsea.

BUILDER.

M. B. Flagler,
Architect and Builder,
Chelsea.

CLERGYMEN.

Wm. B. Holt,
Member of Detroit Conference,
Chelsea.

Benjamin Franklin,
Pastor of Congregational Church,
Chelsea.

EXPRESS AGENT.

W. F. Hatch,
Express Agent,
Chelsea.

FARMER.

Thomas Taylor,
Farmer,
Chelsea.

Foundry & Machinists.

J. W. Bolsford,
Manu'fr. of Plows, Ag'l Implements,
and Castings of all kinds to order.
Chelsea.

HOTEL.

T. McKeene,
Proprietor of Mc'Keene House,
Chelsea.

Justice of the Peace,

Orin Thatcher,
Justice of the Peace & Conveyancer,
Chelsea.

H. A. Smith,
Justice of the peace,
Chelsea.

MANUFACTORIES.

Curran White,
Cider & Vinegar Manufactory,
and Planing Mill,
Chelsea.

T. M. Codey,
General Merchant, and Manufacturer and Dealer,
in Cut Stone and Heading.
Chelsea.

Augustus Newburger,
Chelsea Marble works.

MERCHANTS,

A. Durand,
General Merchant,
Chelsea.

B. F. Tuttle,
Dealer in Agricultural Implements,
Chelsea.

James Taylor,
Dealer in Agricultural Implements,
Chelsea.

George H. Burroughs,
Dealer in Dry goods, Groceries,
Boots & Shoes, Drugs, Medicines &c.
Chelsea.

PHYSICIANS.

R. V. Gates,
Physician & Surgeon,
Chelsea.

G. V. Armington,
Eclectic Physician,
Chelsea.

TEACHER.

Miss M. A. Van Tyne,
Teacher in Union School,
Chelsea.

BUSINESS CARDS OF PATRONS IN MILAN.

DENTIST.

H. L. Tewksbury,
Dentist,
Saline and Milan.

FARMERS,

Monroe Allen,
Farmer and Engineer,
Milan.

M. C. Edwards,
Farmer, 81 acres,
Milan.

George Warner,
Farmer, 80 acres,
Milan.

John C. Dahmer,
Farmer, 130 acres,
Milan.

M. C. Brooks,
Farmer, 40 acres,
Milan.

Daniel Murray,
Farmer, 118 acres,
Milan.

G. L. Van Wormer,
Farmer,
Milan.

F. A. Young,
Farmer, 80 acres,
Milan.

William H. Burnham,
Steam Mill, Lumber Manufacturer, & Farmer,
130 acres,
Milan.

Nelson Taylor,
Farmer, 80 acres,
Milan.

Peter Hamlin,
One of the first settlers.
Farmer 156 acres,
On the farm stands St. Mary's Church.

John D. Olcott,
Steam Saw & Shingle Mill, & Farmer of
200 acres. Supervisor of Town of Augusta.

Thomas H. Fuller,
Farmer, 120 acres,
Stony Creek.

PHYSICIAN.

Edward E. Bigelow, M. D.,
Milan.

PLANING MILL.

Stephen W. Andrus,
Planing Mill & Shingle Manufacturer,
Milan.

MERCHANT.

A. B. Hanum,
Dealer in Dry Goods, Groceries,
Ready-made Clothing &c.
Milan.

AGENT.

J. C. Montgomery,
Station Agent L. S. & M. S. R. R.
Manchester.

Agricultural Implements.

R. R. Porter,
Dealer in Reapers, & Mowers, Drills, Threshers &c.
and a general line of Agricultural Implements.
Manchester.

ATTORNEYS.

A. D. Crane,
Attorney at Law,
Dexter.

G. R. Palmer,
Attorney at Law,
Manchester.

D. A. Stephens,
Attorney at Law,
Saline.

BANKERS.

Peoples Bank,
Incorporated under the general banking law of
the State of Michigan.
J. D. Watkins, Pres.   O. F. Hall, Cash.
Manchester.

German American Bank,
Mack, Schmid & Co., Bankers,
Manchester.

W. H. Davenport, & Co.,
Bankers,
Saline.

CARPENTER.

Henry Harbeck.
Carpenter,
Sharon tp., Manchester P. O.

CLERGYMEN.

J. B. Gilman,
Clergyman,
Manchester.

Jacob Horton,
Pastor M. E. Church,
Saline.

J. C. Lesson,
Pastor Baptist Church,
Salem tp., Summit P. O.

Wm. C. Way,
Detroit Conference,
Sharon tp., Manchester P. O.

DENTISTS.

S. L. Jenney,
Dentist,
Dexter.

A. H. Miller,
Surgeon Dentist,
Dexter.

E. Hunter,
Dentist,
Manchester.

W. S. Stowell,
Dentist,
Manchester.

W. C. Carr,
Dentist,
Saline.

FARMERS.

L. F. Sears,
General Farmer, 183 acres, Sec. 30,
Ann Harbor P. O., Northfield.

Wm. Burnham,
General Farmer, 93 acres, Sec. 26,
Delhi Mills P. O., Webster.

H. B. Jones,
Farmer & Breeder of Pure Short Horned Cattle
and Improved Berkshire Hogs, Sec. 32,
Dexter.

W. H. Wilsey,
General Farmer, 124 acres, Sec. 32,
Dexter.

H. N. Johnson,
General Farmer, 180 acres, Sec. 29,
Dexter.

W. E. Stevenson,
General Farmer, 250 acres, Sec. 18,
Dexter.

N. Howell,
General Farmer, 120 acres, Sec. 28,
Dexter.

C. Howell,
General Farmer, 120 acres, Sec. 28,
Dexter.

A. Taylor,
General Farmer, 240 acres, Sec. 24,
Dexter.

Henry Warner,
Breeder & Dealer in Pure Blood Short
Horned Cattle,
Dexter.

John Stanhope Reade,
General Farmer, 133 acres, Sec. 11,
Dexter P. O.,   Webster.

Wm. H. Scadin,
General Farmer, 155 acres, Sec. 26,
Dexter P. O., Webster.

Edwin Ball,
General Farmer, 160 acres, Sec. 22,
Dexter P. O., Webster.

G. Williams,
General Farmer, 200 acres, Sec. 27,
Dexter P. O., Webster.

Phelps Bro's,
Breeders of Pure Short Horned Cattle as a specialty.
Dexter P. O., Webster.

James Winton,
Fruit, Garden & Evergreen Nursery,
27 acres, Sec. 31, N. W.
Freedom tp., Manchester P. O.

Joseph Wels,
Farmer, 800 acres, Sec. 34, N. W.,
Freedom tp., Manchester P. O.

Walter Webb,
Farmer, 113 acres, Sec. 34, N. W.,
Lyndon tp., Chelsea P. O.

Daniel Barton,
Farmer, 205 acres, Sec. 3, N. E.,
Lyndon tp., Unadilla P. O.

Parmenas W. Watts,
Farmer, 200 acres, Sec. 13, N. E.,
Lyndon tp., Unadilla P. O.

O. A. Howell,
Farmer, 150 acres, Sec. 25, S. W.,
Lyndon tp., Chelsea P. O.

Hugh Cassidy,
Farmer, 800 acres, Sec. 33, N. E.,
Lyndon tp., Chelsea P. O.

Geo. Rowe,
Farmer, 120 acres, Sec. 29, N. W.,
Lyndon tp., Waterloo P. O.

S. A. Collins,
Farmer, 290 acres, Sec. 18, S. W.
Lyndon tp., Waterloo P. O.

W. E. Wessel,
Farmer, 896 acres, Sec. 19, S. E.,
Lyndon tp., Waterloo P. O.

John H. Mumby,
Farmer, 90 acres, Sec. 8, S. E.,
Lyndon tp., Unadilla P. O.

Spencer Boyce,
Farmer, 300 acres, Sec. 17, N. W.,
Lyndon tp., Chelsea P. O.

B. C. Boyce,
Farmer, 240 acres, Sec. 5, N. W.,
Lyndon tp., Chelsea P. O.

Parker H. Bott,
Farmer, 98 acres, Sec. 6, S. W.,
Lyndon tp., Chelsea P. O.

Elbridge G. Taylor,
Farmer, 120 acres, Sec. 7, N. E.,
Lyndon tp., Chelsea P. O.

Einathan Skidmore,
Farmer, 280 acres, Sec. 17, S. E.
Lyndon tp., Chelsea P. O.

John Clark,
Farmer, 410 acres, Sec. 21, N. W.
Lyndon tp., Chelsea P. O.

J. Lawrence Shanlan,
Farmer, 449 acres, Sec. 19, N. W.,
Lyndon tp., Chelsea P. O.

J. H. Collins,
Farmer, 300 acres, Sec. 4, S. E.
Lyndon tp., Unadilla P. O.

A. G. Collins,
Farmer, 160 acres, Sec. 4, N. E.,
Lyndon tp., Unadilla P. O.

W. H. Collins,
Farmer, 95 acres, Sec. 8, N. E.
Lyndon tp., Unadilla P. O.

James Little,
Farmer, 246 acres, Sec. 10, N. E.,
Lyndon tp., Unadilla P. O.

Andrew F. Bott,
Farmer, Carpenter & Joiner 20 acres, Sec. 10, N. W.
Lyndon tp., Unadilla P. O.

George Goodwin,
Farmer, 220 acres, Sec. 9, S. W.
Lyndon tp., Chelsea P. O.

Andrew Smith,
General Farmer, 80 acres, Sec. 8,
Northfield tp., Ann Arbor P. O.

Brown Bro's,
General Farmer, 237 acres, Sec. 7,
Northfield tp., Ann Arbor P. O.

Thomas Moe,
General Farmer, 165 acres, Sec. 7,
Northfield tp., Ann Arbor P. O.

Frederick Kempf,
General Farmer, 184 acres, Sec. 33,
Northfield tp., Ann Arbor P. O.

Geo. Sutten,
General Farmer, 295 acres, Sec. 34,
Northfield tp., Ann Arbor P. O.

W. B. Thompson,
Farmer & Manufacturer of Tile.
135 acres Sec. 19,
Salem tp., Ann Arbor P. O.

John Peebles,
General Farmer, 54 acres, Sec. 50,
Salem tp., Ann Arbor P. O.

C. P. Walker,
General Farmer, 80 acres, Sec. 19,
Salem tp., Ann Arbor P. O.

Huson Alsbro,
General Farmer, 120 acres, Sec. 8,
Salem tp., Ann Arbor P. O.

R. M. Simmons,
General Farmer, 40 acres, Sec. 17,
Salem tp., Ann Arbor P. O.

M. S. Nichols,
General Farmer, 109 acres, Sec. 8,
Salem tp., Ann Arbor P. O.

Scott Cook,
General Farmer, 150 acres, Sec. 8,
Salem tp., Summit P. O.

J. O. Bennett,
General Farmer, 150 acres, Sec. 15,
Salem tp., Summit P. O.

Wm. Murray,
General Farmer, 160 acres, Sec. 15,
Salem tp., Summit P. O.

John S. Rider,
General Farmer, 160 acres, Sec. 2,
Salem tp., Summit P. O.

E. A. Simmons,
General Farmer, 45 acres, Sec. 9,
Salem tp., Summit P. O.

John P. Simmons,
General Farmer, 80 acres, Sec. 9,
Salem tp., Summit P. O.

John Crandall,
General Farmer, 210 acres, Sec. 4,
Salem tp., South Lyons P. O.

Alfred S. Waterman,
General Farmer, 190 acres, Sec. 3,
Salem tp., Northville P. O.

P. C. Murray,
General Farmer, 160 acres, Sec. 15,
Salem tp., Summit P. O.

Thomas Wood,
Fruit & Thorough-bred Stock Farmer,
265 acres,   Saline.

Arthur Covert,
General Farmer, 195 acres, Sec. 16,
Superior tp., Ann Arbor P. O.

Averill Burnett,
General Farmer, 165 acres, Sec. 10,
Webster.

John M. Williams,
Manuf'r. of Clarified Cider and Cider Vinegar,
Dexter P. O.
Webster.

W. Blodgett,
Farmer & Breeder of Short Horned Cattle.
204 acres, Sec. 21, Dexter P. O.
Webster.

FLOURING MILLS.

Evarts & Co.,
Proprietors of Dexter Mills. Dealers in Flour, Grain
and Feed, Plaster and Lime,
Dexter.

BUSINESS CARDS OF PATRONS IN WASHTENAW COUNTY.

FARMERS.

E. P. Downer,
Farmer, 210 acres, Sec. 7, N. E.
Lima tp., Chelsea P. O.

Nathan Peirce,
Farmer, 265 acres, Sec. 8, S. W.,
Lima tp., Chelsea P. O.

Garret Yereance,
Farmer, 100 acres, Sec. 10, N. W.,
Lima tp., Dexter P. O.

Elias Westfall,
Farmer, 200 acres, Sec. 9, S. E.
Lima tp., Chelsea P. O.

I. C. Cooper,
Farmer, 120 acres, Sec. 10, N. E.
Lima tp., Dexter P. O.

Robt. Buchanan,
Farmer, 120 acres, Sec. 10, N. E.
Lima tp., Dexter P. O.

A. M. Freer,
Farmer, 120 acres, Sec. 18, N. W.
Lima tp., Chelsea P. O.

C. W. Brown,
Farmer, 330 acres, Sec. 17, S. W.
Lima tp., Chelsea P. O.

J. M. Betts,
Farmer, 235 acres, Sec. 17, S. E.
Lima tp., Chelsea P. O.

Warren Cushman,
Farmer, 182 acres, Sec. 9, S. W.
Lima tp., Chelsea P. O.

Erastus Whaley,
Farmer, 206 acres, Sec. 18, N.W.,
Lima tp., Chelsea P. O.

Peter Fletcher,
Farmer, 110 acres, Sec. 19, S.W.
Lima tp., Chelsea P. O.

Jesse Scott,
Farmer, 164 acres, Sec. 82, S. W.,
Lima tp., Chelsea P. O.

Levi Whipple,
Farmer, 120 acres, Sec. 33, S. W.,
Lima tp., Chelsea P. O.

James McLaren,
Farmer, 313 acres, Sec. 34, S. W.,
Lima.

E. H. Keyes,
Farmer, 160 acres, Sec. 34, N. W.
Lima.

Byron Whitaker,
Farmer, 240 acres, Sec. 23, S. E.,
Lima.

Geo. M. Mitchell,
Farmer, 160 acres, Sec. 28, N. E.,
Lima.

Irving Storms,
Farmer, 80 acres, Sec. 22, N. W.,
Lima.

S. Stocking,
Farmer, 80 acres, Sec. 21, N .E.,
Lima tp., Chelsea P. O.

Alva Freer,
Farmer, 158 acres, Sec. 16, S. E.,
Lima tp., Chelsea P. O.

Samuel C. Freer,
Farmer, 80 acres, Sec. 21, S. W.,
Lima tp., Chelsea P. O.

Chas. A. Guerin,
Farmer, 160 acres, Sec. 14, N.W.,
Lima tp., Dexter P. O.

E. A. Nordman,
Farmer, 200 acres, Sec. 11, S. E.,
Lima tp., Dexter P. O.

John Pratt,
Farmer, 180 acres, Sec. 2, N. W.,
Lima tp., Dexter P. O.

Geo. Goodrich,
Farmer, 160 acres, Sec. 1, S. E.
Lima tp., Dexter P. O.

David K. Dixon,
Farmer, 160 acres, Sec. 13, S. W.,
Lima tp., Dexter P. O.

Oscar Easton,
Farmer, 160 acres, Sec. 13, S. W.,
Lima tp., Dexter P. O.

Godfrey Lewick,
Farmer, 160 acres, Sec. 22, S. E.,
Lima.

Geo. R. Williams,
Farmer, 258 acres, Sec. 15, S. E.
Lima.

Chas. B. Palmer,
Farmer, 108 acres, Sec. 23, N. W.,
Lima.

Linval Ward,
Farmer, 176 acres, Sec. 23, N. W.
Lima.

Sampson Parker,
Farmer, 220 acres, Sec. 24, N. E.,
Lima tp., Dexter P. O.

Chas. Clements,
Farmer, 200 acres, Sec. 24, S. E.,
Lima tp., Dexter P. O.

Thos. Jewett,
Farmer, 120 acres, Sec. 30, N.W.,
Lima tp., Chelsea P.O.

D. R. Jenks,
Farmer, 140 acres, Sec. 29, S. W.,
Lima tp., Chelsea P. O.

Consider Cushman,
Farmer, 280 acres, Sec. 29, N. E.,
Lima tp., Chelsea P. O.

Chas. Whitaker,
Farmer, 313 acres, Sec. 19, S. E.
Lima tp., Chelsea P. O.

Thomas Young,
Farmer, 200 acres, Sec. 17, N. E.
Lyndon tp., Chelsea P. O.

Sylvester N. Clark,
Farmer, 337 acres, Sec. 21, N. E.
Lyndon tp., Chelsea P. O.

F. Everett,
Farmer, 250 acres, Sec. 2, S. E.,
Sharon tp., Chelsea P. O.

Wm. Graham,
Farmer, 188 acres, Sec. 24, S. W.,
Sharon tp., Manchester P. O.

J. C. McGee,
Farmer, & Stock Dealer, 550 acres, Sec. 27, N. W.
Sharon tp., Manchester P. O.

Wm. F. Hall,
Farmer, 210 acres, Sec. 30, N.W.,
Sharon tp., Norvell P. O.

Mowry A. Pierce,
Farmer, 350 acres, Sec. 22, N. W.,
Sharon tp., Manchester P. O.

Wm. Bowers,
Farmer, 175 acres, Sec. 37, S. E.,
Sharon tp., Manchester P. O.

Mrs. Polly Tallman,
Farmer, 40 acres, Sec. 11, S. W.,
Sharon tp., Manchester P. O.

Jay Everett,
Farmer, 280 acres, Sec. 2,
Sharon tp., Chelsea P. O.

J. B. Lemm,
Farmer, 236 acres, Sec. 7, N. W.,
Sharon tp., Grass Lake P. O.

Chas. Dorr,
Farmer 40 acres, Sec. 9, S. E.,
Sharon tp., Grass Lake P. O.

Cyrenus Rhoads,
Farmer, 140 acres, Sec. 9, N. E.,
Sharon tp., Sylvan P. O.

G. Edwin States,
Farmer and Millwright, 75 acres, Sec. 3, S. W.
Sharon tp., Sylvan P. O.

Harvey Blackman,
Farmer, 160 acres, Sec. 21, N. E.,
Sharon tp., Manchester P. O.

Amos Bullard,
Farmer, 260 acres, Sec. 31, S. E.,
Sharon tp., Manchester P. O.

Walt Peck,
Farmer, 200 acres, Sec. 33, S.W.,
Sharon tp., Manchester P. O.

R. G. Perry,
Farmer, 160 acres, Sec. 33, N. W.,
Sharon tp., Manchester P. O.

E. J. Rice,
Farmer, 120 acres, Sec. 32, N. W.,
Sharon tp., Manchester P. O.

Richard Wheeler,
Farmer, 140 acres, Sec. 31, N. W.,
Sylvan tp., Chelsea P. O.

Ellen Guthrie,
Farmer, 80 acres, Sec. 15, N. W.,
Sylvan.

James Tyndall,
Farmer, 120 acres, Sec. 15, S. W.,
Sylvan.

George Taylor,
Farmer, 77 acres, Sec. 15, N.W.,
Sylvan tp., Chelsea P. O.

E. A. Peirce,
Farmer, 216 acres, Sec. 24, N. W.,
Sylvan tp., Chelsea P. O.

C. Z. Chipman,
Farmer, 100 acres, Sec. 24, S. W.,
Sylvan tp., Chelsea P. O.

W. H. Davidson,
Farmer, 112, acres, Sec. 36, N. W.,
Sylvan tp., Chelsea P. O.

Freeman W. Baldwin,
Farmer, 160 acres, Sec. 22, S. E.,
Sylvan tp., Chelsea P. O.

W. W. Riggs,
Farmer, 280 acres, Sec. 31, N. E.,
Sylvan.

Samuel C. Cooper,
Farmer, 173 acres, Sec. 31, S.W.,
Sylvan tp., Franciscoville P. O.

Milo Baldwin,
Farmer, 160 acres, Sec. 11, N. E.,
Sylvan tp., Chelsea P. O.

Hiram Peirce,
Farmer, 450 acres, Sec. 13, N. E.,
Sylvan tp., Chelsea P. O.

James M. Congdon,
Farmer, 200 acres, Sec. 12, S. E.
Sylvan tp., Chelsea P. O.

C. T. Conklin,
Farmer, 209 acres, Sec. 29, N. E.
Sylvan.

Wm. Judson,
Farmer, 102 acres, Sec. 34, N. W.,
Sylvan.

P. Hathaway,
Farmer, 125 acres, Sec. 34, S. E.,
Sylvan.

W. A. Begole,
Farmer, 120 acres, Sec. 26, S. E.,
Sylvan tp., Chelsea P. O.

Romayn P. Chase,
Farmer, 120 acres, Sec. 25, N. E.,
Sylvan tp., Chelsea P. O.,

John Cook,
Farmer, 133 acres, Sec. 24, S. E.
Sylvan tp., Chelsea P. O.

Chas. H. Wines,
Farmer, 100 acres, Sec. 24 S. E.,
Sylvan tp., Chelsea P. O.

FLOURING MILL.

John H. Evarts,
Proprietor Dexter Flouring Mills,
Dexter.

Furniture Manufactory.

John Costello,
Furniture Manufacturer,
Dexter.

HOTELS.

J. C. Demosh,
Proprietor Belleville Hotel,
Belleville, Wayne County.

Henry Landon,
Proprietor Farmers Home Hotel,
Belleville, Wayne County.

Goodyear House,
Henry Goodyear Proprietor,
Manchester.

Kanouse & Clark,
American Hotel,
Saline.

Justices of the Peace.

George E. Page,
Justice of the Peace,
Dexter.

I. Bailey,
Justice of peace & Carriage Manu'fr.
Dexter.

MERCHANTS.

Lewis H. Weir & Son,
Dealers in Hardware,
Manchester.

BUSINESS CARDS OF PATRONS IN WASHTENAW COUNTY.

Smith & Keal,
Dealers in Dry Goods, Groceries, Notions &c., Dexter.

Ross & Bruegel,
Dealers in Hardware, Stoves, and Agricultural Implements, & Manuf'rs of Copper Tin & Sheet Iron Ware, Manchester.

W. H. Bessac,
Dealer in Dry Goods, Groceries, Hardware, Drugs, Medicine &c. Manchester.

G. W. Doty,
Dealer in Groceries, Drugs, Medicines, Notions, Boots & Shoes, Hats & Caps, Manchester.

Geo. S. Wheeler,
County Sup't Public Instruction, & Dealer in Dry Goods and Groceries. Salem tp., Summit P. O.

John K. Fowler,
General Merchant, Saline.

NEWSPAPERS.

Lansing Journal,
Geo. P. Sanford, Editor and Proprietor. Also Real Estate, and Insurance Ag't, Insurance Capital represented, over $45,000,000, Lansing, Ingham Co.

Manchester Enterprise,
Mat. D. Blosser, Editor & Proprietor, Manchester.

PHYSICIANS.

Daniel Forbes, M D.,
Physician & Surgeon, Bellville.

H. A. Carr, M. D.,
Physician and Surgeon, Lima.

SHOEMAKER.

Geo. Gutekunst,
6 acres, Sec. 28 S. E., Lima tp., Chelsea.

SAW-MILL & LUMBER.

E. M. Ford,
Saw-mill & Lumber, Bellville.

TEACHERS,

Frank Emerick,
Principal of School, Bellville.

N. A. Barrett,
Principal Public Schools, Saline.

Alice E. Fox,
Teacher, Sylvan.

Phebe G. Mohr,
Teacher, Sylvan tp., Chelsea P. O.

Miss Ida E. Poole,
Teacher, Sharon.

WAGON MAKER.

Chas. Guerin,
Wagon Maker, Lima.

BUSINESS CARDS OF PATRONS IN WAYNE COUNTY.

AGENTS.

E. D. Howe,
Agent M. C. R. R. and American Express Co., Dearbornville.

W. U. Thayer,
Agent D. L. & L. M. R. R. and Lumber Dealer, Plymouth.

O. S. Wells,
Shipping Agent, Wyandotte.

ATTORNEYS.

Jerome T. Johnson,
Attorney at Law, Plymouth.

Geo W. Coomer,
Attorney at Law, Wyandotte.

BANKS.

E. J. Penniman,
President of the first National Bank, Plymouth.

Holly Merchants National Bank,
Capital $100,000, S. S. Wilhelm, Cash. Holly, Oakland Co.,

BLACKSMITH.

R. A. Savage,
Repairing and Horse Shoeing, Bellville.

CARPENTERS.

Otis E. Warren,
Carpenter and Builder, Wayne.

R. H. McKinstry,
Carpenter & Joiner Sec. 8, Van Buren tp., Canton P. O.

CITIZENS.

John Bennett,
Citizen, Wyandotte.

S. D. Morse,
Citizen, Wyandotte.

CLERGYMEN,

C. Zimmerman,
Clergyman, Wyandotte.

Theodor Wettenberg,
Priest of the R. C. Church. Wyandotte.

Wm. De Bever,
Priest of the R. C. Church. Wyandotte.

ENGINEERS.

F. H. Pitcher,
Engineer and Sawyer, Wayne.

R. H. Ford,
Engineer and Machinist, Wyandotte.

FARMERS.

Johiael Burt,
Farmer 280 acres, Bellville.

Betsey Jewett,
Farmer 840 acres, Bellville.

Wm. E. Warner,
Farmer, 157 acres, Sec. 29, Bellville.

Thomas Phillips,
Farmer, 100 acres, Bellville.

Jared Stephens,
Farmer, 36 acres, Sec. 21, Canton.

J. D. Harrison,
Farmer, Lumberman & Professional Engineer, 257 acres, Sec. 30, Canton.

J. S. Lyon,
Lumberman 60 acres, Sec. 19, Canton tp., Denton's P. O.

H. O. Hanford,
Farmer, 290 acres, Sec. 8, Canton tp., Plymouth P. O.

D. D. Cady,
Farmer, 120 acres, Sec. 4, Canton tp., Plymouth P. O.

Hiram Murray,
Farmer, 191 acres, Sec. 6, Canton tp., Plymouth P.O.

Ira E. Kluyon,
Farmer, 320 acres, Sec. 6, Canton tp., Plymouth P. O.

C. R. Pattengell,
Farmer & Secretary of F. M. Fire Ins Co. of Monroe and Wayne Co's, 145 acres, Sec. 16, Canton tp., Plymouth P. O.

John Tillotson,
Farmer, 160 acres, Sec. 3, Canton tp., Plymouth P. O.

B. F. Wright,
Farmer, 80 acres, Sec. 4, Canton tp., Plymouth P. O.

S. Harmon,
Farmer, 55 acres, Sec. 8, Canton tp., Plymouth P. O.

D. Tuller,
Farmer, 80 acres, Sec. 23, Canton tp., Wayne P. O.

Geo. Berdan,
Farmer, Carpenter & Joiner, 102 acres, Sec. 13, Canton tp., Wayne P. O.

R. P. Clark,
Farmer, 70 acres, Sec. 24, Canton tp., Wayne P. O.

B. Hodgekinson,
Farmer, 27 acres, Sec. 25, Canton tp., Wayne P. O.

S. Cobb,
Farmer, 100 acres, Sec. 20, Canton tp., Ypsilanti P. O.

Wm. Holmes,
Farmer, 80 acres, Sec. 19, Canton tp., Ypsilanti P. O.

John Huston,
Farmer, 130 acres, Sec. 20, Canton tp., Ypsilanti P. O.

A. C. Harrison,
Grain, Stock and Hay Farmer, 120 acres, Sec. 31, Clayton tp., Flint P. O., Lenawee Co.

A. Lapham,
Hay, Grain, Stock, Beef and Pork, 40 acres, Dearbornville.

Alfred Moore,
Farmer, 270 acres, Sec. 7, Plymouth P .O.

Walter Scotten,
Wool, Stock, Grain &c., 80 acres, Sec. 35, Plymouth.

Peter Trinkaus,
General Farmer, 80 acres, Plymouth.

C. C. Allen,
Wool, Stock, Grain &c., 120 acres, Plymouth.

D. C. Shattuck,
Stock, Grain & Fruits 110 acres, Sec. 26, Plymouth.

N. T. Sly,
Stock, Grains, &c., 163 acres, Sec. 24, Plymouth.

T. Warren,
Farmer, 135 acres, Sec. 1, Sumpter tp., New Boston P. O.

J. R. Clark,
Farmer, 136 acres, Sec. 23, Van Buren tp., Bellville P. O.

F. L. Robb,
Farmer, 112 acres, Sec. 23, Van Buren tp., Bellville P. O.

Obed Coy,
Farmer, 120 acres, Sec. 24, Van Buren tp., Bellville P. O.

Jos. A. Spear,
Farmer, 123 acres, Sec. 14, Van Buren tp., Bellville P. O.

Cyrel C. Potter,
Farmer, 89 acres, Sec. 14, Van Buren tp., Bellville P. O.

Thomas Quirk,
Farmer, 171 acres, Sec. 21, Van Buren tp., Bellville P. O.

Dunham P. Riggs,
Farmer, 346 acres, Sec. 25, Van Buren tp., Bellville P. O.

Henry H. Rosenkrans,
Farmer, 100 acres, Sec. 36, Van Buren tp., Bellville P. O.

Wm. Renton,
Farmer, 160 acres, Sec. 36, Van Buren tp., Bellville P. O.

Chas Danes,
Farmer, 100 acres, Sec. 3, Van Buren tp Bellville P. O.

Geo. Elwell,
Farmer, 103 acres, Sec. 34, Van Buren tp., Bellville P. O.

Isaac Pearl,
Farmer, 53 acres, Sec. 5, Van Buren tp., Bellville P. O.

BUSINESS CARDS OF PATRONS IN WAYNE COUNTY.

Jonathan Miller,
Farmer, 89 acres, Sec. 20,
Van Buren tp., Bellville P. O.

F. W. Moon,
Farmer 100 acres, Sec. 17,
Van Buren tp., Bellville P. O.

Thos. Leonard,
Farmer, 70 acres, Sec. 18,
Van Buren tp., Bellville P. O.

Oliver Westfall,
Farmer,
Van Buren tp., Bellville P. O.

George M. Thirkittle,
Farmer, 120 acres, Sec. 10,
Patentee of Thirkittle's Champion Grain-drill,
Van Buren tp., Bellville P. O.

Horatio A. French,
Farmer, 90 acres, Sec. 12,
Van Buren tp., Wayne P. O.

Peter P. Terhune,
Farmer, 86 acres, Sec. 14,
Van Buren tp., Bellville P. O.

W. Lee Yost,
Farmer, 120 acres, Sec. 3,
Van Buren tp., Canton P. O.

William H. Mc Kinstry,
Farmer, 88 acres, Sec. 3,
Van Buren tp., Canton P. O.

Arch'd Mc Kinstry,
Farmer, 175 acres, Sec. 2,
Van Buren tp., Canton P. O.

S. Y. Denton,
Farmer, 500 acres Sec. 5, general store & saw-mill,
Van Buren tp., Denton P. O.

A. M. Van Tassel,
Farmer, 40 acres, Sec. 5,
Van Buren tp., Denton P. O.

Thomas Barton,
Farmer, 35 acres, Sec. 6,
Van Buren tp., Denton P. O.

E. B. Warner,
Farmer,
Van Buren tp., Bellville P. O.

Wm. E. Warner Jr.,
Farmer,
Van Buren tp., Bellville P. O.

Woodbury Clark,
Farmer, 67 acres, Sec. 22,
Van Buren tp., Bellville P. O.

Gilbert Riggs,
Farmer, 191 acres, Sec. 22,
Van Buren tp., Bellville P. O.

Joseph Voorheis,
Farmer, 100 acres Sec. 22,
Van Buren tp., Bellville P. O.

Loren Riggs,
Farmer, 105 acres, Sec. 53,
Van Buren tp., Bellville P. O.

R. P. Clark,
Farmer, 100 acres, Sec. 23,
Van Buren tp., Bellville P. O.

Amos Bradshaw,
Farmer, 40 acres, Sec. 83,
Van Buren tp., Bellville P. O.

Chas. Ferguson,
Farmer, 180 acres, Sec. 22,
Van Buren tp., Bellville P. O.

N. W. Pierson,
Farmer, 40 acres, Sec. 81,
Van Buren tp., Rawsonville P. O.

Perrin Brown,
Farmer, 110 acres, Sec. 31,
Van Buren tp., Rawsonville P. O.

Alex. Robb,
Farmer, 80 acres, Sec. 27, Carpenter & Joiner,
Van Buren tp., Bellville P. O.

Solomon Haigley,
Farmer, 40 acres, Sec. 27,
Van Buren tp., Bellville P. O.

Wm. Sands,
Farmer, 75 acres, Sec. 27,
Van Buren tp., Bellville P. O.

James G. Mc Quald,
Farmer, 40 acres Sec. 27,
Van Buren tp., Bellville P. O.

Wilkinson Dean,
Farmer, 80 acres, Sec. 27,
Van Buren tp., Bellville P. O.

J. J. Palmer,
Farmer,
Wayne.

FLOURING MILL.

Wyandotte City Flouring
Mill Company.

FRUIT CULTURIST.

T. T. Lyon,
Fruit Culturist,
Plymouth.

FURNITURE.

John F. W. Then,
Furniture Dealer and Manuf'r of
Sash Doors & Blinds, Wyandotte.

HOTELS.

L. D. Van Bleck,
Proprietor of Hotel,
Holly, Oakland Co.

Frank Varney,
Wayne Hotel.

LIVERY.

A. C. Perrin,
Livery and Sale Stables,
Fort Wayne, Indiana.

LUMBER.

E. M. Ford,
Saw Mill & Lumber,
Bellville.

James Stewart,
Lumberman, 60 acres, Sec. 36,
Van Buren tp., Bellville P. O.

James T. Hurst,
Lumber Dealer, Contractor & Builder,
Wyandotte.

MANUFACTURERS.

Cody & Ainsley,
Manuf'rs & Wholesale Dealers in Stairs & Heading.
Also Steam Saw Mill,
Bellville.

Samuel P. Duffield, Ph. D., M. D.,
Consulting and Manufacturing
Chemist, Dearbornville.

Joseph Girardin,
Mann'fr. of Buggies, Wagons,
Cutters & Sleighs, Wyandotte.

E. D. Sheldon,
Manufacturer of Boots & Shoes,
Dearbornville.

West & Kenyon,
Manu'frs. of Washing Machines,
& Corn Shellers, Plymouth.

Wyandotte
Agricultural & Stove Works,
Elisha Mix, Secretary & Treasurer, John D.
Miller, Superintendent. Wyandotte.

MECHANICS.

Orin B. Carpenter,
Wayne Mills, Morgan and Carpenter,
Dearbornville.

R. C. Conwell,
Master Mechanic,
Wyandotte.

Albert Brown,
Foreman in Plate Mill,
Wyandotte.

Joseph Hicks,
Refiner of Iron,
Wyandotte.

MERCHANTS.

J. A. Sexton,
Merchant—General Dealer,
Dearbornville.

E. H. Stone & Co.,
General Merchants,
Holly, Oakland Co.,

Thos. P. May,
Dealer in Dry Goods & Groceries,
Plymouth.

Geo. A. Starkweather,
Dry Goods & Groceries. Dealer in Real Estate,
Plymouth.

I. N. Hedder,
Farmer & Dealer in Hardware, Hay & Grain.
Farm 45 acres, Plymouth.

G. D. Hibbard & Son,
P. M. and Merchant Tailor,
Wyandotte.

J. A. Morgan,
Merchant Tailor, and Dealer in Ready Made
Clothing, Hats, Caps, &c.,
Wyandotte.

A. Leakey,
Merchant, Groceries & Provisions,
Wyandotte.

PHOTOGRAPHER.

Frank March,
Photographer,
Wyandotte.

PHYSICIANS.

E. S. Snow,
Physician and Surgeon,
Dearbornville.

W. C. Clemo,
Physician and Surgeon,
Plymouth.

A. Bostwick,
Physician and Surgeon,
Trenton.

POSTMASTER.

David Hoburt,
Postmaster,
Holly, Oakland Co.

PUBLISHERS.

Griffill & Nellis,
Publisher "Wyandotte Enterprise "
Wyandotte.

REAL ESTATE.

Giles B. Slocum,
Real Estate,
Trenton.

D. H. Roberts,
Real Estate, Insurance Agent, Agricultural
Implements, Bank Building, Room No. 3,
Wyandotte.

SHIP BUILDERS.

Wyandotte Iron Ship Building Works,
Kirby Bro's, Proprietors.
Wyandotte.

SHOE MAKER.

A. G. Evans,
Shoemaker,
Bellville.

TEACHERS.

Miss Ella Edmonds,
Teacher of Belleville Union School,
Bellville.

Frank Emerick,
Principal of School,
Bellville.

Miss Emma Miller,
Teacher of Music, & Belleville
Union School, Bellville.

Hugh Conklin,
Principal Public School,
Trenton.

Mary E. Limbocker,
Assistant in Public School,
Trenton.

Mary E. Lackey,
Principal High School,
Wyandotte.

Mrs. Nettie Denman,
Assistant Teacher in Public School,
Wyandotte.

Nellie E. Knight,
Principal 1st Ward School,
Wyandotte.

Hattie Loselle,
Assistant Teacher in 1st Ward School,
Wyandotte.

Helen Daly,
Principal in 3rd Ward School,
Wyandotte.

Eliza Jackson,
Assistant Teacher in 3rd Ward School,
Wyandotte.

John Walt,
Teacher of the Evang. Luth. School,
Wyandotte.

WAGON MAKER.

E. R. Roys,
Wagon Maker,
Bellville.

ATTORNEYS.

Daniel C. Marsh,
Attorney, and Counselor at Law,
Brighton.

B. F. Button,
Attorney at Law, & Real Estate Ag't.
Handy tp., Fowlerville P. O.

BLACKSMITH.

B. R. Root,
Blacksmith,
Brighton.

CAPITALIST.

William Williamson,
Capitalist,
Howell.

CLERGYMAN.

G. W. Jenks,
Pastor Baptist Church,
Brighton.

FARMERS.

L. D. Fonda,
Farmer, 280 acres, Sec. 33,
Brighton.

L. B. Stewart,
Farmer, 320 acres, Sec. 53,
Brighton.

Wm. S. Conely,
Farmer, 463 acres, Sec. 18,
Brighton.

J. B. Thurber,
Farmer & Supervisor 200 acres Sec. 4,
Brighton.

Wheaton Hicks,
Farmer, 204 acres Sec. 21,
Brighton.

Melzer Bird,
Farmer, 200 acres, Sec. 14,
Brighton.

J. B. Collins,
Farmer, 120 acres, Sec. 14,
Brighton.

John Carter,
General Farmer, 320 acres, Sec. 11,
Brighton tp., Milford P. O.

Henry T. Ross,
Farmer, and Breeder of pure Merino Sheep, also
keeps a Park of Elks, 467 acres, Sec. 2,
Brighton tp., Milford P. O.

G. B. Flansburg,
General Farmer, 413 acres, Sec. 2,
Brighton tp., Milford P. O.

Geo. Pierson,
General Farmer, 100 acres, Sec. 10,
Brighton tp., Milford P. O.

A. T. Frisbee,
Farmer, 414 acres, Sec. 26,
Cohoctah tp., Oak Grove P. O.

Moses Jones,
Farmer, 517 acres, Sec. 25,
Cohoctah tp., Oak Grove P. O.

W. P. Stow,
Farmer & Builder, 240 acres, Sec. 30,
Conway tp., Fowlerville P. O.

E. W. Grant,
Farmer, 140 acres, Sec. 38,
Conway tp., Fowlerville P. O.

Geo. Phillips,
Farmer,
Conway tp., Fowlerville P.O.

C. Bush,
Farmer,
Conway tp., Fowlerville P. O.

O. H. Benedict,
Farmer and Dealer, in Agricultural Implements,
124 acres, Sec. 16, Genoa tp., Howell P. O.

Henry Hartman,
General Farming, 14 acres, Sec. 14,
Genoa.

Richard Behrens,
Farmer, and Dealer in Stock,
400 acres, Sec. 14, Genoa.

Hiram Kellogg,
General Farming, 212 acres, Sec. 11,
Genoa tp., Brighton P.O.

Joseph Rider,
Farmer and Dealer in fine Sheep and Stock,
271 acres, Sec. 17, Genoa tp., Howell P. O.

Geo. E. Beurman,
Farmer, 170 acres, Sec. 27,
Genoa tp., Brighton P. O.

Chas. E. Beurman,
Farmer and Stock Dealer,
200 acres, Sec. 34, Genoa tp., Brighton P. O.

Geo. W. Dean,
General Farmer, 194 acres, Sec. 26,
Green Oak.

H. & G. Lee,
Gen'l Farmers, 242 acres, Sec's. 19 & 20,
Green Oak tp., Brighton P. O.

D. M. Caldwell,
General Farmer, 60 acres, Sec. 32,
Green Oak tp., Whitmore Lake P. O.

A. C. Cady,
General Farmer, 115 acres, Sec. 4,
Hamburg.

Jonathan Burnett,
General Farmer, 80 acres, Sec. 19,
Green Oak tp., Hamburg P. O.

Wm. Ball,
Farmer, and Supt. Public Instruction,
440 acres, Sec. 20, Hamburg.

C. Dunning,
General Farmer, 280 acres, Sec. 15,
Hamburg tp., Pettysville P. O.

Adolph Buck,
General Farmer, and Dealer in Blooded Horses,
880 acres, Sec. 9, Hamburg tp., Brighton P. O.

Ralph Fowler,
Retired Farmer, and Dealer in Village Lots,
Handy tp., Fowlerville P. O.

Seth H. Judd,
Farmer and Dealer in Sheep, 120 acres, Sec. 20,
Handy tp., Fowlerville P. O.

Isaac Page,
Farmer and Horse Painter, 100 acres, Sec. 28,
Handy tp., Fowlerville P. O.

O. Swift,
General Farmer, 40 acres, Sec. 18,
Handy tp., Fowlerville P. O.

Isaac T. Wright,
General Farmer, 160 acres, Sec. 27,
Handy tp., Fowlerville P. O.

H. B. Davis,
General Farmer, 60 acres, Sec. 28,
Handy tp., Fowlerville P. O.

D. W. Disturff,
General Farmer, 220 acres, Sec. 12,
Handy tp., Fowlerville P. O.

Geo. Lovely,
Farmer and Dealer, in all kinds of Stock & Produce,
160 acres, Sec. 26, Handy tp., Fowlerville P. O.

D. Case,
Farmer, Sup't of Poor, and Insurance Agent,
120 acres, Sec. 22, Howell.

D. C. & A. D. Kneeland,
Farmers and Dealers, in Fine Wool Sheep,
450 acres, Sec. 18, Howell.

D. J. Filkins,
General Farmer, 200 acres, Sec. 12,
Howell.

S. Hildebrant,
General Farmer, 175 acres, Sec. 10,
Howell.

S. E. Howe,
General Farmer, 160 acres Sec. 15,
Howell.

Geo. Coleman,
General Farmer, 200 acres, Sec. 22,
Marion.

Josephus Lare,
General Farmer, 140 acres, Sec. 9,
Osceola tp., Howell P. O.

E. J. Hardy & Son,
Farmers, and Dealers in Fine Cattle and Sheep,
572 acres, Sec. 26, Osceola Centre P. O.

Edward Browning,
General Farmer, 360 acres, Sec. 34,
Osceola.

John W. Botsford, & Sons,
General Farmers and Stock Raisers,
708 acres, Sec's. 10 & 22, Osceola.

Roswell Pettibone,
General Farmer, 80 acres, Sec. 33,
Osceola tp., Howell P. O.

A. B. Hosley,
General Farmer, and Breeder of Full Blooded Stock
240 acres, Sec. 16, Osceola tp., Howell P. O.

C. M. Wood,
Farmer, 373 acres, Sec. 16,
Putnam tp., Pinckney P. O.

S. G. Ives,
General Farmer, 200 acres, Sec. 34,
Unadilla.

Christopher Taylor,
General Farmer, 240 acres, Sec. 8,
Unadilla.

W. A. Williams,
General Farmer, 120 acres, Sec. 33,
Unadilla.

Wm. S. Bird,
General Farmer, 290 acres, Sec. 19,
Unadilla.

Mrs. A. Marshall,
Farmer, 305 acres, Sec. 34,
Unadilla.

I. S. Davis,
General Farmer, 120 acres,
Unadilla.

G. J. Daniels,
General Farmer, 157 acres, Sec. 21,
Unadilla.

John Green,
Farmer,
Unadilla.

R. Woodworth,
General Farmer, 380 acres, Sec. 15,
Unadilla tp., Plainfield P. O.

J. B. Foster,
General Farmer, 185 acres Sec. 3,
Unadilla tp., Plainfield P. O.

Wm. R. Coleman,
General Farmer, 240 acres, Sec. 12,
Unadilla tp., Pinckney P. O.

FLOURING MILLS.

Albright & Thompson,
Brighton Flouring Mills,
Brighton.

Calvin Wilcox,
Flouring Mill, Flour and Feed for Sale,
Howell.

MANUFACTURER.

W. W. Starkey,
Manufacturer of Sugar, Molasses, & Rum Shooks,
Handy tp., Fowlerville P. O.

MERCHANTS.

Geo. W. Palmerton,
Dealer in General Merchandise,
Handy tp., Fowlerville P. O.

O. H. Obert & Co.,
Dealers in Dry Goods, Groceries, Hats & Caps,
Boots and Shoes &c., Unadilla.

John Dunning,
Dealer in Dry Goods, Groceries, Paints, Oils, &c.,
Unadilla.

M. Topping & Son.
General Merchants & Dealers in Staves, & Barrels,
and owners of Plainfield Mills, Unadilla.

NOTARY PUBLIC.

W. H. Pullen,
Post Master, Notary Public &
Dealer in Books, Handy, Fowlerville.

PHYSICIANS.

Byron Defendern,
Homeopathic Physician,
Handy tp., Fowlerville P. O.

James Canon, M. D.,
Physician,
Unadilla tp., Iosco P. O.

BUSINESS CARDS OF PATRONS IN MUSKEGON COUNTY.

Architect and Builder.

Asahel G. Hopkins,
Architect and Builder, & Justice of the Peace,
Whitehall.

ATTORNEYS.

Frank Brocella,
Attorney at Law,
Muskegon.

Hodges & Elsworth,
Attorneys, Counselors and Solicitors,
Whitehall.

Henry Slater,
Counselor and Attorney at Law.
Refer to Exchange Bank,
Whitehall.

BANKER.

F. Blackmarr,
Banker,
Whitehall.

DENTIST.

Benj. Treat,
Dentist,
Whitehall.

DRUGGIST.

A. Malcolm,
Druggist,
Montague.

ENGINEER.

G. Mears,
Mechanical Engineer,
Whitehall.

FARMERS & FRUIT GROWERS.

Daniel Upton,
Farmer and Fruit Grower,
Lake Harbor.

Robert Card,
Fruit Grower and Engineer,
Lake Harbor.

Nathan E. Fisk,
Fruit Grower,
Lake Harbor.

A. S. Cobb,
Horticulturist,
Lake Harbor.

Milo Rowe & Son,
General Farmers and Fruit Growers,
Lake Harbor.

J. O. Antisdale,
Extensive Fruit Grower,
Lake Harbor.

Wm. Churchill,
General Farmer and Fruit Grower,
Lake Harbor.

Edward L. Page,
Fruit Grower,
Lake Harbor.

David Swarthout,
Fruit Grower and Carpenter,
Lake Harbor.

F. F. Bowles,
Fruit Grower and Millwright,
Lake Harbor.

H. A. Winslow,
Farmer and Horticulturist,
Lake Harbor.

M. O'Hara,
Extensive Fruit Grower,
Lake Harbor.

Ambrose Hood,
Dealer in Live Stock,
Whitehall.

HOTELS.

Cosmopolitan Hotel,
M. Dodge & Son, Proprietors.
Livery Stable connected with the House,
Whitehall.

Harwood House,
H. N. Wilcox, Proprietor,
Whitehall.

INVENTOR.

E. C. Dicey,
Inventor of Proprietor of Dicey's Improved, Patent
Gang Edger and Ripping Machine, and Dicey's
Patent Log Turner, Whitehall.

LIVERY STABLES.

Partridge Brothers,
Livery Stable,
Montague.

Thos. Merrill,
Livery Stable,
Muskegon.

LUMBERMEN.

Chapin & Foss,
Manuf'rs & Dealers in Lumber. Yard's Cor. of
Van Buren and Carroll St's., Chicago.
Chicago and Muskegon.

D. C. Bowen & Co.,
Manuf'rs of Shingles and Lumber,
Montague.

Wm. H. Bigelow & Co.,
Manuf'rs. of Lumber,
Muskegon.

O. P. Pillsbury,
Lumberman,
Muskegon.

Wm. Glew & Co.,
Manuf'rs. of Lumber and Lath,
Muskegon

E. Emerson,
Lumberman,
Muskegon.

C. C. Thompson,
Real Estate and Lumberman,
Whitehall.

Staples & Covell,
Manuf'rs. of Lumber and Lath,
Whitehall.

J. Alley & Co.,
Manuf'rs & Dealers in Lumber, Lath, & Shingles,
Mills at Whitehall and Alleyton,
Whitehall.

Geo. M. Smith,
Lumberman,
Whitehall.

Jesse D. Pullman,
Lumberman,
Whitehall.

Fisher & Keller,
Manuf'rs. of Lumber,
Whitehall.

Geo. W. Franklin,
Manuf'r & Dealer in Lumber,
Whitehall.

A. M. Thompson,
Lumberman & Farmer,
Whitehall.

W. M. Thompson,
Lumber Dealer,
Whitehall.

W. F. Wafer,
Lumber Inspector,
Whitehall.

Peter Hobler,
Lumberman,
Whitehall.

Johnson & Hagman,
Manuf'rs. of Shingles,
Whitehall.

James Dalton Jr. & Bro.,
Manuf'rs of Lumber, Lath & Pickets,
Whitehall.

Heald, Avery & Co.,
Manuf'rs of Lumber, Lath & Pickets. Mills at
White River and Maple Grove, Whitehall.

Frank H. White & Co.,
Manuf'rs of Lumber, Lath & Pickets,
Whitehall.

Weston Brothers,
Manuf'rs & Dealers in Lumber, Lath
and Pickets, Whitehall.

MANUFACTURERS.

Stewart & Beals,
Whitehall Marble Works, Manuf'rs of Tombstones,
Monuments &c., Whitehall.

Moog, Hill & Co.,
Manuf'rs and General Dealers in Furniture and
House Furnishing Goods, Whitehall.

Utley & Ockobock,
Manuf'rs of Wagons, Carriages, Sleighs, &c.,
Horse Shoeing a Specialty, Whitehall.

Young, Collier & Co.,
Manuf'rs of Wagons, Carriages, &c. Horse Shoeing
and Jobbing, Montague.

Wilson & Hendrie,
Proprietor's of Montague Iron Works, Manuf'rs
of Dicey's Parallel Edgers, Montague.

C. E. Dowling,
Secretary White River Log and Booming Company,
Montague.

MERCHANTS.

John Widoe,
Merchant Tailor, and Dealer in Ready Made
Clothing, Whitehall.

K. F. Morse,
Dealers in Hardware,
Whitehall.

S. H. Lasley & Co.,
Dealers in General Merchandise,
Montague.

Barrows & Goodno,
General Dealers in Hardware,
Montague.

Henry Worth,
General Dealer in Groceries and
Provisions, Montague.

C. M. Boughton,
Salesman,
Whitehall.

Watson Smart,
Salesman,
Whitehall.

S. P. Hartshorn,
Tonsorial Artist, & Dealer in Tobacco
and Cigars, Whitehall.

J. J. Howden,
Supt. Gas Company,
Muskegon.

PHYSICIANS.

J. F. Cooper,
Physician and Surgeon,
Whitehall.

J. A. Wheeler,
Physician and Druggist,
Whitehall.

J. H. Johnson,
Physician and Surgeon,
Whitehall.

Z. Mizner,
Physician and Druggist,
Whitehall.

A. W. Squiers, M. D.,
Whitehall.

POSTMASTER.

Peter Jeannot,
Postmaster,
Lake Harbor.

PUBLISHER.

C. P. Nearpass,
Publisher of Whitehall Forum,
Book & Job Printer, Whitehall.

RAILROAD AGENT.

J. W. Hutty,
Railroad Agent
Montague.

Restaurants and Boarding Houses.

Nelson Patterson,
Restaurant and Boarding House,
Cor. Colby and Lake Sts. Whitehall.

H. Harwood,
Dining Hall,
Whitehall.

BUSINESS CARDS OF PATRONS IN MECOSTA COUNTY.

AGENTS.

E. P. Dana,
Agent of G. R. & I. R. R.
Big Rapids.

G. L. Perkins,
Insurance Agent,
Big Rapids.

ARCHITECT.

Geo. W. Fairfield,
Architect and Builder,
Big Rapids.

ATTORNEYS.

Fuller & Parsons,
Lawyers,
Big Rapids.

M. Brown,
Attorney at Law,
Big Rapids.

C. W. Nottingham,
Lawyer,
Big Rapids.

B. F. Lockwood,
Attorney and Loan Agent,
Big Rapids.

J. G. Murdock,
Attorney at Law,
Big Rapids.

Frank Durnow,
Lawyer,
Big Rapids.

W. L. Roberts,
Attorney and Loan Agent,
Big Rapids.

BANKS.

F. D. Brown,
Exchange Bank of Big Rapids,
Big Rapids.

Geo. M. Burr,
Northern Nat. Bank of Big Rapids,
Big Rapids.

CIVIL ENGINEER.

V. Cornwell,
Civil Engineer,
Big Rapids.

County Officers.

J. Irving Latimer,
County Treasurer,
Big Rapids.

L. G. Palmer,
Co. Superintendent of Schools,
Big Rapids.

J. T. Escott,
County Sheriff,
Big Rapids.

M. D. Ford,
Deputy Sheriff,
Big Rapids.

James M. Colby,
Register of Deeds,
Big Rapids.

DENTIST.

A. W. Eldridge,
Dentist,
Big Rapids.

FARMERS.

N. H. Vincent,
Stock, Grain and Hay, 300 acres,
Big Rapids.

Chas. W. Whitfield,
Stock, Grain & Fruit, 147 acres, Sec. 31,
Green.

HOTEL.

H. S. Johnson,
Pacific House,
Big Rapids.

LIVERY.

Wm. E. Worden,
Livery,
Big Rapids.

MANUFACTURERS.

J. K. Klesner,
Manufacturer of Carriages & Wagons,
Big Rapids.

W. E. Graves,
Manufacturer of Carriages & Wagons,
Big Rapids.

Tioga M'f'g. Co.,
Lumber, Lath and Shingles,
Big Rapids.

Peninsular Hardware and Manuf'g Co.
of Big Rapids,
Big Rapids.

H. B. Wood,
Manuf'r Sash, Doors and Blinds
and Planing Mill,   Big Rapids.

MERCHANTS.

G. W. Crawford,
Grocer,
Big Rapids.

S. G. Webster,
Grocer,
Big Rapids.

D. K. Stearns,
Dry Goods, Notions, etc.,
Big Rapids.

W. E. Conant,
Merchant,
Big Rapids.

F. O. Vandersluis,
General Merchandise,
Big Rapids.

Y. W. Bruce,
Books, Stationery & Paper Hangings,
Big Rapids.

NEWSPAPERS.

Charlie Gay,
"Mecosta County Pioneer,"
Big Rapids.

E. O. Ross,
"Big Rapids Magnet,"
Big Rapids.

PHYSICIANS & SURGEONS.

F. B. Wood,
Physician and Surgeon,
Big Rapids.

S. P. Phelps,
Physician and Surgeon,
Big Rapids.

J. L. W. Young,
Physician and Surgeon,
Big Rapids.

W. S. Springsteen,
Physician and Surgeon,
Big Rapids.

Henry A. Whitfield,
Physician & Surgeon, & Homeopathist,
Big Rapids.

PRINTERS.

D. G. Marvin,
Printer,
Big Rapids.

W. Seymour Stevens,
Printer, and Notary Public,
Big Rapids.

REAL ESTATE.

J. O. Rose,
Real Estate,
Big Rapids.

Thos. Lamell,
Dealer in Real Estate, and Post Master,
Big Rapids.

G. W. Warren,
Dealer in Real Estate and Lumber,
Farm 200 acres, Big Rapids.

Chas. Shafer,
General Agency, Real Estate,
Big Rapids.

TEACHER.

D. E. Thomas,
Principal of Public School,
Big Rapids.

CARDS OF PATRONS IN CHARLEVOIX AND LEELANAU COUNTIES.

ATTORNEY.

S. C. Moffat,
Attorney at Law,
Northport, Leelanau Co.

BLACKSMITH.

S. W. Wilson,
Blacksmith,
Northport, Leelanau Co.

CARPENTERS.

E. F. Dame,
Carpenter and Joiner,
Northport, Leelanau Co.

James Washburn,
Ship Carpenter,
Northport, Leelanau Co.

Samuel W. Lee,
Carpenter and Builder,
Charlevoix, Charlevoix Co.

County Officer,

John S. Dixon,
County Clerk and Sup't of Schools,
Charlevoix, Charlevoix Co.

DRUGGIST.

G. W. Grouter,
Druggist and Chemist,
Charlevoix, Charlevoix Co.

HOTELS.

R. Cooper,
Proprietor Fountain City House,
Charlevoix, Charlevoix Co.

Wm. M. Franklin,
Proprietor Traverse Bay Hotel,
Northport, Leelanau Co.

MACHINIST.

O. S. Washburn,
Machinist,
Charlevoix, Charlevoix Co.

MERCHANTS.

Fox, Rose & Butters,
Dealers in General Merchandise,
Charlevoix, Charlevoix Co.

W. C. Newsman,
General Merchant and Real Estate Dealer,
Charlevoix, Charlevoix Co.

MILL.

Robert Lee,
Manu'fr of Flour and Lumber,
Northport, Leelanau Co.

REAL ESTATE.

E. H. Green,
Real Estate and Law Office,
Charlevoix, Charlevoix Co.

PHYSICIAN.

F. J. Hutchinson,
Physician and Surgeon,
Northport, Leelanau Co.

BUSINESS CARDS OF PATRONS IN GRATIOT COUNTY.

ATTORNEYS.

C. E. Williams,
Attorney and Counsellor at Law,
Ithica.

J. W. Caldwell,
Attorney at Law,
Ithica.

James Wright,
Attorney at Law,
St Louis.

Leonard and Scott,
Attorneys at Law, and Solicitors in Chancery,
St. Louis.

A. J. Utley,
Attorney at Law, and Solicitor, in Chancery,
St. Louis.

BAKERY.

O. L. Vantassel,
Bakery and Saloon,
Alma, St. Louis.

BANKS.

Gratiot County Bank,
A. B. Darragh, Cashier,
St. Louis.

Brick Yard.

H. Peabody,
Proprietor of Brick Yard,
St. Louis.

BUILDERS.

W. H. Brown,
Builder, Engineer and Millwright,
St. Louis.

Elias Sutphim,
Carpenter and Builder,
St. Louis.

J. Marks,
Carpenter and Joiner,
St. Louis.

CLERGYMEN.

Theo. Nelson,
Pastor Baptist Church,
Ithica.

D. C. Woodward,
Pastor Methodist Church,
Ithica.

N. L. Otis,
Pastor Congregational Church,
Ithica.

CLERKS.

Enos B. Bailey,
Clerk in Store,
St. Louis.

C. C. Mc Collom,
Clerk in Store,
St. Louis.

CLOTHING HOUSE.

A. G. Newton,
Clothing House,
St. Louis.

DRUGGIST.

W. E. Fiero,
Apothecary and Druggist,
St. Louis.

FARMERS.

Joel Rowley,
Farmer, 120 acres Sec. 29,
Bethany.

Elmer Chase,
Farmer, 40 acres, Sec. 6,
Emerson.

Henry O. Burt,
Farmer, 66 acres, Sec. 10,
Carson City, North Shade.

Elizabeth C. Harlow,
Farmer, 80 acres, Sec. 17,
Carson City, North Shade.

Wm. Brice,
Farmer & Supervisor, 160 acres, Sec. 17,
Carson City, North Shade.

Frank S. Everett,
Farmer and School Teacher, 80 acres, Sec. 20,
Carson City, North Shade.

Thomas Franklin,
Wool & Grain Farmer, 80 acres, Sec. 19,
Carson City, North Shade.

Joseph Roberts,
Wool & Grain Farmer, 80 acres, Sec. 29,
Hubbardston, North Shade.

Henry Louka,
Farmer, Mechanic and Apiarian, 80 acres, Sec. 32,
Hubbardston, North Shade.

Harvey Silvernail,
Farmer, 62 acres, Sec. 82,
Hubbardston, North Shade.

E. Goodrich,
Farmer, 140 acres,
Alma, Pine River.

Geo. Nutte,
Farmer,
St. Louis.

FURNITURE.

A. J. Harrington,
Wholesale & Retail Dealer in Furniture of every description. Undertakes Goods constantly on hand.
St. Louis.

St. Louis Manuf'g Co.,
Wholesale & Retail Dealers in
Furniture, St. Louis.

HOTELS.

Eastman House,
Taylor and Truesdale, Proprietors,
St. Louis.

Paige House,
H. H. Gale, Proprietor,
St. Louis.

LUMBER.

J. P. Kroll,
Dealer in Pine Land, Logs & Lumber,
St. Louis.

MANUFACTURER.

J. S. Eagor,
Manufacturer of Fine Boots,
St. Louis.

MEAT MARKET.

Simon Vogt & Schlichtle,
Dealers in Fresh, Salt & Smoked Meats and Sausages, St. Louis.

MERCHANTS.

John Jeffery,
Retail Dealer in General Merchandise & Real Estate
Ithica.

E. R. Gibbs & Co.,
Dry Goods, Fancy Goods, & Millinery,
St. Louis.

Kipp & Swayne,
Grocers,
St. Louis.

PHOTOGRAPHER.

Almon Bisbee,
Photographer. All styles of Pictures taken in the best manner. Frames for Sale. St. Louis.

PHYSICIAN.

Jahob Meyer,
Homeopathic Physician,
St. Louis.

REAL ESTATE.

N. Church,
Real Estate Dealer and Money Broker,
Ithica.

Aaron Wessels,
Dealer in Real Estate and Hardware,
St. Louis.

James Paddock,
Real Estate and Insurance Agent,
St. Louis.

STATION AGENT.

Robert Sproul,
Station Agent Saginaw Valley & St. Louis R. R.
St. Louis.

TINSMITH.

Oscar F. Jackson,
Tinsmith,
St. Louis.

BUSINESS CARDS OF PATRONS IN MIDLAND COUNTY.

ATTORNEYS.

G. W. Hitchcock,
Attorney at Law,
Midland.

Henry Hart,
Attorney at Law,
Midland.

M. H. Stanford,
Attorney at Law,
Midland.

James Vanbloek,
Attorney at Law,
Midland.

Geo. F. Hemingway,
Attorney at Law, Midland.

BANKERS.

C. E. & G. Will. Ball,
Bankers, Midland.

CLERGYMAN.

F. W. May,
Clergyman, Midland.

CONFECTIONER.

Geo. C. Thompson,
Confectioner, Midland.

DRUGGISTS.

Nate J. Andrews,
Druggist, Midland.

Anderson Brothers,
Druggists, Midland.

FARMER.

G. B. Butts,
General Farmer, 40 acres, Sec. 28,
Warren.

HOTELS.

Thomas Moore,
Proprietor of Moore's Hotel,
Edenville.

Alexander Findlater,
Proprietor of International Hotel,
Midland.

MANUFACTURERS.

L. W. Hubbell,
Manuf'r of & Dealer in Lumber and
Shingles, Coleman.

J. Shultz,
Lumber & Shingle Manuf'r & Dealer,
Coleman.

D. K. Wise,
Manuf'r of Lumber, Lath and Shingles,
Coleman.

James S. Allen,
Manuf'r & Dealer in Boots and Shoes,
Midland.

MERCHANTS.

Geo. A. James,
Dealer in Hardware,
Midland.

William Patrick,
Hemlock Extract,
Midland.

NEWSPAPERS.

Burton Brothers,
Proprietors of the Independent,
Midland.

Geo. W. Hughes,
Newsdealer, Bookseller, Stationer,
Printer, & Editor of Times, Midland.

OFFICERS.

Wm. Plumber,
County Clerk,
Midland.

Alfred Avery,
Sheriff of Midland County,
Midland.

Asa Bacon,
Register of Deeds,
Midland.

J. H. Whitehouse,
Pension Surgeon,
Midland.

BUSINESS CARDS OF PATRONS IN IOSCO COUNTY.

ATTORNEY.

Robert White,
Attorney and Real Estate Agent,
East Tawas.

BANKERS.

C. P. Bragg & Co.,
Bankers,
Au Sable.

DRUGGIST.

J. W. King, Jr.,
Druggist and Grocer,
Tawas City.

ENGINEERS.

Henry G. Rothwell,
Civil Engineer and Architect,
Au Sable.

Samuel Barnell,
Engineer,
Au Sable.

HOTELS.

Miner & Smith,
Proprietors Miner's Hotel,
East Tawas.

John Curry,
Proprietor American Hotel,
East Tawas.

Justice of the Peace.

Cornelius Dietz,
Justice of the Peace, Real Estate and
Insurance Agent, Au Sable.

LIVERY STABLE.

Mackie & Cunningham,
Livery Stable, Au Sable.

LUMBERMEN.

John Miller Jr.,
Lumberman,
Au Sable.

Geo. D. McKay,
Lumberman,
Au Sable.

Geo. A. Lone,
Lumberman,
Au Sable.

M. Wilbur,
Lumberman,
East Tawas.

W. M. Locke & Co.,
General Dealers,
East Tawas.

O. Newman,
Lumberman,
East Tawas.

MANUFACTURERS.

Colwell, Smith & Lanystaff,
Lumber Manufacturers,
Au Sable.

Backus & Brother,
Manufacturers & Dealers in Lumber,
Au Sable & Detroit.

Geo. Orth,
Manuf'r & Dealer in Boots & Shoes,
Au Sable.

Loud Gay & Co.,
Lumber and General Merchandise,
Au Sable.

Wm. G. Grant & Son,
Manuf'rs of & Dealers in Lumber,
and Salt. Au Sable.

Moore, Tanner & Co.,
Manuf'rs & Dealers in Lumber,
Au Sable, Oscoda.

Adams, Jolly & Co.,
Manuf'rs and Dealers in Lumber,
East Tawas.

H. P. Smith & Sons,
Dealers in Long and Short Pine Lumber & Masts.
East Tawas & Tonawanda N. Y.

Tawas Mill Co.,
Manuf'rs Lath &c.,
East Tawas.

Staats & Quackenbush,
Manuf'rs Sash, Doors, Blinds, Window, and
Door Frames &c. East Tawas.

S. & C. D. Hale,
Manuf'rs & Dealers in Lumber,
Tawas City.

C. M. Whittemore,
Manu'fr of Lumber, Lath & Shingles
Tawas City.

MERCHANTS.

Stanley, Kuopfgen & Co.,
Dealers in Groceries, Provisions
and Meat, Au Sable.

Felix O' Tool,
Dealer in Fish & General Merchandise,
Banking &c, Au Sable.

John Geo. Betz,
Merchant Tailor,
Au Sable.

N. H. Dupraw,
Dealer in Fresh & Salt Meats, Hams, Shoulders.
Lard &c. East Tawas.

Joseph Dimmick,
General Dealer in Dry Goods, Boots &
Shoes, Groceries &c., East Tawas.

Wm. O. Taylor.
Hardware and Stoves.
Tawas City.

MECHANICS.

J. S. Duncan,
Mill Foreman,
Au Sable.

F. H. Davis,
Manager W. U. Telegraph Co.,
Au Sable.

Joshua Brown,
Millwright,
Oscoda.

PHYSICIAN.

J. M. Taggart,
Physician and Surgeon,
Au Sable.

POST MASTER.

Geo. P. Warner,
Post Master,
Au Sable.

BUSINESS CARDS OF PATRONS IN NEWAYGO AND OCEANA COUNTIES.

ABSTRACT OFFICE.

Edward Edwards,
Abstract Office,
Newaygo.

Agricultural Implements,

Francis M. Crandell,
Farmer and Dealer in Agricultural Implements.
160 acres, Sec. 2, Newfield.

ARCHITECT.

John Pittwood,
Architect and Builder,
Newaygo.

ATTORNEYS.

Horace M. Lillie,
Attorney at Law,
Newaygo.

Wm. D. Fuller,
Attorney at Law,
Newaygo.

BOOK KEEPER,

J. Bennett,
Bookkeeper,
Newaygo.

BUILDERS.

Ernest H. B. Forbes,
Carpenter & Builder,
Denver.

R. D. Miller,
Carpenter and Builder,
Newaygo.

Conveyancer and Collector.

J. W. Dunning,
Conveyancer and Collecting Agent,
Hesperia.

County Official.

M. S. Angell,
County Treasurer,
Newaygo.

DRUGGIST.

H. C. Hawley,
Druggist and Physician,
Hesperia.

FARMERS.

Sylvanus Reed,
Farmer, 200 acres, Sec. 4,
Dayton.

Melvin W. Scott,
Farmer, 160 acres, Sec. 6,
Dayton.

P. Monroe,
Farmer, 262 acres, Sec. 5,
Dayton.

Shinar Preston,
Farmer, 240 acres, Sec. 9,
Dayton.

E. R. Haight,
Farmer, 90 acres, Sec. 31,
Denver.

John Maynard,
Farmer, 475 acres, Sec. 27,
Denver.

M. D. Bull,
Farmer, 170 acres, Sec. 34,
Denver.

N. D. McCumber,
Farmer, 220 acres, Sec. 27,
Denver.

Shepherd Tibbetts,
Farmer, 262 acres, Sec. 28,
Newaygo.

James Strobridge,
Farmer & Lumberman, 400 acres,
Sec. 22, Newfield.

FLOURING MILLS.

Geo. Backart,
Flouring Mill,
Croton.

John Rooks,
Proprietor of Flouring Mill,
Denver.

HOTEL.

A. Courtwright,
Proprietor of Brooks House,
Newaygo.

Justice of the Peace.

Timothy Edwards,
Justice of the Peace,
Newaygo.

LUMBER.

John M. Simonds,
Lumberman,
Newaygo.

F. Skinner,
Sash and Door Manufacturer,
Newaygo.

MERCHANTS.

A. J. Spencer,
General Merchant, Denver.

A. J. Stone,
General Dealer, Hesperia.

S. Atherton,
General Dealer, Hesperia.

C. D. Shoemaker,
Merchant, Newaygo.

E. J. Hawn,
Groceries and Provisions,
Newaygo.

PHYSICIAN.

R. M. Lutin, M. D.,
Physician and Surgeon,
Newaygo.

SALOONS.

J. W. Haist,
Saloon Keeper, Newaygo.

Richard Surplice,
Saloon Keeper, Newaygo.

SAW MILL.

Wm. Rice,
Saw Mill, Croton.

C. D. Webster,
Saw and Planing Mill, Denver.

BLACKSMITH.

L. C. De Wolf,
General Blacksmithing,
Jackson P. O. Tompkins tp

CARPENTERS.

Charles Outcalt,
Carpenter and Joiner,
Sec. 36. N. E.
Jackson P. O. Blackman tp.,

Sydney S. Johnson,
Joiner,
Henrietta.

Edward Blackmore,
Carpenter and Joiner,
Henrietta P. O. Rives tp.

E. G. Lyman,
Joiner,
Leslie P. O. Rives tp.,

COOPER.

Edwin E. Baker,
Cooper,
Leslie.

FARMERS.

N. Hairs,
Farmer, 150 acres, Sec. 14, N. E.,
Jackson P. O. Blackman tp.

R. C. Karr,
Farmer, 80 acres, Sec. 14, S. E.,
Jackson P. O. Blackman tp.

S. L. French,
Farmer, 160 acres, Sec. 14, N. E.,
Jackson P. O. Blackman tp.

Alfred Bamel,
Farmer, 352 acres, Sec. 1, S. W.,
Jackson P. O. Blackman tp.

John Todd,
Farmer, 87 acres, Sec. 36, S. E.
Jackson P. O. Blackman tp.

Peter La Bue,
Farmer, 120 acres, Sec. 31, N. E.,
Jackson P. O. Blackman tp.

A. H. Laverty,
Farmer, 210 acres, Sec. 31, S. W.,
Jackson P. O. Blackman tp.

Frank Maynard,
Farmer,
Jackson P. O. Blackman tp.

R. W. Chamberlin,
Farmer, 170 acres, Sec. 14, S. E.,
Jackson P. O. Blackman tp.

Charles Wood,
Farmer, 80 acres, Sec. 25, N. W.,
Jackson P. O. Blackman tp.

D. R. Peck,
Farmer,
Jackson P. O. Blackman tp.

L. M. Chanter,
Farmer, 240 acres, Sec. 28, N. E.,
Jackson P. O. Blackman tp.,

William Roberts,
Farmer, 36 acres, Sec. 24, S. E.,
Jackson P. O. Blackman tp.

George V. Wing,
Farmer, 136 acres, Sec. 11, S. E.,
Jackson P. O. Blackman tp.

Samuel Woodworth,
Farmer, 224 acres, Sec. 22, S. W.,
Jackson P. O. Blackman tp.

F. G. Fifield,
Farmer, 40 acres, Sec. 15, N. W.,
Jackson P. O. Blackman tp.

J. T. McConnel,
Farmer, 130 acres, Sec. 15, N. E.,
Jackson P. O. Blackman tp.

James J. Vanderlyn,
Farmer, 208 acres, Sec. 10, S. E.,
Jackson P. O. Blackman tp.

Nathaniel Morrill,
Farmer, 320 acres, Sec. 10, N. W.,
Jackson P. O. Blackman tp.

Orril Noe,
Farmer,
Jackson P. O. Blackman tp.

George M. Mills,
Farmer, 160 acres, Sec. 10, N. E.,
Jackson P. O. Blackman tp.

Alva True,
Farmer, 65 acres, Sec. 3, S. E.,
Jackson P. O. Blackman tp.

J. A. Houseman,
Farmer, 150 acres, Sec. 9, N. W.,
Jackson P. O. Blackman tp.

B. F. Green,
Farmer, 80 acres, Sec. 9, N. W.,
Jackson P. O. Blackman tp.

Thomas J. Smith,
Farmer, 100 acres, Sec. 4, N. W.,
Jackson P. O. Blackman tp.

D. C. Bond,
Farmer, 82 acres, Sec. 5, N. W.
Jackson P. O. Blackman tp.

J. R. Pool,
Farmer, 175 acres, Sec. 28, N. W.
Jackson P. O. Blackman tp.

T. S. Barringer,
Farmer & Railroad Contractor, 78 acres,
Jackson P. O. Blackman tp.

M. S. Hitchcock,
Farmer, 220 acres, Sec. 22, N. W.,
Jackson P. O. Blackman tp.

Walter A. Higgins,
Farmer, 156 acres, Sec. 21, S. W.,
Jackson P. O. Blackman tp.

Jonathan Wood,
Farmer, Sec. 31, N. W.,
Jackson P. O. Blackman tp.

James R. Fleming,
Farmer, 237 acres, Sec. 16, S. W.
Henrietta.

Owen Hankerd,
Farmer,
Henrietta.

Wm. S. Pixley,
Farmer and Justice of the Peace,
Henrietta.

John A. Hall,
Farmer,
Henrietta.

C. V. Bockoven,
Sec. 1, S. E. 1-4,
Otter Creek P. O.

Calvin Ketchum,
Farmer, 60 acres, Sec. 9, S. E.,
Leslie P. O. Rives tp.

E. Flanigan,
Farmer, 106 acres, Sec. 16, N. E.,
Rives Junction P. O. Rives tp.

H. G. Cole,
Farmer, 108 acres, Sec. 21, N. E.,
Rives Junction P. O. Rives tp.

John H. King,
Farmer, 150 acres, Sec. 16, S. W.,
Rives Junction P. O. Rives tp.

Parson King,
Farmer, 40 acres, Sec. 16, S. W.,
Rives Junction P. O. Rives tp.

Abram Howell,
Farmer, 203 acres, Sec. 9, S. E.,
Rives Junction P. O. Rives tp.

Daniel T. Perrins,
Farmer, 204 acres, Sec. 8, S. E.,
Rives Junction P. O. Rives tp.

Gideon G. Dunham,
Farmer, 110 acres, Sec. 5, N. E.,
Leslie P. O. Rives tp.

Clement Higdon,
Farmer, 77 acres, Sec. 8, N. W.
Leslie P. O. Rives tp.

James Shaw,
Farmer, 190 acres, Sec. 1, S. W.,
Leslie P. O. Rives tp.

Wm. Blackmore,
Farmer, 80 acres, Sec. 12, S. E.,
Henrietta P. O. Rives tp.

Wm. Westren,
Farmer, 120 acres, Sec. 11, S. E.,
Henrietta P. O. Rives tp.

Wm. H. Allen,
Farmer, 160 acres, Sec. 13, S. W.,
Jackson P. O. Rives tp.

Levi Buck,
Sec. 12, S. E. 1-4,
Tompkins P. O. Springport tp.

J. M. Gillett,
Sec. 25, S. E. 1-4,
Parma P. O. Springport tp.

Myron Gillett,
Sec. 14, N. E. 1-4,
Parma P. O. Springport tp.

John Nottingham,
Sec. 14, N. E. 1-4,
Otter Creek P. O. Springport tp.

George J. Townley,
Sec. 19, S. W. 1-4,
Parma P. O. Tompkins tp.

J. C. Southworth,
Sec. 21, S. E. 1-4,
Tompkins P. O.

Jotham Wood,
Sec. 22, S. E. 1-4,
Tompkins P. O.

Wm Hall,
Sec. 22,
Tompkins Centre P. O.

K. P. Wade,
Sec. 16. N. W. 1-4,
Tompkins P. O.

E. W. Ford,
Sec. 18, N. E. 1-4,
Tompkins P. O.

L. W. Cranson,
Sec. 18, N. W. 1-4,
Tompkins P. O.

George N. Jones,
Sec. 2, S. E. 1-4,
Onondaga P. O. Tompkins tp.

Wm. Smith,
Sec. 28, N. E. 1-4,
Rives Junction P. O. Tompkins tp.

Richard Townley,
Sec. 19, S. E. 1-4,
Parma P. O. Tompkins tp.

MERCHANTS.

Wm. Balch,
Dealer in Groceries,
Jackson P. O. Blackman tp.

Wm. Marsh,
General Dealer in Dry Goods,
Groceries &c., Henrietta.

PHYSICIAN.

J. L. Conant,
Physician and Surgeon,
Henrietta.

TEACHERS.

Edward Sager,
Teacher,
Jackson P. O. Leoni tp.

Thomas G. Hunt,
Teacher,
Leslie P. O. Rives tp.

H. C. Rankin,
Teacher,
Rives tp.

Helen F. Livingston,
Teacher,
Parma P. O. Sandstone tp.

Nancy E. Parks,
Teacher,
Waterloo.

Trout Breeder.

Jackson Crouch,
Breeder of Speckled Brook Trout.
Small Fry for stocking Ponds $25 per thousand.
Yearlings $4.00 per hundred.
South Jackson.

BUSINESS CARDS OF PATRONS IN NORTH BRANCH.

Agricultural Foundry.

Wm Butler,

Agricultural Foundry,

ATTORNEY.

George Mott,

Attorney at Law.

BLACKSMITH.

Hugh Mc Lean,

General Blacksmithing, Wagon and Carriage Making.

CARRIAGE MAKERS.

Sanford & Ira H. Bradshaw,

Carriage Makers.

CARPENTER.

Jeremiah Winn,

Carpenter, Farm on Sec. 36, Arcadia.

CLERGYMAN.

F. J. Galbraith,

Pastor Methodist Episcopal Church.

DRUGGIST,

Geo. B. Bence,

Druggist and Grocer.

FARMERS.

Willmot Brazee,

Farmer, Sec. 12.

Samuel B. Scott,

Farmer and Local Preacher, Sec. 5.

L. H. Darling,

Farmer, Sec. 18.

T. J. Dennis,

Farmer, Sec. 2.

Wm. Smith,

Farmer, Sec. 16.

M. W. Fahey,

Farmer, Sec. 16.

D. C. Watties,

Farmer, Sec. 10.

John C. Wade,

Farmer, & Lumberman, Sec. 9.

Wm. Lucas,

Farmer, Sec. 15.

Henry S. Shell,

Farmer, Sec. 1.

William H. Day,

Farmer, Sec. 2.

Charles Magill,

Farmer, Sec. 4.

W. W Coffeen,

Farmer and Lumberman, Sec. 10.

Paul Harrington,

Farmer, Sec. 1.

Osro J. Castle,

Farmer, Sec. 6.

S. S. Lee,

Lumbering and Farming, Residence in Flint.

M. Price,

Farmer, Sec. 28, Kingston tp., Tuscola Co.

Wm. Mc Cromick,

Miscellaneous.

HOTELS.

M. M. Moore,

Moore House.

Henry Gallinger,

North Branch Exchange.

MANUFACTURERS.

Geo! Sicklesteel,

Flour & Grist Mill, Saw Mill, and Sash and Door Factory.

A. Moyer,

Lumber & Stave Manuf'r, and Farmer.

Adam Catlin,

Lumberman.

MERCHANTS.

Ballard & Sholes,

Dry Goods.

Horace C. Weston,

General Merchant and Farmer.

William H. Haddrill,

Grocer and Farmer.

John H. Swalls,

General Merchant and Farmer.

Jonathan Weston,

General Merchant and Farmer. Farm on Sec. 29, Burlington.

Levi H. M. Comstock,

Stoves and Hardware.

D. C. Briggs,

Merchant.

Andrew W. Bradley.

Furniture, Farm on N. E. qr., Sec. 8.

MILLINERS.

A. A. Clover & Co.,

Dealers in Millinery and Fancy Goods.

MILL WRIGHT.

Wm. O Nell,

Mill Wright.

Geo. M. Case,

Miscellaneous.

MONEY DEALERS.

Charles Ballard,

Money Dealer.

O. P. Weston,

Money Dealer.

PAINTER.

T. R. Conklin,

Painter.

PHOTOGRAPHER.

T. M. Goodman,

Photographer.

PHYSICIANS.

W. W. French,

Physician.

A. L. Scott,

Physician.

W. E. Best,

Physician.

W. J. Mc Curdy,

Physician and Surgeon.

BUSINESS CARDS OF PATRONS IN HADLEY.

CLERGYMEN.

C. M. Anderson,

Pastor Methodist Episcopal Church.

N. P. Barlow,

Pastor Baptist Church.

CLERK.

Alva Bentley,

Clerk.

FARMERS.

B. H. Shotwell,

Farmer, Sec. 2.

Homan Palmerlee,

Farmer, Sec. 3.

C. P. Goodrich,

Farmer, and Clergyman Sec. 28.

Chas. Burlingham,

Farmer, Sec. 13.

L. Fitch,

Farmer, Sec. 3.

John W. Campbell,

Farmer, Sec. 18, Goodrich.

Aaron Brigham,

Farmer, Sec. 18, Goodrich.

John Brigham,

Farmer, Sec. 19, Goodrich.

Gardner Dexter,

Farmer, Sec. 19, Goodrich.

David Mills,

Farmer, Sec. 4 (of the firm of Webster and Mills, Agricultural Implements, Lapeer City.)

Calvin Wickham,

Farmer, Sec. 24, Rural Vale.

Fidila Shimans,

Farmer, Sec. 24, Rural Vale.

Curtis Stimson,

Farmer, Sec. 25, Rural Vale.

HOTEL.

C. L. Geer,

Proprietor of Hadley Hotel.

INSURANCE.

Michigan State Insurance Company, Adrian, Lenawee Co., Assets $ 282,051.21, Jan. 1873.

MANUFACTURER.

Proctor Bros.,

Carriage and Wagon Shop, and Agricultural Foundry.

MERCHANTS.

Mills & Hutton,

Dealers in Clothing, Hardware, Dry Goods, Groceries, Drugs &c.

A. S. Little,

Dealer in Dry Goods, Groceries &c.

J. H. Hemingway & Son,

Dealers in Hardware, Farming Implements, and Sewing Machines.

Wm. Kelser,

Dealer in Boots and Shoes.

E. D. Matteson,

Dealer in Dry Goods, Drugs, Medicines, Yankee Notions &c., Davisonville, Genesee Co.

PHOTOGRAPHER.

C. E. Baldwin,

Travelling Photographer.

PHYSICIAN.

L. D. Whitney,

Physician.

SCHOOL.

Cyrus S. Stockwell,

Principal Union School.

BUSINESS CARDS OF PATRONS IN MACOMB AND WAYNE COUNTIES.

Agricultural Implements.

M. J. Monfore,
Dealer in Agricultural Implements,
Disco, Shelby township.

ATTORNEY.

A. L. Canfield,
Attorney at Law,
Mount Clemens.

BLACKSMITHS.

H. N. Orcutt,
Blacksmith,
Disco.

Alfred Waters,
Blacksmith,
Disco.

BUILDER.

James Travis,
Builder,
Dearbonville, Wayne Co.,

CARPENTER.

Milo Bacon,
Carpenter and Joiner,
Disco.

CARRIAGE MAKERS.

J. H. Bell,
Manufacturer of Carriages,
Disco.

George Brown,
Manufacturer of Wagons & Sleighs,
Disco.

CLERGYMEN.

Rev E. McGregor,
Pastor Methodist Episcopal Church,
Disco.

Rev J. F. Wetherald,
Pastor Methodist Episcopal Church,
Disco.

Samuel Phillips,
Pastor Presbyterian Church,
Disco.

FARMERS.

Jonathan Harris,
Farmer, 100 acres, Sec. 11,
Disco.

W. A. Wales,
General Farming, 188 acres Sec. 17,
Disco.

John Keeler,
General Farmer, 60 acres, Sec. 9,
Disco.

Martin C. Beam,
Farmer, 77 acres, Sec. 8,
Disco.

G. Lafayette Norton,
Farmer, Sec. 10,
Disco.

Wm. S. McCracken,
Farmer, Sec. 10,
Disco.

John Adams,
General Farmer, 125 acres, Sec. 9,
Disco.

Wm. Noe,
General Farmer, 80 acres, Sec. 10,
Disco.

Abraham Wilson,
Farmer, 68 acres, Sec. 10,
Disco.

Jacob Hicks,
Farmer, 80 acres, Sec. 4,
Disco.

Alfred Carlton,
Farmer, 117 acres, Sec. 2,
Disco.

Jude S. Preston,
Stock & Wool Farmer, 80 acres, Sec. 1,
Disco.

James M. Payne,
General Farmer & Fruit Grower,
100 acres, Sec. 10,
Disco.

Wm. M. Smith,
Farmer & Stock Raiser, 122 acres, Sec. 2,
Disco.

Riley S. Preston,
Farmer, 80 acres, Sec. 12,
Disco.

Peter B. Lambert,
Farmer, Fruit, Wool and Grain, 90 acres, Sec. 24,
Disco.

David Summers,
Farmer, 158 acres, Sec. 28,
Disco.

John J. Harvey,
Farmer, Sec. 18,
Disco.

Henry Decker,
Farmer, 60 acres, Sec. 28,
Disco.

James M. Ewell,
Farmer, 124 acres, Sec. 17,
Disco.

S. Lintz,
Farmer, 85 acres, Sec. 17,
Disco.

Andrew Evitt,
Farmer, 242 acres, Sec. 18,
Disco.

James S. Lawson,
Farmer & Surveyor, 80 acres, Sec. 9,
Disco.

Frederick Sweitzer,
Farmer, 120 acres, Sec. 8,
Disco.

D. G. Bacon,
Farmer and Teacher, Sec. 8,
Disco.

N. M. Price,
Farmer, 210 acres, Sec. 7,
Disco.

Axford Price,
Farmer, 249 acres, Sec. 7,
Disco.

H. D. Runyan,
Farmer, 60 acres, Sec. 22,
Disco.

J. A. Bloomburg,
Farmer & Fruit Grower,
20 acres, Sec. 16,
Disco.

Almira Granger,
Farmer, 36 acres, Sec. 21,
Disco.

Miron Bixby,
Farmer & Machinist, 86 acres, Sec. 21,
Disco.

John Broughton, Jr.,
Farmer, 60 acres, Sec. 6,
Disco.

Lafayette Warren,
General Farmer, 110 acres, Sec. 1,
Macomb P. O.

D. A. Harlow,
Farmer, 96 acres, Sec. 33,
Plymouth, Wayne Co.

A. McLaughry,
Farmer, 160 acres, Sec. 7,
Wayne P. O. Romulus tp.,
Wayne Co.

Edward Reynett,
Farmer, 60 acres, Sec. 7,
Romulus tp., Wayne Co.

HOTEL.

David Akin,
Proprietor of Disco Hotel,
Disco.

INSURANCE.

Daniel Wooden,
United States Pension Agent, Notary Public,
and Insurance Agent,
Romeo.

MANUFACTURERS.

E. B. Potter,
Sash, Doors and Blinds,
Mount Clemens.

Potter & Lewis,
Manufacturers of Sash, Doors & Blinds,
New Haven.

MERCHANTS.

John W. Cannon,
Dealer in General Merchandise,
Disco.

Levi H. Cannon,
Merchant and Surveyor,
Disco.

M. B. Salter,
Dealer in General Merchandise,
Disco.

Frost & Flammerfelt,
Dry Goods & Groceries, Hats, Caps,
Boots & Shoes,
Romeo.

D. H. Rowley,
General Merchant,
Romeo.

Sumners Leech,
Grocer,
Utica.

PHYSICIAN.

A. E. Bacon,
Physician and Surgeon,
Disco.

Railroad Contractor.

Edward Harris,
Railroad Contractor,
Disco.

SAW-MILL.

George W. Griffeth,
Manufacturer of Hard-wood Lumber,
Disco.

BUSINESS CARDS OF PATRONS IN LAPEER COUNTY.

ATTORNEY.

V. Rich,
Attorney at Law, Sec. 22,
Lapeer P. O., Mayfield.

BLACKSMITHS.

H. E. Skinner,
Blacksmith,
Millville, Lapeer P. O., Mayfield.

James Cowel,
Blacksmith and Wagon Maker,
Deanville, Burnside.

Davidson & Tuskey,
Wagon & Carriage Shops, Horse
Shoeing & Gen'l. Jobbing,
Burnside P. O., Deanville.

Joseph J. Rupert,
Dryden Village.

BOOK AGENTS.

Harry Marsh,
Book Agent, Sec. 7,
Burnside P. O.

Alex McKillop,
Book Agent, Sec. 19,
North Branch P. O., Burlington.

CARPENTERS.

Thomas Emmet,
Carpenter, Sec. 30,
Lapeer P. O., Mayfield.

A. D. Nichols,
Carpenter and Joiner,
Attica

EATING HOUSE.

George Griswold,
Proprietor of Railroad Eating House,
Elba Village.

FARMERS.

Arvin Barber,
Farmer, Sec. 2,
Lapeer P. O., Attica.

Washington Schell,
Farmer, Sec. 8,
Lapeer P. O., Attica.

O. C. Niece,
Farmer, Sec. 5,
Attica.

Benjamin Spencer,
Farmer, Sec. 26,
Imlay P. O., Attica.

James F. Smith,
Farmer, Sec. 29,
Imlay P. O., Attica.

H. J. Folsom,
Farmer, Sec. 24,
Imlay City P. O., Attica.

George H. Kingsbury,
Farmer, Sec. 29,
Attica.

Hiram Watkins,
Farmer, Sec. 20,
Attica.

Newel T. Watkins,
Farmer, Sec. 20,
Attica.

James Watkins,
Farmer, Sec. 30,
Pool P. O., Attica.

Lewis Y. Struble,
Farmer, and Agent for C. J. Nall's Panning Mill,
Sec. 31, Pool P. O., Attica.

James Brown,
Farmer, Sec. 1,
Imlay P. O., Arcadia.

Calvin Wagor,
Farmer & Lumberman, Sec. 30,
Lapeer P. O., Arcadia.

Samuel Bevins,
Hotel Keeper & Farmer, Sec. 34,
Attica P. O., Arcadia.

Oscar M. Dodge,
Farmer, Sec. 23,
Attica P. O., Arcadia.

J. B. Wilson,
Farmer & Lumberman, Sec. 31,
Lapeer P. O., Arcadia.

Peter Stiver,
Farmer, Sec. 16,
North Branch P. O., Burlington.

Wm. Eveland,
Farmer, Sec. 17,
North Branch P. O., Burlington.

John Appelman,
Farmer, Sec. 16,
North Barnch P. O., Burlington.

Amos Bradshaw,
Farmer, & Lumberman Sec. 17,
North Branch P. O., Burlington.

Thomas McGloughlin,
Farmer, Sec. 34,
North Branch P. O., Burlington.

Robert Dey,
Farmer, Sec. 34,
North Branch P. O. Burlington.

Lester J. Weston,
Farmer and Lumberman, Sec. 25,
North Branch P. O., Burlington.

Levi Page,
Farmer, Sec. 10,
North Branch P. O., Burlington.

R. B. Albertson,
Farmer and Carpenter, Sec. 20,
Burnside.

David Smith,
Farmer, Sec. 22,
Burnside.

Charles Cole,
Farmer, Sec. 18,
Burnside.

James W. Dickie,
Farmer, Sec. 14,
Burnside.

John M. Pringle,
Farmer, Sec. 36,
Goodland P. O., Burnside.

Lyman J. Lintz,
Farmer, Sec. 16,
Burnside.

G. E. Curry,
Farmer, Sec. 21,
Burnside.

Alexander Sinclair,
Farmer, Sec. 5,
Burnside P. O.

Franklin Keeler,
Farmer, Sec. 8,
Burnside P. O.

S. P. Gates,
Farmer, Sec. 7,
Burnside P. O.

James Lewis,
Farmer, Sec. 18,
Burnside P. O.

Bruce & Webster,
General Merchants & Farmers,
Burnside P. O.

Andrew Murray,
Farmer and Carpenter and Joiner,
Sec. 6, Burnside P. O.

J. B. Butler,
Lumberman, Farmer and Merchant,
Sec. 32, Burnside P. O.

Joel P. Colvin,
Farmer, Sec. 18,
Marathon P. O., Deerfield.

Wesley Main,
Farmer, Sec. 7,
Watertown P. O., Deerfield.

Abner C. Folsom,
Farmer, Sec. 6,
Watertown P. O., Deerfield.

George Swadling,
Farmer, Sec. 3,
Watertown P. O., Deerfield.

John F. Cook,
Farmer, Sec. 5,
Watertown P. O., Deerfield.

Elihu Woodrow,
Farmer, Sec. 4,
Watertown P. O., Deerfield.

Thomas Craig,
Farmer, Sec. 4,
Watertown P. O., Deerfield.

Oliver Carter,
Farmer, Sec. 5,
Watertown P. O., Deerfield.

Walter Johnson,
Farmer, Sec. 1,
North Branch P. O., Deerfield.

Wm. M. Dodge,
Physician & Farmer, Sec. 5,
Watertown P. O., Deerfield.

John Tuzer,
Farmer & Lumberman Sec. 2,
North Branch P. O., Deerfield.

James P. Henry,
Farmer, Sec. 2,
Lapeer P. O., Deerfield.

J. A. Todd,
Farmer, Sec. 24,
Dryden.

Adam Watson,
Farmer, Sec. 36,
Almont P. O., Dryden.

B. R. Emmons,
Farmer, Sec. 12,
Dryden.

Geo. B. Terry,
Farmer, Sec. 25,
Almont P. O. Dryden.

Daniel Sanborn,
Farmer, Sec. 25,
Almont P. O., Dryden.

Peter Ulrich,
Farmer, Sec. 14,
Dryden.

J. N. Miller,
Farmer, Sec. 25,
Almont P. O., Dryden.

F. Newton,
Farmer, Sec. 30,
Thornville P. O., Dryden.

A. Hosmer,
Farmer, Sec. 31,
Oxford P. O., Dryden.

John Clinansmith,
Farmer, Sec. 32,
Thornville P. O., Dryden.

Henry Bartlett,
Farmer, Sec. 15,
Dryden.

Joseph Buxton,
Thornville P. O., Dryden.

Elijah Bartlett,
Farmer, Sec. 9, Dryden.

Marshal Mahaffy,
Farmer, Sec. 7,
Thornville P. O., Dryden.

Richard Barnes,
Farmer, Sec. 18,
Thornville P. O., Dryden.

D. Cooley,
Farmer, Sec. 28,
Dryden.

Samuel Utley,
Farmer, Sec. 8,
Dryden.

E. D. Race,
Farmer, Sec. 14,
Dryden.

J. A. Porter,
Farmer, Sec. 12,
Dryden.

John Davenport,
Farmer, Sec. 35,
Hadley P. O. Elba.

E. Yilas,
Farmer, Sec. 28,
Hadley P. O., Elba.

Perry Stimson,
Farmer, Sec. 28,
Hadley P. O., Elba.

Henry Gibson,
Farmer, Sec. 27,
Lapeer P. O., Elba.

John T. Rich,
Farmer, Sec. 20,
Elba.

John R. Hammond,
Farmer, Sec. 17,
Elba.

Warren Perry,
Farmer, Sec. 26,
Lapeer P. O., Elba.

Joseph Pierson,
Farmer, Sec. 10,
Lapeer P. O., Elba.

Philander B. Norton,
Farmer,
Lapeer P. O., Elba.

Philo J. Bristol,
Farmer, Sec. 10,
Lapeer P. O., Elba.

BUSINESS CARDS OF PATRONS IN LAPEER COUNTY.

BLACKSMITH.

Robert Bowden,
Blacksmith Sec. 25,
Oregon.

CARPENTER.

Johnie Shepard,
Carpenter & Joiner, Sec. 17,
Almont P. O. Berlin tp., St. Clair Co.

ENGINEER.

Julius Sicklesteel,
Engineering,
Residence Lapeer City.

FARMERS.

James Henderson,
Farmer, Sec. 11,
Lapeer P. O. Elba.

John N. Briggs Jr.,
Farmer, Sec. 11,
Lapeer P. O. Elba.

John Flanagan,
Farmer, Sec. 36,
Farmer's Creek P. O. Elba.

Horace F. Horton,
Farmer, Sec. 36,
Farmer's Creek P. O. Elba.

Joseph Treadway,
Farmer, Sec. 8,
Elba.

Alanson Hammond,
Farmer, Sec. 17,
Elba.

David Godfrey,
Farmer, Sec. 5,
Elba.

Benjamin B. Harrington,
Farmer and Lumberman, Sec. 29,
Goodland P. O.

Geo. Van Wagoner,
Farmer & Lumberman, Sec. 5,
Goodland P. O.

Willard Harwood,
Farmer, Sec. 4,
Goodland P. O.

H. K. Buchanan,
Farmer, Sec. 21,
Goodland P. O.

Robert Courter,
Farmer, Sec. 2,
Goodland P. O.

William M. Abbott,
Farmer, Sec. 8,
Goodland P. O.

M. B. Tucker,
Farmer, Sec. 22,
Goodland P. O.

D. Mixter,
Farmer and Hotel Keeper, Sec. 15,
Goodland P. O.

Byron Wilcox,
Farmer, Sec. 14,
Goodland P. O.

Frederick Shelber,
Farmer, Sec. 24,
Goodland P. O.

Harry Allison,
Farmer, Sec. 16,
Goodland P. O.

Elbridge De Long,
Farmer, Sec. 30,
Imlay P. O. Goodland.

Thomas Barnes,
Farmer, Sec. 25,
Imlay City P. O. Goodland.

Wm. H. Inman,
Farmer, Sec. 32,
Imlay City P. O. Goodland.

Oscar F. Black,
Farmer, Sec. 7,
Imlay.

James Fairweather,
Farmer, Sec. 29,
Imlay City.

Chester Hall,
Farmer, Sec. 19,
Imlay City.

R. A. McRoy,
Farmer, Sec. 30,
Imlay City.

Ira Dodge,
Farmer, Sec. 33,
Imlay City.

H. B. Martin,
Farmer, Sec. 19,
Imlay City.

Amasa Ross,
Farmer, Sec. 34,
Almont P. O. Imlay.

A. W. Farley,
Farmer, Sec. 34,
Almont P. O. Imlay.

F. M. Dodge,
Farmer, Sec. 33,
Almont P. O. Imlay.

Oscar Spencer,
Farmer, Sec. 28,
Almont P. O. Imlay.

Alexander Taylor,
Farmer, Sec. 28,
Imlay City P. O.

Joseph B. Bennett,
Farmer, Sec. 21,
Imlay City P. O.

John H. Bolton,
Farmer, & Carpenter & Joiner, Sec. 7,
Imlay City P. O.

Robert B. Rice,
Farmer, Sec. 20,
Imlay City P. O.

Lawrence Freeman,
Farmer, Sec. 15,
Imlay City P. O.

Orrn Reed,
Farmer, Sec. 21,
Imlay City P. O.

Wm. Hulsart,
Farmer, Sec. 7,
Imlay City P. O.

John Keene,
Farmer,
Residence in Lapeer City.

John P. Cady,
Farmer, Sec. 27,
Lapeer P. O. Mayfield.

Thomas Cliff,
Farmer, Sec. 27,
Lapeer P. O. Mayfield.

R. R. Jones,
Farmer, Sec. 31,
Lapeer P. O. Mayfield.

Samuel Arms,
Farmer, Sec. 19,
Lapeer P. O. Mayfield.

John Thomas,
Farmer, Sec. 18,
Lapeer P. O. Mayfield.

Henry Lee,
Farmer, Sec. 18,
Lapeer P. O. Mayfield.

G. W. Carpenter.
Farmer, Sec. 19,
Lapeer P. O. Mayfield.

Edwin A. Weston,
Farmer, Sec. 34,
Lapeer P. O. Mayfield.

Christopher Farnsworth,
Farmer, Sec. 28,
Lapeer P. O. Mayfield.

J. B. Redhead,
Farmer, Sec. 28,
Lapeer P. O. Mayfield.

Lewis Peck,
Farmer, Sec. 21,
Lapeer P. O. Mayfield.

E. A. Goodale,
Farmer, Sec. 29,
Lapeer P. O. Mayfield.

John Matteson,
Farmer, Millwright and Lumberman,
Sec. 21, Lapeer P. O. Mayfield.

James P. Sculley,
Farmer, Sec. 22,
Lapeer P. O. Mayfield.

Charles Dingman,
Farmer, Sec. 22,
Lapeer P. O. Mayfield.

W. H. Bassett,
Farmer, Sec. 34,
Lapeer P. O. Oregon.

Wm. S. Graves,
Farmer, Sec. 36,
Lapeer P. O. Oregon.

S. K. Woodward,
Farmer, Sec. 36,
Lapeer P. O. Oregon.

J. D. Pope,
Farmer, Sec. 36,
Lapeer P. O. Oregon.

Wm. Wigglesworth,
Farmer, Sec. 36,
Lapeer P. O. Oregon.

Thomas R. Cushing,
Farmer, Sec. 25,
Lapeer P. O. Oregon.

Nelson Perkins,
Farmer, Sec. 25,
Lapeer P. O. Oregon.

Orlando Elliott,
Farmer, Sec. 24,
Lapeer P. O. Oregon.

Thomas Weaver,
Farmer, Sec. 15,
Lapeer P. O. Oregon.

Edward Vermilya,
Farmer, Sec. 5,
Columbiaville P. O. Oregon.

S. P. Colvin,
Farmer, Sec. 5,
Columbiaville P. O. Oregon.

Edward McGunegle,
Farmer, Sec. 15,
Lapeer P. O. Oregon.

Ezra Braymer,
Farmer, Sec. 5,
Columbiaville P. O. Oregon.

David C. Halsey,
Farmer, Sec. 16,
Lapeer P. O. Oregon.

Alfred Cliff,
Farmer, Sec. 20,
May P. O. Rich.

S. A. Gilbert,
Farmer, Sec. 16,
May P. O. Rich.

George Crankshaw,
Farmer, Sec. 8,
May P.O. Rich.

Matthew Rump,
Farmer, Sec. 18,
May P. O. Rich.

N. K. Lawrence,
Farmer, Sec. 6,
May P. O. Rich.

Wm. A. Johnson,
Farmer and Carpenter, Sec. 1,
May P. O. Rich.

Louis Seyforth,
Farmer, Sec. 2,
May P. O. Rich.

Charles Ayers,
Farmer, Sec. 11,
May P. O. Rich.

J. B. McIntyre,
Farmer, Sec. 4,
May P. O. Rich.

Lewis Wilcox,
Farmer, Sec. 4,
May P. O. Rich.

Daniel Weaver,
Farmer, Sec. 32,
Watertown P. O. Rich.

Cohn Bros.
General Merchants Sec. 36,
Goodland P. O. Sharpsville.

Robert Hughson,
Farmer, Sec. 16,
Maple Valley Sanilac Co.,

FOUNDRY.

Armstrong & Brophy,
Agricultural Furnace,
Dryden Village.

HOTELS.

James McDougall,
Hotel Keeper,
Burnside P. O.

BUSINESS CARDS OF PATRONS IN LAPEER COUNTY.

S. S. Bates,
Hotel Keeper,
Burnside.

William Graves,
Hotel Keeper,
Imlay.

Justice of the Peace,

W. B. Churchill,
Justice of the Peace, and Dealer in
Agricultural Implements. Imlay City.

LUMBERMEN.

T. H. Rice,
Lumberman, Sec. 4,
Attica P. O., Arcadia.

P. H. La Forest,
Lumber Dealer & Manuf'r. Sec. 32,
Attica P. O., Arcadia.

I. N. Jennes & Co.,
Lumbermen and Merchants,
Attica.

Arthur H. Fish,
Lumberman,
Attica.

William Williams & Sons,
Lumbermen,
Attica.

Abner Hall,
Lumberman,
Attica.

Varnum & Hodges,
Proprietors Excelsior Mills,
Attica.

Daniel W. Laffity,
Lumberman, Sec. 11,
North Branch P. O., Burlington.

Almon W. Lyman,
Lumberman Sec. 9,
Clifford P. O., Burlington.

E. B. Van Master,
Lumberman, Sec. 22,
Lapeer P. O., Deerfield.

Asa H. Curtis,
Lumberman,
Dryden Village.

Joseph Darwood,
Lumberman, Architect & Builder,
Dryden Village.

Chas. S. Marshal,
Lumberman,
Imlay.

T. M. Peterson,
Lumberman Sec. 4,
Lapeer P. O., Mayfield.

Thomas Parker,
Lumberman Sec. 4.
Lapeer P. O., Mayfield.

C. E. Vaughan,
Manufacturer of Lumber,
Millville, Lapeer P. O., Oregon.

E. L. Thompson,
Lumberman,
Elba P. O., Oregon.

J. S. Peterson,
Lumberman Sec. 14,
May P. O., Rich.

MANUFACTURERS.

John Dean,
Manuf'r. of Lumber, Flour, Feed &c.
Burnside.

Alex. Johnson, Jr.,
Shingle Manuf'g Sec. 23,
Lapeer P. O., Deerfield.

George Cliff,
Shingle Manuf'r Sec. 35,
Lapeer P. O., Deerfield.

C. H. Cliff,
Shingle Maker, Sec. 35,
Lapeer P. O., Deerfield.

E. B. Leman,
Pump Maker,
Dryden Village.

MERCHANTS.

David Donaldson,
Dry Goods, Groceries, Boots Shoes &c.,
Attica.

Fannie Clemons,
Dry Goods, Groceries and Patent Medicines,
Sec. 10, Clifford P. O., Burlington.

Bentley & Black,
Groceries and Hardware,
Imlay City P. O., Deanville.

Joseph Manwaring,
Dealer in Dry Goods, Drugs, Groceries,
Boots and Shoes, Dryden Village.

John Weaver,
Dealer in Dry Goods, Groceries,
Boots and Shoes, Dryden Village.

John Winship,
Merchant,
Elba Village.

P. Losey & Son,
Dry Goods and Groceries,
Imlay P. O.

Geo. Levalley,
Travelling Merchant,
Flint P. O., Oregon.

MILLERS.

M. E. Robinson,
Miller,
Burnside.

George B. Bently,
Miller, Oat Meal and Feed,
Imlay City.

Ara Johnson,
Miller, Sec. 36,
North Branch P. O., Rich.

Geo. Slade,
Manufacturer of Flour, Feed &c.,
Millville, Lapeer P. O., Oregon.

MILL-WRIGHT.

Mines Fuller,
Mill-Wright,
Attica.

PHYSICIANS.

J. D. Minard,
Physician and Surgeon, & Dealer in
Drugs and Medicines, Attica.

S. A. Manyer,
Physician and Surgeon,
Attica.

Milton M. Tucker,
Physician and Surgeon,
Burnside.

W. J. Taylor,
Physician and Surgeon,
Burnside.

John S. Calkins,
Physician,
Thornville P. O., Dryden.

S. S. Stearns,
Physician.
Dryden Village.

Pulaski Middleditch,
Physician and Surgeon,
Imlay City.

SAW MILL.

S. P. Robinson,
Saw Mill,
Burnside.

SAWYERS.

Wm. J. Brown,
Sawyer,
North Branch P. O., Burlington.

A. M. Rogers,
Sawyer, Sec. 25,
North Branch P. O., Burlington.

D. Weaver,
Sawyer, Sec. 31,
Watertown P. O., Tuscola Co.

N. Mott,
Sawyer, Sec. 32,
Lapeer P. O., Attica.

SUPERVISOR.

Wm. Quartermass,
Supervisor.
Imlay City.

TEACHERS.

George S. Maynard,
Teacher, Residence in Almont.

Ann & Hattie Carpenter,
Teachers, Imlay City.

Jno. H. Miller,
Teacher, Sec. 34,
Lapeer P. O., Oregon.

WAGON MAKER,

Wm. W. Tomlinson,
Wagon Maker & General Repairing.
Sec. 36, Lapeer P. O., Oregon.

BUSINESS CARDS OF PATRONS IN ELK RAPIDS, ANTRIM CO.

ATTORNEYS,

Williams & Parkinson,
Attorneys at Law.

BOOKSELLER.

S. W. Stacy,
Bookseller, Stationer, & News Dealer.

CARPENTER.

Wm. N. King,
Carpenter & Builder.

Carriage Manufacturer.

John E. Cooper,
Carriage & Wagon Manufacturer.

County Officer.

Cuthbert Parkinson;
County Clerk, and Register of Deeds.

DRUGGISTS.

Bayot & Bailey,
Drugs, Groceries, &c.

ENGINEER.

Wm. H. Morgan,
Mechanical Engineer.

HOTELS.

S. Mitchell,
Proprietor American Hotel.

E. H. Pearl,
Proprietor Eagle Hotel.

Hussey & Davis,
Proprietors of North Western Hotel.

F. J. Lewis,
Proprietor of Palmer House.

Perry Andress,
Proprietor Mancelona House,
Mancelona, Mich.

MANUFACTURERS.

Dexter & Noble,
Manuf'rs of Charcoal Pig Iron,
Lumber Dealers, & General Merchants.

F. H. Head,
Manufacturer of Charcoal Iron.

E. S. Noble,
Manufacturer of Charcoal Iron.

G. W. Cunningham,
Sup't. in Dexter & Noble's Iron Works.

John H. Silkman,
Manufacturer & Dealer in Lumber.

C. F. Read,
Foreman in Silkman's Mill.

MERCHANTS.

R. W. Coy,
Dealer in General Merchandise,
Spencer Creek, Mich.

Silas W. Spencer,
Dealer in Groceries, and Provisions.

James Williams,
Proprietor Eastport Exchange.

BUSINESS CARDS OF PATRONS. ADDENDA.

AGENTS.

N. P. Taylor,
Real Estate and Insurance Agent,
Ionia.

W. W. Lyons,
Stave Agent,
Ray P. O., Macomb Co.

ATTORNEYS.

Shaw & Pennington,
Attorneys at Law,
Offices at Charlotte and Eaton Rapids.

George H. White,
Attorney at Law,
Grand Rapids.

Samuel B. Horne,
Attorney at Law,
Grand Rapids.

Farr & Lillie,
Atty's & Counselors, Collectors & Real Estate Agents, Grand Rapids, Kent Co.

W. W. Mitchel,
Attorney at Law,
Ionia.

James Van Kleeck,
Attorney at Law,
Midland City.

J. P. Drouillard,
Attorney at Law,
Wenona.

BANKERS.

Danagh & Co.,
Bankers,
Grand Rapids.

BUILDERS.

A. M. Edwards,
Carpenter,
Flint.

H. M. Odell,
Builder,
Grand Rapids.

W. Johnson Sligh,
Carpenter,
Grand Rapids.

Charles H. Galusha,
Contractor and Builder,
Olivet, Eaton Co.

George A. Davis,
Carpenter and Builder,
Roxand, Eaton County.

CLERGYMAN.

A. H. P. Wilson,
Clergyman and Professor of Dead Languages, Grand Ledge, Eaton Co.

CONFECTIONERS.

Wm. Thun & Kuhn,
Confectioners, No. 20 Monroe St.,
Grand Rapids.

ENGINEER.

A. S. Edwards,
Engineer,
Flint.

FARMERS.

Stephen Carpenter,
Farmer and Carpenter,
Adrian.

Geo. S. Brumm,
Farmer, 60 acres, Sec. 20,
Charlotte P. O., Benton tp.

S. W. Harmon,
Farmer, 120 acres, Sec. 16,
Charlotte P. O., Chester tp., Eaton Co.

C. A. Ingalls,
Farmer, 100 acres, Sec. 21,
Portland P. O. Danby tp., Ionia Co.

W. F. Jennison,
Farmer, Sec. 22, Eagle, Clinton Co.

E. A. Hebard,
Farmer and Physician,
Grand Rapids.

Luman Preston,
Farmer, 148 acres,
Macomb Co.

A. Wells.
Farmer, Stock, Grain and Wool,
Macomb Co.

James Thompson,
Farmer, Grain, Stock & Wool,
260 acres, Macomb Co.

P. M. Bently.
Stock, Grain & Wool, 270 acres,
Macomb P. O.

Richard Roe,
Farmer, Stock, Grain & Wool, 40 acres,
Sec. 10, Grand Ledge P. O. Oneida tp., Eaton Co.

Geo. S. Draper,
Farmer, 80 acres, Sec. 19,
Onondaga tp., Ingham. Co.

Wm. Cryderman,
Farmer, 120 acres, Sec. 3,
Roxand, Eaton Co.

Mary Campbell,
Farmer, Stock, Grain & Fruit,
Shelby, Macomb Co.

Edwin J. Bryan,
Farmer, Tecumseh.

M. Walworth,
Farmer, Sec. 3, 80 acres,
Vermontville P. O.

HOTELS.

Joseph Nagele,
Proprietor Michigan House,
Grand Rapids.

W. R. Barnard,
Proprietor Barnard House,
Grand Rapids.

Valentin Richter,
Proprietor Ohio House,
Grand Rapids.

Justice of the Peace.

H. V. Staley,
Justice of the Peace,
Muir.

LUMBERMEN.

W. J. St. Clair,
Lumberman,
Bay City.

A. Stevens & Co.,
Lumbermen,
Bay City.

Potter, Beattie & Co.,
Dealer in General Merchandise, & Lumber Manuf'rs
Grand Rapids.

Henry Hadley,
Lumberman,
Hastings, Barry County.

Joshua Dunn,
Lumberman,
Ionia.

L. H. Douglas,
Lumberman,
Muir.

Wagar & Fox,
Lumbermen,
Muir.

E. Emerson,
Lumberman,
Muskegon.

John McGraw & Co.,
Manuf'rs and Dealers in rough and Dressed Lumber, Shingles, Lath and Salt,
Portsmouth, Bay County.

Dimmick Bennett,
Lumberman,
Saginaw City.

LAND LOOKER.

E. T. Andrews,
Land Looker,
Bay City.

MANUFACTURERS.

Reuben Wheeler,
Manuf'r of Doors, Sash and Blinds,
44 Mill Street Grand Rapids.

Chas. H. Bacon,
Manu'fr of Faucets, Curtain Rollers & Slats,
Trunk Strips and Vinegar Shavings,
Grand Rapids.

Krum, Smith & Co.,
Manuf'rs, Jobbers & Dealers in all kinds of Dressed Lumber, Mouldings and Scroll Sawing, Office cor. Canal & Trowbridge Sts., Grand Rapids.

MERCHANTS.

S. W. & J. H, Campbell,
Merchants,
Bellville, Mich.

H. G. Hall,
Hardware & Agricultural Implements,
Carson City, Montcalm County.

E. H. Bailey,
Dealer in Pianos, Organs, Books, Stationery, Wall Paper, Jewelry, &c., Charlotte Eaton Co.

E. J. Wallace,
Dealer in Wines & Liquors,
Jackson.

James E. Price,
General Dealer in Merchandise,
Romeo, Macomb Co.

D. E. Hallenbeck,
Merchant and Postmaster,
Roxand, Eaton Co.

MILL WRIGHT.

W. M. Straight,
Millwright,
Grand Rapids.

NEWSPAPER.

Wm. J. Ward,
Wenona Herald,
Wenona.

PHYSICIANS.

H. M. Purinton,
The World renowned Lung Physician,
Adrian, Lenawee Co.

R. B. Rawson M. D.
Physician and Surgeon,
Woodland, Barry Co.

George Hendry M. D.
Physician and Surgeon,
Zilwaukie.

SAWYER.

C. S. Walker,
Sawyer,
Bay City.

SUPERVISOR.

Jacob Wright,
Supervisor,
Zilwaukie.

TEACHERS.

L. L. McDougal,
School Teacher,
Adrian.

R. J. Welkins,
School Teacher,
Grand Rapids.

J. L. McDougal,
School Teacher,
Adrian.

Sophia Warren,
Teacher,
Macomb P. O., Macomb Co.

TINSMITH.

George W. Bidwell,
Tinsmith,
Lapeer, Lapeer Co.

CARDS OF PATRONS IN MARATHON TOWNSHIP, LAPEER COUNTY.

CARPENTERS.

Herman Hazelton,
Carpenter.

James W. Hazelton,
Builder,
Drayton Plains, Oakland Co.

ENGINEER.

H. Knowiton,
Engineer,
Otter Lake P. O.

FARMERS.

G. B. Farquharson,
Farmer, Sec. 8,
Otter Lake P. O.

C. T. Collins,
Farmer, Sec. 16,
Marathon P. O.

E. A. Brown,
Farmer, Sec. 20,
Columbiaville P. O.

D. W. Allen,
Farmer, Sec. 29,
Columbiaville P. O.

F. M. Oliver,
Farmer, Sec. 26,
Columbiaville P. O.

J. Jennings,
Farmer, Sec. 86,
Columbiaville P. O.

George W. Chaplin,
Farmer, Sec. 12,
Watertown.

Chauncey Maxfield,
Farmer, Sec. 28,
Columbiaville P. O.

Archibald Raymond,
Farmer, Sec. 28,
Columbiaville P. O.

J. Hollenbeck,
Farmer, Sec. 20,
Columbiaville P. O.

Wm. M. Aurand,
Farmer, Sec. 17,
Columbiaville P. O.

Wm. Hollenbeck,
Farmer, Sec. 21,
Columbiaville P. O.

I. L. Hemingway,
Farmer, Sec. 9,
Columbiaville P. O.

H. L. Hemingway,
Farmer, Sec. 9,
Columbiaville P. O.

A. B. Snyder,
Farmer, Sec. 8,
Columbiaville P. O.

Andrew Aurand,
Farmer, Sec. 17,
Columbiaville P. O.

Geo. W. Aurand,
Farmer, Sec. 17,
Columbiaville P. O.

Rufus Pierson,
Farmer, Sec. 22,
Marathon P. O.

Frank McGarry,
Farmer, Sec. 2,
Watertown P. O.

Edward Salsberry,
Farmer, Sec. 1,
Watertown P. O.

Francis Markle,
Farmer, Sec. 32,
Columbiaville P. O.

Daniel K. Roberts,
Farmer, Sec. 2,
Watertown P. O.

Level Hurd,
Farmer, Sec. 31,
Davison, Genesee Co.

John Clark,
Farmer, Sec. 34,
Columbiaville P. O

Ephraim Clute,
Farmer, Sec. 33,
Columbiaville P. O.

Benj. J. Harris,
Farmer,
Columbiaville.

Thomas Branch & Sons,
Butchers, Builders, and Farmers, Tp. of Forest,
Sec. 29, Otisville P. O. Genesee.

HOTELS.

Mary Farroll,
Proprietor Farroll House,
Columbiaville.

M. M. Larkin,
Proprietor of Hotel, & Steam Shingle & Grist Mill,
Sec. 6, Otter Lake P. O.

Orin W. Gooch,
Manager of Boarding House,
Otter Lake.

INSURANCE.

J. T. Wheeler,
Insurance Agent and Auctioneer,
Sec. 20, Columbiaville P. O.

LABORER.

L. D. Cutting,
Loading Cars,
Columbiaville.

LUMBERMEN.

Asa Richards & Bro.
Lumbermen and Millers,
Columbiaville.

D. G. Lawrone,
Lumberman and Merchant,
Columbiaville.

A. C. Carpenter,
Lumberman,
Columbiaville.

Peter Carpenter,
Lumberman,
Columbiaville.

C. B. Benson,
Lumber Manuf'g. Sec. 7; 6,000 acres,
Otter Lake.

S. J. Lewis,
Lumber Inspector,
Otter Lake.

John Canniff,
Lumber Foreman,
Otter Lake.

Simpson Chapman,
Lumber Foreman,
Otter Lake.

B. F. Hoover,
Lumber Sealer,
Columbiaville P. O.

John Wadley,
Shingle and Grist Mill, Sec. 22,
Marathon P. O.

MERCHANT.

Wm. S. P. Wheeler,
Dry Goods, Groceries, Boots & Shoes &c.
Columbiaville.

PHYSICIANS.

Wm. B. Hamilton,
Physician and Surgeon,
Columbiaville.

L. M. Congdon,
Physician,
Columbiaville.

SAWYERS.

Edward Anthony,
Sawyer,
Otter Lake.

R. K. Sheldon,
Sawyer,
Otter Lake.

S. A. Fuller,
Sawyer, Sec. 9,
Columbiaville P. O.

SALOON KEEPER.

Mart Valentine,
Saloon Keeper,
Marathon P. O.

BUSINESS CARDS OF PATRONS IN METAMORA TOWNSHIP.

BLACKSMITH.

Isaac H. Lewis,
General Blacksmithing,
Thornville.

FARMERS.

Wm. Sage,
Farmer, Sec. 28,
Metamora P. O.

Adam Winegar,
Farmer, Sec. 20,
Metamora P. O.

Andrew Johnson.
Farmer, Sec. 35,
Oxford P. O.

James Mc Gregor,
Farmer, Sec. 3,
Metamora P. O.

Andrew Mair,
Farmer, Sec. 3,
Metamora P. O.

C. R. Chapman,
Farmer, Sec. 11,
Metamora P. O.

Leroy Thomas,
Farmer, Sec. 10,
Metamora P. O.

C. A. Fricke,
Farmer and Dealer in Agricultural Implements,
Sec. 15, Metamora P. O.

Alex. Doherty,
Farmer, Sec. 18,
Metamora P. O.

Thomas Caley,
Farmer, Sec. 5,
Hunter's Creek P. O.

Chas. W. Brown,
Farmer, Sec. 6,
Farmer's Creek P. O.

Orvil Sage,
Farmer, Sec. 92,
Oxford P. O.

Tobias Price,
Farmer, Sec. 28,
Metamora P. O.

M. C. Babcock,
Farmer, Sec. 18,
Farmer's Creek P. O.

Abraham Hunt,
Farmer, Sec. 31,
Oakwood P. O.

Jesse Lee,
Farmer, Sec. 38, Oxford P. O.

HOTELS.

Lorenzo Hoard,
Proprietor of Metamora House.

B. P. Ackerman,
Hotel Keeper, Metamora.

MILLER.

John Morton,
Flour and Feed, Oatmeal and Pearl Barley,
Thornville.

MERCHANT.

H. Townsend,
Dealer in General Merchandise,
Metamora.

PHYSICIANS.

D. F. Stone,
Physician and Surgeon,
Metamora.

J. S. Comstock,
Physician & Surgeon, Sec. 6,
Farmer's Creek P. O.

PRODUCE DEALERS.

M. N. Kelley,
Dealer in Produce,
Metamora.

Geo. W. Snover,
Dealer in Grain, Plaster, Lime and Salt,
Farmer, Sec. 8, Metamora P. O.

BUSINESS CARDS OF PATRONS IN MANISTEE, MANISTEE COUNTY.

ATTORNEYS.

A. W. Fowler,
Attorney at Law,
Manistee.

Dovel & Morris,
Attorneys at Law,
Manistee.

Ramsdell & Benedict,
Attorneys at Law,
Manistee.

N. W. Nelson,
Attorney at Law,
Manistee.

Bullis & Cutcheon,
Attorneys at Law,
Manistee.

Alex. H. Dunlap,
Attorney at Law,
Manistee.

BANKERS.

Charles Secor & Co.,
Proprietor Manistee City Bank,
Manistee.

S. S. Conover,
Money Broker,
Manistee.

BLACKSMITH.

Peter H. Peterson,
Blacksmith,
Manistee.

BOILER MAKERS.

Kirsh & Paulus,
Manistee Steam Boiler Works,
Manistee.

Andrew Jack,
Proprietor Union Boiler Works,
Manistee.

ENGINEERS.

Henry S. Udell,
Surveyor & Civil Engineer, Explorer
and Estimator of Pine Timber, Manistee.

J. B. Lahr,
Mechanical Engineer,
Manistee.

J. N. Gunsoley,
Mechanical Engineer,
Manistee.

W. C. Brown,
Mechanical Engineer,
Manistee.

Peter Branan,
Mechanical Engineer,
Manistee.

S. A. Bass,
Mechanical Engineer,
Manistee.

John Martin,
Mechanical Engineer,
Manistee.

D. W. C. Blackmer,
Mechanical Engineer,
Manistee.

J. M. Davis,
Mechanical Engineer,
Manistee.

John A. Wilson,
Mechanical Engineer,
Manistee.

Chas. Roberts,
Mechanical Engineer,
Manistee.

HOTELS.

City Hotel,
Gregory Bro's, Proprietors, & Dealers
in General Merchandise, Manistee.

Milwaukie House,
Baxter & Fitch, Proprietors,
Manistee.

United States Hotel,
Lorenzo Magoon, Proprietor,
Manistee.

Eagle Hotel,
John Miller, Proprietor,
Manistee.

Lake House,
Peter Niehoven, Proprietor,
Manistee.

LUMBERMEN.

Nell Leitch,
Manu'fr & Dealer in Lumber,
Manistee.

Gifford, Ruddock & Co.,
Manufacturers of Lumber, Bridge, Car, and Build-
ing Timber, cut to order,
Office & Yard, 2623 Water St., Chicago.

G. Wiborn,
Foreman in Gifford, Ruddock & Co's
Mill.

Cushman, Calkins & Co.,
Manuf'rs of Lumber, Lath &c. Dealers
in Dry Goods & Groceries, Manistee.

Wm. Moore,
Foreman in Cushman Calkins & Co's
Mill, Manistee.

Engelmann, Babcock & Salling,
Manuf'rs of Lumber, Lath & Pickets,
Manistee.

Dennett & Dunham,
Manuf'rs of Lumber,
Manistee.

Filer & Sons,
Manuf'rs of Lumber, & Dealers in
General Merchandise, Filer City Mich.

D. W. Filer,
Lumberman,
Filer City.

A. Magnau,
Lumber Manufacturer,
Stronach Mich.

R. G. Peters & Co.,
Manuf'rs of Lumber & Shingles,
Manistee.

Chas. Puggeot,
Manuf'r of Lumber, & Dealer in Gen'l
Merchandise, Stronach Mich.

Chas. Reitz & Bro.,
Mf'rs of Lumber, Lath, Shingles &c.,
Yard 27 N. Canal St. Chicago Mich.

J. N. Zimmerman,
Foreman in Reitz Bro's Mill,
Illinois.

Geo. Sambeeck,
Foreman & Filer in Reitz Shingle Mill,
Manistee.

Louis Sands,
Lumber Manufacturer,
Manistee.

Horace Tabor,
Lumber Manufacturer,
Manistee.

M. F. McMillen,
Foreman in Tabor & Co's Mill,
Manistee.

Wheeler, Magill & Co.,
Manuf'rs of & Dealers in Lumber,
Manistee.

John Lee,
Foreman in Wheeler, Magill & Co's
Mill, Manistee.

D. W. Mowatt,
Foreman in Canfield & Wheeler's
Mill, Manistee.

A. W. Briggs,
Shingle Manufacturer,
Manistee.

E. W. Worden,
Foreman in Briggs' Shingle Mill,
Manistee.

Tyson, Sweet & Co.,
Manuf'rs Lumber, Lath & Pickets,
Manistee.

H. S. Goss,
Foreman in Tyson Sweet & Co's Mill,
Manistee.

G. Young,
Lumber Inspector,
Manistee.

E. W. Secor,
Farmer and Lumberman,
Manistee.

Hopkins Bros.,
Jobbers & Dealers in Pine Land, and
Timber, Manistee.

Chas. F. Ruggles,
Dealer in Pine Lands & Timber, on the Stump,
Locator of Government & State Lands, Manistee.

MANUFACTURERS.

S. C. Overpack,
Manuf'r of Wagons & Carriages,
Manistee.

H. Woodrow,
Contractor and Builder,
Manistee.

B. E. Baxter & Co.,
Prop'r of City Mills. Manuf'rs of Flour & Feed,
Manistee.

MERCHANTS.

Norgaard & Hanson,
Dealers in all kinds of Furniture; House, Sign,
Plain & Ornamental Painters. Agents for Tickets
to and from all parts of Europe, Manistee.

Wheeler & Johnson,
Machine Shop, Forwarding and
Commission, Manistee.

E. Buckley & Co.,
Dealers in Hardware, House Furnishing Goods,
and General Mill supplies, Manistee.

G. L. Russell & Co.,
Wholesale & Retail Dealers in Hardware & House
Furnishing Goods, Manistee.

R. W. Weymouth,
Gen'l Dealer in Groceries, Provisions,
&c., Manistee.

H. M. Davenport,
Market Gardening,
Manistee.

Kirkland & Bedford,
Forwarding & Commission,
Manistee.

MILL WRIGHTS.

E. T. Davis,
Millwright,
Manistee.

E. Sheldon,
Millwright,
Manistee.

T. S. Currier,
Millwright,
Manistee.

J. A. Jamison,
Millwright,
Manistee.

W. W. Chapin,
Millwright,
Manistee.

NEWSPAPERS.

Orland H. Godwin,
Editor & Pub. of Manistee Standard,
Manistee.

R. Hoffman,
Editor & Pub. of Manistee Times,
Manistee.

E. G. Thompson,
Foreman in Times Office,
Manistee.

OFFICERS.

T. B. Collins,
City Recorder,
Manistee.

Peter A. Yous,
Sheriff of Manistee County,
Manistee.

L. S. Ellis, M. D.,
Postmaster,
Manistee.

PHOTOGRAPHER.

E. E. Donville,
Photographer,
Manistee.

PHYSICIANS.

R. T. Mead,
Physician & Surgeon,
Manistee.

W. F. Fisher,
Physician & Surgeon,
Manistee.

T. O. Siqueland,
Physician & Surgeon,
Manistee.

J. Kinsley,
Physician & Druggist,
Manistee.

TANNERS.

W. D. Ramsdell & Co.,
Tanners & Curriers, Dealers in Hides
& Leather, Manistee.

BUSINESS CARDS OF PATRONS IN GREENVILLE, MONTCALM COUNTY.

ATTORNEYS.

J. H. Tatem,
Attorney & Conveyancer at Law, Montcalm,
Kent, Mecosta, Isabella, Newaygo, and
Muskegon Counties.

D. T. Zapp,
Attorney and Solicitor.

John Lewis,
Lawyer.

BANKERS.

W. H. Norton & Co.,
Bankers.

Wm. J. Just,
Cashier First National Bank.

BUTCHERS.

Chas. Serviss & Co.,
Butchers.

CLERGYMAN.

C. E. B. Armstrong,
Pastor Baptist Church.

CONTRACTORS.

Peck & Brown,
Railroad Contractor.

DRUGGISTS.

Wm. H. Conover.
Druggist.

Graham Bros.,
Druggists.

G. R. Slawson,
Druggist and Jewelry.

ENGINEER.

Daniel Hammond,
Steam Fire Engineer.

FARMERS.

E. R. Pierce,
Stock, Grain & Fruit, 50 acres, Sec. 21,
Eureka tp.

Martin L. Baker,
Grain & Fruit Farmer, 71 acres, Sec. 28,
Eureka tp.

S. G. Sayer,
Grain, Stock & Fruit Farmer, 80 acres,
Sec. 28, Eureka tp.

Eli Wissler,
Grain Farmer, 40 acres, Sec. 8,
Eureka tp.

Charles L. Baker,
Grain, Stock & Fruit Farmer, 100
acres, Sec. 8, Eureka tp.

Wm. Backus,
Grain & Hay Farmer, 140 acres, Sec. 17,
Eureka tp.

Daniel Horton,
Farmer, 155 acres.

John A. Fargo,
Grain, Stock & Fruit Farmer, 440 acres,
Sec. 30, Eureka & Fairplain tps.

John R. Tallman,
Grain, Stock, & Fruit Farmer, 40 acres,
Sec. 24, Eureka tp.

A. M. Gravelle,
Farmer & Dairyman, 114 acres, Sec. 21,
Eureka tp.

D. G. Slawson,
Stock, Grain, & Fruit Farmer,
207 acres, Eureka tp.

A. W. Maynard,
Stock, Grain, & Wool Farmer, 130
acres, Sec. 14, Eureka tp.

Moses A. Berridge,
Stock, & Grain Farmer, 160 acres,
Sec. 18, Eureka tp.

Henry Berridge,
Stock, Grain, & Wool Farmer, 160
acres, Sec. 18, Eureka tp.

John Huff,
Stock, Wool, Grain, & Fruit Farmer,
120 acres, Sec. 23, Eureka tp.

Enoch Wilcox,
Grain, & Hay Farmer, 160 acres,
Sec. 23, Eureka tp.

Jerome Fargo,
Retired Farmer, Sec. 14,
Eureka tp.

Geo. Holmden,
Grain, Fruit & Hay, 60 acres, Sec. 11,
Eureka tp.

Wm. De Graw,
Stock, Grain, Wool & Fruit Farmer,
280 acres, Sec. 2, Eureka tp.

Henry Vanallen,
Grain, Stock, Fruit & Wool Farmer,
160 acres, Sec. 1, Eureka tp.

Stephen Bossman,
Gardner, 2 acres, Sec. 3,
Eureka tp.

Ezra Satorice,
General Farming, 155 acres, Sec. 7,
Eureka tp.

Jas. Satorice,
Farmer, Sec. 7,
Eureka tp.

M. A. Lawson,
Mixed Farming, 120 acres, Sec. 20,
Eureka tp.

C. C. Hodges,
Farmer, 40 acres, Sec. 20,
Eureka tp.

H. O. Hodges,
Farmer, 80 acres, Sec. 21,
Eureka tp.

David D. Bartch,
Grain, Stock & Fruit Farmer, 80 acres,
Sec. 7, Eureka tp.

T. H. Story,
Wheat, & Hay Farmer, 80 acres,
Sec. 7, Eureka tp.

A. McKinnon,
Farmer & Lumberman, 230 acres,
Sec. 7, Eureka & 12, Day tp.

Lyman Demorest,
Wheat, Wool, & Fruit Farmer, 100
acres, Sec. 18, Eureka tp.

R. C. Miller & Son,
Grain, Stock, Wool & Fruit Farmers,
400 acres, Sec. 18, Fairplain tp.

D. B. Crawford,
Stock, Grain, Wool & Fruit Farmer,
890 acres, Sec. 18, Fairplain tp.

Lester B. Miller,
Grain, Stock, & Wool, 440 acres,
Sec. 20, Fairplain tp.

E. N. Crippen,
Grain, & Fruit Farmer, 80 acres,
Sec. 22, Fairplain tp., Amsden P. O.

W. Y. Starks,
Grain, Stock, & Hay Farmer, 90 acres,
Sec. 6, Fairplain tp.

A. E. Sanford,
Grain, Stock & Wool Farmer, 80 acres,
Sec. 8, Fairplain tp.

S. H. Tobey,
Grain, Wool & Stock Farmer, 240 acres,
Sec. 7, Fairplain tp.

I. P. Shoemaker,
Farmer & Manufacturer, Saw Mill, Grist Mill,
Shingle Mill, & Store, 1640 acres, Fairplain tp.

Chas. Barnes,
Grain, Stock & Fruit Farmer, 280 acres,
Sec. 21, Fairplain tp., Amsden P. O.

C. W. King, M. D.,
Farmer, Physician & Surgeon, 218
acres, Sec's. 15 & 16, Pierson tp., Isabella Co.

J. C. Mann,
Grain, Stock, & Fruit Farmer, 80 acres,
Sec. 22, Montcalm tp.

A. Dart,
Grain, & Stock Farmer, 80 acres,
Sec. 26, Montcalm tp.

C. P. Baker,
Grain, Stock & Wool Farmer, 80 acres,
Sec. 20, Montcalm tp.

Jackson Carr,
Grain, Stock, & Fruit Farmer, 226
acres, Sec. 33, Montcalm tp.

A. H. Roffroe,
Grain, Stock & Wool Farmer, 120
acres, Sec. 28, Montcalm tp.

Geo. Bellamy,
Mixed Farming, 120 acres, Sec. 16,
Montcalm tp.

L. E. Griffith,
Grain, Stock & Wool Farmer, 80 acres,
Sec. 23, Montcalm tp.

H. J. Pixley,
Grain, Stock, & Fruit Farmer,
Montcalm tp.

L. B. Skermerhorn,
Wool, Stock, & Grain Farmer, &
Supervisor of Montcalm, 80 acres, Sec. 33.

Henry S. Sharp,
Farmer & Lumberman, 120 acres,
Sec. 32, Montcalm tp.

Isaac Underwood,
Mixed Farming, 240 acres, Sec. 27,
Montcalm & 22, Eureka tp.

Wesley Sprague,
General Farmer, 80 acres, Sec. 24,
Oakfield tp., Kent Co.

Henry Watson,
Farmer, 170 acres, Sec's. 1, 2 & 24,
Oakfield tp., Kent Co.

Wm. Holmden,
General Farming, 100 acres, Sec. 24,
Oakfield tp., Kent Co.

HOTELS.

J. Fleming,
Proprietor of Joy House.

G. M. Keith,
Proprietor of Keith's Exchange Hotel.

INSURANCE.

John Ross,
Fire & Life Insurance Agent, &
Farmer, 85 acres, Sec. 16, Eureka tp.

MANUFACTURERS.

S. M. Waters,
Manuf'r of Lumber & Shingles,
Sec. 6, Cato tp.

D. D. Bennett,
Lumberman.

L. J. Macumber,
Dealer in Pine Lands, & Manuf'r
of Lumber.

Henry Hart,
Manufacturer of Lumber.

Fuller & Gowen,
Lumber & Shingle Mills.

Luke Palmer,
Manuf'r of Lumber.

A. Bracy,
Farmer, & Manuf'r of Lumber, 40
acres, Sec. 15,

Joseph M. Fuller.
Manuf'r of Lumber, Shingles, & Lath.

Clark Rhinesmith & Co.,
Manufacturers, & Dealers in Lumber,
Lath, & Shingles.

L. W. Lobdell,
Manuf'r of Lumber, & Lath.

A. W. Dodge,
Manuf'r of Lumber, Lath & Shingles,
Gowen.

F. S. Peck,
Manufacturer of Brooms.

W. H. Vanderhuyden,
Proprietor of Brick Yard, Sec. 16,

Cummings & Co.,
Manuf'r of Lumber, Lath, & Shingles,
Lake Mills, near Sheridan.

Crosby & Son,
Farmers, & Manuf'rs of Lumber, &
Lath, 258 acres, Sec. 13, Montcalm tp.

Horace Shepard,
Manuf'r of Lumber & Shingles, 205
acres, Sec. 24, Spencer tp., Kent Co.

MARSHALL.

N. Y. Brothers,
City Marshall.

BUSINESS CARDS OF PATRONS IN GREENVILLE, MONTCALM COUNTY.

MERCHANTS.

J. W. Belknap,
Dry Goods, etc.

H. Densmore & Sons,
Dry Goods, & Groceries.

Spring & Ashley,
Dry Goods, Carpets, Oil Cloths, etc.

Hiram B. Fargo,
Merchant.

W. P. Strickland,
Dealer in Pianos, Organs, and
Musical Merchandise, Greenville.

Lorell Bros, & Green,
Hardware.

E. Butan & Co.,
Hardware, Paints, Oils, etc.

Daniel Horton,
Dealer in Hardware, Agricultural
Implements, Paints Oils, &c.

John F. Gott,
Dealer in Stoves, and Tinware.

S. B. Stevens,
Manuf'r & Dealer in Boots, & Shoes.

Chas. A. Northrup,
Dealer in Boots, & Shoes, Hats, & Caps.

F. L. Spencer,
Merchant.

Clark Brothers,
Wholesale & Retail Dealers in
Dry Goods.

MILLERS.

L. Porter,
Miller.

E. Middleton & Son,
Millers.

S. Smith,
Dealer in Grain, Flour, and Feed.

R. C. Miller Sons,
Wholesale & Retail Dealers in Flour,
Feed, and Grain.

MONEY LOANER.

Julius E. Crosby,
Money Loaner.

NEWSPAPERS.

E. F. Grabill,
Publisher of the "Independent."

J. Wesley Griffith,
Publisher Greenville Democrat.

NURSERY.

Chas. Ashley,
Nurseryman & Fruit Grower,
57 acres, Eureka tp.

PHOTOGRAPHER.

Milo Hiler,
Artist & Photographer, Private and
Public Views. Lowell, Kent Co.

PHYSICIANS.

THE PRESENT AGE.
The Successful Physicians, For Chronic
Diseases, of all kinds, are now permanently
located in rooms over J. Griffith's Store.
Greenville, Mich., N. B. —Consultation Free.
NO TIME SHOULD BE LOST. Know Thyself.
MONTGOMERY & CARVER,
Physicians, Surgeons, Oculists, and Opticians.
Greenville.

Chas. F. Morgan,
Physician and Surgeon.

E. Fish,
Physician and Surgeon.

Jno. Avary,
Physician and Surgeon.

REAL ESTATE.

J. J. Shearer & Co.,
Hardware & Real Estate.

N. Slaght,
Lumberman and Real Estate.

E. H. Jones, & Co.,
Real Estate and Abstracts.

STABLE.

W. H. Landers,
Sale Stable.

School Superintendent.

E. H. Crowell,
County Supt. of Schools for
Montcalm County.

SURVEYOR.

Francis A. Palmer,
Surveyor,
Westville.

TEACHER.

J. Mac Magrath,
Principal of Public Schools.

UNDERTAKER.

Frederick Boenigk,
Undertaker.

WELL DRIVER.

Harvey L. Mc Nutt,
Farmer and Well Driver, 80 acres.

BUSINESS CARDS OF PATRONS IN BLOOMER, MONTCALM CO.

ATTORNEYS.

Cagwin & Greenhoe,
Attorneys at Law,
Carson City.

Geo. P. Stone,
Attorney at Law,
Carson City.

BLACKSMITH.

Geo. B. Gibbs,
Blacksmith and Wagon Maker,
Carson City.

CARPENTER.

Isaac Burt,
Carpenter & Joiner & Farmer,
Carson City.

CLERGYMAN.

Samuel Sessions,
Pastor of Congregational Church,
Carson City.

FARMERS.

Thomas Cliffe,
Wool & Grain Farmer, 90 acres,
Sec. 21, Bloomer Center P. O.

A. A. Richardson,
Wool & Grain Farmer, 110 acres,
Sec. 20, Bloomer Center P. O.

A. K. Richardson,
Stock & Wool Farmer, 80 acres,
Sec. 21, Bloomer Center P. O.

C. R. Dickinson,
Farmer & Supervisor, 160 acres,
Sec. 28, Bloomer Centre P. O.

M. J. Miner,
Farmer & Dealer in Durham Cattle,
204 acres, Sec. 28, Bloomer Centre P. O.

Hiram Barrett,
Farmer, 30 acres, Sec. 23,
Bloomer Centre P. O.

C. K. Dickerson,
Thresher,
Bloomer Centre.

John Dingler,
Farmer, 53 acres, Sec. 22,
Bloomer Center P. O.

James Corlile,
Wool and Grain Farmer, 80 acres,
Sec. 23, Bloomer Center P. O.

Benjamin S. Carey,
Farmer, 80 acres, Sec. 7,
Bushnell tp., Vickoryville P. O.

G. W. Depew,
Farmer, 200 acres, Sec. 26,
Carson City P. O.

Charles D. King,
Farmer, 200 acres, Sec. 17,
Carson City P. O.

G. J. Chandler,
Grain & Stock Farmer, 40 acres,
Sec. 8, Carson City P. O.

A. A. Dakin,
Farmer & Dealer in Real Estate, 40
acres, Sec. 13, Carson City.

H. P. Miller,
Farmer and Money Loaner,
Carson City P. O.

H. M. Roop,
Farmer & Apiarian, 80 Swarms Pure
Italian Bees, 70 acres, Sec. 11,
Carson City P. O.

Orlando Goldthrite,
Farmer & Lumberman, 102 acres,
Sec. 18, Carson City.

Albert W. Townsend,
Farmer, 80 acres, Sec. 24,
Carson City P. O.

Charles Barrett,
Farmer, 40 acres, Sec. 10,
Carson City P. O.

Aaron Lyon,
Farmer, 80 acres, Sec. 10
Carson City P. O.

Henry F. Deal,
Farmer, 80 acres,
Carson City P. O.

Geo. W. Palmer,
Farmer, Wool, Butter & Cheese' a
Specialty, 120 acres, Sec. 24,
Carson City P. O.

Mrs. Della Miner,
Village lots for sale, 18 acres, Sec. 13,
Carson City.

Isaac Dickason,
Farmer, 60 acres, Sec. 10,
Carson City P. O.

Judson Barrett,
Wool & Grain Farmer, 40 acres,
Sec. 34, Hubbardston P. O.

Martin Eagen,
Farmer, 150 acres, Sec. 34,
Hubbardston P. O.

A. W. Holmes,
Farmer, and Justice of the Peace,
Hubbardston P. O.

Samuel Andrews,
Grain and Wool Farmer, 80 acres,
Sec. 27, Hubbardston P. O.

Stephen J. Smith,
Farmer, 100 acres, Sec. 37,
Hubbardston P. O.

Philander Paine,
Farmer & Lumberman, 40 acres,
Sec. 27, Hubbardston P. O.

HOTEL.

Wm. W. Ferris,
Proprietor of Ferris's Hotel,
Carson City.

MANUFACTURERS.

J. G. Lacy,
Dealer & Manuf'r Sash, Doors, and
Lumber, Carson City.

John A. Taft,
Manu'fr of Short Siding,
Carson City.

MERCHANTS,

J. H. Cressinger,
Wholesale & Retail Druggist,
Carson City.

Daniel Reichard,
Dealer in Drugs and Medicines,
Carson City.

O. B. Sines,
Dealer in Groceries, and Provisions,
Carson City.

Titus Stover,
Dealer in General Merchandise,
Carson City.

A. Proctor,
Dealer in Groceries, & Purchaser of
Farm Produce, Carson City.

Wm. Brown,
Dealer in Groceries & Farm Produce,
Carson City.

A. D. McGill,
Family Groceries,
Carson City.

Cummings & Thayer,
General Merchants & Purchasers of
Farm Produce, Carson City.

Henry E. Hall,
Dealer in Wines, Ales, Liquors,
Cigars & Oysters, Carson City.

O. H. Heath,
Dealer in Hardware, & Agricultural
Implements, Carson City.

Musical Instruments.

Hiram O. Brower,
Dealer in Musical Instruments,
Sheet Music and Books.

PHYSICIANS.

T. B. Colton,
Physician, Lumber Manuf'r, and
Farmer, Carson City P. O.

Dr. J. Tenant,
Physician,
Carson City.

SHERIFF.

Fred E. Scott,
Deputy Sheriff,
Carson City.

STABLE.

Luce & Wakely,
Proprietor of Livery & Sale Stables,
Carson City.

SURVEYOR.

W. A. Sweet,
Surveyor & Real Estate Agent,
Carson City.

TEACHERS.

Anna Allison,
School Teacher,
Carson City.

W. W. Dalglish,
Teacher and Farmer, 80 acres, Sec. 5,
Maple Rapids P. O.

BUSINESS CARDS OF PATRONS IN MONTCALM COUNTY.

ATTORNEYS.

A. P. Thomas,
Attorney & Counselor at Law,
Howard City.

W. N. Rodgers,
Att'y at Law & Dealer in Real Estate,
Lake View.

John C. Mattison,
Attorney and Justice of Peace,
Stanton.

Geo. A. Smith,
Lawyer,
Stanton.

Lyman C. Moore,
Attorney at Law,
Stanton.

Geo. W. Stonebnrner,
Attorney and Solicitor,
Stanton.

Harmon Smith,
Lawyer,
Stanton.

BANKERS.

Mowe & Chapin,
Bankers,
Stanton.

BLACKSMITHS.

Geo. A. Reed,
Blacksmith & Manuf'r of Wagons,
Lake View.

Henry Vale,
Blacksmith & Farmer, 40 acres,
Lake View.

Boarding House.

John Morse,
Proprietor of Boarding House,
Stanton.

CLERGYMAN.

M. V. Bork,
Pastor Methodist Episcopal Church,
Stanton.

County Officers.

D. Barry,
Town Clerk.
Coral.

C. V. Vining,
Town Clerk and Builder,
Lake View.

H. E. W. Palmer,
County Surveyor & Real Estate Agent,
Stanton.

H. Irving Garbutt,
County Clerk,
Stanton.

FARMERS.

Geo. W. Odonnell,
Farmer & Contractor, 140 acres,
Sec. 23, Arcada tp.

E. H. Stryker,
Farmer & Justice of the Peace,
116 acres, Sec. 22, Cato.

L. W. DeClare,
Farmer, & Proprietor of Cato House,
Cato.

Calvin Reynolds,
Farmer, 80 acres, Sec. 20,
Cato.

S. P. Youngman,
Farmer, 120 acres, Sec. 29,
Cato.

Solon Farror,
Farmer, 90 acres, Sec. 20,
Cato.

S. J. Youngman,
Farmer, 120 acres, Sec. 29,
Cato.

C. Richards,
Farmer, 80 acres, Sec. 21,
Cato.

James Vrooman,
Farmer, 40 acres, Sec. 6,
Lake View P. O., Cato tp.

Elan Sanborn,
Farmer, 160 acres, Sec. 7,
Lake View P. O., Cato tp.

John Butler,
Farmer, 100 acres, Sec. 8,
Newago Co. Lake View P. O. Croton tp.

S. H. Warren,
General Farming, 160 acres, Sec. 34,
Otisco P. O., Eureka tp.

W. C. Booker,
General Farmer, 160 acres, Sec. 34,
Otisco P. O., Eureka tp.

Benjamin S. Bigley,
Farmer, 140 acres, Sec. 32,
Otisco P. O., Eureka tp.

James A. Bryant,
Farmer, Lake View.

Cacob Pintler,
Farmer, 80 acres, Sec. 18,
Coral P. O., Maple Valley tp.

Asher R. Parks,
Farmer, 80 acres, Sec. 18,
Coral, Maple Valley tp.

E. B. Ferguson,
Farmer, 240 acres, Sec, 18,
Coral, Maple Valley tp.

W. M. Althouse,
Farmer, 80 acres, Sec. 8,
Coral, Maple Valley tp.

W. R. Holcomb,
Farmer, 40 acres, Sec. 8,
Coral, Maple Valley tp.

E. J. Blanding,
Farmer, 147 acres. Sec. 7,
Coral, Maple Valley tp.

G. V. Snyder,
Farmer, 160 acres, Sec. 4,
Otisco P. O., & tp.

L. E. Fellows,
Farmer & Builder, 80 acres,
Smyrna P. O., Otisco tp.

M. N. Baker,
Farmer, 80 acres, Sec. 14,
Pierson.

J. S. Lores,
Farming, 140 acres, Sec. 2,
Maple Hill P. O., Pierson tp.

Kaleb B. Rice,
Farmer, 385 acres, Sec. 2,
Maple Hill P. O., Pierson tp.

J. D. Pardee,
Farmer & Stock Raiser, 620 acres,
Sec. 21, Pierson.

Orison A. Pierson,
Farmer, 280 acres, Sec. 21,
Pierson.

Thomas S. Peck,
Farmer, 80 acres, Sec. 26,
Pierson.

Geo. M. Pratt,
Grain & Hay Farmer, 80 acres, Sec. 26,
Pierson.

Edward Neve,
Grain & Hay Farmer, 80 acres, Sec. 27.
Pierson.

John Edwards,
Stock, Grain & Hay Farmer, 120 acres,
Sec. 26, Pierson.

E. O. Schermerhorn,
Farmer & Livery Stable, 80 acres,
Sec. 14, Pierson.

David S. Pierson,
Stock & Grain, 188 acres, Sec. 26,
Pierson.

J. J. Reinshagen,
Farmer & Lumberman, 40 acres,
Sec. 12, Rockford P. O., Pierson tp.

Henry O. Wood,
Farmer & Lumberman, 240 acres,
Sec. 16, Rockford P. O., Pierson tp.

Byron H. Weed,
Grain & Hay Farmer, 160 acres, Sec. 33,
Rockford P. O., Pierson tp.

I. C. Carpenter,
Grain & Hay Farmer, 120 acres,
Sec. 24, Rockford P. O., Pierson tp.

Thomas Huckleberry,
Farmer & Lumberman, 140 acres,
Sec. 34, Rockford P. O., Pierson tp.

T. M. Pierson,
Grain & Hay Farmer, 40 acres, Sec. 33,
Rockford P. O., Pierson tp.

Richard Huckleberry,
Farmer & Lumberman, 140 acres,
Sec. 34, Rockford P. O.

H. C. Smith,
Farmer, 455 acres, Sec. 12,
Lake View P. O., Winfield tp.

Isaac Gillies,
Farmer, 140 acres, Sec. 12,
Lake View P. O., Winfield tp.

Daniel E. Knight,
Farmer, 160 acres, Sec. 12,
Winfield tp.

BUSINESS CARDS OF PATRONS IN MONTCALM COUNTY.

HOTELS.

H. J. Horton,
Proprietor Lake View House,
Lake View.

B. H. Briggs,
Proprietor Exchange Hotel,
Langston.

D. H. Bailey,
Proprietor of Bailey House,
Stanton.

Justice of the Peace.

R. P. McLaughlin,
Justice of the Peace, & Dealer in
Flour & Feed, Langston.

LUMBERMEN.

Allen Macomber,
Lumber Dealer, 120 acres, Sec. 1,
Lake View P. O. Cato.

J. C. Richards,
Staves & Heading,
Coral.

Daniel Shively,
Manuf'r of Lumber, Lath, & Shingles,
Coral.

A. C. Fisher,
Manuf'r of Lumber & Lath,
Coral.

Dodge & Aker,
Manuf'rs of Lumber & Shingles,
Coral.

W. Leighton,
Lumberman,
Coral.

Henry B. Gee,
Lumberman,
Crystal.

S. P. Swartz,
Dealer in & Manuf'r of Lumber,
No. 9, State Street, Grand Rapids.

David Botsford,
Manuf'r Lumber, Laths & Shingles,
Howard City.

Oscar A. Adams,
Lumber Dealer, 80 acres, Sec. 8,
Lake View.

E. A. Heath,
Manuf'r of Lumber,
Lake View.

Clinton W. Ross,
Lumberman,
Lake View.

P. H. Crawford,
Proprietor of Langston Mills, Manuf'r of
Lumber, Shingle, &c., Langston.

David W. Morse,
Manuf'r of Lumber,
Langston.

Hart, Oaks & Co.,
Manuf'r of Lumber, Lath & Shingles,
5500 acres, Maple Valley tp.

D. H. Hastings,
Manuf'r of Lumber. 360 acres,
Coral, Maple Valley tp.

Seth Beal,
Farmer & Lumberman, 1500 acres,
Maple Valley tp.

Wm. C. Ingerham,
Lumberman, 60 acres, Sec. 20,
Maple Valley.

John N. Kennedy,
Lumberman, Sec. 26,
Pierson P. O.

David Heron,
Dealer in Pine Lands,
Pierson.

L. H. Dolph,
Manuf'r of Lumber, Sec. 27,
Rockford, Pierson tp.

Smith, Hunter & Co.,
Manuf'rs of Lumber, 2000 acres,
Pierson P. O.

Pearl Brothers,
Manuf'rs of Staves, Heading,
& Shingles, Pierson P. O.

Ira Cone,
Lumberman, 100 acres, Sec. 2,
Maple Hill P. O., Pierson tp.

Z. E. Briggs,
Lumbering, 400 acres,
Langston, Pine tp.

H. H. Hinds,
Gen'l Merchandise, Lumber,
& Shingles, Stanton.

James Hartman,
Manuf'r of Lumber,
Stanton.

E. A. Moffat,
Manuf'r of Lumber & Lath,
Stanton.

Turner Bros.,
Manuf'rs of Lumber,
Stanton.

C. C. & F. K. Winsor,
Manuf'rs of Lumber & Shingles,
Stanton.

Geo. C. Wallace,
Groceries & Provisions, Lumber
& Shingles, Stanton.

Benham & Wales,
Planing Mill, & Manuf'rs of Shingles,
Stanton.

MARSHAL.

A. P. Waterhouse,
Marshal,
Pierson P. O.

MERCHANTS.

Daniel Shook,
Dry Goods & Groceries, & Notary
Public, Coral.

John Holcomb,
Dry Goods & Groceries and P. M.
Coral.

H. & R. S. Cowelen,
General Merchants,
Coral.

Stover & Hill,
General Merchants,
Crystal.

O. E. Mitchell,
Boot and Shoe Merchant,
Lake View.

L. S. Bissell,
General Merchant,
Lake View.

E. R. Sexton,
General Merchant,
Lake View.

J. N. Clark,
Grocer & Postmaster,
Pierson.

Henry Martin,
Merchant Tailor,
Pierson.

R. F. Sprague,
General Merchant, & Farmer,
Sec. 26, Pine tp.

H. W. Rice,
General Merchant,
Stanton.

MILLER.

E. Wright,
Dealer in Flour, Feed, & Provisions,
Howard City.

NEWSPAPER.

E. B. Powell,
Montcalm Herald,
Stanton.

PHYSICIANS.

Barry Brothers,
Physicians & Surgeons,
Coral.

Just & Martin,
Physicians & Surgeons,
Coral.

Charles O. Adams Miller,
Physician, & Surgeon,
Lake View.

Hugh Hubbard,
Physician & Druggist,
Langston.

C. M. Slauson,
Physician & Merchant,
Maple Valley.

D. Shook,
Physician,
Pierson.

H. M. Holden, M. D.
Physician & Surgeon,
Rockford, Pierson tp.

Donald A. Mc Lean,
Physician, Surgeon & Druggist,
Stanton.

REAL ESTATE.

Charles Parker,
Real Estate Dealer, & Farmer. 300
acres, Sec. 7, Maple Valley tp.

Moore & Shepard,
Real Estate Agents,
Stanton.

Finch & Fenn,
Real Estate Agents,
Stanton.

RESTAURANT.

L. W. Gerard,
Restaurant,
Pierson.

SAWYER.

Harmon Smith,
Sawyer,
Stanton.

SURVEYOR.

H. N. Caulkin,
Surveyor & Land Agent,
Langston.

WAGON MAKER.

R. P. Everett,
Wagon Maker,
Lake View.

BUSINESS CARDS OF PATRONS IN MONTCALM COUNTY.

ATTORNEY.

J. F. Corel,
Attorney at Law, P. O. Crystal
or Stanton.

BOOTS & SHOES.

George Griffin,
Boot & Shoe Maker,
Sheridan.

CARPENTER.

George H. Peters,
Carpenter and Joiner,
Dean's Mills.

CLERGYMAN.

Samuel Sessions,
Pastor Congregational Church,
Carson City, Bloomer tp.

DRUGGIST.

Daniel Reichard,
Dealer in Drugs and Medicines,
Bloomer tp., Carson City.

ENGINEER.

L. Swift,
Engineer,
Pierson.

FARMERS.

Benjamin S. Carey,
Farmer, 80 acres, Sec. 7,
Vickeryville P. O., Bloomer tp.

Chas. D. King,
200 acres in Sec. 17, Bloomer tp., also 80 acres
Pine Timber, Sec. 31 & 2, Carson City P.O., Ferris tp.

Guy J. Chandler,
Farmer, Grain & Stock 40 acres, Sec. 8,
Bloomer tp., Carson City P. O.

Isaac Burt,
Farmer, Carpenter & Joiner, 40 acres,
Sec. 13, Carson City P. O., Bloomer tp.

George W. Palmer,
Farmer, Wool Butter & Cheese, 120
acres, Sec. 24, Bloomer tp., Carson City P. O.

Albert W. Townsend,
Farmer, 80 acres, Sec. 24,
Carson City P. O., Bloomer tp.

John Dingler,
Farmer, 53 acres, Sec. 22,
Bloomer Centre P. O., Bloomer tp.

James Coville,
Farmer, Wool & Grain, 80 acres, Sec.
23, Bloomer Centre P. O. Bloomer tp.

Charles Barrett,
Farmer, 40 acres, Sec. 10,
Carson City P. O., Bloomer tp.

Aaron Lyon,
Farmer, 80 acres, Sec. 10,
Carson City P. O., Bloomer tp.

Henry F. Deal,
Farmer, 80 acres, Sec. 3,
Carson City P. O., Bloomer tp.

Isaac Dickason,
Farmer, Wool & Grain, 80 acres, Sec.
10, Carson City P. O., Bloomer tp.

Judson Barrett,
Farmer & Lumberman, Wool & Grain,
40 acres, Sec. 34, Hubbardston P. O. Ionia Co.
Bloomer tp.

Thomas Cliffe,
Farmer, Wool & Grain, 90 acres, Sec.
21, Bloomer Centre P. O., Bloomer tp.

George A. Wood,
Farmer, 90 acres, Sec. 20,
Palo P. O., Ionia Co., Bloomer tp.

A. A. Richardson,
Farmer, Wool & Grain, 110 acres, Sec.
20, Bloomer Centre P. O., Bloomer tp.

Edwin H. Stevens,
Farmer, 200 acres, Sec. 34,
Bushnell tp., Palo P. O.

Richard Low,
Farmer & Stock Grower, 160 acres,
Sec. 13, Bushnell tp , Vickeryville P. O.

Wm. R. Hodges,
Farmer & Stock Raiser, 80 acres, Secs.
20 & 29, Bushnell tp., Fenwick P. O.

U. E. Miller,
Farmer & Stock Raiser, 120 acres,
Sec. 24, Bushnell tp., Palo P. O.

Robert Eastman,
Farming, Grain a speciality, 60 acres,
Sec's. 35 & 36, Bushnell tp., Palo P. O.

Wm. Howorth,
Farmer, 150 acres, Sec. 36,
Bushnell tp., Palo P. O.

Prescott Varnum,
Farmer, 80 acres, Sec. 15,
Bushnell tp., Dean's Mills P. O.

Wm. Castil,
Farmer, 343 acres, Sec. 21,
Bushnell tp., Palo P. O.

Alvin Morse,
Farmer, 80 acres, Sec. 9,
Bushnell tp., Dean's Mills P. O.

Jo. Hanchett,
Farmer & Stock Raiser, 80 acres, Sec.
27, Bushnell tp., Bushnell Center P. O.

Abner Lewallen,
Farmer, Grain & Stock, 320 acres,
Sec. 4, Crystal.

Francis F. Hawkins,
Farmer, Alderney cattle a speciality,
120 acres, Sec. 4, Crystal.

John White,
Farmer, Grain & Hay, 80 acres, Sec. 3,
Crystal.

Samuel Starkey,
Grain, Hay and Fruit Farmer,
204 acres, Sec. 9, Crystal.

Gilbert Ward,
Farmer & Surveyor, 160 acres,
Sec's. 18 & 19, Crystal.

Abner Lenallen,
Farmer, Grain, Stock, Fruit, Wool 320 acres, Sec.
4, Crystal tp., Crystal P. O.

John Mason,
Farmer, Grain, Stock, Fruit, Wool
Crystal tp., Crystal P. O.

Francis P. Hawkins,
Farmer, Dealer in Alderney Cattle,
120 acres, Sec. 4, Crystal tp., Crystal P. O.

John White,
Farmer, Grain, Stock, & Hay, 80 acres,
Sec. 3, Crystal tp., Crystal P. O.

Samuel Starkey,
Farmer, Grain, Hay, Fruit, 204 acres,
Sec. 9, Crystal tp., Crystal P. O.

Samuel Rhoad,
Farmer, 86 acres, Sec. 4,
Crystal tp., Crystal P. O.

R. H. Mason,
Farmer, 40 acres, Sec. 34,
Crystal tp., Crystal P. O.

C. D. Dunshee,
Grain, Hay, & Fruit Farmer, 120 acres,
Sec. 5, Crystal.

C. D. Dunshee,
Farmer, Grain & Hay, 120 acres, Sec. 5,
Crystal P. O., and tp.

Charles W. Rockwell,
Farmer, Grain and Hay, 80 acres, Sec's. 30 and 31
Crystal P. O., and tp.

James Case,
Farmer, 80 acres, Sec. 16 Crystal tp., Crystal P. O.
190 A Pine Sec. 24, tp. 21 R. 2 W. Roscommon Co.

Peter Lee,
Farmer, 110 acres, Sec. 14,
Stanton P. O., Douglas tp.

James Lee,
Farmer, 120 acres, Sec. 3,
Westville P. O., Douglas tp.

D. P. Blood,
Farmer, 390 acres, Sec. 14,
Westville P. O., Douglas tp.

Judson Spitler,
Farmer, and Lumberman and Foreman, Greenville
P. O. Eureka tp., 80 acres, Sec. 19, Winfield tp.

W. McDonald,
Laborer, Elm Hall P. O. Gratiot Co.
Ferris tp., Montcalm Co.

Sylvester S. Rivett,
Farmer, 40 acres, Sec. 26, Sumner
P. O. Gratiot Co. Ferris tp.,

R. H. Mason,
Farmer, Grain, Stock & Hay, 40 acres, Sec. 34,
Ferris tp., Crystal P. O.

Alexander Cowaner,
Farmer and Dealer in Pine Lands,
Grattan tp., Grattan Center P. O.

Wm. C. Morris,
Farmer, 40 acres, Sec. 6,
Maple Valley tp., Coral P. O.

John Ashley,
Grain, Stock & Fine-wool sheep, 320 acres Sec 36.
Oakfield tp. Greenville P. O., Kent County.

Henry M. Carpenter,
Grain & Hay Grower, 80 acres, Sec. 15,
Pierson tp., Wood Lake P. O.

W. R. Stewart,
Farmer, Grain, Hay, and Wool, 80 acres, Sec. 14,
Pierson tp., Wood Lake P. O.

J. A. Field,
Hay & Stock Raiser, 127 acres, Sec 28,
Pierson tp., Wood Lake P. O.

O. J. Mosher,
Hay and Grain, 120 acres, Sec. 14,
Pierson tp., Wood Lake P. O.

Henry M. Carpenter,
Farmer, Grain & Hay, 80 acres, Sec.15,
Wood Lake P. O., Pierson tp.

John White,
Farmer, Grain, Stock, & Hay, 80 acres,
Sec. 3, Crystal tp., Crystal P. O.

Samuel Starkey,
Farmer, Grain, Hay, Fruit, 204 acres,
Sec. 9, Crystal tp., Crystal P. O.

Samuel Rhoad,
Farmer, 86 acres, Sec. 4,
Crystal tp., Crystal P. O.

R. H. Mason,
Farmer, 40 acres, Sec. 34,
Crystal tp., Crystal P. O.

C. D. Dunshee,
Grain, Hay, & Fruit Farmer, 120 acres,
Sec. 5, Crystal.

Elon G. Kingman,
Farmer and Grain Dealer, 160 acres,
Sec. 20, Howard City P.O. Reynolds tp.

Elon G. Kingman,
Farmer and Grain Dealer, 160 acres, Sec. 20,
Reynolds tp., Howard City P. O.

John Moore,
268 acres, Sec's. 6, 31 & 36,
Reynolds tp., Ensley P. O.

Wm. Dozenbery,
Farmer & Stock Raiser, 40 acres,
Sec. 31, Reynolds tp., Maple Hill P. O.

James Stevenson,
Farmer, Grain, Stock & Hay, 80 acres, Sec. 32,
Winfield tp., Howard city P. O.

J. B. Wetherby,
Farmer, Grain, Stock & Hay, 120 acres,
Sec. 20 Winfield tp., Howard city P. O.

Robert Bertram,
Farmer, 120 acres, Sec. 29,
Winfield tp., Howard City P. O.

HARDWARE.

M. G. Hall & Co.,
Hardware & Agricultural Implements,
Carson City

Hoop Dealers & Manufacturers.

Samuel Mc Neil,
Hoop Dealer,
Bushnel Center.

L. W. Nestel,
Manufacturer of Flour Barrels, Hoops, &c.,
Pierson tp., Wood Lake P. O.

HOTELS.

Orson R. Bush,
Hotel Proprietor,
Pierson.

S. H. Bailey,
Hotel Keeper,
Stanton P. O. Day tp.

O. N. Hoisington,
Proprietor Lake House,167 acres,
Sec. 7, Stanton P. O. Home tp.

H. H. Steffey,
Proprietor Eagle Hotel, Crystal P. O. Farmer and
Lumberman, 120 acres, Sec. 18 Crystal tp.

JEWELER.

Wm. B. Wells,
Jeweler, &
Greenville.

LUMBER.

John F. Chubb,
Manufacturer of Lumber, Lath and Shingles,
Howard City.

BUSINESS CARDS OF PATRONS IN MONTCALM COUNTY.

Henry Bromley, I. C. Quinsley & Co.,
Lumber Dealers,
Gaines, Kent County.

A. D. Hewett,
Manufacturer of Lumber,
Greenville.

D. D. Davis,
Lumberman, 80 acres, Sec. 32,
Trufant P. O., Maple Valley tp.

A. D. Hewett,
Lumberman,
Wood Lake P. O., Pierson tp.

J. G. Morgan,
of J. G. Morgan and Quick,
Dealers in Lumber, Lath & Shingles, 360 acres,
Pine Lands Sec. 35, Reynolds tp., Howard City P.O.

MERCHANTS.

O. D. Sines,
Dealer in Groceries & Provisions,
Carson City P. O., Bloomer tp.

Cummings & Thayer,
General Merchandise, & Purchasers of all kinds of
Farm Produce, Bloomer tp., Carson City P. O.

A. Proctor,
Dealers in all kinds of Groceries, & Purchasers of
all kinds of Produce, Bloomer tp., Carson City P.O.

William Brown,
Dealer in Groceries, & Purchaser of all kinds of
Farm Products, Bloomer tp., Carson City P. O.

A. D. McGill,
Family Groceries,
Carson City, Bloomer tp.

L. C. Jenks,
Merchant and Post Master,
Vickeryville.

MUSIC DEALER.

Hiram O. Brower,
Dealer in Musical Instruments, Sheet Music and
Books, P. O. Box 150, Carson City, Bloomer tp.

NEWSPAPER.

Wayne E. Morris,
Publisher of Howard City Record,
Howard City.

NOTARY PUBLIC.

A. M. Mack,
Notary Public and Postmaster, at Carson City
Bloomer tp., 80 acres in Sec. 10 New Haven tp.,
Gratiot Co.

PHYSICIAN.

J. P. Young,
Physician and Surgeon,
Crystal. tp. & P. O.

REAL ESTATE.

A. A. Dakin,
Farmer and Dealer in Real Estate, 40 acres Sec. 13,
Carson City P. O., Bloomer tp.

Mrs. Della Miner,
Village Lots, for sale, 18 acres, Sec. 12,
Carson City P. O., Bloomer tp.

SURVEYOR.

Gilbert Ward,
Surveyor, 150 acres, Sec's 18 & 19,
Crystal P. O. & tp.

TEACHERS.

Anna Allison,
Teacher,
Carson City, Bloomer tp.

Miss Maggie Aldrich,
Teacher,
Westville P. O., Douglass tp.

W. W. Dalgliesh,
Farmer & Teacher, P. O. Maple Rapids, Clinton Co.
80 acres, Sec. 5, Fulton tp., Gratiot Co.

N. E. Keith,
Principal of Public School,
Howard City.

J. G. Morgan & Quick,
Manufacturers of Lumber, Lath and Shingles,
360 acres Pine Land,
Howard City P. O.

THRESHER.

C. D. Dickerson,
Thresher, Sec. 26,
Bloomer Centre P. O., Bloomer tp.

WAGON MAKER.

George R. Gibbs,
Manufacturer of Wagons & all kinds of Blacksmithing, Carson City P.O., Bloomer tp.

WINES, LIQUORS &C.

Henry E. Hall,
Dealer in Wines Ales, Liquors, Cigars & Oysters,
Carson City P. O., Bloomer tp.

CARDS OF PATRONS IN CLARE, INGHAM AND WAYNE COUNTIES.

ATTORNEYS.

F. D. Wheaton,
Attorney at Law,
Clare, Clare County.

D. C. Warner,
Attorney and Counsellor at Law,
Chase, Lake County.

BANKER.

J. S. Lapham,
Banker,
Northville, Wayne Co.

CARPENTER.

John Cooper,
Carpenter and Joiner,
Farwell, Clare Co.

CLERGYMAN.

James Dubuar,
Pastor of Presbyterian Church,
Northville, Wayne Co.

ENGINEER.

J. L. Littlefield,
County Surveyor & Civil Engineer,
Farwell, Clare Co.

FARMERS.

A. Doble,
Farmer, & Dealer in Stock, 295 acres,
Sec. 10, Mason P. O., Alaedon tp.

James Wiley,
Farmer, 100 acres, Sec. 17,
Holt P. O., Alaedon tp.

J. M. Hudson,
Farmer & Veterinary Surgeon, 80 acres,
Sec. 18, Holt P. O., Alaedon tp.

E. Dell,
Farmer, 160 acres,
Mason P. O., Alaedon tp.

Porter Randall,
General Farming,
Clare, Clare Co.

James Thorburn,
Farmer, 140 acres, Sec. 25,
Holt P. O., Delhi tp.

Wm. Summerville,
Farmer and Breeder of choice Short Horned Stock,
224 acres, Sec. 25, Holt P. O., Delhi tp.

John Thorburn,
Farmer and Dealer, in choice Short Horn Stock
480 acres, Sec. 24, Holt P. O. Delhi tp.

Calvin Handy,
Farmer, & first settler in township of
Handy, Livingston Co.

A. T. Ingalls,
Farmer, & Owner of Six Charlie, & Dealer in Sin-
gle and Matched Horses, 124 acres, Sec. 9,
Leslie P. O. and tp.

Richard Coshun,
Farmer, 56 acres, Sec. 33,
Leslie P. O., and tp.

John Saltmarsh,
Farmer and Breeder of choice Stock, 180 acres Sec.
13, Okemos P. O., Meridian tp.

S. E. Jeffres,
Gen'l Farming, 200 acres, Sec. 12,
Okemos P. O., Meridian tp.

H. G. Proctor,
General Farmer, and Builder,
Okemos P. O., Meridian tp.

R. W. Surby,
Proprietor of Pine Lake Grove, Hall &
Boats, Okemos P.O., Meridian tp.

Phebe Hicks,
Farmer, 160 acres, Sec. 24,
Locke P. O., Meridian tp.

Enos Northrup,
Farmer, 200 acres, Sec. 23,
Mason P. O., Vevay tp.

Amos F. Wood,
Choice Shorthorn Cattle, Long Wool Sheep, Essex
Swine and improved Poultry,
Mason, P. O., Vevay tp.

Alton Rowe,
General Farmer, 154 acres, Sec. 7,
Mason P. O., Vevay tp.

M. A. Hawley,
Sheep & Dairy Farm, 320 acres,
Sec. 14. Mason P. O., Vevay tp.

James Fuller,
General Farmer, 160 acres, Sec. 16,
Mason P. O., Vevay tp.

Ira J. Teall,
Farmer and Miller, 236 acres, Sec. 28,
Mason P. O., Vevay tp.

Reubin Kendall
Farmer, 100 acres, Sec. 26,
Eden P. O., Vevay tp.

A. M. Chapin,
Farmer, 280 acres, Sec. 23,
Eden P. O., Vevay tp.

W. M. Rayner,
Dairyman & Surveyor, 280 acres, Sec. 9,
Mason P. O., Vevay tp.

HOTELS.

Henry Woodruff,
Proprietor of Farwell House,
Farwell, Clare Co.

N. H. Stevens,
Proprietor of Nicholls' Hotel,
Clare, Clare Co.

MANUFACTURERS.

I. M. Armstrong,
Manufacturer of Boots and Shoes,
Farwell, Clare Co.

S. P. Baker,
Lumberman,
Farwell, Clare Co.

A. Linton,
Manuf'r of Lumber, Lath & Staves,
Farwell, Clare Co.

Martin & Waldo Brothers,
Manuf'rs of Shingles, and Lumber,
Grant tp., Clare Co.

MERCHANTS.

E. A. Nichols,
Millinery and Fancy Goods,
Clare, Clare Co.

James Callam,
Dealer in General Merchandise,
Clare, Clare Co.

N. D. Todd,
Dealer in Hardware and Furniture,
Farwell, Clare Co.

F. R. Beal,
School Furniture & Hardware,
Northville, Wayne Co.

E. S. Horton,
Drugs, Medicines & Groceries,
Northville, Wayne Co.

A. E. Rockwell,
Jewelry, Solid Silver and Plated Ware.
Practical Watchmaker and Engraver,
Northville, Wayne Co.

OFFICERS.

Wm. Parrish,
Sheriff and Proprietor of Livery Stable,
Clare, Clare Co.

George L. Hitchcock,
County Treasurer,
Farwell, Clare Co.

W. H. Graves,
County Clerk & Proprietor of Livery
& Sale Stable, Farwell, Clare Co.

C. C. Casterlin,
Real Estate & Abstract Office, and
Register of Deeds, Farwell, Clare Co.

PHYSICIAN.

W. G. Wilkinson,
Physician and Surgeon,
Farwell, Clare Co.

PUBLISHER.

J. S. Holden,
Publisher of the Register,
Farwell, Clare Co.

BUSINESS CARDS OF PATRONS IN ST. CLAIR COUNTY.

AGENT.

Alfred J. West,
Deputy Sheriff and Real Estate and Collection Agent,
Capac Village, Mussey Township.

ATTORNEY.

D. C. Walker,
Attorney at Law,
Capac Village, Mussey Township.

BUTCHER.

Joseph Locke,
Butcher,
Capac Village, Mussey Township.

CLERGYMEN.

John L. Walker,
M. E. Minister, Sec. 10,
Brockway Centre P. O.

R. J. Doyle,
Pastor of Capac F. B. Church,
Capac Village, Mussey Township.

John W. Currier,
Pastor of 1st Methodist Church,
Capac Village, Mussey Township.

ENGINEERS.

Henry G. White,
Engineer,
Brockway Centre Village and tp.

Geo. Morris,
Engineer,
Capac Village, Mussey Township.

FARMERS.

J. B. Hamilton,
Farmer and Teacher Sec. 31,
Almont P. O., Berlin tp.

Geo. Edgerton,
Farmer and Teacher, Sec. 9,
Almont P. O., Berlin tp.

Albert Doty,
Farmer, Sec. 12,
Belle River P. O., Berlin tp.

A. D. McGeorge,
Farmer and Agent for American Sewing Machine,
Capac P. O., Berlin tp.

Joseph Reid,
Farmer, Sec. 18,
Almont P. O., Berlin tp.

H. L. Ives,
Farmer, Sec. 20,
Almont P. O., Berlin tp.

Henry J. Sweet,
Farmer, Sec. 29,
Almont P. O., Berlin tp.

Robert M. Muttart,
Farmer,
Berville P. O., Berlin tp.

S. S. Gould,
Farmer,
Berville P. O., Berlin tp.

Reubin Shaver,
Farmer, Sec. 35,
Armada P. O., Berlin tp.

Peter Hagle,
Farmer, Sec. 34,
Berville P. O., Berlin tp.

Henry Abeel,
Farmer, Sec. 31,
Berville P. O., Berlin tp.

A. C. Ferguson,
Farmer and Hop Grower, Sec. 31,
Berville P. O., Berlin tp.

Abram Coddington,
Farmer, Sec. 15,
Belle River P. O., Berlin tp.

Thomas Hannan,
Farmer, Sec. 15,
Belle River P. O., Berlin tp.

William C. Huggett,
Farmer, Sec. 9,
Belle River P. O. Berlin tp.

Charles Hobden,
Farmer, Sec. 4,
Capac P. O., Berlin tp.

Charles Lester,
Farmer and Miller,
Belle River P. O., Berlin tp.

John Berk,
Farmer, Sec 32,
Almont P. O., Berlin tp.

N. F. Churchill,
Farmer, Sec. 29,
Almont P. O., Berlin tp.

William Anderson,
Farmer, Sec. 19,
Almont P. O., Berlin tp.

H. W. Leonard,
Farmer,
Belle River P.O., Berlin tp.

O. P. Chamberlain,
Farmer,
Brockway Centre Village and tp.

Levi Morrill,
Farmer and Lumberman, Sec. 3,
Brockway Centre P. O.

Robert W. Rix,
Farmer, Sec. 10,
Brockway Centre P.O.

Robert Ricks,
Farmer, Sec. 3,
Brockway Centre P. O.

Thomas Morrill,
Farmer, Sec. 2,
Brockway Centre P. O.

John Keywerth,
Farmer, Sec. 4,
Brockway Centre P. O.

John Young,
Farmer, Sec. 9,
Brockway Centre P. O.

Alexander Adams,
Farmer, Sec. 20,
Brockway Centre P.O.

S. J. Welch,
Farmer Sec. 13,
Brockway Centre P. O., Brockway tp.

John Holden,
Farmer, Sec. 13,
Brockway Centre P. O., Brockway tp.

John Mc Farlane,
Farmer, Sec. 13,
Brockway Centre P.O., Brockway tp.

Samuel Carson,
Farmer, Sec. 18,
Brockway Centre P. O., Brockway tp.

George W. Barrett,
Farmer, Sec. 14,
Brockway Centre P. O., Brockway tp.

M. G. Chase,
Farmer and Joiner, Sec. 24,
Brockway P.O., and tp.

Nathaniel Townsend,
Farmer, Sec. 28,
Brockway Centre P.O., Brockway tp.

Richard Newkirk,
Farmer, Sec. 25,
Brockway P. O. and tp.

Albert Mc Kenney,
Farmer, Sec. 27,
Brockway P. O. and tp.

John D. Jones,
Farmer and Lumberman, Sec. 4,
Merrillville P. O., Brockway tp.

Robert Jones,
Farmer, Sec. 35,
Brockway.

William Lee,
Farmer, Sec. 32,
Brockway.

Abram E. Shearer,
Farmer, Sec. 35
Brockway P. O.

David Lindsey,
Farmer, Sec. 34,
Brockway P. O.

James W. Stewart,
Farmer and Teacher, Sec. 34,
Brockway P. O.

Henry Phillips,
Farmer, Sec. 8,
Merrillville P. O., Brockway tp.

Wm. H. K. Smith,
Farmer and Lumberman, Sec. 1,
Brockway P. O., Emmet tp.

James Griffin,
Farmer, Sec. 1,
Brockway P. O., Emmet tp,

Nathan Vanorman,
Farmer, Sec. 1,
Brockway P. O., Emmet tp.

Dennis Carney,
Farmer, Sec. 2,
Brockway P. O., Emmet tp.

David Donohue,
Farmer, Sec. 25,
Emmet.

James Downey,
Farmer, Sec. 25,
Emmet.

James Kennedy,
Farmer, Sec. 14,
Emmet.

John Haley,
Farmer, Sec. 14,
Emmet.

Sylvester Kennedy,
Farmer, Sec. 14,
Emmet.

Michael Reedy,
Farmer, Sec. 11,
Brockway P. O., Emmet tp.

Duncan Mc Kinzie,
Farmer, Sec. 15,
Brockway P. O., Emmet tp.

Henry Morgan,
Farmer, Sec. 24,
Lynn P. O. and tp.

John McMurtrie,
Farmer, Sec. 13,
Lynn P. O. and tp.

R. R. Wood,
Farmer, Sec. 15,
Lynn P. O. and tp.

John D. Watt,
Farmer and Stave and Timber dealer,
Lynn P. O. and tp.

E. B. Sprague,
Farmer, Sec. 23,
Lynn P. O. and tp.

James Le Gear,
Farmer, Sec. 7,
Lynn P. O. and tp.

William Allen,
Farmer, Sec. 4,
Lynn P. O. and tp.

Joseph J. Collins,
Farmer, Sec. 4,
Merrillville P. O.

Samuel M. Holcomb,
Farmer, Sec. 5,
Merrillville P. O.

Lansing Bridleman,
Farmer, Sec. 5,
Merrillville P. O.

John Burt,
Farmer, Sec. 28,
Capac P. O. Mussey tp.

Richard Shutt,
Farmer, Sec. 14,
Capac P. O. Mussey tp.

G. W. Curtis,
Farmer, Sec. 14,
Capac P. O. Mussey tp.

Thos. G. Woodward,
Farmer, Sec. 15,
Capac P. O. Mussey tp.

Warren D. Churchill,
Farmer, Sec. 9,
Capac P. O. Mussey tp.

Frederick Ross,
Farmer,
Capac Village, Mussey Township.

C. Simmons,
Farmer, Sec. 33,
Memphis P. O., Riley tp.

Samuel Thompson,
Farmer, Sec. 29,
Memphis P. O., Riley tp.

John Van Deusen,
Farmer, Sec. 34,
Memphis P. O., Riley tp.

Johnson Van Marter,
Farmer, Sec. 34,
Memphis P. O., Illley tp.

William W. Ross,
Farmer, Sec. 13,
Memphis P. O., Riley tp.

George B. Spencer,
Farmer, Sec. 32,
Memphis P. O., Riley tp.

Patrick Nowell,
Farmer, Sec. 1,
Emmet P. O., Riley tp.

George Laforge,
Farmer, Sec. 1,
Emmet P. O., Riley tp.

Thomas Parker,
Farmer, Sec. 10,
Emmet P. O., Riley tp.

Martin Blinwood,
Farmer, Hops & Dairying, Sec. 18,
Riley Centre P. O., Riley tp.

Thomas Davis,
Farmer,
Riley Centre.

John Cawthorn,
Farmer, Sec. 16,
Riley Centre P. O., Riley tp.

James Corpron,
Farmer, Sec. 5,
Riley Centre P. O., Riley tp.

David Lown,
Farmer, Sec. 13,
Memphis P. O., Riley tp.

A. H. Blynd,
Farmer Sec. 14,
Memphis P. O., Riley tp.

A. G. Lordly,
Farmer, Sec. 24,
Memphis P. O., Riley tp.

HOTELS.

Burr Stewart,
Hotel-keeper and Farmer, Sec. 4, three miles south of Capac,
Capac P. O., Berlin tp.

Oliver H. Ross,
Hotel-keeper, Berlin House, Sec. 21.
Almont P. O., Berlin tp.

BUSINESS CARDS OF PATRONS IN ST. CLAIR COUNTY.

Furgureon House,
Frank Bettis, Proprietor,
Brockway Centre Village and tp.

Northern Hotel,
Ebenezer Smith, Proprietor,
Brockway Centre Village and tp.

Brockway Hotel,
J. T. S. Minnie, Proprietor,
Brockway Village and P. O. Brockway tp.

Sunnet House,
E. & M. Gallagher, Proprietors,
Emmet.

Lynn Hotel,
Robert Reid, Proprietor,
Sec. 3. Lynn tp.

Lafayette Alverson,
Proprietor Alverson House,
Capac Village, Mussey Township.

LIVERY STABLE.

Miles Hagle,
Marine City Livery, Sale and Boarding
Stable, at Demond House.

MANUFACTURERS.

J. A. Morrill,
Lumber Manufacturer and Farmer,
Brockway Centre Village and tp.

Wm. D. Wear,
Woolen Manufacturer and Farmer,
Brockway Centre Village and tp.

Ira Groen,
(Lapeer City) Woolen Manufacturer,
Brockway Centre Village and tp.

Oscar Mills,
Lumberman, Sec. 10,
Lynn P. O. and tp.

MECHANICS.

William O'Connor,
Blacksmith, Sec. 36,
Berville P. O., Berlin tp.

William R. Gillett,
Carpenter, Sec. 11,
Belle River P. O., Berlin tp.

Hiram Ingraham,
Carpenter and Joiner, Sec. 31,
Berville P. O., Berlin tp.

A. A. Smith,
Proprietor Sawmill, and Builder,
Belle River P. O., Berlin tp.

W. & J. Harris,
Carriage and Wagon Manufactory and
General Blacksmithing,
Brockway Village and P. O. Brockway tp.

T. J. High,
Cabinet Maker,
Brockway Centre Village and tp.

William Darcy,
Carriage Maker,
Brockway Centre Village and tp.

Joseph Effrick,
Blacksmith,
Brockway Centre Village and tp.

Thomas Darcy,
Blacksmith,
Brockway Centre Village and tp.

C. D. Bryce,
Carpenter, Sec. 4,
Brockway Centre P. O.

James Cogley,
Carriage & Wagon Manufactory. All kinds
of blacksmithing, Emmet.

John Howet,
Joiner,
Capac Village, Mussey Township.

Hezekiah Allen,
Mason,
Mussey tp.

Albert Raymond,
Blacksmith,
Capac Village, Mussey Township.

John N. Warn,
Carriage and Wagon Manufacturer,
Capac Village, Mussey Township.

Julius Raymond,
Blacksmith,
Riley Centre.

MERCHANTS.

G. Leith,
General Merchant,
Belle River P. O., Berlin tp.

Francis W. Frost,
Dry Goods and Groceries,
Belle River P. O., Berlin tp.

J. S. Duffie,
General Dealer, Dry Goods and Groceries,
Brockway Centre Village and tp.

Gunselus & Makolim,
Groceries, Hardware, Notions, &c.,
Brockway Centre Village and tp.

Moore & Ard,
General dealers in Dry Groceries, Drugs, &c.
Brockway Village and P. O. Brockway tp.

William H. Balentine,
General Dealers, Dry Goods, Groceries, Hardware, Patent Medicines,
Brockway Village and P. O. Brockway tp.

Orid P. Brown,
Harnesses, Saddles, Trunks, Valises,
Whips, &c.
Brockway Centre Village and tp.

Thos. H. Bottomley,
Dealer in Dry Goods, Groceries, Boots, Shoes,
Hats, Caps, Drugs, Medicines and
General Merchandise,
Capac Village Mussey Township.

A. F. Seidel,
General Merchant and Dealer in Flour Barrel Hoops and Tight Barrel Staves.
Capac Village, Mussey tp.

Andrew Millspaugh,
Groceries and Provisions,
Capac Village, Mussey tp .

Benjamin Felker,
Dealer in General Merchandise,
Riley Centre.

MILLERS.

Brockway Mills,
John Trainer, Proprietor, Flour, Feed, &c,
Brockway Village and P. O. Brockway tp.

Brockway Centre Mills,
Jas. Ferguson, Proprietor,
Brockway Centre Village and tp.

James H. Bandfl,
Flour, Gristmill and Sawmill,
Capac Village, Mussey tp.

PHYSICIANS.

Daniel Jones,
Physician, Sec. 32,
Almont P. O., Berlin tp.

Cornelius Mills,
Physician and Surgeon,
Brockway Centre Village and tp.

William Gowan.
Physician and Surgeon,
Brockway Village and P. O., Brockway tp.

Charles E. Ross,
Homeopathic Physician,
Capac Village, Mussey tp.

James H. McGurk,
Physician and Surgeon,
Capac Village, Mussey tp.

TEACHERS.

H. F. Smith,
Teacher, Sec. 11,
Belle River P. O., Berlin tp.

David McArthur,
Teacher,
Brockway Centre Village and tp.

Josephine Johnson,
Teacher,
Sec. 34, Brockway Centre P. O.

O. M. Stephenson,
Teacher, Sec. 20 Columbus tp. and P. O.
Brockway tp.

Mary Allen,
Teacher, Sec. 13,
Ruby P. O. Keneeke tp.

J. D. Frink,
Teacher,
Capac Village, Mussey tp.

BUSINESS CARDS OF PATRONS IN GRATIOT COUNTY.

ATTORNEYS.

Francis Palmer,
Attorney at Law, and Real Estate Agent,
Alma.

Wm. B. Vinton,
Attorney Judge of Probate & Farmer, 300
acres, Sec. 33, Ithica P. O., Arcade tp.

E. L. Drake,
Attorney and Notary Public, 50 acres, Sec. 7,
and 29, Sumner P. O. and tp.

BLACKSMITHS.

Geo. L. Spicer,
Blacksmith and Wagon Maker,
Alma.

J. H. Brown,
Carriage Maker and Blacksmith, River St.
near Bridge St. Grand Ledge, Eaton Co.

Charles R. Smith,
Blacksmith,
Ithica.

Bradley H. Johnson,
Blacksmith, ½ acres, Sec. 8,
Summerton P. O., Pine River tp.

Henry B. Smith,
Blacksmith,
Pompeii.

Ringonborg & Co.,
Wagon Makers, and Blacksmiths,
St. Louis.

A. A. Minor,
Blacksmith and Wagon Maker,
Sumner P. O. and tp.

H. L. Alexander,
Wagon Maker and Blacksmith, 12 Lots,
Sec. 5, Elm Hall P. O., Sumner tp.

John Fowler,
Horse Shoeing,
Sumner P. O. and tp.

BREWER.

George Bahlke,
Brewer and Manufacturer of Beer and
Mineral Water, Alma.

CLERGYMAN.

Carlos Spaulding,
Pastor of M. E. Church,
Portland, Eaton Co.

FARMERS.

A. Bailey.
Stock and Grain Farmer and Manufacturer
of Brick and Drain Tile, 80 acres, Sec. 11,
Alma P. O., Arcada tp.

Edson P. Spink,
Grain, Wool and Stock Farmer, 116 acres,
Sec. 4,
Alma P. O., Arcada tp.

Ralph Ely,
Farmer, Dealer in Pine Lands and Lumber,
1000 acres, Sec. 3,
Alma P. O., Arcade tp.

Darwin Ely,
Farmer and Mechanic, 103 acres, Sec. 11,
Alma P. O., Arcade tp.

A. M. Wiley,
Farmer, Grain, Stock and Wool, 83 acres,
Sec. 5,
Alma P. O., Arcada tp.

J. G. Thompson.
Stock, Grain and Wool Farmer, 45 acres,
Sec. 18,
St. Louis P. O., Bethany tp.

Julia Ann Snook,
Farmer, Grain, Stock and Wool, 80 acres,
Sec. 4,
St. Louis P. O., Bethany tp.

Elias W. Smith,
Farmer and Lumberman, 125 acres, Sec. 10,
St. Louis P. O., Bethany tp.

Gilbert E Hall,
Grain, Stock and Wool Farmer, 40 acres,
Sec. 29,
St. Louis P. O., Bethany tp.

Meritt C. Wilcox,
Farmer, Grain and Stock, 99 acres, Sec. 29,
St. Louis P. O., Bethany tp.

E. W. Growett,
Grain, Stock, and Wool Farmer, and Dealer
in Real Estate, 120 acres, Sec. 18,
St. Louis P. O., Bethany tp.

J. H. Redman,
General Farmer, 196 acres, Sec. 19,
St. Louis P. O., Bethany tp.

Norman D. Vincent,
Farmer and Carpenter, 80 acres, Sec. 29,
St. Louis P. O., Bethany tp.

C. W. Hicks,
Grain, Stock and Wool Farmer, 40 acres,
St. Louis P. O., Bethany tp.

John T. Shuman,
Lumberman, Sec. 30,
Carson City P. O.

Thomas Franklin,
Wool and Grain Farmer, 80 acres, Sec. 19,
Carson City P. O.

Charles Chick,
Wool and Hop Farmer, 80 acres, Sec. 6,
Carson City P. O.

Irvin McCall,
General Farmer, 107 acres, Sec. 19,
Carson City P. O.

Geo. H Phillips,
Farmer, 80 acres, Sec. 34,
Carson City P. O.

D. R. Sullivan,
General Farmer and Dealer in Pine Lands and Lumber, Alma.

James Beattie,
Grain Stock and Wool Farmer, 80 acres, Sec. 14, Arcada tp., Ithica P. O.

E. C. Farrington,
Farmer, Stock, Grain, Fruit and Wool, 60 acres, Sec. 11, Ithica P. O., Emerson tp.

M. S. Lewis,
Grain and Stock Farmer, 40 acres, Sec. 2, St. Louis P. O., Emerson tp.

B. & W. E. Lewis,
Farmer, Grain, Stock and Wool, 40 acres, Sec. 30, Ithica P. O., Emerson tp.

John Mull,
Farmer, Grain and Stock, 80 acres, Sec. 5, St. Louis P. O., Emerson tp.

S. A. Osborne,
General Farmer, 80 acres, Sec. 4, St. Louis P. O., Emerson tp.

W. Coston,
Farmer, 40 acres, Sec. 11, St. Louis P. O., Emerson tp.

F. W. Curtis,
Farmer, 120 acres, Sec. 2, St. Louis P. O., Emerson tp.

Elijah A. Booker,
Grain, Stock and Wool Farmer, 160 acres, Sec. 11, St. Louis P. O., Emerson tp.

Stewart Edgar,
Grain, Stock, & Wool Farmer, 122 acres, Sec. 2, St. Louis P. O., Emerson tp.

Albro Curtis,
Grain, and Stock Farmer, 160 acres, Sec. 12, St. Louis P. O., Emerson tp.

Waldo Curtis,
General Farmer, 120 acres, Sec. 2, St. Louis P. O., Emerson tp.

Patrick Brewer,
Farmer, Grain, Stock, & Wool, 160 acres, Sec. 15, Ithica P. O., Emerson tp.

Charles E. Webster,
Farmer and Stock Raiser, 160 acres, Sec. 11, Pompeii P. O., Fulton tp.

O. F. Baker,
Stock, Wool, & Grain Farmer, 120 acres, Sec. 12, Spring Brook P. O., Fulton tp.

John Kallar,
Grain, Stock, and Wool Farmer, 100 acres, Sec. 24, Bridgeville P. O., Fulton tp.

H. W. Musser,
Farmer, Grain, Stock, & Wool, 40 acres, Sec. 22, Spring Brook P. O., Fulton tp.

W. K. Miller,
Stock, Grain, and Wool Farmer, 100 acres, Sec. 22, Maple Rapids P. O., Fulton tp.

Thomas W. Davis,
Farmer, and Raiser of Stock, 45 acres, Sec. 16, Spring Brook P. O., Fulton tp.

Edward C. Bassett,
Stock, Grain, & Wool Farmer, 70 acres, Sec. 16, Spring Brook P. O., Fulton tp.

George Dodson,
Grain, Stock, and Wool Farmer, 80 acres, Sec's. 3 and 4, Pompeii P. O., Fulton tp.

Albert A. Eagleston,
General Farmer, 150 acres, Sec. 3, Pompeii P. O., Fulton tp.

James H. Lewis,
Farmer, Grain, Stock and Wool, 85 acres, Sec. 10, Fulton tp., Pompeii P. O.

M. H. Baker,
General Farmer & Dealer in Sewing Machines 40 acres, Sec. 21, Fulton tp., Maple Rapids P. O.

F. Sheridan,
Stock and Grain Farmer, 80 acres, Sec. 21, Fulton tp., Maple Rapids P. O.

B. F. Brown,
Stock and Grain Farmer, 40 acres, Sec. 5, Union House P. O., Clinton Co. Greenbush tp.

Sarah J. Dubois,
Grain and Stock Farmer, 50 acres, Sec. 8. Greenbush, Clinton Co.

James Dalton,
General Farmer, 72 acres, Sec. 19, Hubbardston P. O.

Geo. E. Walker,
Hay and Grain Farmer, 160 acres, Sec's. 30 and 31, Hubbardston P. O.

B. Looks,
Wool and Grain Farmer, 130 acres, Sec. 31, Hubbardston P. O.

Samuel Newton,
Grain, Stock and Wool Farmer, 80 acres, Sec. 21, Ithica P. O.

V. Payne,
Grain and Stock Farmer, 45 acres, Sec. 29, Ingham tp., Dansville P. O.

Wm. T. Depew,
Grain, Stock and Wool Farmer, 160 acres, St. Louis P. O., Midland Co., Jasper tp.

Charles W. White,
Stock and Grain Farmer, 80 acres, Sec. 6, Ashton P. O., Lincoln tp.

Roman Tyler,
Farmer, 120 acres, Sec. 24, North Shade tp., Maple Rapids P. O.

Jason Kingman,
Grain and Stock Farmer, Sec. 20, Fulton tp., Maple Rapids P. O.

Dwight Stilt,
General Farming, 160 acres, Sec. 30, Fulton tp., Maple Rapids P. O.

Charles E. Barnhart,
Stock, Grain, and Wool Farmer, 150 acres, Sec. 32, Maple Rapids P. O.

Albert I. Wilcox,
Stock, Grain, & Wool Farmer, 80 acres, Sec. 28, Maple Rapids P. O.

John T. Packer,
Farmer and Justice of the Peace, 80 acres, Sec. 5, Summer P. O., New Haven tp.

Solomon Bruce,
Farmer, 80 acres, Sec's. 18 and 19, New Haven P. O.

Charles H. Morse,
Farmer and Representative of Gratiot Co., 360 acres, Sec's. 20 and 29, New Haven P. O.

Wm. Standish,
General Farmer, 320 acres, Sec. 9, New Haven P. O.

James W. McGinley,
Farmer and Town Clerk, 40 acres, Sec. 29, New Haven P. O.

W. G. Everest,
General Farmer, 160 acres, Sec. 11, New Haven Centre P. O.

N. A. Lect,
General Farmer, 80 acres, Sec. 9, New Haven Centre P. O.

Andrew J. Allen,
Farmer, Grain, Stock, and Wool, 200 acres, Sec. 34, Pompeii P. O., Newark tp.

James Wood,
Farmer, Grain, Stock and Wool Raiser and selling organs, 100 acres, Sec. 80, Newark tp., and P. O.

Samuel W. Nichols,
Farmer and Carpenter and Joiner, 120 acres, Sec. 17, Newark tp., and P. O.

E. W. Kellogg,
General Farmer, 400 acres, Sec. 30, Newark.

Gideon Teachworth,
Raiser of Grain, Wool and Stock, 40 acres, Sec. 3, Newark tp., Pompeii P. O.

Edwin K. Stow,
Farmer and Teacher, 80 acres, Sec. 85, Newark tp., Pompeii P. O.

B. P. Eldred,
Farmer, Grain and Stock, 146 acres, Sec. 36, Maple Rapids, P. O., Northshade tp.

E. C. Cook,
Stock and Grain Farmer, 180 acres, Sec. 31, North Star tp., Pompeii P. O.

John W. Chappin,
Stock and Grain Farmer, 80 acres, Sec. 30, North Star tp., Pompeii P. O.

L. G. White,
Farmer, Grain, Stock and Wool, 80 acres, Sec. 16 and 22, Forest Hill P. O., Pine River tp.

Silas Moody,
Grain, Stock and Wool Farmer, 160 acres, Sec. 9. St. Louis P. O., Pine River tp.

S. T. Sprague,
General Farmer, 80 acres, Sec. 3 and 10, St. Louis P. O., Pine River tp.

Valmore Hoyt,
Grain, Stock and Wool Farmer, 160 acres, Sec. 19, St. Louis P. O., Pine River tp.

John Vanderback,
General Farmer, 360 acres, Sec. 15, St. Louis P. O., Pine River tp.

Orson Briggs,
Farmer, 333½ acres. Sec's. 26 and 35, St. Louis P. O., Pine River tp.

Charles A. Kipp,
Farmer, Sec. 25, St. Louis P. O., Pine River tp.

John Westbrook,
Farmer and Millwright, 40 acres, Sec. 12, St. Louis P. O., Pine River tp.

Simon Cahoon,
Farmer, Stock, Grain and Wool, 200 acres, Sec. 34, Alma P. O., Pine River tp.

John H. Orwig,
Farmer and Fruit Dealer, 40 acres, Sec. 5, Forest Hill P. O., Pine River tp.

N. B. Willis,
General Farmer, 80 acres, Sec. 1, Fulton tp., Pompeii P. O.

J. N. Vanaier,
General Farmer and Dealer in General Merchandise, St. Johns, Clinton Co.

A. C. Welch,
Farmer and Dealer in Groceries and Provisions, 236 acres, Sec's. 23 and 26, Coe tp., St. Louis P. O.

Cornelius Holliday,
Stock, Grain and Wool Farmer, 200 acres, St. Louis P. O.

Perry Estes,
Stock, Grain and Wool Farmer, 160 acres, Salt River P. O., Isabella Co.

Noah Scory,
Farmer, 100 acres, Sec. 3, Fulton tp., Grain, Sheep and Wool for sale, Spring Brook P. O.

H. Prichard,
Farmer, Grain, Stock and Wool, 200 acres, Sec's. 1 and 2, Alma P. O., Sumner tp.

H. L. Townsend,
Farmer, Grain, Stock and Wool, 80 acres, Sec. 11, Alma P. O., Sumner tp.

M. T. Rice,
Stock, Grain and Wool Farmer, 160 acres, Sec. 12, Alma P. O., Sumner tp.

Sylvester Vanleuven,
Farmer, Justice of the Peace and Notary Public, 520 acres, Sec. 4, Sumner P. O.

Wm. A. Tomlin,
Farmer, 80 acres, Sec. 27. Sumner P. O., and tp.

Westley Harvey,
General Farmer, 100 acres, Sec. 33, Sumner P. O., and tp.

Job C. Wolford,
General Farmer, 80 acres. Sec. 88. Sumner P. O., and tp.

Mrs. C. A. Stoughton,
Grain and Wool Farmer, 320 acres, Sec. 33, Sumner P. O., and tp.

David Fry,
General Farmer, 120 acres, Sec. 23, Sumner P. O., and tp.

Joseph Lovell,
General Farmer, 40 acres, Sec. 16, Sumner P. O., and tp.

Wm. J. Gargett,
Farmer and Highway Commissioner, 120 acres, Sec. 16, Sumner P. O., and tp.

George Rookafellow,
General Farmer, 120 acres, Sec. 10, Alma P. O., Sumner tp.

Leonard M. Post,
Pump Manufacturer and Farmer, Union House, Clinton Co.

William Lang,
Farmer, Grain, Stock and Wool, 125 acres, Sec. 18, Pompeii P. O., Washington tp.

Horton Smith,
Farmer and Carpenter, 80 acres, Sec. 20, Washington tp.

Sampson Ovendon,
Farmer, Grain, Stock and Wool, 120 acres, Sec. 19 and 30, Bridgeville P. O., Washington tp.

William Carothers,
Grain, Wool, and Stock Farmer, 42 acres, Sec. 19, Bridgeville P. O., Washington tp.

Samuel Loddick,
Blacksmith and Farmer, 15 acres, Sec. 30, Washington tp.

Charles Wood,
Grain, Stock, & Wool Farmer, 160 acres, Sec. 31, Wheeler tp.

B. B. Goodnough,
General Farmer, Drain and Road Commissioner and Justice of the Peace, 220 acres, Sec. 29, Wheeler P. O., and tp.

Alfred S. Atwood,
Grain and Stock Farmer, 40 acres, Sec. 35, Wheeler P. O., and tp.

David Byar,
Farmer, Grain and Stock.

Road C. Lattimer,
Farmer, Grain Stock and Wool, 84 acres.

Zack Whipple,
Grain and Stock Farmer, 80 acres.

BUSINESS CARDS OF PATRONS IN GRATIOT COUNTY.

Wm. S. Nelson, Grain, Stock, & Fruit Farmer, 860 acres, Sec. 13, also Dealer in Pine Lands & Lumber, Ithaca P. O., Arcade tp.

F. E. Brond, Farmer and Dealer in Stock and Grain, 80 acres, Sec. 30, Ithaca P. O., Emerson tp.

Henry R. Wilcox, Farmer & Supervisor, 140 acres, Sec. 7, Lafayette P. O. and tp.

Samuel Wheeler, Farmer, 143 acres, Sec. 18, Breckenridge P. O., Lafayette tp.

Asa F. Boam, Farmer, 120 acres, Sec. 18, Lafayette P. O. and tp.

Thomas Franklin, Farmer, Wool and Grain. 80 acres, Sec. 19, Carson City P. O., North Shade tp. Montcalm Co.

Charles Chick, Farmer, Hops, Wool & Grain, 80 acres, Sec.0, Carson City P. O., North Shade tp, Montcalm Co.

Aaron Sebin, Farmer and Sawyer, 80 acres, Sec't. 15 & 8, Summerton P. O., Mecosta tp.

Harvey Cady, Farmer, and Stock Dealer, 40 acres, Sec. 1, Ithaca P. O., Newark tp.

N. Arminous Loot, Farmer, 80 acres, Sec. 9, New Haven P. O. and tp.

W. S. Everest, Farmer, Supervisor and Minister, 100 acres, Sec. 11. New Haven P. O. and tp.

George H. Phillips, General Farming, 80 acres. Sec. 34, Carson City P. O., New Haven tp.

Solomon Bruce, Farmer, Justice, Carpenter, and Preacher, 80 acres, Sec's 18 & 19, New Haven Centre P. O., New Haven tp.

William Standish, General Farming, 320 acres, Sec. 9, New Haven Centre P. O., New Haven tp.

James W. Mc Ginley, Farmer and Town Clerk, 40 acres, Sec. 29, New Haven Centre P. O., New Haven tp.

James Crispell, Farmer, Wheat, Wool, and Grain, 160 acres, Sec. 9, Sumner P. O., New Haven tp.

Moses White, Farmer, 120 acres, Sec. 33, New Haven Centre P. O., New Haven tp.

Joseph Wiles Jr. Farmer and Township Treasurer, 320 acres, Sec. 21, New Haven Centre P. O., New Haven tp.

Emanuel Wiles, Farmer, 40 acres, Sec. 16, New Haven Centre P. O., New Haven tp.

Alvin E. Shepard, Farmer, Stave Maker & Jobber, 160 acres, Sec's. 26 & 36, Maple Rapids P. O., New Haven tp.

Mrs. Clarissa A. Husted, General Farming, 80 acres, Sec. 25, Maple Rapids P. O., New Haven tp.

Samuel Y. Dickinson, Farmer & Justice, 80 acres, Sec. 25, Maple Rapids P. O., New Haven tp.

Proctor Shepard, General Farming, 100 acres, Sec's 24 & 25, Maple Rapids P. O., New Haven tp.

Esra Austin, General Farming, 80 acres, Sec. 14, New Haven Centre P. O., New Haven tp.

Robert Gager, General Farming, 80 acres, Sec. 14, New Haven Centre P. O., New Haven tp.

George P. Steadman, General Farming, 80 acres, Sec. 24, Newark P. O., New Haven tp.

John Pool, Farmer, 160 acres, Sec. 13, Newark P. O., New Haven tp.

John T. Packer, Farmer and Justice, 80 acres, Sec. 5, Sumner P. O., New Haven tp.

Irving Mc Coll, General Farming, 107 acres, Sec. 7, Carson City P. O., North Shade tp.

James Dalton, General Farming, 72 acres, Sec. 10, Hubbardston P. O., North Shade tp.

George E. Walker, Farmer, Hay and Grain, 100 acres, Sec. 81, Hubbardston P. O., North Shade tp.

Bezaleel Locke, Farmer, Wool and Grain. 130 acres, Sec. 31, Hubbardston P. O., North Shade tp.

A. B. Loomis, Farmer, Wool and Grain, 102½ acres, Sec. 36, Hubbardston P. O., North Shade tp.

A. Terwilliger, Farmer, Wool and Grain, 120 acres, Sec. 5 & 6, Hubbardston P. O., North Shade tp.

Samuel F. Cranson, Farming and Grazing, 320 acres, Sec. 33, Hubbardston P. O., North Shade tp.

John Dobson, Farmer, 200 acres, Sec. 24, Maple Rapids P. O., North Shade tp.

Alonzo F. Kellogg, Farmer, 40 acres, Sec. 10, Hubbardston P. O., North Shade tp.

M. A. Vanvranken, Farmer, Carpenter and Joiner, 24 acres, Sec. 7, Ithaca P. O., North Star tp.

T. Fuller, Farmer and Hop Grower, 20 acres, Sec. 5, Ithaca P. O., North Star tp.

J. H. Mellinger, Farmer, 120 acres, Sec. 9, Ithaca P. O., North Star tp.

Sidney Thompson, Farmer, 140 acres, Sec. 8, Ithaca P. O., North Star tp.

Elmer N. Riffner, Farmer, 100 acres, Sec's. 16 and 17, Ithaca P. O., North Star tp.

James L. Shults, Farmer, & Justice of the Peace, 160 acres, Sec. 11, Forest Hill P. O., Seville tp.

Patrick D. Egan, Farmer and Town Clerk, 160 acres, Sec. 1, Summerton P. O., Seville tp.

David Mc Laughlin, Farmer and Lumberman, 120 acres, Sec. 2, Summerton P. O., Seville tp.

John B. Mallory, Farmer, 40 acres, Sec. 24, Alma P. O., Seville tp.

George W. Newcomb, Farmer, 160 acres, Sec. 24, Alma P. O., Seville tp.

Wm. H. Kilzinger, Farmer and Mechanic, 80 acres, Sec. 35, Alma P. O., Seville tp.

Wm. G. Falknor, Farmer, 80 acres, Sec. 27, Alma P. O., Seville tp.

C. B. Fisher, Farmer, 200 acres, Sec. 33 and 34, Alma P. O., Seville tp.

N. K. Strayer, Farmer and Blacksmith, 160 acres, Sec. 33, Elm Hall P. O., Seville tp.

Frederick Dunn, Farmer, 200 acres, Sec. 18, Beaver Creek P. O., Seville tp.

Alfred Dundas, Farmer and Lumberman, 160 acres, Sec. 31, Elm Hall P. O., Seville tp.

Job C. Wolford, Farmer, 80 acres, Sec. 32, Sumner P. O. and tp.

Mrs. C. A. Stoughton, Farmer, Wool and Grain, 320 acres, Sec. 32, Sumner P. O. and tp.

David Fry, General Farming, 120 acres, Sec. 28, Sumner P. O. and tp.

Joseph T. Lovell, General Farming, 40 acres, Sec. 16, Sumner P. O. and tp.

William I. Gargett, Farmer & Highway Commissioner, 120 acres, Sec. 18, Sumner P. O. and tp.

George Rockafellow, Farmer, 120 acres, Sec. 16, Alma P. O., Sumner tp.

Samuel C. Zettor, Farmer, 80 acres, Sec. 18, Elm Hall P. O., Sumner tp.

George Older, Farmer and Preacher, 67 acres, Sec. 7, Elm Hall P. O., Sumner tp.

Wm. H. Morrill, Farmer, 160 acres, Sec. 9, Elm Hall P. O., Sumner tp.

Wm. D. Clark, Farmer, 120 acres, 'dee's. 12 and 13, Alma P. O., Sumner tp.

Jonathan Courter, Farmer, 570 acres, Sec. 12, Alma P. O., Sumner tp.

Thomas Gifford, Farmer and Bricklayer, 111 acres, Sec. 30, Sumner P. O. and tp.

Benjamin Fowler, Farmer, 160 acres, Sec. 31, Sumner P. O. and tp.

G. S. Bell, Farmer, 160 acres, Sec. 31, Sumner P. O. and tp.

Arnold Worden, Laborer, Sumner P. O. and tp.

Christopher Cleverdon, Farmer and Merchant, 280 acres, Sec's 20 & 29, Sumner P. O. and tp.

Samuel Story, Farmer, 120 acres, Sec. 19, Sumner P. O. and tp.

Jesse Trapp, Farmer, 180 acres, Sec. 6, Elm Hall P. O., Sumner tp.

Isaac B. Ward, Farmer, 80 acres, Sec. 20, Sumner P. O. and tp.

William A. Tomlin, Farmer, 80 acres, Sec. 27, Sumner P. O. and tp.

Wesley Harvey, Farmer, 160 acres, Sec's. 28 and 33, Sumner P. O. and tp.

N. B. Bradley, Farmer and Lumberman, 320 acres, Sec. 30, Elm Hall P. O., Seville tp, and 1000 acres, Pine, in Seville and Richmond tps, Isabella Co.

Barney Swope, Farmer and Justice, 120 acres, Sec. 21, Wheeler P. O. and tp.

Enos Partee, Farmer, 160 acres, Sec. 17, Wheeler P. O. and tp.

Jacob Bishop, Farmer, and Road Commissioner, 80 acres, Sec. 23, Elsie P. O., Clinton Co., Elba tp.

Andrew Hall, Farmer, 86 acres, Sec's. 27 and 28, Elsie P. O. Clinton Co., Elba tp.

J. B. Kneeland, Farmer & Supervisor, Elsie P. O. Clinton Co. 64 acres, Sec. 23, Elba tp. Gratiot Co.

Jerie A. Gleason, Farmer, Elsie P. O., Clinton Co. Elba tp. Gratiot Co.

Abram Sebring, Farmer, Elsie P. O., Clinton Co. 105 acres, Sec. 33, Elba tp., Gratiot Co.

William C. Wooley, Farmer, Elsie P. O., Clinton Co. 320 acres, Sec. 33, Elba tp. Gratiot Co.

William L. Ball, Farmer and Postmaster, 40 acres, Sec. 31, Stella P. O., Hamilton tp.

Wm. Barton, Farmer, Justice and Postmaster, 80 acres, Sec. 3, Bad River P. O. Hamilton tp.

Harvey L. Curtis, Farmer, Bad River, P. O., Hamilton tp.

Henry O. Burt, Farmer, 66 acres, Sec. 19, Carson City P. O., North Shade tp.

Elizabeth C. Marlow, Farmer, 80 acres, Sec. 17, Carson City P. O., North Shade tp.

William Brice, Farmer, 100 acres, Sec. 17, Carson City P. O., North Shade tp.

Frank S. Everest, Farmer and School Teacher, 80 acres Sec. 20, Carson City P. O., North Shade tp.

Joseph Roberts, Farmer, Wool and Grain, 80 acres. Sec. 29, Hubbardston P. O.,Ionia Co., North Shade tp.

Henry Lenka, Farmer, Apiarian and Mechanic, 80 acres, Sec. 32, Hubbardston P.O., Ionia Co., North Shade tp.

Harvey Silvernail, Farmer, 63 acres, Sec. 32, Hubbardston P.O., Ionia Co., North Shade tp.

Lorenzo Squire, Farmer & Supervisor, 240 acres, Sec's. 20 and 21, Ithaca P. O., North Star tp.

George W. Bolding, Farmer, 140 acres, Sec. 33, Pompeii P. O., North Star tp.

Luther I. Dean, Farmer and School Teacher, 82 acres, Sec.15, North Star P. O. and tp.

J. M. Luther, Farmer, 120 acres, Sec. 11, North Star P. O. and tp.

Hiram Brady, Farmer, 158 acres, Sec. 2, North Star P. O. and tp.

Gilbert G. Gahrion, Farmer, 85 acres, Sec. 19, North Star P. O., Hamilton tp.

M. H. Mills, Farmer, 120 acres, Sec. 36, Stella P. O., North Star tp.

Charles L. Carr, Farmer, Bridgville P. O., Washington tp.

www.ingramcontent.com/pod-product-compliance
Lightning Source LLC
Chambersburg PA
CBHW030320270326
41926CB00010B/1442